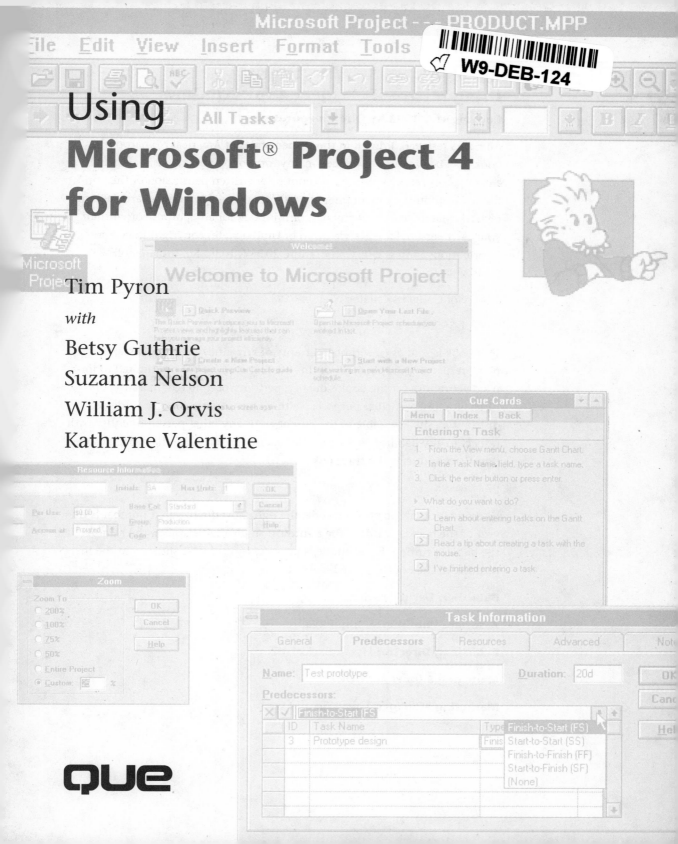

Using
Microsoft® Project 4 for Windows

Tim Pyron

with

Betsy Guthrie

Suzanna Nelson

William J. Orvis

Kathryne Valentine

que

Using Microsoft Project 4 for Windows

Copyright © 1994 by Que® Corporation

Library of Congress Catalog No.: 94-65883

ISBN: 1-56529-594-3

97 96 95   6 5

Interpretation of the printing code: the rightmost double-digit number is the year of the book's printing; the rightmost single-digit number, the number of the book's printing. For example, a printing code of 94-1 shows that the first printing of the book occurred in 1994.

Publisher: David P. Ewing

Associate Publisher: Corinne Walls

Publishing Director: Lisa A. Bucki

Managing Editor: Anne Owen

Marketing Manager: Greg Wiegand

Dedication

This book is dedicated to Gerlinde K. Pyron. Partly in appreciation of the sacrifices she made without complaining as I focused on this project, and for the loving things she continued to do when the tight schedule was rough on the both of us. That is the nurturing part. But she also is a remarkable Renaissance woman of the nineties, and I am indebted to her for her many advanced insights about business and the need for enlightened management. She has contributed to this book directly because she has taught me more valuable lessons about business than I learned in graduate school in the MBA program.

Credits

Acquisitions Editor
Nancy Stevenson

Product Director
Steven M. Schafer

Production Editor
Phil Kitchel

Editors
Audra Gable
Patrick Kanouse
Heather Kaufman

Technical Editors
Frank Gumino
Michael Watson

Editorial Assistant
Theresa Mathias

Book Designer
Amy Peppler-Adams

Cover Designer
Dan Armstrong

Production Team
Stephen Adams
Jeff Baker
Angela Bannan
Cameron Booker
Brook Farling
Dennis Clay Hager
Carla Hall
Joy Dean Lee
Jay Lesandrini
Andrea Marcum
Tim Montgomery
Aren Munk
Nanci Sears Perry
Linda Quigley
Caroline Roop
Dennis Sheehan
Becky Tapley
Michael Thomas
Sue VandeWalle
Donna Winter
Lillian Yates

Indexers
Charlotte Clapp
Johnna VanHoose

Composed in *Stone Serif* and *MCPdigital* by Que Corporation

About the Author

Tim Pyron is the Consulting Coordinator for Productivity Point International in San Antonio, Texas. Productivity Point has locations across the United States and Canada and is the leading provider of computer training and support services in North America, specializing in hands-on training and consulting in the entire range of PC and Macintosh software products. For information on course content, consulting services, and the Productivity Point facility nearest you, contact:

Productivity Point International
45 NE Loop 410, Suite 300
San Antonio, Texas, 78216
1-800-394-8724
(210)342-6500 Voice
(210)340-5177 Fax

Tim's undergraduate degree is in Music, but his Master's and Ph.D. are in Economics from Louisiana State University. He regularly provides consulting services and conducts training in Microsoft Project and in spreadsheet and database applications.

Trademarks

Acknowledgments

The first time you write a book you are astonished to find out just how inadequate this page of the book really is. The familiar phrases "couldn't have done it without..." and "...made it all possible" are not social niceties—they are literally true. It is difficult to share your sense of indebtedness without sounding like a protracted Academy Awards acceptance speech. But a successful book is entirely a team project, and the author is just one link in the chain that stretches from the family through the publishing house to the reader. The difference is, the author gets to write this page and thank the others.

This book owes everything to the ingenious folks at Microsoft who create applications like Microsoft Project that are so rich in features that the rest of us want to know how to use them. The Microsoft Project 4.0 team, led by **Jeff Camp**, has made major advances in project management software with this release. **Christian Stark**, who will lead the effort for the next revision of Microsoft Project, took the better part of a day to be a genial host to me at Microsoft headquarters and explain the early testing release of the product. **Adrian Jenkins**, **Stephen Bridgeland,** and **Scott Chytil** were patient and helpful in providing support when I needed answers about the developing product. Christian and the rest of the development team for Microsoft Project 5.0 are anxious to hear about your wishes for improvements and new features. Call them at (206) 936-9474 to register your preferences for enhancements.

I also want to thank Que Corporation for its continuing series of highest quality computer books; and, for this book, I want to single out **Nancy Stevenson** and **Steve Schafer** who have had to struggle with us and the uneven results that writers oftentimes produce. Those are the two who really put this book together. **Don Roche**, thanks for being the one who made it possible for me to write the first edition of this book.

There were several consultants and writers who helped write and edit *Using Microsoft Project 4 for Windows*, and I want you to know about them.

Betsy Guthrie has over 13 years of experience in computer training and support. As an independent consultant in Novato, California, she has helped users use and adapt project management software to their own business needs in companies all over the United States. Betsy has an undergraduate degree from Cornell University and a graduate degree in education from Smith College.

Suzanna Nelson is currently an instructor/consultant with Productivity Point International in Austin, Texas. She has a BBA in Management Information Systems from the University of Texas at Austin and more than six years of programming experience on both mainframes and PCs. She is also a Microsoft Certified Instructor who specializes in teaching Microsoft Project, MS Access, and MS Visual Basic.

William J. Orvis is an electronics engineer at the University of California's Lawrence Livermore National Laboratory, where he is involved in the large-scale numerical modeling of solid-state devices, development of micron-sized vacuum microelectronic devices, and computer security research. (He describes himself as a computer virus smasher.) He is a member of CIAC, the Department of Energy's computer incident response team. Orvis received both his B.S. and M.S. degrees in Physics and Astronomy at the University of Denver of Colorado. He is the author of several computer books and has written for magazines. He has contributed his expertise with Visual Basic to this and other Que books.

Kathryne Valentine is an independent computer trainer/consultant based in Annapolis, Maryland. Her degree is in Psychology and Education. She also graduated from New York University's Building Trades Association. She has been involved in numerous projects, both in the construction industry and in software development and training as well. She regularly teaches project management, database and spreadsheet applications in the Washington/Baltimore metropolitan area. She also works frequently in hardware/software conversions in the legal community.

Finally, I want to thank my two "partners" and dear friends, **Vangie Bazan** and **Mary Weaver**, for their continuing support and faith in my efforts to write this book. Though they did not write a word directly, they contributed much with their encouragement and enthusiasm for the project.

Contents at a Glance

Project Management

Shared Project Data

Views and Reports

Project Interface

Appendixes

Contents

10 Auditing the Task Schedule   243

11 Resolving Problems in the Project Plan   261

19 Placing Text and Graphics on the Gantt Chart   551

20 Using and Customizing Reports   563

IV Microsoft Project Interface   595

21 Creating and Using Macros   597

22 Customizing Toolbars, Menus, Forms, and Cue Cards   615

Introduction

Project management encompasses all stages of a project, from the planning stages through the completion and drafting of final reports that summarize the completion of the project.

As soon as you determine your project goals, you can get started with Microsoft Project. Microsoft Project is an invaluable tool for the following work:

- Organizing the plan
- Scheduling the tasks
- Assigning resources and costs to tasks
- Fine-tuning the plan to satisfy constraints
- Preparing reports to communicate the final plan to all who must approve or execute the plan

After you begin work on the project, you can use Microsoft Project for the following ongoing tasks:

- Monitoring actual performance
- Projecting the impact on the project schedule when changes occur that threaten the success of the project
- Revising the plan to meet contingencies
- Producing final reports on the success of the project

The techniques used by Microsoft Project were developed by different people and organizations during the earlier part of the twentieth century. Following World War II, the Department of Defense and associated contractors contributed much to the area of project management because of the size and complexity of military projects. The development of electronic computers during the same period made feasible the calculations needed for scheduling many thousands of tasks and resources.

Project management tools have been applied to large and small projects alike, and the personal computer now makes project management tools available to all managers. Although project management techniques are traditionally used in the defense and construction industries, in recent decades these techniques have also been applied in manufacturing, in service industries, and in government. The high-tech computer hardware and software companies are using project management techniques in ever-increasing numbers.

Recent developments in management models show that project teams are an essential, functional unit in the workplace, and project management is being examined for guidelines for task group management.

If you are responsible for the successful completion of a project, you can reap significant benefits from using Microsoft Project.

Who Should Read This Book?

Using Microsoft Project 4 for Windows is written for and organized around the needs of a wide range of readers, including those who have used project management software in the past, and those who have used earlier versions of Microsoft Project or project management software from other sources.

If you are new to project management, this book can guide you through all phases of project management. If you are new to using computer tools in project management, this book can teach you how to use Microsoft Project to tap the computational and presentation capabilities of the computer. If you are new to Windows, you should review Que's *Using Windows 3.1* or *Windows 3.1 QuickStart*.

If you used previous versions of Microsoft Project for Windows, this book brings you up to date on the new and improved features. If you already have experience with Microsoft Project for Windows, Release 4, this book offers detailed explanations of advanced features and ways to customize the program to enhance your use of the product.

What's New in Microsoft Project 4?

Microsoft Project 4 contains major improvements in the user interface, in the sophistication of its connectivity with other computer applications, and in the facilities for automating tasks and creating controlled applications.

Expanded and Enhanced Views and Reports

There are important enhancements in the way your project data can be viewed and printed. The Gantt Chart, which is now a full-screen default view, has a cleaner, more readable look. Task bars are bigger, and text is easier to read. Dependency links between tasks can now be shown on the Gantt Chart, and the default display now includes resource names next to task bars and dates next to milestones. Non-working days now have a shaded background on the timescale, and you can bring the shading to the forefront to hide the task bar on non-working days. The timescale can now show week numbers that are consistent with the international convention. You can now place additional information on the Gantt Chart in the form of free text, graphics, logos, and charts. And individual task bars can be hidden or given special formats.

The new Calendar View provides an easily understood model for creating, modifying, and reporting project details. Tasks can be created and moved directly on a conventional calendar layout.

The PERT chart can now be zoomed without losing the task details. The lines showing dependency links have rounded corners when you choose right-angled lines.

New Learning Aids with Intelligence

It is now easier than ever to learn Microsoft Project. ToolTips defines a button on the toolbar when the mouse pauses over it. Cue Cards are available to give you step-by-step instructions for even the most complicated tasks. You can create your own Cue Cards to help others in your organization create project documents that follow the conventions in your organization. The PlanningWizard monitors your actions and provides helpful warnings or tips for better use of the software and better planning of your project. The printed manual is smaller, because most of its material is now in readily accessible on-line help.

Major Improvements in Ease of Use

Perhaps the most significant improvements are found in the changes that make Microsoft Project easier to use. The main menu has been normalized to match the new Microsoft Office menu standards. The menu looks the same as the menus in Microsoft Word 6.0, Microsoft Excel 5.0, and Microsoft PowerPoint 4. Shortcut menus have been added to speed the selection of commands that are relevant for the item that is currently selected.

One of the major inconveniences of earlier releases was the distribution of project data among multiple files (the Calendar file, the View file, the Winproj.INI file, and the project file itself). Microsoft Project 4 saves *all* pertinent information about a project in the project file itself. A single file, GLOBAL.MPT, contains all the default features. Your customized views and calendars reside in the project file itself. You can use the new Organizer to copy a customized item into the GLOBAL.MPT file so that other projects can take advantage of the custom feature.

There are eight new standard toolbars (plus the Microsoft Project 3.0 toolbar), and you can display or hide them at will. You can also easily customize each toolbar or create new custom toolbars, placing standard buttons anywhere you choose or creating new buttons, with custom color faces, to execute commands or run your macros.

You can now save a project file as a template to serve as a starter for future projects. The template can have custom views, macros, and toolbars as well as standard task groups or a resource pool. The template also can contain customized Cue Cards to instruct users on using the template.

You can now create recurring tasks, such as a staff meeting that is scheduled for 8:30 AM every Monday morning. You specify the frequency, the duration of each event, and the time span during which the recurring tasks will take place.

This release introduces the Drag-and-Drop technology that is so popular in spreadsheets and word processors. You can now use Drag and Drop in all the major views to create tasks, to move tasks to a different position in the task list, to change the indention level of a task in an outline, to assign resources to a task, and to create dependency links for tasks.

The list of standard reports has been expanded significantly, with standardized variations of reports that focus on common reporting needs, as well as innovative report forms such as timesheets, crosstab summaries of work and costs, and a new ability to summarize resource work and costs by groups.

Printing views and reports is now much more efficient with options to fit the report to a page, to omit empty pages in a large Gantt Chart or PERT chart spread, and to repeat identifying columns on each page of a GANTT Chart.

Beefed Up Power

You can now consolidate for reviewing or printing up to 80 projects, and you can have up to 80 projects that share the same resource pool. OLE2 is fully implemented in Microsoft Project 4, including the ability to Drag and Drop data between applications. Your project data can be saved now in the new ODBC (Open Database Connectivity) format. In this database format your project can be combined with large numbers of other projects for consolidation and analysis.

The information sharing ability of Windows for Workgroups has been built into the new release. If Windows for Workgroups is installed, you can have task assignments automatically transmitted to the appropriate resources for confirmation and acceptance of the assignment. Once they accept the assignment, the tasks are placed automatically on their Scheduler. You can have requests for progress reports sent automatically to those same resources once the project is underway, and the responses can be automatically incorporated into the tracking of the project, with their comments attached automatically to the task as notes.

Fully Programmable

This release includes a macro recorder and a full-fledged programming language. Use the macro recorder to automate your maintenance tasks. Edit the macro to include interactive prompts and branching features. Use Visual Basic for Applications to develop complete project management applications and integration with other applications.

The Organization of This Book

This book is divided into four parts, which take you from an overview of project management and Microsoft Project through creating macros and customizing the interface. Here's a brief overview of these parts and the chapters you find in each part:

Part I: Project Management

Part I teaches you the basics of project management, introducing the features of Microsoft Project as appropriate for each phase of project management and including cross-references to the reference material in later parts of the book for more advanced treatment. This is the section where you learn how to create a project document.

The chapters in Part I are designed to follow the usual order of creating a project. In this manner, a beginner can follow the chapters in sequence while learning to use Microsoft Project. The chapters in Part I introduce and explain the most commonly used views and reports for developing and managing a project. The reader can turn to Part III for a comprehensive presentation of the variety of available views and reports.

Chapter 1, "Introducing Project Management," introduces project management concepts and the major phases of managing a project with Microsoft Project.

Chapter 2, "Learning the Basics of Microsoft Project," introduces you to the Microsoft Project workspace. In this chapter, you learn to navigate the screen display, use project files, scroll and select data, and select different views of the project.

In Chapter 3, "Setting Up a New Project Document," you review the preliminary steps you take when creating a project. You learn how to specify the calendar of working days and hours, how to enter basic information about the project, and how to specify the planned date for starting or finishing the project. You also learn how to adjust the most critical of the default values that govern how Microsoft Project displays and calculates a project.

Chapter 4, "Creating a Task List," explains how you define and enter the tasks, milestones, and recurring tasks that must be completed to successfully finish the project. You also learn how to enter the task list in outline form in accordance with top-down planning principles. You learn how to edit the data in a project and how to use different forms for editing the task data.

Chapter 5, "Entering Scheduling Requirements," shows you how to define the special conditions that govern the scheduling of tasks in your project: specific deadlines and sequencing requirements for the tasks.

Chapter 6, "Working with the Calendar View," explains the use of the new Calendar view for entering, editing, and viewing your project.

Chapter 7, "Working with the PERT Chart," shows you how to understand and manipulate the PERT Chart. You learn how to enter project details directly into the PERT Chart view and how to change the presentation and layout of the PERT chart.

Chapter 8, "Defining Resources and Costs," shows you how to define the resource pool that you plan to use in the project and how to define the working and non-working times for those resources. You learn how to sort, filter, and print the resource list. You learn also how to save the resource pool as a template for use in other project documents.

Chapter 9, "Assigning Resources and Costs to Tasks," shows you how to associate resources and costs with specific tasks. You also learn how to assign overtime for resources and how to assign fixed costs to parts of the project. By reading this chapter, you gain an understanding of the way in which Microsoft Project calculates changes in the project schedule when you assign or change the assignment of resources to a task. Finally, you learn how to view the resources, costs, and task assignments in useful ways for auditing the project plan and how to print the standard views and reports.

Chapter 10, "Auditing the Task Schedule," introduces features that help you review your task schedule for completeness and accuracy. You learn how to get an overview of the project to see if you can complete the project plan in a timely fashion and at an acceptable cost. You also learn how to view the task list through filters that focus on important aspects of the project and to sort and print the task list. You learn how to spell-check the schedule and how to view the summary statistics for the project.

In Chapter 11, "Resolving Problems in the Project Plan," you learn how to recognize and respond to problems that involve resource workloads, conflicting time constraints, missed deadlines, and excessive costs. This phase of project management is where you refine the project plan, prior to submitting the plan for approval.

Chapter 12, "Managing the Project," deals with your role as project manager after work on the project begins. You learn how to save a copy of the finalized project plan to use as a baseline. The baseline can then be compared with actual experience after work on the project begins. This chapter teaches you how to track the actual beginning and ending dates for tasks, the actual work amounts, and the actual costs. You learn how to compare the baseline plan with the revised schedule that Microsoft Project calculates from the actual data you have entered in order to anticipate and deal with problems in meeting the project goals while you still have time available to take corrective action.

Part II: Shared Project Data

Chapter 13, "Working with Multiple Projects," explains how to link one or more subprojects to a master or summary project and how to link an individual task in one project to a task in another project. You also learn how to consolidate multiple projects and how to manage multiple projects that share a common resource pool. You learn how to display tasks from multiple projects in a single window for viewing or for printing reports.

Chapter 14, "Exchanging Data with Other Applications," explains how to exchange project data with other applications. You learn to export and import task, resource, and cost data with other applications and file formats, including the ODBC database format. You learn how to establish dynamic links with other Windows applications, so that changing a value in another application can change this same value in Microsoft Project. You learn also how to use OLE2 with Microsoft Project to embed objects from one Windows application in another application.

Chapter 15, "Using Microsoft Project in Workgroups," shows you how to take advantage of the communications, scheduling, and file sharing facilities of Windows for Workgroups to share your project data with members of your group. You learn also how to use the automated features that notify group members of their task assignments and ask them for progress updates.

Part III: Views and Reports

The chapters in Part III teach you how to take advantage of the extensive options that Microsoft Project provides for customizing the application's views and reports to suit your specific reporting needs, one of the exceptional strengths of Microsoft Project. Some of the views and reports are mentioned in Part I at appropriate points. This section provides a comprehensive reference to all the major views and reports.

Chapter 16, "Printing Views and Reports," brings together in one place a reference for the steps used in printing views and reports. This chapter covers all the details of how to use the Microsoft Project page and printer setup.

Chapter 17, "Using and Creating Views," explains the many options for customizing the way in which tables, forms, graphic images, and filters display your project in a View. You also learn how to manage the views, reports, and other customized aspects of your installation in project files.

Chapter 18, "Formatting Views," assembles in one place a reference for the formatting options for all of the major views. Procedures, including tips and techniques, for changing the appearance of graphic elements and text display for categories of items as well as for individual items are explained.

Chapter 19, "Placing Text and Graphics on the Gantt Chart," shows you how to place free text and graphic figures on a view. This is one of the new features of Microsoft Project 4. You learn how to use the Draw toolbar and how to anchor the objects to specific tasks or resources.

Chapter 20, "Using and Customizing Reports," explains how to use the standard reports and how to design supplemental reports.

Part IV: Microsoft Project Interface

The chapters in Part IV cover more advanced topics that you may want to explore after you learn to use the basics of Microsoft Project.

Chapter 21, "Creating and Using Macros," shows you how to record and edit macros to automate procedures that you use frequently in Microsoft Project.

Chapter 22, "Customizing Toolbars, Menus, Forms, and Cue Cards," explains the options for customizing the way Microsoft Project works. You learn how to change the standard tool bar buttons and how to attach commands and macros to a button. You learn also how to customize the Microsoft Project menus and how to create your own forms for data entry and review. You also learn how to create your own Cue Cards for explaining business rules or internal procedures to users.

Chapter 23, "Using Visual Basic for Applications," shows you how to use the subset of Visual Basic that is included in the new releases of Microsoft Office products.

Appendixes

Appendix A, "The Microsoft Project Field Dictionary", defines all of the fields in the task, resource, and resource assignment database. A knowledge of the fields is needed to create filters, design views, and to write Visual Basic applications.

Appendix B, "Shortcut Keys," provides a reference for all the shortcut keys provided in Microsoft Project.

Appendix C, "Glossary," provides brief definitions of the special terms used in project management in general and in Microsoft Project in particular.

Part I

Project Management

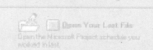

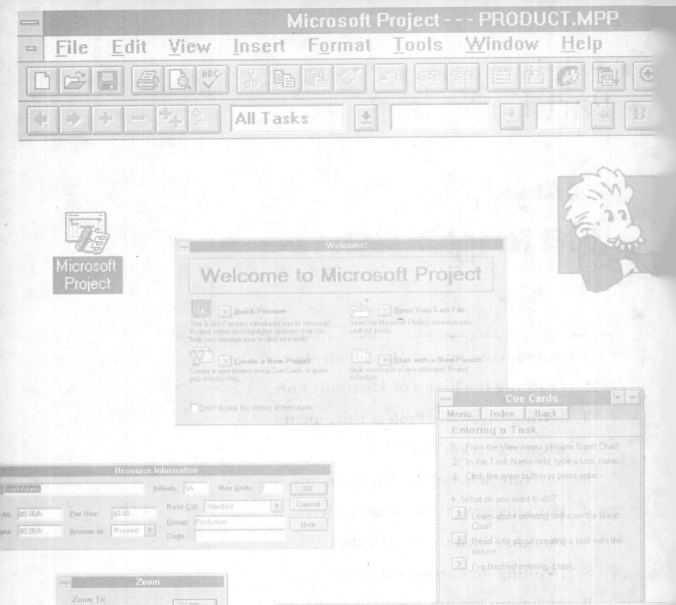

Chapter 1

Introducing Project Management

In this chapter, you learn

- What activities in the organization are appropriate for project management tools.

- The functions of the project manager.

- The advantages of using project management and project management software.

- General guidelines for project managers.

- The general steps you should take in developing a project with Microsoft Project.

- How project schedules are calculated by the computer.

- The essential vocabulary of project management.

Managing projects differs somewhat from more general management assignments. This chapter gets you acquainted with the unique problems of project management and outlines the benefits you can gain from using a project management software product like Microsoft Project. General guidelines for successful project management are included, as well as a brief explanation of the methodology used in project scheduling. Also included is a checklist of the major steps you follow in using Microsoft Project to plan and manage a project.

What Is a Project?

Project management differs from conventional management in that a *project* is a limited concept that is usually more narrowly focused than traditional management goals, such as managing an ongoing organization to assure the success and survival of the organization. The following list shows several features that distinguish projects from other managerial assignments:

- **Projects are temporary.** A project involves a temporary, one-time goal or objective. Managing a department is an ongoing assignment that extends into the foreseeable future, perhaps for the life of the organization. Problems and challenges come and go; providing continuity is an inherent aspect of departmental management.

  A project, on the other hand, is a short-term assignment relative to the life of the organization, lasting only until the project's objectives are achieved. A project has a defined start and finish date.

  Selecting and installing a new word processor, for example, is a project; ongoing management of the word processing pool is not a project.

- **Project objectives are specific and measurable.** Project goals are stated in terms of specific performance objectives, not in vague generalities that call for unspecified improvements.

  You can measure the success or failure of a project by the degree to which the performance satisfies the specifications in the goal.

- **Projects are subject to the immediate constraints of performance, time, and budget.** A project exists to deliver a specific performance objective, and the quality of the performance must be met within the confines of other constraints.

  Projects are constrained by time commitments. Usually, either the project start date or the finish date (or both) must meet some time requirement. The overall time constraint needs to be explicitly incorporated into the project goal statement. Individual tasks within the project also may be subject to time constraints.

  Projects are subject to resource and cost constraints because of the financial limits of how much money you can spend to achieve the project objectives.

Projects require resources—usually resources that are already in demand elsewhere within the organization. The project manager must compete for resources with other projects and with the ongoing activities of the organization. Resources usually are the main source of costs for a project.

■ **Projects must be managed so that the immediate goals are achieved without damaging the long-term viability of the organization.** A project is a short chapter in the ongoing life of the organization. Just as a society should not pursue short-term goals while neglecting to account for the long-term impact of the decisions that are made, the project manager must not lose sight of the larger goals of the organization. If a project meets its immediate goals, but does so without also promoting other projects and commitments of the organization, the project is not really a success. If a project is undertaken for internal purposes, you must include maintaining the healthy fabric of the work environment as another constraint. If you undertake a project for a customer, you must include consideration of good customer relations as another constraint.

Considering these attributes of a project, project management studies usually define a *project* as a collection of activities and tasks designed to achieve a specific but temporary goal of the organization, with specific performance or quality requirements, all the while subject to time and cost constraints.

A successful project must meet deadlines, stay within budget, and deliver performance according to specifications.

What Is Project Management?

The term *project management* refers to managing the activities that lead to the successful completion of a project.

Project management is the application of management principles to plan, organize, staff, control, and direct resources of an organization in pursuit of a temporary or one-time specific goal.

The project manager is responsible for planning the actions or tasks that will achieve the project objectives and for organizing the resources of the organization to carry out the plan.

Project Management

The staffing function for project management is more often a question of negotiating resource commitments with line managers than of recruiting new employees. The personnel often come from the existing work force, and the facilities and equipment often must be shared with the regular operations of the organization. Moreover, the project manager is not necessarily the supervisor for the resources used in a project—this function usually is the job of a line manager.

Defining projects and project management by the terms *temporary* and *short-term* is meant in a relative sense. A sales project may have a life of two weeks, and a project to build a nuclear power plant may have a life of fifteen years. But when compared to the life span of the organization, it is temporary.

Project management techniques evolved continually throughout the twentieth century, but the most rapid developments grew out of the rapidly increasing technology of the defense industry after World War II. Recent developments in general management theory and practice have sparked a renewed surge of interest in project management methods. Leading management specialists are advocating that the organization's work force be organized into more fluid work groups that approach many of the traditional functions of the organization as a series of projects. This approach has led managers to study the methodology of project management from a different point of view as they attempt to find guidelines for successful management strategies.

The Advantages of Using Project Management Software

Project management helps you achieve your project goal on time and on budget. Computer software can aid significantly in project management as a tool for recording, calculating, analyzing, and preparing presentations to help communicate the details of the project. However, the software cannot produce or even guarantee a successful project plan any more than a word processor can produce or guarantee a successful novel, or an accounting program can produce a profitable fiscal year.

Despite the preceding caveat, project management software can be a helpful tool in managing a project. Here are some of the most important advantages afforded by project management software:

Project management software helps you develop a better plan.

- Because the software requires you to specify precisely the tasks necessary for meeting the project goal, you are forced to think carefully about the details of the project. The discipline imposed by the software helps you organize a better plan.

- The screen views provide an organized presentation of the details of your plan, which can improve your ability to visualize, organize, and refine the plan.

Project management software makes calculated projections easier and more reliable.

- Based on the data you enter, the computer calculates a schedule that shows when each task should begin and end and when specific resources are scheduled to perform specific tasks. This schedule also shows the probable costs of the project.

Project management software helps you detect inconsistencies and problems in the plan.

- The computer detects when resources are scheduled for more hours than are available or when deadlines are impossible to meet. If you provide the data in a knowledgeable way, the computer helps you resolve resource overallocations and deadline commitments.

Project management software helps you communicate the plan to others.

- The software provides printed reports that make selling the plan to upper-level management, who must approve the plan, an easier task.

- The printed reports also improve communications about the plan to supervisors or workers, which makes securing their approval and cooperation easier.

Project management software helps you track progress and detect potential difficulties.

- After the project is under way, you replace the projected dates for the scheduled tasks with actual dates as tasks are begun and completed. The computer then revises the schedule to incorporate the actual dates, predicting new completion dates and costs. This new projection provides you with valuable advance warning of potential delays or cost overruns, so you can take corrective measures if necessary.

■ If circumstances change after the project is underway, the computer makes it easier to adjust the plan, and see the consequences of this adjustment.

It cannot be stressed too much, however, that project management software, like accounting software, is only as useful as the reliability and completeness of the data that you supply.

General Guidelines for Project Managers

The following guidelines are offered as aids to successful project management. Most of these guidelines are common-sense management techniques, but reviewing them is always a useful exercise.

■ Keep in mind at all times that your success as a project manager depends largely on your ability to motivate people to cooperate in the project. No computer program or well-designed plan can compensate for ineffective people skills. Computers may respond to logic, but people respond to all that is positive and negative about human emotions.

■ Establish your authority as project manager and your role as coordinator of project planning at the outset. If you are appointed to this role, ask the officer making the appointment to issue a statement that validates your authority.

■ Make the planning stage a group effort as much as possible. You will reap the benefits of a wider base of experience and expertise, and you will find it much easier to secure approval of the plan and get people committed to the final project plan.

■ Set a clear project goal.

State the goal of the project precisely and simply in a manner that everyone associated with the project (supervisors who must approve the project, managers who work with the project, and others who must do the work) can read and understand. To this end, prepare a concise summary statement of the goal of the project.

State your goal in terms that you can measure. If the goals are realized, measuring success then becomes possible.

Secure agreement on the goal by all who must approve the project or who must provide supervision during the execution of the project.

State the goal in realistic and attainable terms.

State a definite time frame in the goal—it should be part of the commitment to the project. The goal "Install a new word processor throughout the company," for example, is ill-defined. "Install new word processor software throughout the company and train all personnel in its use by June 1" is more inclusive and more specific.

Define the performance requirements and specifications carefully.

Nail down all fixed deadlines or time constraints.

Determine the budgetary limitations of the project.

State the performance or quality specifications of the project with great care. Write and then distribute these specifications, in a Statement of Work, to the creators of the specifications, and also to the supervisors and workers. Make sure that no misunderstanding exists about what you expect from the people you are managing. Misunderstood specifications can prove extremely costly.

■ Organize the tasks of the project into major phases or components and establish *milestones*, or interim goals, to mark the completion of each of these phases. These milestones serve as check points by which everyone can gauge how well the project is on target after the work begins. This *top-down* approach helps to provide organization for the project plan from the outset.

For example, the conversion to a new word processing product may involve the following phases and milestones:

Determine the features required of the software.

Review available products.

Select the product to be used.

Software selected (milestone)

Buy the software.

Set up help desk.

Install software.

Software installed (milestone)

Train all users.

Conversion complete (milestone)

- List the tasks that must be completed to reach each milestone and estimate the duration of each task.

- Diagram the flow of activity to show the instances where tasks must be performed in a specific sequence.

- Distribute the project plan to all who are responsible for supervising or doing the work. Secure their agreement that the assumptions of the plan are sound and that all involved are willing to do their part. Revise the plan as needed to secure supervisory agreement.

- Distribute printed copies of the revised schedule with charts and tables to identify clearly the scope of the project and to identify clearly the responsibilities of all who must contribute to making the project a success.

- Secure firm commitments from all responsible parties to contribute as outlined in the finalized plan.

- After work on the project is under way, monitor the work's progress by tracking actual performance and results, which is the best way to discover problems early so that you can take corrective actions.

- Tracking these performance details also helps document problems and explain the results if the project goals are not met.

- If problems arise that make finishing the project on time or within budget unlikely or impossible, you can give superiors ample warning so that expectations regarding the project can be adjusted.

- After the project is completed, acknowledge and thank all participants who made the project a success.

A Checklist for Using Microsoft Project

Microsoft Project is so rich with options you can easily lose your sense of direction when you start working. The following list is intended as an overview of using Microsoft Project to plan a project.

Preliminaries

Before you start entering tasks into the computer, it is a good idea to define some basic parameters that govern how Microsoft Project treats your data. (These topics are covered in Chapter 3, "Setting Up a New Project Document.") To set up the preliminaries, take the following steps:

1. Define working days, non-working days, and regular working hours in Microsoft Project's scheduling calendar.

2. If necessary, adjust the number of hours that Microsoft Project uses for the time units of *day* and *week*. These definitions determine how Microsoft Project calculates the duration of tasks and, therefore, the duration of the project.

3. Enter the basic data that describes the project: the project name, company name, project manager, and the expected start date or finish date.

4. List the resources used in the project, define the costs, and create resource calendars for all resources that show the exceptions to the general calendar of working days and hours. You can include this step as easily in the Planning section as in the Preliminaries section. It is placed here because many users maintain a template of the organization's resources to use for entering new projects. For these users, the resource list already exists when they begin the project planning.

Planning

Planning is the phase in which you outline the project plan, review the plan, and after refining the plan, distribute the finalized plan to all who are involved in the project. These topics are discussed in Chapters 4 through 9. To start planning the project, take the following steps:

1. List the major phases of the project in outline form and then fill in the detailed tasks and milestones in the project. Estimate each task's duration. This is the topic of Chapter 4, "Creating a Task List."

2. If the start or finish date of a task is in any way constrained to a fixed date, enter the date at this point. Define the required sequencing of

tasks—where tasks must be scheduled so that the start or finish is linked to the scheduled start or finish of other tasks. These topics are covered in Chapter 5, "Entering Scheduling Requirements."

3. Assign resources to the tasks. Defining and assigning resources is covered in Chapter 8, "Defining Resources and Costs," and Chapter 9, "Assigning Resources and Costs to Tasks."

4. Assign all fixed costs to the tasks. Costs are also covered in Chapter 9.

5. Review the schedule that Microsoft Project has calculated so far, and correct all problems by taking the actions discussed in the following list:

   Identify and resolve scheduling problems where fixed date commitments are in conflict or where resources are assigned to do more work than can be done in the time period allowed.

   Identify costs that are over budget and try to find ways to lower the costs.

   If the time constraint for the overall project is not met by the schedule, you must find ways to revise the schedule to meet the requirements of the project goal.

   Previewing and refining the schedule are covered in Chapter 10, "Auditing the Task Schedule," and Chapter 11, "Resolving Problems in the Project Plan."

6. Print and distribute the project schedule for review by the managers who must approve the plan and by project supervisors and workers. Basic printing instructions are provided in Chapters 9 and 10. More comprehensive information about printing is provided in Chapter 16, "Printing Views and Reports."

7. Revise the plan, if necessary, to accommodate the requested suggestions or changes.

8. Print and distribute the final schedule to all parties for final approval, and secure from each party a firm commitment to the plan.

Managing the Project

In this phase, you monitor progress on the project, recording actual experience and calculating new schedules when actual dates fail to match the planned dates. These topics are covered in Chapter 12, "Managing the Project." To handle the task of monitoring work on the project, follow these steps:

1. Make a copy of the final schedule plan as a basis for comparison purposes after the project gets under way.

2. Track actual start dates, finish dates, percentage of work completed, and costs incurred, and enter these details into Microsoft Project. The computer will revise the schedule to incorporate these actual events into the remaining planned schedule.

3. Review the revised schedule for problems and, if possible, take corrective measures. Notify all participants of changes in the scheduled date and time of tasks for which each participant is responsible.

4. After the project is completed, print final reports as documentation to show the actual work and costs and to show comparisons with the original plan.

Project Management Scheduling Techniques

The methods used for scheduling tasks and resources in project management include several techniques that you need to understand in order to use Microsoft Project effectively. Although the implications of these methods are reviewed where needed in upcoming chapters, gaining an overview can be useful before you get into the details of planning and coordinating a project.

The Critical Path Method

The fundamental scheduling method used in project management is the Critical Path Method (CPM). To use the CPM model, you must identify all the tasks that need to be completed, stipulate how long each task is expected to take (the task's *duration*), and define all sequencing requirements that govern when you can schedule a task. A *sequencing requirement* means that a task cannot begin until another task is completed or at least has already begun. When you build a house, for example, you don't start framing the walls until the foundation is laid.

The CPM method takes into account all the task data, and calculates the overall duration of the project by calculating the combined durations of the tasks, when all tasks are chained together in the required sequences.

Figure 1.1 illustrates a simple project that contains six tasks. Tasks A, B, and C must be performed in sequence; tasks X, Y, and Z must also be performed in sequence. Both sequences can go on at the same time; however, both sequences must be finished before the project is complete.

Fig. 1.1
The longest sequence of tasks determines the finish date for the project.

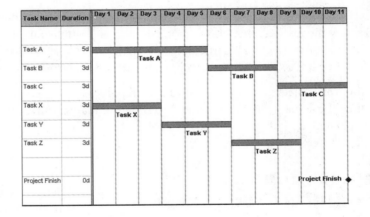

If parallel task sequences are in progress at the same time, the overall duration of the project is the duration of the longest of these task sequences. In Figure 1.1, the sequence A-B-C takes 11 days, and the sequence X-Y-Z takes nine days. It takes 11 days—the duration of the longest sequence—to complete the project.

You cannot complete the project on schedule unless the tasks on the longest sequence are finished on schedule. These tasks, known as *critical tasks*, are vital to keeping the overall project on schedule. The sequence of critical tasks is a *critical path*.

In the figure 1.1, tasks A, B, and C are critical tasks, and the sequence A-B-C is the critical path. The X-Y-Z tasks are not critical. You could delay the completion of any one of these tasks for up to two days without causing a delay of the overall project. The X, Y, and Z tasks are said to have *slack*.

Critical tasks have no slack. These tasks cannot be delayed if the project is to finish on schedule, which is the operational definition of a critical task.

Identifying the critical tasks is an important step in managing a project. Suppose that you need to shorten the duration of the overall project (commonly known as *crashing* the schedule), and you are looking for some task durations that you can try to shorten. You need to focus attention on the critical tasks and not on the noncritical tasks. Cutting time from noncritical tasks is of no use—it's just a waste of time. This knowledge can save you a great deal of time in analyzing ways to crash the project.

Resource-Driven Scheduling

Some tasks have a *fixed duration* in the sense that, no matter how many workers or resources you assign to the task, the duration still remains unchanged. The task to deliver a small package to a nearby city, for example, requires a driver and a truck. You probably won't shorten the duration of the task by placing two drivers in the truck. If, however, the task is to deliver a truckload of packages, a second driver could reduce the time it takes to load and unload the packages. If changing the quantity of resources assigned to a task leads to a change in the duration of the task, the task is said to be a "resource-driven" task. The schedule for the task is driven or determined by the quantity of resources assigned.

Microsoft Project assumes that tasks are resource driven, that they are *not* fixed duration tasks. If a task has a fixed duration, you must define the task explicitly as fixed duration. The program assumes that you can shorten the duration of a task if you increase the number of resource units you assign to do the work.

The Calendar Used for Scheduling

Microsoft Project uses the factors outlined in the previous sections (the start date, the duration of tasks, and the sequencing of tasks) to calculate a schedule for tasks, and consults a calendar of days and hours during which work can be scheduled as part of the calculation. The default calendar assumes that any task can be worked on for up to eight hours a day, five days a week.

You must customize the calendar to represent the work days and shifts of your organization. If the organization has non-working days or hours, you must enter these in the calendar so that Microsoft Project cannot schedule tasks during these times.

You also can create calendars for individual resources. The resource calendar identifies exceptions to the standard calendar that apply to a resource. When you assign a resource to do the work on a task, Microsoft Project examines the resource's calendar and schedules the work to take place on the days and during the times that the resource is available.

Scheduling Constraints

When calculating a schedule of dates for tasks, Microsoft Project schedules each task to begin as soon as possible, considering the task's position in the sequence of tasks. However, if a task must start or finish by a specific date, you can enter this requirement as a constraint on the scheduling of the task.

Unless absolutely necessary, do not enter start and finish constraints for individual tasks. Let the program calculate the start and finish dates for tasks.

From Here...

In this chapter, you had an overview of what project management is all about and how to go about planning a project in a general way. You also were introduced to some important terminology and concepts in project management.

- For an introduction to the Microsoft Project 4 interface, go on to Chapter 2, "Learning the Basics of Microsoft Project."

- If you are ready to jump right in and begin a project, see Chapter 3, "Setting Up a New Project Document," or Chapter 4, "Creating a Task List."

- If you are interested in how to print your project data, see Chapter 16, "Printing Views and Reports."

- If you want to know how to customize the views used by Microsoft Project, go to Chapter 17, "Using and Creating Views."

Chapter 2

Learning the Basics of Microsoft Project

In this chapter you learn how to work in the Microsoft Project software environment. Specifically, you learn how to

- Interpret and navigate the screen display.
- Use the menu commands.
- Open and save project files.
- Display different views of the your project data.
- Select tasks, resources, or individual task fields.

Starting and Exiting Microsoft Project

When you install Microsoft Project, the Setup program places a program icon named Microsoft Project within the Microsoft Office program group (by default if chosen during setup). Figure 2.1 shows the Microsoft Project program icon.

Fig. 2.1
The Microsoft Project 4 program icon.

You can double-click this program icon or press Enter to start Microsoft Project. The program first displays a new project window in the background, with a blank document named Project1 (see fig. 2.2) and a Welcome! window in the foreground. The list below describes the choices in the Welcome! dialog box.

Fig. 2.2
The initial
Welcome!
window.

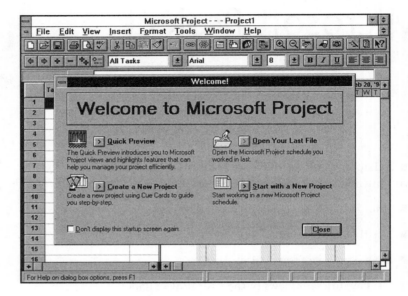

- Choose **Q**uick Preview for a tutorial and demonstration of the major features of Microsoft Project.

- Choose **U**p and Running Tutorial to display Cue Cards from the on-line Help system that guide you through setting up a new Project1 document.

- Choose **O**pen Your Last File to automatically open the file you were working on at the end of your last Microsoft Project session.

- Choose **S**tart a New Project to close the Welcome! window and begin working in Microsoft Project on your own.

In addition to the four main choices, you also can fill the check box labeled "**D**on't display this startup screen again" if you want to bypass the display of the Welcome! window the next time you start Microsoft Project. Use the Close button to close the Welcome! window without selecting any of the above choices.

After closing the Welcome! window, you will see a Tip of the Day dialog box. These tips appear each time you start Microsoft Project unless you clear the **S**how Tips at Startup check box at the bottom of the dialog box. Choose the **N**ext Tip button to see another tip. Choose the **M**ore Tips button to see a Help screen with a list of all of the Tips categories. You can choose any category and read all of the tips in that category. If you choose to see More Tips, you should close the Help screen to return to Microsoft Project. Choose the **F**ile menu and then the E**x**it command to exit Help. When you are finished reading Tips, choose the OK button to start using Microsoft Project.

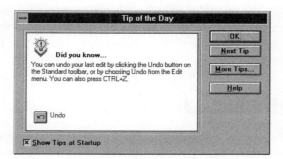

Fig. 2.3
Tips of the Day
are an easy way
to learn a new
Microsoft Project
feature or skill each
time you use
Microsoft Project.

You can exit Microsoft Project by choosing E**x**it from the **F**ile menu. Or you can double-click the application's Control button in the upper left corner of the application window. You can also use the Alt+F4 quick-key combination to close Microsoft Project.

When you exit the application, all open project files close. If any project files have changed since you last saved the file, a dialog box prompts you to save the changes before closing the file. Choose the **Y**es button to save the changes, or choose the **N**o button to close without saving the changes. Choose the Cancel button if you want to return to work on the project.

Saving a Baseline Copy

If the Planning Wizard asks you about saving a *baseline* when you save a file, you can safely choose the OK button and let the Planning Wizard create the baseline for you. The *baseline* is a static copy of the way the schedule looked at a moment in time. You can fill the **D**on't tell me about this again check box to avoid seeing the warning every time you close a file.

The *schedule* of tasks in your project will change as you modify the list of tasks or change the durations of tasks in the list. You can compare the baseline with the current schedule to see how the project plans have changed. This comparison is especially useful once actual work on the project begins and you enter the actual durations and completion dates for tasks. You'll want to be able to compare what actually happened with a baseline copy of what you had planned to happen.

► "Managing the Project," p. 319

You must remember to create the baseline copy *before* you start entering what has actually happened on the project because entering the actual data changes the schedule and then the schedule no longer shows the original plan. The Planning Wizard helps you remember to save the baseline by displaying a warning each time you close the project without having saved or updated the baseline.

Using the On-Line Learning Aids

Microsoft Project has an extensive on-line help facility, with several special aids to help users learn how to use its features. The learning aids include Cue Cards, the Planning Wizard, the Tip of the Day, and ToolTips.

Using On-Line Help

There are four ways to access Help in Microsoft Project:

■ Use the **H**elp option on the main menu bar to display the Help menu. Microsoft Project must be in Ready mode to access the main menu.

■ When the main menu is unavailable, you can press the F1 key to display the Help Contents screen.

■ Press Shift+F1 to access context-sensitive help. If the menu is active, the Help program goes directly to a message about the highlighted command. If the menu is inactive, the mouse pointer changes into a question mark and an arrow. Choose a menu command or point to an area of the screen about which you want help, and click the mouse button. The Help program goes directly to a screen about the command or about the area of the screen on which the pointer rests.

■ Dialog boxes feature Help buttons to provide more details about the subject of the dialog box. Choose Help to view the Help screens about the topic.

The Help menu offers the following choices:

■ **Contents**   Choose **C**ontents for a general starting point in the Help application.

■ **Search for Help On**   Choose **S**earch for Help On to find help topics that match a word or phrase that you type.

■ **Index**   Choose **I**ndex for an alphabetized list of specific topics.

■ **Quick Preview**   Guides you through a demonstration of project management and Microsoft Project.

■ Tip of the **Day**   Choose Tip of the **D**ay to see a tip or suggestion (as shown in fig. 2.3) about how to best use Microsoft Project. If the **S**how Tips at Startup check box is filled, you will see a new Tip each time you start Microsoft Project.

■ **Cu**e Cards

■ **Technical Support**   Choose **T**echnical Support for suggestions about where to go for answers you don't find in the Help screens.

■ **A**bout Microsoft Project   The **A**bout Microsoft Project choice shows information about the Microsoft Project copyright and the user's license, and also details about hardware and memory usage.

Using the Cue Cards

Choose **Cu**e Cards from the **H**elp menu if you want guidance on how to start and complete an activity (see fig. 2.4). The Cue Cards list specific actions for you to take and offer you choices for the next activity to be explained.

When finished with a Cue Card, you can choose another card from the suggested list on the card, use the Back button to go back to the previous card, use the Index button to see the Index of help topics, use the Menu button to go to the main menu of Cue Card topics (labeled "The Project Planning Process"), or close the Cue Cards.

Tip

You can access Cue Cards with the Cue Card button on the Standard toolbar.

Fig. 2.4
Cue Cards stay visible on the workspace to guide you through the steps for an action.

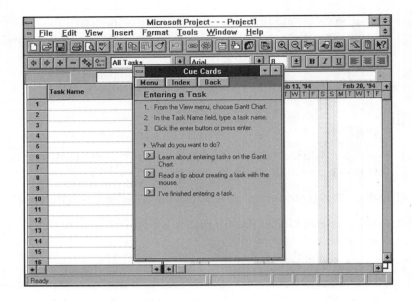

Working with the Wizards

There are still more learning aids than those accessed with the Help menu. The Planning Wizard continuously monitors your work and suggests tips for easier ways to do things, or intercepts actions that may cause problems and offers you solutions for avoiding the problems. For example, the message in figure 2.5 appears when Planning Wizard detects that a task is being moved to a non-working day and suggests appropriate ways to complete the procedure.

Fig. 2.5
The Planning Wizard helps you avoid errors, or provides tips for easier ways to do things.

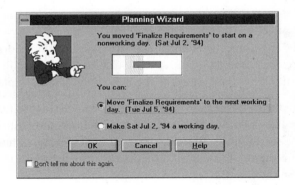

There are other Wizards that are available during specific activities to guide the user through complex tasks. For example the Gantt Chart Wizard helps you customize the graphics features of the Gantt Chart, and the Template Wizard can be used to provide customized help for preparing projects from a Template.

Opening, Saving, and Closing Files

Use the **F**ile command on the menu to open, save, and close files. Each project file resides in its own document window, and you can easily activate different project windows with the **W**indow selection on the main menu. You can have up to twenty windows open at the same time in Microsoft Project.

Creating a New File

Use the **F**ile **N**ew command to create a blank project file. All new files use generic document titles: Project1, Project2, and so on. When you issue the command to save a new file, the program opens the Save **A**s dialog box, which enables you to change the file name (see "Saving a File," later in this chapter).

Opening an Existing File

Use the **F**ile command to copy existing project files from disk into memory— which is commonly called "opening" a file. When you choose the **F**ile pull-down menu, at the bottom there is a list of up to four of the most recently used project files, with the most recent file first in the list. If you worked on a project file recently and that file you want to open is listed, choose the file name to reopen the file.

From the **F**ile menu, choose **O**pen to display the Open dialog box (see fig. 2.6). The Open dialog box displays all the Microsoft Project data files found in the current directory. The current directory is selected in the center of the Open dialog box. Use the Dri**v**es and **D**irectories boxes to choose a new current directory. Project files that contain task, resource, and cost data have the default extension .MPP. Open a project by double-clicking a file with an .MPP extension, or click the project and choose OK.

Project Management

Fig. 2.6

Choose one of the .MPP files to open a project data file.

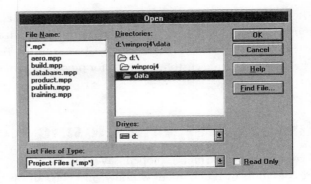

The File **N**ame list may contain files with extensions other than .MPP. Beneath the File **N**ame list is the List Files of **T**ype field. The default selection for this field is Project Files (*.MP*), which selects all project data files, template files, calendar files, view files, and workspace files. If you want to limit the display of file names to only one file type, you can designate other file extensions. For example, you can choose Projects (*.MPP), Templates (*.MPT), Calendars (*.MPC), Views (*.MPV), or Workspace (*.MPW) to restrict the File **N**ame list to just these types of files. See Chapter 14, "Exchanging Data with Other Applications," for descriptions of the other extensions.

When you open a file, you are by default given the reserved right to save changes in the file under the original file name. During the time you have the file open, other users can open the file but cannot save changes to it without saving their copy of the file under a new name. These users see a message that states their copy is a *read-only* copy of the file, and that the file cannot be saved under the original name. This option protects shared files on a network. If you attempt to save a read-only file, you are asked to change the name first. If you want to open a file without reserving the save-rights to the file, choose the **R**ead-Only check box. Then another user is allowed to open the file and save changes in the original file name. If you make changes, you have to save these changes under a new name.

If a project already is open on-screen when you open a new file, the new file resides in a separate document window and becomes the active window. See the upcoming section, "Using the Window Command," to see how to activate different files currently open.

Saving a File

When you save a file, you will see a warning from the Planning Wizard that refers to the *baseline* (see fig. 2.7). Choose OK and Microsoft Project will add the baseline to your project for you. See Chapter 12, "Managing the Project," for a description of the baseline and how to use it.

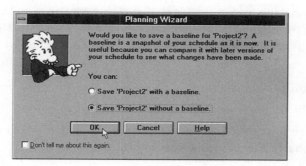

Fig. 2.7
The Planning Wizard warns you about steps you have omitted and may offer to execute them for you.

The first time you save a file, the Save As dialog box appears, in which you can specify how you want to save the file (see fig. 2.8). Give the file a distinctive name (instead of project1, project2, and so on) and, if you want, choose a different disk drive or directory in which to save the file. You must use the File Save As command to change a file's name, to save a file in a new directory or disk drive, to save a file with password protection, as a read-only file, as a file in a different format (for example, as a template), or to save a file in the format of another application (such as Excel or dBASE).

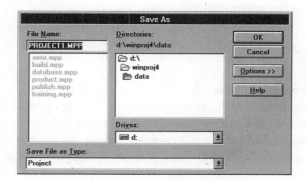

Fig. 2.8
Use the Save As dialog box to change any aspect of the way in which a file is saved.

After you use the File Save As command to establish how to save the file, you can use the File Save command to save the file immediately—with its current name—without going through the Save As dialog box.

Providing Security for Saved Files

When you save a file using the Save As command, you can choose the Options button on the dialog box to choose among the following four security features (see fig. 2.9):

- You can password protect the file so that no one can view the data without knowing a password.

- You can write protect the file so that others may open and view the file under the original name—but not save any changes to it. This feature protects the data you placed in the file, yet allows others to view the data.

- You can save the file with a warning message saying that you prefer users open the file as a read-only file.

- You can force Microsoft Project to make a backup copy of the previous version of a file every time you save the file.

Fig. 2.9
You can save a file in an encrypted form and require a password to open it.

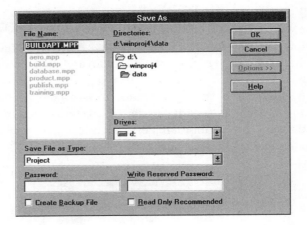

Password-Protecting a File

Protect a file by choosing the **P**assword field and typing up to 17 characters as a password. You can enter any character, including numbers and keyboard symbols. Note that the password is case-sensitive: if you enter capitals in the password, you must use capitals when you supply the password to open the file. As you type the password, each character is represented on-screen by an asterisk. When you choose OK, you are prompted to confirm the password by typing it again.

When you open the file, you are required to enter the password exactly as typed when the password was saved. If you do not enter the password correctly, including the upper- and lowercase of individual characters, you cannot use the file. It is a good idea to write down your password and store it in a safe place.

The password remains with the file each time the file is saved. To remove a password, use the Save **A**s command, and choose the **O**ptions button. Delete all characters from the password field, and choose OK.

Saving a Read-Only File

You also can save a file with a **W**rite Reserved Password. This enables all users to open the file, but a warning appears stating that the file is write reserved. If the user supplies the correct password in the password field, the file opens and the user has the right to save the file under the same name. If the user doesn't supply the correct password, the user still can open the file but as a read-only file. A read-only file can be saved only under a new name, not under the original name. Saving a file with a **W**rite Reserved Password ensures that, unless the user has the password, no one can replace the data in this file.

Saving a File as Read Only Recommended

If you mark the **R**ead Only Recommended check box, users who try to open the file are warned that you prefer the file is opened only as a read-only file. A user with write privileges, however, still can open the file. This option doesn't effectively prevent users from replacing the data in the file, but it does warn the users that the file is shared with others.

Exercising the Create Backup File Option

If you mark the Create **B**ackup File check box, the copy of the file on the disk is renamed by changing the extension from .MPP to .BAK. The active file is then saved under the original name with the .MPP extension. This procedure retains a copy of the original version of the file on disk.

Saving the Workspace

The **F**ile Save **W**orkspace command saves a small file that contains a list of the names of all the files currently open in memory. When a workspace file is opened, all the files contained in the related list of file names are also opened.

Suppose you're working on two project files when you go to lunch. If you use the Save **W**orkspace command before you save and close the individual files, after lunch you can restore all the files to the screen just by opening the one workspace file.

When you choose the Save **W**orkspace command, Microsoft Project first prompts you to save all open files that changed since the last save. You will also see the Planning Wizard warning about saving a baseline if tasks have been added that have not been added to the baseline. After you answer these prompts, the program displays the Save Workspace As dialog box. Workspace file names have the extension .MPW. Microsoft Project suggests a default workspace file name of RESUME.MPW, but you can change the name in the File **N**ame text box. Unless you choose another drive or directory, the workspace file is saved in the current directory.

Use the **F**ile **O**pen command to open a workspace file and all the files contained in its list of file names.

Saving and Using Templates

A *template* is a project file that contains a typical or standard set of tasks, resources, or other information that is used as a basis for creating new project files similar to the template. Microsoft Project provides sample templates, and you also can create your own. The *Template Wizard* can be invoked when a template is opened to provide structured guidance in using the template.

To save the active file as a template, choose **F**ile Save **A**s. Enter the File **N**ame you want to use, and from the Save File as **T**ype list, choose Template. The file-name extension is changed to .MPT automatically. When a template file is opened, the extension is changed to .MPP automatically so that the customized file will be saved as a regular project file.

Removing Files from the Workspace

Use the **C**lose command to remove the active file from memory. If the file has been changed since you last saved it, you are prompted to save the contents before closing. Choose **Y**es to save before closing. Choose **N**o to close without saving. Choose Cancel to cancel the request to close the file.

Using the Find File Command

The Find File command is a powerful new feature in Microsoft Project 4.0 that enables you to search for files by file name, location, author, and the date the files were created or last saved. Alternatively, you can use the information you enter in the Summary Info dialog box (refer to "Providing Summary Information about the New Project" in Chapter 3). You also can search for specific text that occurs in a project document. You can specify search criteria as broadly or narrowly as you want. The more you narrow the search, the fewer files that will be found.

The files found by using the criteria you specified are listed in the Find File dialog box (see fig. 2.10). From there, you can browse through the directories that you included in the search, sort the files in the list, and preview any file without opening it in Microsoft Project. Further, you can view information about a file, specifically the file name, title, size, author, and date last saved, or you can view the summary information that is entered for a file.

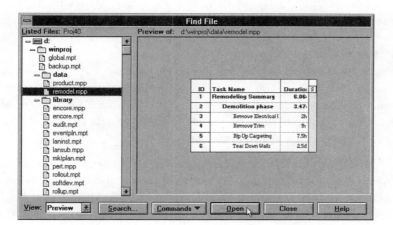

Fig. 2.10
All the files that meet the search criteria you specify are listed in the Find File dialog box.

You can accomplish many other file-related tasks from the Find File dialog box. You can select as many files as you want in the list, and then open, print, copy, or delete the files. The capability of working with multiple files is a powerful feature of the Find File command and a great timesaver.

When you save a file, you give it a file name and then decide where you want to store the saved file. As the number of files you create in Microsoft Project increases, you may want to come up with some system for organizing files. The easiest way is to set up directories on the hard disk that contain related files. For example, you might have one directory for new construction projects and another one for remodeling projects. You also might have a directory for each of the projects on which you are working. When you save a project file, be sure that you do so in the appropriate directory. In this way, it is easier to retrieve the project if you need to work with it again.

After you have decided where to store your files, you still need to locate them when you want to work with them again. If you haven't worked with a project for a long time, you can easily forget its name or location when you want to reopen it. Or you may want to look over a group of related projects without having to open each one in Microsoft Project. You can use the Find File command to bring together a list of related files or to find a specific file.

Project Management

After you have found all the files that match the criteria you specified, you can browse through the directories and files found by the search until you find the file or files with which you want to work. You can preview any file to make sure that it is the one you want and then open, print, copy, or delete the file. To act on several files at once, you can select them first and then issue one of the commands that acts on these files. You can select a group of files, for example, and then copy them to a floppy disk to back them up, or print several files at once without opening the files in Microsoft Project.

Finding Files

Before you can use the Find File commands that manage files, you need to find the files with which you want to work. The search can be narrow; for example, you can look for a particular file with a familiar file name. You also can search for a group of files that match whatever criteria you specify. This section shows you the ways you can search for files.

 You begin a search for files by choosing the File Find File command. Alternatively, you can choose the Find File button in the Open dialog box. There is also a button on the Workgroup Toolbar to activate File find. To find files, you must specify the *search criteria* that Find File uses to look for the files. The first time you use the Find File command, Microsoft Project displays the Search dialog box so that you can describe the files or directory you want to search. After you complete the first search with Find File, subsequent uses of the Find File command will display the Find File dialog box with the list of files that match the criteria for which you last searched.

Fig. 2.11
You specify the criteria for a simple file name or directory search in the Search dialog box.

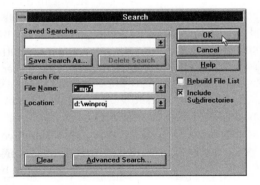

To change the found files shown in the listing, you must specify new or additional criteria and then initiate a new search in the Search dialog box (see fig. 2.11). You can limit the search to a file with a specific file name; to all Microsoft Project files that end with the extension .MP*; or to all types of files, regardless of extension. To limit the scope of the search to one disk drive or to certain directories on a disk, you can specify the location for the search.

Using the **A**dvanced Search command, you can narrow the list of files that must be found (see fig. 2.12). You do this by specifying additional criteria, such as the file creation or save date, author name, summary information, or specific text strings (such as a word or phrase).

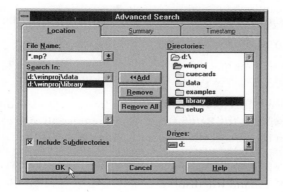

Fig. 2.12
You can enter additional search criteria in the Advanced Search dialog box.

After you specify search criteria, you initiate a new search by choosing OK in the Search dialog box. If you must cancel a search before it is completed, choose Cancel. The files meeting the new search criteria are listed in the Find File dialog box. For instructions on how to view file information and preview the files in the list, see the upcoming section, "Viewing Project and File Information."

Searching Different Drives or Directories

If you know where the files you are looking for are located, you can indicate specific directories to search. This technique speeds up the process of finding the files because Find File does not have to search the entire hard disk. For example, you may know that the files you want to find are in one or more of the subdirectories of the \WINPROJ directory. In this case, you can limit the search to these subdirectories. You also can specify a different drive for a search, such as a floppy drive.

To specify the directories to search, follow these steps:

1. Choose the **F**ile **F**ind File command, or the **F**ind File button in the Open dialog box. The Find File dialog box appears, listing the files that meet the current search criteria (refer to fig. 2.10).

2. Choose the **S**earch button in the Find File dialog box. The Search dialog box appears (fig. 2.11).

3. From the **L**ocation list, select the drive you want to search.

4. Choose the **A**dvanced Search button, and select the **L**ocation tab. The Location tab of the Advanced Search dialog box is displayed (see fig. 2.12).

   The directories that are currently searched are listed in the S**e**arch In list.

5. To add a directory to the S**e**arch In list, select the directory in the **D**irectories box, and choose the **A**dd button.

6. To remove a directory from the S**e**arch In list, select the directory in the list, and choose the **R**emove button. To remove all directories from the Search In list, choose the Re**m**ove All button.

   If you are connected to a network, you can use the Net**w**ork button to connect to a network drive and then select the network drive from the Dri**v**es list. The directories for the network drive are listed in the **D**irectories list, and you can select which directories you include in the search as described in steps 5 and 6. If you aren't connected to a network, the Net**w**ork button doesn't appear.

7. To include all the subdirectories of the directories listed in the S**e**arch In list, select the Include Su**b**directories check box.

8. Choose OK in the Advanced Search dialog box, and then choose OK in the Search dialog box to begin the search.

The files matching the location criteria and other criteria specified are listed in the Find File dialog box.

Searching for Specific Files or Different File Types

By default, Microsoft Project searches for all project files in the specified directories (or on the entire drive if no path has been specified). However, you also can search for a specific file or different types of files. If the files are compatible with Microsoft Project, you can open or print the files; you can copy or delete the files you find, even if they are not compatible with Microsoft Project.

To search for different file types, follow these steps:

1. Choose the **F**ile **F**ind File command, or the **F**ind File button in the Open dialog box. The Find File dialog box appears, listing the files that meet the current search criteria (refer to fig. 2.10).

2. Choose the **S**earch button. The Search dialog box appears (refer to fig. 2.11).

3. In the File **N**ame box, type the name of the file for which you want to search. Be sure to include the file extension.

4. To search instead for a file type, pull down the **F**ile Name list, and select the type of file for which you want to search.

   In the File **N**ame box, type also the extension of the file type for which you want to search. If necessary, you can use wild-card characters. An asterisk (*) represents any string of characters; you can search for all files ending with the extension .MPP by typing *.MPP. A question mark (?) represents any one character; you can search for SUBDIV*.MP? to find all files named SUBDIV1.MPP, SUBDIV23.MPP, SUBDIV.MPT, and so on.

   By default, Microsoft Project replaces the existing file list with a new list of files matching the current search criteria. To add the files that match the new criteria to the existing list, choose the **A**dvanced Search button, and select the **S**ummary tab. Next select Add Matches to List from the Options list, and choose OK.

5. Choose OK.

Searching by Summary Information or Text in the File

One of the biggest advantages to including summary information in all Microsoft Project files is that you can search for files by text contained in any of the summary information fields. You can add a title to a project, for example, and then use it to search through files. In this way, Microsoft Project enables you to override the DOS limitation of an eight-character file name. You also can search for a file based on any of the text contained in it.

▶ "Providing Summary Information about the New Project," p. 74

To search by summary information or any text in the file, follow these steps:

1. Choose the **F**ile **F**ind File command, or the **F**ind File button in the Open dialog box. The Find File dialog box appears, listing the files that meet the current search criteria (refer to fig. 2.10).

2. Choose the **S**earch button to display the Search dialog box (refer to fig. 2.11).

3. Choose the **A**dvanced Search button. The Advanced Search dialog box appears (refer to fig. 2.12).

4. Select the **S**ummary tab. The Summary tab appears (see fig. 2.13).

Fig. 2.13
A partially complete Summary tab.

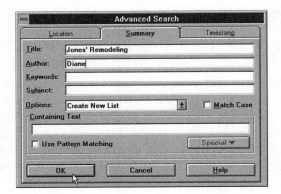

5. In the appropriate text boxes, type the summary information for which you want to search:

Text Box	Searches For
Title	Text you enter in the Title box
Author	Text you enter in the Author box
Keywords	Text you enter in the Keywords box
Subject	Text you enter in the Subject box

6. Select **M**atch Case to match upper- and lowercase exactly.

7. To search the contents of a project file, enter the text to search for in the **C**ontaining Text box. To add special symbols or wild cards to the search text, select the Use Pattern Matching check box, and choose the

Sp**e**cial button to display a list of special characters. Select a character to insert in the search text.

8. From the Options list, select one of the the following options:

    Create New List   Replaces the existing list.

    Add Matches to List   Adds the new list to the exiting list.

    Search Only in List Searches for criteria only in the existing list. (This option doesn't apply when you search a different drive or directory.)

9. Choose OK twice.

A few rules exist for searching files by summary information or text in the file. You can type as many as 255 characters in any of the summary information fields in the Summary tab (shown in fig. 2.13). You can use partial words or any combination of upper- and lowercase letters. If you type **an** or **An** in the Title field, for example, you get a list of files that contain the words *annual* or *bank*, as well as any other files that have the letters *an* in their titles. (Select the **M**atch Case option to match upper- and lowercase exactly.) To search for a phrase, such as *subdivision finished*, enclose it in double quotation marks, as in "subdivision finished." You can use wild cards in the search, and you can combine words, as the following examples show:

To Search for	Type in the Text Box
Any single character *Example:* type **an??** to find *annual* or *Andy*.	? (question mark)
Any string of characters *Example:* type **an*** to find any word that begins with the letters *an*.	* (asterisk)
A phrase (such as *bank loan*) *Example:* type "bank loan."	" " (quotation marks enclosing the phrase)
One word or another word *Example:* type **subdivision,county** to find files containing *subdivision* or *county*.	, (comma)
One word and another word *Example:* type **subdivision & county** or **subdivision county** to find files containing *subdivision* and *county*.	& (ampersand or space)
Files not containing *Example:* type **subdivision~county** to find files containing *subdivision* but not *county*.	~ (tilde)

Searching by Date Saved or Created

You can search for files based on the last date you created or saved the file. This feature is convenient, especially when used with other search criteria. You can search for files, for example, containing the title words *subdivision* and *county* that were created between June 1 and June 30 of last year.

To search for files by date created or saved, follow these steps:

1. Choose either the **F**ile **F**ind File command, or the **F**ind File button in the Open dialog box. The Find File dialog box appears, listing the files that meet the current search criteria (refer to fig. 2.10).

2. Choose the **S**earch button to display the Search dialog box (refer to fig. 2.11).

3. Choose the **A**dvanced Search button. The Advanced Search dialog box appears (refer to fig. 2.12).

4. Select the Timestam**p** tab. The Timestamp tab appears (see fig. 2.14).

Fig. 2.14
Use the Timestamp tab to establish date criteria for a search.

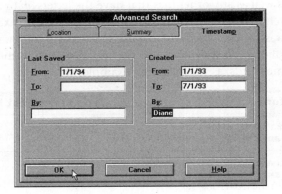

5. To search for files by date last saved, in the **F**rom box type the beginning date of the range of dates for which you want to search. In the **T**o box, type the ending date. Use the format *mm/dd/yy* (for example, 6/1/93).

   To search for files last saved on a specific date, enter the same date in both the **F**rom and **T**o boxes. To search for files saved since the **F**rom date, leave the **T**o box empty. To search for files saved before the **T**o date, leave the **F**rom box empty.

6. To search for files by the date the file was created, in the **F**rom box type the beginning date of the range of dates for which you want to search. In the **T**o box, type the ending date. Use the format *mm/dd/yy* (for example, 6/1/93).

   To search for files created on a specific date, enter the same date in both the **F**rom and **T**o boxes. To search for files created since the **F**rom date, leave the **T**o box empty. To search for files created before the **T**o date, leave the **F**rom box empty.

7. You can specify the author of the file by typing the name in either the **B**y or the B**y** box.

8. Choose OK.

Saving Search Criteria

If you have entered a set of search criteria and you want to reuse it for future searches, you can save the criteria with a name. When you want to reuse the criteria, you select the named set of criteria from the Search dialog box and then initiate a new search.

To save search criteria, follow these steps:

1. Choose either the **F**ile **F**ind File command, or the **F**ind File button in the Open dialog box. The Find File dialog box appears, listing the files that meet the current search criteria (refer to fig. 2.10).

2. Set up the search criteria you want, as outlined in the preceding sections.

3. Choose the **S**ave Search As button in the Search dialog box. The Save Search As dialog box appears (see fig. 2.15).

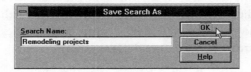

Fig. 2.15
You can give a name to a set of search criteria so that you can reuse it.

4. In the **S**earch Name text box, type a name for the search criteria.

5. Choose OK.

6. To start a search with these criteria, choose OK.

To reuse saved search criteria, follow these steps:

1. Select the set of criteria you want to use from the Saved Searches list in the Search dialog box.

2. Choose OK to begin the search using the saved criteria.

The name of the set of search criteria used in the search appears at the top of the listed files.

Viewing Project and File Information

After you find the files with which you want to work, you can sort the list of found files and view file information or preview a file. Viewing file information and previewing files can help you manage your project files. You can preview a file, for example, before you open or print it so that you know you are working with the right project. You also can view file information to find out which is the most recent version of a project on which you are working.

Using Find File To View Projects and File Information

After you complete a search by using the criteria you specify, all the files matching the criteria are listed in the Listed Files box in the Find File dialog box (see fig. 2.16). The matching files are listed by directory, starting with the root directory. Each directory that contains files that match the criteria is represented by a folder in the Listed Files box. The name of the directory appears on the right side of the folder icon. Closed folders have a plus sign (+) beside them and can be opened to display the files in the folder. To do this, click the plus sign or use the arrow keys to move the highlight to the folder, and press Enter. Open folders are displayed with a minus sign (–) next to them. To close a folder, click the minus sign or use the arrow keys to move the highlight to the folder, and press Enter.

Before you can view a file or its information, you must select the file. To select the file, click the file name with the mouse or press the Tab key until the focus (the dotted lines) is in the box with the list of files. Then use the up- and down-arrow keys to select the file.

The rest of this section describes how to sort a list of files, preview a file, and view file information.

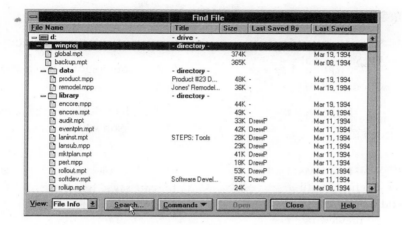

Fig. 2.16
The Find File dialog box displays a list of files matching your search criteria.

Sorting File Lists

If the list of files in a directory is long, you may want to sort the listed files. You can sort by file name, author, size, creation date, or date last saved. You also can sort by using the name of the person who most recently saved the file. You can list the files by file name or by the title entered in the Summary Info dialog box.

To sort a list of files, follow these steps:

1. Choose the **F**ile **F**ind File command, or the **F**ind File button in the Open dialog box.

2. Choose the **C**ommands button in the Find File dialog box. Then choose Sor**t**ing. The Options dialog box is displayed (see fig. 2.17).

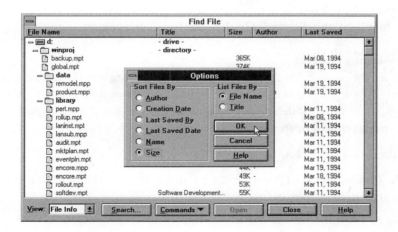

Fig. 2.17
In the Options dialog box, you can select how you want to sort and list files.

3. In the Sort Files By list, select one of the following sorting options:

Author	Sorts alphabetically by author.
Creation **D**ate	Sorts chronologically by creation date.
Last Saved **B**y	Sorts alphabetically by the name of the person who last saved the file.
Last Saved Date	Sorts chronologically by the date files are saved (most recent date first).
Name	Sorts alphabetically by File Name or Title depending on the option button you select in the List Files By area.
Si**z**e	Sorts numerically by file size, smallest to largest.

4. Select one of the following List Files By options:

Filename	Lists files by file name.
Title	Lists files by title used in the Summary Info for each file.

5. Choose OK.

The files in all the directories in the Find File dialog box are sorted.

Previewing Projects

Among the most useful features in the Find File dialog box is the capability of previewing a project. When you make decisions about what files you want to open, copy, print, or delete, it is helpful to preview files' contents quickly, without having to open them.

To preview a file, follow these steps:

1. Choose **F**ile **F**ind File from the menu, or the Find File button in the Open dialog box.

2. From the **V**iew list in the Find File dialog box, select Preview (see fig. 2.18).

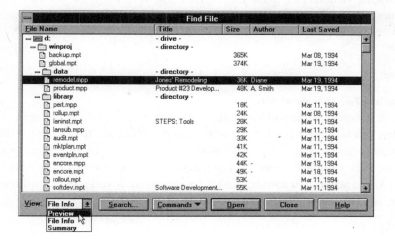

3. Select the file you want to preview from the list of files. A reduced view of the file contents is displayed in the Preview Of box (see fig 2.19).

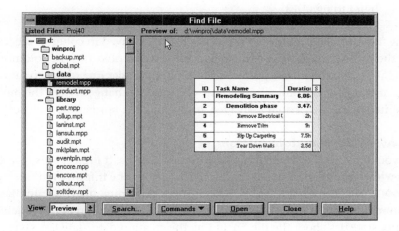

Note

Selecting Preview as the view in the Find File dialog box can slow you down if you don't have a fast computer because the Preview area is redrawn each time you select a new document from the file list. Use the File Info or Summary view to speed up things.

Viewing File Information

You can view information for a file rather than view the file's contents. When you select the File Info view, information for each file in the file list is displayed next to the name of the file. You see different information, depending on how you have sorted the file list. For example, if you sort by name, the title, size, author, and date last saved are displayed. If you sort by creation date, the Last Saved field is replaced by the Created field.

To view file information, follow these steps:

1. Choose the **F**ile **F**ind File command, or the **F**ind File button in the Open dialog box.

2. Select File Info in the **V**iew list at the bottom of the Find File dialog box (refer to fig. 2.18).

The file information for each file in the list is displayed in columns adjacent to the list (see fig. 2.20). You can change the width of any of the columns. To do this, move the mouse pointer over the right border line of the column heading for the column whose width you want to change. When the mouse pointer changes to a double-headed arrow, drag the border to a new position.

Viewing Summary Information

If you chose to add summary information to Microsoft Project files, you can view this information in the Find File dialog box. The information can include title, author name, subject, keywords, and comments you enter in the Summary Info dialog box. The summary information automatically includes other statistics about the file, including the creation date, date last saved, and size of the file. Therefore, even if you don't add summary information when you save the file, you see some information when you view the summary information.

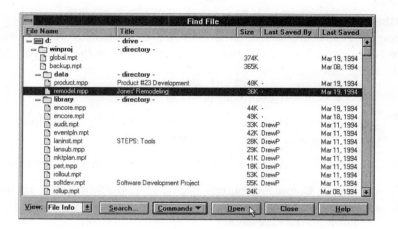

Fig. 2.20
You can use the
File Info view to
view information
about the files
listed in the Find
File dialog box.

To view summary information, take these steps:

1. Choose the **F**ile **F**ind File command, or the **F**ind File button in the
   Open dialog box.

2. Select Summary in the **V**iew list at the bottom of the Find File dialog
   box (refer to fig. 2.18).

The summary information and document statistics are displayed for the file
selected in the Listed Files box (see fig. 2.21).

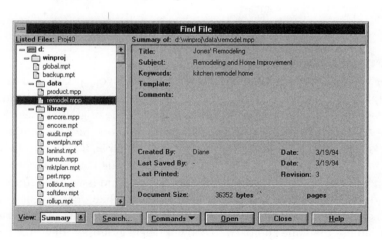

Fig. 2.21
You can view the
summary informa-
tion for a file in
the Find File
dialog box.

Editing and Adding Summary Information

If you didn't add summary information to a project file when you created or saved it, or if you want to edit the summary information for a file, you can do so from the Find File dialog box.

To edit or add summary information, follow these steps:

1. Choose the **F**ile **F**ind File command, or the **F**ind File button in the Open dialog box. The Find File dialog box appears.

2. From the **L**isted Files box, select the file with which you want to work.

3. Choose the **C**ommands button, and then choose **S**ummary from the submenu. The Summary Info dialog box from Microsoft Project is displayed for the selected file.

4. Fill in or edit any of the fields. Include as much information (up to 255 characters) or as little as you want.

5. Choose OK.

> **Note**
>
> Use the Summary Info box to attach a descriptive title to all the Microsoft Project documents. Then list the files by title in the Find File dialog box. This makes it easier to identify your files in the file list, and helps you work around the eight-character limitation for DOS file names.

Working with Files

After you find the files that meet the search criteria you specify, you can accomplish many tasks with these files by using the commands in the Find File dialog box. You can open, print, copy, or delete a file or group of selected files—all from this dialog box. Selecting more than one file at a time from the **L**isted Files list is a tremendous timesaver. For example, if you want to print several files at once, you can find all of them with the Find File command. Then you can select all the files you want to print and issue one print command. This approach is much simpler and quicker than opening each of the files, one by one, from within Microsoft Project and printing them separately. You can use the same approach to copy or delete groups of files. This capability, along with being able to preview the contents of a file without having to open it, greatly facilitates the process of managing your files.

Selecting Files with Which To Work

Before you issue various commands to manage files, you need to select one or more of the files with which you want to work. To select a file with the mouse, click the name of the file you want; or press and hold down the Ctrl key and click multiple file names (see fig. 2.22). If you want to select several sequential files, press and hold down the Shift key, and then click the first and last file you want. (Press and hold down the Ctrl key, and click a second time to deselect any file you select by mistake.)

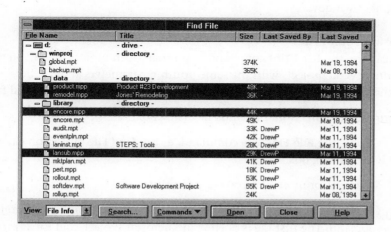

Fig. 2.22
Multiple files selected in the file list.

To select a file with the keyboard, press the Tab key until the focus (the dotted line) is in the Listed Files box. Then use the up- or down-arrow key to move to the file you want to select. To select multiple files that are not contiguous, press Shift+F8. Then move to each file you want to select, and press the space bar. Press Shift+F8 again to turn off the multiple-selection mode. To select multiple contiguous files, press the up- or down-arrow key to select the first file. Next, press and hold down Shift, and then press the up- or down-arrow key to extend the selection.

Opening Found Files

After you use the Find File command to find and select a file, you can open it from the Find File dialog box. You can also open more than one file.

To find and open documents, take these steps:

1. Choose the File Find File command, or the Find File button on the Open dialog box.

2. Select the file or files you want to open.

3. Choose the Open button.

4. If you want to prevent yourself from modifying any of the files you open, choose the **C**ommands button. Then choose the Open **R**ead-Only command from the submenu.

When you choose the Open button, all files open, each in a separate document window.

Printing Found Files

▶ "Printing Views and Reports," p. 443

You can use the **F**ile **P**rint command to print an open project file. If you want to print several projects with the same printing parameters at once, however, use the **F**ind File command to first find and then print multiple selected files.

To print documents from the Find File dialog box:

1. Choose the **F**ile **F**ind File command, or the **F**ind File button on the Open dialog box.

2. Select one or more files you want to print.

3. Choose the **C**ommands button and then the **P**rint command from the submenu. The first file is opened in Microsoft Project, and the Print dialog box appears for you to select print options and print. Project files are opened in the view in which they were saved.

4. Select the printing options for each file and print.

5. Select the printing options and print each file as it is opened in succession.

> **Note**
>
> If you routinely need to print the same set of projects, such as the projects you use in a report, set up a search criteria that finds only these files. Then save the search criteria set. When you need to print these documents, select the set of criteria from the Saved Searches list. Next, run the search and select all the found files. Then issue the **P**rint command.

Copying Found Files

You can use Find File to copy selected files from one location to another. Similarly, you can use a combination of techniques to move files. You must first copy them to their new locations and then delete them from their original locations.

To find and copy files, follow these steps:

1. Choose the **F**ile **F**ind File command, or choose the **F**ind File button on the Open dialog box.

2. Select one or more files you want to copy.

3. Choose the **C**ommands button, and then select the **C**opy command from the submenu. The Copy dialog box appears (see fig. 2.23).

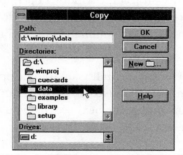

Fig. 2.23
You can copy files to another location using the Copy dialog box.

4. If the destination is on another drive, select the drive from the Drives list.

5. If you want to create a new directory to copy the files to, select the directory you want the new directory to be a subdirectory of, and choose the **N**ew button. Type the name for the new directory, and choose OK.

6. In the **D**irectories box, select the directory to which you want to copy the file(s), or type the path name in the **P**ath text box.

7. Choose OK.

Files are copied to a new location with their original name and extension.

Deleting Found Files

To find and delete files, follow these steps:

1. Choose the **F**ile **F**ind File command, or choose the **F**ind File button on the Open dialog box.

2. Select the files you want to delete.

3. Choose the **C**ommands button and then the **D**elete command from the submenu. A dialog box asks you to confirm the deletion.

4. Choose **Y**es to delete the files, or choose **N**o if you don't want to erase them. (Select Help to learn more about deleting files.)

Using the Window Command

You can have up to twenty project file windows open in memory at the same time. You can place one file at a time on-screen for viewing, or you can place all the files on-screen for simultaneous viewing using the **A**rrange All command.

The Microsoft Project **W**indow menu lists up to nine open file windows at the bottom of the pull-down menu (see fig. 2.24). A dot indicates the currently active file. You can choose the next file that you want to activate by choosing a file from the list.

Fig. 2.24
Select the next project file to view by selecting it from the Window menu.

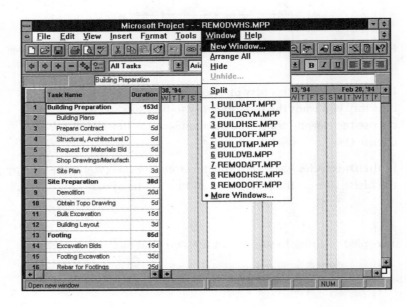

If more than nine file windows are open in memory, the **M**ore Windows command appears at the bottom of the **W**indow menu. Choose the **M**ore Windows command to access the Window Activate dialog box (see fig. 2.25). The Window Activate dialog box enables you to choose the window you want from a scroll list. Choose the file you want to activate, and choose the OK button.

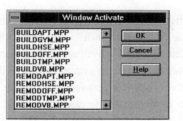

Fig. 2.25
Use the Window Activate dialog box if you have more than nine files open.

You also can use Ctrl+F6 to activate the next window. Pressing Ctrl+F6 returns you to the window that you most recently left; press the key combination again to return to the window you left before that, and so on. See Chapter 13 for more information on working with multiple files.

Exploring the Microsoft Project Window

When Microsoft Project first starts, you see the Microsoft Project title bar at the top of the screen, along with the Microsoft Project menu, two toolbars, and an entry bar. The Status bar is visible at the bottom of the screen, and the data area in the center of the screen will display the project data.

The display in the data area is a known as a *view*. The term view refers to the way that the project data is displayed. The default view is the Gantt Chart, which shows a list of task names on the left and a timescale on the right (where a bar chart will show the beginning and ending of each task). Some views are *forms* that show many details about one task or resource at a time. Some views are *graphics images*, like the Gantt Chart, that present data in bar charts or network diagrams. Some views are *spreadsheets* that show data in columns and rows. Still other views are combinations of these basic types.

The Menu Bar

The Microsoft Project menu is almost identical to the menus in the other Microsoft Office products (Word, Excel, and PowerPoint). The menu commands will be defined and described in detail in later chapters, as the functions that they perform are discussed.

The Toolbars

Appearing below the menu bar, the toolbars contain buttons that you can activate with the mouse to provide shortcut access to frequently used menu choices or special functions. The individual buttons on the toolbar are described as you encounter them in the chapters that follow. A brief description appears beneath toolbar buttons if you rest the mouse pointer over a toolbar for several seconds. For more complete descriptions of the toolbar buttons, use the Microsoft Project **H**elp menu. From the **H**elp menu, choose **C**ontents. From the Contents screen choose Reference Information and then the Toolbars and Buttons item from the General Reference category.

There are nine toolbars provided in Microsoft Project. The two displayed initially are the Standard toolbar and the Formatting toolbar. You can add and remove toolbars and create your own custom toolbars.

Showing and Hiding Toolbars

To show additional toolbars, or to hide one that is currently displayed, choose the **V**iew **T**oolbars command. The Toolbars dialog box appears (see fig. 2.26). Choose the toolbar you want to show, and choose the **S**how button. If you choose a toolbar that is already displayed, the **S**how button is replaced by a **H**ide button. Choosing the **H**ide button hides that toolbar.

Fig. 2.26
Use the Toolbars dialog box to show or hide toolbars.

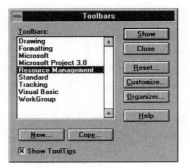

You also can use the toolbar shortcut menu to show and hide toolbars.
Position the mouse pointer over one of the visible toolbars and click the
secondary mouse button to display the shortcut menu (see fig. 2.27). Toolbars
that are checked are currently displayed. Choose a checked toolbar to hide it;
choose an unchecked toolbar to show it.

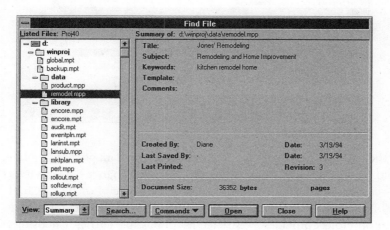

Fig. 2.27
Use the toolbars
shortcut menu to
quickly show or
hide a toolbar.

The Entry Bar

The Entry bar is on the line below the toolbars (see fig. 2.28). The Entry bar
performs the following functions:

- The left end of the Entry bar displays progress messages that let you
  know when Microsoft Project is engaged in calculating, opening and
  saving files, leveling resources, and so on.

- The center of the Entry bar contains an entry area where data entry
  and editing takes place. During Entry and Editing modes, Cancel and
  Enter boxes also appear. When the data being entered or edited has
  an entry list available, an entry-list arrow appears at the far right of
  the text area.

Fig. 2.28
When the data area has an entry list, the entry list arrow appears at the right of the Edit Bar.

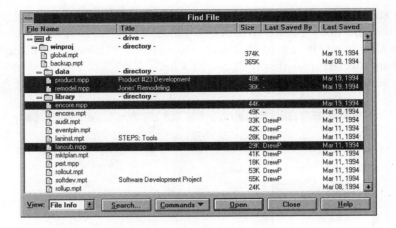

Use the entry area to enter data in a field or to edit data previously placed in a field. You use the entry area primarily when you change data in views that show a spreadsheet table or when you enter task data in the PERT Chart. The entry-list arrow appears only when you choose a field of data for which Microsoft Project provides a restricted list of possible entries. Choosing the entry-list arrow causes an entry-list to appear. Selecting an item in the entry list places this value in the entry area. You can use the Cancel box in place of pressing the Esc key to cancel an editing event, and you can use the Enter box in place of pressing Enter to conclude an editing event.

To enter data in the project, choose the field where you want the data to appear and begin typing. The entry area is activated and displays the typed data as you proceed. In the entry area, you can make changes to data before you place the data in the field. To enter the data, either press Enter, choose the Enter box to the left of the entry area, or use the mouse or keyboard to select another field. To cancel the data entry and leave the selected field unchanged, click the Cancel box or press Esc.

To edit data, select the field to edit and activate the Entry bar by clicking in the entry area or by pressing the F2 function key. The contents of the current field are displayed in the entry area so that you can make changes.

The appearance of an entry-list arrow on-screen indicates that you can display an entry list to help fill the field. To display the entry list, select the entry-list arrow or press Alt+down arrow (see fig. 2.28). To choose an item from the list, select the item, or use the arrow keys to highlight the choice and press Enter. For example, when you assign resources to tasks, you can activate the Entry bar list to display the list of currently defined resources.

Note

When the entry bar is active, many features of Microsoft Project are unavailable. Most menu commands, toolbar buttons, and quick keys are also unavailable. Be sure that you close the entry bar by pressing Enter or by selecting the Enter box after entering or editing data in a field.

The Status Bar

The Status bar is located at the bottom of the window and shows the status of special keys, displays advisory messages, and describes the current menu choice when the menu is active (see fig. 2.28).

- At the left end of the Status bar is the mode indicator. This indicator displays "Ready" when Microsoft Project is waiting for you to begin an operation. The mode indicator displays "Enter" when you enter data and "Edit" when you edit a field entry.

   When you activate the menu, the mode indicator displays a description of the menu choice currently highlighted.

- The middle of the Status bar is used to display warning messages in cases when recalculation is needed, when resources are over-allocated, and when circular relationships are created while linking tasks. (See Chapter 5, "Entering Scheduling Requirements," for more information about circular relationships.)

- The far right end of the Status bar is used to indicate the status of the Extend, Add, Caps Lock, Num Lock, Scroll Lock, and Insert keys. When you turn on one of these keys, the key name appears in the Status bar.

   The Extend (F8) and Add (Shift+F8) keys are used when you use the keyboard to extend the selection of data to multiple fields before you initiate some action on those fields. See the section, "Selecting Data Fields in Tables," at the end of this chapter for more information about these keys.

   The Caps Lock key forces the alphabet keys to produce capital letters without holding down the Shift key and to produce lowercase letters if you apply the Shift key.

The Num Lock key activates the numbers on the keys in the number key pad area of the keyboard (the far right section of most key boards).

The Scroll Lock key is used in views that have a spreadsheet table display. When activated, the Scroll Lock key causes the arrow keys to drag the selected field around the screen while keeping the same field selected.

The Insert key is used when using the entry area in the Entry bar. When the entry area is active, you can press the Insert key to switch from Insert mode to Overstrike mode. (The OVR indicator appears in the Status bar as long as Overstrike mode is active.) Press the Insert key again to return to Insert mode.

Introducing the Gantt Chart View

The default view of a new project is the Gantt Chart view (shown in fig. 2.29). The Gantt Chart view is the most often used view for listing the project tasks.

Fig. 2.29
The Gantt Chart is the default view for Microsoft Project.

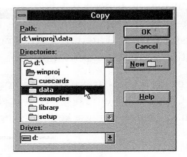

The Gantt Chart View

The Gantt Chart view is a graphical view that contains a spreadsheet table on the left side and a bar chart on the right side. The table displays the task list, which includes the name and duration of each task. Additional columns, hidden behind the bar chart, are also included in the table. You can scroll the additional fields into view with the arrow keys or with the scroll bar beneath the table. The task list can be created in an outline format to show the major phases of a project with subordinate details indented to the right.

The bar chart on the right displays a timescale at the top and a horizontal bar beneath for each task. The position of the bar indicates when the task starts and finishes. Use the scroll bars below the bar chart to scroll through the timescale. If you drag the horizontal scroll button on the timescale, an information box appears to identify the time as you scroll forward and backward. The scroll bar to the right of the Gantt Chart enables you to scroll up and down the task list without affecting the selected task. If you drag the vertical scroll button, an information box appears to tell you the task you will locate when you release the button.

The Gantt Chart and most other views may fill the entire window (as the Gantt Chart does in the initial display), or a combination of views may appear together—one in the top pane of the window and one in the bottom pane. Microsoft Project refers to these combination views as *dual-pane* views.

The view in figure 2.30, for example, is a dual-pane view. The top pane, shows the same Gantt Chart. The bottom pane is called the Task Form, and it shows more detail about the task that is selected in the top pane. This particular combination, the Gantt Chart over the Task Form, is called the Task Entry View. To add the Task Form to the Gantt Chart, choose the **S**plit command from the **W**indow menu.

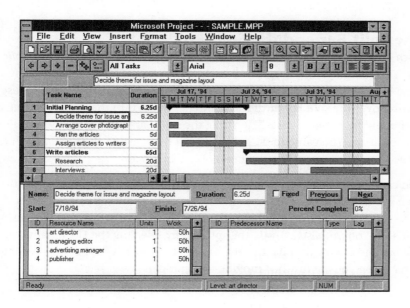

Fig. 2.30
The Task Entry view is a popular dual-pane view.

The bottom pane of combination views always displays details about the task you select in the view in the top pane. Therefore, the top view of a combination view is the main view, and the bottom view shows extra detail or a different perspective for the task selected in the top view. The same principle holds true when the top view displays resources rather than tasks; the bottom view shows details for the resource selected in the top view.

Use F6 to switch between panes in a combination view, or click the mouse pointer anywhere in the pane you want to activate.

The Task Form

The task form includes fields that do not appear on the standard spreadsheet table in the Gantt Chart. The form also displays Resource assignments and Predecessor task relationships in small tables at the bottom of the form.

The Active View Bar

The Active View bar is a narrow vertical strip along the left edge of both top and bottom panes (see fig. 2.31). The purpose of the Active View bar is to signal which pane is active. When a pane is active, the corresponding Active View bar displays the same color as the window title bar. When the pane is inactive, the bar is clear.

The Split Bar and the Split Box

With combination views, the top and bottom panes are separated by a *split bar*. You can move the split bar up or down to change how much of each pane is displayed. You activate the split bar by moving the tip of the mouse pointer over the split bar until the pointer changes into the shape illustrated in the middle of figure 2.31. Then drag the split bar with the mouse to its new position. You can also drag the split bar by dragging the *split box*, which is the short black bar at the right end of the split bar.

You can also use Shift+F6 to activate the split bar from the keyboard, and then use the arrow keys or the mouse to resize the panes. You must press Enter or click the left mouse button to finish moving the split bar after using Shift+F6. You can also activate the split bar by selecting the Document control bar and choosing Spli**t**. Use the mouse or arrow keys as before, pressing Enter when you are finished moving the split bar.

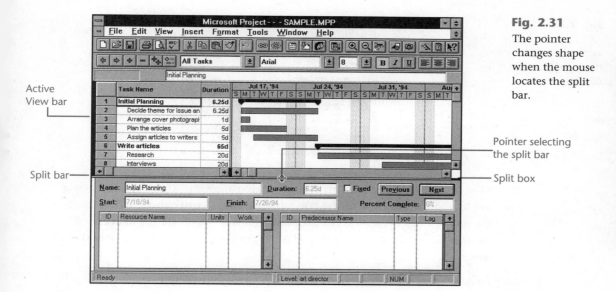

Fig. 2.31
The pointer changes shape when the mouse locates the split bar.

Active View bar

Split bar

Pointer selecting the split bar

Split box

Some panes also have a vertical *divider bar*. The Gantt Chart, for example, has a vertical divider bar between the spreadsheet area and the timescale. You can relocate the vertical divider bar just as you do the horizontal split bar by dragging with the mouse or by using Shift+F6 and the arrow keys. This action enables you to display more of the spreadsheet or the timescale area.

If you double-click the split bar or the split box, a combination view becomes a single-pane view (which displays only what was formerly in the top pane), and the split box is relocated at the bottom right of the screen. Double-clicking the split box in a single-pane view returns you to a dual-pane view. When a single pane view is displayed, the mouse pointer does not activate the split bar. You must use the **W**indow **S**plit command, the split box, the Shift+F6 keys, or the Document Control button and the Spli**t** command to activate the split bar.

Changing Views

Many views are available for displaying a project. The **V**iew menu lists the most often used views, but all of the views are displayed if you choose **M**ore Views from the **V**iew menu. Figure 2.32 shows the More Views dialog box that appears.

Fig. 2.32
All of the defined
views are listed in
the More Views
dialog box.

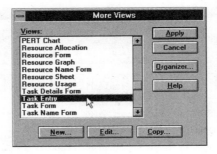

Most views listed in the menu display single-pane views that you can choose to place in the top pane or the bottom pane. When you choose a view from the menu, the view appears in the pane that was active when you accessed the menu. The Task Entry view and other combination views replace both panes.

To display the Task Sheet view in the top pane, for example, follow these steps:

1. Activate the top pane.

2. Choose **M**ore Views from the **V**iew menu.

3. Scroll through the list of views to **T**ask Sheet.

4. Choose Task Sheet.

5. Choose the Apply button.

Scrolling and Selecting Data Fields

Unless a project is very small, you probably won't see more than a small part of all the data on-screen at one time. There are several ways to scroll through all the data fields in a project.

Scrolling through the data fields differs from *moving* through the data fields. Scrolling changes the screen display to show new data fields without changing the field selected for data entry or editing. Moving changes the selected data field. Scroll bars are provided on all views except the forms.

The most widely used scrolling and moving methods are presented in this section. More specific methods are presented in the chapters that introduce the different views. For example, see Chapter 4 for details about using the various Task views and Chapter 8 for the Resource views.

Using the Scroll Bars

You use the vertical scroll bar along the right side of a view to scroll through the rows of tasks or resources displayed in the view. If you drag the scroll box, you will see a small box next to the top of the scroll bar that displays the task or resource that will become active when you release the mouse button.

When a view displays data in rows and columns, you can use a horizontal scroll bar along the bottom of the view to scroll through the columns of data. When a view displays data in a timescale, you can use the horizontal scroll bar beneath the timescale to scroll to different dates. If you drag the scroll box, you see a small box next to the scroll bar that shows the date that will be displayed when you release the mouse button.

Scrolling the Timescale with the Keyboard

You can change the date displayed on the timescale by using the Alt key and the cursor movement keys. These key combinations and their functions, are shown in the following list:

Key Combination	Result
Alt+Home	Beginning of project
Alt+End	End of project
Alt+left arrow	Left 1 unit
Alt+right arrow	Right 1 unit
Alt+PgUp	Left one screen
Alt+PgDn	Right one screen
Ctrl+Shift+F5	Beginning of selected task bar

Tip
Use the Goto Selected Task button on the Standard toolbar to scroll the timescale to the beginning of the selected task.

Finding Tasks or Resources by Name

If you are looking for a task by name, you can use the **E**dit **F**ind command (or the Ctrl+F shortcut key combination). The Find dialog box (shown in fig. 2.33) provides a text field you can use to enter a key word that is part of the task name. Choosing the **N**ext button initiates the search down the task list for the next task that contains the value you entered within its name. Choosing the **P**revious button starts the search up the task list. If a task is found that matches your search criterion but is not the task you were looking for, press the Shift+F4 key to continue searching down the task list or Ctrl+Shift+F4 to search up the task list.

Fig. 2.33
You can locate a
task or resource if
you know any part
of the text that
makes up its
name.

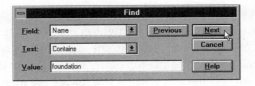

Selecting Data Fields in Tables

You must select a data field if you want to enter data, if you want to edit the
existing data in the field, or if you want to copy, move, or delete the data in
the field. You can select data fields in views and dialog boxes by clicking the
mouse pointer on a field in any view or dialog box. You also can use the
arrow keys to select fields in the spreadsheet views.

You can use the cursor movement keys to move through the project data,
and the movement selects new data fields. The following keys function in
the same way in all views except forms:

Key Combination	Result
Up arrow	Up one row
Down arrow	Down one row
Left arrow	Left one field
Right arrow	Right one field
Home	Left end of a row
End	Right end of a row
PgUp	Up one screen
PgDn	Down one screen
Ctrl+PgUp	Left one screen
Ctrl+PgDn	Right one screen
Ctrl+Home	First field in first row
Ctrl+End	Last field in last row

You can extend the selection to include multiple data fields when in a table view by dragging the mouse pointer through all fields that you want to select. You also can hold down the Shift key as you use the arrow keys to extend the selection. Pressing the Extend key (F8) allows you to extend the selection without holding down the Shift key. When you press F8, EXT appears in the Status bar. Use the arrow keys to extend the selected data fields. Then carry out the action that you want to apply to all the selected data fields.

If you want to add fields that are not adjacent to the current selection to this selection, use the Ctrl key as you select the additional fields with the mouse. You also can use the Add key (Shift+F8) to extend the selection. Pressing the Add key keeps the current selection from going away while you move to the next fields that you are adding to the selection. After pressing the Add key, move to the next field that you want to add to the selection. The Status bar displays Add in place of EXT. Then press the Extend key again and extend the selection, use the Shift key with arrow keys to extend the selection, or drag with the mouse to extend the selection.

Scrolling and Selecting Fields in Forms

Form views display details about one task or one resource at a time. You can move through the project's tasks or resources with the Previous and Next buttons that appear in most forms. Use the Tab and Shift+Tab keys in forms and dialog boxes to move to and select successive fields. The text next to each field in a form has an underlined character. Using the Alt key with the underlined letter moves the selection directly to this field. You cannot extend the selection in forms.

From Here...

This chapter introduced you to the screen elements and menus in Microsoft Project and to techniques that you use to work with these elements. To work on specific parts of a project, see the following chapters:

- Chapter 3, "Setting Up a New Project Document," shows you how to get started with the preliminary settings in a new project document.

- Chapter 4, "Creating a Task List," is the first in a series of four chapters that show you how to define the tasks in a project.

■ Chapter 8, "Defining Resources and Costs," is the first of two chapters that show you how to define resources and assign them to tasks.

■ Chapter 10, "Auditing the Task Schedule," is the first of two chapters that deal with auditing the final project plan.

■ Chapter 12, "Managing the Project," shows you how to track actual performance on the project.

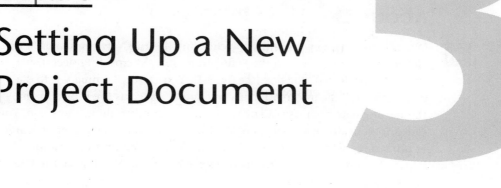

Chapter 3

Setting Up a New Project Document

Creating a project with Microsoft Project is a flexible process. You are not bound to a rigid order of steps in entering and defining the project. You can begin by jotting down some ideas about tasks that you think may be required, and you can later adjust the scheduling calendar, enter the basic project information, revise the calculation and display options, and define the resources. In fact, you can execute all of the preceding steps in any order.

The topics covered in this chapter are preliminaries: You should consider these topics before you start entering tasks and resource assignments into a project file. By starting with the preliminary measures, you are more likely to find your data processed by Microsoft Project in a way consistent with your expectations. Moreover, you still can change these preliminary settings after you enter the project data without suffering loss or distortion of data.

In this chapter, you learn how to

- Provide summary information about the specific project you are starting.

- State your preferences among the environment options for calculating and displaying data.

- Define the calendar of working days and hours that you plan to use for scheduling work on the project.

Providing Summary Information about the New Project

When you start a new file either by choosing the **F**ile **N**ew command or by clicking the New button on the Standard toolbar, Microsoft Project displays the Summary Info dialog box (see fig. 3.1). You use the Summary Info dialog box to record basic information about a project, such as the project name, the starting date, the base calendar to be used for scheduling, and so on. You can automatically place several fields from this form in the header or footer of printed reports for the project (see Chapter 16, "Printing Views and Reports"). You can access this dialog box at any time by choosing the **F**ile Summary **I**nfo command.

Fig. 3.1

The Summary Info dialog box has two tabbed sheets for summarizing your project.

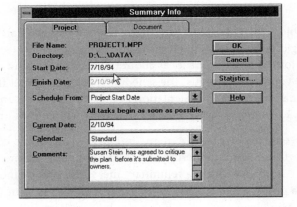

The fields for Summary Info are grouped on two tabbed sheets. Select the Project tab to enter scheduling information about the project. Select the Document tab to enter names and descriptions associated with the project.

While working in the Summary Info dialog box, use the Tab and Shift+Tab keys to advance from field to field, or move directly to a field by pressing the Alt key plus the underlined letter in the field name. Using either of these methods selects the current entry in the field, as well as the field, and you can begin typing the new entry to replace the old contents of the field. The left and right arrow keys move the insertion point for editing within the current entry.

You also can use the mouse to select a field, but you must double-click the old entry to select it for replacement.

Avoid the temptation to press Enter after you type a new field entry; pressing Enter selects the OK button and closes the Summary Info dialog box. The only exception to this rule is the Comments text box. You can press Enter in the Comments box to start new lines of text.

To enter project information in the Summary Info dialog box, follow these steps:

1. From the File menu, choose Summary Info. The Summary Info dialog box appears (see fig. 3.1).

2. Choose the Start Date field to define a specific date on which the project should be scheduled to start. If the project must be scheduled to finish on a specific date, choose the entry list arrow to the right of the Schedule From field and select Project Finish Date. You can then type a specific date into the Finish Date field above it. See the section "Understanding the Start and Finish Date Fields," later in this chapter for more information about these fields.

3. Select the Current Date field to change the date used on reports or to enter tracking information that should be entered as of a different date. (See the following section, "Understanding the Current Date Field," for more information about the Current Date entry.)

4. Select the Calendar field if you want to change the name of the base calendar to use for scheduling the project. (See the section "Scheduling with Calendars," later in this chapter.)

   Select the entry list arrow to the right of the Calendar field to view the list of base calendars that are already defined. Then select a base calendar from the list by clicking the calendar's name, or by using the arrow keys to highlight the name and pressing Enter.

   If the base calendar you want to use is defined in a different project file, you must use the Organizer to copy that calendar into the current project file before you can select it. (See the section "Working with Calendar Files," later in this chapter.)

5. Select the **C**omments field at the bottom of the dialog box to type memos or notes about the project. These notes can be printed on the Project Summary report. (See Chapter 16, "Printing Views and Reports," for instructions on printing the Project Summary report.)

The **C**omments field holds almost 2,500 characters. Text typed into the **C**omments field word-wraps from line to line as you type. If you want to start a new line or paragraph, simply press Enter.

Choose the Document tab (shown in fig. 3.2) to enter descriptive names and titles for the project.

Fig. 3.2
Use the Document tab to supply project titles and names, as well as information to identify the document file in searches.

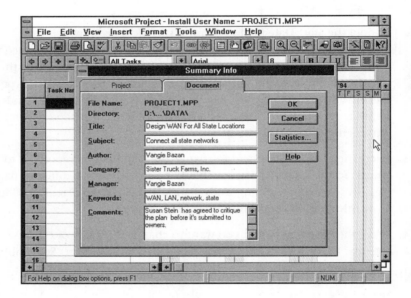

1. Choose the **T**itle field and type the project's name. The project name can contain up to 256 characters; make this name more descriptive than the eight-character file name. The **T**itle can be displayed automatically in report headers and footers.

2. Choose the **S**ubject field if you want to enter a short descriptive statement about the project that won't be printed as part of the title on reports. This field can hold only 49 characters. You can search the **S**ubject field with the **F**ile **F**ind File command.

3. Choose the **A**uthor field and enter your name. This field can be searched with the **F**ile **F**ind File command to locate project documents by author. The default name is the user name you entered when Microsoft Project was installed or the user name you have entered into the Options dialog box. (See the section "Selecting the Environment Options" later in this chapter.)

4. Choose the Company field and type the company's name. This name can be placed automatically in report headers and footers. The default entry for this field is the organization name you entered when you installed Microsoft Project.

5. Choose the **M**anager field and type the name of the person who will serve as project manager. This field can be printed automatically in report headers and footers.

6. Choose the **K**eywords field if you want to supply some identifying words to search for when you use the **F**ile **F**ind File command to locate project files.

7. Choose the OK button when you finish entering the project information to close the dialog box.

Understanding the Current Date Field

The computer's internal clock initially determines the date listed in the Current Date field. Changing this field has several implications.

■ The date in this field determines the location of the dashed (current) date line on the Gantt Chart timeline.

■ The Current Date appears in the header of the Summary Info standard report as an As Of date. You also can display the Current Date field in headers or footers on other reports by typing the appropriate code in the header or footer definition.

■ You can use the Current Date to track the progress of the project, specifically to record the progress of all tasks scheduled to be in progress or finished as of the date in the Current Date field. See Chapter 12, "Managing the Project," for a full description of tracking progress.

Understanding the Start and Finish Date Fields

Tip
After you enter
all the tasks in
a project, you
may want to
enter the **F**inish
date deadline
temporarily,
just to see
when the
project must
begin if you are
to meet this
deadline. You
then can return
to a scheduled
Start date for
working within
the project
plan.

You enter either a **S**tart date or a **F**inish date in the Summary Info dialog box to function as an anchor point for scheduling the tasks in the project. If you enter the **S**tart date, Microsoft Project schedules the first task in the project to begin at that time and calculates the project's finish date based on that starting date.

If you enter the **F**inish date, Microsoft Project schedules the tasks at the end of the project first and works backward. The final task is scheduled to end by the finish date; the task that precedes the final task is scheduled to end in time for the final task to begin, and so on. By the time Microsoft Project schedules all tasks to end in time to meet the **F**inish date requirement, the program calculates a **S**tart date (the date by which the first task must begin for the project to be completed by the specified finish time).

You enter only one of these two dates in the dialog box, either the **S**tart date or the **F**inish date, and Microsoft Project computes the other date. You cannot specify both a start date and a finish date in this dialog box.

Although most project goal statements are probably set in terms of a **F**inish date deadline, you may find that designating a **S**tart date—and then having Microsoft Project calculate the resulting finish date—usually is more advantageous. You retain more flexibility in your schedule with this method.

Selecting the Environment Options

You can change the operating characteristics of Microsoft Project to suit your needs with the **T**ools **O**ptions command. Microsoft Project displays the Options dialog box (see fig. 3.3). The options are conveniently organized into categories on separate tabs. Some options, such as those on the View tab, let you choose default display characteristics and formats (for dates and money amounts, for example).

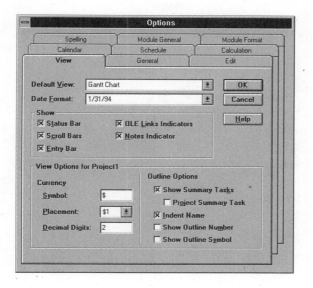

Fig. 3.3
The Options dialog box contains most of the environment settings on separate tabs.

The options on the General tab (shown in fig. 3.4) govern how Microsoft Project uses the Tips and Planning Wizard features. Other options, such as those on the Calendar tab, govern basic definitions, such as the number of hours in your work week, the starting month of your fiscal year, and the time unit in which task durations will be displayed (see fig. 3.5). You can customize most of the Options by filling check boxes or by choosing items from entry lists. If the selected item has an entry list available, the entry list arrow appears to the right of the text box for the item.

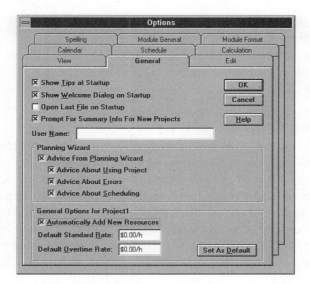

Fig. 3.4
The General tab of the Options dialog box regulates the display of on-line learning tools.

Fig. 3.5
The Calendar tab has options to let you tell Microsoft Project such things as the start of the fiscal year and the default time for work to begin each day.

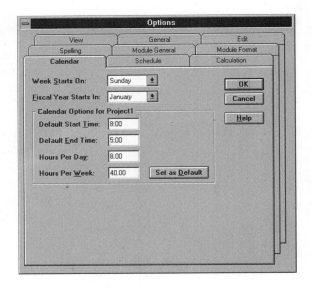

The following discussion focuses on a few Options dialog box choices that are critical in defining any project and a few options of general interest that can be explained at this point without knowledge of more advanced topics.

Most of the options affect the way all projects will be viewed. Those options that are enclosed in a group box labeled with the project name affect only the current project. For example, the setting for the start of the fiscal year in figure 3.5 affects all projects that you may work on. The setting for the default start time of work each day affects only Project1.

Note

All changes you make in the Options dialog box are saved in a file named WINPROJ4.INI that is located in the Windows directory.

Reviewing Critical Options

The two most critical Options settings are those that define the meaning of the basic task duration units, *day* and *week*. The fundamental unit of time in Microsoft Project is the *hour*, and when the user enters days and weeks, these terms are converted internally into hours based on the definitions in the Options dialog box. Therefore, the items Default Hours/Day and Default Hours/Week are crucial to the interpretation and display of your entries for task durations. Be certain that these settings are appropriate for your organization.

> **Note**
>
> If you change the definitions for a day or a week after entering the project data, Microsoft Project doesn't redefine the hour duration of tasks, but merely displays these hours as a different number of days or weeks.

The name of the month that begins the fiscal year also is a critical option. This choice affects displays and reports that show annual and quarterly amounts. If the fiscal year begins in July, for example, you probably want all reports to include the July through September figures in the first quarter totals and the annual figures to be calculated by using the July through June figures.

To set these critical preferences, follow these steps:

1. From the **T**ools menu, choose **O**ptions.

2. Choose the Calendar tab.

3. If your fiscal year does not start in January, choose the **F**iscal Year Starts In entry list arrow and select the correct month.

4. If your work day doesn't start at 8:00 AM, use the Tab key to advance to that field and enter the appropriate time. You can enter time in the 12-hour or 24-hour format. If you use the 12-hour format, be sure to add PM to hours past noon.

5. Change the Hours Per Da**y** or Hours Per **W**eek if necessary to accurately represent your organization. For example, if your office is open 8 hours a day during the week and 4 hours on Saturdays, change the Hours Per **W**eek to 44.00. Then you can estimate a task to take a week, and Microsoft Project will interpret your estimate to mean 44 working hours.

Changing the values in the last four fields on the Calendar tab affects only the current project unless you choose the Set As **D**efault button. Choosing that button makes your entries in those fields the default values for all new projects—but it doesn't change the values in those fields for projects that have already been created with different values.

Changing the starting month for the fiscal year, however, changes the fiscal year start for all projects, even those you created earlier.

Setting Other Useful Options

There are other settings that you can change to make your data entry easier. It is a good idea to review the current settings in the Options dialog box for each of the items in the following partial listing.

- Choose the Schedule tab (shown in fig. 3.6) to select the time unit you plan to use most often when estimating task durations. Choose the Show Duration In field and use the entry list arrow to select **M**inutes, **H**ours, **D**ays, or **W**eeks.

  This setting provides Microsoft Project with instructions about the unit of time to use in case you enter a task duration without specifying the unit of time. For example, if the default duration unit is days and you just enter the number 2 in the Duration field, the computer records the task duration as 2d (two days).

Fig. 3.6
Set the default duration and work units to those you most commonly use.

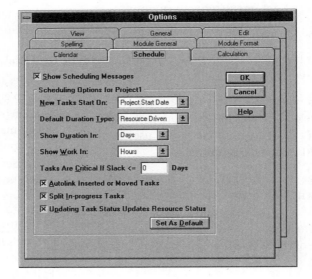

- Choose the View tab to change the Default view if you want a view other than the Gantt Chart to appear when you start a new project.

- Choose Date **F**ormat on the View tab to specify how dates are to be displayed. The default format displays the date without the time for task starts and finishes. The entry list provides alternative format options (such as, for example, the date and time together or the day of the week along with the date).

■ Choose the Currency **D**ecimal Digits field to specify the number of decimal points to use in displaying money amounts. The preset value is 2 decimal points, but you also can select 0 or 1.

Note

In the previous release of Microsoft Project, you also had the option of selecting your choice of the "international" date and time formats or those used in the United States. That choice is now made in the Windows Control Panel instead of in the Microsoft Project application. To change the date and time formats, open the Main group in the Program Manager and choose Control Panel; then choose the International icon. Choose the Change button for either Date Format or Time Format, and choose the way long and short displays of dates and times will be presented.

■ The **A**utomatically Add New Resources field on the General tab determines how Microsoft Project treats unrecognized resource names that you try to assign to a task. If this check box is filled, unrecognized resource names will be assigned to the task and automatically added to the resource pool. Although you might consider that a convenience, it also allows misspelled resource names to go undetected and to be added to the pool as additional resources. You will probably save time in the long run by clearing the **A**utomatically Add New Resources check box. (Clearing the check box only changes this option for the current project. Choose the Set As **D**efault button to make the change the default for all future new project documents.)

■ When you are entering data into a sheet column in Microsoft Project, the Enter key causes the selection to advance automatically to the cell below. You can cut this feature off if desired by clearing the **M**ove Selection After Enter check box on the Edit tab.

I

Project Management

Defining a Calendar of Working Time

Microsoft Project contains an internal Standard calendar that defines the default working and non-working days that are used for scheduling tasks in your projects. The standard calendar assumes five working days per week, Monday through Friday, with eight hours of work per day (including an hour off for lunch). The default schedule is 8:00 AM to 12:00 PM and 1:00 PM to 5:00 PM. No designated holidays are set in the original standard calendar.

All projects are assigned to a base calendar, and the default assignment is to the Standard calendar. You can edit the Standard calendar or create other base calendars and assign the project to one of them if you want.

You can edit the Standard calendar to reflect your organization's regular working and non-working days and hours. You also can designate the exceptions to the normal workdays. You can designate holidays, for example, or time periods when the plant will be closed for remodeling, a company-wide meeting time when no work should be scheduled, and so on.

Base calendars also are used as the basis for resource calendars. Each resource has its own calendar, and the resource calendar is linked to a designated base calendar (by default the Standard calendar). The resource calendar inherits all the standard days and hours of its base calendar, as well as all the holidays and other exceptions in its base calendar. The resource calendar then can be edited to record the days and hours when the availability of the resource differs from the normal working times found in the base calendar. Examples of resource exceptions may be vacation days, sick leave, unusual hours on particular days, and so on. See the section "Defining Resource Calendars" in Chapter 8 for more information about resource calendars.

As an example, the base calendar for an organization in the United States may show that Thanksgiving Day is a company holiday. Suppose that a maintenance worker is scheduled to work on Thanksgiving Day and to have the following Friday off. The resource calendar for this worker will initially show the company holiday, Thanksgiving Day, as a non-working day and the next Friday as a working day. For this maintenance worker only, the resource calendar needs to be edited to reverse the status of both days.

If a resource has only a few exceptions to the Standard calendar, it is easy to edit the resource calendar. If the resource has working times that are radically different from the Standard working times, the editing job can require a lot of work. If there are several resources with the same unique set of working times, it's easier to create a base calendar that has those unique working times and link each unique resource to that base calendar. For example, night and weekend security guards have unique days and hours. Instead of greatly altering a number of Standard base calendars, it's easier to create a Security Guard base calendar to reflect the special working times for security guards. Then link each newly employed security guard to that base calendar.

Scheduling with Calendars

Microsoft Project uses the base calendar and the resource calendars to schedule the start dates for tasks. When Microsoft Project schedules a task, it notes the earliest possible starting date, based on when the predecessors to the task will be completed. If no resources are assigned to work on the task, the project's base calendar is used to schedule the start and finish of the task. Otherwise, Microsoft Project checks to see which resources are assigned to work on the task and when the resource calendars for these resources show them available for work. The task then is scheduled to start on the next available working hour for the assigned resources.

▶ "Defining Resources and Costs," p. 177

Editing the Standard Calendar

Changing the working days and hours on the Standard calendar will affect the scheduled work times for all tasks that have no resources assigned to them and for all tasks whose resources are linked to the Standard base calendar.

Changing Working and Non-Working Days

The original calendar shows all weekdays, Monday through Friday, as working days and all Saturdays and Sundays as non-working days. You can change the status of any day to make the day working or non-working, and you can specify the number of hours available for work on any day by defining the starting and ending times for work shifts on that day.

To edit the Standard calendar, choose the Tools menu and choose Change Working Time. The Change Working Time dialog box appears (see fig. 3.7). The Change Working Time dialog box can display a calendar of working and non-working times for any of the base calendars and resource calendars defined for the project.

Fig. 3.7

Use the Change Working Time dialog box to define the days and hours when work can be scheduled by Microsoft Project.

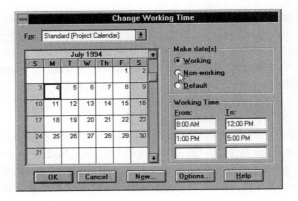

The dialog box contains a monthly calendar form on the left, daily working times on the right, and buttons to change the calendar. Non-working days are shaded gray on the calendar, and working days are clear. Use the scroll bar to the right of the calendar to change months and years. The calendar spans the period from January, 1984, to December, 2049.

Buttons to the right of the calendar form enable you to change a calendar day to **W**orking or **N**on-working. Fields on the right side of the dialog box enable you to define the Working Time for different work shifts.

To change the status of a single day or a consecutive period of days from working to non-working or vice versa, select the day by using the mouse or arrow keys. You can select consecutive days by clicking and dragging or by pressing the Shift key and using the arrow keys. You can select multiple days that are not consecutive by pressing the Control key as you click on the extra dates. To make the selected day(s) non-working days, select the Non-working button; to make the selected day(s) working days, select the **W**orking button.

You also can change the working status of any day of the week for all weeks throughout the year. If your organization works on Saturdays, for example, you will want to make all Saturdays working days.

To change the working status of a day for all weeks, select the day of the week by clicking on the day letter at the top of the calendar, or by using the up arrow key to select the day letter and then selecting the **W**orking or **N**on-working button.

Changing the Standard Working Hours

You can define the work periods for each day by supplying up to three work periods in the Working Time fields of the Change Working Time dialog box. Each work period has a **F**rom field and a **T**o field. The default eight-hour work time periods are 8:00 AM to 12:00 PM and 1:00 PM to 5:00 PM.

To change the Hours fields for working shifts, follow these steps:

1. Select the **F**rom time field for the first time period you want to change. If you use the Alt+F key, Microsoft Project selects the first **F**rom time entry. Use the Tab key to advance to the other time fields. Use Shift+Tab to return to previous fields.

2. Enter a time in the Working Time field that you want to change.

3. Tab to successive fields to change other work period times.

4. Tab to the end of the Working Time fields or click to select another date.

> **Note**
>
> Microsoft Project checks all time entries for consistency. Each successive time must be later in the day than the preceding time field.
>
> You cannot leave a work period blank and put data in a work period beneath it. Therefore, the top pair of work period fields must be used first; then you can fill the middle pair for a second work period; only then can you fill the bottom pair of fields for a third work period.

Entering Time Formats

You can use several formats for entering times in these fields. You can use either the 12-hour clock or the 24-hour clock to enter times. If you enter times based on the 12-hour clock, make sure that you use the AM and PM suffixes to ensure that the program understands your intent. If you enter a time without using an AM or PM suffix, the computer uses the first instance of the time following 8:00 AM (or whatever time you designate as the Default Start **T**ime on the Calendar tab of the Options dialog box).

If you enter 3:30 without a suffix, for example, the computer assumes that

Tip
To record a 24-hour workday, enter 12 AM in both the From and To fields of the first time period in the Hours fields.

you want to use 3:30 in the afternoon and attaches the PM suffix. If you want to set a work shift to start at 5:00 in the morning, enter 5 AM instead of 5:00 because the program interprets 5:00 to mean 5:00 PM. (If the time you want to enter is on the hour, simply enter the hour number. For example, 10:00 AM can be entered as 10, and 5:00 PM can be entered as 5 PM.)

Note

Noon is entered as 12:00 PM, and midnight is entered as 12:00 AM.

Removing Work Periods from the Hours Fields

To remove a work period from the Hours fields, you need to delete both the start time and the finish time for the period.

1. Select the entry in the From field for the work period to remove.

2. Use the Delete key to make the field blank.

3. Repeat for the To field for that time period.

Resetting a Calendar

You can use the Default button to cancel changes you have made for calendar days, returning to the standard definitions for those days. Selecting individual days and choosing Default returns those days to the working hours for those days of the week. Selecting the day of the week letters at the top of the calendar returns all days in the column(s) selected to the standard 8-hour day, 8 AM to 5 PM. Selecting all the weekday letters at the top of the calendar and choosing Default returns the entire calendar to the initial Standard calendar with no holidays and a 40-hour week.

Creating a New Calendar

Suppose some of your resources work a night shift, from 5:00 PM to 1:00 AM. You should create a Night Shift calendar to use as a base calendar for all of those resources. The regular shift begins at 5:00 PM and continues to 1:00 AM the following day. A half-hour break is scheduled from 9:00 PM to 9:30 PM.

Create a new base calendar by following these steps.

1. Choose the New button at the bottom of the Change Working Time dialog box to create a new base calendar. The Create New Base Calendar dialog box will appear (fig. 3.8).

2. Choose the N**a**me field and type a distinctive name, such as Night Shift, for the new calendar.

3. Choose the Create **n**ew base calendar button if you want to start with no holidays and the standard 40-hour week. Alternatively, choose the **M**ake copy of button to start with a copy of an existing base calendar and all its holidays and exceptions. Choose the entry list arrow and select an existing base calendar from the list. If you have already defined all regular company holidays on the Standard calendar, start with a copy of the Standard calendar so you don't have to enter those holidays again.

4. Choose OK to start defining the new calendar.

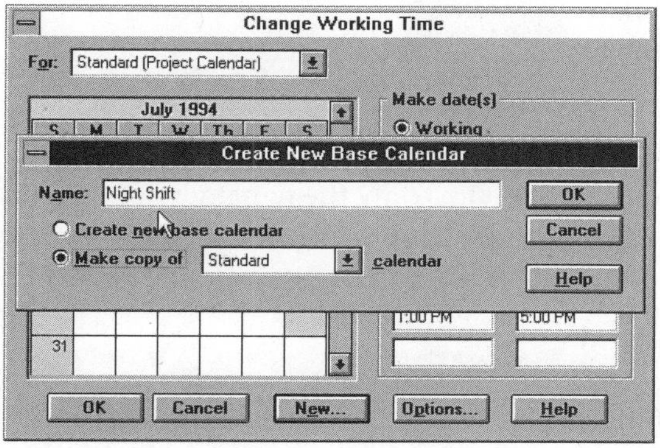

Fig. 3.8
Create a new base calendar from a fresh start or by copying an existing calendar and modifying it.

Figure 3.9 illustrates the definition of Monday Working Times for the Night Shift calendar. The hours for Mondays are 5:00 PM to 9:00 PM and 9:30 PM to 12:00 AM. The remainder of the shift is defined on the Working Time schedule for Tuesdays.

Fig. 3.9
Night Shift workers begin the week at 5 PM on Mondays.

The Tuesday through Friday schedules require three shifts, as shown in figure 3.10. The first shift is the continuation of the previous evening's shift. The second and third shifts show the periods for the day's shift.

Fig. 3.10
The Tuesday through Friday schedule begins at midnight with the last leg of the previous work day and starts again at 5 PM.

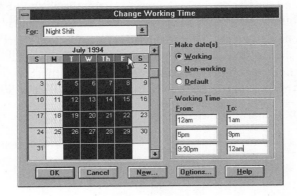

The Saturday schedule contains only the remainder of the Friday evening shift (see fig. 3.11). Although there is only one hour of work scheduled on Saturdays, that's enough to make Saturdays working days.

Fig. 3.11
The Saturday schedule merely completes the Friday work day.

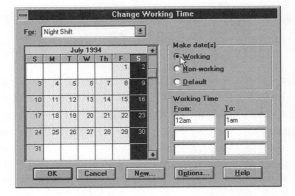

Saving or Cancelling Your Changes

To finish editing base calendars and save the changes you have made, choose the OK button at the bottom of the Change Working Time dialog box. Choosing the Cancel button causes all changes to be lost.

Working with Calendar Files

All of the calendar information is saved along with the task and resource information in the same project file. In earlier releases of Microsoft Project, the calendars were saved in a separate file named CALENDAR.MPC, and there was potential for confusing mistakes when the user copied project files from one computer to another. Now you can copy a calendar from one project file to another, or you can copy calendars into the GLOBAL.MPT template that is used by default as the basis for all new project files. The calendars in the GLOBAL.MPT file are automatically included in any new project file.

Note

The GLOBAL.MPT template is stored in the directory with the Microsoft Project program files.

The Organizer is a new feature that is used to copy calendars from one project or template to another. You also must use the Organizer to delete or rename a base calendar in a project. To make a customized Standard calendar the default Standard calendar for all new projects, you must do two things:

- Define the working times, holidays, and special hours in a project file's Standard calendar.

- Use the Organizer to copy the customized Standard calendar to the GLOBAL.MPT file, replacing the existing Standard calendar in the GLOBL.MPT file.

The Organizer can copy not only calendars from one project or template to another, but also other customized elements (such as views, reports, macros, forms, tables, filters, toolbars, and menu bars). Therefore, the Organizer can be activated from several different points in Microsoft Project—but not from the Change Working Time dialog box where calendars are defined. The steps that follow access the Organizer through the Toolbars dialog box.

To copy a calendar to the GLOBAL.MPT template:

1. Choose the **V**iew **T**oolbars command to display the Toolbars dialog box.

2. Choose the **O**rganizer button to display the Organizer dialog box (shown in fig. 3.12). The calendars in the GLOBAL.MPT file are listed on the left, and those in the current project file are listed on the right.

Project Management

Fig. 3.12
Use the Organizer
to copy custom
elements like
calendars
between project
documents.

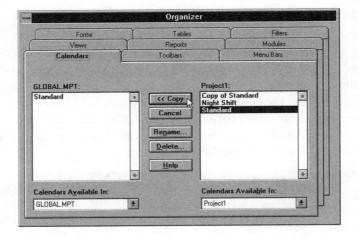

3. Choose the Standard calendar in the project file on the right.

4. Choose the << Copy button. Since there is already a calendar by the same name in the GLOBAL.MPT file, you are asked to confirm your intentions (see fig. 3.13).

Fig. 3.13
You must confirm
that you want
to replace a
calendar in the
GLOBAL.MPT
template.

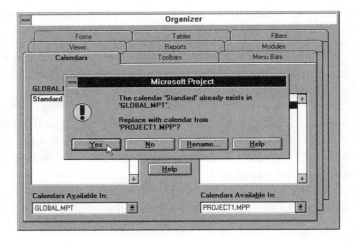

5. Choose the **Y**es button to replace the GLOBAL.MPT Standard calendar with your customized Standard calendar. Alternatively, you can use the **R**ename button to change the name of the calendar file in the current document and then copy the customized calendar into the GLOBAL.MPT template without replacing the existing Standard calendar.

6. Choose the Close button to close the dialog box.

> **Note**
>
> You cannot edit the calendars in the GLOBAL.MPT template directly. To edit
> a calendar in the GLOBAL.MPT template, copy it to a project file with the
> Organizer. Edit the calendar in the project file, and then use the Organizer to
> copy it back to the GLOBAL.MPT template.

Using Calendars from Microsoft Project 3.0

If you have a calendar from Microsoft Project 3.0 that you want to use in
release 4.0, you must open the CALENDAR.MPC file (or any other .MPC file)
from Microsoft Project 3.0 with the **F**ile **O**pen command. You can then copy
the calendars into the GLOBAL.MPT file with the Organizer.

Printing the Base Calendars

You can print a report to show the details of each of the base calendars in the
active project file (see fig. 3.14). Printing reports is covered in detail in Chapter 16, "Printing Views and Reports," and customizing the reports is covered
in Chapter 20, "Using and Customizing Reports." This section is designed to
give you a quick reference for printing a standard report.

BASE CALENDAR:	STANDARD
Day	Hours
Sunday	Nonworking
Monday	8:00 AM - 12:00 PM, 1:00 PM - 5:00 PM
Tuesday	8:00 AM - 12:00 PM, 1:00 PM - 5:00 PM
Wednesday	8:00 AM - 12:00 PM, 1:00 PM - 5:00 PM
Thursday	8:00 AM - 12:00 PM, 1:00 PM - 5:00 PM
Friday	8:00 AM - 12:00 PM, 1:00 PM - 5:00 PM
Saturday	Nonworking
Exceptions:	
Date	Hours
1/17/94	Nonworking
2/21/94	Nonworking
5/30/94	Nonworking
7/4/94	Nonworking
9/5/94	Nonworking
10/10/94	Nonworking
11/23/94	8:00 AM - 12:00 PM
11/24/94	Nonworking
12/23/94	8:00 AM - 12:00 PM

Fig. 3.14
The Working Days
report prints a
separate page for
each base calendar,
showing the
standard working
days and times and
a list of exceptions.

To print the base calendar report, follow these steps:

1. From the **V**iew menu, choose **R**eports. The Reports gallery shown in figure 3.15 appears.

2. Choose the **O**verview reports, and from that gallery choose the **W**orking Days reports.

3. Choose the **S**elect button to preview the report.

4. Choose the **P**rint button to send the report to your printer. Choose the **C**ancel button to return to the project workspace.

Fig. 3.15
The Reports gallery offers ready-made reports about every aspect of your project.

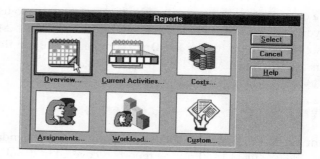

The report shows the standard working hours for each day of the week, followed by a list of the exceptions for individual days. Each base calendar prints on a separate page.

From Here...

This chapter has shown you how to prepare Microsoft Project for the task and resource definitions that you will enter in a project. You can proceed from here to the following chapters:

■ Chapter 4, "Creating a Task List," is the first of four chapters that deal with defining tasks and task relationships.

■ Chapter 8, "Defining Resources and Costs," is the first chapter to deal with resources and resource assignments. You can enter resources before you create the task list if you prefer.

■ Chapter 16, "Printing Views and Reports," offers instructions for printing the calendars and general project information as well as the views that show tasks and resources.

Chapter 4

Creating a Task List

Planning a project always begins with the creation of a concise but comprehensive goal statement. If the goal of the project is not clearly in focus from the outset, the task list very likely may need extensive revisions and can entail far more work in the long run. After the goal is agreed upon, the next major planning function is to draw up a list of activities that must be undertaken to achieve the project goal.

Using Microsoft Project to help create the task list can save a great deal of time and effort. At this stage of the process, the major contribution of the computer is as a word processing tool to help you enter, revise, and rearrange your ideas. The computer facilitates editing and reorganizing that always accompanies the initial stages of project planning.

This chapter begins with the simple mechanics of drawing and rearranging the order of the task list. After entering the task names, you must define the duration for your tasks. Microsoft Project can then calculate a preliminary schedule with start and finish dates for each task and for the project as a whole. This chapter shows alternative ways to enter, edit, and display the task list. The chapter ends with instructions for printing the project plan that you develop using the procedures in this chapter.

In Chapter 4, you learn how to

- Approach the planning process.

- Enter and edit project tasks.

- Utilize the various task sheets and forms.

- Outline the task list.

Approaching the Planning Process

Project planning can begin with a top-down approach or a bottom-up approach. If you use a top-down approach, you start by identifying the major phases of the project. Then you fill in the components of each phase in greater detail until you create an outline of all the tasks that the project requires. This method is probably the most common approach to project planning.

All the entries in an outlined project are *tasks*. All tasks that have subordinate detail tasks indented under them are *summary tasks*, and they are treated differently from the tasks that have no subordinates (in other words, the tasks where the work actually gets done).

If you use the bottom-up approach, you begin by listing all the task details. You then arrange the details into an orderly progression, and you also may finish by creating an outline.

Microsoft Project simplifies both the top-down and the bottom-up approach. You can follow the top-down approach by entering the major phases as tasks and creating subordinate tasks under the major tasks. Microsoft Project supports up to nine levels of indented subordinated detail. You also can follow the bottom-up approach, first entering all the detail tasks, then inserting summary items for groups of tasks to create summary tasks and indented subordinate tasks.

You can create a complete project plan without using outlining. Using outlining has numerous advantages, however, and it significantly enhances your project's usefulness.

- Outlining facilitates an orderly planning process, with less likelihood of leaving out crucial steps.

- Outlined projects can be displayed with different levels of detail. You can collapse the outline to major topics only, or to any level of detail. You can easily tailor reports to any needed level of detail.

- The summary tasks in outlined projects automatically provide subtotals for the detail tasks under them, showing the duration, costs, and amount of work involved for all the detail tasks taken as a whole.

Outlining produces an organizational form that has traditionally been called the *Work Breakdown Structure*. The Work Breakdown Structure identifies major components of a project and shows multiple levels of detail under each major component. Work Breakdown Structure (WBS) codes are traditionally used to label each task in such a way that the code identifies where the task fits into the hierarchical structure, and these codes are identical to the outline numbers provided automatically by Microsoft Project. The outlining feature of Microsoft Project automatically supplies outline numbers that serve well as WBS codes. A WBS field exists for each task that can be viewed on the Task Information Form (introduced later in this chapter), and Microsoft Project automatically places the outline number in this field.

Entering and Editing Tasks in the Gantt Chart

The initial view in Microsoft Project is the Gantt Chart view (see fig. 4.1). If the Gantt Chart view is not on-screen, select the **V**iew menu and choose the **G**antt Chart command.

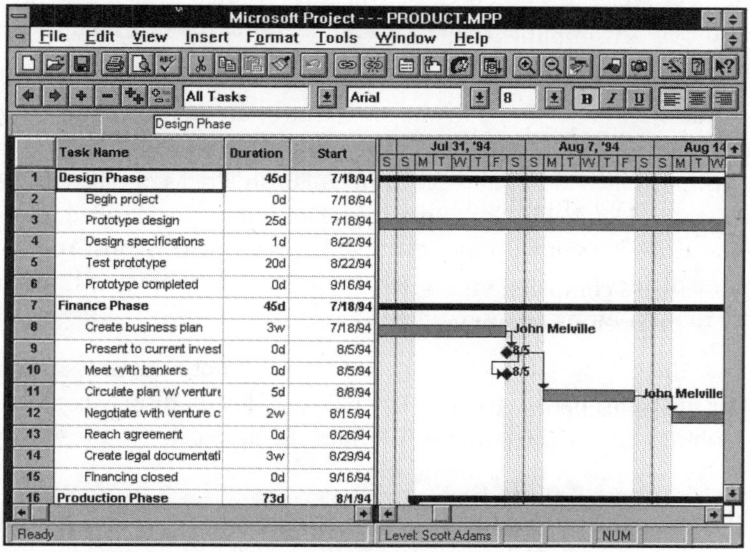

Fig 4.1
The Gantt Chart view of the PRODUCT project.

In the early 19th century, Henry Gantt popularized a modeling technique now known as the Gantt Chart. The Gantt Chart displays a spreadsheet table on the left side of the screen and a timescale with a bar chart on the right side of the screen for showing task dates and durations. The spreadsheet table is ideal for creating and editing the task list. The bar chart shows graphically the duration of each task and the chart's temporal relationship to other tasks. In addition, the bar chart shows the resources assigned to each task at the end of the task bar. The link between two tasks is graphically illustrated by an arrow drawn between the tasks. (See Chapter 5, "Entering Schedule Requirements," for more details on linking tasks.) The timescale shows a vertical dashed line as an indicator of today's date, unless you disable this feature.

> **Note**
>
> You can access other views and commands available for entering greater detail about a particular task. Several of these options are discussed later in this chapter.

You can enter a maximum of 9,999 tasks in a single project, and 9,999 rows are available in the task table. If you want to visually separate groups of tasks, you may leave blank rows in the task list. The ID numbers at the left of the table are record numbers in the database that Microsoft Project uses for storing your project details. If you move a task to another location in the list, the task takes on the ID number of the new location. You usually use the current ID number to refer to a task because you are permitted to create duplicate task names in the task list. The task ID number, not the task name, identifies each task uniquely.

The spreadsheet table on the left of the Gantt Chart view contains more columns than just the ID, Name, and Duration fields that you initially see. The other columns (Scheduled Start, Scheduled Finish, Predecessors, and Resource Names) are hidden behind the timescale chart but can be scrolled into view with the arrow keys or with the scroll bar beneath the columns. You also can move the divider bar between the spreadsheet columns and the timescale to display more columns or more timescale.

▶ "Working with the PERT Chart," p. 165.

The Task Sheet view is a spreadsheet table view without the timescale and bar chart of the Gantt Chart view (see fig. 4.2). The default display contains the same columns as the Gantt Chart. Without the timescale on-screen, you can see all the columns at the same time.

You also can use the Program Evaluation and Review Technique (PERT) Chart view to enter and edit tasks (see fig. 4.3). Each task is represented on the PERT Chart by a box or node, and a line is drawn from each predecessor task to its successor.

Entering Tasks in the Gantt Chart

Create a task by typing a task name in one of the rows of the spreadsheet table of the Gantt Chart view. As soon as you enter the task name, Microsoft Project supplies a default duration for the new task in the Duration field, and displays a task bar under the timescale in the Gantt Chart to the right. Unless you define a different start or finish date in the Summary Info dialog box, the start date of the project is today's date.

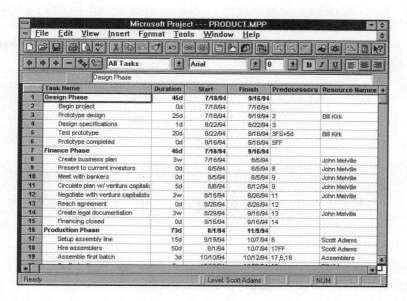

Fig. 4.2
A Task Sheet view of the SAMPLE project.

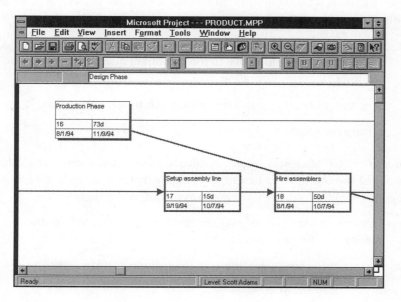

Fig. 4.3
A PERT Chart view of the SAMPLE project.

To enter a task name, perform the following steps:

1. Select a cell in the Name column.

2. Type the task name, using any combination of keyboard characters and spaces. Task names can contain up to 255 characters. Task names do not have to be unique; you can use the same name for multiple tasks in the same project.

3. Complete the cell entry by pressing Enter, by clicking the Enter button in the entry bar, or by selecting another cell. You can cancel the cell entry by pressing the Esc key or by clicking the Cancel button in the entry bar. The field will revert to its former contents.

Note

If you first select a range of cells, you can type the list of task names without selecting each new cell. The cell selector moves down to the next row as you press the Enter key after you type each task name.

Adjusting the Column Widths in the Gantt Chart

If the task name is too long to see in the Name column, you can adjust the width of the column. To change the width of a column, follow these steps:

1. Move the mouse into the column headings for the spreadsheet table. To widen the Name field, move to the column divider line between the headings Name and Duration.

2. Drag the column border to the right or left to suit your needs.

3. Release the mouse.

You also can tell Microsoft Project to calculate the widest entry in the column and adjust the column to a best fit for the data that you entered. To adjust the column width to the best fit, perform the following steps:

1. Move the mouse pointer over the divider line to the right of the column heading for the column you want to adjust.

2. Double-click the divider line, and the column adjusts.

Note

If your placement of the mouse pointer is not exactly on the divider line, double-clicking the mouse activates the Column Definition dialog box (shown in fig. 4.4). You can select the **B**est Fit button to have Project adjust the column width. You also can type a specific column width.

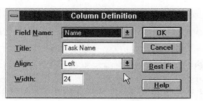

Fig. 4.4
The Column Definition dialog box.

Adjusting the Height of Task Rows

For long task names, you may want to use two or more lines for each task name. Task names are word-wrapped by Project if extra lines are both needed and available for displaying task names. Figure 4.5 shows word-wrapped task names.

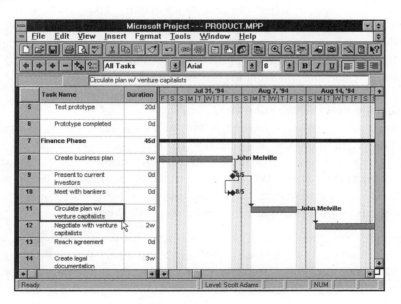

Fig. 4.5
Using two rows for the Task Names field in the Gantt Chart.

▶ "Using and Creating Views," p. 463.

To adjust the number of lines displayed for each task name, position the mouse on the row divider line in the Task ID column, and drag the divider line downward to increase the width of the task rows. A menu command also is available for adjusting row heights.

Entering Task Durations

When you create a task name, Microsoft Project assigns the task a default duration. The default duration is always one day (eight hours of work), but you can change the units in which the day is expressed (for example, 8 hours, .2 week) with the **T**ools **O**ptions command (see Chapter 3, "Setting Up a New Project Document"). You can type over the default duration to define the duration, as described in the upcoming section, "Entering the Duration."

The duration bar for the task appears under the timescale, and the bar starts at today's date unless you previously designated a different start date for the project. If the project start date is not today's date, the task bar may not be visible until you scroll to the date for the start of the project. Use Alt+Home to jump to the start date of the project on the timescale or use Alt+End to move to the finish date of the project.

You can enter an estimate of the task duration as you create the task names. The task bars instantly reflect this new duration entry. You can continue creating the project by entering the task names and duration, or you leave the default durations for later so that for the moment you can focus on organizing the list of tasks. This chapter follows the first course and discusses the duration field before finalizing the task list entries.

Understanding the Duration Field

The duration of a task is measured in units of minutes, hours, days, or weeks. The abbreviations m, h, d, and w refer to minutes, hours, days, and weeks respectively. A duration estimate of 45m means 45 minutes, and an estimate of 3w means three weeks. When you enter a duration estimate in day or week units, Microsoft Project internally converts these units to hours, based on the definitions for these terms as set using the **T**ools **O**ptions command.

When you set a duration of 12 hours, you mean that it will take twelve consecutive work hours on the base calendar to complete the task. If the original Standard calendar is the base calendar for a project (with five eight-hour days per week), and a 12-hour task is started at 8:00 AM, the task will be completed at 12 PM on the following workday. If work starts at 4 PM on a Friday, the task is completed after the next 12 regular working hours—by 11 AM on the following Tuesday.

The task bar on the Gantt Chart starts at the scheduled start time and stretches to the scheduled finish time for a task. If the task duration spans a weekend or other non-working time period, the bar is longer than if no intervening non-working time were present.

For some processes that may be entered as tasks, the process continues around the clock. If a chemical process takes five hours, for example, and is scheduled to start at 3 PM, five hours will elapse—by the clock, not after five regular working hours as dictated by the base calendar—before the process is complete. Duration estimates for tasks like this are entered as *elapsed* time. The letter 'e' is inserted between the number of units and the unit abbreviation. The duration estimate for the chemical process, for example, is 5eh.

Note

Microsoft Project makes fixed-duration tasks of all tasks that you define with elapsed durations. (See the following discussion on fixed-duration tasks.)

The duration for a summary task is calculated by Microsoft Project, based on the durations of the subordinate tasks under the summary task. You cannot enter a duration for a summary task. The summary task start date is the earliest start date of any of the subordinate tasks, and the summary task finish date is the latest finish date of any of the subordinate tasks. The duration of the summary task is the amount of work time on the base calendar between that earliest start date and that latest finish date. The summary task duration isn't measured in elapsed clock time (24 hours a day), but in elapsed base calendar time (8 hours a day, usually). Therefore, a summary task that starts at 8 AM one day and finishes at noon the next day would have a duration of 12 hours (12 working hours) instead of 28 hours (28 clock hours).

Estimating the Task Duration

When estimating durations, you should consider past experience with similar tasks, the experience and skill level of the resources you plan to use, and the number of resources you plan to use. When you assign the resources to the task, Microsoft Project will assume that the number of resource units you enter is the number you had in mind at the time you entered the duration.

Entering the Duration

The default duration supplied when you enter a task name is always one day. Use the **T**ools **O**ptions command to change the default unit for measuring durations. If the default duration unit is "day," and you want to enter a duration estimate of three days, you only have to enter the number 3 and the default duration unit will be applied.

To type a different duration estimate for a task, perform the following steps:

1. In the Duration column of the spreadsheet portion of the Gantt Chart, select the duration field for the task you want to change.

2. Type the duration, using the following abbreviations for the time units:

Abbreviation	Meaning
m or em	Minutes or elapsed minutes
h or eh	Hours or elapsed hours
d or ed	Days or elapsed days
w or ew	Weeks or elapsed weeks

3. Complete the entry by pressing Enter or by selecting another field.

Locating the Current Task Bar on the Gantt Chart

If the task bar for a task is not visible on the Gantt Chart, you can force the computer to scroll to the beginning date for the task by pressing Ctrl+Shift+F5. You can scroll instantly to the start date of the project by pressing Alt+Home. Scroll instantly to the finish date for the project by pressing Alt+End.

You also can use the Go to command to go directly to a specific date on the timescale. To scroll the timescale directly to a specific date, perform the following steps:

1. Press F5 (the Goto key) or select the Edit menu and choose Goto. The Go To dialog box appears (see fig. 4.6).

2. Tab to the Date field and enter the date to which you want to move.

    You also can enter the words "today" and "tomorrow" to jump directly to these dates. If you enter a three-letter weekday abbreviation, such as Tue., Wed., and so on, Microsoft Project jumps directly past today's date to the next occurrence of that weekday.

3. Select OK.

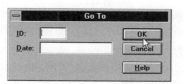

Fig. 4.6
The Go To
dialog box.

Project Management

Defining Fixed Duration Tasks

If the duration of a task is known to be fixed (so that the number of resources working on the task has no effect on its duration), mark the task as a Fixed Duration task.

To define a fixed duration task with the mouse, use a combination view with the Gantt Chart or Task Sheet in the upper pane and the Task Form in the bottom pane. The Task Entry view will give you this combination.

To display the Task Entry view, follow these steps:

1. Select the **V**iew menu.

2. Choose the **M**ore Views command.

3. Select the Task Entry view from the dialog window and click the **A**pply command.

To define a fixed duration task, follow these steps:

1. Select the task in the top pane in the spreadsheet table.

2. Mark the Fi**x**ed check box on the Task Form in the bottom pane.

3. Select OK or press Enter.

To use the keyboard, follow these steps:

1. Select the task in the top pane in the spreadsheet table.

2. Use F6 to activate the Task Form in the bottom pane.

3. Use Tab or Alt+X to select the Fi**x**ed field.

4. Use the Spacebar to toggle the X mark on and off. An X in the check box defines the task as a fixed task.

5. Select OK or press Enter.

Entering Milestones

One special task, the milestone, is defined by entering a duration estimate of zero. A *milestone* is a significant landmark, development, or turning point in the life of the project. Commonly, you use milestones to mark the completion of a major segment of the project. Milestones do not represent doing the work; they signal that the work has started or is completed. Milestones represent a point when something happens, whereas the ordinary tasks stretch out over time and represent continuing activity.

You may want to create milestone tasks at points that you want to monitor closely in the project. In a project to construct a building, for example, one milestone might be the completion of all the tasks involved in laying the foundation. The milestone might be named *Foundation Complete* and have a duration of zero. If you enter a zero in the duration field for a task, Microsoft Project makes the field a milestone.

▶ "Formatting Views," p. 497.

The Gantt Chart displays a milestone as a diamond shape, without a duration bar, as shown in figure 4.7. You can modify the symbol for a milestone and for all other task bars with the **F**ormat Bar **S**tyles command for the Gantt Chart view.

To enter a milestone task, enter the task name as described in the previous paragraphs, and then type **0** in the **D**uration field.

Fig. 4.7

Milestones, as shown in the Gantt Chart.

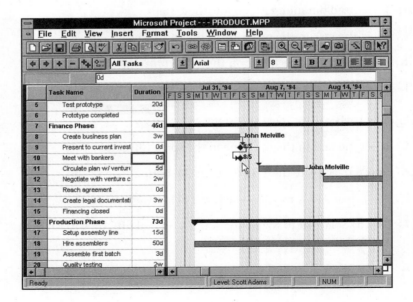

Entering Recurring Tasks

Occasionally, you will need to add a task to your project that will be repeated several times throughout the life of the project. Microsoft Project allows you to create these as recurring tasks. A status meeting with duration of two hours every Monday morning is a good example of a recurring task.

To insert a recurring task into your task list, perform the following steps:

1. Select the task name field on the row where the recurring task should be inserted.

2. Select the Insert **R**ecurring Task command from the **I**nsert menu.

3. Type the task name and duration in the appropriate boxes on the Recurring Task Information dialog box (see fig. 4.8).

Fig. 4.8
The Recurring Task Information dialog box.

4. Choose the This Occurs option that applies to the task, and then select exactly when the task will occur (see fig. 4.9).

Fig. 4.9
The Monthly occurrence option on the Recurring Task Information dialog box.

5. Define the length of the recurring task by defining the dates in which it should continue or by specifying the number of times it will occur.

6. Click OK or press Enter to complete the task entry.

Once entered, the recurring task is placed in the task list as a summary task, with the duration of the task being the total duration of the recurring task. The task bars for the recurring task are also placed in the timeline on the appropriate dates (see fig. 4.10).

Fig. 4.10
A recurring task item in the task list.

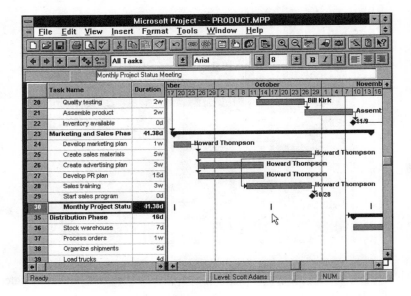

Editing the Task List

You can edit the list of task names and task durations in several views. The Gantt Chart and Task Sheet, either with or without the Task Form in the bottom pane, are probably the most useful views for organizing the tasks into an orderly list or into an outline.

Undoing Changes in the Task List

While you're revising the list, you can undo nearly any change made in the task list with the **U**ndo command in the **E**dit menu. Only the most recent change, however, can be undone. Most of the time you also can Redo (re-store) the last change just undone, and when this is the case, the **U**ndo command will be replaced by the **R**edo command on the **E**dit menu.

To undo or redo a change, perform the following steps:

1. Select **U**ndo from the **E**dit menu or press the Ctrl+Z shortcut key to reverse the most recent change in the project (if Undo is available).

2. Select **E**dit **R**edo to reverse the Undo that you just executed.

Inserting, Clearing, and Deleting Tasks

As you revise a project, you will need to be able to insert new tasks or remove tasks from the task list.

To insert a task between other tasks, select a cell in the row where you want to insert the new task. If you want to insert several tasks at the same location, extend the selection to include the requisite number of rows. All the details of the tasks included in the selection are shifted down to make room for new blank rows. Select the **I**nsert **I**nsert Task command or press the Insert key. You also can use the shortcut key Ctrl++ (the plus key on the numeric key pad) to insert rows.

Deleting a task is different from clearing the data from one or more cells of the task. The **E**dit **C**lear command merely erases the contents of the selected cells, but does not delete the remaining task details. The **E**dit **D**elete Task command deletes all details about the selected task(s). The Delete key is the shortcut for the Delete Task command.

The **E**dit **C**lear command gives you several choices for clearing the contents of the selected cell. You may choose to clear the **F**ormats only of the cell, the **C**ontents, the **N**otes, or **A**ll of the selected cell. The **E**ntire Task option will clear all of the cells for the task, but does not delete the task row.

To clear only the active cell while many cells are selected, perform the following steps:

1. Select the cells.

2. Use the Enter key or the Tab key (or their Shift combinations) to make the cell you want to clear the active cell.

3. Press Ctrl+Backspace. This clears the active cell and activates the editing area of the entry bar so that, if you want, you can type a replacement entry.

4. Type a replacement entry for the active cell if desired.

5. Press Enter or Tab to activate another cell without losing the range selection.

> **Note**
>
> Clearing a name cell and leaving a task with no name is possible. However, this is not advised.

To delete one or more entire tasks, select at least one cell in each of the tasks to be deleted and select the **Edit Delete** Task command or press the Delete key. The rows for the selected tasks are removed from the task list, and the remaining tasks will close the gaps.

Moving and Copying Tasks

You can use the Windows Clipboard if you want to copy or move one or more tasks to another location in the task list or to another project file. For both moving and copying, you first must select the tasks or the cells you want to use. Then you use the **Cut** command to move the selection or the **Copy** command to just copy the selection. Both commands place a copy of the selection in the Windows Clipboard. Finally, select the new location for the data and use the **Paste** command to copy the data from the Clipboard to the new location.

▶ "Working with Multiple Projects," p. 357.

You must be careful when selecting the data cells for the **Cut** and **Copy** commands. If you want to cut or copy an entire task or group of tasks, you must select the task ID number. Use the mouse to select the ID number, which selects all cells in the task. You also can use Shift+Spacebar to select the entire row for a task. If you select a limited number of cells within a task or group of tasks, only the data in these cells copies to the Clipboard.

To move a task or group of tasks, follow these steps:

1. Select the original task entries by clicking the ID number(s) for the tasks. You also can use Shift+Spacebar to select all cells in a task row.

   Use click-and-drag to select multiple task ID numbers that are next to each other.

2. Select the **Edit Cut** command or use the Ctrl+X key to cut the original data from the task list to the Clipboard.

3. Select the task row where the data is to relocate. Even if you are moving more than one task, you select only the first row of the new location.

If a task already resides on the row you selected, this task and all tasks below it shift down to make room for the task or tasks that you are moving.

4. Select the **E**dit **P**aste command or press Ctrl+V to paste the Clipboard contents into the task list at the selected row. The **P**aste command inserts a new row or rows at the target selection point and copies the tasks in the Clipboard into the inserted rows.

To copy a task or group of tasks, take the following steps:

1. Select the original task entries by clicking the task ID number for the tasks. You also can use the combination Shift+Spacebar to select all cells in a task row.

   Use click-and-drag to select multiple task ID numbers that are next to each other.

2. Select the **E**dit **C**opy command or press Ctrl+C to copy the selected data to the Clipboard.

3. Select the task row where you want the data duplicated. Even if you are copying more than one task, you select only the first row at the new location.

   If a task already exists on the row you select, that task (and all tasks below it) are shifted down to make room for the new task or tasks that you are copying.

4. Select the **E**dit **P**aste command or press Ctrl+V to copy the Clipboard contents into the task list at the selected row. The Paste command inserts a new row or rows at the target selection point and copies the tasks in the Clipboard into the inserted rows.

After task data is copied to the Clipboard, you can paste the data into many locations. The task data remains in the Clipboard until another copy or cut operation replaces the current Clipboard contents with new data.

If you select just the Name field for a task (rather than the entire task) before a cut or copy procedure, the **P**aste command doesn't insert a new row to create a new task at the target location. Instead, **P**aste copies the text from the Name cell into the existing target cell. If no task exists on the target row, the new entry creates a new task with a default duration.

> **Caution**
>
> Be sure that you select the entire task or tasks *before* you begin a cut or copy operation if you intend to create new tasks at the paste site.

In addition to the cut-and-copy method for moving and copying tasks within the project, Microsoft Project also includes a drag-and-drop feature to perform the same commands.

To move a task or group of tasks using the drag-and-drop feature, follow these steps:

1. Select the original task entries by clicking the ID number(s) for the tasks. You also can use the Shift+Spacebar to select all cells in a task row.

   Click and drag to select multiple task ID numbers that are next to each other.

2. Move the mouse pointer over the ID number for any one of the tasks selected.

3. Hold down the mouse button and drag the mouse pointer directly below where you wish to insert the selected tasks. A shadowed line will follow as you drag the pointer to its destination (see fig. 4.11).

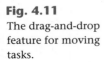

Fig. 4.11
The drag-and-drop feature for moving tasks.

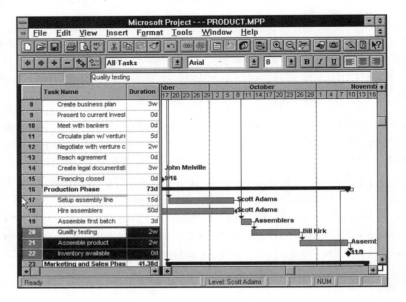

4. Release the mouse button, and the selected task(s) move into the new position.

Note

You cannot move or copy noncontiguous groups of tasks.

To copy a task or group of tasks using the drag-and-drop feature, follow these steps:

1. Select the original task entries by clicking the ID numbers for the tasks. You also can use the Shift+Spacebar to select all cells in a task row.

   Click and drag to select multiple task ID numbers that are next to each other.

2. Move the mouse pointer over the ID number for any one of the tasks selected.

3. Hold down the Ctrl key and the mouse button together and drag the mouse pointer directly below where you wish to copy the selected tasks. When you hold down both the Ctrl key and the mouse button, a small plus symbol is attached to the mouse pointer. This symbolizes a copy command using the drag and drop feature, rather than a move. A shadowed line will follow as you drag the pointer to its destination.

4. Release the mouse button, and the selected task(s) will be copied to the new position.

Entering Additional Data in the Task Information Form

The Task Information Form is a pop-up dialog box displayed when you select the Task Information tool on the toolbar (see fig. 4.12). The fields displayed in the Task Information Form are categorized using folder tabs along the top of the dialog window. The five tabs contain additional detail fields about the task selected on the current view. These fields are not immediately available on the Gantt Chart or Task Sheet views. Most of these extra fields will be explained in later chapters when the topic they address is covered. Some of the commonly used fields can be covered here, however.

Fig. 4.12
The Task Information Form dialog box.

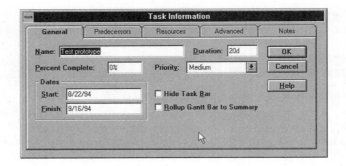

You can mark a task as a milestone by selecting the **M**ark as a Milestone check box on the Advanced tab. When you enter a duration of zero, a task is automatically marked as a milestone. You can mark any task as a milestone by filling this check box, even if the task's duration is not zero. You also can remove the milestone status by clearing this check box.

The Resources tab contains several fields used to enter resource information. The Resource names and number of units assigned to the task will appear in the Resources section of the dialog window.

▶ "Entering Scheduling Requirements," p. 131.

The Predecessors tab contains fields used to list the predecessors to the selected task. The predecessor name, dependency type, and lag/lead time are entered and displayed here.

▶ "Assigning Resources and Costs to Tasks," p. 205.

An important feature of the Task Information Form is its capability to make an identical change in several tasks at once. If you select multiple tasks before activating the form, the Multiple Task Information Form dialog box appears, with all fields empty (see fig. 4.13). Any entry you make in a field will be copied to all of the tasks that were selected when you activated the form.

Fig. 4.13
The Multiple Task Information Form dialog box.

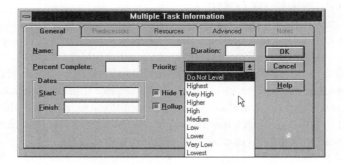

Navigating and Entering Data on the Task Information Form

To enter data on the Task Information Form, you must first select the folder tab that contains the fields you want to edit. To activate a folder tab, click the mouse on the tab name. You may then move from field to field on the Task Information Form with the Tab key and Shift+Tab keys. Move directly to a field by clicking the field. You also can move directly to a field by using the Alt key plus the underlined letter in the field name. Use Alt+D, for example, to move directly to the **D**uration field on the General tab.

When you are finished typing data into the form, and filling in or changing as many fields as you choose, click the OK button or press the Enter key to enter the changes. To cancel all the changes you made, choose the Cancel button or press Esc.

Entering Task Notes

You can use the Notes tab on the Task Information Form to enter and display notes about each task (see fig. 4.14). These notes may be of use to you at this stage of planning the project.

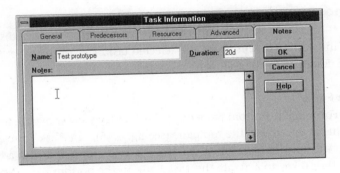

Fig. 4.14
The Notes option on the Task Information Form.

To enter notes about a task, select the Notes tab on the Task Information Form, position the cursor in the Notes field (by pressing the Tab key until the field is active or by pressing Alt+T), and type the note. Notes can contain up to 3,071 characters.

Microsoft Project word-wraps within the Notes field. If you want to force a new line or start a paragraph, use the Enter key. Use the following keys to move through the note field:

Key	Effect
Home	Moves to the beginning of the current line.
End	Moves to the end of the current line.
Ctrl+Home	Moves to the beginning of the note.
Ctrl+End	Moves to the end of the note.
Ctrl+left arrow	Moves one word to the left.
Ctrl+right arrow	Moves one word to the right.

▶ "Printing Views and Reports," p. 443.

▶ "Formatting Views," p. 497.

You can display Notes in customized views or print them as part of standard reports.

Viewing Other Task Forms

The Task Information Form is only one of four forms that you can display for entering and editing details about the selected task. Two of the other three forms are described in the following sections.

The Task Form

The Task Form in the bottom pane of the Task Entry view shows details for the task that is selected in the top pane (see fig. 4.15). The Task Form always appears in the bottom pane when you use the Split command with a task view. Use the F6 key to activate the Task Form in the bottom pane. You may also show the Task Form in a full-screen view rather than in the bottom pane of a combination view, but you only see the information for a single task at a time when viewing the Task Form full screen.

The Task Form has entry or editing fields for the task **N**ame, the **D**uration, and other fields that do not immediately appear on the spreadsheet table in the Gantt Chart. The start and finish dates that Microsoft Project currently has scheduled for the task are shown on the form. There are also fields to identify tasks that have fixed durations and to register the percent complete when you begin tracking the actual work done on the task.

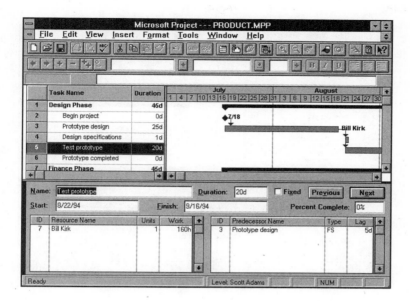

Fig. 4.15
The Task Form
view in the
bottom pane.

Note

Do not enter dates in the Scheduled **S**tart and Scheduled **F**inish date fields unless the task *must* start or finish on these dates. These fields are placed on the form solely for entering constraints on the scheduling of the task. If you enter a date in either field, the date becomes a Start No Earlier Than or a Finish No Later Than constraint date for the task. See the section on task constraints for more information.

You can customize the bottom of the Task Form to display different kinds of information. Initially, the form displays entry tables for resource assignments and for predecessor relationships. The predecessor tasks are these tasks whose scheduled dates must be considered before the current task can be scheduled.

▶ "Entering
Scheduling
Requirements,"
p. 131.

The Task Details Form

The Task Details Form, shown in figure 4.16, can be viewed in the bottom pane to display many more fields of data about the task than the Task Form shows. However, the Task Details Form compresses the area at the bottom of the form devoted to the optional detail tables and fields. To display the Task Details Form, choose **V**iew from the menu and choose the **M**ove Views command. Select the Task Details Form from the Move Views dialog box and choose **A**pply to display it.

▶ "Formatting
Views,"
p. 497.

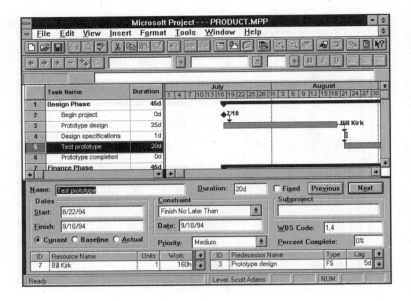

Fig. 4.16

The Task Details Form view in the bottom pane.

Outlining the Task List

Outlining usually is thought of in terms of its visual effect: you indent detail topics under major topics (see the task list in fig. 4.17). The major topics control and summarize the subordinated detail topics. In project management, the subordination of a task is called *demoting* the task, and the task that you demote is a *subordinate* task. The task under which the task is subordinated automatically becomes a *summary* task that both controls and summarizes the subordinate tasks. Microsoft Project displays subordinate tasks indented beneath the summary tasks, unless you choose to display them differently.

A summary task serves one primary function: to summarize the duration, cost, and amount of work expended on its subordinate tasks. When a task is transformed into a summary task, the task's start date is determined by the start date of the subordinate that starts first, and the finish date is determined by the finish date of the subordinate that finishes last. You cannot enter a scheduled start date or finish date for a summary task. These dates can be calculated only from the related subordinates. The costs and amount of work associated with the subordinate tasks are summarized in the cost and work fields of the summary task.

If you demote a summary task, the related subordinate tasks are demoted even further. In fact, all actions you apply to a summary task also are applied to the related subordinate tasks. If you delete, copy, move, promote, or demote a summary task, all of the subordinates, including subordinated summary tasks and their subordinates, are deleted, copied, moved, promoted, or demoted along with the summary task.

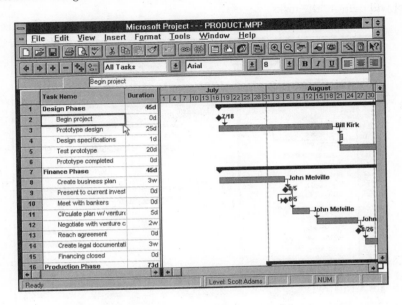

Fig. 4.17
An outlined task list.

You can *promote* tasks already indented by shifting these tasks to the left. When an indented task is promoted, the tasks immediately beneath the promoted task are affected in one of these ways:

- If the tasks below are at the same level of indentation as the new promoted task, the tasks become subordinates to the new summary task.

- If the tasks below are subordinates of the promoted task, these tasks remain subordinates but shift to the left to follow the summary task.

- If the tasks below are at a higher outline level (already further to the left than the promoted task), these tasks are unaffected by the promotion.

If you want to introduce a new task into the task list and make the new task a summary task, you must insert the task just above the intended subordinates. You can then demote the subordinate tasks or, if the new summary task is inserted within an already subordinated list of tasks, you can promote the summary task rather than demoting the subordinates.

Microsoft Project provides quick keys and outlining tools at the left side of the entry bar (see fig. 4.18). The right-arrow tool is the Indent tool, and the left-arrow tool is the Outdent tool. The key combination Alt+Shift+right arrow is the indent quick key. The key combination Alt+Shift+left arrow is the outdent quick key. The outdent tool will promote the tasks, and the indent tool will demote the tasks.

Fig. 4.18
The outlining tools.

Outlining tools—

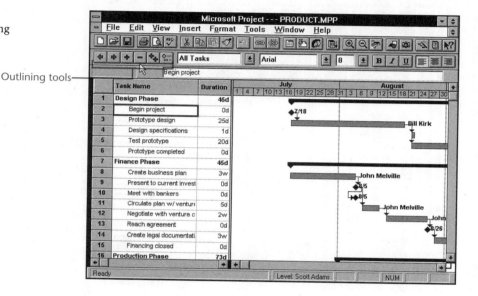

Indenting and Outdenting Tasks

To indent or outdent a task or group of select tasks, select the task(s) and use the Indent or Outdent button on the Formatting toolbar or choose **T**ools from the menu and choose O**u**tlining, **I**ndent or **O**utdent. You also can drag a single task to the right or left in the task list with the mouse. Place the mouse pointer over the first letters of the Task Name field until it becomes a double-arrow. Drag the pointer to the right or left to change the Indent or Outdent level of the task.

Collapsing and Expanding the Outline

A major advantage of outlining is that it enables you to collapse the outline to view only the major components of the project (see fig. 4.19). Collapsing an outline merely suppresses the display of the subordinate tasks, leaving just summary tasks.

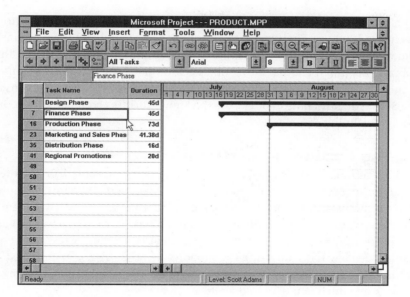

Fig. 4.19
The PRODUCT
outline, collapsed.

You also can collapse all but one part of the outline to show how the details
of the part fit into the overall picture (see fig. 4.20).

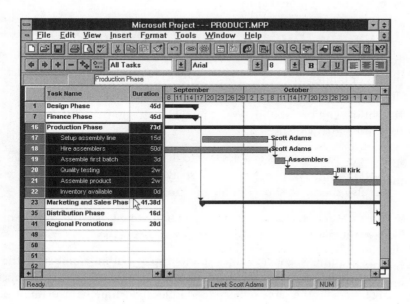

Fig. 4.20
The PRODUCT
outline with one
section expanded
and all others
collapsed.

To hide subtasks, select the summary task and use the Hide Subtasks button or choose from the Tools menu the Outlining command and then choose Hide Subtasks. To display subtasks, select the summary task and use the Show Subtasks button or choose Show Subtasks from the Tools, Outlining command. To show all subtasks throughout the project, select any task and use the Show All Tasks button or choose the Show All Tasks command from the Tools, Outlining command.

Editing Outlined Projects

When a summary task is deleted, copied, cut, pasted, promoted, or demoted, all subordinate tasks are included in the same operation. Therefore, if you delete a summary task you also delete all the subordinate tasks. If you demote a summary task, you further demote its subordinate tasks. If you want to use one of the operations listed above on a task that is a summary task, and you want to do so without affecting the subordinate tasks, then you must first promote the subordinates so that these tasks no longer are summarized by the task on which you plan to operate.

A task that was demoted can be *promoted* easily to a higher level. All tasks immediately below this task on the same or on a lower level become subordinates to the new promoted task.

Selecting the Display Options for Outlining

Select the Tools menu and choose Options to change the formatting options for outlining. The Outline options are displayed under the View tab in the Options dialog box (see fig. 4.21).

In the Outline Options section, you can make four choices, which are described in the following list:

- Show Summary Tasks enables you to display summary tasks (the default) or suppress them from the display. When they are displayed, you can also choose to show or hide the Project Summary Task.

- Indent Name enables you to indent subordinate tasks (the default) or leave them left justified like top level summary tasks.

- Show Outline Number enables you to display outline numbers to the left of each task or to leave them off (the default). The outline numbering scheme is the same scheme used in legal documents. The number for each task includes the position number for each of the summary tasks under which it is subordinated (see fig. 4.22).

Outline numbers are ideally suited for use as Work Breakdown Structure (WBS) codes. Whether you choose to display outline numbers or not, the outline numbers are placed in the WBS Code field for all tasks. You can view and edit this field on the Task Details Form. If you desire, you can replace the outline number with your own WBS codes.

I

Project Management

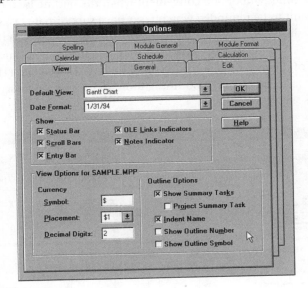

Fig. 4.21
The Outline options.

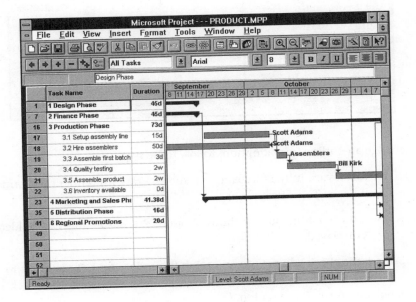

Fig. 4.22
Displaying outline numbers.

■ Show Outline Symbol enables you to display outline symbols to the left of each task or to leave them off (the default). The outline symbols are a plus sign and a minus sign. Summary tasks have a plus sign and all other tasks have a minus sign.

The outline symbols are convenient when the outline is collapsed and you want to be reminded which tasks have subordinate tasks not currently displayed. In figure 4.23, the tasks with plus signs to the left have detail tasks hidden from view. You may also turn the outline symbols on or off by using the outline symbol tool on the toolbar. (This tool is to the far right of all the outlining tools and shows a plus sign and a minus sign.)

Fig. 4.23
Displaying outline
symbols.

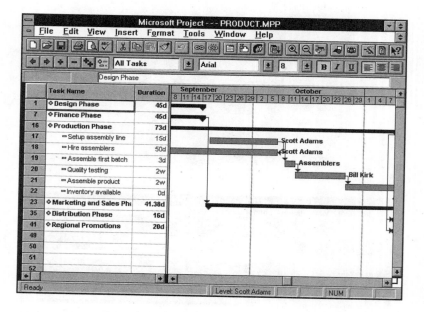

To change an outline format option, follow these steps:

1. Activate a view in the top pane that shows a task list (either the Gantt Chart or the Task Sheet view).

2. Select the **T**ools menu and choose **O**ptions. Make sure the View folder tab is displayed.

3. Mark the check box next to an option to produce an X if you want to turn on the option or to remove the X if you want to clear the check box and turn off the option.

4. Select OK when all options are set to your liking, or select Cancel to close the dialog box without making any changes.

Printing the Project Task List

You can print the task list in a number of ways to suit your purposes. You can print the Gantt Chart, the PERT Chart, or the Task Sheet view, all of which appear on paper much like they appear on-screen. You also can choose from among several standard, printable report forms. The task forms and the Task PERT, however, cannot be printed.

▶ "Printing Views and Reports," p. 443.

Chapter 16 explains how to control the results of printing the views and the standard reports. Chapter 18 explains how to customize views and reports. The steps below outline how to send a report to the printer.

▶ "Formatting Views," p. 497.

Printing the Task Views

To print one of the views, perform the following steps:

1. Display the view in the top pane or full-screen; the view prints no matter which view you select.

2. Select all filters or perform all sorting that you want in the printed report.

3. To preview how the report is going to look, select the Print Preview tool or select the File menu and choose Print Preview (see fig. 4.24).

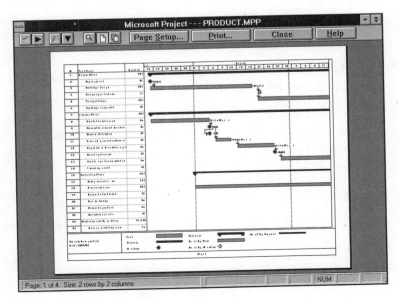

Fig. 4.24
The Print Preview screen.

4. Select the Multi-page button (the button that shows a *stack* of paper) to get an overview of the full report. Figure 4.25 shows an overview of the full report.

Fig. 4.25
The multi-page print preview.

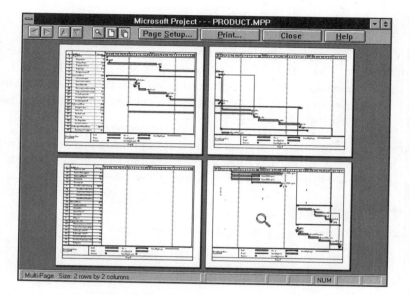

5. Place the pointer over any page of the report, and the pointer changes to a *zoom pointer*, an image of a magnifying glass that replaces the standard mouse pointer (refer to fig. 4.25). Click to view the page in a full-screen view.

6. Use the arrow buttons in the upper left corner of the screen (not the arrow keys) to scroll to different pages.

7. Click the zoom mouse pointer on any section of a page to see that section in greater detail (see fig. 4.26).

8. Choose the Page Setup button to change the page features of the report. The Page Setup dialog box shown in figure 4.27 appears. Make all needed changes and choose OK.

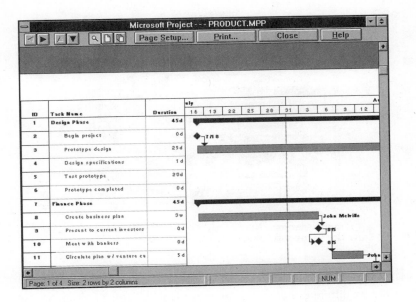

Fig. 4.26
The Print Preview
screen in Zoom
view.

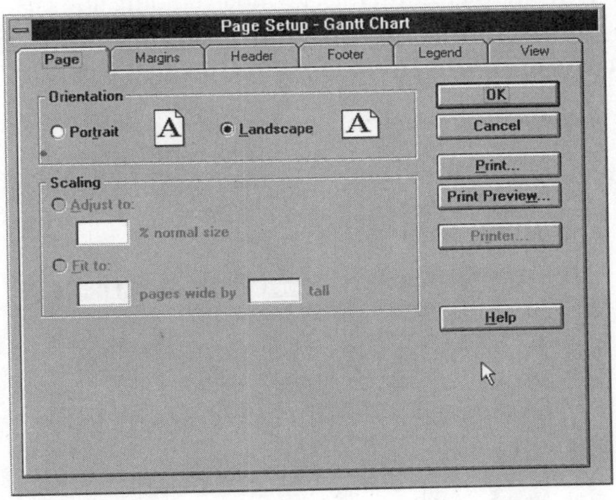

Fig. 4.27
The Page Setup
dialog box.

Project Management

9. Choose the **P**rint button to send the report to the printer. The Print
   dialog box appears as shown in figure 4.28.

Fig. 4.28
The Print dialog
box.

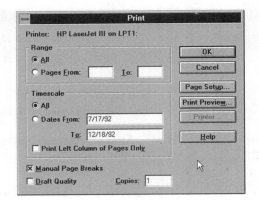

▶ "Printing Views
and Reports,"
p. 443.

10. To start the print job, select the OK button.

Printing the Standard Task Reports

There are six different report categories available for printing standardized and custom reports in Microsoft Project. Understanding and customizing these reports is covered in Chapter 20, "Using and Customizing Reports," but is mentioned here in case you want to print a standard report.

To print one of the standard reports, perform the following steps:

1. Select the **V**iew menu and choose the **R**eports command. The Reports dialog box appears as shown in figure 4.29.

Fig. 4.29
The Reports dialog
box.

2. Choose the report type you want to print from the six categories and click **S**elect.

3. Click on the report you want to print and choose the **S**elect button. This will show you the selected report in the Print Preview window (see fig. 4.30).

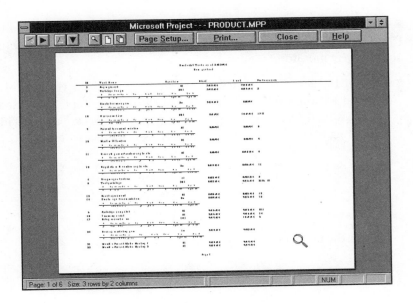

Fig. 4.30
The Print Preview screen for a selected report.

Project Management

4. Select the **P**rint button in Print Preview to print the report.

▶ "Using and Customizing Reports," p. 563.

From Here...

In this chapter, you learned how to create and edit the task list, as well as how to estimate and enter durations for the tasks. You viewed the various task forms used to enter additional task information. Finally, you learned how to outline the task list and the basic steps needed to print task reports.

Now that you know how to create the basic task list, you can investigate the scheduling tools available in Microsoft Project. These chapters will provide you with the additional information you need to complete your project:

■ Chapter 5, "Entering Scheduling Requirements," discusses the various task constraints available, as well as how to understand and create dependency relationships between the tasks—thus creating a link for each task.

■ Chapter 10, "Auditing the Task Schedule," discusses the different tools and techniques available to audit the schedule for correctness and to filter and sort the tasks and resources.

- Chapter 16, "Printing Views and Reports," discusses in depth the various reports and views that can be used to produce professional reports for project monitoring.

- Chapter 18, "Formatting Views," covers the various ways you can format and sort the standard or customized views. Some topics discussed include formatting the text display, formatting timescales, and specific formatting techniques for the commonly used standard views.

Chapter 5

Entering Scheduling Requirements

Once the project tasks have been defined and entered, the scheduling portion of project management becomes important. Up to this point, we have used Microsoft Project as a basic word processor—entering tasks and their durations into one of the various task sheets and forms available. In this chapter, we take a look at how these tasks can be sequenced and linked, thus providing a calculated preliminary schedule.

The sequencing and linking of tasks in the schedule is based on several factors. One group of factors is the internal or external constraints that limit when the task can be scheduled for completion. Another important set of factors are the scheduling requirements that link the scheduled start or finish of the task to the start or finish of other tasks.

In this chapter, the discussion focuses on

- Understanding and creating task constraints.

- Understanding the task dependencies.

- Defining and establishing task links.

Entering Deadline Constraints for Tasks

When you add a task to a project, Microsoft Project marks the task as one scheduled to start as soon as possible. This means that the program considers any sequencing requirements that determine when the task's predecessors will be completed, then schedules the task to begin as soon as possible after the preceding tasks are completed.

Some tasks, however, may be subject to deadlines from outside the project—imposed by customers, contractors, government, or even internal company policies. Some situations are shown in the following examples:

- The financial task of preparing payroll reports is constrained by pay dates and tax reports.

- A manufacturing contract may call for delivery no later than a stated date.

- A vendor may stipulate that he can start work no sooner than a certain date.

When a task is constrained, Microsoft Project cannot schedule the task by considering only when the task's predecessors are completed. The date constraints also must be considered. Consider a case where you stipulate that a task must start on a certain date, but Microsoft Project calculates that the preceding tasks cannot be completed in time to meet this deadline. If a date constraint conflicts with the scheduling of predecessors, you see a message that states that Microsoft Project cannot reconcile the conflicting requirements you imposed on the project.

▶ "Auditing the Task Schedule," p. 243

One of the most common mistakes a novice user of Microsoft Project makes is to accidentally impose constraints that make the schedule impossible to reconcile. Task Constraints are created any time you specify the scheduled Start or Finish dates for a task by entering, for example, the dates on the Task Information form or by creating a task by dragging in the Gantt Chart or the Calendar view.

Understanding the Types of Constraints

Constraint classifications exist that describe the constrained status of a task. These classifications are described in the following list:

Classification	Status
As Soon As Possible	This labels a task as unconstrained.
As Late As Possible	This task should be delayed as long as possible, without holding up the finish of the project.

Classification	Status
Start No Later Than	This task must be started on or before the designated date.
Must Start On	This task must start exactly on the designated date.
Start No Earlier Than	This task cannot start until the designated date or later.
Finish No Later Than	This task must be completed on or before the designated date.
Must Finish On	This task must finish exactly on the designated date.
Finish No Earlier Than	This task must not be completed before the designated date.

Entering Task Constraints

You can record the task constraints on the Task Details Form or on the Task Information Form. After you activate the form you prefer, the procedure is the same for both forms. The Task Information Form is a dialog box that you activate with the Information tool after you select a task. The Task Details Form is a view that you must activate in a window pane. This form usually is placed in the lower pane to display details about the task that you selected in the upper pane. The upper pane usually contains the Gantt Chart or Task Sheet.

To enter task constraints on the Task Details Form, perform the following steps:

1. Activate the lower pane of a combination view by pressing F6 or by clicking in the lower pane. The Gantt Chart or Task Sheet should be in the upper pane.

2. Open the **V**iew menu and choose **M**ore Views. The More Views dialog box appears (see fig. 5.1).

3. Scroll toward the bottom of the list of views and select the Task Details Form.

4. Choose the **A**pply button to display the form.

5. Select the **C**onstraint field.

6. Activate the entry list (shown in fig. 5.2) by clicking the entry list arrow or by pressing Alt+down arrow.

7. Select the appropriate constraint type.

Fig. 5.1
The More Views
dialog box.

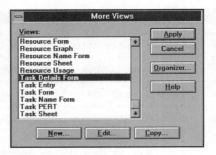

Fig. 5.2
The Task
Constraint
Entry List.

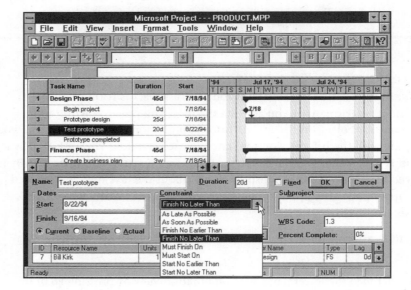

8. Enter the constraint date, if required, in the Date field just below the constraint type (see fig. 5.3). The As Soon As Possible and As Late As Possible constraints do not require a constraint date.

9. Complete the entry by clicking OK or by pressing Enter.

To enter task constraints on the Task Information Form, follow these steps:

1. Select the task to constrain.

2. Activate the Task Information Form by clicking the Information tool or by selecting the Task Information command from the Insert menu.

   You could also activate the Task Information Form by double-clicking the mouse on the task to be constrained.

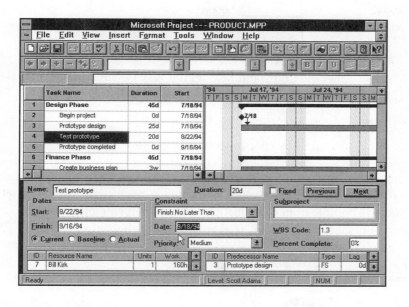

Fig. 5.3
The constraint type and date entered.

Project Management

3. Select the Advanced folder by clicking on the folder tab.

4. Select the Constraint Task Type field in the dialog box.

5. Display the entry list (shown in fig. 5.4) by clicking the entry list arrow or by pressing Alt+down arrow.

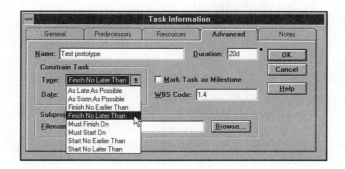

Fig 5.4
The Task Information Form Constraint list.

6. Click on the constraint type that you want or highlight it with the arrow keys and press Enter.

7. Select the Constraint Task Date field just below and enter the constraint date, if required. The As Soon As Possible and As Late As Possible constraints do not require a constraint date.

8. Select OK or press Enter to complete the entry.

To remove a task constraint, perform the following steps:

1. Select the task.

2. Select either the **C**onstraint field on the Task Details Form or the Constraint Task Ty**p**e field on the Task Information Form.

3. Select As Soon As Possible from the entry list.

4. Enter the change by choosing OK or by pressing Enter.

▶ "Auditing the Task Schedule," p. 243

In this case, if you wanted to return several tasks to an unconstrained status, you could select all the tasks you plan to change, activate the form, and select As Soon As Possible from the Constraint field. When you select OK, the changes are made in all the selected tasks.

Linking Tasks in Sequence

It's difficult to imagine a project in which no sequencing requirements exist for the tasks. Invariably, one or more tasks must be scheduled based on when some predecessor task is completed or at least started. This relationship between tasks is known as a *dependency relationship* in project management: the scheduled start or finish of one task is dependent on the scheduled start or finish of another task. If a painting project calls for applying two coats of paint, for example, you should schedule the task of applying the second coat to start *after* the task of applying the first coat is completed.

The dependent task usually is known as a *successor* task, and the task upon which this task depends is its *predecessor*. This taxonomy, although useful, can be misleading. Cases occur when the dependent task must be scheduled for completion in time for its predecessor to begin! The key to understanding this paradox is to remember that the terms predecessor and successor were chosen for the most common cases, where one task does in fact precede the other in time. It's less confusing to use the terms *independent* task and *dependent* task. Remember that the point of this exercise is to identify the tasks whose scheduling should be done to coincide in some way with the scheduled start or finish of some other task or tasks.

Often deciding which of two tasks is the predecessor and which is the successor is self-evident. Obviously, the second coat of paint is the successor task because you cannot apply the second coat until the first coat is applied. But, what if the final coat of paint is applied by an artist, and the artist is in such demand that you have to let her do her part *when* she says she can do it? If painters for the first coat are relatively easy to find, then you can schedule the completion of the first coat in time for the artist to begin. If the artist's schedule changes, you can reschedule the first coat task more easily than you can reschedule the artist to accommodate the less-skilled painters. Here, you make the task of applying the first coat of paint the dependent task, so that the scheduling accommodates the task of applying the final coat.

The decision as to which task should be the predecessor and which the dependent or successor task hinges on which task you have more control over. If you have equal scheduling control over both tasks, make the task that must come first the predecessor and let the later task be the dependent. But, in cases where one task is less easily rescheduled than the other, you may want to arbitrarily make the more flexibly scheduled task the dependent task— regardless of which task actually must come first.

Dependency relationships may be defined to allow for lag time when the successor task must be delayed somewhat beyond its predecessor date. Framing the walls of a house, for example, may be the successor task to pouring the foundation slab. However, you may want to allow some lag time to allow the concrete to dry and cure before the carpenters begin.

You also can allow for lead time in cases where the successor task overlaps the predecessor. Loading the moving van, for example, may be the successor task to packing the boxes, but you don't have to wait until all the boxes are packed to start loading the van. With some lead time, the loading task can overlap the packing task.

Understanding the Types of Task Dependencies

Four kinds of dependency relationships exist. In each type, the definition references a date for the predecessor task, followed by a date for the dependent task (see fig. 5.5). The dates are merely stated as start or finish. Therefore, the most common dependency relationship, where the finish of the predecessor task determines the start of the dependent task, is known as the *Finish-to-Start relationship*.

The four dependency relationships, and the two-letter codes used by Microsoft Project to designate these relationships, are shown in the following list:

Finish-to-Start (FS)   The finish date of the predecessor determines the scheduling of the start date of the dependent task; you cannot start a different task until the current one is finished. For example, starting the framing of a house is dependent on having the foundation finished.

Finish-to-Finish (FF)	The finish date of the predecessor determines the scheduling of the finish date of the dependent task; you schedule the two tasks to finish at the same time. For example, the mixing of the concrete to pour a swimming pool should be scheduled to finish when the forms for the walls of the pool are completed.
Start-to-Start (SS)	The start date of the predecessor task determines the scheduling of the start date of the dependent task; you schedule the two tasks to start at the same time. For example, when moving a company to a new office, schedule the movers to start loading the vans fairly soon after the packers start disassembling the furniture.
Start-to-Finish (SF)	The start date of the predecessor task determines the scheduling of the finish date of the dependent task; the finish date of the dependent task must be scheduled to coincide with the start date of the predecessor. For example, when preparing for an important test, most students schedule studying to finish approximately when testing begins.

Fig. 5.5

The four dependency relationship types.

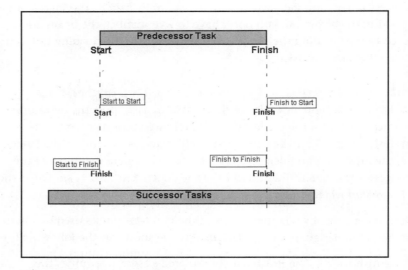

Using Leads and Lags

Besides defining the kind of dependency relationship that exists between tasks, you also must account for any lag time or lead time that you think is appropriate in the relationship. In the painting project, for example, the second coat of paint should be applied only after the first coat is completely dry. Therefore, you must not only define the relationship between these tasks, but you also must inform Microsoft Project about the lag time that must be built into the schedule between finishing the first coat (the predecessor) and starting the second coat (the successor).

In some dependency relationships, you may want to define a lead time: you can schedule the dependent task date to precede the actual predecessor date by some appropriate amount of time. The painting project, for example, also must schedule a cleanup task. When you start the cleanup should depend on when you finish the second coat. However, you may feel that you can begin cleaning up when the painters have only two hours of painting left to do. So, you can schedule the cleanup with a Finish-to-Start dependency on the second coat task, but with a two-hour lead time.

Lag time is expressed as a number followed by one of the same time code letters that you use for entering durations (m,h,d,w). A two-day lag is entered as 2d. You also can express lag time as a percent of the predecessor's duration. Therefore, if the successor task can be started after its predecessor is ninety-percent complete, you enter a Start-to-Start relationship (SS) with a ninety-percent lag.

Lead time is entered in the lag field as a negative number or percentage.

> **Note**
>
> Identifying the task relationships where overlap between tasks is possible is among the best approaches to take when trying to shorten the overall time it takes to finish a project. Look for dependency relationships where lead time is possible, and where the relationship can be defined as Start-to-Start or Finish-to-Finish.

Entering Dependency Relationships

You can define task dependencies in Microsoft Project in several ways. If the dependency is a Finish-to-Start relationship, you can simply select the tasks and use the Link Tasks tool on the toolbar, or you can use the **L**ink Tasks command on the **E**dit menu. If the relationship is more complex, you may need to use a task editing table or form for typing the kind of relationship and the lead or lag times, if applicable.

You can edit or remove task relationship definitions with any of the task editing forms or spreadsheet tables.

Using the Link Tasks Command

One way to link tasks is to select the tasks and then use the Link Tasks command or tool to define the dependency relationship. Only the simplest kind of dependency, the Finish-to-Start, can be defined with this method. Moreover, the predecessor task always remains the higher task on the task list (the tasks with lower task ID numbers). The Link Tasks command assumes that the tasks you selected to link are listed in sequential linking order.

No limit exists to the number of tasks that you can link in the same execution of the linking command. You can link just one predecessor and one successor at a time or you can link all the tasks in the project in the same operation. The order in which you add tasks to the selection makes no difference in defining the relationship; tasks higher up on the task list (with lower ID numbers) are always the predecessor when linked to tasks lower on the list (with higher ID numbers).

Tip

To select all tasks in the project, select a column heading name in the spreadsheet table. Select the column heading (Name, for example), and all tasks are selected.

To select multiple tasks in the task list, select the first predecessor task, and then select the successor task(s). For tasks that are adjacent in the task list, use the Shift+down arrow or Shift+up arrow key combinations or drag the mouse pointer to extend the selection to as many tasks as you want to link. For non-adjacent tasks, add tasks to the selection by pressing and holding the Ctrl key while clicking additional tasks. Or you can click and drag on additional groups of tasks.

To link the selected tasks with the menu or with the Link Tasks tool on the toolbar, follow these steps:

1. Select the tasks to be linked using one of the previously discussed selection methods.

2. Select the **Edit Link** Tasks command or select the Link Tasks tool, and the task links are established automatically.

Using the Unlink Tasks Command

Tasks that you linked in a dependency relationship can be unlinked with relative ease. Select the tasks to unlink and use the Unlink Tasks tool on the toolbar or the U**n**link Tasks command on the **E**dit menu. You also can use one of the task editing forms or tables to remove the task relationship.

You can unlink two tasks or all tasks in one operation. You select the tasks for unlinking in the same manner that you select tasks for linking. The unlinking operation works on all task relationships, not just the simple Finish-to-Start relationship.

To unlink selected tasks with the toolbar, select the tasks that you want to unlink and choose the Unlink Tasks tool. To unlink selected tasks with the menu, select the tasks that you want to unlink, select the Edit menu, and select Unlink Tasks.

To unlink all project tasks, select all tasks by clicking a field name (a column heading) in the spreadsheet table, and choose the Unlink Tasks tool or use the Unlink Tasks command in the Edit menu.

Defining Task Links with the Task Information Form

The Task Information Form can also be used to link tasks to one another. It provides a text field for typing the predecessor codes. To create the dependency relationship using the Task Information Form, perform the following steps:

1. Select the successor task.

2. Activate the Task Information Form by clicking the Information tool or by selecting the Task Information command from the Insert menu.

3. Activate the Predecessors folder by clicking on the Predecessor folder tab.

4. Enter the predecessor Task ID, Name, Dependency Type, and lead or lag time in the appropriate fields (see fig. 5.6).

   You can use the entry list down arrow to select the Task Name and Dependency Type information from a list of available IDs and dependency types without having to type the information in the appropriate fields.

5. Select OK or press Enter to complete the entry.

Defining Task Links in the Gantt Chart

You can enter, delete, and revise dependency relationships in the Gantt Chart by selecting a task and defining the related predecessor relationship(s) in the Predecessor field. The simplest relationship, the Finish-to-Start, can be entered by just entering the task ID number for the predecessor task in the Predecessor field.

Fig. 5.6
Entering predeces-
sors on the Task
Information Form.

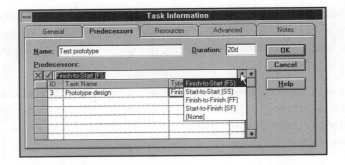

To enter one of the other relationships, you must enter the task ID number
followed immediately by the abbreviation for the relationship. Leads and lags
are entered after the relationship type. Begin a lag with a plus sign and a lead
with a minus sign. For example, to enter a Start-to-Start relationship with a
two-day lag, in which the predecessor for a task is task number 3, type
3SS+2d. If a task has more than one predecessor, separate the predecessor
definitions by commas. Continuing the example above, a field entry of
3SS+2d,6FS–1h indicates that task 6 also is a predecessor and that the relationship is Finish-to-Start with a one-hour lead time.

To see the additional Gantt Chart spreadsheet fields, click on the right arrow
on the horizontal scroll bar at the bottom of the Gantt Chart. The Predecessor field will be one of these additional fields.

To enter the predecessor relationship, select the Predecessors field in the row
for the successor task, and then enter the codes for the relationship, as described in the preceding paragraphs (see fig. 5.7).

Note that if you do not remember the task ID for the predecessor task, you
can use the following steps to scroll the task list to find the ID number:

1. Activate the edit bar by pressing F2 or by clicking in the editing area.
   You will see the Cancel and Enter boxes appear.

2. Use the scroll bar if necessary to find the predecessor task.

3. When the predecessor task is visible on-screen, click the mouse in any
   field on the row for the predecessor task, and the ID number will be
   placed in the editing area.

4. Type the remainder of the predecessor relationship code if necessary.

5. Press Enter or select the Enter box to complete the entry.

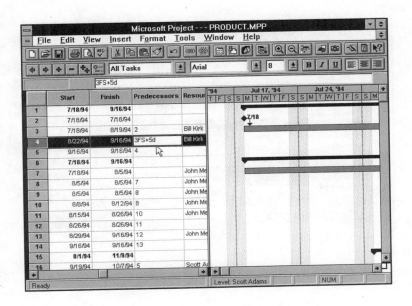

Fig. 5.7
Entering predecessors in the Gantt Chart.

Project Management

Defining Task Links with the Task Form

You can use the Task Form in the bottom pane of the Task Entry view to define the predecessor and successor relationships for the currently selected task. This is the easiest location in Microsoft Project to use for defining the more complex dependency relationships—relationships that contain leads or lags or that are not Finish-to-Start relationships.

The Format menu enables you to choose the entry fields that appear at the bottom of the form. The form usually displays entry tables for Resources and Predecessors. You also can display entry tables for the task's successors. If the tables for defining task relationships are not placed on the task form, use the Format menu to select the desired display.

To place the Resources and Predecessors editing tables on the Task Form, follow these steps:

1. If the Task Entry view is not the current view, select the **V**iew menu and choose **M**ore Views.

2. Select the Task Entry View from the list and choose **A**pply.

3. Activate the bottom pane by pressing F6 or by clicking anywhere in the bottom pane.

4. From the menu, select F**o**rmat and choose **D**etails. From the Details drop-down list, select Resources & Predecessors (see fig. 5.8).

Fig. 5.8
The Details list for
the Task Form.

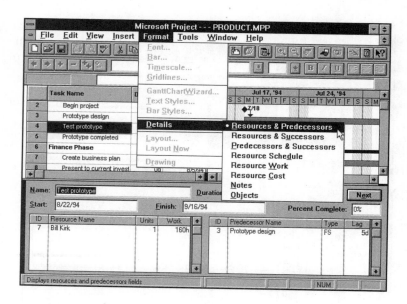

To define a predecessor for the current task, perform the following steps:

1. Select the dependent task by clicking the task row in the Gantt Chart
   display. You also can choose the N**e**xt and Pre**v**ious buttons in the Task
   Form to select the task that you want to define as the dependent task.

2. Select either the ID field or the Predecessor Name field in the Predecessors table on the Task Form.

3. Type the predecessor's ID number or Name, depending on the field you
   selected, and press Enter to complete the entry in the cell. The Task
   Form still displays OK because the Enter key only completed the cell
   entry. Click OK to complete the entry and define the relationship as
   Finish-to-Start (see fig. 5.9).

4. By selecting OK, you define the relationship as Finish-to-Start. To
   change the relationship type, select the Type field in the Predecessor
   box and type the two-letter code for the relationship. (The codes are FS,
   FF, SS, and SF.) Complete the entry by choosing OK.

5. Type the lag time (a positive number) or lead time (a negative number)
   in the Lag field. If the lead or lag is expressed as minutes, hours, days,
   or weeks you must use the same one-letter code that you used for durations. For example, type **2h** for a two-hour lag or **–3d** for a three-day
   lead time. For percentage expressions of lead or lag, just type a number

with a percent sign (%). For example, if a lag is equal to 25% of the duration of the predecessor, type **25%**. If the successor can start when the predecessor is 80% finished, you could type the lead as **–20%** (from the finish of the predecessor). Complete the entry by pressing OK.

6. Repeat steps two through five for each predecessor you want to record.

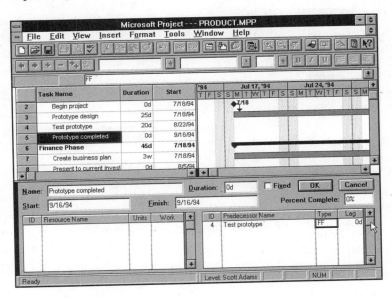

Fig. 5.9
Entering predecessors on the Task Form.

Note that when you edit a field in one of the tables at the bottom of a form, the Entry bar at the top of the screen is activated. You must complete the action in the Entry bar by entering or canceling the entry or by choosing another field in the Task Form. Until you choose the OK button though, all changes which have been made to the Task Form are not completed. After choosing the OK button, the additional predecessor data will be displayed.

To delete dependency definitions on the Task Form, follow these steps:

1. On the Gantt Chart in the top pane, select the dependent task.

2. Select a field in the Predecessor row in the Predecessors table, on the Task Form in the bottom pane.

3. Press the Delete key to delete the row in the Predecessors table.

4. Complete the change by either choosing the OK button or switching to the top pane.

Working with the Automatic Linking Option

Microsoft Project has a feature known as *automatic linking* that manages the impact of cutting and inserting tasks when the task list is already linked. If you cut a task from a chain of linked tasks, auto link keeps the chain intact by linking the former predecessor and successor to each other. If you insert a task into a chain of linked tasks, automatic linking initiates two actions: automatic linking breaks the existing link at the point of insertion by removing the dependency relationship between the tasks on either side of the insertion point, and then links the new inserted task to the task above and below the new task.

Automatic linking is activated or deactivated by the **A**uto Link Inserted or moved tasks setting on the Schedule tab of the Options dialog box. By default, automatic linking is enabled, but you can disable it by removing the X in its setting box.

Linking Outlined Task Lists

Linking in outlined task lists is more complicated than in non-outlined lists because more options are available. You can link the summary tasks to each other, or you can link the subordinate tasks in one summary group directly to the subordinate tasks in the predecessor and successor summary groups.

Linking Summary Tasks

If you enter the tasks for a new project in an outline format and choose to link all the tasks at the same time by selecting all tasks and using the linking tool, Microsoft Project links the summary tasks to each other and links the subordinate tasks separately within each summary group.

The first subordinate task of each summary group is implicitly linked to its summary task, and the remaining subordinate tasks are linked to the first subordinate task. The first subordinate task in the group does not have to have any explicitly named predecessor tasks; it is implicitly linked to the summary task, which is linked to the end of the previous summary task. Similarly, the last subordinate task in the group does not have to have any explicit successor tasks; it is implicitly linked to the summary task, which is linked to the end of the previous summary task.

The advantage of this method of linking outlined tasks is that you can change the structure of the detail tasks within a summary group without worrying about the linking to other summary groups. If you add new detail tasks at the end of a summary group, for example, you do not have to worry about the link to the first detail task in the next summary group.

You can link summary tasks only in Finish-to-Start relationships that have no lead or lag time. If you need a different relationship or if you need to define lead or lag time, define the first detail task in the summary group with the relationship you need. The summary task will reflect the effects of the relationship.

If automatic linking is enabled and you rearrange an outline, review carefully the links that result each time you move a task or group of tasks within the outline. You may have to adjust the automatic results to reflect exactly the relationship to be defined.

Leaving Summary Tasks out of the Linking Chain

The other method of linking tasks in an outline is to ignore the linking summary tasks and link only the detail tasks. The predecessor for the first detail task in a summary group is a detail task in a previous summary group. This method of linking is harder to maintain because if you add tasks at the beginning or end of a group, you must be concerned with maintaining the proper link to other groups.

Auditing the Task Links

The PERT Chart (Program Evaluation Review Techniques) is a view that shows the task relationships as a graph. Each task is represented by a small box known as a *node*, and the nodes for related tasks are linked by a line. Of the two linked tasks, the task to the right or below is the successor task.

▶ "Working with the PERT Chart," p. 165

The Task PERT view shows the predecessors and successors for just the selected task (see fig. 5.10), and is useful for confirming that you defined the task relationships as intended. You display the Task PERT view in the bottom pane while selecting tasks in the Gantt view or the Task Sheet view. The selected task is represented by a box or node in the center of the Task PERT view, with predecessors pictured on the left and successors on the right. The relationship is defined between the task nodes.

The Task PERT view is a display-only view. You can make no changes on this view screen, nor can you print the Task PERT view.

From Here...

This chapter showed you how to impose and remove date constraints for tasks when needed. It also introduced and explained the four types of dependency relationships, as well as how to use lead and lag time. In addition, you saw the various ways these task relationships can be imposed and defined.

Fig. 5.10
The Task PERT
view.

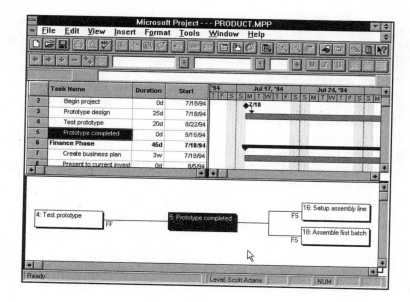

Now that the project tasks have been defined and their dependency relationships completed, the following chapters will give you the additional tools you
need to refine and complete your project:

- Chapter 6, "Working with the Calendar View," teaches you how to
  understand and work with the Calendar view. You will also learn how
  to edit the project and use the layout options available within the Calendar view.

- Chapter 10, "Auditing the Task Schedule," discusses the different tools
  and techniques available to audit the schedule for correctness and to
  filter and sort the tasks and resources.

Chapter 6

Working with the Calendar View

In this chapter, you learn how to

- Apply the Calendar view to your project data.

- Find and display task data in the Calendar view.

- Use the Calendar view to create and edit the tasks in your project.

- Link tasks in the Calendar view.

- Assign resources to tasks in the Calendar view.

You will often find it useful to be able to display your project on the familiar calendar background. After creating a project file using the other views provided by Microsoft Project, it can be very helpful to distribute reports showing all tasks or selected tasks in the calendar format. Although it may not be the best view for designing and creating lengthy or complex projects, the Calendar view can be used to create simple short duration projects.

Display the Calendar view by choosing from the **V**iew menu the **C**alendar command. The standard Calendar view is displayed in figure 6.1.

Fig. 6.1
The Calendar view presents your project in a familiar format.

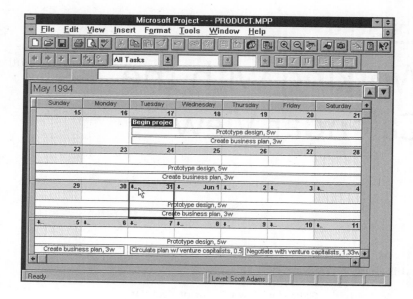

Understanding the Calendar View

▶ "Formatting
Views," p. 497

The Calendar view features a Month title above a calendar that shows one or more weeks of dates with task bars stretching from their start dates to their finish dates. The default display shows four weeks at a time and includes bars or lines for all tasks except Summary tasks. You can elect to include Summary tasks and you can change many other features of the display by customizing the Calendar view.

In some cases there is not enough room in the calendar to display all the tasks whose schedules fall on a particular date. When this is the case, you will see an overflow indicator at the left of the gray band that appears at the top of the date box. The overflow indicator is a small downward pointing black arrow followed by an ellipsis to indicate "more is available." For example, see the dates in the last week in figure 6.1.

You can see all the tasks that are scheduled on a given date by displaying a pop-up Task List for the date. To display the Task List for a specific date, either double-click the gray band at the top of the date box, or follow these steps:

1. Position the mouse pointer over any portion of the gray band at the top of the date box. The day number appears at the right of this gray band in the default calendar layout.

2. Use the right mouse button to display the Shortcut menu for dates.

3. Choose Task List from the Shortcut menu. The Tasks occurring on: dialog box will be displayed for the specific date that you were pointing to (see fig. 6.2).

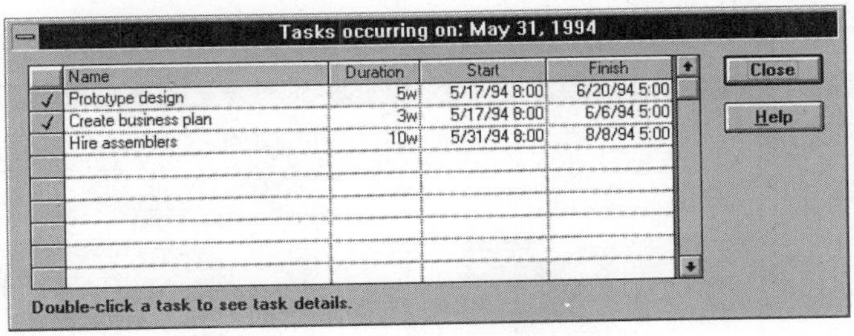

Fig. 6.2
All tasks occurring on a specific date are shown in a list. Double-click any of them to see details for that task.

4. After reviewing the list of tasks, choose the Close button to close the dialog box.

The Tasks Occurring On dialog box lists all tasks whose schedule dates encompass the date you have selected. Those tasks whose bars appear in the calendar have a check mark at the left of the listing. To increase the number of tasks that appear on the calendar, you can use the Zoom command (see the section "Using Zoom" later in this chapter) or else you must make changes in the calendar format.

▶ "Formatting the Calendar," p. 522

The Calendar View, like other views, has a number of Shortcut menus available. One way to approach learning about this view is to just start right-clicking in different spots on the view. There are navigation options like Go To and Zoom on Shortcut menus. Additional Shortcut menus offer access to the Task Information dialog box, access to a list of tasks occurring on specific dates, and formatting options for virtually every element of the calendar.

Moving Around in the Calendar View

As with other views, your effective use of the Calendar View depends on your ability to move around and find the information that you want to focus on. It is also helpful to know how to change the display of the calendar to show only selected information.

Scrolling the Calendar

Use the standard scroll bars to move forward and backward in time on the calendar. Note that when you drag the scroll box on the vertical scroll bar, a date indicator pop-up box helps you locate a specific date (see fig. 6.3). The beginning and end points on the scroll bar are approximately the start and end dates of the project.

Fig. 6.3

Drag the scroll box to move quickly to a specific date.

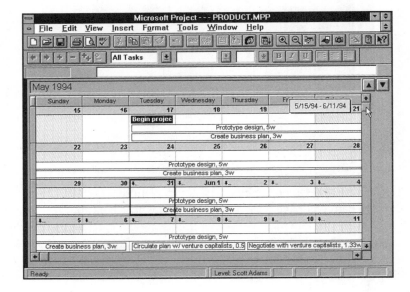

Use Alt+Home and Alt+End to jump to the beginning and ending dates of the project, respectively. You also can use the PageUp and PageDown keys to scroll through the display showing successive weeks in the life of the project.

Scroll through the months of the year with the up and down arrow buttons on the right side of the month title row. As you scroll through the months, the beginning of each successive month appears in the first row of the calendar, no matter how many weeks you have chosen to display in the view. The Alt+Up Arrow and Alt+Down Arrow keys also scroll by months through the project calendar.

Locating a Specific Task or Date

You can quickly move to a specific date anywhere in the calendar, including dates outside the date range of the project. You also can locate specific tasks by specifying their task ID number or by searching for tasks by name.

Using the Go To Command

Use the Go To command to move directly to a specific task ID or date. You can access the Go To function by pointing to the month title area, or anywhere but directly on a task bar, and right-clicking to display the Shortcut menu. You also can access the Go To command by choosing **E**dit from the menu and choosing **G**o To. When you choose Go To, the Go To dialog box appears, as shown in figure 6.4.

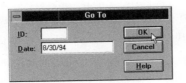

Tip

As with many Windows applications, you also can access the Go To feature by pressing F5.

Fig. 6.4
Use the Go To dialog box to move to a specified date or task ID.

> ## Caution
>
> The Go To command (and the Find command described below) will not select tasks for which task bars are not displayed in the Calendar view. Therefore, since summary tasks are not displayed in the default display, you cannot Go To a summary task unless you change the task bar styles. See the section "Formatting the Calendar" in Chapter 18, "Formatting Views", for instructions on changing the task bar styles.

If you type an ID number for a task whose task bar is not displayed because there are too many tasks on its date, the task will be selected and its beginning date will scroll into view—but you won't see the task or a selection marker to indicate which date is the beginning date. Nevertheless, since the task is selected, you can choose the Information button on the toolbar to view its Task Information dialog box. The task start date is displayed on the General tab. You can close the Task Information dialog box by choosing the Cancel button and then clicking on the Start date for the task to see the other tasks that are scheduled on that date.

Using the Find Command

You can use the Find command to locate tasks by their field values, usually by the value in the Name field. As with the Go To command, if the task you find is not currently displayed in the calendar, you will not see it even though it is selected.

> **Note**
>
> You can use the Find command in the Calendar view only if you have selected a task bar.

To find a task by searching for one or more characters in its name, follow these steps:

1. Select any task. If you want to search from the beginning of the task list, use Ctrl+Home to select the first task in the project and then select a task bar.

2. From the **E**dit menu, choose **F**ind (or use the Ctrl+F shortcut key). The Find dialog box will appear (see fig. 6.5).

Fig. 6.5
Search for a task by name with the Find command.

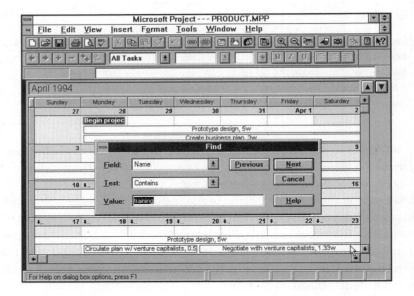

3. Type the characters you want to search for in the **V**alue field. You can enter whole words or phrases or only parts of words.

4. Choose the **N**ext button to search for the value among tasks with higher ID numbers (tasks that are toward the bottom of the task list but not necessarily later in the calendar). Choose the **P**revious button to search for the value among tasks with lower ID numbers (tasks that are toward the top of the task list but not necessarily earlier in the calendar). Project will find the next occurrence of the value.

I

5. Use Shift+F4 to search further toward the end of the task list, or Ctrl+Shift+F4 to search further toward the beginning of the task list.

> ### Note
>
> If the bar for the task is not visible, try using the Zoom In button to see more task bars for each day or use the Task Information button to see details for the task. Both of these features are described in the following sections.

Using Zoom

You will often want to look at your calendar from different perspectives, backing away at times to see the big picture (although this has practical size limitations) or zooming in on the details for a specific week. To accomplish this task, choose the **V**iew menu and select the **Z**oom command, or use the Zoom In and Zoom Out buttons on the Standard toolbar.

The calendar in figure 6.6, for example, is zoomed in to a two-week view to get a good feel for the tasks that are going on during that time.

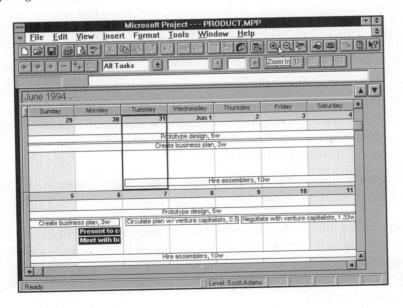

Fig. 6.6

Click the Zoom In tool twice to display only two weeks.

The buttons will cycle through displays for 1, 2, 4, and 6 weeks. As is often the case, you have more options when accessing the dialog box for a feature than you do when using the toolbar buttons. With the Zoom dialog box, you also have options for zooming to a custom level specified in weeks or **F**rom one date **T**o another (see fig. 6.7). The Zoom option is also available on the Shortcut menu that you access by right-clicking the date box header or footer section.

Fig. 6.7
The Zoom dialog box offers more specific choices for zooming.

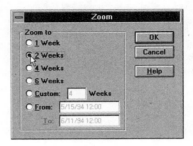

Using Filters To Clarify the Calendar View

For a project with many overlapping tasks, the Calendar view can quickly become very cluttered. As previously discussed, you can zoom in to see more detail, but you may also find it useful to use filters to narrow down the list of tasks that are displayed at any one time. Use the **T**ools **F**iltered for command to narrow down the tasks displayed by any one of many categories offered.

To apply a filter to a Calendar View, do one of the following:

- From the **T**ools menu, choose the **F**iltered for command and choose from the predefined filters.

- If you would like to simply highlight a particular category of tasks, choose the **T**ools **F**iltered for command as above and then choose the **M**ore Filters option. Choose the filter you want to apply and then choose the Hi**g**hlight button.

All Tasks

- Use the Filter tool on the Formatting toolbar. Choose from the available filters on the pull-down list.

▶ "Using and Creating Filters," p. 478

▶ "Formatting the Calendar," p. 522

When you are trying to focus on the deadline and, therefore, the critical path, filter by Critical Tasks. When you want to give each resource a list of its assigned tasks, choose the Using Resource filter. After the project is underway and you want a record of what has been accomplished so far, the Completed Tasks filter is handy.

Editing the Project in the Calendar View

As mentioned at the beginning of this chapter, it is not recommended that you try to use the Calendar view to create a complex project. This view is really more useful for reviewing and printing tasks and the time frames during which they are calculated to occur. Therefore, this section starts with various techniques for looking up and modifying task information. It could be helpful, for example, to be able to add and modify task notes when re-viewing the calendar.

Viewing Task Details in the Calendar View

The display of information about individual tasks is minimized in the Calendar view. You can view and edit details about a task by selecting the task and then activating the Task Information dialog box. Alternatively, you can use the Calendar as the top part of a dual pane view, selecting tasks in the Calendar and viewing details for the tasks in the lower pane.

You can activate the Task Information dialog box (see fig. 6.8) for a task in the Calendar view in several ways. Any of the four methods listed below can be used for tasks whose task bars are displayed. If the task bar is not displayed, you must use one of the last two methods.

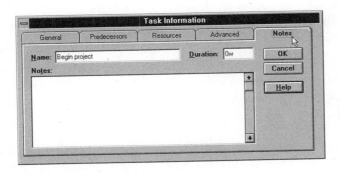

Fig. 6.8
The familiar Task Information dialog box offers easy access to most of the tasks information fields.

To display the Task Information dialog box for tasks whose task bars are displayed, use one of these methods:

- Double-click the task bar to both select the task and display the Task Information dialog box.

- Right-click the task bar to both select the task and display the task Shortcut menu (see fig. 6.9). From the Shortcut menu choose Task Information to see the General tab of the Task Information dialog box, or choose Task Notes to go directly to the Notes tab of the dialog box.

Fig. 6.9

The Shortcut menu for a task is helpful for getting at task information.

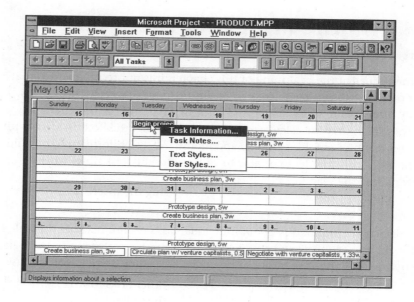

If the task bar is not displayed, you must first select the task using the Go To command or the Find command as described in the earlier section "Locating a Specific Task or Date." Once the task is selected, you can use either of these methods to display the Task Information dialog box.

■ Once the task is selected, choose **I**nsert from the menu and then choose the Task **I**nformation command. Choose the Task **N**otes command instead if you want to go directly to the Notes tab of the dialog box.

■ Once the task is selected, you can choose the Information button on the Standard toolbar to view the General tab of the Task Information dialog box, or choose the Attach Note button if you want to go directly to the Notes tab.

Another way to view task details is to combine the Calendar View with another view in the bottom pane. For example, the Task Form placed in the bottom pane would display task information for whatever task was selected in the Calendar View. The Task PERT displayed in the bottom pane would illustrate task dependencies for the task that is selected in the calendar. You can split the view window into two panes using any of the following methods:

■ From the **W**indow menu, choose **S**plit.

■ Access the Shortcut menu by right-clicking on anything in the Calendar except a task and then choose Split.

■ Access the Control menu for the Project file and choose Split.

The Task Form is the default view that is placed in the bottom pane when you use the Split command. You can replace the Task Form with any other view that you want (except the PERT Chart, which cannot be displayed in a bottom pane).

Inserting and Deleting Tasks in the Calendar View

In addition to viewing the project, you also can edit the task list in the Calendar view. You can insert, delete, and change tasks in this view.

Creating Tasks in the Calendar View

You can create tasks in the Calendar view by using the Insert Task command on the menu or by dragging the mouse to create a new task bar in the calendar. Although it is easy to create tasks in the Calendar view, you will probably choose not to do so for two reasons:

- Unlike the Gantt Chart and other views where you can insert a new task ID in the middle of the project near other tasks to which the new task is related, when you create a task in the Calendar view it will always be given the highest ID number in the project. When viewed in the Gantt Chart or any view with a table, the task will be at the bottom of the list, even if its dates fall in the middle of the project or you link it to tasks in the middle of the task list.

- The task that is created in the Calendar view will often be automatically given a date constraint. Although the constraints that are automatically assigned are not the rigid "Must Start On" or "Must Finish On" constraint types, they can still produce problems in the schedule and you will usually want to remove the constraint as soon as you create a task in the Calendar view. Otherwise, you may see schedule conflict messages like figure 6.10.

Fig. 6.10
Task constraints can result in scheduling conflict messages. Do not leave unwarranted constraints on tasks.

Caution

Adding tasks to the project in the Calendar view can result in task constraints that, unless removed, may needlessly produce scheduling conflicts like that illustrated in figure 6.10.

Whether tasks created in the Calendar view are constrained or not depends on what is selected when you create the new task: a task or a date.

- If a task is selected and you insert the new task with the menu or the Insert key, the new task will not be constrained—its constraint type will be "As Soon As Possible."

- If a date is selected when you create the new task, or if you create the task by dragging with the mouse (which automatically selects the date where you start dragging), the new task will be constrained.

If the task is constrained when you create it, the constraint type will depend on whether you have elected to schedule your project from a fixed Start Date or a fixed Finish Date. If you create the task by dragging with the mouse, the constraint type will also depend on the direction you drag the mouse—from start to finish or from finish to start. Attempting to remember what each combination of these factors does to the constraint type is not worth the effort. Just remember to check the Constraint Type of any task you create in the Calendar view (following the steps that are outlined below) and change it appropriately.

To insert a task with the menu, follow these steps:

1. Select the date for the start of the task if you want the Start date constrained, or select any task if you do not want the task to be constrained.

2. From the **I**nsert menu choose **I**nsert Task. Or, simply press the Insert key that is the shortcut key for the Insert Task command. Either way, a new task with no name is inserted into the project with a default duration of one day. Since the task has no name yet, its task bar will only display its duration. If there is no room to display the bar for the new task, it will seem to disappear. However, the new task is selected, whether you can see it or not.

3. Choose the Information button on the Standard toolbar, or from the **I**nsert menu choose Task Information, to display the Task Information dialog box.

4. Provide a name for the task and any other task information you want to enter. For example, you will probably need to enter the Duration. You may also want to choose the Notes tab and type comments about the task.

5. Since most tasks that are created in the Calendar view are automatically given a date constraint, choose the Advanced tab and change the entry in the Constrain Task Type field as appropriate.

6. Choose the OK button to close the dialog box.

To insert a task with the mouse, follow these steps:

1. Scroll the Calendar so that you can see the Start date (or Finish date) for the task.

2. Drag the mouse from the Start date to the Finish date for the task (or from the Finish date to the Start date).

3. Choose the Information button to display the Task Information dialog box and supply the task Name and any other information you want to specify.

4. Choose the Advanced tab and correct the Constrain Task Type as appropriate.

5. Choose the OK button to close the dialog box.

Deleting Tasks in the Calendar View

To delete a task, simply select it and choose **E**dit **D**elete Task or just press the Delete key. If the task bar is not displayed, you must use the Go To command or the Find command to select it. (See the section "Locating a Specific Task or Date," earlier in this chapter.) If you accidentally delete a task, use the Undo feature by selecting **E**dit **U**ndo or by pressing Ctrl+Z (the shortcut key combination). You must do this right away though, because Undo can only undo your last action.

To remove an unintended constraint, access the Task Information dialog box either by using the Shortcut menu or by double-clicking the task name. Choose the Advanced tab and select the As Soon As Possible constraint type from the entry list arrow.

◄ "Understanding the Types of Constraints," p. 132

Creating Links between Tasks in the Calendar View

There are several methods for creating task dependency links in the calendar view. One method is to select the tasks that you want to link using the Ctrl key to add tasks to the selection. Then choose the Link button on the Standard toolbar.

Alternatively, you can use the mouse. Simply click in the center of the bar for the predecessor task and hold the mouse button until the mouse assumes the shape of chain links, and then drag to the intended successor task. The mouse pointer will first change to a shape of a link, and once you start dragging a pop-up box will appear that indicates the creation of a Finish-to-Start relationship between the two tasks.

◄ "Linking Tasks in Sequence," p. 136

In order to change to a different kind of relationship or to add lag or lead time, you must display the Task Information dialog box for the dependent (successor) task and choose the Predecessors tab.

Assigning Resources to Tasks in the Calendar View

► "Assigning Resources and Costs to Tasks," p. 205

You can review resource assignments as well as add them to tasks in the Calendar View. You can access the Task Information dialog box to review the current assignments to a task. You can also choose the Resource tab in that dialog box to make resource assignments.

You can also use the Resource Assignment button, which appears on both the Standard toolbar and the Resource Management toolbar, to display the Resource Assignment dialog box. The benefit of this approach is that the dialog box has the ability to float on the surface of the desktop; it is not automatically closed when you make an assignment. You can simply select another task in the calendar in the background and either review or make additional assignments.

Troubleshooting

■ If the Find command is dimmed on the Edit menu, you do not have a task bar selected. You can use the Find command in the Calendar view only if you have selected a task bar.

■ If you attempt to link tasks in Calendar view and a warning message appears advising you about moving a task, choose to Cancel the move and start over. This time, be sure that the mouse pointer is in the middle of the task bar before you start to drag to the successor task.

From Here...

By this point you have created a project file, entered task information, and viewed it from a variety of perspectives. This chapter introduced to the possibilities of reviewing and editing task information in the Calendar view.

Depending on the nature of your project and your priorities, you could be ready to look at several different topics. First you could be interested in further exploring the formatting options of the calendar. On the other hand, you might want to look at your project from a different perspective— focusing on task dependencies, for example. Finally, you might want to assign resources to the tasks, deciding who is going to do what. Depending on your priorities, refer to the following chapters:

- Chapter 7, "Working with the PERT Chart."

- Chapter 8, "Defining Resources and Costs."

- Chapter 18, "Formatting Views."

Working with the PERT Chart

The PERT Chart is a graphic display of the tasks in a project, in which each task is represented by a small box or node, and the nodes are connected by lines to show the task dependencies. The PERT Chart is most useful for an overall view of how the task details fit together. You also can use the PERT Chart as the original entry view.

While in the PERT view, you cannot filter the task list, and you cannot use the Clipboard to copy or move entire tasks. You can, however, use the Clipboard to cut, copy, and paste individual field entries.

In Chapter 7, the topics discussed include:

- Understanding the PERT Chart

- Editing the task data in the PERT nodes

- Formatting the PERT Chart layout options

Understanding the PERT Chart View

The PERT Chart is named for the Program Evaluation and Review Technique (PERT), a project management methodology introduced by the Special Projects Office of the U.S. Navy in 1958. The PERT Chart has evolved into several species of network diagrams. The popular version used in Microsoft Project reveals information about the individual task, as well as information about the task's place in the flow of activity.

Each task is represented by a box or node and is connected to predecessors and successors by lines. In the diagram, dependent (successor) tasks are always placed to the right of or beneath the predecessors. Different border styles or colors distinguish summary tasks, critical tasks, and milestones. Subordinate tasks are placed below and to the right of the summary tasks.

The following list describes a few of the borders for task nodes:

Tasks	Node borders
Critical tasks	Red borders
Milestones	Double borders
Summary tasks	Shadow box behind border

► "Formatting Views," p. 497.

The default format for task nodes displays five fields for the task: the Name, ID, Duration, Scheduled Start, and Scheduled Finish. You can select other fields to display.

To view the PERT Chart, perform the following steps:

Tip
To get the full PERT Chart, use Shift as you select **V**iew and choose **P**ERT Chart.

1. If the PERT Chart is to be only a half-screen display, select the top pane.

2. Select the **V**iew menu and choose **P**ERT Chart from the list.

> **Note**
>
> You cannot display the PERT Chart in the bottom pane.

Zooming the PERT Chart View

The **V**iew menu contains an option to zoom the PERT Chart in or out so you can view more or less of the data at a glance. Select the **Z**oom command from the **V**iew menu to see the zoom options available (see fig. 7.1). To change the zoom percentage, select the percentage in the Zoom window and choose the OK button. The 100% zoom is the normal default view.

You can also zoom the PERT Chart by choosing the Zoom In and Zoom Out tools on the toolbar. The Zoom In and Zoom Out tools increment and decrement the zoom percentage by 25 percent each time you choose the tools. The supported zoom range is from 25 percent to a maximum of 400 percent.

Fig. 7.1
The Zoom dialog
window.

Scrolling and Selecting in the PERT Chart

You can use the scroll bars or selection keys (the arrow keys, PgUp, PgDn, Home, and End) to scan through the PERT chart. However, the rules for each method are quite different.

Scrolling does not change the currently selected node. Therefore, after scrolling, you probably cannot see the selected node, although the name remains in the edit bar.

To put the selected node back in the center of the screen, press the Edit key (F2) as though you plan to change the selected node. To cancel the editing, press the Esc key. To select one of the visible nodes after scrolling, just select the node.

You also can use the selection keys (the arrow keys, PgUp, PgDn, Home, and End) to move around the PERT Chart, selecting different nodes as you go. However, the rules that the selection keys follow in selecting the next node are not at first apparent, as shown in the following list:

- Right arrow selects nodes to the right until no more nodes lie directly to the right. Then selects the next node down and to the right and continues to the right.

- Down arrow selects nodes directly below until no more nodes lie directly below. Then selects the next node that is down and to the right and continues down.

- Left arrow selects nodes to the left until no more nodes lie directly to the left. Then selects the next node up and to the left and continues to the left.

- Up arrow selects nodes directly above until no more nodes lie directly above. Then selects the next node above and to the left, and continues up.

The following keys simulate repeated use of the arrow keys. The new selected task name appears in the Edit bar. If the selected task is not visible after the move, press the Edit key (F2), then press Esc to place the selected task in the center of the screen.

- PgDn simulates repeated down arrow for one screen.

- End simulates repeated down arrow until it reaches the bottom row of the PERT Chart.

- PgUp simulates repeated up arrow for one screen.

- Home simulates repeated up arrow until it reaches the top row of the PERT Chart.

- Ctrl+PgDn simulates repeated right arrow for one screen.

- Ctrl+End simulates repeated right arrow until it reaches the last column of the PERT Chart.

- Ctrl+PgUp simulates repeated left arrow for one screen.

- Ctrl+Home simulates repeated left arrow until it reaches the first column of the PERT Chart.

To move to the beginning of the PERT Chart, press Ctrl+Home and Home. You also can use the **G**o To command and select task ID number one, assuming you haven't left a blank row at the top of the task list.

To go to the start of the project, follow these steps:

1. Press the F5 (Go To) key or select **E**dit and choose **G**o To.

2. Type the ID number for the first task in the project (usually number 1).

3. Choose the OK button.

Editing the Project in the PERT Chart

You can use the PERT view to change task data, to add and delete tasks, and to create and modify task links.

Changing Task Data in the PERT Chart

To change the field data displayed in a task node, follow these steps:

1. Select the task to edit by clicking the mouse pointer on the task node or by using the arrow keys.

2. Select the field to edit using the Tab and Shift+Tab keys or by clicking the field.

3. In the edit bar, type the new data or edit the existing data.

4. Complete the change by pressing Enter, by selecting the Enter box in the edit bar, or by selecting a different field or node.

If you want to change data in fields that do not appear in the task node (such as constraints, fixed duration, and so on), you can use the Task Information Form.

1. Select the node for the task to edit.

2. Double-click the task node to display the Task Information Form.

3. Make the changes you want using the folder tabs.

4. Choose the OK button.

Adding Tasks in the PERT Chart

You can add tasks directly to the project in the PERT view. To add a new task, perform the following steps:

1. If possible, select the task that you want as the predecessor to the new task. This step just ensures that the new task node is placed to the right of the predecessor.

2. Press the Insert key to insert a blank node to the right of the selected task, or select the **I**nsert Task command from the **I**nsert menu. The ID number for the new task is one greater than the selected task, and all existing tasks with ID numbers higher than the selected task are increased by one. The new task will be inserted directly on top of the task node to the right of the selected task (see fig. 7.2). See the section, "Moving Task Nodes in the PERT Chart," to move the new task.

Fig. 7.2
Adding tasks in the
PERT Chart using
the Insert method..

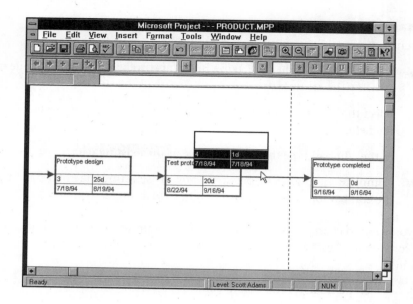

3. Type the data for the new task. Use Tab to move from field to field.

You also can create a new task node by dragging the mouse pointer to form a rectangle in an empty area of the PERT chart.

> **Note**
>
> Automatic linking of tasks is not enabled while tasks are added, deleted, or moved in the PERT Chart.

Deleting Tasks in the PERT Chart

You can delete tasks while in the PERT view. Note, however, that you cannot delete summary tasks in the PERT view. If you delete a task, you must manually relink the predecessors and successors.

To delete a task, select the task, and press Delete or select the **E**dit menu and choose **D**elete Task.

Linking Tasks in the PERT Chart

You can create task links in the PERT Chart by dragging the mouse from the predecessor to the successor task. The task relationship will be a Finish-to-Start relationship with no lead or lag. If you want to change the relationship, enter lead or lag time, or delete the task link, you must double-click the line that links the tasks. The Task Dependency dialog box appears, and you can redefine the task relationship.

To link tasks in the PERT Chart, drag from the center of the predecessor task node to the successor task and release the mouse in the successor task node (see fig. 7.3). A line is drawn to connect the tasks, with an arrowhead at the successor task end.

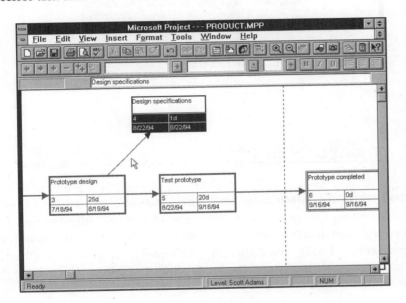

Fig. 7.3
Linking tasks in the PERT Chart.

To redefine a task relationship in the PERT Chart, follow these steps:

1. Double-click the line that links the tasks, and the Task Dependency dialog box appears (see fig. 7.4).

2. Change the relationship or enter a lead or lag.

3. Choose the OK button to complete the change.

To delete a task dependency in the PERT Chart, double-click the line that links the tasks. This action displays the Task Dependency dialog box. Then select the **D**elete button. This selection removes the line that links the tasks.

Fig. 7.4
The Task Dependency dialog box.

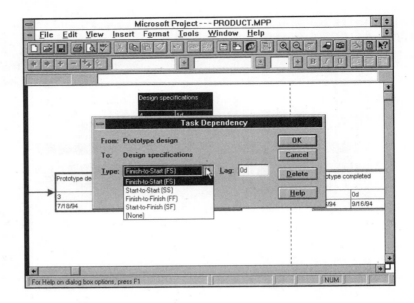

Moving Task Nodes in the PERT Chart

You can change the layout of the PERT Chart by moving individual task nodes or groups of task nodes to new positions in the PERT Chart view. If you move a group of nodes simultaneously, the nodes retain position relative to each other as you move them. The linking lines also follow task nodes to the new locations.

Tip
You may find Zoom out useful to see an overview as you redesign the layout of the PERT Chart.

To move a task node with the keyboard, select the task and then hold down the Ctrl key as you press the arrow keys to move the node. To move the task node with the mouse, move the mouse pointer to the border of the task node, hold down the primary mouse button, and drag the node to the new location. A gray border surrounds the node, even after you release the mouse button (see fig. 7.5).

To move a group of task nodes together, perform the following steps:

1. Select the border of the first node of the group that is to be moved.

2. Select other nodes to be moved at the same time by pressing the Ctrl key as you select their borders.

3. When all nodes are selected, hold down the primary mouse button and drag the border of one of the nodes. They will all move together to the new location (see fig. 7.6).

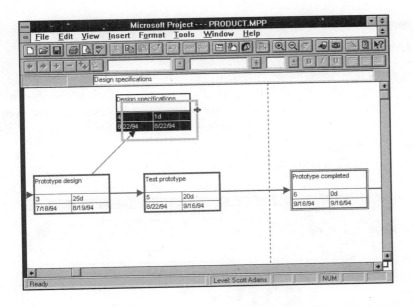

Project Management

Fig. 7.5
Moving a node
with the mouse.

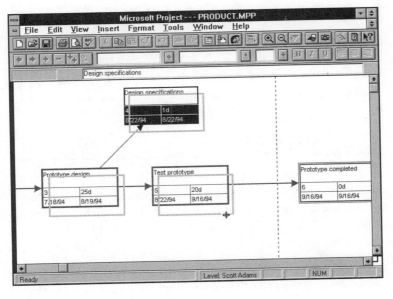

Fig. 7.6
Moving a group of
nodes in the PERT
Chart.

You also can select nodes to be moved as a group by drawing a selection box
around them. To select multiple nodes with a selection box, follow these
steps:

1. Visualize a rectangle that encloses the nodes you are selecting.

2. Move the mouse pointer to a corner of this rectangle.

3. Hold down the mouse button and drag the mouse pointer diagonally to the opposite corner of this rectangle, creating the rectangle as shown in figure 7.7. Then release the mouse button. All task nodes that fall even partly within the area of the rectangle are selected for moving.

4. Drag the border of one member of the selected group, and the entire group moves to the new location.

Fig. 7.7
Using a selection box with task nodes.

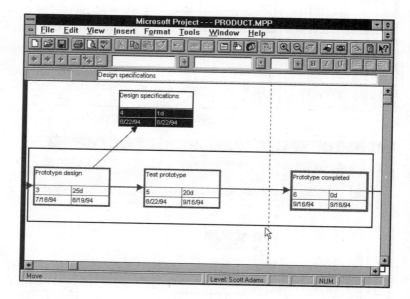

You can quickly select all of a summary task's subtasks by holding down the Shift key as you click the border of the summary task. You also can select all of a normal task's successor tasks by holding down the Shift key as you click the border of the predecessor task. Drag the border of any task in the selected group to move the entire selected group.

When you rearrange the PERT Chart, you want to see the page break lines so that you don't place a task node on a page break. If you do so, part of the node prints on one page and the remainder prints on another page.

Using the Layout Dialog Box

You can customize the layout of the PERT view with the choices in the Format Layout dialog box (see fig. 7.8). The following four choices are available:

- By default, the dependency lines usually are drawn diagonally from predecessor to successor tasks. If you prefer, with the **L**inks option, you can choose orthogonal lines so that only right angles are used to display the dependency line (see fig. 7.8).

- The Show **A**rrows option enables you to show or remove the arrow tips from the successor end of the dependency lines. Removing the tips leaves lines with no explicit direction.

- You can disable the Show **P**age Breaks option so the dotted page break lines do not appear on the PERT chart display.

- With the A**d**just for Page Breaks option, you can adjust task nodes to the page breaks so that no task node is split by a page break. If a node must be adjusted, the node is moved to the right or down until it fits entirely on the next page.

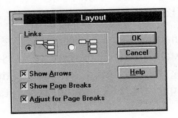

Fig. 7.8
The Layout
dialog box.

To change one or more of the Layout options, follow these steps:

1. From the Fo**r**mat menu, choose **L**ayout.

2. Select the button beside the **L**inks style that you want to use.

3. Turn the other three options on or off by marking the check box to Show **A**rrows, Show **P**age Breaks, or Adjust for **P**age Breaks. A mark in the check box indicates that the feature is turned on.

4. Select the OK button to activate your choices. The **L**inks choice, the Show **P**age Breaks choice, and the Sh**o**w **A**rrows choice are implemented as soon as you choose OK. The Adjust for **P**age Breaks choice is not implemented until the next time you choose Layout **N**ow from the Fo**r**mat menu (covered in the next section).

Using Layout Now

The Layout **N**ow command forces Microsoft Project to redraw the PERT Chart. All changes you made by moving task nodes are lost. To have Microsoft Project redraw the PERT Chart, choose Layout **N**ow from the F**o**rmat menu.

▶ "Formatting Views," p. 497.

Microsoft Project enables you to control more custom features for displaying the PERT Chart.

From Here...

This chapter taught you the basics of using and understanding the PERT chart view. You saw the zooming features, the node selection techniques, and the editing techniques used in the PERT chart.

The following chapters will provide you with additional techniques and information you can use to further complete and format your project:

- Chapter 8, "Defining Resources and Costs," shows how to create a list of the resources available to work on a project, how to define the costs associated with each resource, how to work with the resource calendars, and how to print the resource information.

- Chapter 18, "Formatting Views," covers the various ways you can format and sort the standard or customized views. Some topics discussed include formatting the text display, formatting timescales, and specific formatting techniques for the commonly used standard views.

Chapter 8

Defining Resources and Costs

In this chapter you examine the association between tasks and the resources and costs that may be assigned to tasks. You see how to define resources and costs and also how to define fixed costs not associated with a particular resource. You learn how to create calendars for resources that Microsoft Project then can use for scheduling resources and, thereby, for scheduling the tasks that these resources are assigned to work on. Throughout this chapter, you see the different views and reports that Microsoft Project provides to facilitate the maintenance of the tasks and the tasks' associated resources and costs. You also see how to filter and sort the resource lists to produce more meaningful and informative reports.

In Chapter 8, you learn how to

■ Identify and define Resources and Costs.

■ Enter Resources into the Resource Views.

■ Modify the Resource working times.

■ Sort and filter the Resource list.

■ Print the Resource list.

Understanding How Microsoft Project Uses Resources and Costs

You can use Microsoft Project to plan projects without adding resources and costs. You can enter the tasks and let Microsoft Project schedule the project based on the duration of the tasks, the task constraints, and the dependency relationships that you define for the list of tasks. When no resources are assigned to a task, Microsoft Project uses the base calendar that you assigned to the project in the Summary Info dialog box and schedules the tasks in the working hours defined in that calendar. You also can assign costs, known as *Fixed Costs*, to the individual tasks without defining resources. If you fail to define and assign resources to tasks, however, you will miss one of the single biggest advantages of using Microsoft Project: the program's capability to advise you that you may have placed competing demands on a resource's time by assigning more work than can be done during the working hours defined for that resource.

If you do use resources in a project, Microsoft Project schedules work according to the availability of the resources assigned to work on each task, and uses the resource calendars to determine when resources are available. When resource assignments are made, Microsoft Project calculates the amount of work or effort each resource may expend on each task, and calculates the cost of the work. The cost is based on a standard cost rate per unit of work time, which you can define when you define the resource.

You can define a comprehensive list of resources at the outset and later assign these resources to the respective tasks. You also can assign undefined resource names to tasks, and Microsoft Project adds these names to the roster of resources. The Automatically Add New Resources switch (available through the **T**ools **O**ptions command) determines how Microsoft Project treats undefined resources that you assign to tasks. If the Automatically Add New Resources switch is enabled, Microsoft Project automatically adds new resources to the resource pool without asking you. If the Automatically Add New Resources switch is disabled, you must confirm each new resource before Microsoft Project can add the resource to the pool. If you confirm that you want to add a resource, Microsoft Project requires that you fill in the details about the resource when you assign the resource to a task. If the Automatically Add New Resources switch is enabled, the resource is added to the pool, but you must remember to fill in the details later.

Understanding the Definitions of Resource and Cost

Resources in your project may include not only the people, but also the facilities, equipment, and supplies that contribute to the work on a task. Resource assignments also can be used to designate the people who have responsibilities for tasks, and to record the outside contractors who provide components of the project. Costs include not only the cost of the resources you assign to tasks, but also all expenses not related directly to resources, such as overhead and fixed costs.

Identifying Resources and Costs

The term *resource* primarily is applied to people and assets that must be assigned to do the work or to facilitate the work that is required to complete a task. Resources can include workers and supervisors, plant and equipment, facilities, and critical supplies or materiel that you deem necessary to complete a task. You also may identify as resources for a task people who do no actual work on the task, or whose work you do not need to measure (such as outside contractors or vendors), but whose name you want associated with the task.

Some resource names that you add to the resource pool will represent a single individual or asset. A person's name, for example, can be used as a resource name, or a single piece of equipment can be named as a resource. Other resource names may represent *groups* of resources that are considered to be interchangeable units. For example, you might define a group of three Assemblers. All individuals in the group must have the same cost rate and must be scheduled by a common resource calendar if you want to define these individuals as a group.

Using group resources keeps you from having to define each individual member of the group. But there is also a more subtle and more powerful reason for using group resources. When you define a group resource, you can increase or decrease the number of units from the group that are assigned to work on a task, and Microsoft Project will recalculate the duration of the task based on the fact that with more resources it should take less time to complete the task, and with fewer resources it should take longer to complete the task. If the task is defined as a Fixed Duration task, of course, no such recalculation will be done.

In contrast to the automatic adjustment of duration when you change the quantity of group resources, Microsoft Project does not adjust the duration of a task when you add an additional resource *name* to the task. The program assumes that the additional named resource is required to work alongside other resources in order to complete the task. The duration of the task is not changed, but the total amount of work expended on the task is increased. There is, however, a macro—the **Effort_Driven** macro—that can be used to reapportion the existing task work among all resources when new resource names are added.

When you assign a resource to a task, Microsoft Project calculates a cost value for the task based on the number of units of work (hours, days, and so on) times the cost rate per unit for the resource. You also can define a *cost per use* that Microsoft Project will charge as a cost once to each task for each unit of the resource assigned. The example usually given for cost per use is the delivery charge incurred when equipment is rented or leased. Both the cost per unit of time and the cost per use are known as the *variable costs* associated with completing a task.

Fixed costs, however, are costs not associated with a particular resource; they are associated with the actual task. An example of a fixed cost would be a vendor's fixed fee for doing the work of a task in the project. For instance, if you hire a contractor to install air conditioning for a fixed amount, the contract price is a fixed cost—whether the contractor has to spend more or less time than originally anticipated. Overhead charges are another example of a cost that may be treated as a fixed cost.

When you define the cost for using a resource, you also must specify (for reporting purposes) when the costs are incurred. Costs may be prorated over the duration of the task, so that as work is done on the task, a proportional amount of the cost is considered as already incurred. Prorating costs is the default method for accumulating costs. You also can stipulate that all the costs be considered incurred as soon as the task is begun. A third option is to count costs as incurred only after all work on the task is completed.

Understanding the Resource Fields

The resource fields are found on several views. You can use the Resource Sheet or Resource Form to define resources. If you assign an undefined resource, Microsoft Project displays the Resource Information Form, shown in figure 8.1, which contains the same fields for you to define the new resource.

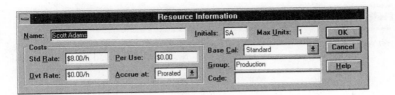

Fig. 8.1
The Resource fields
on the Resource
Information Form.

Project Management

When you define a resource, you must provide a resource name. You may fill
in data for the remaining fields as described in the following list, or you can
leave the fields with the default zero or blank values:

Field	Purpose
ID	When you add a resource to the resource pool, Microsoft Project assigns the next available resource ID number to the resource. As with tasks, resources are identified by their ID number. You cannot assign the ID number; an ID number is assigned by Microsoft Project. The ID field appears on the Resource Sheet but not on the Resource forms.
Name	Always identify the resource with a name. The name can contain any characters except the comma and the square brackets ([ ]). Resource names can be up to 255 characters long, but they do not have to be unique because resources are identified by their ID numbers. However, if you assign a resource name to a task, Microsoft Project uses the first resource with that name in the resource list. You can distinguish resources that use the same name with different initials.
Initials	To save space, you can use the initials on Gantt Charts and PERT Charts rather than the full names. You also can use initials when assigning resources in the Task Form view to save the time of typing the full resource name.
Max Units	You use the Maximum Units field to define the maximum number of units of a resource available for assignment at the same time in the project. The default value is one (1), but you can enter any value between zero (0) and one hundred (100). For a single unit resource, enter one (1) if the resource is available full-time or a fraction if the resource can only work part-time on tasks in this project. For example, enter **.5** if the resource is to work no more than half of each day on any task in this project.
	You also can enter fractional values. If you have two full-time writers and one part-time writer, for example, you can type 2.5 in the maximum units field.
	Microsoft Project uses this field to advise you when a resource is overallocated. Because resources can be assigned to multiple tasks (even to multiple projects), it is possible to assign the same resource to multiple tasks that

(continues)

Field	Purpose
	are scheduled at the same or overlapping times. If the total number of resource units called for by all the tasks combined at a given moment exceeds the entry in the Maximum units field, the program warns you at the bottom of the screen that you need to level the resource. This means that the requirements for the resource must be leveled out; the tasks that demand the resource must be spread out so that the resource can accomplish the required work.
Std Rate	The standard rate is the cost per unit of time to charge for the use of the resource. Type the standard rate as a number, type a slash, and then type one of the following time unit letters: m (minute), h (hour), d (day), w (week), or y (year).
	If you don't include a time unit, Microsoft Project uses the amount as an hourly rate. For example, type 600/w for $600 per week, 35000/y for $35,000 per year, and 15.5 for $15.50 per hour.
	When you assign the resource to a task, the standard rate is converted to an hourly rate and is applied to the number of hours of work it takes to complete the task. For annual rates, the hourly rate is calculated by assuming 52 weeks, and the number of hours per week is derived from the entry in the Options dialog box for default hours per week.
Ovt Rate	The Overtime rate is used when overtime hours are added to the work schedule. If the rate for overtime work is the same as the regular rate, you must enter this amount again in the Overtime rate field or overtime hours will be charged at the zero default rate.
Per Use	The Per use cost is a charge added once for each unit of the resource assigned to any task. Assume that the per use charge is $100 and that one unit of the resource is assigned to Task A for 15 minutes of work. The per use charge for Task A is $100. If two units of the same resource are assigned to Task B for 50 weeks, the per use charge for Task B is $200.
	The cost of the task derived from the cost of resources (the variable cost) is the sum of the standard rate charges, the overtime charges, and the per use charges.
Accrue at	This field has three possible entries: Start, End, and Prorated. The accrual method determines how Microsoft Project calculates actual costs after you enter a start date or begin work on a project.
	The default accrual method is Prorated, which means that, after work on a task is underway and you enter the actual amount of work done (or the percentage done), Microsoft Project calculates actual costs for the proportion of the work already done.

Field	Purpose
	If you choose Start, when you enter an actual start date for the task, Microsoft Project calculates the entire cost of the task as actual cost as of the start date.
	If you choose End for the accrual method, Microsoft Project defers recognition of the actual cost until you enter a finish date or until the task is 100 percent complete.
	The significance of the accrual selection is found in interim reports. If a task was 20 percent completed when a cost report was printed, the Prorated option would show 20 percent of projected costs as Actual Costs (already incurred); the Start option would show all of the costs as Actual Costs; and the End option would show zero Actual Costs.
Base Calendar	The entry in the base calendar field identifies the base calendar for this resource. Use the entry list to select one of the base calendar names.
Group	The Group field provides a place to enter an identifying code word or number that you can use for sorting and filtering resources. You can identify all management personnel, for example, with the entry Management; all equipment resources with the entry Equipment; and all vendors and contractors with the entry Vendors. With these entries in the Group field, you then can use the Group resource filter to view the data for only one of the group categories, such as Management.
	You can enter any kind of information in this field—not just a group name. You can enter any combination of letters, numbers, spaces, or other characters, up to 255 symbols in length. Do not confuse this field with the concept of resource groups, which are multiple units of interchangeable resources identified with one ID and Name. This is a resource field named Group that provides a field for entering code words that you can use to organize the resource names into meaningful groupings.
Code	In the Code field, similar to the Group field, you can enter any kind of information, and can use any combination of symbols for up to 255 characters. The most common use of the Code field is to place accounting codes so that you can group task cost information by accounting codes for exporting to other applications.

Understanding the Fixed and Total Cost Fields

Besides the costs derived from the cost of using resources, you also can attach a lump-sum cost figure directly to a task. This cost is known as Fixed Cost because the amount of the cost doesn't change as the amount of work on the task changes. An important example of fixed cost is the fixed fee paid to vendors or contractors to complete a task. The Fixed Cost field is displayed on the Cost table, which can be applied to the Gantt Chart and to the Task Sheet views. Figure 8.2 shows the Task Sheet with the Cost table. To display the Task Sheet as a full-screen view as shown in figure 8.2, select the **View** menu and choose **More Views**. In the More Views dialog box, choose Task Sheet from the view list and choose **Apply**. To apply the Cost table, select the **View** menu and choose the **Table** command. Select Cost from the drop-down menu of table options.

Fig. 8.2

The Fixed and Total Cost fields.

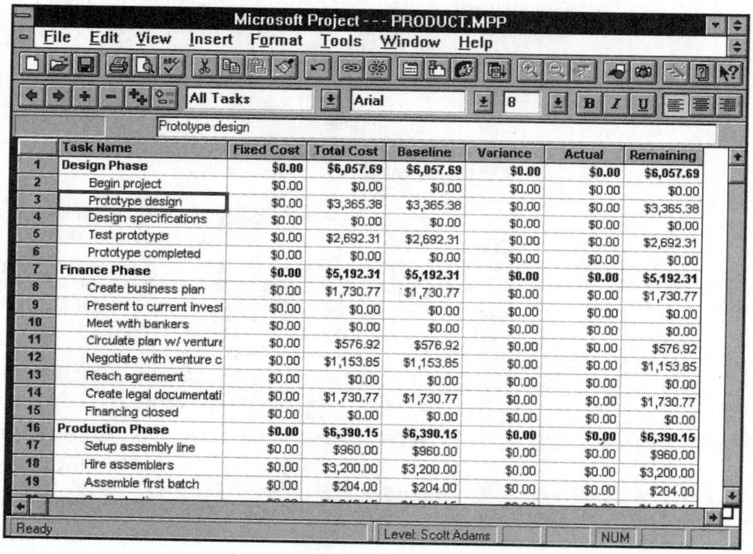

	Task Name	Fixed Cost	Total Cost	Baseline	Variance	Actual	Remaining
1	**Design Phase**	**$0.00**	**$6,057.69**	**$6,057.69**	**$0.00**	**$0.00**	**$6,057.69**
2	Begin project	$0.00	$0.00	$0.00	$0.00	$0.00	$0.00
3	Prototype design	$0.00	$3,365.38	$3,365.38	$0.00	$0.00	$3,365.38
4	Design specifications	$0.00	$0.00	$0.00	$0.00	$0.00	$0.00
5	Test prototype	$0.00	$2,692.31	$2,692.31	$0.00	$0.00	$2,692.31
6	Prototype completed	$0.00	$0.00	$0.00	$0.00	$0.00	$0.00
7	**Finance Phase**	**$0.00**	**$5,192.31**	**$5,192.31**	**$0.00**	**$0.00**	**$5,192.31**
8	Create business plan	$0.00	$1,730.77	$1,730.77	$0.00	$0.00	$1,730.77
9	Present to current invest	$0.00	$0.00	$0.00	$0.00	$0.00	$0.00
10	Meet with bankers	$0.00	$0.00	$0.00	$0.00	$0.00	$0.00
11	Circulate plan w/ venture	$0.00	$576.92	$576.92	$0.00	$0.00	$576.92
12	Negotiate with venture c	$0.00	$1,153.85	$1,153.85	$0.00	$0.00	$1,153.85
13	Reach agreement	$0.00	$0.00	$0.00	$0.00	$0.00	$0.00
14	Create legal documentati	$0.00	$1,730.77	$1,730.77	$0.00	$0.00	$1,730.77
15	Financing closed	$0.00	$0.00	$0.00	$0.00	$0.00	$0.00
16	**Production Phase**	**$0.00**	**$6,390.15**	**$6,390.15**	**$0.00**	**$0.00**	**$6,390.15**
17	Setup assembly line	$0.00	$960.00	$960.00	$0.00	$0.00	$960.00
18	Hire assemblers	$0.00	$3,200.00	$3,200.00	$0.00	$0.00	$3,200.00
19	Assemble first batch	$0.00	$204.00	$204.00	$0.00	$0.00	$204.00

To see how this process works, enter a cost amount in the Fixed Cost field. The amount you enter is added to the variable costs—the resource costs—to calculate the Total Cost.

The Total Cost field is a calculated field that sums the resource costs and the fixed costs and is displayed to the right of the Fixed Cost field on the Cost table. For clarity, the Cost field is labeled Total Cost on the Cost table, but the field name is Cost. If resource costs are not defined, you can enter cost figures for tasks directly into the Total Cost field or in the Fixed Cost field. If resource costs do exist, any entry you make in the Total Cost field is ignored.

Defining the Resource Pool

The list of resources available for work on a project is known as the *resource pool*. The resource pool usually is defined within each project. You also can stipulate, however, that a project will use the resource pool already defined in another project.

▶ "Working with Multiple Projects," p. 357.

Many users create a project template that contains no tasks but has all the standard company resources and costs previously defined. When you create a new project file, the project is created from this template file of resources. The upcoming section, "Creating a Resource Template," covers the steps for creating a resource template file.

You can create the resource pool before you define the tasks or attempt to assign resources to tasks. You can view either the Resource Sheet or the Resource Form and use either view to add resources to the pool.

You also can add resources to the pool automatically, as you attempt to assign the resources to tasks. You can use any task view that has a field for resource assignments to assign and define resources. When you assign a resource name to a task, Microsoft Project checks the resource pool for the name you enter. If the name is not yet defined, Microsoft Project attempts to add the resource to the list. If you disabled the Automatically Add New Resources switch (through the **T**ools **O**ptions command), you are asked to decide whether or not to add the resource to the resource pool. If you confirm that you want to add the resource, you are asked to fill out the Resource Form immediately. If you enabled the Automatically Add New Resources option, the new resource is added to the resource pool without your confirmation, and you can fill in the details about the resource at a later time.

> **Caution**
>
> You are not reminded that the resource definition was not completed. You must remember to go back and fill in the resource definition.

Entering Resources in the Resource Sheet

Use the Resource Sheet view to enter many resources at one time. The fields in this view are the same fields described in the earlier section, "Understanding the Resource Fields."

To enter the resource pool on the Resource Sheet, as shown in figure 8.3, follow these steps:

1. Select the **V**iew menu and choose Resource **S**heet. The Resource Sheet view appears.

2. Fill in the field information as described in the upcoming section, "Filling in the Resource Fields."

Fig. 8.3
The Resource Sheet.

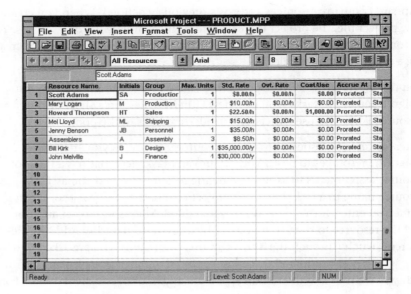

	Resource Name	Initials	Group	Max. Units	Std. Rate	Ovt. Rate	Cost/Use	Accrue At	Bas
1	Scott Adams	SA	Production	1	$8.00/h	$0.00/h	$0.00	Prorated	Sta
2	Mary Logan	M	Production	1	$10.00/h	$0.00/h	$0.00	Prorated	Sta
3	Howard Thompson	HT	Sales	1	$22.50/h	$0.00/h	$1,000.00	Prorated	Sta
4	Mel Lloyd	ML	Shipping	1	$15.00/h	$0.00/h	$0.00	Prorated	Sta
5	Jenny Benson	JB	Personnel	1	$35.00/h	$0.00/h	$0.00	Prorated	Sta
6	Assemblers	A	Assembly	3	$8.50/h	$0.00/h	$0.00	Prorated	Sta
7	Bill Kirk	B	Design	1	$35,000.00/y	$0.00/h	$0.00	Prorated	Sta
8	John Melville	J	Finance	1	$30,000.00/y	$0.00/h	$0.00	Prorated	Sta
9									
10									
11									
12									
13									
14									
15									
16									
17									
18									
19									

Entering Resources in the Resource Form

The Resource Sheet displays the resource data in a spreadsheet arrangement. You also can enter the resource pool by filling in the fields on the Resource Form for each resource. To enter the resource pool on the Resource Form, as shown in figure 8.4, perform the following steps:

1. Select the **V**iew menu and choose the **M**ore Views option.

2. From the More Views dialog box, choose Resource Form and choose **A**pply.

3. To enter notes about the resources, choose the **D**etails command from the **F**ormat menu.

4. Select the Notes option from the Details drop-down menu.

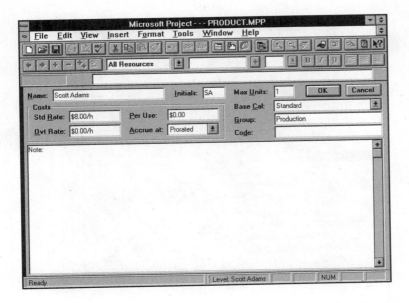

Fig. 8.4
The Resource Form
with the Notes
field.

5. If some resources are already in the pool, you need to choose the N**e**xt button until a blank form for adding a new resource appears.

6. Fill in the fields, as described in the upcoming section, "Filling in the Resource Fields."

7. To save the new resource, choose the OK button; to get a blank form for the next resource, select the N**e**xt button.

Editing Resource Data in the Resource Information Form

You use the Resource Information Form to define the resource when you assign an undefined resource to a task. The setting of the Automatically Add New Resources switch (available through the **T**ools **O**ptions command) determines how Microsoft Project reacts when you assign an undefined resource.

To set the Automatically Add New Resources option for automatic addition of resources, as shown in figure 8.5, perform the following steps:

1. From the **T**ools menu, choose **O**ptions. The Options dialog box appears.

2. Click the General folder tab to display the Automatically Add New Resources option at the bottom of the dialog box.

Fig. 8.5
The Options dialog
box with the
option for adding
resources.

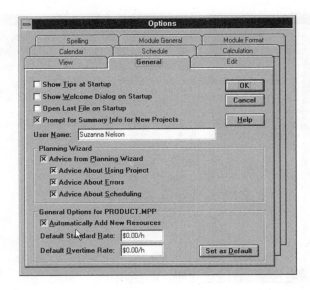

3. Choose the **A**utomatically Add New Resources option until an X appears (indicating that the switch is enabled) if you want Microsoft Project to add resource names to the resource pool without asking you to fill in the details about the resource. (You must remember to perform this action later.) Or, choose the **A**utomatically Add New Resources option until the X disappears (indicating that the switch is disabled) if you do not want Microsoft Project to add resources without waiting for the resource details.

   You should generally disable the Automatically Add new Resources option. If it is enabled, then mistyped resource names are automatically added to the resource pool and assigned to tasks without any warning. When the option is disabled, Microsoft Project warns you that the resource doesn't exist and asks if you want to add the new name to the resource pool. If you respond **Y**es, the Resource Information form pops up for you to define the fields for the new resource.

To add resources to the pool as you assign them to tasks, perform the following steps:

1. Enter the resource name in the Resource Name field in one of the views where resource assignments are possible. Figure 8.6, for example, illustrates how to use the Task Entry view to enter the resource name.

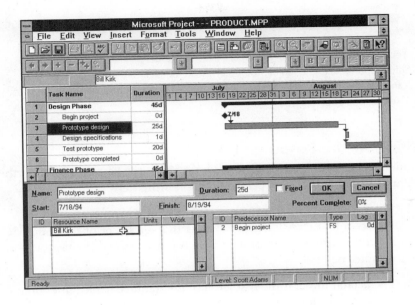

Fig. 8.6
Assigning a
Resource in the
Task Entry view.

I

2. Define the Units or Work as necessary. See Chapter 9, "Assigning Resources and Costs to Tasks."

3. Choose OK to execute the resource assignment.

4. Microsoft Project displays the warning that the resource name is not in the resource pool (see fig. 8.7).

Fig. 8.7
The Undefined
Resource warning.

5. Choose **Y**es to view the Resource Information Form and fill in the resource definition fields. Choose **N**o if you do not want this resource name added to the resource pool.

6. Fill in the fields as described in the upcoming section, "Filling in the Resource Fields."

7. Choose OK to complete the resource definition. You are returned to the view you were using to assign resources.

Filling in the Resource Fields

To fill in the resource fields in the Resource Sheet, the Resource Form, or the Resource Information Form, perform the following steps:

1. Enter a name of up to 255 characters. Although you can use either upper- or lowercase letters, remember that reports print the names exactly as entered. You cannot use a comma or square brackets ([ ]) in resource names.

2. The default initial is the first letter of the resource name. Enter unique initials for each resource if you want to use initials on Gantt Charts, calendars, or PERT Charts or as a shortcut for naming the resource when assigning the resource to a task. Microsoft Project doesn't reject duplicate initials, but if you use duplicates, it results in confusion.

3. Enter a Group identifier for the resource, and you can sort or filter resources according to the identifiers you enter in this field. (You can enter any kind of information in this field—not just a group name, but any combination of letters, numbers, spaces, or other characters up to 255 characters in length.)

4. Enter the maximum number of units of the resource available at any one time to work on one task or a combination of tasks simultaneously. The default value is one (1), but you can enter any value between zero (0) and one hundred (100), except when entering a single person resource. A single person resource can only have a maximum value of one (1).

   You also can enter fractional values. If, for example, two full-time workers and one part-time worker are available in a group, type **2.5** in the maximum units field.

5. Enter the standard rate for charging cost to tasks on which the resource works. Type the standard rate as a number, type a slash, and then type one of the following time unit letters: **m** for minute, **h** for hour, **d** for day, **w** for week, or **y** for year.

   If you enter a number but do not include a time unit, Microsoft Project uses the number as an hourly rate. For example, type **600/w** for $600 per week, **35000/y** for $35,000 per year, and **15.5** for $15.50 per hour.

6. Enter the overtime rate. The overtime rate calculates resource cost when overtime hours are entered in the work schedule. If the rate for overtime work is the same as the regular rate, you must enter this amount again or overtime hours are charged at the zero default rate.

7. Enter the Per Use cost, a charge added once per task per unit of the assigned resource.

8. Select the accrual method for calculating actual costs: from the entry list, select Start, End, or Prorated.

9. Enter the Base Calendar to use for scheduling the resource. By default, the Resource Calendar for this resource inherits all the standard working days and hours of the base calendar and all the exceptions, both non-working days and extra working days.

10. Enter a Code for the resource, and you can sort or filter resources according to the entries in this field. You can use any combination of up to 255 symbols. The most common use of the Code field is to place accounting codes so that cost information for the task can be grouped by accounting codes for exporting to other applications.

Changing Working Times for Resources

You use the resource calendar to record details about the working availability of individual resources. Each resource calendar is tied to one base calendar, and the resource calendar inherits all the information in the base calendar: the standard working hours and days and the exceptions to these standard working times (the holidays, the extra work days, so on). You then adjust the resource calendar for each resource defined to show the working times, holidays, and so on for each resource.

Understanding Resource Calendars

Resource calendars are edited to indicate the exceptions to the base calendar that apply to each resource. You can edit Resource calendars by choosing the Change Working Times option from the Tools menu.

If several resources have similar exceptions to the base calendar used in the project, creating a base calendar for use by each resource in the group is worthwhile. Therefore, if a night shift of workers is working on the project, and they all have the same basic schedule of night work hours, creating a base calendar for night-shift work and then using the base calendar for all workers who have the same hours saves you time. With this method, you only define the hours once.

> **Note**
>
> If you create several base calendars for use by resources, you must remember to make company-wide changes in working days and hours to all base calendars. If the Board of Directors decides to make December 24 a new holiday, for example, you need to edit each base calendar used by resources to apply the holiday to all resources.

Changing the Resource Calendar

After you add a resource to the resource pool, you can edit the resource's calendar to change their working times.

To edit the resource calendar for a resource, follow these steps:

1. Optionally, you can select the resource name in a field on one of the views (see fig. 8.8). If you do this, the calendar for this resource appears in the next step.

2. From the Tools menu, choose Change Working Time. The Change Working Time dialog box appears (see fig. 8.9).

3. If the resource you want to edit is not the currently displayed calendar, click the entry list arrow or use Alt+down arrow to activate the For entry list. Then select the resource you want to edit.

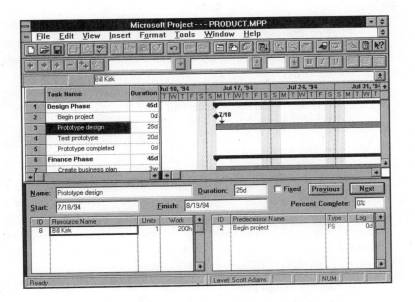

Fig. 8.8
The Resource
Name selected for
defining the
calendar.

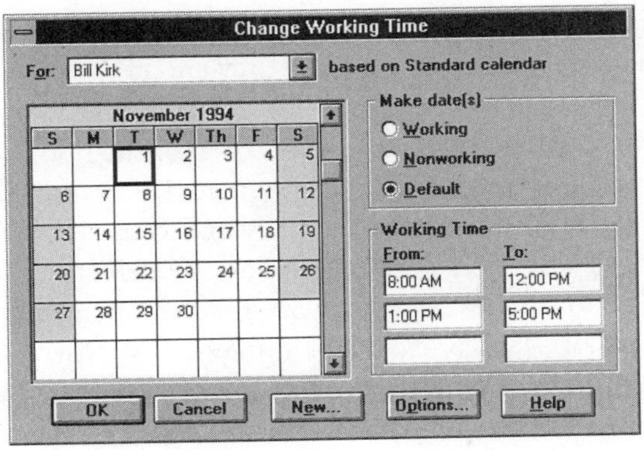

Fig. 8.9
The Change
Working Time
dialog box.

4. Edit the calendar and hours, using the same techniques described in
   Chapter 3, "Setting Up a New Project Document," for editing the base
   calendar.

You use the **W**orking and N**o**nworking buttons in the Change Working Time box to mark days for which the resource's work schedule differs from the base calendar. If November 24 and 25 are holidays on the base calendar, these dates are shaded as non-working days on the resource calendar. If a worker has agreed to work on the 25th, you use the **W**orking button to show that the worker will work this day, regardless of what the base calendar shows (see fig. 8.10). Similarly, you use the N**o**nworking button to mark vacation or sick days when the resource cannot work, regardless of what the base calendar shows.

Use the **D**efault button when you want to undo an exception on the resource calendar. If a day is marked N**o**nworking on the resource calendar, but you need the day to be a Working day that is not an exception (reverting to the base calendar's original setting), set the day with the **D**efault button. If you reset the day as a Working day, the worker is expected to work on this day, even if the base calendar date subsequently was changed to a N**o**nworking day. The **D**efault button enables the base calendar to determine the status of the day.

The days marked as non-working days on the base calendar are shaded gray on the resource calendar, just as they are on the base calendar. Exceptional days, however, have colored shading. Working days on the base calendar that are marked non-working for the resource are shaded, but with cyan color added to the day square. For example, in figure 8.10, November 11 appears shaded in cyan because Bill Kirk takes it as a non-working day. Non-working days on the base calendar that are working days for the resource have no shading, but are colored cyan on the resource calendar. For example, in figure 8.10, November 25 appears in cyan because Bill Kirk is taking it as a working day to make up for his day off on November 11.

5. Choose the OK button to record the changes in the resource calendar, or choose Close to abandon the changes.

You can make whole months non-working days by dragging the mouse from the first square on the calendar to the last square. This procedure selects all the month's days, and you then can select the N**o**nworking button. Advancing to the next month with the scroll bar leaves all days selected, allowing you to easily mark long periods of time as non-working by selecting the N**o**nworking button on each month in the period.

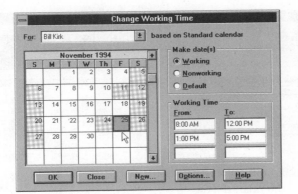

Fig. 8.10
Shading differ-
ences on the
Resource Calendar.

You can make the same weekday a non-working day throughout all months
and years of the calendar by selecting the weekday letter above the calendar
and choosing the **N**onworking button. Reverse the procedure by selecting
the weekday and choosing the **D**efault button.

> **Note**
>
> When planning a long-term project, you may need to show that the maximum units
> in a resource group will increase at specified hire dates. You need to make each
> group of new hires a separate resource group. To keep Microsoft Project from sched-
> uling these groups for work prior to the actual hire date, you must make all their
> days prior to the hire date non-working days.

Sorting Resources

You can sort the resource list for special purposes. For example, you may
want an alphabetical listing of resources (see fig. 8.11). Or if you apply the
Cost table to the Resource Sheet, you can sort the resources by the Total Cost
with the most costly resource assignments listed first (see fig. 8.12).

Fig. 8.11

An alphabetical listing of resources.

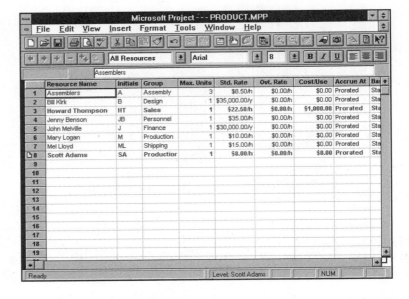

	Resource Name	Initials	Group	Max. Units	Std. Rate	Ovt. Rate	Cost/Use	Accrue At	Bas
1	Assemblers	A	Assembly	3	$8.50/h	$0.00/h	$0.00	Prorated	Sta
2	Bill Kirk	B	Design	1	$35,000.00/y	$0.00/h	$0.00	Prorated	Sta
3	Howard Thompson	HT	Sales	1	$22.50/h	$0.00/h	$1,000.00	Prorated	Sta
4	Jenny Benson	JB	Personnel	1	$35.00/h	$0.00/h	$0.00	Prorated	Sta
5	John Melville	J	Finance	1	$30,000.00/y	$0.00/h	$0.00	Prorated	Sta
6	Mary Logan	M	Production	1	$10.00/h	$0.00/h	$0.00	Prorated	Sta
7	Mel Lloyd	ML	Shipping	1	$15.00/h	$0.00/h	$0.00	Prorated	Sta
8	Scott Adams	SA	Production	1	$8.00/h	$0.00/h	$0.00	Prorated	Sta

Fig. 8.12

Resources, sorted by Cost, in decreasing order.

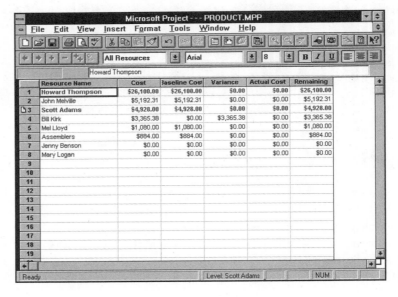

	Resource Name	Cost	Baseline Cost	Variance	Actual Cost	Remaining
1	Howard Thompson	$26,100.00	$26,100.00	$0.00	$0.00	$26,100.00
2	John Melville	$5,192.31	$5,192.31	$0.00	$0.00	$5,192.31
3	Scott Adams	$4,928.00	$4,928.00	$0.00	$0.00	$4,928.00
4	Bill Kirk	$3,365.38	$0.00	$3,365.38	$0.00	$3,365.38
5	Mel Lloyd	$1,080.00	$1,080.00	$0.00	$0.00	$1,080.00
6	Assemblers	$884.00	$884.00	$0.00	$0.00	$884.00
7	Jenny Benson	$0.00	$0.00	$0.00	$0.00	$0.00
8	Mary Logan	$0.00	$0.00	$0.00	$0.00	$0.00

To produce a view with the resource list that shows the cost fields sorted by Cost in decreasing order, perform the following steps:

1. Select the **V**iew menu and choose Resource **S**heet.

2. Select the **V**iew menu and choose the **T**able command. Select Cost from the Table drop-down list.

3. From the **T**ools menu choose the **S**ort command. Select **S**ort By from the Sort drop-down list.

4. In the Sort dialog box, choose the Sort By field (see fig. 8.13).

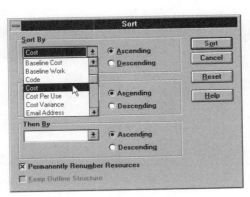

Fig. 8.13
The Sort dialog box.

5. Scroll the field name list to find the Cost field. (You can type the letter **c** to quickly move to the first field name that begins with the letter c.) From the list, select Cost.

6. Choose the **D**escending button to the right.

7. Choose the **S**ort button to execute the sort.

Note

The By Cost option in the Sort drop-down list will sort the resource list in Descending order. To sort in Ascending order, you must choose the Sort By command.

Strategically sorting your lists can greatly enhance the list's usefulness as a report. After examining the list in figure 8.12, for example, management may look for resources on the list who could be substituted for Howard Thompson to possibly reduce the cost of the project and to correct his overallocated time.

Fig. 8.14
Using the
Overallocated
Resource filter.

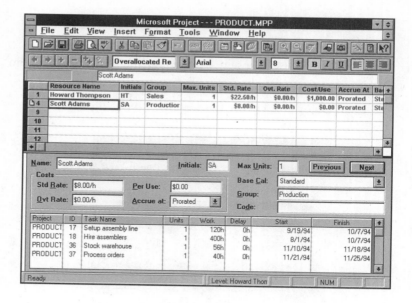

Filtering Resources

Several filters already are prepared for restricting the listing of resources or for highlighting resources that match the filter criteria. A common use of filters for resources, for example, is the Overallocated Resources filter. This filter displays only resources scheduled to work on more than one task at the same time (the resources whose time is overallocated). Figure 8.14 shows the Resource Sheet in the top pane with the Overallocated Resources filter applied. Only Howard Thompson and Scott Adams are overallocated resources. The bottom pane shows the Resource Form, with the tasks assigned to the selected resource.

To display this view, follow these steps:

1. If the Resource Sheet is not in the top pane, select the top pane, open the **V**iew menu, and choose Resource **S**heet.

2. Filter the resource names by choosing the **T**ools menu, selecting the **F**iltered for command and choosing **O**verallocated Resources. You could also choose the Filter list box from the Formatting toolbar to see the standard filters available for the resources (see fig. 8.15).

3. If no bottom pane is visible, use the **W**indow, **S**plit command.

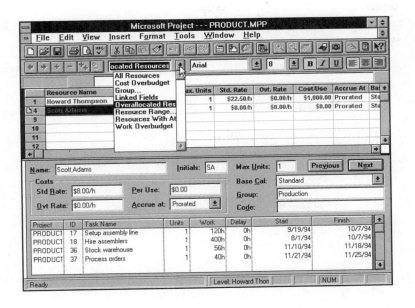

Fig. 8.15
The Formatting
toolbar with the
Filter list box.

4. Activate the bottom pane.

5. Place the Resource Form in the bottom pane by selecting **M**ore Views
   from the **V**iew menu.

6. Choose Resource Form from the More Views dialog box and choose
   Apply.

7. Activate the top pane and select a resource name. The task details
   appear for the selected resource in the bottom pane.

The view shown in figure 8.14 is a good device to determine the tasks that
contribute the most to the costs of particular resources.

Creating a Resource Template

In some cases, you may have a group of resources who are defined and used
across several different projects. It is a good idea to define these resources and
their associated costs in an empty project file and save that project as a template file. When you open the template file, a new project is opened based on
the template file data. You may now add your tasks for the project, without
having to define the project resources and costs.

To save a project file containing resources as a template, perform the following steps:

1. Enter the resource information and related costs into an empty project file.

2. Select the Save **A**s command from the **F**ile menu.

3. Type the project file name in the File **N**ame box.

4. In the Save File as **T**ype list box, choose Template. When you save a project file as a template file type, the file extension is .MPT.

5. Click OK or press Enter to save the project file.

To open a resource template into a new project file, perform the following steps:

1. Choose the **O**pen command from the **F**ile menu or click the Open File tool on the standard toolbar to activate the Open dialog box.

2. From the List Files of **T**ype list box choose Templates (*****.MPT).

3. Select the template file name from the file list box.

4. Choose OK or press Enter to open a new project file based on the template you selected.

Printing the Resource List

You can print the Resource Sheet view described in this chapter with the **F**ile **P**rint command. Follow the same guidelines described in Chapter 4, "Creating a Task List," for printing task views. Printing the Resource Sheet view will give you a listing of the resources used in the project along with their associated costs.

To print one of the views, follow these steps:

1. Display the view either in the top pane or full-screen.

2. Select filters or perform the sorting that you want in the printed report.

3. To preview how the report is going to look, select the Print Preview tool. Or, open the **F**ile menu and choose Print Pre**v**iew.

4. To get an overview of the full report, click the Multi-page button (see fig. 8.16).

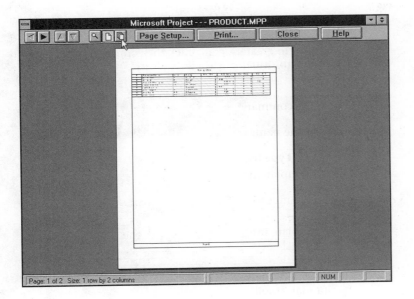

Project Management

Fig. 8.16
Selecting the
Multi-Page Print
Preview.

5. Place the mouse pointer over any page of the report and, when the
   pointer changes to a zoom pointer (see fig. 8.17), click to view the page
   in a full-screen view.

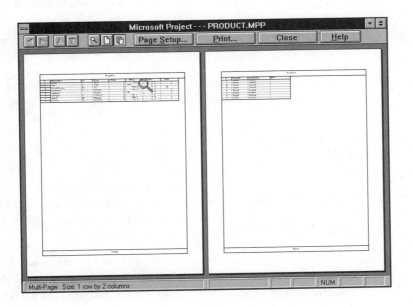

Fig. 8.17
Selecting the Zoom
view of multiple
pages.

6. Use the arrow buttons to scroll to different pages.

7. To see the section in greater detail, click the zoom mouse pointer on any section of a page (see fig. 8.18).

Fig. 8.18
Print Preview,
Zoom view.

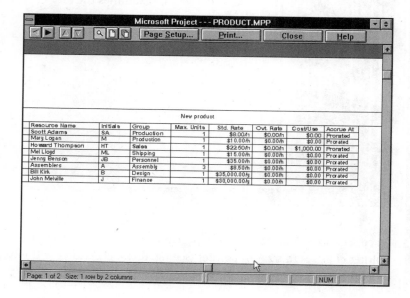

8. Choose the **S**etup button to change the page features of the report. The Page Setup dialog box appears.

▶ "Printing Views and Reports," p. 443.

9. Choose the **P**rint button to send the report to the printer. The Print dialog box appears.

From Here...

Chapter 8 described how to create the list of resources for the project. You also saw how to sort and filter the resource list to provide better management reports. To learn more about defining the resources for the project and to assign resources to tasks, refer to the following chapters:

■ Chapter 9, "Assigning Resources and Costs to Tasks," shows how to assign resources and costs to the project tasks. You will also learn how to change the individual elements of the resource assignments for both resource-driven and fixed tasks.

■ Chapter 13, "Working with Multiple Projects," will discuss in greater detail how you can use the resource file template to create a global resource pool used across several projects.

■ Chapter 16, "Printing Views and Reports," examines the different print options for the standardized reports and views through Microsoft Project. In this chapter, you will see the various reports available for providing thorough, yet concise project data for management.

Chapter 9

Assigning Resources and Costs to Tasks

Assigning a resource to a task usually signifies that the resource does some or all of the work for the task. You also can assign a resource in order to signify that this resource is associated with the task, although no work is measured for the resource on this task. You may want to, for example, associate the name of a management person whose association isn't charged to the task. You may want to associate the name of a contractor whose work is not measured (because this calculation is the contractor's responsibility) but who gave you a fixed price for delivering the completed task.

Resources can be assigned to tasks in several views. The Task Entry view, with the Task Form at the bottom, usually displays the Resources and Predecessors entry areas. The Resource entry area has columns for the resource ID, Name, Units, and Work. You can also assign resources on the Task Details Form, the Task Information Form, the Task Sheet, and the Resource Assignment Form. Each of these screens is discussed in the following sections, but first the resource assignment fields are described. These fields appear at the bottom of the Task Form when the Resources entry area is applied.

In this chapter, you learn how to

- Create Resource-Driven and Fixed Duration Tasks.

- Assign Resources to the Scheduled Tasks.

- Modify the Resource Assignment Data.

- Assign Overtime Work.

- Print the Resource and Cost Reports.

Understanding the Resource Assignment Fields

When you assign a resource to a task, you must name the resource, indicate the number of resource units to dedicate to the task, and optionally specify the amount of work that the combined units of the resource are expected to perform. The fields in which you enter this information are shown in the following list:

Name   You must identify the resource by resource ID number or by name. When you assign resources with the Task Form using the Resources entry table, you can also identify the resource with the resource's initials.

Units   This value is the quantity of resource units dedicated to the task per day. The default value is 1, but you can enter any value between 0 and 100. You may enter 0 units when you do not want to measure the amount of work performed on the task by the resource, nor do you want to measure the cost of this work. Use zero units when you assign a contractor to a task and the contractor agrees to complete the task for a fixed fee, which you enter as a fixed cost.

If only part of a resource's time per day is devoted to the task, enter a fraction that represents the amount of time that this resource works on the task each day. If a worker spends half-time on the task, for example, type **.5** in the Units field. You can enter fractional amounts in tenths or hundredths of a unit, but no smaller division is permitted. If you want to specify that a worker spends no more than one hour per day on a task (one-eighth or .125 of a day), you cannot type .125 units of the worker's time, but must type **.12** or **.13** unit.

Work   The amount of work is measured in hours and is calculated from the duration (measuring duration in hours) and the number of resource units. The formula for calculating work is *Work=Duration*Units*.

If the duration is one day (8 hours) and the number of units is 2, then the amount of work is 16 hours (1 day . 2 units). If the duration is 4 days, and the resource is only assigned half-time to the task, the amount of work is 16 hours (4 days . 8 hours . .5). The calculated work is denominated in hours, no matter what time unit you use for the duration.

If you enter the work amount and the task is not a fixed duration task, Microsoft Project recalculates the duration according to the formula derived from the previous formula *(Duration=Work/Units)*.

Understanding Resource-Driven and Fixed Duration Scheduling

When you first enter a duration, Microsoft Project assumes that you already decided on the number and quality of the resources that you plan to assign to the task. When you make the resource assignments, Microsoft Project uses the duration to calculate how much work each assigned resource does during the duration of the task.

When you designate a task as having a fixed duration, the duration is not altered by Microsoft Project, even if the resource units assigned to the task change. By default, however, Microsoft Project doesn't assume that new tasks are fixed duration tasks. Instead, the normal task status is to determine the duration by the amount of work and the number of resource units assigned to do the work. The formula for determining the duration is *Duration=Work/ Units*.

If you enter the work for a Fixed Duration task, Microsoft Project doesn't change the duration estimate. If the amount of work you entered cannot be completed by the resource unit(s) within the given duration, Microsoft Project displays the warning shown in figure 9.1. This message means the schedule needed for the resource to complete the work on the task requires that the resource work beyond the dates scheduled for the task duration. When you get the warning, you have several options. You can cancel the change to avoid a scheduling conflict, or you can continue and allow the conflict to exist. At the bottom of the dialog box window, you have the option of turning the warning message off so that in the future you are not notified of these potential conflicts.

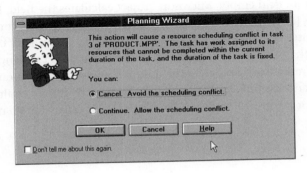

Fig. 9.1
The Work greater than Duration warning dialog box.

If a task is designated as a fixed duration task (if you checked the Fixed box in the Task Form, for example), Microsoft Project doesn't recalculate the duration if resource units and work are inconsistent with the duration. As long as the work can be done within the estimated duration, no problems arise. If the work cannot be completed within the allowed duration, the warning message shown in figure 9.1 appears.

Resource-driven scheduling means that Microsoft Project recalculates the duration of a task to be consistent with the number of units and the amount of work these units must accomplish. When a resource assignment (including the number of units) is first entered, Microsoft Project calculates the work amount by multiplying the duration and the units. If you enter the work amount, however, Microsoft Project recalculates the duration by dividing the work by the number of units.

After the amount of work is established for the task, changes in the number of resource units assigned to do this work result in an automatic recalculation of the task duration. The phrase *after the amount of work is established* is an important part of the definition. The first time that you assign a resource to a task, Microsoft Project defines the work associated with the task by multiplying the duration times the number of resource units. Thereafter, when you change the number of resource units, Microsoft Project calculates the appropriate duration for the new units to accomplish the defined amount of work. If you subsequently change the amount of work, Microsoft Project recalculates the duration that accommodates this amount of work, given the number of units.

When multiple resources are assigned to a task, not all the resources do the same amount of work. As with the first resource assigned to a task, if you leave the work field empty, Microsoft Project calculates the field. If the resource does less or more work than the duration provides time for, however, you may enter the amount of work for the resource. If this work takes less work time than the duration provides, the duration doesn't change. If the work takes more work time than the duration allows, the duration is adjusted to provide enough time for this amount of work. The resources already entered and for whom the amount of work already is calculated do not change.

Using the Resource Assignment Form

You can assign resources in views other than the Task Entry View, but you cannot easily make entries in the work field in these views, nor can you use the resource initials or the resource ID number as a shortcut for entering the resource name. The views that include the resource assignment field are the Resource Assignment Form, the Task Information Form, and the Task Sheet—with the Entry table.

You can use the Resource Assignment Form to assign resources to one or more selected tasks (see fig. 9.2). You activate the Resource Assignment Form by choosing Resource **A**ssignment from the **I**nsert menu or by selecting the Resource Assignment tool on the toolbar.

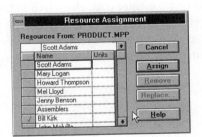

Fig. 9.2
The Resource Assignment Form.

Adding Resource Assignments to a Task or Group of Tasks

Unlike the Multiple Task Information Form, you can make selected changes in multiple tasks at the same time with the Resource Assignment Form. You can add one or more resources to the selected tasks; you can remove one or more resources from selected tasks; and you can replace one resource at a time for all selected tasks that are assigned to the resource. The Resource Assignment Form is a versatile tool for changing the resource assignments for a single task as well as multiple tasks.

To add a resource assignment to a selected task or group of tasks, perform these steps:

1. Select the task or tasks to which you want the resource assigned.

2. Activate the Resource Assignment Form by choosing Resource **A**ssignment from the **I**nsert menu or by clicking the Resource Assignment tool on the toolbar.

Project Management

3. Click on the Name field and, from the list of names, select the resource name to assign to the task.

4. Select the Units field and type the resource units to assign to the task (see fig. 9.3). The default for the Units field is 1 unit. If this entry is appropriate, you may leave the Units field without entering a value, and Microsoft Project supplies the default value when you choose **As**-sign. Remember that you can enter any value between 0 and 100, and that a fractional amount means that a resource devotes only this fractional part of each day to the task. If you enter 0 as the units value, neither work nor resource cost is calculated for this resource for this task. Use the Fixed Cost field to record costs for the tasks that do not depend on the amount of work of a resource.

   The units should be no greater than the maximum units available for this resource. If you do not know or remember the maximum units amount, double-click the resource name field to see the Resource Information Form.

Fig. 9.3
Entering the resource units on the Resource Assignment Form.

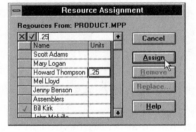

5. Select the **A**ssign button or press Enter to assign the resource and unit information to the selected tasks.

6. If you are adding more resources to the same tasks, select the next resource name to be assigned, type the number of units to assign in the Units field, and select **A**ssign to assign this resource to the selected tasks (see fig. 9.4).

7. After the resource list is completed, select the Close button to close the Resource Assignment Form.

Note

When you select the **A**ssign button on the Resource Assignment Form, a check mark is placed to the left of the resource that was assigned, as shown in figure 9.4.

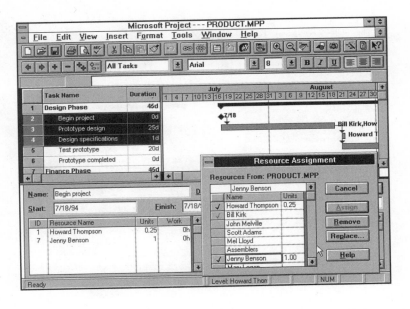

Fig. 9.4
Adding multiple
resources in the
Resource Assign-
ment Form.

You can assign resources to the tasks using the drag-and-drop method as well. An advantage to using the drag-and-drop assignment feature in the Resource Assignment Form is that you do not have to select the task for which a resource should be assigned. So this provides a quick and efficient way of assigning different resources to several tasks at one time.

To assign resources to a task using the drag-and-drop feature, perform the following steps:

1. Activate the Resource Assignment Form by choosing Resource **A**ssignment from the **I**nsert menu or by clicking the Resource Assignment tool on the toolbar.

2. Select the resource by clicking in the Name field.

3. Position the mouse pointer in the gray rectangle to the left of the Name field. The Resource Assignment graphic will appear below the mouse pointer (see fig. 9.5).

4. Hold down the mouse button and drag the mouse pointer to the task for which the resource should be assigned.

5. When the task is highlighted, release the mouse, and the resource is assigned (see fig. 9.6).

Fig. 9.5
The Resource
Assignment
pointer used to
drag and drop
resource assign-
ments to tasks.

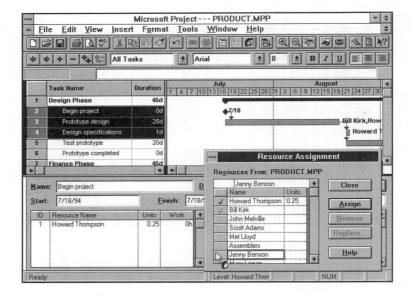

Fig. 9.6
The Resource
Assignment made
using the drag and
drop feature.

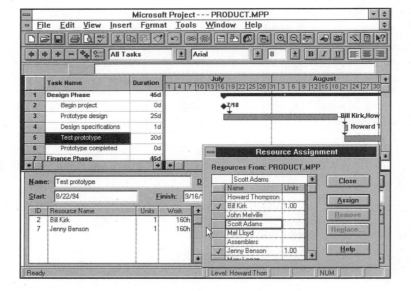

> **Note**
>
> By default, the units field is set to 1 when using the drag-and-drop method. Once assigned, this unit value can be changed in the Resource Assignment Form to reflect the correct number of units to assign to the task.

To assign multiple resources to a task using the drag-and-drop feature, hold down the Ctrl key while selecting the resource names in the Resource Assignment Form (see fig. 9.7). When you drag the mouse pointer to the task, all selected resources will be assigned at once.

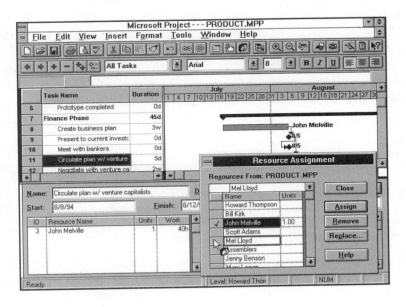

Fig. 9.7
Assigning multiple resources to a task using the drag and drop feature.

To assign the resource(s) to a group of tasks, select the tasks before activating the Resource Assignment Form, and then perform the drag-and-drop steps outlined above.

Removing Resource Assignments from One or More Tasks

To remove a resource assignment from one or more selected tasks, perform the following steps:

1. Select the task or tasks assigned to the resource.

2. Activate the Resource Assignment Form with the **I**nsert Resource **A**ssignment command or using the Resource Assignment tool on the toolbar.

3. The currently assigned resources will have a check mark beside them. Select the one to remove by clicking the check mark or the Name field. To remove a group of resources from the selected tasks, hold down the Ctrl key while you select the resources.

4. Choose the **R**emove button. All the selected tasks with the resource or resources assigned are edited, and the resource names are removed from the respective assignment lists.

Changing Resource Names and Unit Assignments

Use the Re**p**lace command on the Resource Assignment Form to change the resource name or unit assignment for one or more tasks. You can replace only one resource name or assignment at a time. Use the Re**p**lace command to change the units assignment for a resource. To change a full-time assignment for Bill Kirk to part-time, for example, replace the unit assignment of 1, with the new unit assignment of .5 (to symbolize part-time).

To replace a resource assignment, perform the following steps:

1. Select the task or tasks to make an identical assignment change.

2. Activate the Resource Assignment Form with the **I**nsert Resource **A**ssignment command or with the Resource Assignment tool.

3. Select the Resource Name or Unit assignment to be replaced.

4. To replace the unit assignment, type the new unit assignment in the Units field, and then select the Re**p**lace button (see fig. 9.8). To replace the resource name, select the Re**p**lace button before making any changes.

Fig. 9.8
Changing the unit assignment in the Resource Assignment Form.

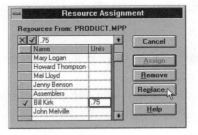

5. To change the resource name, select the new resource, and select OK or press Enter (see fig. 9.9). If only the unit assignment needed to change, select OK or press Enter to complete the change.

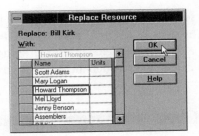

Fig. 9.9
Changing the
resource name in
the Resource
Assignment Form.

Note

Changing the number of resource units assigned to a task causes Microsoft Project to recalculate the task duration (unless the task is a fixed duration task). See the following section for more information about the effects of changing the resource assignment.

Assigning Resources with the Task Information Form

You can use the Task Information Form to assign resources to the task or tasks in the current selection. The assignment entry used here will be different from the format described in the preceding section, "Using the Resource Assignment Form."

To change the resource assignments for a task with the Task Information Form, perform the following steps:

1. Select the task in any field in which it appears on-screen.

2. Activate the Task Information Form by selecting the **I**nsert menu and choosing Task In**f**ormation or by selecting the Information Form tool on the toolbar. The fields in the form show the current data for the task (see fig. 9.10).

3. Select the Resources folder tab to assign or view the resource information for the selected task.

4. In the Resource Name field, edit any existing entry. To add or change the resource, type the resource name or activate the resource list (as shown in fig. 9.11) and choose a resource.

You may then select the Units field and type the unit assignment for the resource. The default for the Units field is 1 unit. If this entry is appropriate, leave the Units field without entering a value, and Microsoft Project supplies the default value when you choose OK after completing the form.

Fig. 9.10
The Task Information Form.

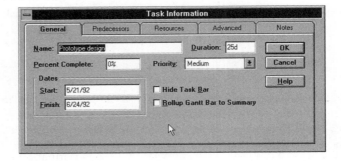

Fig. 9.11
The drop-down Resource Name list in the Task Information Form.

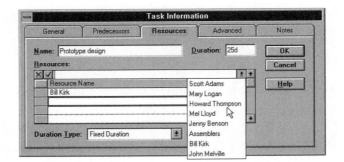

Note

To add additional resources to the selected tasks, choose the next Resource Name field and repeat the steps above.

5. After you complete the entry, choose the OK button.

You can use the Task Information Form to add, change, and delete the resource assignment information for the selected task. You also can use the Task Information Form to add the same resource assignment to multiple tasks. Select all the tasks to which the assignment is to be made before you select the Multiple Task Information Form. You can only add resource assignments on the Multiple Task Information Form; you cannot change existing resource assignments with this form.

To assign resource(s) to multiple tasks with the Multiple Task Information Form, follow these steps:

1. Select the task or tasks to which the resource assignment is to be made.

2. Choose Task Information from the Insert menu or select the Information Form tool from the toolbar to activate the Task Information Form. When multiple tasks are selected, all fields on the Multiple Task Form are blank.

3. Select the Resource Name field and type the resource name to assign, or activate the resource list and choose a name from the list.

4. Type the unit assignment information.

5. After you complete the entry, choose the OK button.

The resource assignment entries you make in the Task Information Form are added to existing resource assignments for the selected tasks. You cannot change the existing resource assignments when you use the Multiple Information Form; you can add to the existing assignments only.

Assigning Resources with the Task and Task Details Forms

Both the Task Form and the Task Details Form can display the Resources entry table at the bottom. The Resources entry table is a convenient place for assigning resources because the fields are separated into columns and are easily identified. The steps outlined below describe the use of the Task Form, but the procedure is identical for the Task Details form.

To assign resources using the Task Form, perform the following steps:

1. From the View menu, choose More Views. Select the Task Entry view and choose Apply.

2. Activate the Task Form in the lower pane.

3. If the Resource entry table is not visible, choose the Format Details command. From the Details list, select an option that contains the Resources information (see fig. 9.12). You find the Resource ID, Name, Units, and Work fields on the Resources & Predecessors, Resources & Successors, Resource Schedule, and Resource Work tables. (The Resource Cost table doesn't show the Work field.)

Fig. 9.12

The Format Detail choices for the Task Form.

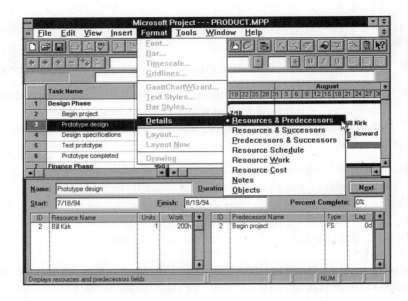

4. Select the Resource Name field.

5. If the resource was already added to the resource pool, you can type either the resource name or the resource initials. If you don't remember the name or initials, select the entry list arrow at the top of the view in the Edit bar for a pull-down menu that lists the resources. Select the resource name you want (see fig. 9.13).

   Whether you type the name or the initials, or use the entry list to select a name, you must press Enter or select another entry field to complete the entry in the Edit bar.

6. Use the right arrow or mouse to select the Units field. The default for the Units field is 1 unit. If this entry is appropriate, leave the Units field without entering a value, and Microsoft Project supplies the default value when you choose OK after completing the form. Otherwise, enter the units that you want to assign to the task.

7. Use the right arrow or mouse to select the Work field. If you want Microsoft Project to calculate the work, leave the field empty.

   If the resource does more or less work than is implicit from multiplying the task duration times the units for this resource, you can enter the amount of work directly in the work field. If the work amount you entered cannot be completed within the original duration (assuming that the task is not a fixed duration task), Microsoft Project recalculates the duration. If other resources already are assigned to the task, the work of these resources is unaffected by a recalculation of the duration.

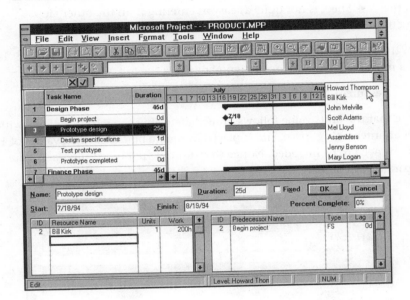

Fig. 9.13
The Resource Name drop-down list from the Entry bar.

8. If you are assigning multiple resources, you can enter these resources in the extra rows of the Resource entry table.

9. After all resource assignments are made for the task, choose the OK button on the Task Form.

If multiple resources are assigned to a task, Microsoft Project assumes that each named resource works for the duration alongside all the other named resources. If you add a second resource name to the assignment, Microsoft Project doesn't assume that the new resource reduces the work load of the first resource. Rather, the assumption is that you originally intended to have both resources working in tandem to complete the task within the duration you estimated.

Assigning Resources on the Task Sheet

You can also use the Task Sheet to assign resources to a task or group of tasks selected on the Task Sheet. However, entering the resource assignment data on the Task Sheet is not quite as easy as entering it on the other views described.

On the Task Sheet, the Resource Name field is a text entry field (see fig. 9.14). You must enter the resource assignment using the following notation:

Resource1 Name[Units],Resource2 Name[Units], and so on

Note that the units value follows immediately after the resource name, without an intervening space, and is placed in square brackets. Units values of 1 do not need to be included. Notice that multiple resource assignments are separated by commas.

Fig. 9.14
Assigning resource information in the Resource Names field on the Task Sheet.

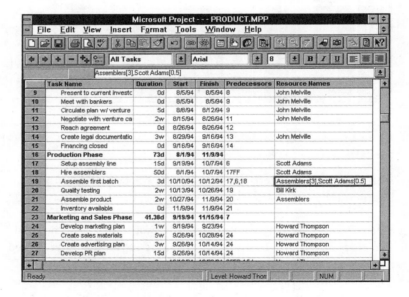

To assign resources to tasks in the Task Sheet view, perform the following steps:

1. Select the **V**iew menu and choose the **M**ore Views command. Choose Task Sheet from the view list and click **A**pply.

2. Select the Resource Names column of the Task Sheet for the task to which you want to assign resources.

3. Enter the resource name. You can select the entry list arrow in the Edit bar to pick the name from the resource list.

4. If the number of units is other than 1, follow the name immediately with the number of units, enclosed in square brackets.

5. If you want to assign more resources to the same task, use a comma to separate each resource.

6. Press Enter or select the Enter box in the Edit bar to complete the cell entry.

Understanding the Effects of Changing Resource Assignments

After you assign a resource to do work for a task, scheduling the task is influenced by the availability of the resource to do the work, and the duration of the task may be influenced by changes in the quantity of resource units assigned to work on the task. Fixed duration tasks are influenced in a different manner from resource-driven tasks. This section is designed to help you see how Microsoft Project reacts to changes in resource assignments.

Changing a Task to Fixed Duration

You can change the status of a task from resource-driven to fixed duration with relative ease by marking the Fixed check box on the Task Form. Clearing the check box makes the task a resource-driven task again. If you try to change the fixed status in the same command with changes in the duration, work, or units values, however, the recalculated values may not be what you had in mind. Always change the fixed status of a task without changing the duration or resource assignments for the task. After the change in the fixed status is assimilated, you can change any other details about the task.

To change a resource-driven task into a fixed duration task, perform the following steps:

1. In any task view, select the task in the upper pane.

2. If either the Task Form or the Task Details Form is in the bottom pane, select the Fixed field and mark the check box, or press the Spacebar to change the box's status. To complete the change in status, choose the OK button.

3. If the Task Form is unavailable, activate the Task Information Form with the **I**nsert Task Information command or click the Information Form tool on the toolbar. Select the Resources folder tab to view the resource assignment data for the selected task.

4. In the Duration **T**ype field, click the entry list arrow to show the duration types: Fixed and Resource (see fig. 9.15). Select the duration type that should be applied for the selected task.

Fig. 9.15
The Resource folder of the Task Information Form with the possible duration types listed.

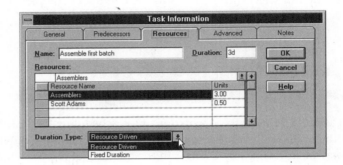

5. Choose OK to complete the change in status.

Changing Fixed Duration Tasks

Changing the resource assignment values for fixed duration tasks never leads to an automatic change in the duration of the task. Moreover, Microsoft Project never recalculates the units value of a resource assignment. However, changes in the amount in the work field must be consistent with the previously set duration and resource units value. If you change the work and units to levels that cannot be completed within the task duration, Microsoft Project warns you that the extra work will be scheduled for the resource, but that the scheduled time is beyond the finish time for the task (see fig. 9.1). Microsoft Project allows you to accept or cancel the inconsistency, and you receive a warning message each time the project is recalculated.

Note

To discontinue error messages and/or warnings, select the **T**ools **O**ptions command and disable the **S**how Scheduling Messages option on the Schedule tab.

Changing the Duration of Fixed Tasks

If you change the estimated duration of a fixed task, Microsoft Project examines the relationship of the duration and the amount of work to do, given the number of resource units, and—depending on the result—responds in one of the following ways:

- If the duration was just sufficient to do the work, Microsoft Project calculates a change in the amount of work proportional to the change in the duration. If you increase the duration by 20 percent, Microsoft Project calculates a 20 percent increase in the amount of work for the resource. If you decrease the duration by 50 percent, the work is decreased by 50 percent.

- If the original duration is longer than needed for the resource units to do the work amount, and if the new duration is still sufficient to do the work, then the work amount remains unchanged.

- If the original duration is longer than needed for the resource units to do the work amount, and the new duration is insufficient to do the same amount of work, a warning appears (refer to fig. 9.1).

Changing the Number of Resource Units

If you change the units of resource assigned to a fixed task, Microsoft Project changes the amount of work for the resource proportionally, with the change in the units.

Assume that one unit of a resource is doing 6 hours of work in a fixed duration task with a duration of 8 hours (the resource is not using the full duration to do the work). If you increase the number of resource units from 1 to 3, the work amount changes to 18 hours (increased by a multiple of 3, like the change in the resource units).

Changing the Amount of Work in Fixed Duration Tasks

If you change the value in the work field, Microsoft Project makes no changes in either the duration or the units fields. If the new amount of work is impossible to complete within the duration by the resource units, you see the warning message shown in figure 9.1.

Changing Resource-Driven Tasks

When you make changes in the duration or the resource variables (units or work) for resource-driven tasks, more recalculation possibilities exist of which you should be aware. Because the duration is not fixed, Microsoft Project can adapt to a change in the resource units, for example, by changing either the duration or the work amount.

Changing the Resource Units

If you change the number of resource units, Microsoft Project assumes that the amount of work to do is unchanged, but that the work now is to be done by a different quantity of resources. So Microsoft Project calculates the duration needed by the new quantity of resources to do the same amount of work.

Because the formula for the duration is *Duration = Work/Units*, the change in the duration is inverse to the change in the units. The change in the duration is the reciprocal of the change in the number of units. A doubling (multiply by 2) of the number of units, for example, results in a reduction in the duration by a half (multiply by 1/2). A 50 percent increase in the units (multiply by 3/2) reduces the duration to two-thirds of the former level (multiply by 2/3).

Changing the Duration or Work Amount

Microsoft Project never changes the number of resource units—only you can make this change. Therefore, if you change the duration, the program changes the amount of work. If you change the amount of work, the program changes the duration. As always, the duration is governed by the maximum duration needed by any one of the resource names to do the assigned work for the task. If you double the duration, for example, the amount of work is doubled automatically by the program.

When multiple resources are assigned to a task, the resulting changes in the work and duration values are calculated in a slightly different manner. The task duration always is determined by the longest duration required for any one resource name to complete the related work assignment: the duration is *driven* by the work load of the resource. If one of the resources is not fully occupied with work for the task during the task duration, an increase in the estimated duration produces no increase in the work for this resource. The work for the resource *driving* the duration, however, increases proportionally with the increased duration.

If you decrease the duration for a task that is assigned multiple resources, the work load for the resources *driving* the duration decreases proportionally. If another resource, which was not previously fully occupied by the task, cannot now do the work in the new duration, Microsoft Project resets the duration to the time needed for this resource to complete the assignment. The *driver* resource will have changed names.

As an example, the resource assignments shown in figure 9.16 for task 18 (Assemble first batch) in the PRODUCT project were augmented to include Bill Kirk and Mary Logan. For this task, both Mary and Bill have lower work loads than the Assemblers resource. The Assemblers resource is the driver resource for the task's duration because the three-day duration is based on the work load of 24 hours for one Assembler. Bill can perform his work in a day and a half, and Mary can do her part in a half day.

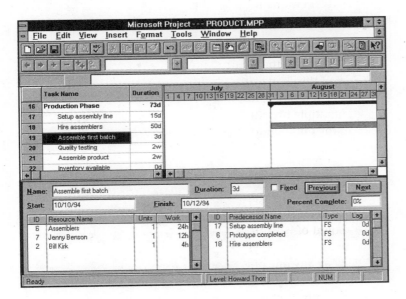

Fig. 9.16
Multiple resource assignments, with a driver resource.

Figure 9.17 shows what happens when a new duration of one day is entered. Microsoft Project calculates that the Assemblers work load is reduced proportionally to 8 hours, (because it was the *driver*). However, Bill's assignment cannot be completed in one day; so Microsoft Project overrides the one-day duration entry and makes the duration 1.5 days (as you see in the duration field of the Task Form). Bill Kirk now is the driver resource. Mary Logan's work load is unchanged in the calculations.

Figure 9.18 shows how the task would be affected if you increased the number of Assemblers to three units (instead of changing the three-day duration). Three Assemblers can do the 24 hours of work in 1 day; therefore, the duration would have been changed to 1 day if the work load for Bill Kirk hadn't required 1.5 days. Because of Bill's work load, the duration is only reduced to 1.5 days. The work load of all resources remains unchanged.

Fig. 9.17
Reducing the task
duration.

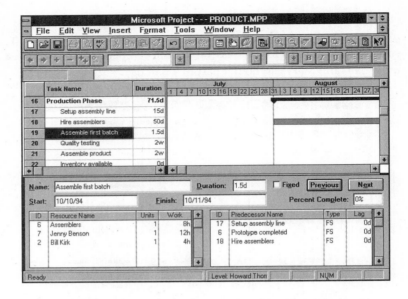

Fig. 9.18
Changing the
number of
resource units
with multiple
resources.

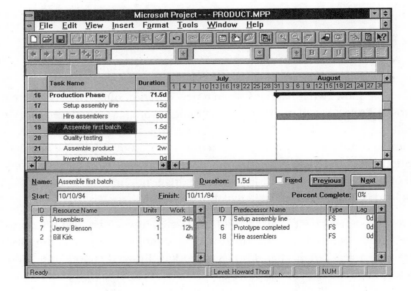

Transferring Part of the Work Load between Resources

When you assign the first resource to a resource-driven task, Microsoft Project calculates the amount of work based on the number of units. If you also enter the work amount, Microsoft Project calculates the duration that makes this amount of work possible.

When you assign more resource names to the task, Microsoft Project assumes that the new resources work in parallel with the first resource. In other words, Project does not assume that the new resource or resources reduce the amount of work that must be done by the first resource. The work load of the first resource is not reduced when new resource names are added.

When you want to substitute the work of one resource for another (usually to reduce the duration of the task), you must enter the revised work load values for both resources.

Note

If you want to redo the task duration and the units and work loads for the resources already assigned to the task, you need to make the task a Fixed Duration task first, and then make all the changes. When the changes are complete, remove the Fixed task mark. Otherwise, as you make multiple changes in the values, Microsoft Project continually recalculates the values, which makes achieving the revised values difficult.

Assigning Overtime Work

Overtime usually means that a resource works at a time outside the normal working schedule. This definition explains how Microsoft Project sees overtime. To Microsoft Project, if part of the work on a task is done in overtime, that much of the task work is not scheduled during the regular working hours.

Understanding How Microsoft Project Schedules and Charges for Overtime

When you instruct Microsoft Project to schedule a certain amount of time in overtime hours, the program just makes a note to reduce the number of regular hours you must devote to the task.

The cost of the overtime hours is calculated by using the overtime rate that you define on the Resource Sheet or Forms. Note that when you enter overtime work hours, you do not designate the exact days and hours when the overtime work takes place, you just tell Microsoft Project that a certain number of hours on the task are overtime hours. Microsoft Project uses this instruction to reduce the number of regular calendar hours scheduled for the task, and notes that the overtime rate is used for costing purposes.

As you see, if you use overtime, providing Microsoft Project with the needed information for assessing the cost of overtime hours is vitally important. If you don't enter an overtime rate when defining the resource (leaving the field with the default zero value), overtime work is charged at the rate of zero. Tasks that use overtime work for which no overtime costs are recorded will appear to use fewer of the limited resources than they actually do. The overtime hours of all resources (even salaried professionals) should be charged as a cost to reflect the opportunity cost of having done one task instead of others.

Another way of recording overtime is to change the calendar of working hours to specify the days and hours when a resource is available, in addition to the regular schedule. You edit the resource calendar and make these days and hours working times rather than non-working times. Be aware, however, that Microsoft Project charges no overtime rate for work done during the regular calendar hours. If you do not pay premium overtime rates, then editing the calendar is satisfactory; indeed, it gives you the capability of stating explicitly when the overtime work takes place. If you pay premium overtime rates, however, you must enter overtime hours in the Overtime field so that costing is done at the overtime rate.

Entering Overtime Work

The Overtime field appears on three forms and, in each case, you must use the Fo**r**mat **D**etails command to apply the Resource Work table at the bottom of the form. You can enter overtime in the following places:

- On the Task **F**orm, with the Resource **W**ork entry table displayed at the bottom of the form.

- On the Task Details Form, with the Resource **W**ork entry table displayed at the bottom of the form.

- On the **R**esource Form, with the **W**ork entry table displayed at the bottom of the form.

> **Note**
>
> If you want to clear an overtime entry, you must enter a 0. You cannot leave the field empty; this field must have a value.

You can see the total overtime worked by a resource for all tasks by viewing the Resource Sheet and applying the Work Table.

Using the Task Form To Enter Overtime

You can use the Gantt Chart, the Task Sheet, or the PERT Chart in the top pane to display and select the task for which you want to record overtime, and use the Task Form in the bottom pane to enter the amount of overtime.

To enter overtime in the Task Entry view, perform the following steps:

1. Select **V**iew from the menu and choose **M**ore Views.

2. Choose the Task Entry view from the view list and select **A**pply. You can use the Gantt Chart, the Task Sheet, or the PERT Chart in the top pane to display and select the task for which you want to record overtime in the bottom pane. You also can use the Task Form in the top pane and not use the bottom pane. See the instructions following this section for details.

3. Select the task for which you want to schedule overtime.

4. Press F6 to activate the Task **F**orm in the bottom pane. If you prefer the Task Details Form, choose **M**ore Views from the **V**iew menu, select the Task Details Form from the view list, and choose **A**pply.

   Of these two options above, the Task Form is the preferable view to use because it does not have as much data on the form.

5. From the Fo**r**mat menu, choose **D**etails and select Resource **W**ork to display the work fields entry table at the bottom of the form (see fig. 9.19).

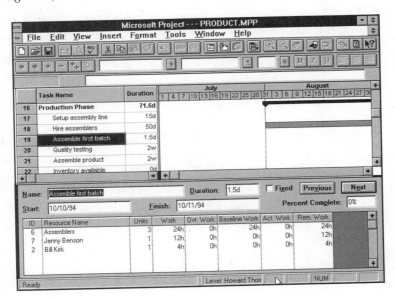

Fig. 9.19
The Resource Work entry table on the Task Form.

6. If the resource already is assigned to the task, select the resource. If not, assign the resource and, in the Work field, enter the total hours of work, including overtime hours.

7. Select the Ovt. Work field and enter the amount of work that you are scheduling in overtime—beyond the regular calendar of work hours. Enter a number followed by a time unit letter (m for minute, h for hour, d for day, or w for week), and then press Enter or click the Enter box on the Edit bar.

Do not reduce the entry in the Work field. The entry must show the total amount of work to be done, including the overtime work (see fig. 9.20).

Fig. 9.20
The Overtime Work entered in the Resource Work fields.

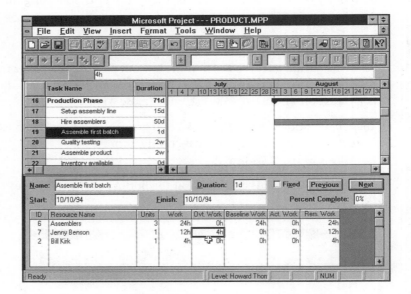

8. Choose the OK button to complete the overtime assignment.

In Figure 9.19, the task is number 19 and the resource is Bill Kirk, whose work load for this task is 12 hours. Remember that this resource was driving the duration of this task in a prior example because Kirk's 12 hours of work takes 1.5 days, and the other resources can complete the work in a day or less. After recording the overtime of 4 hours for Bill Kirk, the task duration is reduced to 1 day (see fig. 9.20). Usually, overtime is scheduled for just this reason, to reduce the overall time taken to complete a task.

To use only the Task Form for recording overtime, perform the following steps:

1. Select the top pane.

2. From the **V**iew menu, choose **M**ore Views. Select the Task Form view from the view list and click **A**pply. Position the mouse pointer on the split bar line in the middle of the screen and double-click the mouse to make this a full-screen view, as shown in fig. 9.21.

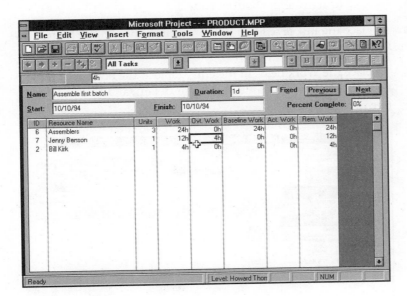

Fig. 9.21
Using the Task Form in a full-screen view to enter overtime.

3. From the Fo**r**mat menu, choose **D**etails and choose Resource **W**ork to display the resource fields at the bottom of the form in an entry table.

4. Use the N**e**xt and Pre**v**ious buttons to locate the task for which you want to record overtime.

5. Enter the amount in the Ovt. Work field, as described in the preceding steps. Type a number followed by a time unit letter (m, h, d, or y), and press Enter or click the Enter box in the Edit bar.

6. To complete the entry, choose the OK button.

Using the Resource Form To Enter Overtime

If you apply the Work fields entry table, you can use the Resource Form to enter overtime hours. To enter overtime in the Resource Form, perform the following steps:

1. From the **V**iew menu, choose **M**ore Views and select the Task Entry view from the view list. In the top pane, select the task to which you want to assign overtime work.

2. Press F6 to activate the bottom pane.

3. To place the Resource Form in the bottom pane, choose **M**ore Views from the **V**iew menu and select Resource Form.

4. To place the Work fields in the entry table at the bottom of the form, select the Fo**r**mat menu, choose **D**etails, and choose **W**ork (see fig. 9.22).

Fig. 9.22
Entering overtime in the Resource Form.

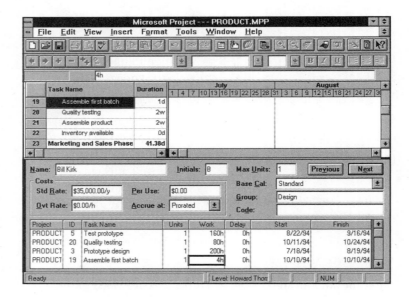

5. Because the resource form shows details for only one resource at a time, you may need to use the N**e**xt or Pre**v**ious buttons to select the resource for which overtime is to be entered.

You also can use the **F**ind command from the **E**dit menu to select the resource. Press Shift+F5, or choose **E**dit **F**ind to display the Find dialog box. Type all or part of the resource name and choose **N**ext to move forward to this resource. If you must search in the opposite direction, choose **P**revious to close the Find dialog box and start the search.

6. The work fields table shows a row for each task to which the resource is assigned. If the task you want to assign overtime to is not visible, use the scroll bar on the right of the form to bring the task into view.

7. Select the Ovt. Work field for the task.

8. Enter the amount of overtime work using a number and a time unit letter (m, h, d, or w), and press Enter or click the Enter box on the Edit bar.

9. Choose the OK button to complete the overtime assignment.

Assigning Fixed Costs and Fixed Contract Fees

For some tasks, you need to assign costs that aren't linked to the task duration or the resource assignment. These costs, known as *fixed costs*, are entered on the Gantt Chart or the Task Sheet with the Cost Table applied.

You also use fixed costs when the work on a task is done by a contractor or vendor at a fixed fee. You do not want Microsoft Project to track the work estimate for this kind of task because the amount of work is important to the contractor or vendor but not to you. (Your cost isn't affected if the work takes more time or money than estimated.) For these tasks, make the task a fixed-duration task and assign the contractor or vendor as a resource to the task, but enter a zero in the units field. The work amount is calculated as zero; therefore, resource cost values from this resource are also zero. Then enter the contract cost in the Fixed Cost field.

Figure 9.23 shows an application of the previously outlined procedure for recording contractors and fixed costs. You want to transfer the Quality testing task (number 19 in the PRODUCT example) to a vendor named Quality Testing Labs. The vendor agrees to a delivery price of $1,000 and agrees to complete the testing within the two weeks originally scheduled for the task's duration. Bill Kirk's work load is reduced to ten hours of coordinating and overseeing the testing process.

Fig. 9.23

Using fixed costs
for contractor fees.

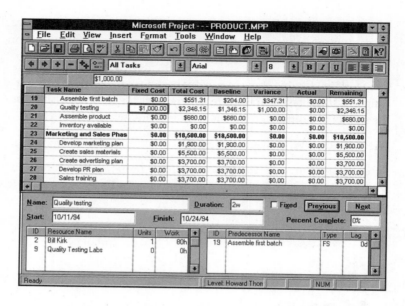

To enter the cost of a fixed contract fee for a task, perform the following steps:

1. Display the Task Entry view by choosing **M**ore Views from the **V**iew menu. Select the Task Entry view and click **A**pply.

   If you want to see the Task Sheet in the upper pane, which shows more fields, select the **V**iew menu, choose **M**ore Views again, and select Task Sheet.

2. Display the Cost table by choosing **T**able **C**ost from the **V**iew menu.

3. Select the task to assign to a contractor or vendor.

4. Mark the **F**ixed check box on the Task Form and choose the OK button to make the task a fixed-duration task.

5. Assign the contractor as a resource in one of the Resource entry fields in the bottom pane.

6. Enter the resource units as zero (0).

7. To complete the resource assignment, choose OK.

8. Activate the top pane.

9. Select the Fixed Cost field for the task.

10. Enter the Fixed Cost amount, and press Enter or select the Entry box in the Edit bar.

The Fixed Cost is added to the resource costs in the Total Cost column, which really is the field named *Cost*.

The task is first made into a fixed duration task because the work is handled outside the company's resources. The vendor name is added to the resource listing, but the units are set to 0. At the same time, Bill Kirk's work load is reduced to 10 hours.

When you choose OK, the vendor's name is added to the resource pool. The vendor quoted a fixed price for this job, but also has quoted the hourly rates and a setup fee charged for most jobs. These rates and charges are entered as illustrated in figure 9.24. Note that the setup charge and standard rates do not affect the cost of this task because the unit assignment is 0. Finally, the $1,000 fixed fee is entered in the Fixed Cost field of the Task Sheet (refer to fig. 9.23).

Fig. 9.24
The Resource Information Form for the Quality Testing Labs vendor.

The manager of this project has already captured an original project plan, and the Baseline column of the cost table shows that the original estimate for this task was $1,346.15. The new cost of the task is $1,168.27 (the vendor's fee plus Bill Kirk's 10 hours at $168.27). Using the contractor has reduced the cost of the task by $177.88, as indicated in the Variance field.

Using Alternate Views of Resources and Resource Assignments

To this point, this chapter showed you how to enter and assign resources and costs in projects to individual tasks or groups of tasks. Several views were used in the data entry explanations, including the Resource Form and the Resource Sheet. Several new tables and format displays also were introduced, including the Cost and Work tables for spreadsheet views of tasks and of resources, and the Cost and Work fields entry tables on the Task Form.

▶ "Resolving Problems in the Project Plan," p. 261.

Besides these tools, several resource views are available that provide interesting insights into the resource work loads in your project. The Resource Usage, Resource Allocation, and Resource Graph views are especially interesting and are briefly described in the following sections.

Understanding the Resource Usage View

The Resource Usage view has a timescale similar to the Gantt Chart, but the Resource Usage view shows number values instead of bars. These numbers are the scheduled amount of work for each resource name during the time unit (see fig. 9.25).

Fig. 9.25
The Resource Usage View beneath the Gantt Chart.

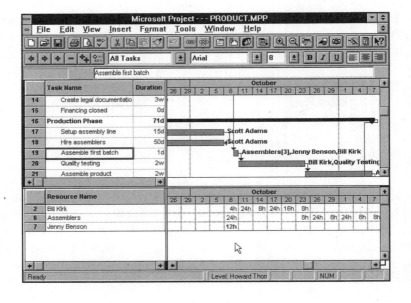

To view the Resource Usage view beneath the Gantt Chart, follow these steps:

1. From the **V**iew menu, choose **M**ore Views and select the Task Entry view.

2. Select the lower pane.

3. From the **V**iew menu, choose Resource **U**sage.

4. Select the upper pane and select the task you want to view. (The resources Bill Kirk and Mary Logan were added to task 18 earlier in this chapter to show multiple resource assignments to one task.)

The Resource Usage table shows the amount of work each resource is scheduled to do during each time unit shown on the timescale. If the resource name appears in the color red, the resource is overallocated at some time period during the project.

> **Note**
>
> You can increase the time span covered in each unit of the timescale with the timescale Zoom Out tool. If the time unit is currently days, selecting the Zoom Out tool twice displays the total amount of work by week for the resources. Press the timescale Zoom In tool to return to the daily timescale. The top pane must be active to use the timescale Zoom tools on the toolbar.

Understanding the Resource Allocation View

The Resource Allocation view is a valuable tool for dealing with overallocated resources, and also is a good view for reviewing the work assignments by resource. Where the Resource Usage view showed the usage of resources for the task selected, the Resource Allocation view puts the Resource Usage view in the top pane and displays all resources. The Resource Allocation view also places a Gantt Chart in the lower pane (see fig. 9.26), which only shows the tasks assigned to the selected resource in the top pane. The Gantt Chart used here is known as the Delay Gantt because of the Delay field. When resources are overallocated, you occasionally need to delay one or more tasks until the resource has the time to do the work. The Delay field shows how much a task has been delayed.

▶ "Resolving Problems in the Project Plan," p. 261.

Fig. 9.26
The Resource
Allocation view.

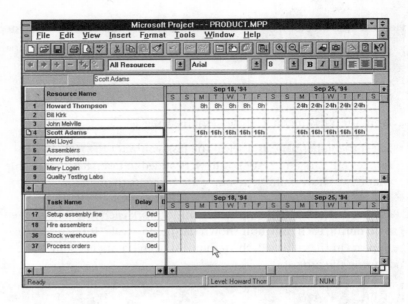

► "Resolving
Problems in the
Project Plan,"
p. 261.

To display the Resource Allocation view, perform the following steps:

1. From the **V**iew menu, choose **M**ore Views.

2. Select Resource Allocation from the list.

3. To activate the view, choose the **A**pply button.

The top pane lists all the resources in the resource pool and shows the timescale, with the scheduled hours of work during each time unit. Select a resource name, and the lower pane shows a list of all tasks on which the selected resource is assigned to work, with a task bar in the timescale to show when the task is scheduled for work. In figure 9.26, for example, Scott Adams is scheduled to work on task number 17, Setup assembly line, among others. To see the task bar for a particular task, select the task in the bottom pane and choose the Go To selected task button.

To review the assigned work schedule for the resource over the life of the project, scroll the timescale. Use Alt+PgDn to move the timescale forward and Alt+PgUp to move the scale back through time.

Understanding the Resource Graph View

The Resource Graph view not only shows the allocation of the resource per time period, but also shows the maximum available units of the resource in the same time frame. You can see the Resource Graph most effectively by placing the graph in the bottom pane, beneath the Resource Usage view (see fig. 9.27).

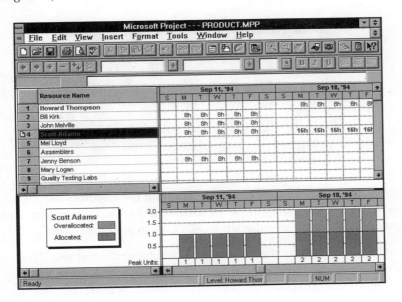

Fig. 9.27
The Resource Graph view beneath the Resource Usage view.

To view the Resource Graph view in the bottom pane, follow these steps:

1. From the **V**iew menu, choose **M**ore Views.

2. Select the Resource Allocation view and choose **A**pply.

3. Press F6 to activate the bottom pane.

4. From the **V**iew menu, choose Resource Graph.

The left half of the Resource Graph view will show the graph legend and resource name. To the right is the timeline that graphically shows the number of units allocated for a resource. The blue bar shows the amount of units allocated; the red bar shows the overallocated units.

▶ "Resolving Problems in the Project Plan," p. 261.

Printing Resource Work and Cost Reports

Available through the **V**iew **R**eport command are several report options to help you monitor and evaluate the scheduled tasks for the resources, as well as the resource costs for the project (see fig. 9.28).

Fig. 9.28
The Reports dialog box shows the available report categories.

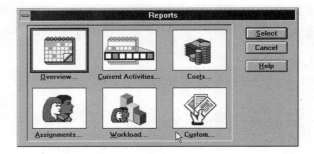

The Co**s**ts reports provide budget information for the resources and tasks, special reports to show only those resources or tasks that are currently over budget, and a report to monitor the weekly cash flow of the project.

The **A**ssignments reports show the resource assignment information for specific resources and/or time periods, including a report showing overallocated resources, and one that contains a weekly to-do list for a specific resource (see fig. 9.29).

Fig. 9.29
A zoomed view of the weekly to-do list for the Scott Adams resource.

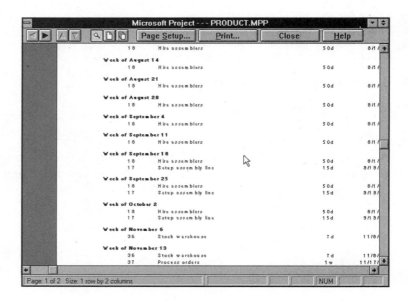

The **W**orkload option has a Resource Usage report, similar to the Resource Usage view, that shows the resources, the tasks assigned to each resource, and their work assignment over a time period (see fig. 9.30).

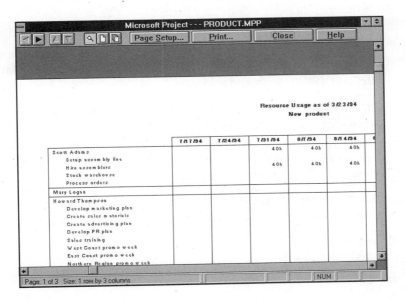

Fig. 9.30
The Print Preview screen for the Resource Usage report in a zoomed view.

To choose one of these report options, select the **V**iew **R**eports command and choose the report category to select from. When you select a report, the report is displayed in the Print Preview window automatically. From this screen, you can zoom the report to see the data close up (refer to fig. 9.30), choose Page **S**etup to format the report layout, and choose **P**rint to send the report to the printer.

► "Printing Views and Reports," p. 443.

From Here...

This chapter described how to assign resources and costs to tasks using the various resource views available in Microsoft Project. You also learned how to distinguish between and assign fixed and duration-driven tasks. The assignment of overtime resources and costs was discussed, as well as several examples of the resource work and costs reports that can be used to monitor the resource progress of the schedule.

Now that the project schedule has been created and the resources and costs have been assigned to the tasks, you are ready to learn more about auditing the project schedule and resolving any scheduling conflicts which have arisen. In the following chapters, you will be introduced to some of these topics:

- Chapter 10, "Auditing the Task Schedule," discusses the different tools and techniques available to audit the schedule for correctness and to filter and sort the tasks and resources.

- Chapter 11, "Resolving Problems in the Project Plan," shows you how to resolve any scheduling conflicts that arose when you assigned resources to the tasks in the project. Different strategies for eliminating overallocation conflicts are discussed, as well as plans for reducing costs.

- Chapter 16, "Printing Views and Reports," discusses in depth the various reports and views that can be used to produce professional reports for project monitoring.

Chapter 10

Auditing the Task Schedule

In this chapter, you will learn how to

- View your project to get the overall picture.

- Use filters.

- Sort task and resource lists.

- Spell-check the project document before printing.

- Use reports that summarize that summarize the project.

After the tasks are defined and the resources and costs that you are using in the project are associated with their respective tasks, you may want to step back from all these details and look at the overall project. You need to evaluate how successfully the project plan meets the objectives of the project as stated in the project goal.

Often, the first draft of a project plan includes costs that exceed budget limits, or the scheduled finish date of the project is later than acceptable. There may also be inconsistencies in the plan. For example, resources may be overallocated, or deadlines for individual tasks may not be met. This chapter shows you how to get an overview of your project. The resolution of inconsistencies and other problems is covered in Chapter 11, "Resolving Problems in the Project Plan."

Looking at the Big Picture

You probably feel a little overwhelmed by the multitude of details in a large project. From time to time, you may find that it's a good idea to step back and look at the overall project to keep a global perspective. You can review the Project Statistics sheet to note specifics about the scheduled start and finish dates and the planned costs. You can collapse the timescale when viewing the Gantt chart to get a macro time perspective. You can filter the summary tasks and milestones or collapse the outline to view and compare the schedules and costs of the major phases of the project.

After you define the tasks, the durations and constraints, the dependency relationships, and the resource assignments, Microsoft Project calculates the scheduled start and finish date for each task, and also the scheduled finish date for the project. You can use the Project Statistics dialog box shown in figure 10.1 to view the scheduled start and finish dates for the project. All the data in the Project Statistics dialog box is calculated—you cannot edit any of the fields on the form.

Fig. 10.1

Examine the Project Statistics dialog box for a quick summary of the project's start and finish dates.

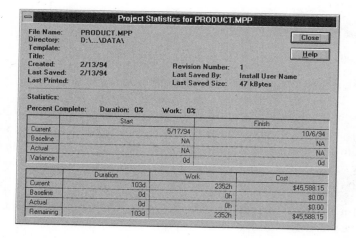

To display the Project Statistics information box, choose the Project Statistics tool on the Tracking toolbar, or use the File Summary Info command to display the Summary Info dialog box and choose the Statistics button.

At a glance, you will see the currently scheduled start and finish dates, the duration for the project, and also the planned amount of work and cost. Later, after you capture the baseline copy of the schedule, you will see the planned start and finish dates. After you start work on the project and enter tracking information, you will see also the actual start of the project.

If the project is scheduled from the start date, use the Project Statistics summary box to identify the currently calculated finish date; if the project is scheduled from the finish date, use the summary box to view the currently calculated start date. If the calculated date is inconsistent with the project goal statement, you need to find ways to shorten the life of the project.

The scheduled cost figure in the Project Statistics summary box tells you at a glance the sum of all resource costs and fixed costs that you previously defined for the project. If this figure is too high to be consistent with the goals of the project, search for ways to reduce costs without sacrificing the time objectives of the project goal.

Compressing the Timescale

You usually can gain an overview of the flow of activity in the project by viewing the Gantt Chart with the timescale compressed. In figure 10.2, for example, the PRODUCT sample project is displayed with the timescale compressed to show weeks as the unit of time. (Resource names have been removed from the task bars.)

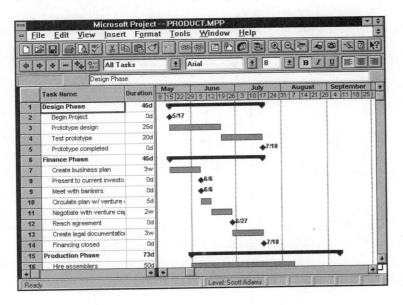

Fig. 10.2
Compress the time scale to get an overall view of the time dimension of the project.

To compress the timescale with the toolbar, select the Zoom Out tool to automatically select larger time units represented in each unit of the timescale. The display of weeks in figure 10.2 is the result of clicking the Zoom Out tool twice. Use the Zoom In tool to subdivide time into smaller units of time.

► See Chapter 18, "Formatting Views."

To make more explicit changes than these tools provide, use the Timescale command on the Format menu. To make references easier to follow in the discussion, for example, the illustrations in this chapter label the days on the timescale with the day number rather than with the weekday letter. See the instructions in Chapter 18, "Formatting Views" to make this change in your project.

Collapsing the Task List Outline

The compressed time display may be more meaningful if you also collapse the outline or filter the task list to view only the summary tasks or the milestones. In figure 10.3, the task list is collapsed to show only the first level summary tasks (all subtasks are hidden). This view provides an overview of the start and finish dates of the major phases of the project. You can collapse the outline to any level of detail by first collapsing the task list to the first level tasks, and then expanding the list to show the next level of subtasks.

Fig. 10.3
Hide the subtasks in an outlined project to focus on the major phases of the project.

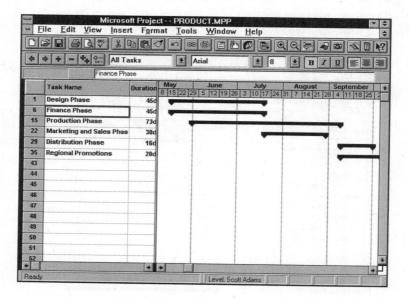

To collapse the outline to the first level, follow these steps:

1. Activate a pane that displays a task list table (the Gantt Chart, for example).

2. Select all tasks by clicking the column headings row of the task list (for example, click on the word Name at the head of the task names). All tasks will show the selection highlight.

3. Use the Hide Subtasks tool (the single minus sign on the Formatting toolbar) to hide all subtasks. You also can choose **T**ools from the menu and then the O**u**tlining command, followed by the **H**ide Subtasks command, to hide all subtasks.

You can use the Show Subtasks tool (the single plus sign on the Formatting toolbar) to open up successive levels in the outline. For example, if your project had five levels in the outline and you wanted to display tasks down to the third level, click the Show Subtasks tool twice. To remove the highlight on all tasks, select any cell in the task list.

Similarly, you may find it constructive to view just the milestones in order to focus on the completion dates of the important sections of the projects. The next section shows you how to filter the display to show just certain tasks or resources.

Filtering the Task or Resource List

When you filter the task list, you impose conditions that must be met in order to display a task. All the tasks that meet the conditions are allowed to filter through to be displayed and are known as *filtered tasks*. All those tasks that fail to meet the conditions are not displayed. You can apply a filter, for example, to display only the milestones (as shown in fig. 10.4) or only the critical tasks, or only the summary tasks. You also can use filters to just highlight the tasks selected by the filter, leaving the rest of the tasks displayed but not highlighted (see fig. 10.5). Filters also can be used in resource views to display certain resources only.

Microsoft Project has many predefined task filters, and you can add custom filters to the list. Some of the filters are interactive filters: when you select the filter, a dialog box appears from which you specify values to use in selecting the filtered tasks. The Date Range filter, for example, prompts you for two dates, and then displays all tasks scheduled to start between those two dates.

Fig. 10.4
The filtered task list showing only milestones lets you focus solely on important completion dates.

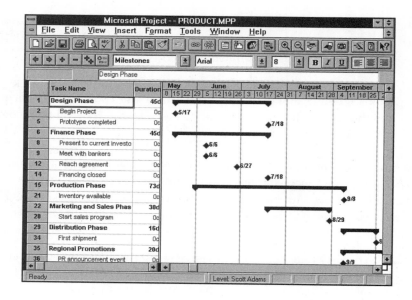

Fig. 10.5
Having filtered tasks appear **highlighted** makes them stand out in the display.

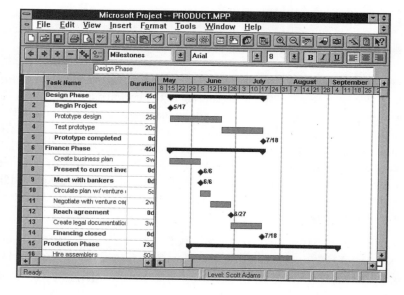

You may find the following partial list of task filters useful for reviewing the project after the tasks are all entered:

Critical	Filters only critical tasks.
Date **R**ange	Filters only those tasks scheduled to start between two dates that you enter when prompted.

Milestones	Filters only milestone tasks.
Summary Tasks	Filters only summary tasks.
Tasks with Fixed Dates	This filter is on the **M**ore Filters list and it filters all tasks that have any date constraint other than As Soon As Possible.

Project Management

Note

The Summary Task filter is not usually a good substitute for collapsing the outline as described in the previous section. The Summary Task filter shows only summary tasks, but all levels in the outline are displayed. Furthermore, if any first level task in the outline is not a summary task, the task will not be included in the list of tasks filtered by the Summary Task filter. If you want to focus only on the tasks to a certain level in the outline, you will find that collapsing the entire outline to that level of tasks is the preferred method.

Using Filters

To filter the task list or the resource list, select the **F**iltered for: menu and choose the filter that you want to apply. If you choose an interactive filter, respond to the prompts by typing the requested information, and then choose the OK button. For example, to view only the milestone tasks for the project, choose the **T**ools **F**iltered for: command and choose Mil**e**stones from the pull-down menu of filters.

If you want the filter to highlight the selected tasks, hold down the Shift key as you select the **F**iltered for: command. You can then select the filter that you want to apply, and it will be implemented as a highlight filter.

Note

Users of Release 3.0 note that Shift must be engaged as you select the **F**iltered for: command, not just as you select the main menu command **T**ools.

You also can display a highlight filter by following these steps:

1. From the **T**ools menu, choose **F**iltered for:.

2. Choose the **M**ore Filters command.

3. Select the filter you want to use in the More Filters dialog box.

4. Choose the Hi**g**hlight button.

Tip

If you edit the tasks or resources while a filter is applied, you may change that element of a task or resource that is tested by the filter. You must then reapply the filter to make the filtered display accurate. The quick key Ctrl+F3 updates the display to accurately reflect the filter criteria.

► See Chapter 11, "Resolving Problems in the Project Plan."

When you finish using the filter, you can remove it by pressing the shortcut key F3, or by selecting the **F**iltered for: command and choosing the **A**ll Tasks filter.

One of the most useful filters is the filter for Tasks With Fixed Dates. This filter is used to identify all the tasks that have constrained dates. Novice users of Microsoft Project often inadvertently place constraints on tasks, then they're plagued with scheduling messages about tasks that cannot be completed in the time allocated (see fig. 10.6). Use the Tasks With Fixed Dates filter to display tasks that have constraints. You can then review the tasks and be certain that the constraints are in fact necessary.

Fig. 10.6
The "Late date before scheduled date" warning may result from accidentally constraining a task's start or finish date.

To apply the filter for constrained tasks, follow these steps:

1. From the **T**ools menu, choose **F**iltered For:.

2. Choose the command **M**ore Filters at the bottom of the command list. The More Filters dialog box is displayed (see fig. 10.7).

Fig. 10.7
Additional filters are listed in the More Filters dialog box.

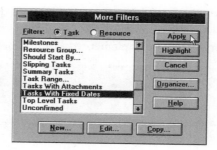

3. Select the Tasks With Fixed Dates filter.

4. Choose the Appl**y** button to activate the filter.

The Overallocated filter is one of the more useful filters for resources. This filter reduces the list of resources to just those that have excessive task assignments during one or more time periods. To apply the Overallocated filter to the Resource Sheet view, follow these steps:

1. From the **V**iew menu, choose Resource **S**heet.

2. From the **T**ools menu, choose **F**iltered for:.

3. Choose **O**verallocated Resources from the list of resource filters.

Viewing the Costs

The Gantt Chart focuses on the time relationships among the tasks. If you want to focus on the costs of the major phases of the project or on the amount of work scheduled for each major phase, view the Task Sheet with the Summary table. Figure 10.8 shows the summary cost, work, and duration of all the tasks in the Product project. Figure 10.9 shows the same information, but with the Summary Task filter applied.

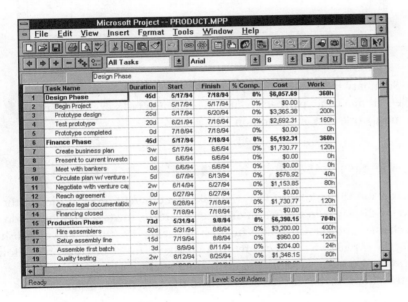

Fig. 10.8
The Summary table shows duration, work, and cost details for the project.

To view the Summary table for the task sheet, follow these steps:

1. View the Task Sheet by choosing the **V**iew **M**ore Views command and scrolling the list of views to select **T**ask Sheet.

2. Choose the **A**pply button to display the view immediately.

3. From the **V**iew menu choose Ta**b**le:, and choose **S**ummary from the pull-down list of tables.

Fig. 10.9
Collapsing the
outline in the
Summary table
focuses on work
and cost amounts
for the major
phases of the
project.

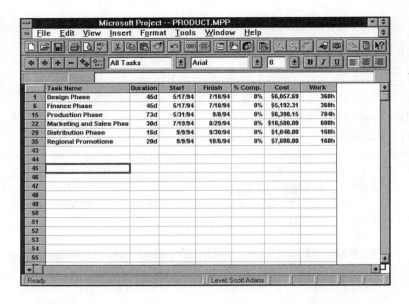

The Summary table view of the project affords an opportunity to see the
project from a larger perspective and to see which tasks or phases entail
the most work, cost, and duration.

Sorting the Task and Resource List

You can sort the task list to view the tasks in a different order. Although the
tasks are displayed in a different order after sorting, the task ID numbers do
not change, and the schedule is unaffected (see fig. 10.10). When you finish
using the sorted order, you can return the task list to the original order. However, you also have the option of instructing Microsoft Project to permanently renumber the task IDs according to the current sort order.

Caution

It's a good idea to save the project immediately before you permanently renumber
the task IDs. You can then return to the previous numbering if the result is not what
you want.

When you sort an outlined project, you can retain the outline structure or
you can ignore the outline structure. If you retain the outline structure, all
tasks at the first outline level are sorted (carrying their subtasks with them);

then within each summary task all subtasks at the next outline level are sorted (carrying their subtasks with them), and so forth. If you choose not to keep the outline structure, subtask groups are broken up and dispersed throughout the task list independent of their summary task. If you do not keep the outline structure, you will probably want to suppress the display of summary tasks and suppress the indentation of subordinate tasks, as shown in figure 10.10.

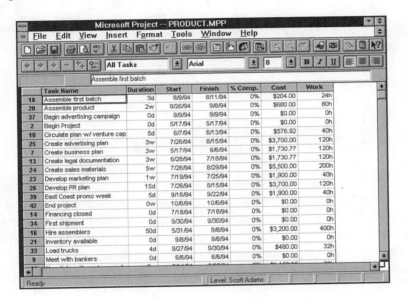

Fig. 10.10
The list of working tasks is sorted here in alphabetical order. Summary tasks have been omitted from the list.

Note

If you choose to ignore the outline structure during sorting, you cannot permanently renumber the tasks to match the new sort order, for that would restructure the outline.

Normally, the task and resource lists are sorted according to the numbers in the ID field, and the sort order is ascending order. When you use the Sort command, you are asked to identify the field to use for sorting and the direction of the sort—whether to sort in ascending (normal) order or in descending (reverse) order. For example, you could sort the resource list by the Standard Rate paid to the resources, with the highest pay rates listed first. The sort field in this instance is Standard Rate, and the order is descending (see fig. 10.11).

Fig. 10.11
Here the resource
is sorted in
descending order
by the pay rate.

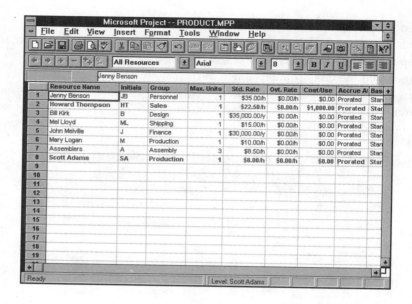

You can use up to three sort fields, which enables you to apply a second and third sort order for groups of tasks or resources that have the same entry in the first sort field. If, for example, you sort tasks by Duration and many tasks have similar estimated durations, you may use the second sort field to sort all the tasks with the same duration by name. If several tasks have the same duration and the same name, you can use a third sort field to arrange the tasks within this similar group according to their scheduled start dates. The process is the same as when you sort a mailing list by state, and within states by city, and within cities by name.

> **Note**
>
> If the tasks are filtered when you sort, or if some tasks are hidden because the outline is collapsed, the suppressed tasks still are not displayed after sorting.

Suppose that you want to sort the task list by Duration (with the longest Durations listed first), and for identical Durations by Name and, for identical names, by Start date, follow these steps:

1. Select the Sort command from the Tools menu and choose Sort by. Some of the most commonly used fields for sorting will appear in a short list. If the field you want to sort on is listed, and you want to sort in normal order, and you want to sort by that field only, choose the

field from the list. If the field you want is not listed, or you want to sort in descending order, or you want to use more than one sort key, choose the **S**ort by command. The **S**ort by dialog box appears (see fig. 10.12).

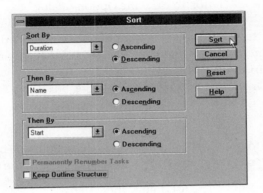

Fig. 10.12
Use the Sort by dialog box to tailor the way the task or resource list is sorted.

2. Choose the **S**ort by field to identify the name of the field that you want to serve as the primary sort key. Choose the entry list arrow to view the field names or type the first letter of the field name (D in this case) to activate the entry list. Scroll to and then choose the field you want to use (Duration).

3. Choose **D**escending order for the first key.

4. Choose the **T**hen by field and choose Name from the field list.

5. Choose As**c**ending order for the second key.

6. Choose the Then **B**y field and choose Start from the field list.

7. Choose Ascending order for the third key.

8. Clear the **K**eep Outline Structure check box to sort tasks independently of their summary task groups. (This also makes it impossible to permanently renumber the tasks.) If you fill the check box, first level tasks in the outline will be sorted, then second level tasks in the outline will be sorted within their summary tasks, and so on.

9. Choose the S**o**rt button to initiate the sort.

If you want to hide the display of summary tasks and to remove the indent from the display of subtasks, follow these steps:

1. From the **T**ools menu, choose the **O**ptions command.

2. Choose the View tab on the Options dialog box.

3. Clear the check boxes for Show Summary Tasks and for Indent Name.

4. Choose the OK button to close the Options dialog box.

After you edit a sorted list, you may want to sort the modified list again to take into account the values that have changed because they may affect the sort order. To sort the list again using the current sort keys, press Ctrl+Shift+F3. Or you can activate the Sort dialog box again. The sort keys still are defined as you last set them, and you can simply select the Sort button again.

To reset the list to normal (ID number) order, press Shift+F3, or access the Sort dialog box and choose the Reset button and then the Sort button.

To permanently renumber a list, follow these steps:

- Choose the sort keys as in the preceding steps. If you are renumbering a task list, be certain that the Keep Outline Structure check box is filled. You cannot renumber tasks unless Keep Outline Structure is turned on.

- Choose the Permanently Renumber Tasks button for tasks or the Permanently Renumber Resources button for resources.

Caution

You can undo the renumbering, provided you act immediately. Choose Edit and then choose Undo Renumber.

Checking for Spelling Errors

Microsoft Project has a spell checker that you can use to verify spelling in one or all of the fields for names, notes, and special text for both tasks and resources.

Using the Spelling Command

To activate the spell checker, select the Spelling tool or select Spelling from the Tools menu. When Project cannot find a word in the dictionary, the Spelling dialog box appears (see fig. 10.13).

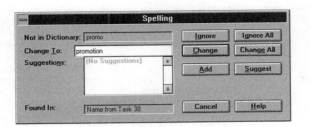

Fig. 10.13
Use the Spelling
dialog box to
decide how to
treat words that
are not in the
dictionary.

The fields on the Spelling dialog box show you the problem word and where the word is found, and offer options for responding to the condition. The fields on the Spelling dialog box are defined in the following list:

Field	Definition
Not in Dictionary	Display-only field that shows the problem word.
Change To	Text entry field in which you type a replacement for the word. If Always Suggest is enabled on the Spelling tab of the Options dialog box, a suggested replacement from the Suggestions list is placed in the field automatically.
Suggestions	Optional list of possible replacements culled from the dictionary (and optionally from your custom dictionary).
Found In	Display-only field that shows the field and task or resource where the problem word is found.

The following list defines the action buttons found in the Spelling dialog box:

Button	Use
Ignore	Select Ignore to ignore the problem word in this instance.
Ignore All	Select Ignore All to ignore the word here and anywhere else it appears.
Change	Select Change to have the entry in the Change To field replace this instance of the problem word.
Change All	Select Change All to have the entry in the Change To field replace this and all other occurrences of the problem word.
Add	Select Add to add the problem word to your custom dictionary. Spell checker ignores this occurrence and all future occurrences with the same exact spelling.

(continues)

Button	Use
Cancel (Close)	Select Cancel to quit the spell checker before any words are changed. If any words have changed, the Cancel button changes to a Close button. Select Close to quit the spell checker immediately. Words that you changed remain changed.
Suggest	Select the **S**uggest button to display a list of suggested alternatives for the problem word when the Suggestions list is not already displayed. This button is only available when the Always **S**uggest option is not selected in the Spelling tab of the Options dialog box (see the following section) or when you type into the Change **T**o field.

Setting the Spelling Options

The Spelling tab of the Options dialog box provides you an opportunity to determine some characteristics of the spell check operation. The Spelling tab, shown in figure 10.14, provides the following option fields:

Fig. 10.14
Use the Spelling tab in the Options dialog box to regulate how spell checking works.

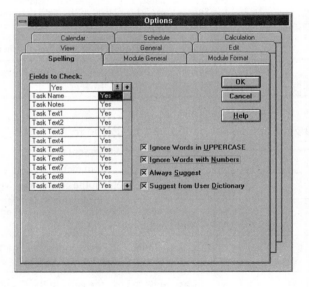

Option	Description
Fields to Check	This field contains a selection list of text fields in the task and resource databases. All fields are initially marked Yes to be included in the spell checking operation. Change any field settings to No if you don't want the field checked.
Ignore Words in **U**PPERCASE	Causes UPPERCASE words to be ignored.
Ignore Words with **N**umbers	Causes words that contain numbers to be ignored.
Always **S**uggest	Activates the Suggestions list each time the spell checker is used.
Suggest from User **D**ictionary	Besides the standard dictionary, checks problem words against the custom dictionary.

To change the spelling options, follow these steps:

1. From the **T**ools menu, choose **O**ptions.

2. Choose the Spelling tab in the Options dialog box and change the options you want to change.

3. Choose the OK button to implement the choices.

Note

The spelling program is a Windows application and is located in the WINDOWS\MSAPPS\PROOF directory. The user's custom dictionary is stored in that directory also, and is named CUSTOM.DIC. You can edit the custom dictionary with a text editor. Be certain, however, that the entries are in alphabetical order before you save the edited file.

Caution

Remember to save the project before you attempt to permanently renumber tasks or resources. To recover the old numbering, Open the same project name and choose to revert to the saved version of the file. Or, you can close the renumbered version of the file without saving it, and then open the saved version.

From Here...

Now that you know how to display the project in ways that summarize the project or that give an overview of the project, you will want to print those views or use them to identify problems in the project.

- See Chapter 11, "Resolving Problems in the Project Plan," to see how to deal with scheduling conflicts for tasks and for resources.

- See Chapter 16, "Printing Views and Reports," for guidelines in printing the project.

- See Chapter 17, "Using and Creating Views," and Chapter 18, "Formatting Views," for more information about ways to customize the presentation of your project.

Chapter 11

Resolving Problems in the Project Plan

After the tasks are defined, and the resources and costs that you are using in the project are associated with their respective tasks, you may want to step back from all these details and look at the overall project. You need to evaluate how successfully the project plan meets the objectives of the project as stated in the project goal. Often, the first draft of a project plan entails costs that exceed budget limits, or the scheduled finish date of the project is later than acceptable.

Even more basic, however, frequent internal inconsistencies exist within the project plan—inconsistencies that reveal that the project plan simply cannot work. The two most prominent of these inconsistencies are shown in the following list:

- Resources are assigned to do more work in specific time periods than is possible.

- Irreconcilable conflicts exist due to conflicting constraints on task dates.

In this chapter, you will learn how to

- Identify and eliminate internal inconsistencies caused by task scheduling constraints.

- Develop strategies to bring the project within the desired time frame.

- Identify resources that are overallocated, during what time periods, and the tasks that are causing the overallocation.

- Solve resource overallocations.

- Apply techniques to bring the project within budget goals.

Resolving Conflicts Caused by Constraints

If you impose date constraints on the tasks in the project, knowingly or not, you eventually encounter the Planning Wizard, as shown in figure 11.1. The function of this Planning Wizard is to warn you about the potential scheduling conflict imposed by your action. You then have a choice of cancelling the action, choosing an alternate constraint, or moving forward regardless of the conflict.

The message in figure 11.1 was created by imposing a Must Start On constraint on task number 39, the successor to task 38, by stipulating that task 39 must start by the currently scheduled start date.

Fig. 11.1
The Planning
Wizard anticipates
scheduling
conflicts.

If you choose Continue, a Must Start Constraint will be set on this task. If subsequent changes require that the Start Date of this task be rescheduled, another Planning Wizard will again alert you to a potential problem (as shown in fig. 11.2). Once again you can cancel the action that would cause the scheduling conflict or continue despite the conflict. This message was created by increasing the duration of Task 38, which is a predecessor to Task 39 by one day. This increase in turn causes Task 39 to start one day later, which violates the Must Start On constraint already placed on it.

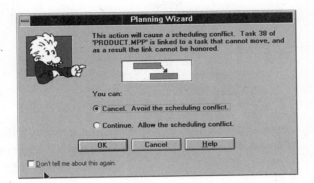

Fig. 11.2
The Planning
Wizard continues
to warn of
potential schedul-
ing conflicts.

Notice that you can discontinue the Planning Wizard by marking the **D**on't tell me about this again check box. This check box refers not only to this particular conflict but all scheduling conflicts. Use the options in the T**o**ols **O**ptions dialog box, General tab, (as displayed in fig. 11.3) to turn the Planning Wizards on or off.

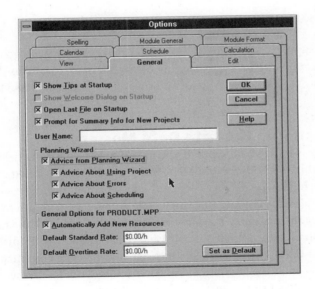

Fig. 11.3
Controlling the
Planning Wizards.

If you turn off the Planning Wizards, you will be alerted to potential scheduling conflicts with another message—one that's not quite as clear as the one you get from the Planning Wizard (see fig. 11.4).

Fig. 11.4
The Late Date
before scheduled
date message.

As described in the numbered steps below, you can also turn off the late date message by changing the **S**chedule option, **S**how Scheduling Messages, to unchecked.

To discontinue the warning messages about the schedule, take the following steps:

1. From the **T**ools menu, choose **O**ptions.

2. Choose the Schedule tab.

3. Uncheck the **S**how Scheduling Messages check box.

4. Choose the OK button.

Obviously, suppressing the messages doesn't make the problem go away. The following sections explain the meaning of this message, as well as the warnings given by the Planning Wizard, and suggest steps you can take to resolve the conflict.

Understanding the Late Date Message

The message is somewhat cryptic if you are unfamiliar with the field names and scheduling methods used in Microsoft Project. The scheduled date is easy enough: it refers to the dates on which the task named in the message is currently scheduled to start and finish. The late date refers to an internal calculation made by the program. The late date is the latest date that the task can start or finish on and still remain consistent with the start and finish of all of the successor tasks. So the Late Date message says that the current scheduled dates are later than the latest dates consistent with dates for the successor tasks and the rest of the project. Apparently, the successor tasks have date requirements inconsistent with the currently scheduled dates for the task named in the message. If the schedule remains as is, you cannot schedule the successor tasks and the rest of the project in accordance with required deadlines.

The cause of this problem almost always is a constrained date for one of the successor tasks. The problem also can be caused by a successor task that already had an actual start date recorded. In either case, the constraint keeps the successor start date from being rescheduled or the existence of an actual start date keeps the start date from being rescheduled; therefore, the late date for the task in the message cannot be moved to accommodate changes in the schedule.

Resolving the Conflict

The task named in the message has one or more successors that have fixed dates—dates that cannot be rescheduled to accommodate changes in the schedule. These dates are fixed either because of constraints on the dates or because the actual event has already happened—and you can't reschedule history.

Three fundamental solutions to the problem exist:

- Change the conditions that make the successor task dates *fixed*.

- Remove the relationship definition so that a relationship successor to the task in the message no longer exists.

- Change the conditions governing the finish date for the predecessor (the task named in the *Late date* message) so that you can schedule the task to finish by the late date.

You need to choose the course of action that makes the most sense in your project. Frequently, a careful review of the tasks, the constraints, and the task relationships reveals that new definitions are called for—conditions may have changed since the original definitions were entered and the definitions are now more restrictive than they need be. If the successor task has a recorded start date, for example, something is seriously wrong with a relationship definition when the predecessor still is being planned and the *successor* has already started.

Your task is to find the successor task causing the problem, identify the nature of the problem, and change the constraints or the relationship definition. If you cannot change the successor tasks, then you need to find ways to make it possible to finish the task named in the message by the late date.

The Task PERT chart is an excellent tool to use for examining the details about the successor tasks. Display the Gantt Chart in the top pane and the Task PERT in the bottom pane. Select the task named in the message in the top pane; you see the successor tasks displayed to the right of the selected task in the bottom pane. You can select the successor task(s) and use the Information tool in the Standard toolbar to view the Task Information dialog and change the constraint or predecessor definition.

To isolate and remedy the cause of a Planning Wizard warning that was ignored or a Late date before start date message, take the following steps:

1. Select the top pane.

2. Place the Gantt Chart (or other task view) in the top pane by choosing **G**antt Chart from the **V**iew menu.

3. Select the bottom pane. (If you are not already viewing a composite view, choose **W**indow **S**plit first.)

4. Display the Task PERT by selecting Tas**k** PERT from the **V**iew **M**ore Views menu (see fig. 11.5).

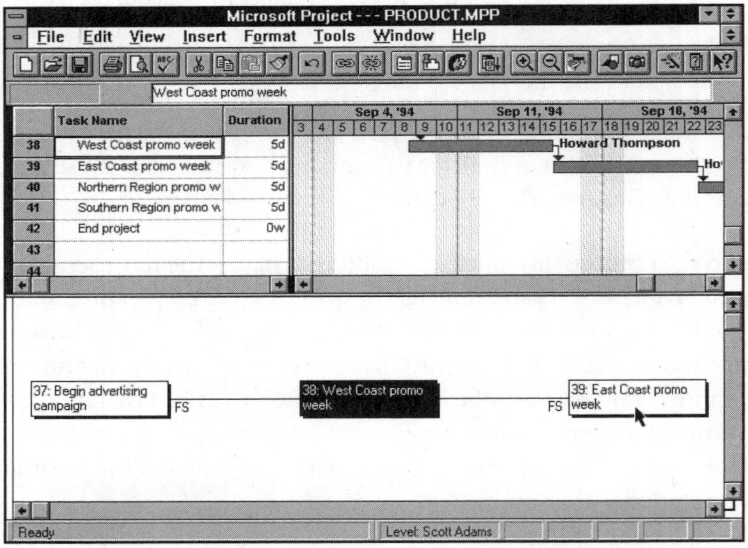

Fig. 11.5
Using the Task PERT to identify scheduling conflicts.

5. Select the top pane and select the task named in the Late date message. You can use the Go To (F5) key or the **E**dit **G**o To command and type the task ID number to find the task quickly. In figure 11.6, the selected task in the top pane is Task 38, but the Task Information dialog box displays details for Task 39, which was selected in the Task PERT.

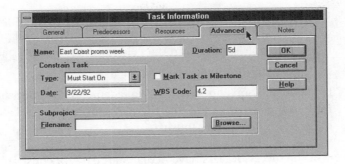

Fig. 11.6
The Task Information dialog box for the successor task.

6. Examine the display in the Task PERT chart to see the names of the successor tasks.

7. Select a successor task by clicking the node in the Task PERT chart.

8. Display the Task Information dialog box for the selected successor task by using the Information tool.

9. Choose the Advanced Tab and examine the constraint type; if it is not As Soon As Possible, examine the constraint date. Changing the date to a later date, if possible, may solve the conflict. Changing the constraint type back to the unconstrained As Soon As Possible certainly removes the conflict (at least as far as this task is concerned).

10. If the task is not constrained, you need to examine whether there has been an Actual date imposed on this task. Use the Tools Tracking menu choice and select Update Tasks. You can also use the Update Tasks tool on the Tracking toolbar. Look to see if an Actual Start date has been inadvertently entered. If no actual date was entered, the Start date field displays the value NA. The Actual start date field is displayed in figure 11.7, but no date is yet entered.

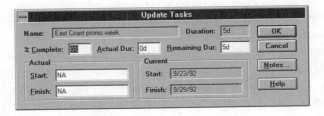

Fig. 11.7
Checking the Actual Dates in the Update Tasks dialog box.

If the task has already started and a date has been entered, then consider redefining the task relationship as described in the following step.

If an Actual Start date was entered by accident, select the current entry (use Alt+S or click and drag across the current entry) and press the Delete key or type **NA** to return the field to an unrecorded status.

11. Examine the task relationship. You can remove the predecessor task to break the relationship. You can also redefine the relationship to allow for lead time to recognize that the successor has started before the predecessor is scheduled to finish.

If none of the successor tasks have Actual Start dates or constraints, then the task in the Late date message must have a summary task that links to a task with fixed dates or to another summary task with fixed dates in one of the subordinate tasks. You need to examine the successor to the summary task. If the successor is another summary task, you must examine all the subordinate tasks for the constraint.

Finally, if none of the previously suggested changes is feasible, you must review the conditions that cause the scheduled date of the date in the message to be later than the Late date, and attempt to find a way to move the scheduled finish date forward in time to match the Late date. For suggestions, see the following section on shortening the critical path.

Shortening the Critical Path

The preceding sections were dedicated to resolving inconsistencies and conflicting task constraints within the project plan. This section addresses one of the most needed skills: reducing the overall duration of the project to schedule the finish date sooner (or the start date later for a project that is scheduled from the finish date). The popular term for this process is *crashing* the schedule.

To reduce the duration of the project, you must reduce the duration of the tasks or overlap the tasks so that the combined duration of all the tasks is not as great. Reducing the duration of individual tasks may be no more complicated than reassessing the estimated duration and entering a more sanguine figure. Often, however, more effort is required. You may need to increase the quantity or quality of the resources assigned to the task. You may be able to schedule overtime to shorten the duration of a task. By changing the relationships among tasks, you may be able to realign the task dates to allow for more overlapping of tasks. You may define lead time for some Finish-to-Start relationships, or you may be able to redefine a Finish-to-Start relationship to be a Start-to-Start or Finish-to-Finish. To the extent that tasks scheduled end-to-end are allowed to overlap in time, you probably can shorten the project schedule by redefining the task relationships.

Of course, working on shortening noncritical tasks, or scheduling these tasks to overlap, would waste time. You should focus your attention only on critical tasks, because only critical tasks count when trying to crash the schedule. Keep in mind that changes that you make in the schedule may change the status of a noncritical task to critical. But at all times you need to focus on the critical tasks.

Identifying the Critical Path

You can use any task view to identify the critical tasks. The basic Task Entry view on the **M**ore Views menu is popular because this view displays, in either the top or bottom panes, many fields relevant to crashing the schedule. (This view is also accessible using the Task Entry view tool on the Resource Management toolbar.) You also can use the PERT Chart to identify the critical tasks. However, it's not as easy to get to all the fields you may want to change as you revise the project.

You can identify the critical tasks most dramatically by filtering the task list in the Gantt Chart view or the Task Sheet view to show only the critical tasks. However, as you redefine the project, some tasks may change from noncritical to critical. The filter does not automatically recalculate, although you can use Ctrl+F3 to quickly reapply the current filter. You also can highlight the critical tasks by choosing a highlight filter, and then all tasks are in view at all times, and the critical tasks are highlighted. The same problem exists, however, in that the highlight filter is not recalculated as you change the project. The most satisfactory results are derived from formatting the text of critical filter names to appear in a highlighted color, because the format choice is constantly updated as the status of a task changes.

To filter the critical tasks, take the following steps:

1. Select the top pane if a combination view is in place.

2. Display a task list view by choosing either **G**antt Chart from the **V**iew menu or **T**ask Sheet from the **M**ore Views menu choice.

3. From the **T**ools menu, choose **F**iltered for and then **C**ritical from the drop-down menu.

To highlight the critical tasks, hold down the Shift key as you perform these same steps. Instead of hiding the tasks that are not critical, Microsoft Project highlights the task name of the critical ones in blue. Otherwise the steps are the same as listed above.

To Format the display of critical tasks to show a highlight color at all times, take the following steps:

▶ "Formatting Text Displays for categories of Tasks and Resources," p. 502

1. Display a task list view in the top pane as shown in the preceding steps.

2. From the Format menu, choose **T**ext Styles. The Text Styles dialog box appears (see fig. 11.8).

3. Select Critical Tasks from the **I**tem to Change list.

Fig. 11.8
Styles dialog box to change the format of critical tasks.

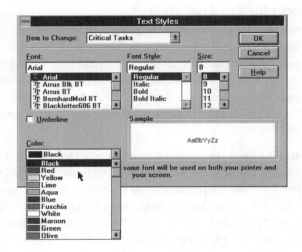

4. Choose the formatting feature to use as a highlight. Select **B**old from the Font St**y**le field, for example, to bold critical tasks, or choose the **C**olor entry list and select a color to use as a highlight.

5. After you make all the desired selections, choose the OK button.

Another popular combination view for crashing the schedule places the Task Details Form in the top pane and the Task Form in the bottom pane (see fig. 11.9), and then displays the Predecessors & Successors fields in the top form and the Resource Work fields in the bottom form. You can filter the top form to display only Critical tasks (but note that you need to recalculate the filter fairly often). Use the Pre**v**ious and N**e**xt buttons in the top pane to change the tasks as you review the task definitions. You can change task definitions, relationship definitions, and resource assignments (including overtime) all on the same screen. You will not have the benefit, however, of the graphical displays that help you keep the project organized in your head.

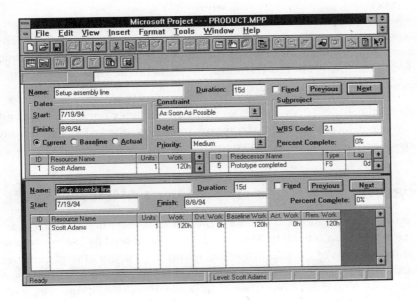

Fig. 11.9
Using two task
forms to crash
the schedule.

I

Project Management

Strategies for Crashing the Schedule

No matter which view you use, move through the project from critical task to critical task, looking for the opportunities in the following list:

- Review with a critical eye to reducing task durations that are unnecessarily long.

- Examine the predecessor and successor relationships and try to identify the relationships that you can change from Finish-to-Start to one of the overlapping relationships (Start-to-Start, Finish-to-Finish, or Finish-to-Start with lead time). This strategy usually is one of the most fruitful because many users hastily define all relationships as Finish-to-Start when more lenient definitions can be applied.

- Increase resource assignments for tasks that are not fixed duration tasks. You can accomplish this increase by finding idle resources, but the change is often necessarily accompanied by hiring additional resources or by increasing the regular working hours on the calendar.

- Schedule overtime to reduce the amount of regular work hour duration that a task may take.

You may find it easier to concentrate on each of these strategies if you go through the project task list once for each of the areas identified in the preceding list. Remembering what you are looking for is sometimes easier if you look for the same thing as you examine task after task. You make one complete pass through the project, looking for duration estimates that you can trim. You then make another pass through the complete list of critical tasks, looking for changes in task relationships. Then, do the same for changing resource assignments and scheduling overtime.

After you make changes, remember that some formerly noncritical tasks now may be critical and that these tasks now should be reviewed along the same lines for possible duration reductions.

Resolving Resource Overallocations

A resource is overallocated when assigned to work more hours during a given time period than is feasible. The feasibility is determined by the maximum number of units of the resource available and the amount of work time defined in the resource calendar. If a single worker is assigned to do two eight-hour tasks, a total of 16 hours' work, in one eight-hour day, this worker is overallocated. By the same token, if Painters is a group resource that represents a team of 10 painters, and a task is scheduled for 15 assigned painters, then Painters is overallocated. As shown in these examples, overallocation can occur when a resource is assigned to multiple tasks at the same time, or when more than the maximum available number of units of the resource are entered in the units assigned field.

Figure 11.10 shows multiple tasks that occur during the same time period. If the same resource is assigned to all these tasks on a full-time basis, then overallocation of the resource is inevitable.

Understanding How Resource Overallocations Occur

Microsoft Project schedules tasks in accordance with your definitions of the tasks—including the estimated durations, the predecessor relationships, and any date constraints—and your defined assignments and resource availability. The scheduled start date for a task is based on the following requirements:

- When the predecessor requirements for the task are met.

- When the next regular work period is defined on the resource calendar(s) for the assigned resources. If no resource assignments exist, the project's base calendar is used.

Microsoft Project schedules a task to begin in the first available time slot on the resource calendar *after* the predecessor relationship requirement is satisfied. No consideration is given, in the normal calculation mode, to the possibility that the resource may already be busy on another task and may not be able to work on the task you are scheduling. The task is scheduled as though the resource calendar is the only requirement to consider. Although you can instruct Microsoft Project to delay tasks automatically until their assigned resources are finished with other tasks and are available for additional work, this mode is not the default mode in which Microsoft Project calculates the project schedule. You usually will find that leaving the default scheduling method is the best approach. Therefore, you must make judgment calls about which tasks have higher priority and should not be delayed. You need to make these decisions yourself.

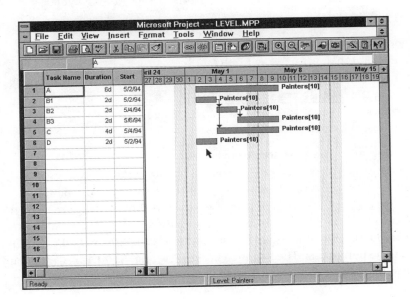

Fig. 11.10
A resource is overallocated when assigned full time to simultaneous tasks.

Identifying Resource Overallocations

Microsoft Project provides an indicator in the center of the status bar at the bottom of the screen to warn you when one or more resources are overallocated. If the painters are overallocated, you see the message Level Painters in the status bar. More resources than just the painters may be overallocated, but you usually can see only one resource name in the warning message; the message cannot be longer than eleven characters. Figure 11.11 is the PRODUCT project displayed in the Task Entry composite view. Notice the message Level: Scott Adams, which serves notice that at least one resource (Scott Adams) is overallocated.

Tip
Click on the Task Entry View tool on the Resource Management toolbar to create the combination view called Task Entry.

Fig. 11.11

At least one resource is overallocated as indicated by the Level message in the Status bar.

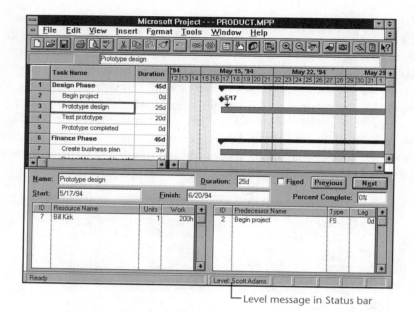

└ Level message in Status bar

Working with the Resource Usage View

To identify all the overallocated resources by name, you need to use a re-source view, such as the Resource Sheet or the Resource Usage view. If a resource is overallocated during any period in the life of the project, the re-source name is highlighted in red in each of these views. You must use a resource view with a timescale if you want to see the time period when the overallocation occurs. The Resource Usage view (see fig. 11.12) is a standard screen that is specifically designed to show resource allocation per time period.

To display the Resource Usage view as shown in figure 11.12, press the Shift key as you choose the **V**iew menu, then choose Resource **U**sage.

As described in Chapter 5, "Entering Scheduling Requirements," the Resource Usage view shows the sum of the work assignments for a resource during each time period that is marked off in the timescale. If a resource is over-allocated during any time period, the related Resource Name will be displayed in red highlighting. Furthermore, the display of the summary work value will be highlighted in red in those time periods where an overallocation exists. If you increase or decrease the unit of time used in the timescale, the values that appear increase or decrease accordingly to show the sums for longer or shorter time periods.

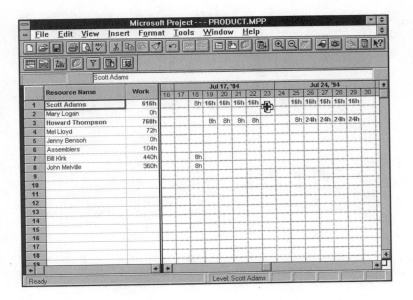

Fig. 11.12
Using the Resource
Usage view to
locate when
resources are
overallocated.

Adding a Gantt Chart View. A useful combination view for dealing with overallocations is the Resource Allocation view, which is the Gantt Chart in the lower pane beneath the Resource Usage view (see fig. 11.13). With this combination you can identify instances of overallocated resources in the top pane and see the list of tasks assigned to the selected resource that are in conflict in the bottom pane.

You can access this view in one of two ways. From the **V**iew menu, you can choose **M**ore Views and then Resource Allocation from the More Views dialog box. For a shorter route, use the Resource Allocation View button on the Resource Management toolbar.

When you select a resource name in the top pane, the Gantt Chart in the lower pane identifies all the tasks on which the selected resource is assigned to work. The Gantt bars overlap if multiple tasks are scheduled for the resource during the same time periods. During periods when an overallocation exists, you can see at a glance the overlapping tasks that contribute to the problem.

Figure 11.13 shows clearly that Scott Adams has multiple task assignments beginning on July 19, with simultaneous assignments to hire assemblers and set up assembly line. The summary work value displayed in the Resource Usage timescale indicates that the assignments on July 19 total 16 hours of work.

Fig. 11.13
Using the
Resource Alloca-
tion View to
identify tasks
assigned to
overallocated
resources.

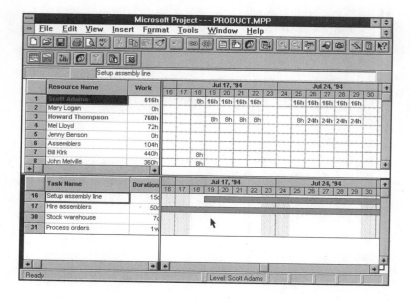

Filtering Overallocated Resources. You can filter the Resource Usage view to display only resources overallocated at one or more time periods during the project (see fig. 11.14).

Fig. 11.14
The Overallocated
filter applied to
the Resource
Usage view.

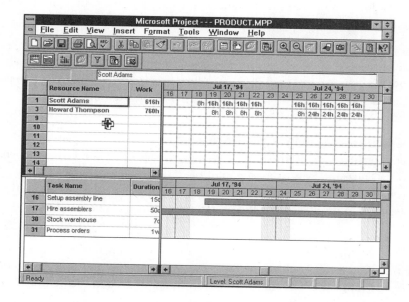

To apply the Overallocated filter, select the top pane view, and then from the **T**ools menu, choose **F**iltered for and then **O**verallocated Resources.

The Overallocated Resources filter restricts only the listings in the top pane. (All filters affect only the top pane, because the bottom pane is already filtered to show details for the top pane selection.) The Gantt Chart in the bottom pane displays all task assignments for the selected resource, whether or not an overallocation is involved in the assignment.

Changing the Overallocation Measure. You can use the timescale section of the Resource Usage view to display any one of eight values per unit of time. The default value displayed in this view is the total hours of assigned work per unit of time. The other field values you can display are selected with the Format Details menu. You can elect to see the amount of the overallocation, for example, by selecting the **O**verallocation field format (see fig. 11.15).

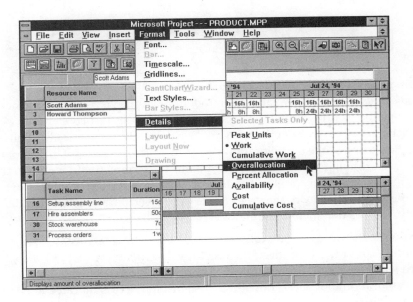

Fig. 11.15
Changing the values displayed in the Resource Usage view.

The resulting display shows only the amount of the overallocation, rather than the total work allocation during each time period (see fig. 11.16). This display shows at a glance how much work you can transfer to other resources to resolve the overallocation. The Overallocated value is useful when the resource has a nonstandard work day and you must know the daily work schedule of the resource to calculate how much of the total work load is overload.

Fig. 11.16
The Overallocated field format for the Resource Usage view displays the size of the overallocation problem.

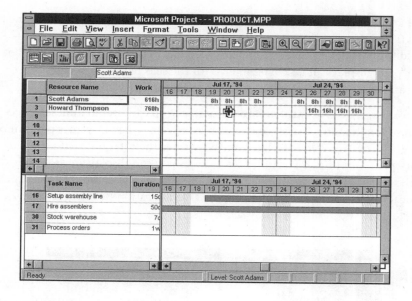

Using the Goto Overallocation Tool

You can use the Goto Overallocation tool in timescale views to find the next time period (starting from the left edge of the timescale display) during which a resource overallocation begins. The timescale automatically scrolls to the beginning of the overallocation period identified by the tool. If you want to search through the entire project, you must first scroll the timescale to the beginning date of the project. Use the Alt+Home key combination to move to the beginning date of the project. The Goto Overallocation tool is available only in views that include a timescale.

If you use the Goto Overallocation tool in a view with a task list, such as the Gantt Chart or the Task Sheet, the task list will scroll to the first task associated with the overallocation and select that task. Successive use of the Goto Overallocation tool selects other tasks assigned to the overallocated resource during the same time period. When all tasks for that time period have been identified, the Goto Overallocation tool will identify the next time period with an overallocated resource and select the first task for that time period. When the last task for the last overallocated time period has been identified, you will see an information dialog box similar to figure 11.17.

If you use the Goto Overallocation tool in a view with a resource list, such as the Resource Usage view, the search for overallocated time periods is limited to those tasks to which the selected resource is assigned. If you select a resource name, the Goto Overallocation tool will find the next time period during which that resource is overallocated. When the last overallocation for that resource is identified, you will see the message illustrated in figure 11.17.

Project Management

Fig. 11.17
The final
overallocation
information box.

If you want to search through the entire project for overallocated resources, select all resources first by clicking on one of the column headings in the resource view, and move to the beginning date of the project with the Alt+Home key combination. When you use the Goto Overallocation tool, the first time period with an overallocation will be identified and the first resource that is overallocated during this time period will be selected in the resource list.

Note that the Goto Overallocation tool can compensate for a potentially misleading feature of the Resource Usage view. If you look for red highlighting of values in the Resource Usage timescale to identify the periods of overallocation, you may not see any time period with highlighting for the resource, or you may see an unhighlighted value in a time period when you know that a resource is overallocated.

The red highlight appears only when the work load is excessive for the time period displayed. Suppose that a resource is overallocated by four hours on a Monday, but the total allocation of work for the week is only 30 hours—well under the 40-hour maximum available for the resource. If the unit of time on the timescale is a day, the overallocated value for the Monday appears in red. If the unit of time is a week, the weekly value is not in red because the value is not an excessive amount of work for a week. Although the display does not show the red highlight, the Goto Overallocation tool still selects the time period as overallocated, and selects the week that contains the overallocated Monday.

The Resource Graph View

The Resource Graph offers still another view of the overallocated resource, showing not only the allocation of the resource per time period, but also showing the maximum available units of the resource in the same time frame and what part of the total allocation is an overallocation. You can use the Resource Graph effectively by placing the graph in the lower pane, beneath the Resource Usage view.

To display the Resource Graph, choose Resource Graph from the list of views in the **V**iew menu.

The Resource Graph is a histogram that represents resource data per time period, as shown in figure 11.18. The default value shown is the Peak Units allocated during the period. The Peak Units value measures the number of units of the resource assigned to all tasks within the time period on the graph. The bar displays the allocation value in blue, up to the maximum available amount of the resource. All allocations over the maximum available during the time period measured in the graph appear in red. Therefore, the existence of red bars in the Resource Graph indicates an overallocated resource.

As an indicator of resource overallocation, the *peak* measurement can mislead you. If a resource is assigned to three one-hour tasks during the same day, the peak units value is 3 (the number of unit-assignments for the day). If only one unit of the resource exists, the resource graph displays a blue bar up to the level of one unit and a red bar from one unit to three units—suggesting an overallocation of the resource. Because all the tasks are each only an hour long, however, the resource is committed to only three hours of work during the day and is not overallocated in terms of work. For this reason, it is best to use the Format command (as described in the following paragraphs) to display the amount of work that the resource is assigned to do rather than the peak number of units allocated.

The Format Details menu offers eight value measurements that can be used in the Resource Graph (see fig. 11.19). Choose either Work or Overallocation, which measures the overallocated amount of work, when using the graph to identify overallocated resources. Figure 11.20 shows the same Resource Graph, using Work as the format value.

Fig. 11.18
The Resource Graph, a histogram, offers a graphical view of resource overallocations.

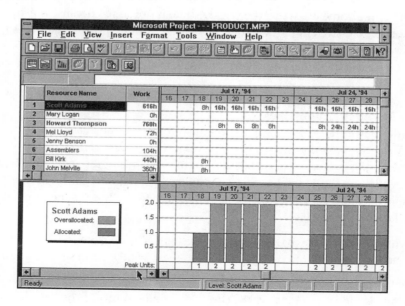

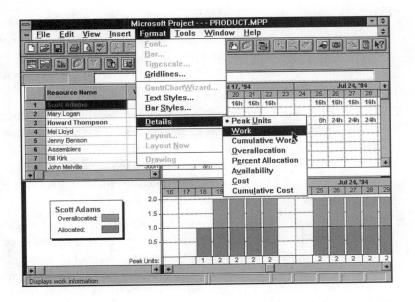

Fig. 11.19
Using the Format Details menu to change the values displayed for the Resource Graph.

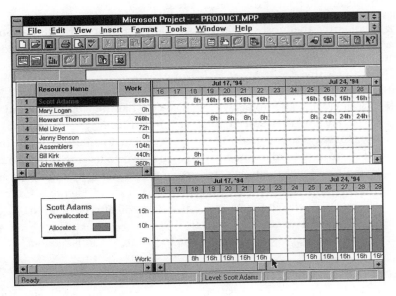

Fig. 11.20
The Resource Graph with the Work value format.

Strategies for Eliminating Resource Overallocations

If overallocated resources exist, you can resolve the conflict in several ways, as shown in the following list:

■ The simplest solution for the planner is to just hire new resources. This option can take several forms; for example, adding new resource names to the pool or increasing the maximum number of available units of group resources. Increasing employment, however, isn't always possible or economically feasible.

■ Overallocation means that more hours are scheduled than the resource calendar provides as part of the regular work load. If the overallocation is not substantial, you can schedule overtime hours for the over-allocated resource. Overtime hours are charged to the task at the overtime rate defined for the resource and, therefore, increase the cost of the task.

Tip

You can access the Resource Information dialog box by double-clicking on the resource name in most views where the resource name is displayed. (The views where this doesn't work are the two Resource form views where displaying the dialog box is probably not necessary.)

■ A somewhat similar solution is to redefine the resource calendar, adding more working hours to the normal work schedule. If the resource agrees to this solution, adding work hours to the normal work schedule is more desirable than scheduling overtime because all hours of regular calendar work are charged at the regular rate to the task, while overtime hours are charged at the overtime rate.

■ Frequently, the most satisfactory solution to resource overallocation is to look for other resources that can do the work and also that are idle during the period when the overallocation occurs. This solution requires more investigative work for the planner.

■ The final strategy is to delay some tasks so that the work load requirements are *leveled*, or spread out over time sufficiently to make it possible for the resource to do all the work assigned while working within the resource calendar schedule. Delaying tasks to level resource loads is known as *leveling* the tasks. This may not be a viable option when deadlines are important because this option may extend the project. If critical tasks are delayed the project finish date will also be delayed.

Each of these strategies is examined in the following sections.

Adding Resources

◄ "Defining the Resource Pool," p. 185

You can add new resource names to the resource pool in several views: the Resource Sheet, the Resource Form, the Resource Usage view, the Task Entry view, and so on.

To add to the maximum number of available units of a resource when in either the Resource Usage or Resource Graph view, take the following steps:

1. Select the resource name. You may have to scroll the list to find the resource name. If the Resource Usage or Resource Graph view is in the bottom pane, you need to scroll the top pane to a task to which the resource is assigned.

2. Click the Information tool to display the Resource Information dialog box (see fig. 11.21).

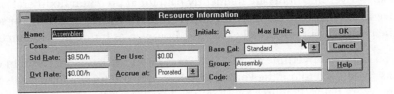

Fig. 11.21
Increasing Maximum Units on the Resource Information dialog box.

3. Select the Max **U**nits field and enter the new value.

4. Choose the OK button to complete the entry.

If the Task Form is displayed, select a task to which the resource is assigned and then select the resource name in the Resource fields at the bottom of the form. You then can choose the Information tool to change details about the resource.

After you define the additional resources as part of the resource pool, you can assign these resources to the overallocated tasks. You must use a view that shows tasks for this purpose. The Task Form, which is the bottom pane of the Task Entry view, is a good choice because the values in the Resource fields displayed at the bottom are separated into columns, making them easier to understand. You also can use the Resource Assignment tool or the Alt+F8 accelerator key combination with any task view to add resources to a task or to increase or decrease the units assigned to a previously assigned resource.

◀ "Assigning Resources and Costs to Tasks," p. 205

Note

The Resource Assignment tool is available on both the Standard and Resource Management toolbars.

Increasing the maximum units of a resource usually isn't the most cost effective way to handle the resource allocation conflict. Hiring or otherwise engaging additional resources is costly and time-consuming.

Scheduling Overtime for the Resource

You also can schedule overtime hours for the resource to supplement the regular calendar working hours. If you enter overtime hours, Microsoft Project subtracts this number of hours from the total amount of work scheduled within the normal working hours of the resource calendar. You must not reduce the total amount of work hours for the task when adding overtime hours; just enter the quantity of hours that will be worked overtime. Of course, overtime hours are frequently paid for at premium hourly rates. Using overtime to solve overallocation problems may be a costly method of solving the problem, but not usually as costly, however, as hiring new resources.

You can enter overtime on the Task Form or on the Resource Form. In either case, you need to use the F**o**rmat **D**etails command for the form to display the Work fields (Resource **W**ork on the Task Form). If you use the Task Form, you see only one task listed at a time. If you use the Resource Form, all tasks on which the resource is assigned to work are displayed in the Work fields table, and you can assign overtime to multiple tasks at the same time.

To enter overtime hours for a task using the Resource Form, take the following steps:

1. Select the pane in which to place the Resource Form. In this example, the bottom pane is used, with the Resource Usage view still in the top pane. From the **V**iew menu, choose **M**ore Views and then choose Resource Form.

2. Make the Resource Form the active pane.

3. From the F**o**rmat menu, choose **D**etails and then **W**ork from the drop-down menu.

    The Resource Work fields are displayed at the bottom of the form (see fig. 11.22).

4. If the Resource Form was placed in the bottom pane, you can select the resource in the top pane or use the N**e**xt and Pre**v**ious buttons until you find the resource. If the Resource Form is in the top pane, use the N**e**xt and Pre**v**ious buttons to select the resource name. Here, Howard Thompson is selected in the top pane.

5. Select the task for which you want overtime hours scheduled. Here, the task is *Create sales materials*, task 24.

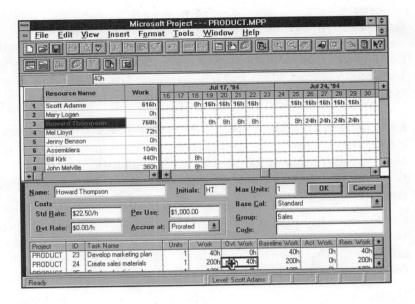

Fig. 11.22
Entering overtime work to solve an overallocation problem.

6. In the Overtime field, type the amount of overtime work. You must use a number, followed by a one-letter abbreviation for time (m,h,d,w). If you don't use a letter for the time period, Microsoft Project assumes that the time unit is *hours*. In figure 11.22, for example, 40 hours of overtime is entered for Howard Thompson on task number 24.

7. Choose the OK button to complete the entry.

Note

Be sure that the resource doesn't have a zero overtime rate in the cost fields of the resource form. Some users mistakenly leave the overtime rate zero if no premium pay exists for overtime hours—if overtime is paid at the same rate as regular hours. If you leave the overtime rate set to zero, however, overtime hours are charged at a zero rate.

Note that the Overtime Rate for Howard Thompson was not entered even though it should have been entered at the same rate as the Standard Rate because Howard Thompson receives no premium pay for overtime work. With the current setting, all of Howard's overtime will not be charged to the project, a potentially damaging mistake.

Exactly when the overtime hours are worked does not matter to Microsoft Project. You cannot specify exactly when the overtime hours are worked. You can specify only on which task the hours are applied, and settling with the resources involved exactly when the hours are worked is a separate matter. Overtime hours do not show up on any schedule. In figure 11.22, Howard Thompson will work 40 of the 200 hours on this task outside usual working hours, which are defined on his resource calendar.

Extending the Working Calendar for the Resource

If resources work extra hours and the overtime rate is the same as the regular rate, you then can adjust the calendar for the resource to show the extra hours. All regular working hours on the calendar are charged at the standard rate for the resource.

If only certain resources work the added hours, make the change on the individual resource calendars. If the added hours are worked by all resources, you can make the change on the base calendar (and on all base calendars used for resources in the project).

To extend the normal working hours for the resource, take the following steps:

1. From the **T**ools menu, choose **C**hange Working Time.

2. Use the List arrow in the **F**or: text box to select the resource whose hours you want to extend.

3. Select the date or dates on which you want the extra hours worked.

4. Enter the extra time in the Hours fields.

5. Choose the OK button to close the dialog box and execute the changed hours.

Figure 11.23 shows Howard Thompson's resource calendar being modified to extend his Tuesday, Wednesday, and Thursday hours during July, 1994 by adding 4 hours a day, starting at 6:00 PM.

Substituting Underused Resources for Overallocated Resources

Probably the most conventional method of dealing with the problem of overallocated resources is to find substitute resources to take some of the load off the overallocated resources. To use this approach in a cost-effective manner, you need to consider the following six things:

■ The list of overallocated resources and their current work loads per time period. (This tells you when the overallocations occur.)

- The tasks that each overallocated resource is currently assigned to work on during the periods of overallocation. (This identifies the tasks for which you should seek substitutes.)

- The work loads of other resources not already fully allocated to other work during the overallocated time periods. (This helps you find resources that may be used as substitutes.)

- The skill level of other resources available to do the work and the time it may take them to learn the tasks that need to be done.

- The cost of using each of the resources. (This tells you the cost of substituting other resources for resources currently assigned to the tasks.)

- The total work commitment for each of the tasks for which resources may be substituted. (This helps you decide which of two tasks to give to a substitute and which to keep for the overallocated resource. You can give the task that involves the most total work to the cheaper resource to keep costs low.)

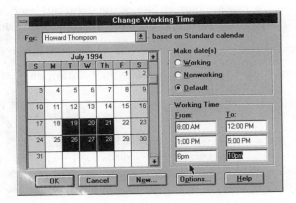

Fig. 11.23
Extending working hours on an overallocated resource's calendar.

Using the Resource Allocation to Substitute Resources

The Resource Allocation View, which you access through the **V**iew **M**ore View menu, provides a good starting point for tackling the problem of finding cost-effective substitute resources. This view also has its own tool on the Resource Management toolbar, offering easy access.

This composite view shows the names and workloads of all resources, and highlights overallocated resources. The bottom pane shows the tasks to which the selected resource name is assigned during any period on the timescale. You can use the Goto Overallocation tool in either pane to pinpoint overallocated resource assignments. In the top pane, the Goto

Overallocation tool identifies resources that are overallocated. In the lower pane, the Goto Overallocation tool identifies tasks that initiate an over-allocation of the resource you selected in the top pane.

 After a task is selected for substituting resource assignments, you can use the Resource Assignment tool to replace one resource with another.

1. Select the task for the substitution. In figure 11.24 the task is *Setup assembly line*.

2. Choose the Resource Assignment tool to initiate the substitution. (You can also use Alt+F8 to call up this same dialog box.) The Resource Assignment dialog box appears (see fig. 11.24).

> **Note**
>
> Because of the view you were in when you accessed this dialog box, the overallocated resource in question should already be highlighted.

3. Choose the Re**p**lace button. Notice the slight difference in the dialog box. The words Replace and With have been added at the top.

4. Select the name of the resource that you want to assign as a substitute.

5. Choose the OK button to complete the substitution.

> **Note**
>
> Be careful when working in this dialog box. It will appear that your substitution was not made because the dialog box is still open, and the resource you were making substitutions for is still listed. Notice, however, that the list of tasks in the Gantt Chart is different now than it was earlier. The task whose resource was replaced is no longer in the list. If you click Mary Logan's name in the Resource Usage view, you will see that she has a new task. The Resource Assignment dialog box will actually stay open until you specifically close it.

> **Note**
>
> The substitution of Mary Logan for Scott Adams in this example is not incorporated in the examples in the remainder of this chapter, so you can work through the examples that follow without having to go back and work through the preceding examples. If you plan to continue experimenting with the examples, you can reverse the substitution of Mary Logan for Scott Adams in the Setup assembly line task.

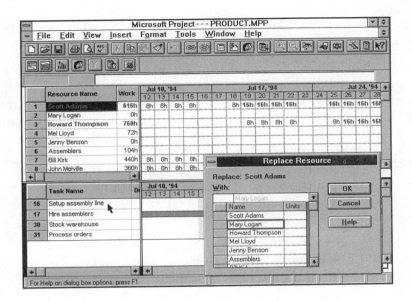

Fig. 11.24
Substituting Mary Logan for Scott Adams as the resource assigned to the Setup assembly line task.

The composite view used in the preceding series of steps provides the first three sets of data that were previously described as essential for choosing resource substitutions in a cost-effective way. First, the view identifies the overallocated resources. Second, it shows the work load for those resources and the tasks to which they are assigned. And third, it points out the availability of substitute resources. The other two important considerations, the unit cost of using each resource and the work commitment entailed in each assignment, are missing. The following section describes how to customize the Resource Allocation view to add these fields. Because the view that you develop is so useful, place this view as a new, defined view on the **V**iew menu. In the process, you learn how to create custom views. The views and tables are developed as new entries in the View and Table menus, leaving the standard views unchanged.

▶ "Using and Creating Views," p. 463

▶ "Formatting Views," p. 497

Creating a New View for Resource Substitution

This section shows you how to create a combination view useful for deciding which resources to substitute for overallocated resources. The new view has two panes, and the view in each pane is new. The table used in the top pane view also is new. The top pane is a variation of the Resource Usage view, although the table that's displayed is different. The bottom pane is similar to the Gantt Chart view, although a different table is used. You define the new table first, then the views that use the new tables, and finally the combination view that uses the new views in the two panes. For the most part, you

start with copies of existing views that come close to that which you are trying to create.

The table used in the Resource Usage view is the Usage table from the **V**iew
Ta**b**le menu and contains only one field, the Resource Names. You can add
more fields to show additional information about each resource. In this case,
you add the Standard Rate so that you can choose among potential substitute
resources, with consideration given to how much money the alternate resources cost. You may also want to add the name of the Group to which each
resource belongs. The Group name can help you identify the resources that
are likely substitutes for one another. In fact, if you sort the resource list by
Group names, you see all the resources from the same groups listed together,
which also makes your job easier.

Adding Fields to the Usage Table. Because the table in the Resource
Usage view is similar to the table you want to develop, you start by copying
the Usage table. Give the new table a new name, and add the fields to the
table that you want to display.

To place the Standard Rate and Group fields in a table similar to the Usage
table, take the following steps:

1. Select the top pane.

2. From the **V**iew menu, choose Ta**b**le, and then select **M**ore Tables.

3. Select the Usage table.

4. Choose the **C**opy button to make a copy of the selected table. The Table
   Definition dialog box is displayed to help you create a new table (see
   fig. 11.25).

Fig. 11.25
After you copy an
existing table, the
initial Table
Definition dialog
box is displayed.

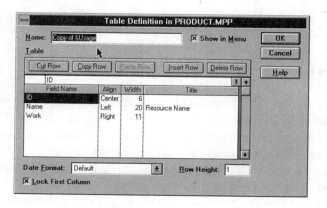

5. In the **N**ame field, type an identifying name, like **Work Loads**. The name should reflect the purpose or contents of the table.

6. In the **T**able fields area, select the first blank cell in the Field Name column (below ID, Name, and Work).

7. The field name to use in this instance is Standard Rate. Type the field name or use the entry list arrow to choose the field from the list of fields. Select Standard Rate from the entry list.

8. You can customize the column title for the new field by typing in a title of your own in the title column of the dialog box. You could give the Standard Rate field the title Rates, for example, by typing that title in the Title column. Otherwise, the column title will be the field name.

9. Select the next blank cell in the Field Name column.

10. Type the field name **Group** or select Group from the entry list.

11. For this view we won't need the work field, so select that row and choose the **D**elete Row button.

12. Because this table is used in a view that you haven't yet named and it doesn't need to appear on the **T**able menu's list of tables, clear the **S**how in Menu check box at the top of the dialog box.

13. Choose the OK button to submit the finished definition of the table (see fig. 11.26).

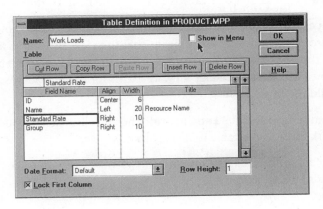

Fig. 11.26
The completed
Table Definition
dialog box.

14. To put the new table to use, choose the Apply button in the More Tables dialog box.

The top pane now contains the Resource Usage view with a different table—the Work Loads table that you just created. You will make this a new view called Resource Work Loads, which is like the Resource Usage view, except that this selection uses the table Work Loads.

Adapting the Resource Usage View. With the customized table defined, you can create a special view to use the table. To create the Resource Work Loads view, take the following steps:

1. From the **V**iew menu, choose **M**ore Views to display the More Views dialog box.

2. Select the Resource Usage view because this view is similar to the view that you want to create.

3. Choose the **C**opy button to display a copy of the Resource Usage definition in the View Definition dialog box (see fig. 11.27).

Fig. 11.27
Creating a new
view with a copy
of an existing one.

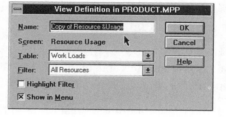

4. Type **Resource Work Loads** in the **N**ame field for the new view.

   You cannot change the **Sc**reen setting because this view shows the Resource Usage screen, which means that the view also shows a table and the timescale, with resource value calculations in each time period. You copied the Resource Usage view as a basis for the new view so that you could use this screen.

5. Choose the **T**able field and activate the entry list. Select your new table. Work Loads is the table to display in this view.

   You don't need to use a filter for this view, so you can leave the **F**ilter field set to All Resources.

6. This view actually is just the top part of a composite view and doesn't need to appear on the **V**iew menu. Unmark the Show in **M**enu check box.

7. Choose the OK button on the View Definition dialog box to save the completed definition of the new view (see fig. 11.28).

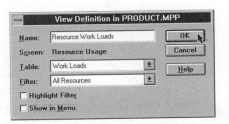

Fig. 11.28
The completed
View Definition
dialog box.

8. Choose the Apply button in the More Views dialog box to use the new view in the top pane.

The top pane now displays the Resource Usage screen but with a different table—the table showing the fields you use to help find substitute resources for overallocated resources. You may need to adjust column widths. To adjust the width of the column, click and drag the column divider to the right of a column name, or double-click the same divider line position to have Microsoft Project calculate the best fit for the width display.

If you sort the table by Group names, all resources in the same group are listed together, which makes identifying potential substitutes an easier job. Use the **T**ools Sor**t** command to sort the table. All format changes become a permanent feature of the view.

To sort the table in the current view (in this case, the Resource Work Loads view), take the following steps:

1. From the **T**ools menu, choose **S**ort, and then select **S**ort by from the drop-down menu.

2. Choose the **S**ort By field and select Group from the entry list that appears (see fig. 11.29).

3. Choose the **A**scending radio button for the normal sort order.

4. Choose the **S**ort button to execute the sort.

Fig. 11.29
Sorting the table
on the Group
name field to
group like
resources together.

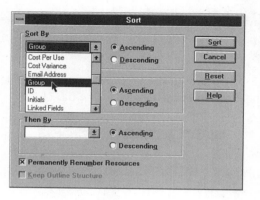

> ## Note
>
> When you choose a different view, even a view with a Resource Work Loads table, the table entries are not sorted unless you execute a sort in the view. When you next return to the Resource Work Loads view, however, the sort by Group name is automatically applied.

Customizing a Gantt Chart for the Bottom Pane. You now have customized the top pane for the composite view that you are going to use for substituting resources. Next, you create a customized Gantt Chart for the bottom pane. After both parts of the composite view are ready, you combine the parts into a view to place on the **V**iew menu for easy access.

To customize the Gantt Chart for the bottom pane of the composite view, take the following steps:

1. Select the bottom pane by clicking anywhere in the pane. If you don't already have a top and bottom pane, you may need to use the **W**indow **S**plit command first.

2. From the **V**iew menu, choose **M**ore Views. The More Views dialog box appears.

3. Select the Gantt Chart view to use as the basis for a new Gantt Chart with a different table.

4. Choose the **C**opy button to copy the Gantt Chart definition to the View Definition dialog box (see fig. 11.30).

5. Change the **N**ame field to **Work Load Gantt** to distinguish this view from other Gantt Chart views. Notice that this view displays a Gantt Chart S**c**reen.

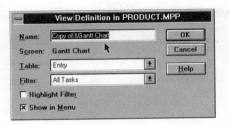

Fig. 11.30
Creating a new
view by copying
the Gantt Chart.

Project Management

6. Select the **T**able field and change the table from Entry to Work by typing **Work** in the field or by activating the entry list and selecting Work
   from the list.

7. Clear the Show in **M**enu check box because this view is designed to be
   used only as a part of a composite view.

8. Choose the OK button to save the completed definition of the view (see
   fig. 11.31).

9. Choose the **A**pply button to set the view in the lower pane.

You now have designed both parts of the composite view, as shown in figure
11.32. The final step is to put a view name on the menu that displays the two
special views that you created.

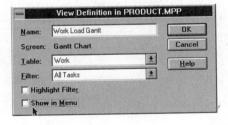

Fig. 11.31
The completed
Work Load Gantt
chart view.

Creating the Combination View. The combination of the two customized views for the top and bottom panes can be defined as a view and listed
on the **V**iew menu for easy access.

To create the combination view, follow these steps:

1. From the **V**iew menu, choose **M**ore Views to display the More Views
   dialog box.

Fig. 11.32
The completed
composite view for
substituting
resources.

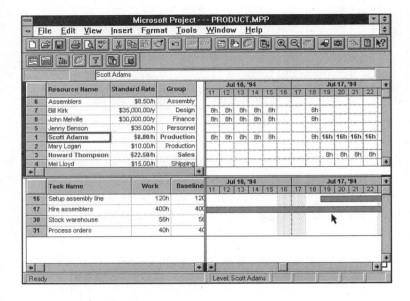

2. Choose the **N**ew button to create a new view. The Define New View
   dialog box appears (see fig. 11.33).

3. Choose the **C**ombination View radio button.

4. Choose the OK button to advance to the View Definition dialog box.

Fig. 11.33
Creating a new
combination view.

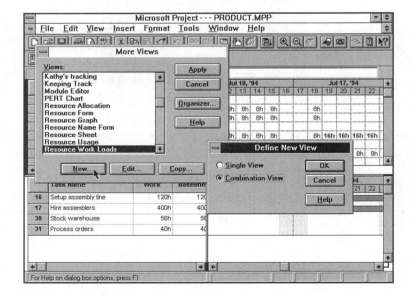

5. Type in the name of the new view. If you plan to place this view on the **V**iew menu, you can designate a selection letter (the letter you press to select this view when the pull-down menu is displayed). Place an ampersand (&) before the letter you want to use, and when the menu is displayed, the letter appears underlined to indicate that it is the selection letter. If you name the view Resource Substitution, for example, and want the letter *e* to be the selection letter, type **R&esource Substitution**. As you can see in figure 11.34, the letter *e* is not already used as a selection letter. (Note: if you use a letter that is already used as a selection letter, you may need to press that letter repeatedly to move between the menu choices that use that letter.)

6. Choose the field **T**op to define the view that goes in the top pane of this composite view. Select the Resource Work Loads view from the entry list.

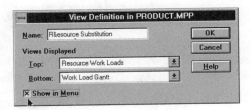

Fig. 11.34
The completed new View Definition dialog box.

7. Choose the field **B**ottom to define the view that goes in the bottom pane of the view. Select Work Load Gantt view from the entry list.

8. Make sure that the Show in **M**enu check box is marked. To toggle between marked and cleared, click the box with the mouse or tab to the field and use the spacebar. This box must be marked for the view name to appear on the **V**iew menu.

9. Choose the OK button to complete the view definition.

10. To close the More Views dialog box and display the new view, choose the Apply button.

The **V**iew menu now includes the R**e**source Substitution listing (see fig. 11.35).

Fig. 11.35

The new view is displayed on the View menu.

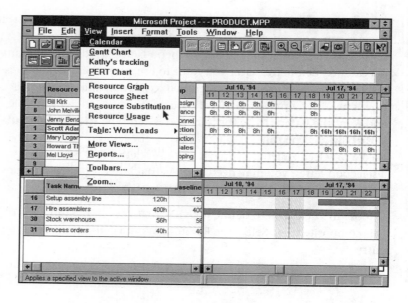

Using the Customized View. To use the new view to help find suitable substitute resources for overallocated resources, follow these steps:

1. From the **V**iew menu, choose R**e**source Substitution.

2. Press Alt+Home to move the timescale to the beginning of the project.

3. Select an overallocated resource. The resource name is highlighted in red. To use the Overallocated Filter, choose the **T**ools menu, choose **F**iltered for, and then choose **O**verallocated Resources from the subsequent drop-down menu. The filtered view enables you to see the list of overallocated resources, but use the filter only temporarily to make a mental note of the resource names because you need to redisplay all resources so that you can pick substitutes for the overallocated resource names.

4. To clear the filter, choose **F**iltered for from the **T**ools menu, and then select **A**ll Resources. The Work Load Gantt in the bottom pane displays all the tasks to which the selected resource is assigned in the project. In the example, the resources are Scott Adams and the four tasks listed in the bottom pane (see fig. 11.35).

5. Activate the bottom pane by using F6 or clicking anywhere in the pane, and use the Goto Overallocation tool to find the next time period when an overallocation begins for the selected resource. Tasks that are concurrent with the overallocated time period display their task bars under the overallocated value, which appears in the top pane.

If the time period that the Goto Overallocation tool displays shows no red highlighting of the work values in the time periods, you may have to zoom in on the timescale to display smaller time units. You must be in the top pane to use the Zoom In tool to change the timescale units.

6. Determine the other resource that you plan to substitute for the overallocated resource.

Look back to the top pane to view other resource allocation values for the time period in question. Look for another resource in the same resource group that's not fully allocated during the time periods. If several potential substitutions are available, compare their standard rates to select the most cost-effective substitution.

In the example in figure 11.36, Scott Adams is overallocated beginning on July 19. Mary Logan is in the same group (Production) and is assigned no hours during the time period covered by the two tasks that cause Scott's overallocation. This is the same situation that was illustrated in figure 11.24. In this example, the cost factors are considered.

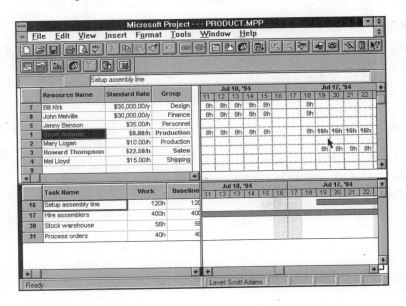

Fig. 11.36
Selecting a substitute resource.

Project Management

7. Select the task for which the resource substitution will be made. Examine the task work amounts in the table in the Gantt Chart in the bottom pane. If the new resource and the old resource have different Standard Rates, consider placing the cheaper resource on the task with more work. Of course, you also must consider how effectively each resource can do the work of the respective tasks. The duration of the task and the quality of the work may be affected by changing the resource assigned to do the work on the task.

In the example in figure 11.36, you can see that Mary Logan is paid a higher standard rate than Scott Adams is. Substituting her for one of the two tasks, therefore, increases the cost of the task and the project. The total work commitment for task number 16, Setup assembly line, is less than half of the other task. Therefore, you may want to select task 16 for the substitution.

8. Select the Resource Assignment tool to effect the substitution. The Resource Assignment dialog box appears.

9. Select the name of the overallocated resource to be replaced on the task (Scott Adams, in the example).

10. Choose the Replace button.

11. The Replace Resource dialog box appears. Select the name of the resource to be assigned as a substitute (in this case, Mary Logan).

12. Choose the OK button to complete the substitution (see fig. 11.37). If you are finished with resource substitutions, choose the Close button to close the Resource Assignment dialog box. Otherwise, it will remain open until you specifically close it.

The result of the resource substitution is that the work load of the overallocated resource is reduced. In figure 11.38, Scott Adams is no longer overallocated, as evidenced by the removal of the red highlight from his name in the top pane. The Setup assembly line task no longer appears among his tasks in the bottom pane. The Level warning in the Status line now references another resource, Howard Thompson, instead of Scott Adams.

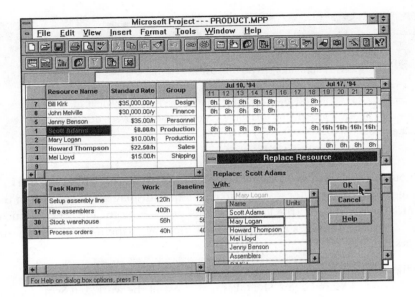

Fig. 11.37
One resource is replaced with another for a specific task.

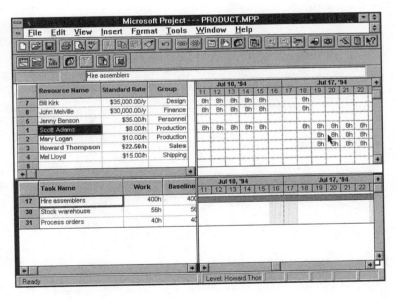

Fig. 11.38
The resource overallocation has been resolved.

Project Management

> **Note**
>
> Changing the values displayed in the timescale cells in the top pane is a useful way to research specific information. To do this, use the Format Details command and then select an option. Use the Availability value to see the number of work hours available for likely substitutes; use the Peak Units value to see how many units of a group resource are assigned during each time period; or use the Overallocation value to see the amount of overallocation per time period.

If you need to substitute another resource for part, but not all, of the work assigned to the overallocated resource on a task, display the Task Form in the bottom pane. Then, in the Resources fields at the bottom, add other resources and apportion the work among these resources by changing the values in the Work field.

In figure 11.39, for example, the task Setup assembly line is not entirely transferred to Mary Logan. She takes over most of the work, but Scott Adams handles the remainder.

Fig. 11.39
Reallocating part but not all of a task assignment by changing hours of work.

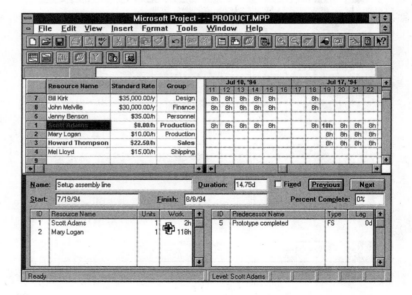

To replace part, but not all, of a task assignment, follow these steps:

1. Select the bottom pane.

2. From the **V**iew menu, choose **M**ore Views, and then select Task **F**orm from the More Views dialog box.

3. If the Resources fields are not displayed, choose the **F**ormat menu and choose **D**etails. Then select **R**esources and Predecessors, Resource **W**ork, or one of the other options that displays resource fields.

4. Add new resources to the list and adjust the amount of work manually for all resources. In the example, Mary Logan is added as a resource to the Setup assembly line task and is assigned 118 of the 120 hours of work on the task. Scott Adams is left with only 2 hours, which does not completely solve the overallocation of his time, but makes the problem more manageable.

5. Choose the OK button to complete the reassignment.

Note that if the unit allocation of Scott Adams' assignment is 1, which assigns him full-time to the task, the schedule dedicates his full attention to the task to finish his assigned two hours on the first day. If Scott's Units field entry is a small fraction, you can spread out the extra time over successive days, reducing the impact on any one single day.

Resolve Overallocations by Delaying Tasks

If resource overallocation is the result of scheduling multiple tasks at the same time, you can delay one or more tasks to level or spread out the demands on the resource over a longer period of time, which reduces the demands on currently overallocated days. You can delay tasks yourself by examining the task schedule and selecting the tasks to delay, or you can have Microsoft Project choose the tasks to delay—either on your command or automatically as tasks are added to the schedule. If you choose to delay tasks yourself, use the Delay field of the task database to enter delays in the start dates for tasks. This field is included on the Delay table, which is the table used by the Delay Gantt on the **V**iews **M**ore Views menu. You can also place this field on any table that you wish.

▶ "Using and Creating Tables," p. 472

Note

If you constrain tasks to be scheduled As Late As Possible—as is the case, for example, if the project is scheduled from a fixed Finish Date—then tasks already are delayed as much as possible and no room exists for resolving overallocation problems by leveling.

Instead of entering delay information on tasks manually, you can use the **T**ools Resource **L**eveling command to have Microsoft Project do that for you. Do not attempt to use leveling until after you enter all the tasks and all the information about each task and resource. If you do use leveling, you will just repeat the leveling operation after you add more tasks or redefine resources and resource assignments.

The **T**ools Resource **L**eveling command provides a dialog box with all your choices for leveling functions provided by Microsoft Project (see fig. 11.40).

Fig. 11.40
The default settings in the Resource Leveling dialog box.

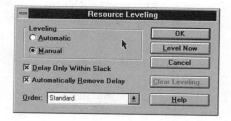

Leveling Resource Work Loads Manually

Use the Resource Allocation view when leveling resource work loads manually (see fig. 11.41). This view displays the Resource Usage view in the top pane to help you select the overallocated resources. The bottom pane displays the Delay Gantt, a Gantt Chart with the Delay field displayed in the table next to the task name. You can enter delay amounts directly in the field in this view. The Delay table also includes the Successors field to give you information about what tasks are directly affected if you delay the selected task.

The Delay field usually is zero, but if you enter a time period in the field for a task, the start of this task is delayed by the amount in the Delay field. The task bars display the names of assigned resources to the right of the bar. You can delay a task as much as the free slack, without affecting the scheduling of other tasks.

The Delay field receives a time value of minutes, hours, days, or weeks. The value in the Delay field is added to the earliest start date of a task—the moment immediately after predecessor requirements are satisfied—to calculate the Scheduled Start date. The Delay field usually is zero for all tasks, and tasks are scheduled to start on the earliest start date. Delay time is displayed in the Delay table as elapsed time.

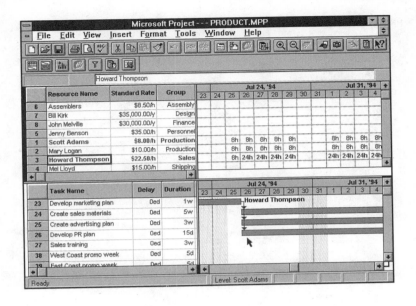

Fig. 11.41
Use the Resource
Allocation view
when leveling
resources manually.

To display the Resource Allocation view, take the following steps:

1. From the **V**iew menu, choose **M**ore Views. The More Views dialog box appears.

2. Select the Resource Allocation view from the **V**iews list.

3. Choose the **A**pply button in the More Views dialog box to activate the Resource Allocation view.

As figure 11.41 shows, Howard Thompson is an overallocated resource. Selecting his name in the top pane causes the tasks to which he is assigned to appear in the bottom pane. After using Alt+Home (to move to the beginning of the project), select the Goto Overallocation tool to locate the first time period during which Howard Thompson is overallocated. The first overallocation occurs on July 22 when tasks 24, 25, and 26 all start at the same time (because these tasks all have task 23 as a predecessor).

In figure 11.42, task 25 is delayed one day and task 26 is delayed five days. Notice that by delaying two of the tasks, July 22 is no longer an overallocated day, and the overallocation on July 25 has fallen from 24 hours to 16 hours. Incidentally, note also that, because the delay field value is always elapsed time, the 5-day delay in task 26 counts weekend days (August 1 and 2) as part of the elapsed period. Entering a delay as **5d** still results in a delay of *5ed*.

Fig. 11.42
Entering Delay
values for selected
tasks.

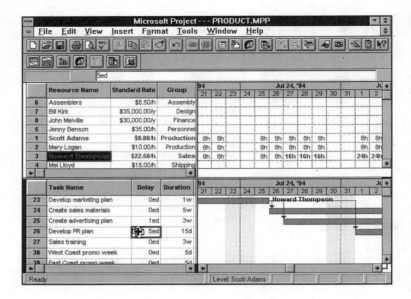

By experimenting with delay values, you can resolve most resource
overallocations (unless task constraints prevent effective delays). Of course, if
you delay tasks beyond the free slack, then other tasks also are delayed; and if
you delay a task beyond the total slack, the whole project is delayed. In the
example, all three conflicting tasks are noncritical tasks. If you delay a task
beyond the total slack, the task becomes critical.

Removing Delays for Tasks

You can use Undo (Ctrl+Z) immediately after entering a delay amount to
restore the previous values to the delay field entries. You also can remove a
delay by entering a zero in the delay field. Note that you cannot delete a
value and then leave the entry blank. A Clear Leveling command also exists
on the Tools Resource Leveling dialog box to reset the Delay field to zero for
the entire project or for just selected tasks.

To return the delay values to zero for a single task or group of tasks, take the
following steps:

1. Select the tasks for which you want to reset the delay to zero. Click and
   drag to select adjacent tasks. Press Ctrl while clicking to select nonadjacent tasks.

2. From the Tools menu, first choose Resource Leveling, and then choose
   the Clear Leveling button. The Clear Leveling dialog box appears (see
   fig. 11.43).

3. Choose the **S**elected Tasks radio button to change the values for only the tasks that you selected. If you want to remove all delay values for all tasks, use the **E**ntire Project radio button.

4. Choose the OK button. All tasks with nonzero delay values are reset to zero delay.

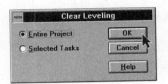

Fig. 11.43
The Clear Leveling dialog box removes delays imposed on tasks.

Enabling Microsoft Project To Level the Project

If the project is scheduled from a fixed Start Date, you also can have Microsoft Project calculate task delays to remove resource overallocations. Remember that the program cannot level a project scheduled from a fixed Finish Date because all tasks already are delayed as much as possible to minimize the duration of the project.

In preparation for letting Microsoft Project do the leveling of tasks, you can assign Priority values to each task.

Setting Task Leveling Priorities. Use the Task Details Form or the Task Information tool to assign priority levels to tasks for leveling purposes. Figure 11.44 illustrates the priority choices. The higher the Priority, the less likely it will be that the task is selected to be delayed in a leveling operation. The highest priority is Do Not Level, and these tasks are never selected for delay.

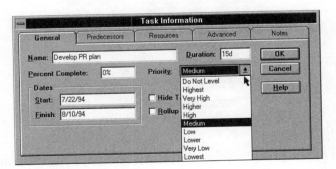

Fig. 11.44
Setting priorities for a task control indicates whether or not it can be delayed.

To assign a priority level to one or more tasks, take the following steps:

1. Activate a task view. If you view the Task Details Form, you can skip to step 4.

2. Select the task or tasks to assign.

3. If you are not in the Task Form view, choose the Information tool to display the Task Information dialog box.

4. Select the Priority field. The default priority is Medium.

5. Select one of the ten priority levels.

6. Choose the OK button to complete the assignment.

Understanding How Automatic Leveling Is Done. When you execute the command to **L**evel Now, Microsoft Project searches for overallocated resources. For the first overallocation problem it encounters, Microsoft Project identifies the tasks causing the overallocation and notes tasks that *cannot* be delayed. These include tasks that have Must Start On, Must Finish On, or As Late As Possible constraints, tasks that have Do Not Level priority assignments, and tasks that are already started.

If more than one task exists that you can delay, Microsoft Project uses a set of rules to select one or more of the tasks to delay. You can specify one of three sets of rules for use in selecting the tasks to delay. Use the Resource Leveling dialog box to control how the delays are calculated, as well as the method used for selecting the tasks to delay (see fig. 11.45).

Fig. 11.45
The Resource
Leveling dialog
box.

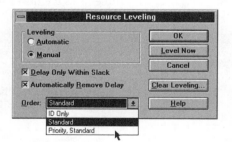

Table 11.1 outlines the choices in the Resource Leveling dialog box and provides a brief description of each choice.

Table 11.1   The Leveling Options

Option	Meaning
Automatic Le**v**eling	Instructs Microsoft Project to level tasks the moment one or more overallocated resources is detected. Automatic leveling takes place as you enter the tasks into the project.
Manual	Leveling is executed only when you choose **T**ools Resource Leveling **L**evel Now. **M**anual is the default status for leveling.
Delay Only Within Slack	If this box is marked, tasks are delayed only within the amount of total slack, and the finish date of the project is not delayed. With this constraint, the leveling operation may not resolve the overallocation problem. If you clear this box, and no task constraints exist to serve as impediments, Microsoft Project can resolve the resource overallocation through leveling.
Automatically **R**emove Delay	If this box is marked, all delay values return to zero before leveling begins. If you are leveling only selected resources, the delay is removed from all tasks in the project that use these resources. Leave this box checked most of the time. If not, you must remember to use the **C**lear Leveling button on the Resource Leveling dialog box before executing the **L**evel Now command. The reason for clearing the box may be that you want to preserve delays you manually entered for certain tasks.

If delay values are not removed before the leveling operation, the existing delay values are treated as unalterable, as though they were lag values associated with the predecessors to the task. Therefore, the opportunities for resolving resource conflicts can be significantly reduced. You may find large gaps in the project schedule if delay values are not reset to zero before leveling. |
| **O**rder | This option provides three choices for establishing how Microsoft Project decides which of several tasks to delay when the tasks cause a resource overallocation conflict. The choices are ID Only, Standard, and Priority. A description of the choices follows in this table, and a detailed explanation of the Standard and Priority choices is shown in Table 11.2. |
| ID Only | If the ID number is used to determine the order for delaying tasks, Microsoft Project chooses the task further down the task list, the task with the higher ID number, as the task to delay. If the task list is chronological—with earlier tasks listed at the top of the list and with one sequence of tasks leading to the finish date—the ID Only scheme essentially delays tasks with the later start dates. Delaying the tasks with later start dates minimizes the number of successor tasks affected by imposing delays. |

(continues)

Table 11.1	Continued
Option	**Meaning**
Standard	The Standard order, which is the default leveling order for Microsoft Project, uses five factors to determine which of several tasks is to be leveled first.
Priority, Standard	The same factors considered in the Standard order are used for the Priority, Standard order. This ranking of the factors, however, is changed to give primary weight to the Priority assignment of each task.

The Standard Order and Priority, Standard choices require more explanation. In both cases Microsoft Project uses the following five criteria for selecting the task or tasks to be delayed in the leveling operation:

- Predecessor relationships

- The amount of total slack (the task with the most total slack is delayed before others)

- The start date (the task with the latest start date is delayed before others)

- The Priority assignment

- Constraints on the tasks

 The criteria for the Priority order are the same, except that the Priority assignment is moved to the top of the list. You can enter Priority assignments on the Task Details Form or the Task Information dialog box accessed with the Information tool.

Table 11.2 defines the default settings for the Resource Leveling dialog box and briefly describes the implications of each option for executing a leveling operation.

Table 11.2	Default Settings for the Resource Leveling Dialog Box	
Option	**Default Value**	**Implication**
Automatic or Manual	**M**anual	Leveling is calculated only when you execute the **L**evel Now command.
Delay Only Within Slack	Cleared	Tasks can be delayed so much that the project finish date is delayed.

Option	Default Value	Implication
Automatically **R**emove Delay	Checked	All delay values are reset to zero before leveling operations begin.
Order	Standard	Standard—the Standard rules as described in Table 11.1 are used to determine the order in which tasks are selected for delay in leveling operations.

Therefore, if you use the **L**evel Now command without changing settings in the Leveling dialog box, all delay values are removed from all tasks before leveling begins, the tasks delayed are the tasks selected by the Standard rules, and the project's finish date may be delayed as a result of the leveling operation.

> **Note**
>
> The default settings for the Leveling dialog box are saved in the WINPROJ.INI file when you exit Microsoft Project.

Using Level Now

After establishing your choices in the Resource Leveling dialog box, you can instruct Microsoft Project to level the project with the Level **N**ow command. If you select this command from a task view, the leveling occurs immediately, without prompts. If you select the command from a resource view, you see the Level Now dialog box (see fig. 11.46).

If you choose **S**elected Resources, only the overallocations for the resources in the selection are reviewed for leveling operations. If you select **E**ntire Pool, all resources and all tasks are reviewed.

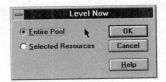

Fig. 11.46
You can level all resources at once or just a selection.

When you choose the OK button, Microsoft Project tries to resolve the resource overallocations by leveling—within the bounds you specify in the Resource Leveling dialog box. If one or more dates where overallocations occur cannot be resolved, you see a message similar to the message in fig. 11.47.

Fig. 11.47
Microsoft Project
can't resolve
all resource over-
allocations.

To respond to the Unresolved Overallocations message, take the following steps:

- Choose **C**ontinue to have Microsoft Project continue looking for and attempting to resolve overallocations with leveling.

- Choose **S**top to stop the leveling process and keep all the delays that have been entered so far.

- Choose **R**evert to stop the leveling process and erase all the delays that have been entered so far.

Appreciating the Caveats Concerning Automatic Leveling

Note that automatic leveling is unlikely to produce the best results possible for your project, especially considering all the information that you cannot put in the database to guide the program to do as you want. You usually will know the situation far better than you can describe to the computer. Review the results of the leveling operation carefully to be sure that you are satisfied with the results.

You also should note that Microsoft Project doesn't *optimize* the leveling strategy. The program doesn't examine all possible combinations of task delays in order to choose the best—actually, the computer cannot know what you consider the best solution.

Remember that you cannot use leveling with projects scheduled from a finish date, and if many date constraints exist on your tasks, you may find gaps in the schedule, or you may find that leveling simply is not a feasible solution to the problem.

Reducing Costs

If the project costs are above expectations, you can examine the project schedule for possible cost savings. Because the variable costs all derive from resource assignments, you may want to focus on ways to reduce the cost of the resources assigned to individual tasks.

Reviewing the Cost Schedule

You can view the task list with the cost and total amount of work for each task if you view the Task Sheet and apply the Summary table. If you want to focus on only tasks with costs in excess of some determined amount, you can create a filter to display only these tasks. If you display the Task Form in the bottom pane and choose the Resource Work fields from the Format menu to appear at the bottom of the form, you can see the resource assignments, including overtime work, in detail.

You also may use the Resource Substitution view developed earlier in this chapter to identify less expensive resource substitutes to assign to tasks.

To display the Summary table in the top pane and the Resource Work table in the bottom pane, take the following steps:

1. Select the top pane if currently displaying a combination view.

2. From the **V**iew menu, choose **M**ore Views. Then select **T**ask Sheet from the More Views dialog box. **A**pply the view.

3. Re-select the **V**iew menu and this time select the **T**able option. Then select S**u**mmary.

4. Select the bottom pane. If you are not currently displaying a combination view, choose **W**indow **S**plit first.

5. From the **V**iew menu, choose **M**ore Tables, and then select **T**ask Form.

6. From the Fo**r**mat menu, choose **D**etails, and then select Resource **W**ork to display the work fields.

To design a filter to display all tasks that cost more than a specified amount, take the following steps:

1. Select the top pane.

2. From the **T**ools menu, choose **F**iltered for and select **M**ore Filters. The More Filters dialog box appears (see fig. 11.48).

3. To define a new filter, choose the **N**ew button. The Filter Definition dialog box appears (see fig. 11.49).

4. Supply a name for the filter in the **N**ame field. If you plan to list the filter in the main Filter menu (and not just in the More Filters menu) remember to use an ampersand before the letter you want to use to select the filter. You must select the Show in **M**enu box at the top of the dialog box to actually include the name in the **F**iltered for menu list.

Fig. 11.48
The More Filters
dialog box.

Fig. 11.49
Defining an
interactive filter
for costs.

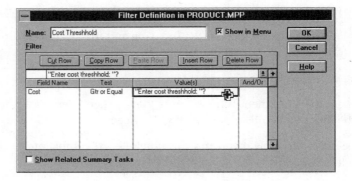

5. Select the first row in the Field Name column.

6. Select the entry list arrow that appears above the And/Or column on the right side of the dialog box and select the field name to test for the filter. Here, the field name is Cost, so select Cost.

7. Select the first row in the Test column.

8. Choose the Entry List arrow to see a list of the possible tests. In this case, you want to choose Gtr or Equal, to test for cost values greater than or equal to the value supplied in the Value(s) column.

9. Select the first row in the Value(s) column.

10. You can place just a number in this column; the filter always tests for costs that exceed this number. The filter is more useful, however, if designed to prompt for a value to use in the filter test. In double quotes, type a prompt to display to the user, followed immediately by a question mark. This combination causes Microsoft Project to display the prompt and wait for a response from the user when this filter is selected.

11. Mark or unmark the Show in **M**enu box at the top of the form, depending on whether you want this filter to appear in the **F**iltered for menu.

12. Choose the OK button to complete the filter definition.

13. Choose the App**l**y button to activate the filter immediately. Alternatively, you may choose the Hi**g**hlight button to highlight the tasks that meet the filter's criteria without hiding the other tasks.

14. A dialog box appears, displaying the filter name in the title bar and the text you typed in double quotes as a prompt. The program pauses, waiting for an entry (see fig. 11.50).

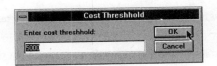

Fig. 11.50
The interactive filter dialog box prompts for a value at the time the filter is applied.

15. Type the minimum cost figure on which you want to focus and choose the OK button.

16. The filter is activated, using the minimum cost value you entered.

The illustration in figure 11.50 shows an entry of $5,000 and, in the background, the filtered list is shown as it appears after the filter is applied.

Strategies for Reducing Costs

Less expensive resources that perform the same quality of work in the same amount of time obviously will lower your costs. You also can reduce costs if you can substitute more expensive but more efficient resources. You can justify the extra cost if the number of hours of work that complete the task is more than reduced proportionally. If the standard rate of the new resource is 20 percent higher than the old resource, for example, but you can reduce the work hours by 25 percent; this substitution would result in a cost savings.

You also may be able to assign tools or equipment to the task and thereby increase the efficiency of the labor so that reduced hours of work result in reduced total labor costs. If the reduction in labor time and costs is enough to match the cost of the tools or equipment, the added capital expense results in a cost savings overall.

Troubleshooting

I think I've inadvertently placed constraint dates on many tasks in my project. How can I find them all and set them back to As Soon as Possible?

Use the Table and Filter feature together to find these tasks. Apply the table called Constraint Dates. You can find this under **V**iew **M**ore Views. If there are many tasks it is also useful to filter the project by Tasks with Fixed Dates. You can find this under **T**ools **F**iltered For More Filters. If you want to set all tasks back to As Soon as Possible, select all tasks in this filtered view, and use the Information tool to bring up a generic form. Any change you make to this form will occur to all selected tasks. Choose the Advanced tab and choose As Soon as Possible from the Constrain Task entry list arrow.

I think there are tasks in my project that don't have a predecessor task assigned. How can I find them?

Apply the Schedule table to the task sheet and look at the Total Slack column. Tasks that have a large slack amount, particularly if the slack amount is the length of the total project, are candidates for tasks with no predecessor. Sort by the Total Slack column and then review those with the largest amount of slack.

I use a variety of composite views to look for and resolve problems in the project plan. This seems tedious and time-consuming.

Save the composite views that you use most often by creating a new view and then place it on the menu. You can even set the table and filter of your choice.

I'm working on resource-overallocation problems. I don't have any idle resources, I can't hire more, and my deadline is important. What can I do?

Look for tasks that have slack. If they are tasks that use resource driven scheduling then you can reduce the number of units allocated to the task. The resulting increase in duration should not matter because they are non-critical tasks. Don't take too many resources away from that task because it can become critical. Use either the Schedule table to see the amount of slack or the Gantt Chart Wizard to modify the task bars to include a line for slack.

From Here...

This chapter dealt with the techniques you need to refine the task definitions and resource assignments to produce a workable plan, without internal inconsistencies, that finishes on time and within costs consistent with the project goal.

You are now ready to implement and begin tracking the project plan. To learn the methods for keeping a project up-to-date, refer to the following chapters:

- Chapter 12, "Managing the Project," deals with making a copy of the final plan so that you can compare the final plan with what actually happens. You see how to track actual performance on the project, recording start and finish dates for tasks, the actual cost of tasks, and the percentage complete for tasks not finished as of the reporting date.

- Chapter 17, "Using and Creating Views," deals with using the building blocks of view, tables, and filters to create custom views to be used for tracking and reporting.

- Chapter 18, "Formatting Views," illustrates many techniques for customizing the way a view appears on-screen and on printouts.

- Chapter 20, "Using and Customizing Reports," describes the many ways you can customize reports to display not only the planned project but also progress as it occurs.

Chapter 12

Managing the Project

Previous chapters showed you how to create a plan for a project. In Chapter 3, you established the background information for the project: naming the project, setting the date objectives, and establishing the calendar. In Chapters 4 and 5, you entered all the tasks and defined their characteristics, in terms of durations, constraints, and task relationships. In Chapters 8 and 9, you added resources to the project file and assigned resources to the tasks. You refined the schedule in Chapters 10 and 11 to remove inconsistencies, and you tweaked the schedule, or plan, to bring it in line with the dates and cost specified in the project goal statement. You now have a finalized plan that meets the project objectives in a workable way. After the plan is finalized, you are ready to begin the work and execute the project.

It's now time to save a copy of the plan for future reference and get to work on the project itself. As the work proceeds on the project, you may often find that changing the plan to more accurately reflect reality is necessary. You may have to add or redefine tasks and resource assignments. You also may find that recording facts about what actually happened on a task by task level is worth your while. If everything happens exactly as you planned, you have no need to reschedule subsequent tasks. If the actual finish dates for tasks differs from the planned dates, however, Microsoft Project can use the real dates to reschedule the remaining tasks in the project. You then can distribute the new schedule to the project members who are affected by the updated schedules. The new schedule also gives you an advance warning if the changes create problems with meeting the project objectives. The sooner you know about problems, the more opportunity you have to avoid missed deadlines or cost overruns.

You may find that crashing the schedule again is necessary if some tasks are not finished on time, and you may be required to cut costs in later tasks to compensate for cost overruns in the earlier tasks.

If you fail to take advantage of the forecasting powers of Microsoft Project you miss some of the greatest benefits that using Microsoft Project can provide.

In this chapter, you learn how to

■ Save a copy of the finalized plan or baseline for future reference.

■ Enter the tracking information that enables Microsoft Project to keep the schedule or plan as accurate as possible.

■ Examine the revised schedule to identify potential problems.

Setting the Baseline or Plan

After you finalize the planning of the project, set aside a copy of the finalized project schedule for future reference. Actually, the *final plan* is final only because the plan shows the final product of the initial planning effort. The copy that you make of the finalized plan is the baseline that you use to compare actual performance with planned performance. As work progresses on the project, you may have to tweak the plan to respond to changing circumstances or as a result of new information. Resource availability can change, duration estimates can change, and so on. You also begin to record the actual start and finish dates for tasks. If actual dates match the planned dates exactly, you performed a miracle. In all probability, some tasks will finish late and other tasks will finish early. As you enter these actual dates, Microsoft Project reschedules successor tasks to reflect the changed circumstances.

Figure 12.1 illustrates the evolution of the schedule. The *planning stage* culminates in a finalized plan, the copy of which is known as the *baseline*. As the *execution stage* gets under way, changes and revisions in the plan often are necessary. As these changes are added to the computer version of the plan, Microsoft Project recalculates the schedule to incorporate the revisions. As work on the project progresses, the actual dates and durations of tasks are entered into the computer version of the plan, and Microsoft Project replaces the calculated start and finish dates with the actual dates and recalculates the remaining schedule. Therefore, as the project goes forward the current schedule is revised by the addition of changes and actual data. You can print reports that show the variances or differences between the planned dates and the actual dates, the planned amount of work and the actual amount of work, the planned cost and the actual cost.

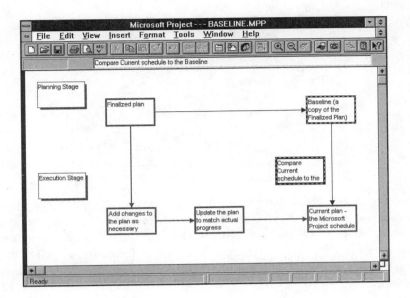

Fig. 12.1
The evolution of
the project plan
schedule.

The baseline is like an architect's final drawings for a building project. After construction gets underway, change orders are penciled in and some features are *whited out*. If changes are significant, new plans are drawn. By setting aside a clean copy of the original plans at the start of construction, you can compare the original intentions with the final result.

In managing your project you can set aside copies of the printouts from the original plan for comparison purposes, but you may find that having an electronic set of the plan dates, planned work, and planned cost is more useful so that the computer can print comparisons or variances to show how work is progressing, how well the plans are being realized, and how likely you are to meet the project goals.

Capturing the Baseline

Microsoft Project provides two ways to capture the baseline once initial planning is complete. The first is with a Planning Wizard. The first time you save a file, the Planning Wizard asks if you want to save the file with a baseline (see fig. 12.2). If you say yes, the Planning Wizard saves a second set of baseline dates, in addition to the currently calculated start and finish dates. Future changes you make to the project file, including tracking actual dates, can then be compared to those frozen baseline dates. Otherwise, you save the file as usual.

Fig. 12.2
The Planning
Wizard stands
ready to save
baseline informa-
tion when you
first save a project
file.

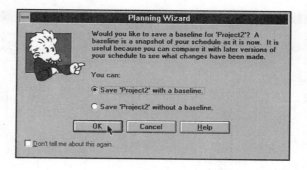

When you close a file without saving first, you are normally prompted for whether you want to save your changes. When you indicate Yes, if there is at least one task that does not have baseline information, the Planning Wizard again prompts whether you want to save baseline information as well as the changes made to the file. As shown in figure 12.3, you have several options at this point.

Fig. 12.3
The Planning
Wizard watches
for changes and
updates all tasks
or just new tasks
with baseline
information.

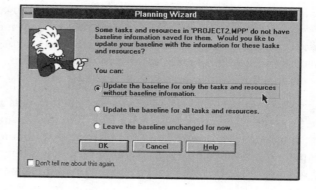

As with other Planning Wizards, you may elect not to be reminded of this in the future. If you mark the **D**on't Tell Me about This Again check box and later want to turn the feature back on again, use the General tab in the **T**ools **O**ptions dialog box. The Advice about **S**cheduling option is unchecked. Re-check the box to once again have the Planning Wizard prompt you for updating the baseline.

The second method of saving the baseline is by using the **T**ools Tr**a**cking **S**ave Baseline command. This command copies the currently calculated start and finish dates and work and cost data into a set of fields known as Baseline Start, Baseline Finish, Baseline Work, and Baseline Cost. You can execute the Save Baseline command from any task view, but not from the resource views.

The Save Baseline command offers an option of copying data for the entire project or for only selected tasks. You use the selected task option when you want to correct mistakes for selected tasks or add data for tasks that you added to the plan after the baseline was captured. You use the entire project option when you create the baseline for the first time or when you want to update the baseline for all tasks.

To save the baseline plan, take the following steps:

1. Activate any task view, such as the Gantt Chart or the Task Sheet. From the **V**iew or **M**ore Views menu choose the view name.

2. From the **T**ools menu, choose Tracking and then **S**ave Baseline. The default settings for the Save Baseline dialog box appear in figure 12.4.

3. Choose the OK button to save the baseline. You see no evidence that the field data was copied until you look at views that display baseline data fields. The following section explains how to view the baseline data.

Fig. 12.4
The Save Baseline dialog box allows you to specifically save the baseline information.

Viewing the Baseline

The fields that are changed with the Save Baseline command are the Baseline Duration, Baseline Start, Baseline Finish, Baseline Work, and Baseline Cost. These fields are displayed in the Task Plan table (see fig. 12.5).

To view the baseline fields in a task view, take the following steps:

1. Be sure that you are in either the Task Sheet view or the Gantt Chart view. If you are in a composite view and you want to see all tasks, you must be in the top pane.

2. From the **V**iew menu, choose Ta**b**les and then choose **M**ore Tables to see the full list of standard tables.

3. From the **T**ables list for Tasks, select the Baseline table.

4. Choose the Apply button to display the table.

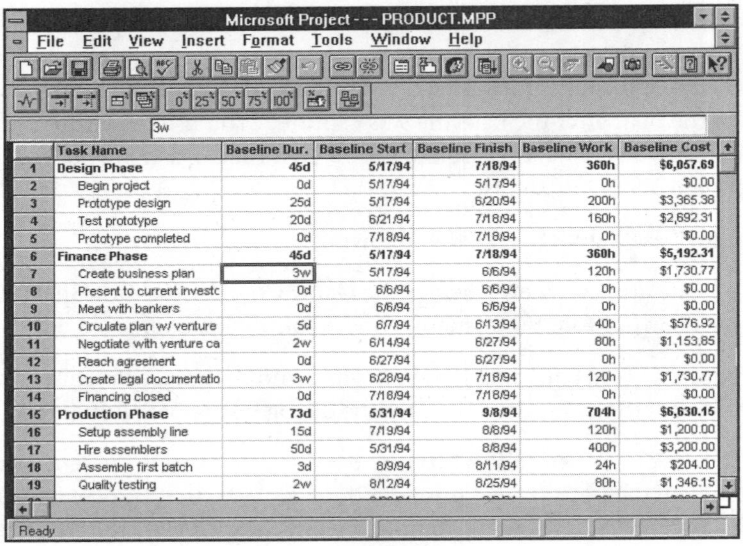

	Task Name	Baseline Dur.	Baseline Start	Baseline Finish	Baseline Work	Baseline Cost
1	**Design Phase**	**45d**	**5/17/94**	**7/18/94**	**360h**	**$6,057.69**
2	Begin project	0d	5/17/94	5/17/94	0h	$0.00
3	Prototype design	25d	5/17/94	6/20/94	200h	$3,365.38
4	Test prototype	20d	6/21/94	7/18/94	160h	$2,692.31
5	Prototype completed	0d	7/18/94	7/18/94	0h	$0.00
6	**Finance Phase**	**45d**	**5/17/94**	**7/18/94**	**360h**	**$5,192.31**
7	Create business plan	3w	5/17/94	6/6/94	120h	$1,730.77
8	Present to current investc	0d	6/6/94	6/6/94	0h	$0.00
9	Meet with bankers	0d	6/6/94	6/6/94	0h	$0.00
10	Circulate plan w/ venture	5d	6/7/94	6/13/94	40h	$576.92
11	Negotiate with venture ca	2w	6/14/94	6/27/94	80h	$1,153.85
12	Reach agreement	0d	6/27/94	6/27/94	0h	$0.00
13	Create legal documentatio	3w	6/28/94	7/18/94	120h	$1,730.77
14	Financing closed	0d	7/18/94	7/18/94	0h	$0.00
15	**Production Phase**	**73d**	**5/31/94**	**9/8/94**	**704h**	**$6,630.15**
16	Setup assembly line	15d	7/19/94	8/8/94	120h	$1,200.00
17	Hire assemblers	50d	5/31/94	8/8/94	400h	$3,200.00
18	Assemble first batch	3d	8/9/94	8/11/94	24h	$204.00
19	Quality testing	2w	8/12/94	8/25/94	80h	$1,346.15

Fig. 12.5
The Baseline table applied to the Task Sheet view displays baseline information.

Correcting the Baseline

If you want to correct the entries for any tasks, or if you need to add tasks to the baseline because the tasks were not in the plan as originally conceived, select the tasks to be added or corrected to the baseline plan and use the **T**ools Tr**a**cking **S**ave Baseline command as outlined above. This time, however, use the Selected **T**asks option on the Save Baseline dialog box rather than use E**n**tire Project.

You also can make changes directly to the Baseline table. Be careful when you use this option, however, because Microsoft Project doesn't check entries for consistency. Typographical or calculation errors are not corrected by the program. If you change the baseline duration, for example, the program doesn't change the baseline finish date. For most changes, the best route is to use the Save Baseline command to be sure that all the data entries are consistent.

You can change the baseline dates in the Task Details Form. In figure 12.6, this form is used to change the baseline start date. Using this method of changing baseline data, you also have to enter the baseline finish date because Microsoft Project doesn't make this change.

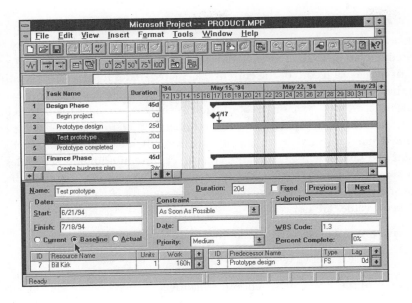

Fig. 12.6
Editing baseline dates on the Task Details form.

If you need to change the baseline work or cost for individual resource assignments, use the Format Details command to view the Resource Work or Resource Cost fields on the Task Details Form, or view the Work or Cost fields on the Resource Form. Figure 12.7 demonstrates adding a resource to a task and includes baseline work as part of the entry.

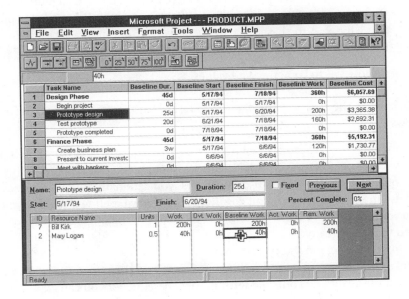

Fig. 12.7
Adding baseline work information for a new resource assigned to a task on the Task Details form.

Saving Interim Schedules

At key points during the project, either during the planning stages before the baseline plan is saved or after work is under way on the project, you may want to make a record of the current (calculated) dates for tasks at this point in the evolution of the project plan. Five sets of baseline date fields are available for each task—five sets of Start and Finish dates—besides the date fields saved in the baseline. Each date set is numbered; therefore, you see fields named Start1 through Start5 and Finish1 through Finish5 for each task. By using the Save Baseline command, you can capture interim date schedules by copying the Current Start and Finish dates in one or more of these sets of date fields. Note that only the date fields are copied for each task—the work and cost values are not copied.

To save interim project dates, take the following steps:

1. Choose a task view.

2. From the **T**ools menu, choose Tra**c**king and then choose **S**ave Baseline.

3. Choose the Save Interim **P**lan radio button. The **C**opy: and **I**nto date fields are then available.

4. Select the E**n**tire Project radio button (although you also can choose to copy only selected tasks).

5. Both sets of date fields have a list of five sets of Start/Finish date fields. Do not use the Planned Start/Finish fields because performing this process wipes out the baseline dates. Choose an appropriate set of dates from each entry list arrow.

6. Choose OK to copy the date values.

You can use the copies of the dates in reports or display them in customized views.

▶ "Using and Creating Views," p. 463

▶ "Formatting Views," p. 497

▶ "Using and Customizing Reports," p. 563

In long projects, the project plan may change so dramatically over time that a new baseline is considered worthwhile. Although you can keep up to five sets of date values for comparison purposes, you can maintain only one set of baseline duration, work, and cost figures. If a new baseline is needed, and you want to preserve the work and cost estimates of the old baseline, you need to find a creative solution to the problem of saving data for which no automatic-saving provision exists. Several avenues are open: you can save a copy of the project file under a different name, and then open the originally named file again and continue setting a new baseline; or you can export the baseline field data to a spreadsheet or database for storage until you need to use the data.

If you only want to preserve the dates of the original baseline and are unconcerned about the work and cost estimates, you can copy the dates to one of the five sets of interim dates.

▶ "Exchanging Data with Other Applications," p. 379

To copy the baseline dates to an interim set of dates, follow the preceding steps for saving interim dates with just one exception—step 4 should read:

4. Choose **C**opy, and select Baseline Start/Finish.

No standard views or reports are available that display the interim date fields. You can create, however, views and reports; or modify any view or report that displays the Baseline dates and substitute the interim dates for the Baseline date fields.

▶ "Using and Creating Views," p. 463

▶ "Using and Customizing Reports," p. 563

Comparing the Baseline with the Current Schedule

The baseline data is displayed beside the currently calculated data in three separate task tables—the Variance table, the Cost table, and the Work table. You can display each table in the Task Sheet or in one of the Gantt Chart views. You can use all three tables to print progress reports.

In each table, the currently calculated field values are displayed along with the baseline field values. Variances are calculated to show the difference between the current and the baseline data.

The current values represent predicted or anticipated values until actual tracking data is entered. Actual data always replaces the currently calculated data, so that the schedule always contains the most accurate information available. Therefore, after tracking begins, the current fields show anticipated values for tasks that have not yet begun and actual values for tasks that already have actual data recorded.

Viewing the Task Variance Table

The Baseline Start and Baseline Finish date fields are displayed in the task Variance table (see fig. 12.8). The Variance table focuses on dates only. The current start and finish dates are changed to equal the actual dates when the actual dates are entered for a task. Therefore, the start variance and finish variance columns show anticipated variances until you enter actual data, and then these columns show actual variances. Incidentally, it is impossible to tell from the Variance table alone whether the current start and finish dates are actual dates or just the currently planned dates.

Fig. 12.8

The Variance table applied to the task sheet concentrates on date differences in the schedule.

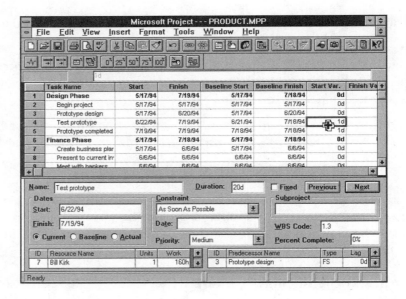

In figure 12.8 the scheduled start for task 4 was changed to one day later than originally planned. Now, the start is a day later than the baseline start, and the variance fields show a resulting one day variance. Note that the delay in task 4 also delays task 5, task 4's successor, and the variance also shows up for task 5. The tasks in the Finance phase group are unaffected because these tasks are not successors to the group that includes task 4.

To display the task Variance table, display the Task Sheet in the top pane by opening the **V**iew menu, by choosing **M**ore Views, and then by choosing **T**ask Sheet. Then display the Variance table by choosing **V**ariance from the **V**iew Ta**b**le menu.

Viewing the Task Cost Table

The Baseline Cost field appears in the task Cost table (see fig. 12.7). The Total Cost values in the Cost table equal the actual values if tracking data was already entered for the tasks, and variances are either anticipated or actual, depending on whether or not actual data was entered.

- For tasks that have not yet begun, the values in the Actual column are zero and the values in the Total column are the currently calculated data. The Remaining cost equals the Total cost.

- For completed tasks, the Total and Actual data is the same and the Remaining cost is zero.

■ For tasks still in progress, the Actual cost plus the Remaining cost equals the Total cost.

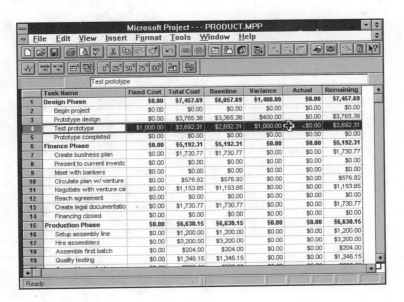

Fig. 12.9
The Cost table applied to the Task Sheet focuses on differences in costs over what was planned.

An unexpected Fixed Cost of $1,000 was entered for task 4, as shown in figure 12.9, and as a result the Total Cost field becomes $1,000 greater than the Baseline Cost, and the Variance field shows the $1,000 disparity. Microsoft Project creates values in the Actual field when tracking data is entered.

To display the task Cost table, display the Task Sheet in the top pane. Then display the Cost table by selecting **T**able from the **V**iew menu and by choosing **C**ost.

Viewing the Task Work Table

The Baseline Work field is displayed in the task Work table (see fig. 12.10). The values in the Work column equal the actual work amounts if tracking data was already entered for the tasks, and variances are either anticipated or actual, depending on whether or not actual data was entered.

■ For tasks that have not yet begun, the Actual work amount is zero and the Work amount is the current baseline amount. The Remaining work equals the value in the work column because all the work remains to be done.

- For completed tasks, the Work and Actual work amounts are the same and the Remaining work is zero. The % W. Comp. (percent of work completed) field is 100 percent.
- For tasks still in progress, the Actual work plus the remaining work equals the Work, and the percent of work completed (%W.Comp.) reflects the completed portion.

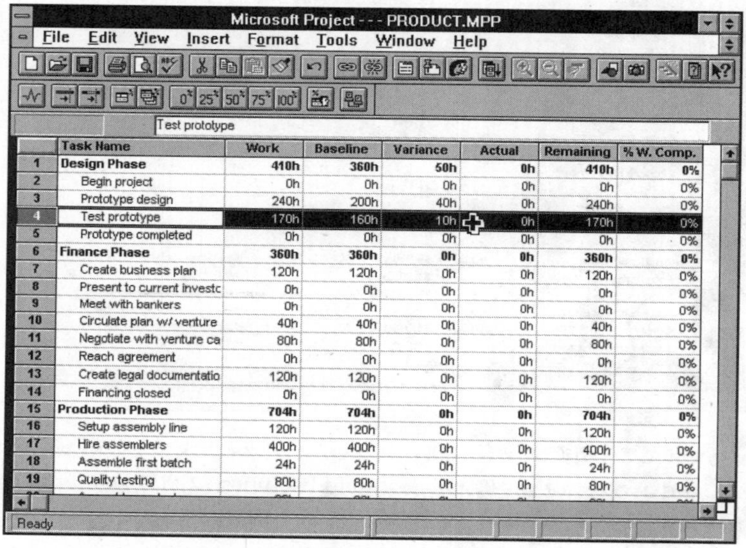
Microsoft Project - - - PRODUCT.MPP
File Edit View Insert Format Tools Window Help
Test prototype
Task Name | Work | Baseline | Variance | Actual | Remaining | % W. Comp.
1 Design Phase 410h 360h 50h 0h 410h 0%
2 Begin project 0h 0h 0h 0h 0h 0%
3 Prototype design 240h 200h 40h 0h 240h 0%
4 Test prototype 170h 160h 10h 0h 170h 0%
5 Prototype completed 0h 0h 0h 0h 0h 0%
6 Finance Phase 360h 360h 0h 0h 360h 0%
7 Create business plan 120h 120h 0h 0h 120h 0%
8 Present to current investc 0h 0h 0h 0h 0h 0%
9 Meet with bankers 0h 0h 0h 0h 0h 0%
10 Circulate plan w/ venture 40h 40h 0h 0h 40h 0%
11 Negotiate with venture ca 80h 80h 0h 0h 80h 0%
12 Reach agreement 0h 0h 0h 0h 0h 0%
13 Create legal documentatio 120h 120h 0h 0h 120h 0%
14 Financing closed 0h 0h 0h 0h 0h 0%
15 Production Phase 704h 704h 0h 0h 704h 0%
16 Setup assembly line 120h 120h 0h 0h 120h 0%
17 Hire assemblers 400h 400h 0h 0h 400h 0%
18 Assemble first batch 24h 24h 0h 0h 24h 0%
19 Quality testing 80h 80h 0h 0h 80h 0%
Ready

Fig. 12.10
The Work table applied to the Task Sheet displays differences in number of hours worked over what was planned.

The Work field was increased for task 4 from 160 hours to 170 hours in the illustration, and because Work is now greater than Baseline work, the Variance field shows the 10 hour difference. The Actual field is updated during tracking of the project.

To display the task Work table, display the Task Sheet in the top pane. Then display the Work table by selecting **T**able from the **V**iew menu and by choosing **W**ork.

Viewing the Tracking Gantt Chart

An extremely informative graphic view of baseline values compared with the current schedule is one created by the Gantt Chart Wizard (see fig. 12.11). This view, often called a Tracking Gantt, is created when you choose the Baseline option on the Gantt Chart Wizard. The view shows two task bars for each task, the upper bar represents the baseline start and finish dates for the same task, and the lower bar represents the currently calculated start and finish dates for the task.

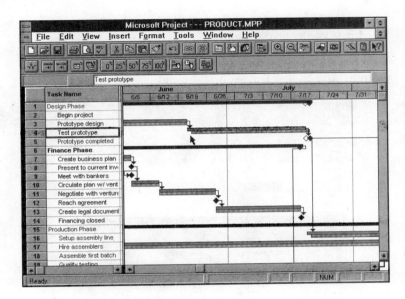

Fig. 12.11
The Tracking Gantt displays two sets of bars for each task, one that you planned and one that reflects reality.

To Create a Tracking Gantt chart follow these steps:

1. Create a new view based on a Gantt chart by choosing **V**iew **M**ore Views. Choose **N**ew and then OK the **S**ingle View choice.

2. Enter a name for the new view, such as **Tracking Gantt**.

3. Make sure that the S**c**reen field has Gantt Chart. If not, choose Gantt using the entry list arrow.

4. Choose a **T**able of your choice from the entry list arrow. The tracking table provides fields for entering actual information.

5. Apply a filter if desired. If you do, you probably want to mark the High-light Filte**r** so that you always see all tasks. If deadlines are important, you may want to highlight Critical tasks.

6. If this is a view that you plan to use often, which you very well may, make sure to mark the Show in **M**enu check box.

7. Choose OK to save the new view.

8. Choose **A**pply to display the new view.

9. Activate the Gantt Chart Wizard by choosing F**o**rmat Gantt Chart **W**izard. You can also use the Shortcut menu or the Gantt Chart Wizard tool on the standard toolbar.

10. Choose the Next> button at the introductory screen, and then choose Baseline from the Step 2 window.

11. Make the rest of your formatting choices in answer to the Wizard's prompts, and choose Format It at the end.

> ### Note
>
> You could also choose the Custom Option at step two, follow all the prompts until you get to step 8. This step offers to draw a Baseline bar, a Total Slack bar or both (see fig. 12.12).

Fig. 12.12
The Gantt Chart Wizard draws baseline bars for you.

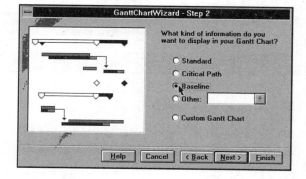

As long as the project proceeds according to the plan, the dates on the two bars match. When the dates of any task deviate from the baseline, however, you can see the discrepancy immediately. In figure 12.11, for example, the delayed start for task 4 is reflected in the shift to the right of the start of the lower bar. The added work that was imposed is reflected in the even further shift to the right of the scheduled finish date. Note that any successor tasks would also be similarly affected.

Printing the Views That Show Baseline Comparisons

Each of these views that display comparisons between baseline values and values in the current schedule can be printed without extensive adjustments. The default print settings are adequate for simple reports.

To print any of these views, display them on-screen and choose **P**rint from the **F**ile menu. For a list of reports that display current activities compared against baseline values, choose **V**iew **R**eports, and then choose the Current Activities option on the Reports dialog box.

▶ "Using and Customizing Reports," 563

Tracking Actual Performance and Costs

After the project gets underway you may find that some tasks start or finish early or late, or that completing a task takes longer or costs more than expected. As you respond to these unexpected changes in the project, you may need to adjust estimated durations for later tasks—based on the experience of the earlier tasks—and you may want to change task relationships. If the cumulative effects of the changes threaten the finish date and cost as set forth in the project goal, you may need to crash the schedule again and find ways to reduce costs.

If you record the actual dates, durations, and work for tasks as events unfold, Microsoft Project uses this data to reschedule tasks affected by the changes. You can see right away the implications for the rest of the project when the actual work doesn't go according to plan. With this knowledge beforehand, you can take corrective measures to minimize unwanted consequences. Therefore, tracking the actual performance and keeping the data entered in the computer on a timely basis can give you the advantage of predicting problems. You also can use the project schedule to try *what-if* tests to measure the effects of alternative compensating actions.

The frequency with which you update the project is determined by how critical the project is. A project plan is like a financial plan or budget—the plan is a blueprint for reaching a goal. If accounting data is not recorded regularly and in a timely fashion, then management does not have the accounting reports that may warn of possible problems in meeting budgeted profits. Similarly, if the project data is not recorded regularly and in a timely fashion, the project manager doesn't have reports that may warn of problems with the project; therefore, the project may not be completed on time and within budget.

Updating the project schedule is a time-consuming task and, probably for this reason, is often neglected by project managers. You may choose to track dates and durations carefully but choose not to spend the time needed to track individual resource work and cost. You must base this decision on the usefulness of the data as opposed to the cost of gathering and entering the information. If you take this route, Microsoft Project still can help warn you about tasks that slip (are not on schedule) and can help you keep the project on course. The cost data, however, will be less accurate because cost is mainly calculated from the work expended by individual resources.

You can view the tracking data in several tables and in the graphics views. The Gantt Chart displays a progress bar in the middle of the task bar for tasks that have already begun. The progress bar is a solid dark bar inside the task bar that represents the percentage complete. Figure 12.13 shows the PRODUCT project with progress already noted for some design phase tasks.

The PERT Chart also can display a record of progress but only in a general way (see fig. 12.14). If a task is completed, the task node shows crossing diagonal lines (as though the node was crossed out). If the task is in progress but not complete, you see a single diagonal line drawn through the node. No diagonal lines appear in tasks that are not yet started.

Fig. 12.13

The progress bars indicate tasks that have already started.

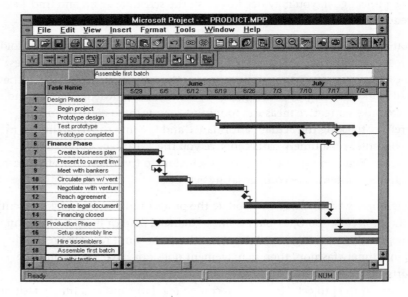

The sections that follow describe the tables that you can use to enter and review actual progress data.

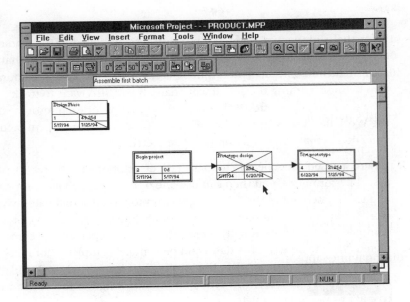

Fig. 12.14
Progress marks on
the PERT Chart
nodes indicate
tasks that have
started or are
complete.

Project Management

Establishing a Procedure for Updating Tasks

The updating procedure is a simple process if work on tasks proceeds according to the schedule. Updating becomes progressively more time consuming
when dates, work amounts, durations, and costs differ from the schedule. A
well-established procedure for gathering actual performance data and regularly updating the computer files is needed to keep the project file current, as
shown in the following steps:

1. First, gather information about the progress on each task, both information about what was actually done and new estimations about tasks yet
   to do. You need to know if duration estimates were revised or if the
   estimated amount of work for a resource on a task was revised. You may
   want to print a progress report form that you distribute to all personnel
   who work on the project. You also may want to require these personnel
   to submit regular updates. This data can provide the basis for the actual
   data that you enter as you track progress.

2. Next, revise the scheduled description of tasks to match the actual
   events or revised estimates before you record that actual work was begun or completed. If the progress reports indicate that the actual duration, amount of work, or cost for a task doesn't match the predicted
   values as outlined in the schedule, change the description of the task in
   the schedule to match the actual events. If the progress reports suggest
   that you should make changes in the planned schedule for unfinished

tasks, enter adjustments to the scheduled duration, work, and costs before you enter actual dates and percentages completed. If the workers on a task, for example, took 30 hours to complete the task rather than the scheduled 20 hours, you can more easily revise the scheduled duration before recording the actual work date. If you also want to track total work and costs effectively, make these entries for each resource on the Work fields table at the bottom of the Task or Resource Form before you enter actual dates and duration completed.

3. Having revised the schedule to make task descriptions fit the reality of actual performance, you then can use one or more of the views, forms, and tools described in the following section to record actual dates when work began and, if completed, when work is finished. If work is not completed, you can optionally record the estimated percentage completed. When you enter the dates and percentage completed for tasks, Microsoft Project can calculate the interim and completed work and cost figures. If necessary, you can enter your own figures for work and cost after tasks are completed.

Understanding the Fields Used in Updating

You can type one or more of the following tracking fields for tasks. Many of these fields are calculated by Microsoft Project when an entry is made in one of the others in the list.

- Actual Start date

- Actual Finish date

- Percentage Completed (percentage of the Duration)

- Actual Duration (to date)

- Remaining Duration

- Revised Scheduled Duration

- Actual Work

- Percentage of Work Completed

- Remaining Work

- Actual Fixed Cost

- Actual Cost (Total Cost)

- Remaining Cost (Total Cost)

No one view displays all these fields—with the possible exception of the Export table. Some of these fields lead to automatic recalculation of other fields. Some fields are calculations only and your entries are ignored. The Work and Cost fields are special cases; if you are tracking work and cost carefully, you do not enter actual in-progress work or costs for the task, but rather you enter the in-progress work for the resources assigned to the task. The work that you enter for the resources are the source of the cost calculations.

You can save time if you understand how these fields are interrelated. You then can select the fields to update and select the view or form that provides the fields you want to use. The tracking fields are described in the following sections, with emphasis on the impact made by entering a change in one of the fields. You become more successful in tracking projects if you understand these relationships.

Actual Start Date

Prior to having an actual date entered, this field's value is NA. When you record actual dates, Microsoft Project changes the current calculated start and finish dates to show the actual dates. Therefore, as the project progresses, your entries of actual dates replace the calculated entries for task dates, and the schedule contains more and more real data.

You can enter the actual start date on all the tracking views and forms either directly or indirectly through setting some other field value. Setting this field changes the current date to equal the actual date but otherwise changes no other field values.

Actual Finish Date

This field displays NA until the task finish date is entered or calculated. You can enter the actual finish date on all the tracking views and forms, either directly or indirectly, by having the finish date calculated. If you enter a date in the actual finish date field, Microsoft Project performs the following procedures:

- Moves the actual finish date to the current finish date.

- Sets the percentage complete (of the duration) to 100 percent.

- Sets the actual start date to equal the current start date, if no actual start date is entered.

- Calculates the actual duration field, and changes the duration, if necessary, to match the actual duration.

- Sets the remaining duration field to zero.

- Calculates the actual work and actual cost fields, based on the actual duration. If the actual duration differs from the original duration, work and cost are adjusted proportionally.

Actually, only the work and cost for the resource or resources that drive the duration of the task change. Resources not fully engaged for the entire duration of the task are unchanged in the calculations, which clearly is one case where redefining the task before recording the task's completion—and being left with inaccurate calculations—is best.

If you want to enter actual work and cost information that differs from the calculated work and cost, make the changes in the calculated data for the individual resources on each task before setting the actual completion date of the task. See the section, "Recording Actual Work and Costs," later in this chapter.

Percentage Completed

After a task is started, you can track the progress of the task by entering the percentage completed on a regular basis. You also can track progress by entering the actual duration to date for the task or by entering the remaining duration. See the "Actual Duration" and "Remaining Duration" sections later in this chapter. The relationship among these three variables (percentage complete, actual duration, and remaining duration) are defined by these equations:

Percentage complete = Actual Duration/Scheduled Duration

Remaining Duration = Scheduled Duration–Actual Duration

When you record a finish date for a task, Microsoft Project displays 100% in the Percentage Complete field for the task. If you want to track interim progress on a task, you can enter partially completed percentage numbers.

You can enter this field on almost all updating views and forms. If you enter a figure in the percentage complete field, Microsoft Project makes changes similar to the changes described under the Actual Finish Date entry in the preceding section.

When the percentage complete field is changed, Microsoft Project performs the following procedures:

■ Sets the actual start date to equal the current start date, unless an actual start date was already entered. If the task did not start on schedule, first update the start date with the actual start date, and then enter the percentage complete.

■ Sets the actual finish date to match the current finish date if 100% is the percentage value that is entered. If the actual finish date is not the same as the calculated date, type the actual finish date rather than entering 100%.

■ Sets the actual duration field to equal the percentage figure times the scheduled duration. Therefore, if a task is marked 60 percent complete when the scheduled duration was 10 hours, the actual duration field is calculated and set to 6 hours.

■ Sets the remaining duration field to equal the scheduled duration minus the actual duration. Using the preceding example, the remaining duration field is calculated as 10 minus 6 and set to 4.

■ Sets the actual work and actual cost fields to match the percentage figure times the scheduled work and cost amounts, but only if the check box for U**p**dating Task Status Updates Resource Status is marked. You can find this check box on the Schedule tab of the **T**ools **O**ptions dialog box.

Note

The U**p**dating Task Status Updates Resource Status option on the Schedule tab of the **T**ools **O**ptions dialog box instructs Microsoft Project as to whether or not it should translate actual duration into actual work and actual work into actual costs. If the option is set to Yes, Microsoft Project calculates the actual work and costs for each task by adding up the actual work and cost for each resource assigned to the task as work on the task progresses. Therefore, you will see prorated cost figures appear as you indicate progress on the task (if the *accrue at* setting for the resources has been set to prorated). See the following section, "Recording Actual Work and Costs."

Actual Duration

This field is available only on the Tracking Table and the Update Tasks dialog box. (You can access the Update Tasks dialog box by choosing **T**ools Tr**a**cking Update Tasks.) When you enter a value in this field that is less than or equal to the scheduled duration, Microsoft Project assumes work on the task is progressing according to plan. Accordingly, the program automatically sets the actual start date as scheduled (unless it has been set previously) and calculates the percentage complete and the remaining duration field by comparing the actual duration with the originally entered or calculated duration.

If you enter an actual duration that is greater than the original duration, Microsoft Project assumes that the task is finished and took longer than scheduled. The current duration is changed to match the new, longer duration, and then the percentage complete and remaining duration fields are set to 100% and 0, respectively, to indicate that the task is complete.

If the Updating Task Status Updates Resource Status option is on, the work and cost figures for resources also are updated based on the task information entered.

Remaining Duration

If you enter a value in the remaining duration field, Microsoft Project assumes that work has begun as scheduled, and that all but this amount of the scheduled duration has been completed. The program calculates and sets the actual duration and the percentage complete based on the new value and the original duration. If not already set, Microsoft Project sets the actual start date as whatever was scheduled. If Updating Task Status Updates Resource Status is on, and the resources were assigned to the tasks, work and costs are updated for the resources and summed for the task.

If you enter **0** in the remaining duration field, it is the same as entering 100% in the Percent Complete field. The actual finish date will be updated as originally scheduled.

If you enter a figure in the remaining duration field that is larger than the existing figure, Microsoft Project assumes that you are simply entering a new estimation of the total duration and not tracking actual progress. If no entry has been made to show that the task has started, this new remaining duration value is simply used to increase the scheduled duration of the task. If the task has already been marked as started, the new remaining duration entry is used to extend the scheduled duration. The new scheduled duration will be equal to the actual duration already shown plus this new estimate of the amount of time left to complete the task. Percentage complete is recalculated to show the actual duration figure as a percent of the new, longer total duration; and the work and cost figures are recalculated proportionally.

For example, suppose that a task with an estimated duration of 10 days has already had 3 days of actual duration recorded. The remaining duration field shows 7 days and 30% displays in the percentage completed field. If the entry in the remaining duration field is changed to 9 days, Microsoft Project takes

that to mean that 9 more days (after the 3 days already recorded) are necessary to complete the task instead of just 7. The total duration is changed
automatically to 12 days, and the percentage completed is reduced to 25
percent (3 days of 12 total days).

The Scheduled Duration

Revised estimates of the scheduled (originally planned) duration can be
entered in any of the locations discussed in previous chapters for defining
a task.

If you change the scheduled duration after a task has already started and
actual duration is greater than zero, the already recorded actual duration is
left unchanged and the percentage completed and remaining duration fields
are adjusted to reflect the new estimate of total duration.

Recording Actual Work and Costs

Work and cost values are calculated by Microsoft Project for individual resources and summed for the tasks to which the resources are assigned. If a
task has no resources assigned, you must manually enter the work and cost
values when the task is completed. You can enter the work and cost values
for individual resources while work is in progress, but you cannot override
the summed work and cost values for the tasks until the tasks are marked as
completed.

To successfully update work and cost amounts, you need to understand the
following points:

- If no resources are assigned to a task or if resources are assigned but
  Updating Task Status Updates Resource Status on the Tools Options
  dialog box, Schedule tab is not marked, you can enter actual work and
  cost amounts directly into the actual work and cost fields for the task,
  just as you can enter actual dates and duration.

- If resources are assigned and Updating Task Status Updates Resource
  Status is marked, Microsoft Project translates actual duration into actual
  work and actual work into actual costs and does so for each resource
  assignment. When this situation exists, you may not enter actual cost
  values into the task tracking fields while the task is in progress (before it
  is marked completed). The values are being calculated from the actual
  work data for each resource, and all entries you make are replaced immediately by the calculated value. After the task is marked as completed, however, you may override the calculated work and cost figures
  with your own entries.

To track work and costs while the task is in progress, you must enter the actual work and cost amounts for the resources individually. The task level actual work and cost fields summarize these entries for you. You use the Task Details Form, or Resource Form, to enter actual work and cost values for each resource. The work and cost fields are available at the bottom of these forms by selecting the appropriate format choice from the menu when the form is displayed. *Note that entries in actual work do not force a calculation of the percentage complete value for the task duration. You also must update the task actual duration.*

Note

If Updating Task Status Updates Resource Status is marked, but you are tracking work and cost details by resource for some tasks, you must not enter the percentage completed value for these tasks because doing so forces a calculation of the work and cost figures based on percentage formulas rather than just adding your detailed actual entries. You must wait until these tasks are completed and then enter the actual finish date. The percentage complete changes to 100%, and the work and cost figures you entered remain unchanged.

Using the Facilities Provided for Updating Tasks

Several views, menu commands, tools, and custom forms are available for updating tasks. This section starts with the facilities that provide the greatest detail and the greatest range of options. The shortcut tools and commands are covered at the end of the section. You should understand the details of the operation and results of using the shortcut tools, and you get this understanding from the review of the tables and forms where the actual field values are presented for you to fill in.

The facilities that can be used for tracking actual performance are described in the following list:

- The Task Sheet, with the Tracking, Variance, Work, or Cost tables applied, provides access to all the fields described in the preceding section. These tables were shown in previous sections. The Tracking table focuses only on the tracking or actual fields. The other tables show scheduled values and baseline values and also the actual, remaining, and variance values.

- The Task Form provides the duration and percentage completed tracking fields. The Task Details Form provides the actual dates fields. Both forms provide entry fields for resource work and resource costs by choosing the appropriate option from the F**o**rmat **D**etails menu.
- The **T**ools Tr**a**cking menu has two commands in addition to saving the baseline for updating individual tasks or updating the entire project. These commands provide a date-sensitive facility for updating the actual dates, duration, and percentage completed for tasks that have scheduled dates that fall before a designated *as of* date.

Fig. 12.15 The Tracking Toolbar gives easy access to updating actual information.

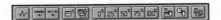

- The Tracking toolbar has a series of buttons that can make tracking progress easier.

Using the Tracking Table

The Task Sheet views can display a Tracking table that provides columns for tracking the percentage complete, actual dates, and so on. To view the Tracking table, open the **V**iew menu, choose **M**ore Views, and then choose **T**ask Sheet. Again open the **V**iew menu, but this time choose Ta**b**le and then choose **T**racking (see fig. 12.16).

Microsoft Project - - - PRODUCT.MPP
File Edit View Insert Format Tools Window Help
60%
Task Name | Act. Start | Act. Finish | % Comp. | Act. Dur. | Rem. Dur. | Act. Cost | Act. Work
1 Design Phase 5/17/94 NA 82% 40.2d 9.05d $5,515.39 344h
2 Begin project NA NA 0% 0d 0d $0.00 0h
3 Prototype design 5/17/94 6/20/94 100% 25d 0d $3,765.39 240h
4 Test prototype 6/22/94 NA 60% 12.75d 8.5d $1,750.00 104h
5 Prototype completed NA NA 0% 0d 0d $0.00 0h
6 Finance Phase 5/17/94 NA 89% 40d 5d $4,615.37 320h
7 Create business plan 5/17/94 6/6/94 100% 3w 0w $1,730.76 120h
8 Present to current inv NA NA 0% 0d 0d $0.00 0h
9 Meet with bankers NA NA 0% 0d 0d $0.00 0h
10 Circulate plan w/ vent 6/7/94 6/13/94 100% 5d 0d $576.92 40h
11 Negotiate with venture 6/14/94 6/27/94 100% 2w 0w $1,153.84 80h
12 Reach agreement NA NA 0% 0d 0d $0.00 0h
13 Create legal document 6/28/94 NA 67% 2w 1w $1,153.85 80h
14 Financing closed NA NA 0% 0d 0d $0.00 0h
15 Production Phase NA NA 0% 0d 73d $0.00 0h
16 Setup assembly line NA NA 0% 0d 15d $0.00 0h
17 Hire assemblers NA NA 0% 0d 50d $0.00 0h
18 Assemble first batch NA NA 0% 0d 3d $0.00 0h
19 Quality testing NA NA 0% 0w 2w $0.00 0h
Ready
NUM

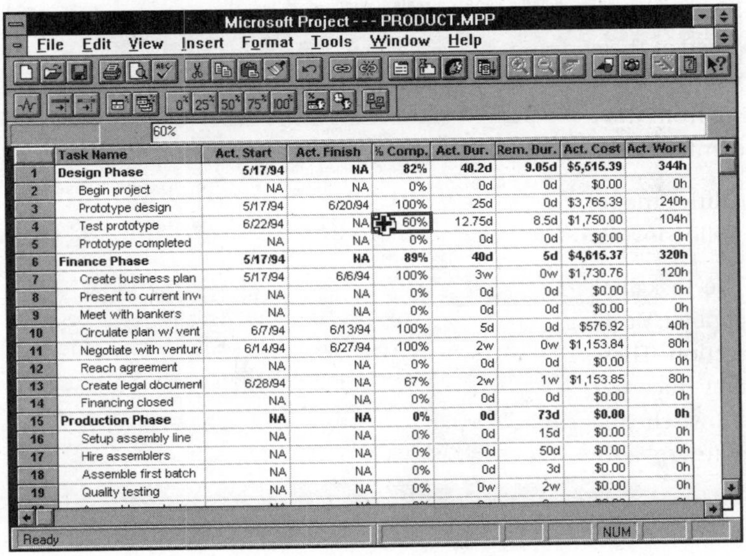

Fig. 12.16 The Tracking Table has fields for entering progress on tasks.

Note that the actual date fields in the Tracking table display NA when no actual date is yet recorded. This table also displays the percentage complete, actual duration, remaining duration, actual cost, and actual work fields. You see the values in these fields calculated immediately after you enter any of the fields that signal work actually done on the task. The calculated entries are the same proportion of their scheduled values as the value displayed in the percentage complete field.

If resources are assigned to tasks and U**p**dating Task Status Updates Resource Status is marked, you cannot change the entries in actual cost until the task is marked as completed. You must enter progress data for the actual work and cost in the individual resource assignments to the individual tasks. Therefore, revise the resource assignment schedule before you update the task actual duration data to have the correct actual work and cost data.

Using the Task Form for Tracking

The Task Form and the Task Details Form both provide fields for entering tracking information although the Task Details form offers much more flexibility, partly because you can enter actual dates here. You must first activate the actual fields by choosing the actual radio button. Figure 12.17 shows the Tracking table applied to the Task Sheet in the top pane and the Task Details Form in the bottom pane.

Fig. 12.17
Combining the Task Sheet with the Tracking table at the same time as the Task Details Form provides many needed fields for tracking.

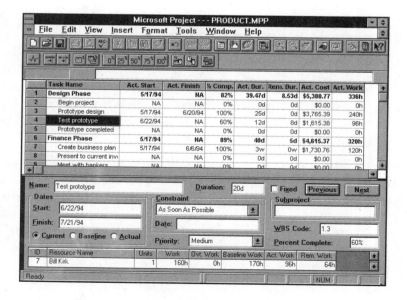

In figure 12.17 the task number 4 was updated to show that the task is 60 percent complete, which means that the duration is 60 percent complete. As a result, in the Tracking table you can see that Microsoft Project calculated that the actual duration is 12 days (60 percent of 20 days), the remaining duration is 8 days, and the Start date has been placed in the Actual Start column. You also notice that the Actual Work field shows that 96 hours of work has been done (60 percent of the 160 hours assigned to Bill Kirk) and the Actual Cost is set to $1,615.38, which is based on the standard rate for Bill Kirk and the actual work value.

You also can display the Resource Work fields at the bottom of the Task Form and Task Details Form and record actual work by resource by individual task (see fig. 12.18). If the Updating Task Status Updates Resource Status option is on, Resource Work fields are one of the few places you can record the work by task by resource. Another place where you can enter resource work and costs is on the Resource Form with the Work fields applied. You must use the Format Details command to select these fields in each case.

▶ "Formatting Views," p. 497

Note that in figure 12.18, the actual work for Bill Kirk was adjusted to 80 hours rather than the 96 hours calculated when the duration was marked as 60 percent completed. The new actual work amount is 80 hours of actually recorded work which is 50 percent of the scheduled work. The percentage of the duration is unchanged since this percentage was set previously as 60 percent. In fact, setting the actual work doesn't affect the percentage of duration completed. The actual cost, however, reflects the new entered actual 80 hours of work.

You use the work data to calculate the resource costs for each task. If actual costs differ from the scheduled cost for the amount of work already entered in the actual work fields, you can display the Resource Cost fields at the bottom of the Task Details Form and record actual costs by resource for each task after the task is marked as completed (see fig. 12.19).

In figure 12.19, a second resource, Mary Logan, was added belatedly to task 4. The task was marked 100 percent complete and the actual cost for Mary Logan exceeded the planned $800 amount. The actual cost of $1,000 for Mary Logan was entered in the cost fields of the Task Form. If you want to make detailed cost entries that differ from the scheduled costs before 100 percent completion, you must turn off the Updating Task Status Updates Resource Status option.

Fig. 12.18
The Resource
Work fields on the
Task Details Form.

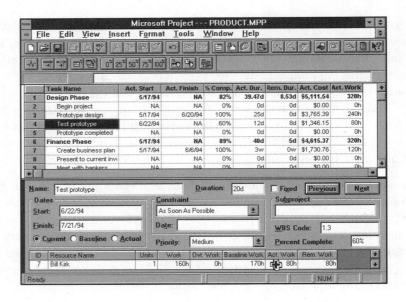

Fig. 12.19
The Resource Cost
fields on the Task
Details Form.

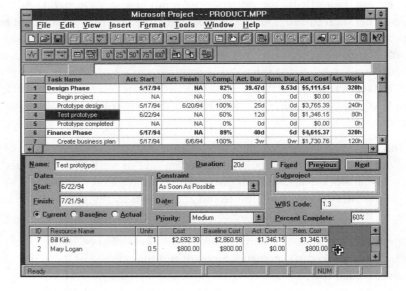

Using the Update Tasks Dialog Box

Access the Update Tasks dialog box by using either the **T**ools Tr**a**cking **U**p-
date Tasks menu command or the Update Tasks button (see fig. 12.20). Use
this dialog box to enter all the tracking fields discussed in this section except
the actual work and cost.

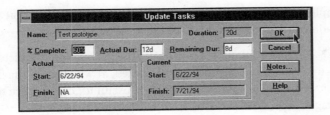

Project Management

Fig. 12.20
Use the Update
Tasks dialog box
for individual or
groups of tasks to
provide actual
information.

If you select several tasks, this form appears blank. Any change you enter here is added to all the selected tasks. You could record, for example, all tasks completed yesterday by selecting the tasks and typing yesterday's date in the Actual Finish Date field.

Using the Percent Completed Buttons

If one or more tasks have started and finished on schedule, you can select the tasks and use the Percent Completed Button to copy the scheduled start and finished dates to the actual dates and to enter the appropriate percentage in the Percentage Completed field.

You also can use the methods described below to mark a task as completed; this tool, however, is the fastest way to show tasks that are on schedule either as completed or in varying stages of completion.

Using the Update Project Command

The Update Project command on the Tools Tracking menu is a convenient way to update a group of tasks scheduled to start and/or finish by a certain date (Update Work As Complete Through). Only the tasks with scheduled activity before the update date are affected by this command. When you choose this command, the dialog box displayed in figure 12.21 is displayed.

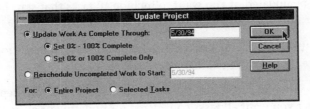

Fig. 12.21
The Update
Project dialog
box offers choices
for updating
tasks that are on
schedule and tasks
that are slipping.

The updating options you can choose in this dialog box are as follows:

■ **S**et 0% - 100% Complete sets the actual dates as originally scheduled and also calculates the percentage completed. The percentage completed is calculated as the percentage of the duration that was scheduled for completion by the update date.

■ **Se**t 0% or 100% complete Only leaves the percentage complete field at zero until the actual finish date is updated, at which time the percentage is set to 100 percent. This option is useful for cases where the percentage complete is to be either 0 percent or 100 percent.

■ **R**eschedule Uncompleted Work to Start as of: reschedules slipping tasks to start on the update date as entered at the top of the dialog box. If the task already has some amount of actual duration recorded for it, the remaining duration is split off from the part already completed and rescheduled to begin on the Update date. If a task has not yet started but should have, Project moves the start of the task to start on the update date.

Note

The check box for Split In-Progress Tasks must be marked on the Schedule tab of the **T**ools **O**ptions dialog box before you can use the third option.

To mark this option take the following steps:

1. From the **T**ools menu, choose **O**ptions and then choose the Schedule tab.

2. Make sure that the Split In-Progress Tasks check box is marked.

3. Choose OK.

To use the Update Project command, take the following steps:

1. Select the task or tasks that you want to update, if only selected tasks are to be updated. If you want to include all tasks that start before the update date, the tasks that you select are of no consequence.

2. From the **T**ools menu, choose Tr**a**cking and then Update Project. The Update Project dialog box appears (see fig. 12.21).

3. Choose the E**n**tire Project or Selected **T**asks radio button, depending on whether you want all tasks considered for updating or only tasks that you selected.

4. Choose the operation that you want performed. Select one of the options as described above.

5. Change the date field to the date you want to use as a cut-off date—all uncompleted tasks *before* the Update Date is processed by the command. By default the Update date is today's date, but you can change this setting to any date using **F**ile Summary Info.

6. Choose OK to execute the update.

The **U**pdate Work As Complete Through option is also available using the Update as Scheduled tool on the Tracking toolbar.

Figure 12.22 shows the results of using this tool. Note that all task bars that lie to the left of the current date line (June 30) show progress bars right up to the update line.

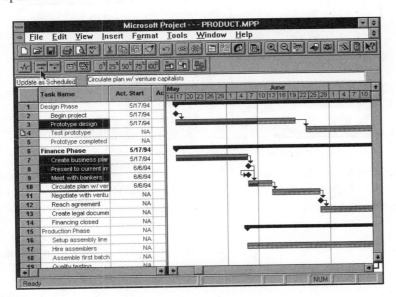

Fig. 12.22
Use the Update as Scheduled tool on the Tracking toolbar to update tasks that are on schedule.

Using the Reschedule Work Tool

The **R**eschedule Uncompleted Work to Start option is also available with the Reschedule Work tool on the Tracking toolbar for the selected task or tasks. If the scheduled start date falls before the current date and the task has not started, the task is rescheduled to start on the current date. If the task has started but the actual duration is less than expected by the current date, the remaining duration of the task is split off and scheduled to start on the current date. The task actually is given a Stop date to mark the point where actual work stopped and a Resume No Earlier Than constraint for the current date.

Notice the Gantt bars for task 17 in figure 12.23 display that the currently calculated start date has been rescheduled to the current date (as identified by the current date vertical line).

Fig. 12.23
Use the Reschedule Work tool on the Tracking toolbar to update tasks that are slipping.

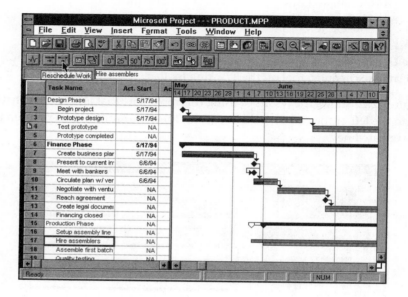

Using the Mouse in the Gantt Chart

You can use the mouse in the Gantt Chart to drag the progress bar from the start date of a task to the percentage completed point on the task bar. To enter percentage complete with the mouse, take the following steps:

1. View the Gantt Chart in the top pane by selecting **V**iew from the menu and choosing **G**antt Chart.

2. Move the mouse pointer to the beginning of the task bar for a task you want to update. The pointer changes to a percent sign (%).

3. Drag the mouse to the right to increase the percentage complete. As you move the mouse, an information box appears to the left of the task bar to indicate the date the task is complete through a certain date which is specified as you drag the mouse. When the correct date is reached, release the mouse button. Drag the mouse all the way to the finish date to indicate 100 percent complete.

   The percentage of work complete changes to the value that you set with the mouse, and the actual start date is set to the date on which the task was scheduled to start.

You can extend the duration of a task by dragging the scheduled end date to the right. Move the mouse pointer to the right end of the task bar until the pointer changes to a right-pointing arrow. As you drag the pointer to the right, an information box appears to let you know the duration that will be set when you release the mouse button.

After you record an actual start date for a task, you can use the mouse to change the date. Move the mouse pointer to the left end of the task bar until it turns into a left-pointing arrow.

Be careful when using the mouse to update tasks on the Gantt Chart. If the mouse is in the middle of the task bar, the pointer turns into a double-arrow symbol, and if you drag the mouse you set a task constraint of Start No Earlier Than. If you move a milestone in this way, the constraint becomes a Must Finish On. These constraints are insidious because you probably will not be aware that you have set a constraint.

If you accidentally start any of these mouse actions in the Gantt Chart and want to escape, you can drag the mouse down from the task bar before releasing the button to prevent any changes. Depending on where you pointed when any of these actions were initiated, the mouse pointer may change to a chain link. If this happens, make sure that you drag to an open space sufficiently away from other task bars so as not to inadvertently create a task link.

The tracking facilities presented so far are used for the more difficult cases, which actually may be the more common cases. When tasks start on time and finish within the scheduled duration, quicker ways exist to record the actual data. You also can update many tasks at the same time (refer to the section, "Using the Update Tasks Dialog Box," earlier in this chapter).

Analyzing the Revised Schedule

Microsoft Project provides several views to help you analyze the updated schedule with an eye toward spotting problems and doing some *preventive maintenance* for avoidable problems. If some tasks are slipping (not on schedule) or if the whole project is running over budget, hopefully, you can discover the problem early enough to take corrective actions.

Start by using the Project Statistics tool on the Tracking toolbar to display the dialog box shown in figure 12.24. You can also access this dialog box by choosing **F**ile Summary **I**nfo and then the Statistics button. This is the big picture of the progress of the project as compared to what you had originally planned. You can check Current dates, compared to the Baseline and Actual dates, with variances calculated. Information about duration, work, and cost variances are also presented in this dialog box.

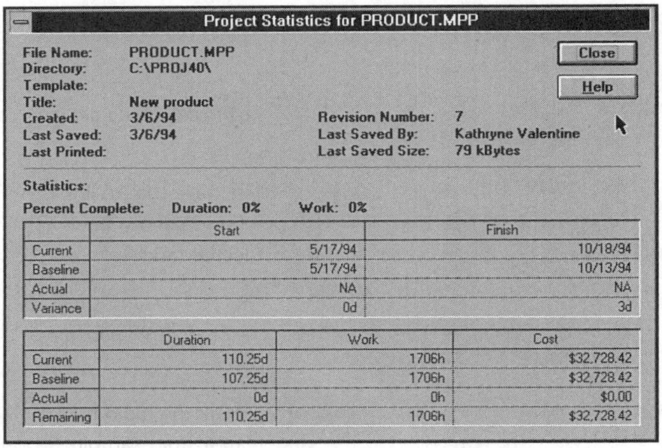

Fig. 12.24
The Project Statistics dialog box offers a big picture overview of the progress of your project.

The task list can be filtered to show the following potential problems:

- Tasks currently scheduled to finish later than their planned finish dates.

- Tasks that should have started but haven't.

- Tasks that are over budget.

Use the Slipping filter to filter tasks that get behind schedule. From the **V**iew menu, choose **G**antt Chart, or from the **V**iew **M**ore Views menu, choose **T**ask Sheet. Then from the **T**ools **F**iltered For menu, choose More Filters, and then choose S**l**ipping Tasks. The task list display contains only the tasks scheduled to finish later than their baseline finish date.

Tip
You can enter the words **today** and **tomorrow** rather than type in the actual dates. For *yesterday*, enter **today-1**.

Use the Should Start filter to select the tasks that have not—but should have—started by a specific date. From the **T**ools **F**iltered For menu, choose Should St**a**rt, which is an interactive filter. You are asked to supply a date.

The Tracking Gantt provides a graphical comparison of the planned, scheduled, and actual dates for a task. You also can use this view to spot tasks that slip. The Detail Gantt shows the amount of slippage as a line at the left of the task bar.

Use the Overbudget filter to find tasks either scheduled to—or that have—run over budget. From the **T**ools **F**iltered For menu, choose **M**ore Filters and then Cost Overbudget. Only tasks for which scheduled or actual costs exceed planned costs are listed.

Troubleshooting

I've already saved the baseline and begun work on the project; then I get a new set of tasks assigned. What do I do?

Add the new tasks in the most appropriate place and make sure to link them to the rest of the project as necessary. Then select the tasks and choose **T**ools Tracking Save Baseline. Make sure to mark the radio button for selected tasks.

The project's baseline has already been saved and initial phases of the project have begun. Then the project is delayed. How can I reset the baseline without loosing the one I have already?

Use **T**ools Save Baseline as before but make sure to mark the radio button for Interim Plan, and then choose one of the alternate sets of dates—for example, Start1, Start2, Start3, and so on.

I get tracking information from people out in the field. How can I provide them with a tool that allows them to capture the information I need?

Print out the project using the task sheet with the tracking table applied. The task sheet has several blank columns where information can be entered as soon as it is available. If the project is long, filter the project for a specific date range.

As I track my project I want to manually track the actual time worked on a project rather than have the software do it, but when I indicate that a task has started, the work and cost fields are filled in and I can't change them.

The option that controls this is found on the Schedule tab of the Tools Options dialog box and is called Updating Task Status Updates Resource Status. When you deselect this option, the work and cost fields are not calculated automatically; you can enter information of your own there.

From Here...

This chapter described how you can use Microsoft Project to manage the project, once actual work gets under way. You have seen how to compare actual experience with the finalized plan for the project and how to track actual dates, duration, work, and cost.

At this point you probably want to print out progress reports for management and staff. You may want to refer to the following chapters:

- Chapter 15, "Using Microsoft Project in Workgroups," explains the techniques offered by Microsoft Project to assist you in tracking a project that many people on a network are also working on.

- Chapter 16, "Printing Views and Reports," discusses the mechanics of printing your views and reports and the options you have to make changes in the manner in which they are printed.

- Chapter 17, "Using and Creating Views," demonstrates how to modify existing views or create views of your own using custom tables and filters, as well as combining different views in new composite views.

- Chapter 22, "Customizing Toolbars, Menus, Forms, and Cue Cards," describes the ways that you can customize the way Microsoft Project appears and works to make it more consistent with your work environment.

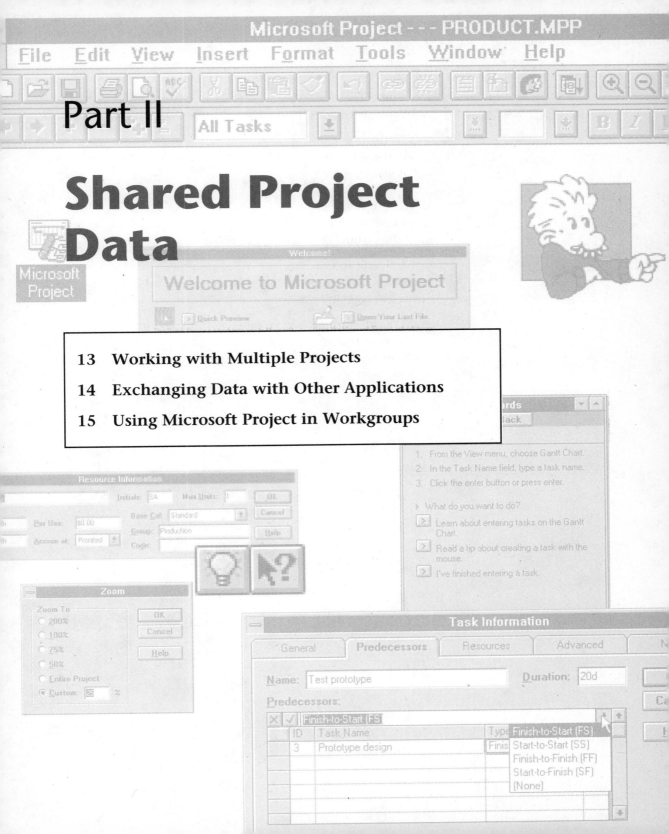

Part II

Shared Project Data

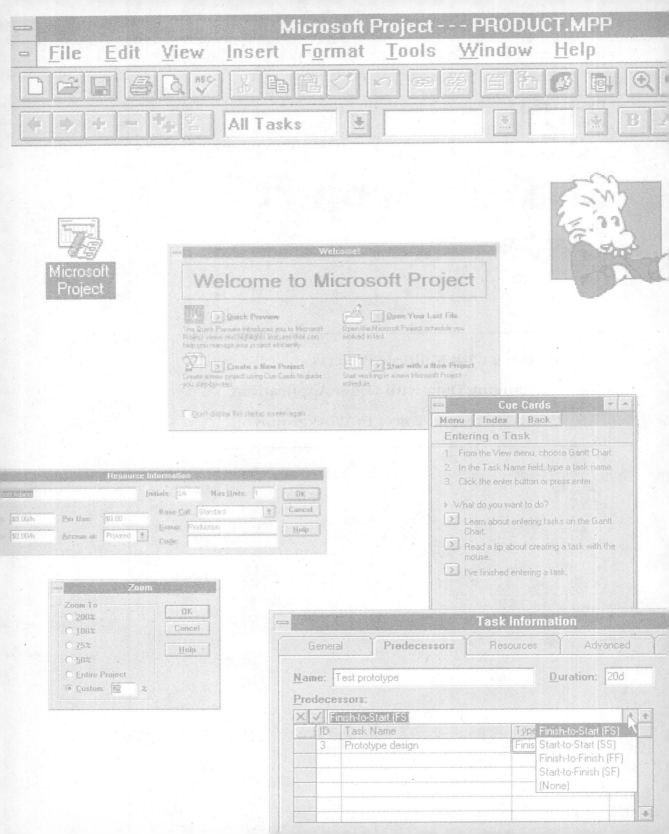

Chapter 13

Working with Multiple Projects

There are several instances where working with only one project does not allow you to accomplish certain objectives. Working in a Windows environment typically offers the capability to work with more than one project file at a time. With this in mind, linking the details between project files can provide the following benefits:

- The value in a field in one project may depend on a value in another project. For example, the start date for one task may need to be linked to the start or finish date for a task in another project.

- Several projects that are managed by different people may be placed under a larger project to provide coordination for the start and finish dates for each of the subprojects.

- A project may be so large that it is easier to organize when broken into separate, more manageable units, which are then linked together as subprojects under a controlling master project. This benefit is similar to outlining, but on a larger scale.

- Several projects may use the same resource pool and need to be linked together to provide for resource leveling.

- A project may be too large to fit into memory at one time. Breaking it into subprojects can overcome the memory limitations.

- Several projects can be printed and viewed simultaneously by consolidating them.

In this chapter, you explore the various ways that are available for working with more than one file at a time: moving from one file to another and working with multiple projects that are linked to each other. You will learn to:

- Move between open projects

- Hide and unhide projects

- Use subprojects for maximum efficiency

- Share a common pool of resources among multiple projects

- Link projects together

Using the Window Command

In keeping with the standard Windows convention, you can have more than one project file open at one time. When there are multiple files open at once, the **W**indow command is used to control and move between the various windows that are open. You can also use the Ctrl+F6 shortcut key combination to move between active project windows. As shown in figure 13.1, a list of open project files appears at the bottom of this menu. A bullet appears in front of the active window. When more than nine files are open at once, there will be an additional More Windows option that, when chosen, displays all project files that are open. Choose the project file that you want to make active. Other files are not closed, they are simply moved to the background. Note that this list of files is different than the one displayed at the bottom of the File menu, which is simply a list of the last four files that were opened; but which are not necessarily open now.

▶ "Creating a Combination View," p. 469

The split command, discussed previously, is used when dividing the screen for a composite view.

Viewing All the File Windows at the Same Time

The **A**rrange All command is useful when you want to view more than one project file in its own distinct window at the same time. Open the projects that you wish to see on the screen at once and then choose this command. Depending on how many project files are open at once, each window will be sized and moved (tiled) so that each file can be seen on-screen simultaneously. The name of each file will be displayed in its title bar, with the active window having the highlighted title bar. This is obviously only practical when a small number of project files are open at once.

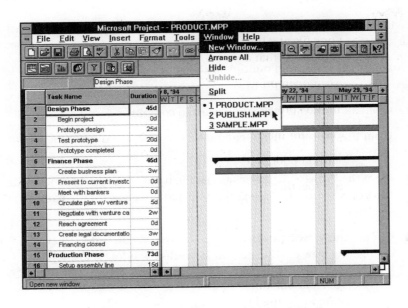

Fig. 13.1
The Window commands with a list at the bottom that you can use to locate other project files that are open.

When you maximize any one window, all other windows will become maximized as well. You won't be able to see them because the active file is covering the full screen, but when you move to any other file it will already be maximized.

Hiding and Unhiding Open Windows

If there are any project files that are open that you don't want included in the Arrange All display, you need only temporarily hide them using the **H**ide Command. To redisplay the hidden window, choose the **W**indow menu once again. If any files have been hidden, an **U**nhide command is now on the menu. When you choose it an Unhide dialog box will be displayed with a list of files that have been hidden. Choose the one you want to unhide and choose OK.

► "Using Subprojects," p.361

Combining Tasks from Different Files into One Window

You can merge multiple project files into one window in order to view or print their tasks or resources in one view. Each task or resource retains its native ID number, so you will see more than one task with ID number 1. You can sort and filter the merged list to display just the tasks from all the projects you want. You can apply any table or view to see the merged view, except the PERT Chart. You can print views or reports from the merged window as though it were a single project file. Although you can change

II

Shared Project Data

individual data fields in the merged window, you cannot delete or add tasks except in the original window.

To combine the tasks from multiple projects in the same view, follow these steps:

1. Open all the projects that you want to combine.

2. From the **W**indow menu, choose **N**ew Window to display the New Window dialog box (see fig. 13.2).

3. From the **P**rojects list, select all the file names you want to include in the new window. Use the Ctrl key to add nonadjacent file names to the selection.

4. Choose the **V**iew field and change the view if you want. You can change the view at will later, once the new window is displayed.

5. To display the new window, choose the OK button.

Fig. 13.2
In the New Window dialog box, choose the projects that you want to combine into one window.

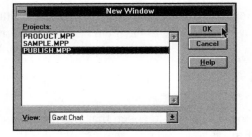

The merged window has the title Multi1, where the 1 is a consecutively assigned number for each time that you create a new window of existing open files. If you asked for another new window after selecting the files that would be in the new window, it would be titled Multi2.

When you open the **W**indow menu, you will see that the Multi1 choice is now a separate entry on the open projects list, while the individual project files have been left open. You can save the merged window for further use with the Save **W**orkspace command on the **F**ile menu. Initially, all the tasks will be grouped by the file from which they come. You can sort or filter the list. If you want to see the project name for each task, add a column to the table to display the Project field, which contains the project name for each task.

You might also use the New Window command when you want to see two window views of the same project. This, in essence, allows you to see more than the standard composite view. For example, you might want to see two views of the same project full-screen and use the Ctrl+F6 key combination to toggle back and forth between them. To do this use the **W**indow **N**ew Window command, but select only one project file. The title bar of the new window will have the project name followed by a colon and a number, indicating the second instance of this project file. You can use either the **W**indow command or Ctrl+F6 to move between them. If these two windows are the only ones open, this key combination has the effect of toggling back and forth between the two different views of the same file.

Any changes that you make and save to one instance of the project file will be saved in the other window as well. There is only one file open here: it's simply displayed in two separate windows, much like the composite views you have already seen.

Using Subprojects

A subproject is a regular project file that contains task and resource assignment details. If the project is part of a larger project, you can include the project file in the *master* project by placing a task in the master project to represent the project file. The representative task has no work assigned to it directly; the task takes its duration, resource assignments, work, and cost data from the subproject file.

Both the Task Information dialog box and the Task Details Form display the Subproject field. Use the Information tool to access the Task Information dialog box, and then choose the Advanced tab.

> **Note**
>
> You can also access the Task Information box using the Shortcut menu. While pointing at the Task Name, press the right mouse button and choose Task Information from the shortcut menu that appears.

There is a distinct advantage to using the Task Information dialog box instead of the Task Details form. In figure 13.3, the Information tool was used while viewing the Task Details form. There, you can see the Su**b**project filed in the top right corner of the Task Details form, while the Subproject box on the Task Information dialog box not only has a field for the subproject name but also has a Browse button. Using this button will allow you to use a dialog box very similar to the **F**ile **O**pen dialog box to find the file. This is convenient when you don't know the exact name or location of the subproject file or you simply don't want to enter the full path and name.

Fig. 13.3

Use the Subproject field to assign a separate project file as a task.

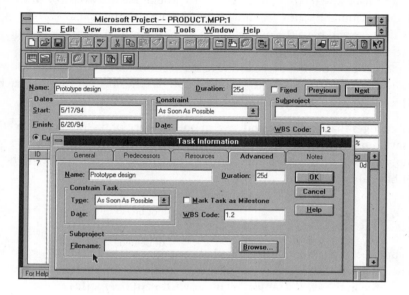

You use the Subproject field to name another file as the source of the task's definition. The only fields defined for the task in the master file are the predecessor and successor relationships. When files are linked in this manner, Microsoft Project schedules the subproject start date based on the predecessors for the representative task. The duration of the subproject is added to the start date to calculate the finish date for the representative task.

When the Su**b**project field for a task contains a project file name, Microsoft Project copies the duration, percent complete, dates, cost, and work from the subproject file into the task. The scheduled Start of the representative task depends on its predecessors. The scheduled Finish for the representative task is calculated by adding the borrowed duration to the scheduled Start date. The scheduled Start of the subproject file is calculated by the master project file.

> **Note**
>
> Both the master project and the subproject must be in memory at the same time for the master project to be able to set the scheduled Start date of the subproject file.

A subproject is scheduled by the master project. The work and cost of the subproject is included in the work and cost of the master project. If you just want to link a project to the scheduled dates of another project, without also counting the work and costs, or if the subproject must be free to schedule a separate start date, you want to link the date fields of the two projects rather than define one field as a subproject of the other. See the upcoming section, "Linking Project Field Values."

Defining a Subproject

To define a subproject, follow these steps:

1. Create both project files.

2. Create a task in the master project to represent the subproject, and link the representative task to its predecessors and successors.

> **Note**
>
> This task's relationship to its predecessor cannot be Finish-to-Finish, or Start-to-Finish. In other words, only the start date for the representative task can be tied to its predecessors. The finish date cannot be tied.

3. Choose the task that you created in step 2. Then choose the Information tool to display the Task Information dialog box, and choose the Advanced tab (refer to fig. 13.3).

4. In the Subproject field, type the name of the subproject file. To be safe, in case you move the master project in the future, also include the full path of the subproject file. If you don't know the name or location of the file, use the Browse button.

   If you type a file name that Microsoft Project cannot find, the Can't Find dialog box appears (which is identical to the Open dialog box), enabling you to search for the file you want to use (see fig. 13.4). Figure 13.4 shows the results if you type **XXXX** as the project file name.

   Select the file that you want to use as the subproject, searching other directories if necessary, and choose the OK button to close the dialog box. If the project was not yet created, you can leave the intended name in this field and create the subproject later. Click the Cancel button to quit searching for a file in the Can't Find dialog box, and leave the unknown definition in place.

Fig. 13.4
Use this familiar
dialog box to
search for the
subproject file
name.

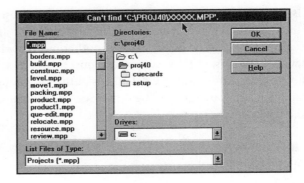

If this dialog box is canceled, the warning dialog box in figure 13.5 is
displayed. If you continue, the subproject link will not be made.

Fig. 13.5
The Unknown
Subproject
warning appears
when you cancel
the Can't Find
dialog box.

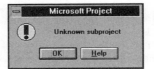

5. To complete the definition of the subproject, choose the OK button in
   the Task Information dialog box, the Task Details form, or the warning
   dialog box. If the warning dialog box was displayed, the link will not be
   made.

You can create subprojects of subprojects; that is, you can create a project
structure with one or more levels of subprojects. Microsoft Project checks to
be sure that no circular references exist within the levels. All the project files
must be open in memory for calculated dates among them to be correct.

Breaking a Large Project into Subprojects

You can create subprojects by moving tasks from the master project into new
project files, and then by defining the new files as subprojects by linking
them to representative tasks. Some preparation is involved in making the
move as easy and successful as possible.

If you move one or more tasks linked to tasks that will remain behind, you
will lose the links and have to redefine them later. It is easier to create the
new representative task first and then move all the task links to the representative task before you make the move.

The first task among those that are to be moved should be at the first or highest level of the outline. If you are moving a group of subordinate tasks, insert a copy of their summary task above the actual summary task. The copy of the summary task will be left behind as the representative task. Transfer all predecessor and successor links to the representative task. Then promote the tasks you are going to move so that the real summary task is a first-level task in the outline.

To move tasks to a subproject file, take these steps:

1. Select the task IDs of the tasks that you plan to move. This ensures that all fields will be selected and that all relevant data will be copied.

2. From the **E**dit menu, choose **C**opy (or press Ctrl+C) to copy the task data to the clipboard.

3. From the **F**ile menu, choose **N**ew to create a new project file. If the Prompt for Summary **I**nfo for New Projects check box has been marked on the General tab of the Tools Options dialog box, you will be prompted to enter general information about the project.

   ◀ "Creating a New File," p. 33.

4. With the Name field of the first task selected in the new file, choose **P**aste from the **E**dit menu. The task data is copied. All tasks are copied at the same outline level they occupied in the source file.

   > **Note**
   >
   > If subordinate tasks exist, there must be at least one summary task at each higher level, all the way up to the first level. Microsoft Project automatically promotes tasks, as needed, in order to create at least one summary task at the higher levels, which is why you promoted the tasks ahead of time in the preparation steps.

5. Save the file under the new name by choosing Save **A**s from the **F**ile menu. Fill in the dialog box to save the file under a new name, and choose the OK button to complete the renaming of the file.

6. Return to the original file by choosing the file name from the list at the bottom of the **W**indow menu. Alternatively, press **Ctrl+F6** until the project document reappears.

7. Select the representative task and define the subproject as described in the preceding section.

II

Shared Project Data

> **Note**
>
> You can test your link by double-clicking on the sub-project task and the sub-project file should appear in the project file window. To return to the original file use the Window menu as described earlier or press Ctrl+F6.

Changing Subproject Links

You can change the name of the subproject that is assigned to a task by changing or erasing the name in the Subproject field on the Task Information dialog box or the Task Details Form. If the new file name exists, it will be used as the subproject file instead of the one just replaced. If the file name is simply deleted, the link between the two projects is severed.

Identifying Tasks with Subprojects

One of the fields in the task database is the Subproject File field (the field on the task form). You can design a table to display that field and thereby identify the tasks. Figure 13.6 shows the Subproject File field substituted for the Resources field.

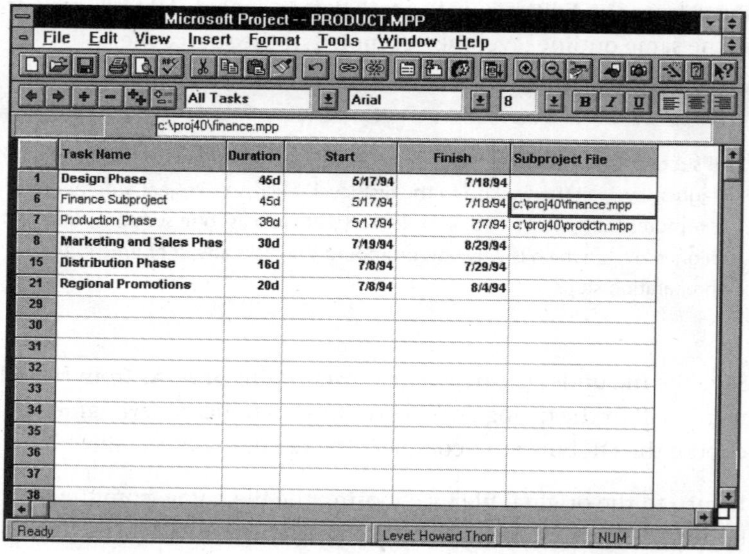

Fig. 13.6
Create a table with a subproject field to see which tasks have subprojects.

	Task Name	Duration	Start	Finish	Subproject File
1	Design Phase	45d	5/17/94	7/18/94	
6	Finance Subproject	45d	5/17/94	7/18/94	c:\proj40\finance.mpp
7	Production Phase	38d	5/17/94	7/7/94	c:\proj40\prodctn.mpp
8	Marketing and Sales Phas	30d	7/19/94	8/29/94	
15	Distribution Phase	16d	7/8/94	7/29/94	
21	Regional Promotions	20d	7/8/94	8/4/94	

▶ "Using and Creating Tables," p. 472.

You can design a filter to select the tasks that have an entry in the Subproject File field. The filter definition condition will be that the field *not equal* a blank value. Figure 13.7 illustrates the filter definition.

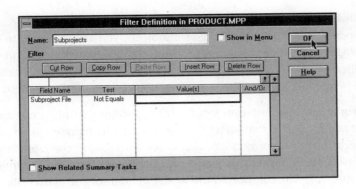

Fig. 13.7
A subproject filter
definition.

▶ "Creating
Custom
Filters,"
p. 484.

When the filter is applied, the list of tasks shows only tasks with subprojects
(see fig. 13.8).

Fig. 13.8
The Task Sheet,
filtered for
subproject tasks.

II

Shared Project Data

	Task Name	Duration	Start	Finish	Subproject File
6	Finance Subproject	45d	5/17/94	7/18/94	c:\proj40\finance.mpp
7	Production Phase	38d	5/17/94	7/7/94	c:\proj40\prodctn.mpp
29					
30					
31					
32					
33					
34					
35					
36					
37					
38					
39					
40					
41					
42					

Working with Subprojects

If you work with a master project and the project's subproject files are open
in memory at the same time, Microsoft Project updates all links between
these files as you work. Changes in the start date of the representative task in
the master project force changes in the start date of a subproject. Changes in
the tasks of a subproject are summarized in the master project. You also can
open and work with a master project without opening the project's subprojects, and you can open and work with a subproject without opening the
master project.

Using Only the Master Project

If you open a project that has linked subprojects, you are prompted to decide whether you want Microsoft Project to read the summary information that the application needs from the subproject files in order to be accurate. If no changes were made in the subproject files, you can ignore this request.

If you work with the master project file while a subproject file is not open, and you make changes that affect the start date of the representative task and subproject, the master project calculates the finish date of the representative task by using the duration that was copied previously from the subproject and by applying that duration to the work calendar for the master file. If the master project and the subproject use different calendars, the results can be inaccurate.

Suppose that a delay is introduced in the start of the subproject because of a delay in the predecessor of the representative task in the master project file. If the resources used in the subproject go on vacation during the new scheduled work time, the results may be inaccurate.

To get truly accurate results, you should load the master file and subproject file at the same time before making any crucial decisions based on the combined schedule. You can open a subproject file by double-clicking its representative task in the Gantt Chart, PERT Chart, or Task Sheet. Select the task row on a table or the task node on the PERT Chart. The subproject file opens automatically and becomes the active file.

Using Only a Subproject File

If you open a file used as a subproject by another project file, you will not be asked to update the links between them, because the linking definition is stored in the master project file. If the start date of the representative task has changed, the subproject file cannot be made aware of that unless both the master file and the subproject file are open in memory at the same time.

Opening Subproject Files from the Master File

You can double-click any task that has a subproject defined for it, and the subproject file is opened automatically. If you want to have all subprojects opened automatically when you open the master project, save them as a Workspace (covered later in this chapter).

Linking Project Field Values

If a task in the project you are defining has a predecessor task or event defined in another project file, you can paste a link between the dates of the task in the other file and the dates of the task you are defining. If the entire project in the other file needs to be represented (the other file's start and finish are important to the project you are defining), you can name the other project as a subproject. That action, however, would cause the subproject file's start date to be determined by the master project, and all the work and costs of the subproject would be summed in the work and costs of the master project.

If you want to include the start and finish dates of another project without declaring that project to be a subproject, you can create a *dummy* task in the file you are defining; the task's only purpose is to represent the other project's dates. In this case, the first task in the source project must be a summary task that summarizes the entire project.

To link both of the date fields of one project to those of another, follow these steps:

1. Create both projects, being sure that the first task in the source project is a summary task that summarizes the entire project.

2. Select the entire task by clicking the ID field of the summary task in the source project.

3. Choose **C**opy from the **E**dit menu, press Ctrl+C, or click the Copy tool on the Standard toolbar.

4. Select the entire row of the representative task in the target project file.

5. From the **E**dit menu, choose Paste Special. Figure 13.9 shows the Paste Special dialog box that will be displayed.

6. Choose the Paste Link radio button, and then choose Text Data from the **A**s: list. Select OK. The task in the target file will display small triangles to indicate the link. Any changes in the source file date fields will be reflected in the target file's schedule.

▶ "Exchanging Data with Other Applications," p. 379

Caution

Any changes made in the project start date of the target file will not be reflected in the Source file. Therefore, you may get error messages about tasks in the source project file starting before the target project. You will need to manually make adjustments in the Source file.

Fig. 13.9
The Paste Special dialog box sets up a link to another project.

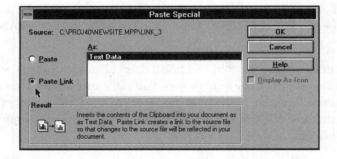

Note

Do *not* fill in the Su**b**project field on the Task Edit Form if you have linked the dates.

Consolidating Projects

Occasionally, you may wish to view and/or print several related projects at once in one window. The Consolidate Projects command, available on the **T**ools Multiple **P**rojects menu, offers you a way to bring several projects together into one window. You can also use the Consolidate Projects tool on the Workgroup toolbar. The maximum number of project files that can be consolidated is 80, limited of course by available memory and system resources.

▶ "Formatting Views," p. 497

▶ "Printing Views and Reports," p. 443

The project files do not need to be open already as with the **W**indow **N**ew Window command. You can choose whether to maintain a link with the individual source files. If you choose to maintain a link, changes in task's data will be reflected in the original source file. Regardless of your choice, any changes made to the formatting of the resulting Multi file will not be reflected in the source files. The advantage of this is that you can make formatting changes to the consolidated project for purposes of printing views and reports, without having those changes reflected in the underlying source files.

To consolidate several projects into one window:

1. Choose **T**ools Multiple **P**rojects **C**onsolidate Projects. The Consolidate Projects dialog box is displayed (see fig. 13.10).

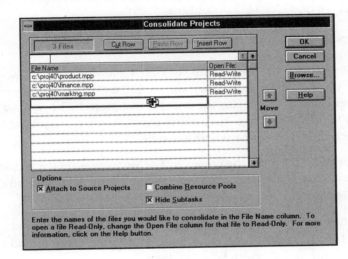

Fig. 13.10
The Consolidate Projects dialog box allows you to combine several projects into one for viewing and printing.

2. Either type the project file names in the **F**ile Name section of the dialog box or choose the **B**rowse button to select from a list. You can choose multiple files in the Browse dialog by pressing the Ctrl key while selecting files.

   Files will originally be listed in the order of their appearance in the Consolidate Projects dialog box. Use the Move button to the right of the File list to rearrange them.

3. By default, files will be opened as Read-Write, but you can change that to read-only if you prefer to protect the original source files. To do this, select the Read-Write column for the appropriate file and then use the entry list arrow to choose the Read-Only option or press F2 to enter Edit mode and then type Read-Only.

4. If you want a link to be retained between the new Multi window and the original source file, leave the **A**ttach to Source Projects check box marked (the default).

5. Mark the check box for Combine **R**esource Pools if you want to track the resources for all the independent projects in this one consolidated project. This option will not be available if you are not maintaining a link to the Source projects as determined by the Attach to Source **P**rojects check box.

6. The Hide **S**ubtasks check box controls whether the individual projects tasks will initially be shown or hidden. You can always hide or show them after consolidating the projects.

7. Choose OK when you are finished making your choices.

The resulting window will have a title of Multi1 and will contain a project summary task for each project which was consolidated. Double-click on the project summary task to display the tasks for that project. The summary task will open to display subtasks, but will not physically open the project file from which those tasks came as with the subproject feature.

If you provided a name for the project in **F**ile **S**ummary Info the project summary task will use that name, otherwise the full project file name and extension will be used.

Because the individual tasks are coming from several different projects, you will have tasks with the same ID number. Use the table feature to add a field or project name to distinguish between them.

After you have consolidated several project files you may wish to add or delete projects to the consolidated window. Simply choose the **T**ools Multiple **P**rojects **C**onsolidate Projects command again. If there is already a consolidated project window open, you will be prompted for whether you want to create a new one or edit the existing one.

You can save the Multi project window as a separate file if you wish. It will initially have the name MULTI# where # is a sequential number assigned automatically. This name can be changed to something more descriptive. You cannot, however, enter Summary Information under the **F**ile menu for this file. All summary information is taken from the individual source files.

Sharing Resources among Projects

If the resources that you assign to work on tasks in one project are also committed to work on other projects, you may want to have Microsoft Project recognize the common resource pool and keep track of the assignments of the resources in all the projects. You do this by designating one of the project files as the *owner* of the common resource pool and instructing the other project files to use the resources defined in the *owner* file.

If projects share the same list of resources, you can open all the projects at the same time and view the allocation of resources across the projects. Microsoft Project will warn you when a resource is overallocated because of conflicting assignments in different projects, and you can use the leveling command to resolve the resource overallocation by delaying tasks in different projects.

Creating the Resource Pool

Any file can be the one that contains the resource pool definitions. You can create a project file that has no tasks defined in it but that defines all your resources. This file can be used to define a common resource pool that is shared by other projects. This file also can be used as a read-only template for starting new project files. When you start a new project, just open the template file and begin defining the project. If the template is saved with a Write Reserved Password (see Chapter 2, "Learning the Basics of Microsoft Project,"), you must open the file as a read-only file, *unless* you know the password. When you attempt to save the new project, you see the Save **As** dialog box to change the name under which the file is saved.

Using the Resource Pool

With the **T**ools Multiple Projects Share Resources command, you can define any project file to use the resources of another project file. If both files have resources defined in them at the time the link is established, the resource pool will be enlarged to include all resources defined in both files. If the same resource is defined in both files and there is a difference in the definition between the two files, you must tell Microsoft Project which file takes precedence in settling definition conflicts. The dialog box that you will use provides a check box for this purpose.

While both files are in memory, you can look at the Resource Sheet in either file to see the complete list of resources, and you can change the resource definitions in either file. When you close the files, each includes a copy of the entire resource pool. In this way, you can open the *pool user* file independently, if needed, to modify and manage that project file.

To define a project file so that this file can use the resources of another file, follow these steps:

1. Open both project files: the one containing the resource pool and the one that is to share that pool. Make sure that the active project is the one that is to use the other project's resources.

2. From the **T**ools menu, choose Multiple Projects and then Share Resources to display the Share Resources dialog box (see fig. 13.11). Choose the **U**se Resources radio button and use the entry list arrow for a list of currently open files from which you can choose the file name.

Fig. 13.11
Use the Share Resources dialog box to use a resource pool from another project file.

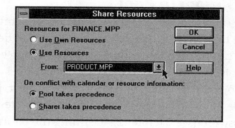

3. Mark the radio button for **P**ool Takes Precedence on Conflict if you want conflicting definitions to be settled by the entry in the file that contains the resource pool. Mark the **S**harer takes precedence radio button if you want resource definition conflicts to be settled by the entry in the file that uses the resource pool.

4. Choose the OK button to complete the link.

When you open a file that uses another project's resource pool, you are advised by a dialog box that its resource pool is not in memory and that you can elect to have the file with the resource pool opened for you (see fig. 13.12). However, you can work on the file even if you do not have the resource pool project open, because a copy of the pool is saved with each file that uses the common resource pool.

Fig. 13.12
Microsoft Project offers to open the file containing the resources.

After a project is defined to use another project's resource pool, changes you make to the resource pool while both files are open are recorded directly into the shared pool and are shared by both files immediately. If you work with the dependent file alone, however, and you make changes in the copy of the resource pool, the changes may not be saved when both files are opened, and the conflicting resource definitions become apparent. If you merely add new resources with different names, the resources are added to the resource pool when both files are open together the next time.

If you change the definition of the resource (for example, the pay rate, maximum units, or working days on the resource calendar), the changes may be lost when both files are loaded in memory together the next time. If you marked the **P**ool Takes Precedence check box in the Resource Sharing dialog box, the changes are lost; if you left the check box unmarked, the changes are recorded in the resource pool. You can mark and unmark this check box at will. If you enter a resource definition change in the sharing file when only this file is opened, and you want to have the change copied to the resource pool, mark the check box before opening the file with the resource pool.

Saving Multiple Files in a Workspace

If you want to open all the files that share the same resource pool at the same time, you can save the workspace in addition to saving the individual files. To save the workspace, follow these steps:

1. From the **F**ile menu, choose Save **W**orkspace.

2. If any files have unsaved changes, you are prompted to save the individual files. In the dialog box that appears, choose the **Y**es button.

3. The Save Workspace as dialog box is displayed. Select the directory and name for the workspace (see fig. 13.13). Workspace files have the extension .MPW. Choose the directory and name the workspace file. The name of the workspace file will initially be "resume" (so that you can resume later with the same files), but you can change it.

4. Choose the OK button to complete the operation.

To open all the files, select **F**ile and choose **O**pen. Select the workspace file and select the OK button.

Discontinuing Resource Sharing

You can discontinue the sharing of resources at any time. Simply open the file that uses another file's resources, open the Resource Sharing dialog box, and choose the Use **O**wn Resources button. The resources in the resource pool will no longer be available to the file. However, any resources that were assigned to tasks in the file will be copied into the file's resource list and will be saved with the file.

Fig. 13.13
Saving a workspace saves time loading multiple files that are used together.

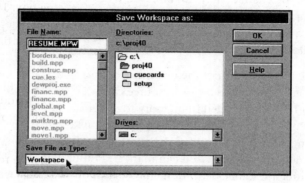

To discontinue a project file's dependence on another file's resource pool, perform the following steps:

1. Open both the file that contains the resource pool and the file that is to become independent (and use its own resources).

2. Make the file that is to use its own resources the active file window.

3. From the **T**ools menu, choose Multiple **P**rojects and then **S**hare Resources.

4. Choose the Use **O**wn Resources radio button in the Share Resources dialog box.

5. Choose the OK button to execute the new definition.

Note

If you were to have the file that contained the resources active when you chose the Tools, Multiple Projects menu option, you would see a different dialog box (see fig. 13.14). In this one, you would see a list of files that are linked to yours, including the one that is sharing resources. After selecting it, you could then choose the Break Link button and then choose OK.

Identifying Resource Pool Links

The resource-sharing connection is recorded in the file that contains the resource pool (it is aware of the other files that share its resource pool) and in the file that uses the resource pool. However, the existence of the link is monitored in different places in the two files.

To verify that a project file uses the resources of another project file, you must view the Resource Sharing dialog box. From the **T**ools menu, select Multiple **P**rojects and then **S**hare Resources to see the dialog box. The radio button for Use **O**wn Resources will be selected if it is an independent file, or if the project uses resources from another file and the name of that file appears in the **F**rom box.

To determine whether a project file's resources are used by other project files, you also use the **T**ools Multiple **P**rojects **S**hare Resources command. When the active file is one whose resources are being used by another project, you will see a different dialog box when using this command.

To view the resource sharing links between the file that owns the resource pool and other files, follow these steps:

1. From the **T**ools menu, choose Multiple **P**rojects and then **S**hare Resources. The Share Resources dialog box is displayed (see fig. 13.14).

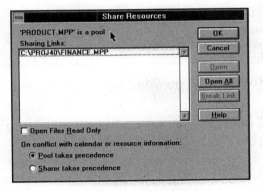

Fig. 13.14
Use the Share Resources dialog box to determine which files are using the resource pool in the current file.

2. You may choose to open one or all of the project files that shares resources with the owner by selecting the file from the Sharing **L**inks list and then choosing either the **O**pen button or the Open **A**ll button.

3. You can choose to **B**reak the Link that currently exists between these project files. This is essentially the same as choosing Use **O**wn Resources in the project file that was using the owner project file's resources.

4. The precedence radio buttons at the bottom of this dialog box exert the same control as described previously in the section on Use Resource Pool.

5. Choose OK to save changes.

Troubleshooting

When I use the Window New Window command, I can't tell which task is from which file, especially if I have sorted the tasks by their start date.

Modify the table that you are using to also display the project file name, most likely just before the ID number for the task. This way you can see the file name and the task ID together to distinguish between files.

I want to be able to link project files together, but I don't want to have the work and cost fields automatically updated. I want to track those changes manually.

Use the Link fields option instead of the Subproject feature. Copy the start and finish dates in one file and then use the Paste Special option instead of just Paste.

When I double-click on a task, I normally get the Task Information dialog box, but when I double-click on a sub-project task I am taken to that file. How do I see the Task Information dialog for a sub-project task?

Access the shortcut menu by pressing the right mouse button which points at the sub-project task. Choose Task Information from the shortcut menu.

When I use the consolidation feature to see several project files at once, I only see the project file name. How can I have something more descriptive?

In the original project files (not the consolidated one), access the File Summary Info dialog box, choose the Document tab, and enter a title.

From Here...

This chapter has dealt with the important issues associated with working with than more than one project file. You learned about moving from one window to another, displaying multiple project files in one window, and linking multiple project files for a variety of reasons. To learn how to link project data with other applications or with other users on a network, refer to the following chapters:

- Chapter 14, "Exchanging Data with Other Applications."

- Chapter 15, "Using Microsoft Project in Workgroups."

Exchanging Data with Other Applications

In this chapter, you learn to

- Import and export data files in different file formats.

- Copy selected data between Microsoft Project and other applications.

- Create dynamic data links between Microsoft Project and other application files.

- Link data between Microsoft Project and other applications as objects.

- Embed external data as objects in Microsoft Project and embed project data objects in other applications.

- Identify the tasks or resources that have external links or objects attached to them.

This chapter is devoted to the methods you can use to exchange data between a Microsoft Project data file and other files, whether the files are project files or documents from other applications. You can transfer data between Microsoft Project and other applications in whole or in part, and as static copies or as linked copies.

- You can copy all essential project information (including calendars and resource assignment details) between Microsoft Project and other project management programs, including earlier versions of Microsoft Project and Microsoft Project for the Macintosh.

■ You can copy all essential project information (including calendars and resource assignment details) to an ODBC database format, in which the details of hundreds of projects can be aggregated for querying and reporting.

■ You can transfer task or resource data between Microsoft Project and other applications in the native format of the other applications. Microsoft Project reads and writes in the native formats of products such as Microsoft Excel, Lotus 1-2-3, Microsoft FoxPro, and Borland's dBASE.

■ You also can save Microsoft Project files in ASCII text formats so that you can transfer the information to other project management products, such as Primavera and Artemis.

■ Using the Windows Clipboard, you can copy selected data values directly from other applications to fields of a project file or from a project file to other applications.

■ You can establish links between selected field values in Microsoft Project and another application that are automatically updated when the data in the other application changes. Microsoft Project also can reciprocate by supplying linked data to other applications.

For example, you can keep the hourly rates of resources in an Excel spreadsheet, and link copies of these rates to the resource pool of a project file. All changes in the Excel document then are automatically reflected by updated values in the Microsoft Project file.

■ You can embed visual *objects*, created and maintained by other applications (such as graphs from Excel, slides generated by PowerPoint, logos created in Microsoft Paintbrush, or memos from Microsoft Word). These objects are visible in selected Microsoft Project views and reports and can be printed along with the data from a project.

■ You also can embed objects created by Microsoft Project into other applications, such as Gantt Charts or Resource Graphs. The possibilities for data exchange are rich indeed.

Importing and Exporting Data Files

You can import and export entire projects, using the **F**ile **O**pen and **F**ile Save **A**s commands to read and write the project data in formats other than the .MPP format that is native to Microsoft Project.

◀ "Learning the Basics of Microsoft Project," p. 27

Using the MPX File Format

Although most users probably think about exchanging project data with a spreadsheet or database, the most comprehensive exchange of data between Microsoft Project and other products is through the MPX (Microsoft Project Exchange) format, which is a standardized protocol for exchanging project data between project management software applications. This protocol allows the exchange of project task definitions, resource definitions, resource assignments, work and cost data, calendars, and other project information. Microsoft Project can open or save one of these files as simply as it can open or save a regular Microsoft Project data file.

Save a Microsoft Project 4 project in the MPX 3.0 format so that it can be read by Microsoft Project 3.0. Save it in the MPX 1.0 format so that it can be read by Microsoft Project 1.0 for Windows or Microsoft Project for the Macintosh. These earlier formats will not contain new features found in Microsoft Project 4 (like recurring tasks and the fields for workgroup communication). Save a Microsoft Project 4 file in the MPX 4 format to save all features of release 4 project files for programs that can read the new format.

> **Caution**
>
> If you are exporting or importing in the MPX format, Microsoft Project uses the Export table. This table is already defined on the Define Tables menu and is designed to match the standard order of fields honored by the participating project management software vendors. Do not redefine the Export table. If you make any changes to this table, the MPX exchanges will fail. You can, of course, redefine a copy of the Export table.

To save a project file in the MPX format, follow these steps:

1. Use the **F**ile Save **A**s command.

2. Change the selection in the Dri**v**es, **D**irectories, and File **N**ame text box if appropriate.

3. Display the entry list for the Save File as **T**ype text box and select MPX

II

Shared Project Data

4. Choose the OK button to execute the command.

To open a file into Microsoft Project that was saved in the MPX format, simply use the **F**ile **O**pen command as usual. All MPX files are included in the file list along with the rest of the "*.MP*" files.

Using the Microsoft MDB Format to Store Project Data

The new Save to Database command gives Microsoft Project 4 the capability to store all of its project data in a Microsoft Access database (MDB format), which is, Because of Microsoft's open database connectivity (ODBC), accessible not only to Microsoft Access but also to other database products through backends like SQL Server, Oracle, or Btrieve. In this way you can place the details of hundreds of projects in one database for enterprise-wide analysis and reporting. You also can open a copy of a project that is stored in the database with the Open from Database command to place its details into a Microsoft Project file for processing by Microsoft Project.

When you save a project with the Save to Database command, a hidden GLOBAL macro creates an Access database with these four tables:

- ■ Projects—Lists all projects contained in the database along with summary information for each project.

- ■ Tasks—Lists all tasks from all projects in the database along with most of the task fields from each project.

- ■ Resources—Lists all resources from all projects in the database along with most of the resource fields from each project.

- ■ Resource Assignments—Lists all resource assignments for all resources from all projects in the database along with most of the resource assignment fields from each project.

You can add other projects to this database, thereby creating a repository of project information for analysis.

Saving Projects to a Database

The individual projects in the database are distinguished by their project title. Although this is an optional field on the Summary Info dialog box, it is not optional if you are saving the project to a database. If the title has not been entered, you are prompted for it when you attempt to save to a database.

To save a project file to a database, follow these steps:

1. Open the project file into Microsoft Project.

2. Open the **T**ools menu and choose **W**orkgroups; then choose the S**a**ve to Database command (or use the Save to Database button on the Workgroups toolbar).

   If you have not supplied a title for the project you see a dialog box that requests the title (see fig. 14.1). The project file name is supplied as the title by default, but you should replace it with a more descriptive title to make identification in the database easier.

Fig. 14.1
If you have not supplied a project title, you must do so before you can save the project in a database format.

3. In the Save to Database dialog box, you must identify the database file that the project will be saved in (see fig. 14.2). Choose one of the Dri**v**es and **D**irectories to locate the database.

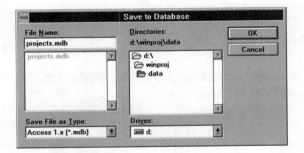

Fig. 14.2
Define the name and location of the database file.

4. Supply a File **N**ame for a new database or select an existing database File Name to append this project to it.

5. Choose the file format from the Save File as **T**ype list. Choose either Access 1.x or Access 2.x format.

6. Click OK to begin saving to the database files.

II

Shared Project Data

When the project has been saved, you see an information box announcing that the project was successfully saved (see fig. 14.3).

Fig. 14.3
The successful
transfer of the pro-
ject to the database
is confirmed with
an information
dialog box.

> **Note**
>
> You should generally avoid using the file name of the project you are saving as the name for the database. Remember that the database will probably hold many projects. The name of the project you are saving will be just one field in a table in the new database. You should generally choose a database name that is appropriate for many projects.

Opening a Project from a Database

Once a project has been saved to a database, it can be loaded into a project window with the Open from Database command. You also can select several projects from the database to be merged into one window.

To open the data for a project from an Access database, follow these steps:

1. Choose the **T**ools **W**orkgroups **O**pen from Database command (or use the Open from Database button on the Workgroups toolbar). The Open from Database dialog box appears (see fig. 14.4).

Fig. 14.4
You must first
locate the database
that contains the
project(s) you
want to load.

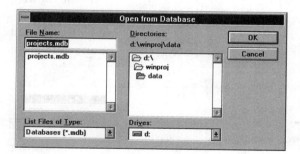

2. Change the selection in the Dri**v**es and **D**irectories boxes if necessary.

3. Select the database name that contains the project. The dialog box changes to display a list of the projects that are contained in the database you selected (see fig. 14.5).

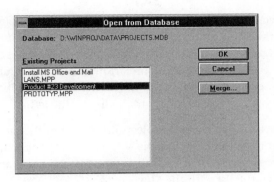

Fig. 14.5
Choose the title of
the project you
want to open.

4. Select the title for the project that you want to copy into Microsoft
   Project from the list of **E**xisting Projects. If you want to merge multiple
   projects from the database, see the instructions that follow this set of
   steps.

5. Click OK to begin importing the data.

A new project file is created with a temporary file name that you can keep or
replace.

Merging Projects from a Database

If you want to merge several projects from the database into one window,
follow these steps:

1. Choose the **T**ools **W**orkgroups **O**pen from Database command and
   locate the database file as in steps 1-3 in the previous steps.

2. When the list of **E**xisting Projects appears, choose the **M**erge button to
   select projects to be merged from the available list (see fig. 14.6). The
   new Open from Database dialog box shows a list of **A**vailable Projects
   and a list of **S**elected Projects, separated by arrows to move project
   names from one list to the other.

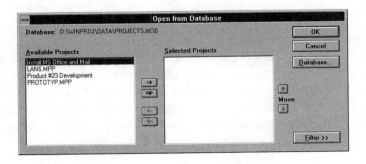

Fig. 14.6
Move projects
from the Available
Projects list to the
Selected Projects
list to consolidate
them into one
window.

II

Shared Project Data

3. Select each project name you want to use in the **A**vailable projects list on the left and click the top arrow between the lists to move it to the **S**elected Projects list. Click the second arrow to move all the projects to the **S**elected Projects list. The third arrow moves individual projects from the **S**elected Projects list to the **A**vailable Projects list, and the fourth arrow moves all projects to the list on the left.

4. The projects in the **S**elected Projects list appear in the merged project in ther order they are listed. Use the Move arrows to the right of the **S**elected Projects list to rearrange the order. Select a name and move it up or down on the list with the Move arrows.

5. You can choose the **D**atabase button to display different lists of **A**vailable Projects, thereby building a list of **S**elected Projects that comes from different databases.

6. If you want help selecting projects by their Author, Manager, Company, or Keywords, choose the **F**ilter button to limit the projects that are included in the **A**vailable Projects list to those that meet specific criteria (see fig. 14.7).

Fig. 14.7
Use the filters to shorten the list of Available Projects to those that meet a specific criteria.

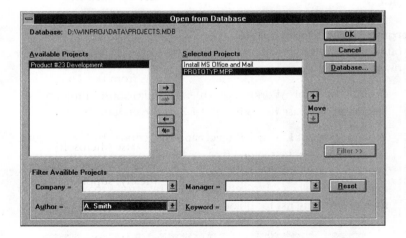

■ To restrict the list of **A**vailable Projects to those for a specific Company, choose the entry-list arrow to the right of the Company field in the Filter Available Projects area and select the Company you want to use. The names in the **A**vailable Projects list are immediately restricted to those for that company. Select and move projects for that company to the **S**elected Projects list as described above.

■ If you want to choose projects by their author, choose the entry-list arrow for the A**u**thor box and select the author's name. This limits the **A**vailable List of projects to those by the chosen author. You can then select and move project names to the **S**elected projects list.

■ Use the entry-list arrow to the right of the Manager box to filter the list of available projects to those having a specific manager.

■ Use the entry-list arrow to the right of the **K**eyword box to choose projects by the entries in their keyword fields.

You can use these criteria in combination to further restrict the list of Available Projects. For example, you could select entries in both the Manager and Keyword boxes to display only those projects having both the specified Manager and Keywords.

Use the **R**eset button to clear all entries in the Filter Available Projects area, thus restoring a complete list in the **A**vailable Projects box.

7. When the list of **S**elected Projects is satisfactory, click OK to begin merging the projects into one window, in the order they are listed in the **S**elected Projects box.

Merging projects from a database produces a single file with the same result as that achieved by choosing **C**onsolidate Projects from the **T**ools Multiple **P**rojects command and then clearing the **A**ttach to Source Projects checkbox.

◄ "Working with Multiple Projects," p. 357

Using the Project Database for Queries

This section does not attempt to teach you how to use Microsoft Access. Instead, the purpose is to illustrate how the project database can be used to answer questions about multiple projects. Specifically, suppose you want to know all of the projects and tasks that Bill Kirk has worked on, including how many hours he spent on each task.

Figure 14.8 shows the list of tables that are contained in the Projects Database that was created in the preceding examples. The list contains four tables: Project, Resource Assignments, Resources, and Tasks.

II

Shared Project Data

Fig. 14.8
The Tables View in Microsoft Access shows the four related tables that are contained in the PROJECTS database.

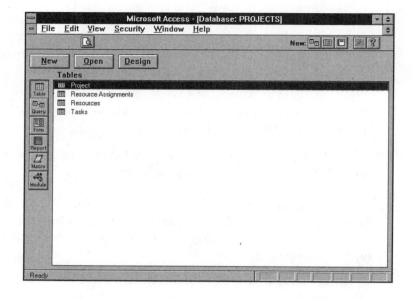

These tables are linked by fields they have in common that contain codes for projects, tasks, and resources. The Query Design that is illustrated in figure 14.9 shows field lists for each of the four tables at the top, with lines connecting the fields that the tables have in common.

Fig. 14.9
The Query Design View in Microsoft Access shows the fields in the four tables, with links indicated by connecting lines.

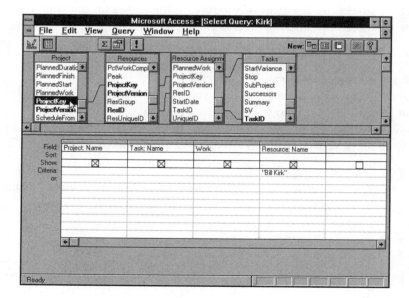

- ProjectKey is a field that contains codes that identify each of the projects. The ProjectKey field appears in all of the tables (although ii is scrolled out of sight in the Tasks table in figure 14.9).

- The ResID (Resource ID) field appears in both the Resources table and the Resource Assignment table and provides a link between the task assignment and the name of the resource.

- The Task ID field appears in both the Tasks table and the Resource Assignment table and provides a link between the task assignment and the name of the task.

The bottom of the Query Design form is used to select the columns that appear in Datasheet View and to express criteria for selecting records to appear in the datasheet. In figure 14.9, "Bill Kirk" is used to select records based on the Resource Name.

Figure 14.10 shows the Datasheet View that results from the query in figure 14.9. Note that tasks from three different Project Names are represented with their Work amounts. The Resource Name column is included just to prove that the records are really those for Bill Kirk. The Work amounts could also be totaled by project or for all projects together.

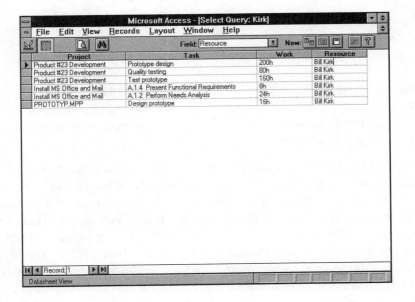

Fig. 14.10
The query result from figure 14.9.

Using the Native Format of Other Applications

You can both export and import project data directly from some applications. You also can import and export ASCII text files and can therefore indirectly exchange data with still more applications. The direct import and export exchange of Microsoft Project data with other applications is more limited than the MPX format method. You can exchange any data that you can display in a task or resource table in a sheet view. You cannot, however, specifically export or import resource assignment data, or their work or cost values.

Both the File Open and the File Save As dialog boxes offer the options of working with other file formats. You can open a file originally created and saved in another application's native format while you are in Microsoft Project. The data translates to Microsoft Project format during the import process. You can save the data from a project file in the native format of another application. Microsoft Project can read and write Excel and Lotus 1-2-3 spreadsheet data as well as dBASE III and IV data.

The following list shows the application formats (and their file name extensions) that Microsoft Project supports for file opening and saving:

Microsoft Excel spreadsheets	XLS
Lotus 1-2-3 spreadsheets	WKS, WK1, WK3
dBASE III or IV	DBF
Microsoft FoxPro	DBF

Importing Data from Other Applications

When you import data to Microsoft Project, it is essential that there be a Microsoft Project table with columns defined in the same order as the columns of the incoming data.

Figure 14.11 shows an Excel spreadsheet named NEWPROD.XLS that contains the same task names as the PRODUCT project file used throughout this book. Only three columns of data exist in this spreadsheet: the Task (Name), the Start (Scheduled Start Date), and the Days (the Duration). If you plan to open this data in Microsoft Project as a project file, a Microsoft Project table must be defined with columns that match the column order of the incoming data. In this example, no Microsoft Project predefined table exists that starts with the task Name, Scheduled Start, and Duration fields. All predefined tables start with the task ID. You would need to either create a new table definition in Microsoft Project or edit the Excel spreadsheet to put the columns in an order that matches one of the Microsoft Project tables.

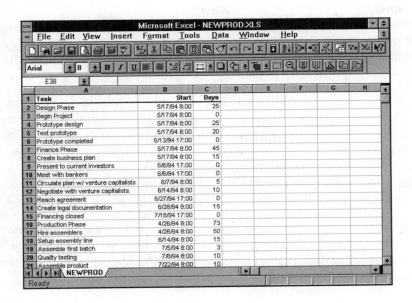

Fig. 14.11
A task list in an Excel workbook can be imported into Microsoft Project to start a new project.

The first row of the spreadsheet is imported as a task. Therefore, you should clear all column headings from the spreadsheet data. Figure 14.12 shows the error message that you see if you try to open the NEWPROD.XLS spreadsheet file with the column headings still in the spreadsheet. The Task Entry view is active in the top pane, and the first three columns are ID, Name, and Duration. The error message indicates that Microsoft Project has found incompatible data in Row 1 (task 1) Column 3 (Duration). The text value in row 1, column 3 (Days) is not a number value, as expected for the Duration field.

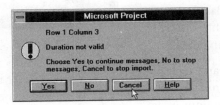

Fig. 14.12
Microsoft Project warns you if the data type for incoming data does not match the data type for the column in the active view.

If you proceed with this import example, the row that presents the problem will be imported with default values substituted for the inappropriate data types. Note that problems with data compatibility may be hard to detect once the data is imported into Microsoft Project.

Tip
Prepare the data
you are importing
before you start
the import pro-
cess. Eliminate
column headings
and any data types
that are not con-
sistent within the
columns of data.

▶ "Using and
Creating
Views," p. 463

When you receive this kind of data error message, you can continue importing the file by choosing either the **Y**es or the **N**o button—but without warning messages if you choose **N**o—or you can discontinue importing the data
by choosing Cancel.

An additional problem with the imported file in this illustration is the fact
that the view on the screen has the task ID in the first column, the task Name
in the second column, and the Duration in the third column. If you continue
to load this file as shown, the project file will attempt to place all the Excel
file Task names in the project ID column (the names are lost because the
default ID numbers prevail), and the dates from the second column of the
Excel workbook will be placed in the task Name field of the project file.

To make importing the NEWPROD.XLS spreadsheet accurate, you must define a new Microsoft Project table that has columns of the correct type to
receive the Excel data. Figure 14.13 shows the Table Definition that provides
a match for the incoming data. The new table is named Copy of Entry.

Fig. 14.13
The Table
Definition dialog
box can be used to
create a Microsoft
Project table with
columns that
match the
imported data.

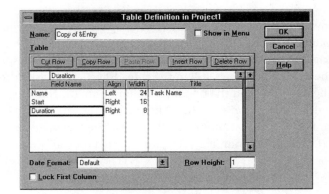

Since the new table resides only in the current project document, the imported data must be merged into the active document for the table to be
available for importing the data. Figure 14.14 shows the new attempt to
import the data, this time with the Copy of Entry table applied to the Task
Sheet in the background.

After you choose the OK button on the Open dialog box, the Import dialog
box appears (see fig. 14.15). You must answer three questions for Microsoft
Project to complete the loading of the file:

- Are the rows of the incoming data **T**asks or **R**esources?

- What T**a**ble is used to match the imported data?

■ Is the incoming data to be a new file or to be merged into the active file, updating tasks (or resources) that have matching ID numbers?

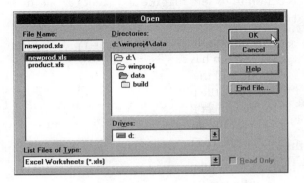

Fig. 14.14
The view in the background shows columns that are appropriate for opening the NEWPROD.XLS data.

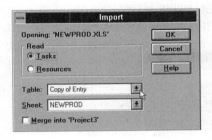

Fig. 14.15
The Import dialog box defines how the imported data will be interpreted.

II

Shared Project Data

Note

The table that will receive the imported data doesn't have to be in the active view at the time the import is executed.

The Import dialog box enables you to select the table name to use for defining the columns of incoming data. If the table is currently applied to the view, its name will appear in the selection field automatically.

The table to be used for importing does not have to be the current table. However, the table must be defined for the project document that will receive the imported data. If you defined the new table in the active document and have not copied it to the GLOBAL.MPT template, you must fill the **M**erge check box at the bottom of the Import dialog box to merge the imported data into the active document. If you have copied the special table to the GLOBAL.MPT template, you can create a new file out of the imported data by clearing the **M**erge check box and choosing the table from the T**a**ble entry list on the Import dialog box.

If a project file is active and you decide to merge the imported data, Microsoft Project 4 writes over the task rows starting at row 1. Therefore, you must take the added precaution to be sure that the task names are in the same order as the imported data when you merge files.

To import a data file from another application as a project file, follow these steps:

1. If necessary, prepare the Microsoft Project table definition that identifies the fields of the imported data. A table must be defined already that has columns defined in the same order as the data you import.

2. From the **File** menu, choose **O**pen. The Open dialog box appears (see fig. 14.14).

3. Select the entry list arrow in the List Files of **T**ype box to select the format of the file to import—unless the file is an .MPX file, in which case the file is listed among the .MPP files. Select the file type, and the list of files in the File **N**ame box is restricted to only files with this extension. In figure 14.14, the Excel Worksheets format is selected.

4. From the File **N**ame entry list, select the file name. In figure 14.14, the NEWPROD spreadsheet is selected.

5. Choose the OK button.

   If you are importing a file with a format other than MPX, you see the Import dialog box shown in figure 14.15. When opening or saving MPX files, Microsoft Project uses the table named Export (on the Define tables list), so you do not need to identify the table to use.

6. In the Read area, choose either the **T**asks or the **R**esources radio button to tell Microsoft Project the kind of project data that you want to create from the imported data.

7. Choose the T**a**ble box, and select from the entry list the name of the table that you want to use to identify the fields in the incoming data (fig 14.16). If you fill the **M**erge check box (see the next step), the list of tables will be those in the current file. If you clear the **M**erge check box, the list of tables will be those in the GLOBAL.MPT template.

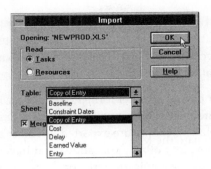

Fig. 14.16
Choose the table
definition that
matches the order
of the data being
imported.

8. Mark the **M**erge into *filename* check box only if you want to add the
   incoming data to the active project file. If you want to create a new file,
   don't mark the check box.

9. To begin importing the data, choose the OK button.

Microsoft Project imports the data (with error messages as described above if
incoming data is of the wrong type for a column). Figure 14.17 shows the
imported Excel file NEWPROD. Note that the first task is actually the column
headings of the spreadsheet and should be deleted from the project.

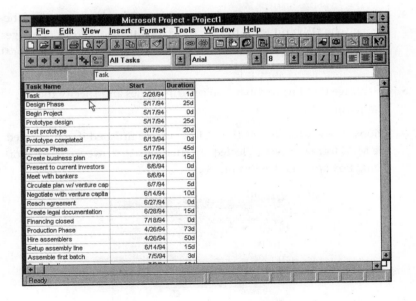

Fig. 14.17
The Excel data has
been successfully
read into Microsoft
Project to create a
new task list with
durations and start
dates.

II

Shared Project Data

Exporting Projects to Other Applications

You export Microsoft Project data to other applications with the **F**ile Save **A**s command. The project data is translated by Save **A**s into a file in the native format of the application you select.

When saving project data in another format, you must select a Microsoft Project Table to define the fields that will be exported. Only the data in fields contained in the table you choose are exported. If you export ASCII text files that you plan to import into other applications that have a fixed field structure, such as an accounting application, the order of the fields is important—as important as including the correct fields. The order of the fields, however, often is not critical when you export to spreadsheet or database files because these applications usually can design a document that accepts the data in the order in which you supply the data.

To export project data in another format, follow these steps:

1. Open the Microsoft Project file you plan to export.

2. From the **F**ile menu, choose Save **A**s to display the Save As dialog box.

3. In the File **N**ame box, type a name for the file.

4. Select the entry list arrow for the Save File as **T**ype box and select the format in which you want to save the data. Microsoft Project changes the extension on the file name to match the standard extension for the format you choose.

5. To change the directory path, select **D**irectories and specify the new path.

6. Choose the OK button. At this point, you are finished if you selected the MPX format. If you selected another format, however, the Export dialog box appears (see fig. 14.18).

Fig. 14.18
The Export dialog box defines what information from the active project file will be exported.

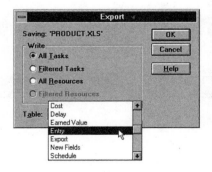

7. Select the button that applies to the kind of data that you want to export. These choices are defined in the following list:

Button	Result
All **T**asks	Exports all tasks, even tasks hidden by any currently active filter.
Filtered Tasks	Exports only tasks not hidden by the current filter.
All **R**esources	Exports all resources, even resources hidden by any currently active filter.
Filtered Resources	Exports only resources not hidden by the current filter.

8. Select the name of the T**a**ble whose column structure defines the fields you want to export. (The MPX export routine uses the Export table, found on the Define Tables menu.)

9. To save the data, choose the OK button.

Using Microsoft Project Data with Other Formats

You also can open and save files in DOS text formats that a wide range of other applications can import or export. Two text formats are supported:

Text—An ASCII format with tabs between the fields

CSV—An ASCII format with commas between the fields (called Comma Separated Value)

When you export a project file as Text or as CSV (a Comma Separated Value document), Microsoft Project creates a line (record) in the resulting text document for each task or resource, and each line contains the fields that are displayed in the current table. If you export to the Text format, the document is given the extension .TXT and field values are separated by the tab character. If you export to the CXV format, the file is given the extension .CSV and field values are separated by commas.

If you import a Comma Separated Value text files into Microsoft Project, the extension must be CSV or Microsoft Project cannot import the data. Text files with tabs separating the fields do not have to have the .TXT extension. For both text file types, you see the Import dialog box illustrated in figure 14.5, and the same conditions apply that apply to importing spreadsheets: the table that is used for the Import must match the field types of the incoming data.

Pasting Static Copies of Data between Applications

If you do not need to transfer all the information in a file (for example, you need just one value or a part of the data in the source document), you can copy and paste the data to the Windows Clipboard from one document (the source) to another (the destination). You can choose to paste only a one-time copy of the current value, or you can establish a dynamic link that not only pastes in the current value, but allows the value in the destination to be updated on demand to reflect changes in the source document (see the next section for creating linked data).

The same condition that applies for importing and exporting data files applies to copying data between files; you must define a Table in Microsoft Project that uses the data fields in the same order as the data that you are transferring. Moreover, when you copy data between applications, the Microsoft Project table must be the current view. If you copy data to a project view, and the data type you copy to a field doesn't match the data type of the field, no change is made in the data in the field.

If you copy data to a calculated field, the calculated value is restored after the next recalculation of the project file.

Copying Data from Other Applications

To copy data from another application into Microsoft Project, follow these steps:

1. Select the source data. You may select a single value or several values. If you select several values, be sure that the order of the values matches the order of the values in the table that you are using in Microsoft Project as the destination.

2. Place the data in the Clipboard by choosing **C**opy from the **E**dit menu or by pressing Ctrl+C (in most Windows applications).

3. Move to Microsoft Project and select a sheet view and a table that has the columns you need to match the order of the data you are copying.

   Do not close the other application if more data is to be moved. Use Alt+Tab to switch between Project and the other open application.

4. Select the task or resource row and the first field in the table to receive the data. If you select blank rows, Microsoft Project creates new tasks or resources with the data you copy in. If you select rows that already contain data, Microsoft Project replaces the existing data with the new copied data.

5. From the **E**dit menu, choose **P**aste.

Paste places a static copy of the current value from the source document in the field that you selected. Microsoft Project cannot update this value if the value in the source document is changed unless you execute another copy and paste.

Copying Microsoft Project Data into Other Applications

To copy data from Microsoft Project to another application, follow these steps:

1. Place a view on-screen with a table that displays the data you want to copy to the other application.

2. Select the source data. You can select a single value, several adjacent values, or whole task or resource rows.

3. Place the data in the Clipboard by choosing **C**opy from the **E**dit menu or by pressing Ctrl+C.

4. Move to the other application and select where you want to place the data.

5. From the **E**dit menu, choose **P**aste.

Paste places a static copy of the current value from the project file. This value is not updated if the value in the Project is changed.

Linking Selected Data between Applications

The copy operations described in the preceding section produce static copies: the copy of the data doesn't change as the original data changes. Establishing links between data fields in one application and data fields in another application is also possible. These links are *Dynamic Data Exchange* (DDE) links.

You can define a link for a field value in Microsoft Project that causes the field to reflect a value stored in another project file or in a document in another application. The file that *supplies* the data is called the *server* document or application. The file that *borrows* the data is called the *client* document or application.

Use the **Edit C**opy command in the *server* document and use the equivalent of the Paste Lin**k** command in the *client* document to create the dynamic link.

Linking Microsoft Project Data to Other Sources

To link Microsoft Project field values to values in other sources:

1. Select the source data, for example, a range of cells in an Excel sheet. You can select a single value or several values. If you select several values, be sure that the order of the values matches the order of the values in the table that you use as the destination in Microsoft Project (see fig. 14.19).

Fig. 14.19

A list of tasks and durations in Excel can be the source of task names and durations in Microsoft Project.

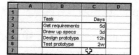

2. Place the data in the Clipboard by opening the **E**dit menu in the original application and choosing **C**opy or, in Windows applications, by pressing Ctrl+C.

3. Move to Microsoft Project and select a sheet view and a table with the columns you need to match the order of the data that you are copying.

4. Select the task or resource row in the table to receive the data. If you select blank rows, Microsoft Project creates new tasks or resources with the data that you are copying into the file. If you select rows in which data already exists, Microsoft Project replaces the existing data with the data being copied.

5. From the **E**dit menu, choose Paste **S**pecial. The Paste Special dialog box appears (see fig. 14.20).

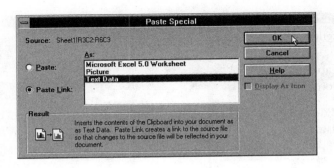

Fig. 14.20
Choose the way
data will be pasted
into Microsoft
Project with the
Paste Special
dialog box.

6. Choose the Paste **L**ink button.

7. In the **A**s box, choose Text Data as the type of link if you want the data
to become text in a table. You must use the Text Data option if you
want to define tasks or resources with the linked data.

   Choose the Worksheet or Picture option if you want the data to be a
   picture in a graphic area. In the GANTT Chart view, for example, both
   those options would create a picture object in the bar chart area of the
   view.

8. Choose the OK button to establish the link.

Tip

Choose the Paste
Link button before
choosing the type
of data in the **A**s
box, because
changing the Link
option may change
the selection in the
As box.

II

Shared Project Data

Figure 14.21 shows the resulting tasks that are defined by the linked Excel
data that was illustrated above. Each field value that is linked to an external
source displays a small triangle in the lower right-hand corner of its cell as a
linked indicator.

> **Note**
>
> Note that pasting dates into the Start or Finish fields creates Constraints for those
> tasks.

Paste **L**ink places a dynamic reference to the source data. You see the current
value displayed immediately; if the source document changes, the displayed
value also changes when the link is refreshed. For more information about
Links, move on to the next section.

Fig. 14.21
The Excel data is used to define four tasks and their durations. Note the linked indicators in each linked field.

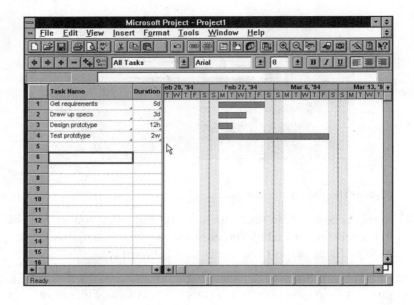

Refreshing Linked Data in Microsoft Project

While the source document and Microsoft Project are both in memory, the linked data in Microsoft Project is refreshed each time the project file is recalculated.

When the source document is not in memory, you can use the Links command to update the link. The source application will not need to be opened for the linked value to be refreshed.

To update the data links to external sources, follow these steps:

1. From the **E**dit menu choose Lin**k**s. All links from other applications are listed in the Links dialog box (see fig. 14.22).

Fig. 14.22
All external sources of linked data in a project document are identified in the Links dialog box.

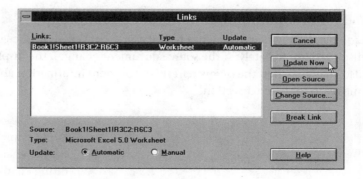

2. Select all links that you want to refresh. To add non-adjacent links to the selection, use the Ctrl key while making the selection.

3. Choose the **U**pdate Now button to refresh all the data links you have selected. Each document that you reference is searched for the current value of the link. If you want to open the application document named in the link reference, choose the **O**pen Source button.

If you want to change the source of the linked data, you can do so in the Change Link dialog box. Choose one of the links in the **L**inks box and choose the **C**hange button. The Change Source dialog box appears (see fig. 14.23), in which you can choose another file to link to. Although you can browse through the files for the file name of the new source, you must know the location within the new source file in order to complete the change.

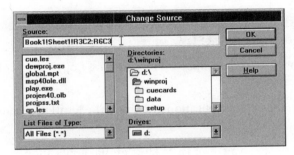

Fig. 14.23
The Change
Source dialog box
lets you redefine
the source of
linked data.

When you open a Microsoft Project document that has links to external sources, an alert box appears (see fig. 14.24) warning you that the file has links and offering to reestablish the links before displaying the data. Choose **Y**es to refresh linked data immediately. Choose **N**o to defer refreshing the links to a later time.

Fig. 14.24
You have the
option to refresh
linked data when
you open files that
contain links.

Deleting Links to Other Sources

If you attempt to type over a field value that is a link to another file, you are warned that the link will be lost; you are offered the opportunity to proceed or to cancel the data entry. If you choose Yes (to proceed with the change), the DDE link reference is lost. Choose No to abandon the editing change and preserve the link.

II

Shared Project Data

To delete the data and its link to an external source, you can select the field whose link you want to remove and choose the Cle**a**r command from the **E**dit menu. Then select the **C**ontents option. You are then asked to confirm the deletion. Click OK to complete the deletion.

You also can use the Links dialog box to delete links without clearing the field value. Choose the links you want to delete and choose the **B**reak link button.

Linking Other Applications to Microsoft Project Data

To copy data from Microsoft Project to another application, follow these steps:

1. Choose a view with a table that displays the data you want to copy to the other application.

2. Choose the source data. You can select a single value, several adjacent values, or entire rows of tasks or resources.

3. Place the data in the Clipboard by choosing **C**opy from the **E**dit menu or by pressing Ctrl+C.

4. Move to the other application and select the location where you want to place the data.

5. Choose the equivalent of Paste Lin**k** in that application.

Paste Lin**k** embeds a dynamic reference to the Microsoft Project data in the other application. You see the current value displayed immediately; if the project document changes, the displayed value in the other application also changes when the link is refreshed.

Displaying Objects

The preceding sections focused on sharing individual data elements between applications. For example, a group of cell entries in an Excel workbook can provide the task names and durations in a Microsoft Project document.

An *object*, on the other hand, is a picture of data (usually a group of data) that exists in another application but whose individual elements are not distinct and cannot become individual pieces of data. The most frequent use of objects is to show graphic data (for example, Excel charts, PC Paint-brush artwork, or special displays like the PERT chart or the GANTT Chart in Microsoft Project) in an application that doesn't normally generate similar graphics images.

For example, if you paste Excel data as text into a project Gantt Chart view, each cell will be placed in a separate field in the table, as in figures 14.21 and 14.25. If you paste the Excel data as a picture object, a mini-spreadsheet will be displayed in the graphics area of the Gantt Chart, complete with gridlines around each cell (see fig. 14.15). You can position and resize the picture within Microsoft Project.

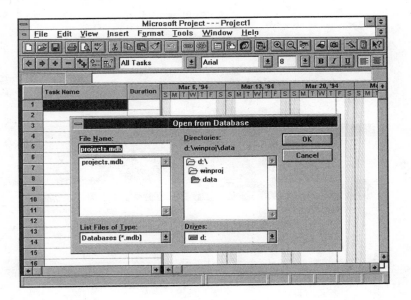

Fig. 14.25
The same block of Excel cells is pasted into the Gantt Chart as **text** in the table columns and as a **picture** in the graphic area.

If task rows from a Gantt Chart in Microsoft Project are pasted into a Microsoft Word document as text, each row of task information will be a text row in the document. If the same task rows are pasted as a picture object, the task fields—along with the task bar and the timescale above the task bar—will be shown as a graphic object in the Word document (see figures 14.26, 14.27, and 14.28).

Fig. 14.26

A Microsoft Word document can show a Microsoft Project image within its page of text.

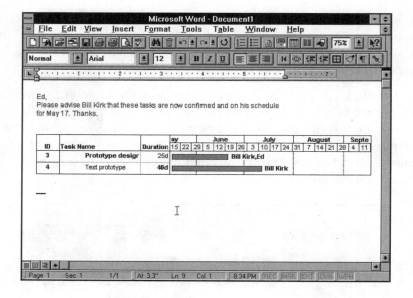

Fig. 14.27

An Excel worksheet can display a Gantt chart image from Microsoft Project as an object in the spreadsheet area.

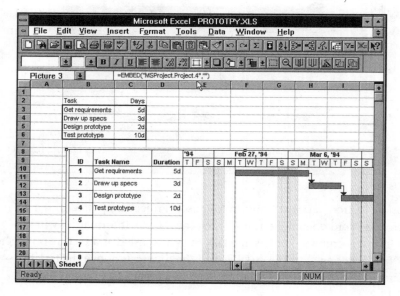

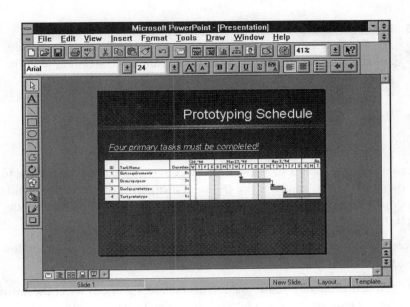

Fig. 14.28
A Powerpoint slide
can use a timeline
generated in
Microsoft Project
to illustrate a
point.

Objects can be pasted whether or not they are linked. If they are not linked, the pasted image cannot be updated to show changes in the source document without pasting the image again.

Pasting Objects

To paste linked or unlinked picture objects from one application into another, follow the same steps as those given for pasting text data: copy the data to the Clipboard in the server (source) document and paste the object from the Clipboard into the client (destination) document. The difference is that when you paste into the client document, you choose the picture or object format instead of the text data format. Picture objects can only be pasted into Microsoft Project in the graphics area of the Gantt Chart or into the Object box of either the resource or task form.

To paste an object into the Gantt Chart, follow these steps:

1. Activate the source (server) application and copy the object to the Clipboard using the **E**dit **C**opy command.

2. View the Gantt Chart.

3. Choose the **E**dit Paste **S**pecial command.

4. In the Paste Special dialog box (shown in figure 14.20), choose the **P**aste button or the Paste **L**ink button as appropriate.

5. In the **A**s box, you may have an option that includes the server application's name, and you will always have the Picture option. Both choices produce picture images that look similar. The option with the server application's name shows more of the special formatting that the server application is capable of displaying. The Picture option is less responsive to special formats and to changes in the formats.

6. Choose the OK button to paste the image.

 When copying an object in Microsoft Project to the Clipboard for pasting to another application, you have the choice of using the **E**dit **C**opy command or the Copy Picture button on the Standard toolbar. Use the Copy Picture button if the application that is to receive the object is not OLE2 compliant.

To copy a Microsoft Project object to an OLE2 compliant application, follow these steps:

1. Select the task or resource data to be included. You can select the entire task or resource rows in a table or just several adjacent fields.

2. Choose the **E**dit **C**opy command.

3. Switch to the client application and choose the equivalent of the Paste or Paste Link command, depending on whether you want a linked relationship.

If the client application is not OLE compliant, use the Copy Picture button to copy the Microsoft Project object to the Clipboard. Then switch to the client application and use the Paste command.

Embedding Objects

In the previous examples, an object in the server application was copied and pasted into the client application, with the advantage being that the special formatting features of the server application data were made available to the client application.

You also can display data that resides only within Microsoft Project but has the formatting features of the server application. In this case, the functionality of the server application is made available to Microsoft Project data.

For example, figure 14.29 shows a Gantt Chart with text formatted by Microsoft WordArt 2.0. The image was created from within Microsoft Project by calling on WordArt to insert a formatted image. You could also call on Microsoft Excel to chart some project data and display it in the Gantt Chart area. These are called *embedded* objects. The data resides solely within the client application, but the functions to process the data are borrowed from another application. This powerful process is made possible by Microsoft OLE and OLE2.

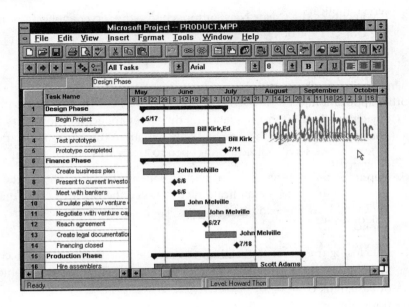

Fig. 14.29
The logo for Project Consultants Inc is displayed as an embedded object on the Gantt Chart.

To embed an object in Microsoft Project, follow these steps:

1. While in Microsoft Project, choose the **I**nsert menu and choose the **O**bject command. The Insert Object dialog box will appear, as shown in figure 14.30.

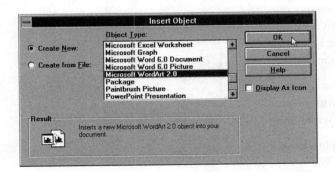

Fig. 14.30
The Insert Object dialog box lets you choose a server application to create an embedded object out of your Microsoft Project data.

2. Choose the Create **N**ew button unless the object has already been saved as a separate file. In that case, choose the Create from **F**ile button and select the file from the file names dialog box that is displayed in that case.

3. If you choose the Create **N**ew button, choose the server application in the Object **T**ype box.

4. Choose the OK button to open the server application on top of Microsoft Project.

5. Prepare the object in the server application. You may have to copy and paste the Microsoft Project data into the server application to begin processing. However, the data will only remain in the server application as long as the server application is open to create this object.

6. When the object is ready to put back in Microsoft Project, choose the **F**ile menu in the server application and choose the **U**pdate option that appears during embedding operations. Then you can exit the server application.

7. On closing the server application, you will be back in Microsoft Project, and the new object will be a graphic object in the Gantt Chart graphics area.

Modifying Embedded Objects in Microsoft Project

You can move and resize embedded objects to suit your needs once they have been embedded, and you can use the objects to activate the applications that created them if you want to edit the contents of the objects. To effect any of these changes, you must first select the object. Simply click the object once to select it. Small black "handles" will appear around the edges of the object (see fig. 14.31).

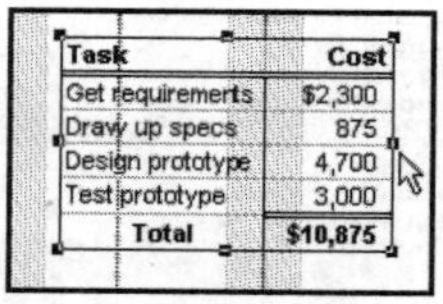

Fig. 14.31
Small black handles appear around the edges of an object to indicate that the object is selected .

Task	Cost
Get requirements	$2,300
Draw up specs	875
Design prototype	4,700
Test prototype	3,000
Total	**$10,875**

To move the object, follow these steps:

1. Select the object by clicking it once.

2. Move the mouse over the object or along its edge, but not over one of the handles. A plus sign appears to be attached to the mouse pointer when it is ready to move the object. If the mouse becomes a thin double-headed arrow, it will resize the object instead of moving it. Figure 14.32 shows both of these pointer images. The "move" pointer is near the lower right-hand corner of the object, and the resize pointer is on the bottom center handle.

3. Drag the object to its new location.

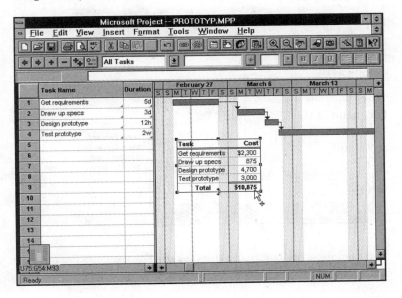

Fig. 14.32
The shape of the mouse pointer determines whether the mouse moves or resizes an object.

Resizing the object may produce undesirable results since the object expands or contracts to fit the new dimensions, and the content of the object may not be as readable or as attractive after the change. This is especially true when the object contains text.

To resize the object, follow these steps:

1. Select the object by clicking it once to make the selection handles appear.

2. Move the mouse over one of the handles until the pointer becomes a thin double-headed arrow. Select one of the side handles to move that edge of the object horizontally. Select the bottom center or top center handle to move that edge vertically. Or, select one of the corner handles to move both adjoining edges simultaneously.

3. Drag the handle to the new size you want.

You also can display the Shortcut menu for objects by moving the mouse pointer over the object and clicking the right mouse button. Figure 14.33 shows the Shortcut menu for embedded objects. In addition to the editing commands to cut, copy, and delete, there are also commands that are unique to objects.

Fig. 14.33

Use the Shortcut menu for objects for access to most operations.

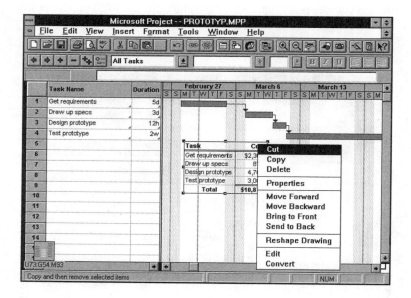

Choosing the Properties command displays the Format Drawing dialog box where you can choose the Line & Fill properties of the object, as well as its Size & Position.

Use the Line & Fill tab (shown in figure 14.34) to define an outline border around the object, including the **C**olor of the line and the **L**ine style. You also can select a color and pattern for the background of the object.

Fig. 14.34

Use Format Drawing's Line & Fill tab to change the style and color of an object's border and fill pattern.

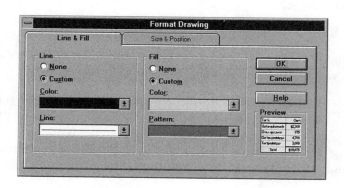

Use the Size & Position tab (shown in figure 14.35) to size the object and to attach it to a position in the Gantt Chart. You can attach it to a specific date on the timescale (which is what you are doing when you move the object with the mouse). In figure 14.35 the object is attached to the **d**ate 3/1/94 and is offset from the timescale by 1.23 inches. You can enter these values, but it is much easier to simply move the object with the mouse to the most visually appealing location. It also it is much easier to Size the object with the mouse than to enter inch dimensions in the Heigh**t** and **W**idth text boxes.

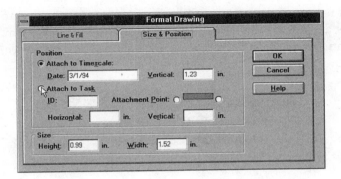

Fig. 14.35
The size and relative position of an object in the Gantt chart can be set with the Size & Position tab.

You also can attach the object to the start or finish of a specific task. As the task bar moves due to changes in the schedule, the object will move with it.

To attach an object to a task bar:

1. Select the object and right-click to display its Shortcut menu. (Or you can choose the F**o**rmat D**r**awing command and select the Properties option to reach the same point.)

2. Choose the Size & Position tab.

3. Choose the Attach to Tas**k** button.

4. Choose the **I**D field and supply the ID number of the task. Note that you must know the task ID number. You cannot browse through the task list at this point to determine which task ID to use.

5. Choose the Attachment **P**oint by choosing the button at either the beginning or the end of the representative task bar.

6. Enter the Horizo**n**tal and Ve**r**tical offset from the task bar attachment by entering inch amounts.

7. Choose the OK button.

▶ "Placing Text and Graphics on the Gantt Chart," p. 551

The Properties menu also offers you the options to move the object forward and backward in the layers of graphic objects (which includes the task bars on the Gantt Chart), or to bring the object all the way to the front or send it all the way to the back. This is more often used with Drawing objects.

At the bottom of the Properties menu, you can choose to Edit the object and to Convert the object. The Edit option activates the server application that created the object, just as double-clicking the object does. The Convert option offers you the choice of replacing the real image of the object with an icon that represents the application. You can double-click the icon to launch the server application and see the data in the object. This choice may make your Gantt Chart less cluttered looking if you have several objects embedded for reference but you don't need to actually see them at all times.

Fig. 14.36

Use the **D**isplay As Icon option to hide an OLE object while still providing quick access to the image.

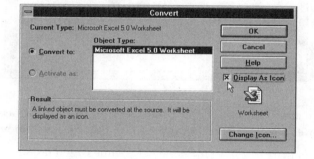

Fig. 14.37

The Excel object shown in figure 14.32 can be displayed on demand by double-clicking the Excel icon.

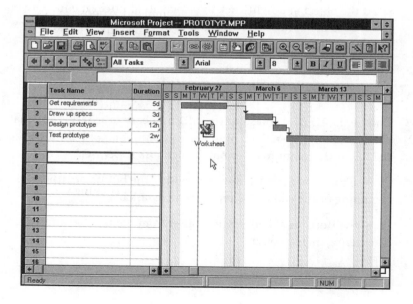

To attach an object to a Microsoft Project task or resource, you must view the object box for the task or resource and paste the object from the other application. To attach an object to a task or resource object box, follow these steps:

▶ "Using and Customizing Reports," p. 563

1. Display the task or resource in a form.

2. Display the Object box by choosing the F**o**rmat **D**etails command and choosing **O**bjects from the list of details that can be displayed.

3. Select the object in the other application and use **E**dit **C**opy to move the object to the Clipboard.

4. Select the object box in the form in Microsoft Project.

5. From the **E**dit menu, choose **P**aste or Paste Lin**k**. If linked, the object can be refreshed to reflect changes in the original source.

Objects that are attached to the Objects box of a resource or task can be printed in task or resource reports by selecting the Objects check box on the Details tab of the Report dialog box.

Identifying Tasks or Resources with Links Attached

You can filter the task or resource list to determine which tasks or resources use linked data from other sources. For either a task view or a resource view, choose the **T**ools menu and the **F**iltered For command. Choose **M**ore Filters to display the More Filters dialog box, and choose the Linked Fields filter. Choose the Appl**y** button to filter out all the tasks or resources that have one or more linked fields.

Similarly, you can determine which tasks or resources have objects attached to their Objects boxes by using a filter. However, you must define this filter because there is no standard filter to identify attached objects. The Objects field for each task and resource contains the number of objects that are attached to that task or resource. You can design a filter to test for values greater than zero in this field to identify the tasks or resources. See Chapter 17, "Using and Creating Views" for information about creating your own filters.

II

Shared Project Data

From Here...

This chapter has dealt with the options you have for sharing data—from whole project files to individual task or resource information—with other applications. The exchange can be static or dynamically linked, and objects can be embedded or linked. Related topics are discussed in the following chapters:

- Chapter 13, "Working with Multiple Projects," shows how to link data between project files within Microsoft Project.

- Chapter 19, "Placing Text and Graphics on the Gantt Chart," shows how to place drawing objects that are generated within Microsoft Project on the graphics views.

- Chapter 15, "Using Microsoft Project in Workgroups," describes the ways in which you can communicate Project data to others on your electronic mail system.

Using Microsoft Project in Workgroups

Projects are almost always group endeavors. You can use Microsoft Project to schedule your own personal projects or agenda; but by far the most frequent use of Microsoft Project is to plan and track projects that involve many planners and many resources who do the work of the project.

In this chapter, you learn how to

- Route a copy of your project for comments and approval.

- Send electronic mail messages about schedule details.

- Notify resources of task assignments and schedule changes, and record their confirmations.

- Request status reports for tasks, and use the reports to update tracking information automatically.

The new workgroup features in Microsoft Project 4 are some of the most impressive enhancements to the program, both technically and in terms of the increase in project management effectiveness.

The technical achievement is the application of Microsoft Mail's *custom message handlers* to Microsoft Project. With this technology, you can automatically send standard messages for specific purposes by selecting tasks and using a menu command or toolbar button.

- The "Send Task Request" command automatically addresses electronic mail messages to the resources you have assigned to tasks, describing the task details and asking for confirmation that they will do the task as sscheduled. They can confirm the tasks as listed, decline them, or offer suggested changes in their reply to you. When you receive their reply, you can automatically update the project to include their response and comments. Task assignments that are confirmed are specially marked to facilitate follow-up communications.

■ Microsoft Project automatically keeps track of those tasks whose schedule details have changed since the last time the task's resources were notified about the task. The "Send Task Updates" command selects all tasks that need updates sent out and prepares messages to their assigned resources describing the new schedule for the tasks.

■ Finally, and perhaps most importantly, you can now use the "Request Task Updates" command to automatically send messages to resources asking for status reports on the tasks that they are assigned to. The message provides a timesheet on which to fill in important tracking information such as when they started the task, how much has been done, how much remains to be done, and any comments (or excuses) about the task status. When the project manager receives this response, the update information can automatically be inserted into the project document. With the onerous task of tracking task status distributed among the resources, one of the most difficult parts of project management is suddenly made far more tractable.

If you are using Microsoft Mail, which uses MAPI (Messaging Application Programming Interface), or one of the mail systems like Lotus Notes or cc:Mail, which use VMI (Vendor Independent Messaging), you can attach a routing slip to a tentative project plan and send preview copies to interested parties for their comments and approval. Each recipient has only to "send" the message, and it is automatically addressed to the next name on the routing slip.

The examples in this chapter assume Mark is the project manager for a Software Development project. He needs to communicate with his superior, Eleanor, and with resources named Ed and Sam, to whom he has assigned to tasks in the project. Windows for Workgroups is installed and the members of the workgroup use Microsoft Mail and Schedule+. Some, but not all, of the features described here would also work with other electronic mail platforms.

Circulating the Project Schedule for Review

Routing your project plan to key managers and technical experts for comments and approval is critical to the success of any project. You need to be sure that the plan is workable and that you have the support you need to complete the project. The Send command will create an electronic mail message for you, with your project file attached. You can address the message as you send it, or you can attach a routing slip that can be used over and over to communicate with the same group or to send the message sequentially to each person on the list.

Using the Send Command

The Microsoft Project Send command is similar to the Send command in the other applications in the Microsoft Office group. The Send command opens the mail system for you to compose and address a message, and the currently active document is automatically attached to the message. Each addressee will get a copy of the project file in Microsoft Project. You can, if you wish, remove the attached project file and send the message without it.

◀ See Chapter 2, "Learning the Basics of Microsoft Project."

The steps that follow assume that you have not previously attached a routing slip to this project and that you must address the message before you can send it. See the next section for information about creating and using routing slips.

To address and send a copy of a project file through electronic mail, follow these steps:

1. Open the project file and activate its window.

2. Open the **F**ile menu and choose Sen**d**, or choose the Send Mail button on the Workgroup toolbar.

3. The Microsoft Mail Sign In dialog box appears if you are not already logged into the mail system (see fig. 15.1). Enter your **P**assword if necessary and choose the OK button to continue.

4. When the form for preparing electronic mail messages appears, there will be an icon in the message area representing the attached project file (see fig. 15.2). You will need to address the message and add appropriate text in the message area.

II

Shared Project Data

Fig. 15.1

Using the Send command automatically activates the electronic mail login if you are not already logged in.

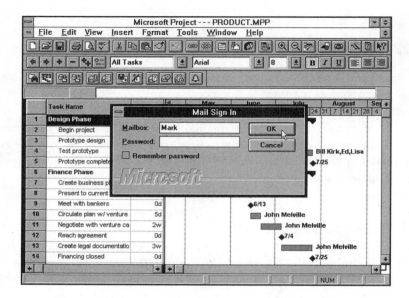

Fig. 15.2

The dialog box for preparing mail messages will have the project file name in its title bar and an icon representing the attached file in the message area.

Attached project file

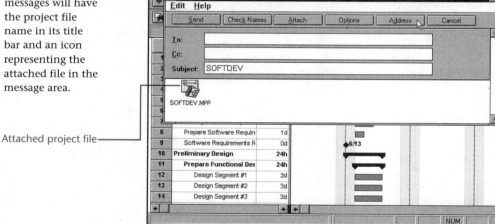

5. Type the names of the people to whom you want to address the message in the **T**o field and the names of those to whom you want to copy the message in the **C**c field. Or you can choose the A**d**dress button and pick the names from the address list. If you type multiple names in either list, you must separate the names with semicolons.

If you choose the A**d**dress button, the Address dialog box (shown in fig. 15.3) will appear. From the list of addresses at the top, select a name, and choose the **T**o button to add the name to the To list or choose the **C**c button to add the name to the copy list. Choose the **O**K button when the addressing is complete.

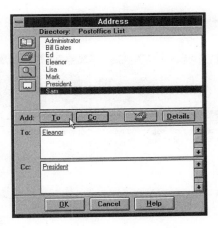

Fig. 15.3
The Address dialog box makes it easy to add names to the address list with accurate spelling.

6. Type the text of your message in the message area at the bottom of the mail form, either before or after the icon for the attached file (see fig. 15.4). If you want, you can select and delete the icon for the attached file, making your message text only.

7. When the addresses and message are complete, choose the **S**end button to transmit the message with the accompanying copy of the project file.

When the addressees receive the message (see fig. 15.5), they can double-click the file icon in the message area to open Microsoft Project with the project file displayed.

Tip
Choose the Chec**k** Names button to verify the accuracy of the address list you type. Names that are found in the mail directory will be underlined. Those that are not found will be selected for you to correct. Using commas instead of semicolons to separate names will cause the name check to fail.

Shared Project Data

Fig. 15.4
Add message text
before or after the
icon for the
attached file.

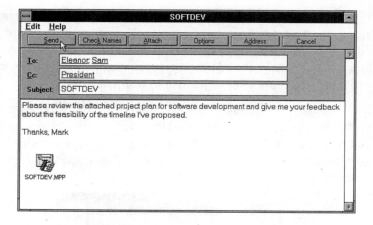

Fig. 15.5
The recipient of
the mail message
can open the
project file by
double-clicking
the file icon in
the message.

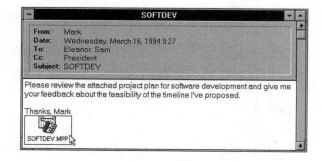

Using a Routing Slip

Tip
You can start
typing the name
you want to use,
and when enough
letters have been
typed to identify
the name, it will
appear selected in
the list. Then you
can press Enter to
place the name in
the To list, or
press Alt+C to
place the name in
the copy list.

If you will be corresponding regularly with the same group about the project,
you will want to prepare a routing slip to attach to the project file. The routing slip can be used repeatedly. One added advantage of a routing slip is that
it circulates the same file from one recipient to another, accumulating suggested changes in the project file. You also will be notified automatically as
each recipient forwards the message and file on to the next person on the
routing slip list. These status notes will keep you informed of the progress
of the message.

You can reuse the routing slip to send later messages and new versions of the
project. You also can change the names on the list and change the message
text. You can choose to have the project and message sent to all names on
the address list simultaneously, or one after another in the order they are
listed. If you route the message one after another, you can choose to have
tracking notices sent to you each time the message is forwarded to the next
name on the list.

To attach a routing slip to a project file, follow these steps:

1. Open the project file and activate its window.

2. Open the **F**ile menu and choose Add **R**outing Slip, or choose the Routing Slip button on the Workgroup toolbar. If there is already a routing slip attached to the file, the command will be Edit **R**outing Slip instead of Add **R**outing Slip.

   The Routing Slip dialog box appears (see fig. 15.6). You can use the Cancel button to close the dialog box without changing anything.

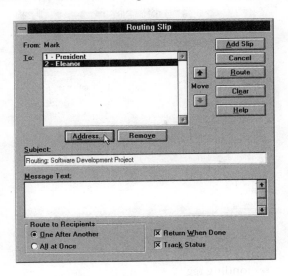

Fig. 15.6
Create a permanent address list and an accompanying message with the Add Routing Slip command.

3. Add to the address list and remove names from the list with the A**d**dress button and the Remo**v**e button. You can remove all names from the list (and clear the message area) by choosing the Cl**e**ar button (see fig. 15.7).

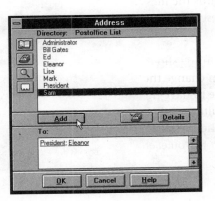

Fig. 15.7
The order in which you choose names for the **T**o list determines their sequence number.

II

Shared Project Data

If you are routing the message to recipients one after another, you can move names up or down in the list to alter the order by which the message will be routed. Move a name by selecting the name and then clicking one of the arrows above or below the Move label. In figure 15.8, the President is currently first on the list to receive the message. President is selected and the down arrow can be used to move President down the list. In figure 15.9, President has been moved to the bottom of the list and will be the last to receive the message, enabling the President to review all comments and changes.

Fig. 15.8
The order of names can be changed with the Move buttons.

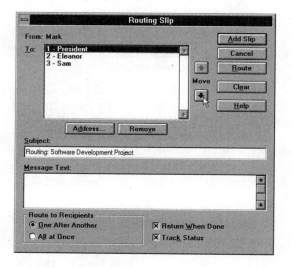

Fig. 15.9
Now the President will be the last to receive the message before it is returned to Mark.

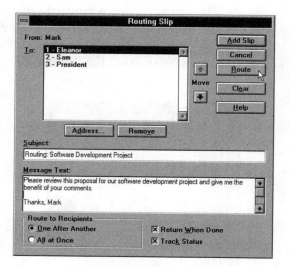

4. Type a subject heading into the **S**ubject text box.

5. Type the message you want delivered with the file in the **M**essage Text box.

6. Choose the method to Route to Recipients. Choose **O**ne After Another to let one copy of the message make the circuit of all recipients, accumulating responses and changes in the project file as it moves down the list in the order you have entered the names. Choose A**l**l at Once to send a separate copy of the message and file to each recipient.

7. If you route the message One After Another, you can choose to receive tracking notices as each recipient passes the message on to the next name on the list. Fill the Trac**k** Status check box to receive progress messages.

8. Fill the check box for Return **W**hen Done if you want the project file, including modifications by the people on the routing list, to be returned to you after all others on the routing slip have seen it.

9. If you are ready to send the message immediately, choose the **R**oute button. If you want to attach the routing slip to the project but are not ready to send the message just yet, choose the **A**dd Slip button.

When you send the message with the routing slip, each recipient will be able to double-click the project file icon to open Microsoft Project and the attached project file. Recipients can make changes in the project if they choose. Figure 15.10 shows the message that Eleanor receives. The message about the routing slip and how to continue the routing is supplied automatically by Microsoft Project and Microsoft Mail.

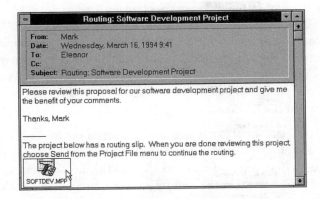

Fig. 15.10
Recipients of routed messages are automatically advised to use the Send command to continue the routing.

II

Shared Project Data

To forward the message and file on to the next name on the routing slip (or back to the originator when the route is complete), the recipient must open the project and use the **F**ile Sen**d** command. The Routing Slip dialog box will appear (see fig. 15.11). You can choose to continue the routing (Sam is the next name on the list), or you can choose to send the project to an address you supply.

Fig. 15.11

The Routing Slip dialog box offers to continue the routing or to let you send a copy to an address you enter.

To review and forward a project you have received as a recipient on a routing slip, follow these steps:

1. Open the mail message that contains the routed project file.

2. Double-click the icon for the Microsoft Project file.

3. Review the project, making changes and adding notes to tasks or resources as you think appropriate.

4. From the **F**ile menu choose Sen**d** to forward the message and the edited file to the next name on the routing slip. The Routing Slip dialog box appears.

5. Choose the button next to **R**oute project to *nextname*, and choose the OK button to send the message.

6. Close the project file and save the changes.

When routing slip recipients forward the message to the next name on the list, a status message is automatically sent to the originator of the routing slip if the Track Status check box is filled on the routing slip. Figure 15.12 illustrates the notice that Mark receives after Eleanor sent the message on to the second name on the list, Sam.

When the last recipient of the routed message sends the file on, the file is returned to the author of the routing slip. The Routing Slip dialog box shows the names who have received the message, and the message text and subject are dimmed to indicate that the routing has been completed (see fig. 15.13). The Clear button has changed to a R**e**set button. Use the R**e**set button to restore the routing slip, clearing the (received) markers and reactivating the text boxes.

You can modify the **M**essage Text and **S**ubject and change the names on the list before using the routing slip again. Choose the **A**dd Slip button to save the reconstituted routing slip. After using the **R**eset button, the button becomes a Cl**e**ar button again. You can use the Cl**e**ar button to remove all names and text from the routing slip. If you want to save the cleared routing slip, choose the **A**dd Slip button.

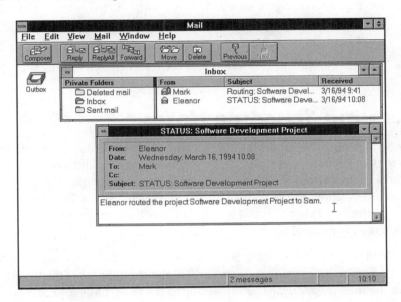

Fig. 15.12
Automatic progress messages keep the message author posted as to how far down the routing list the project has gone.

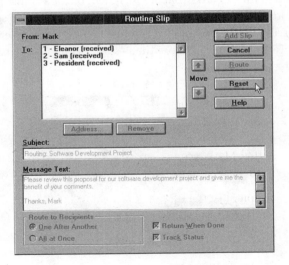

Fig. 15.13
A completed routing slip shows the names that received the message and dims the text to indicate that it is no longer waiting to be sent.

Shared Project Data

To reset an expired routing slip, follow these steps:

1. From the **F**ile menu, choose Edit **R**outing Slip.

2. Choose the R**e**set button to restore the original routing slip.

3. You can leave the routing slip like it was originally, or change it for the next routed message. Choose the Cl**e**ar button if you want to clear all settings from the routing slip. Edit the name list and text areas if you want to revise the routing slip.

4. Choose the **A**dd Slip button to save the reconstituted routing slip.

Sending Schedule Notes

The Send command described in the section above sends the entire project file to the recipients of the message. If you would like to send a message about a limited selection of tasks, or if you want to send a special copy of the project file without losing your routing slip, you can use the Send Schedule Note command. This command is found on the **T**ools menu, under the **W**orkgroup command.

The Send Schedule Note dialog box (shown in fig. 15.14) will appear to offer you choices about creating the message. Fill the check boxes at the top to have the message addressed automatically to the Project **M**anager, the assigned **R**esources for the tasks that are included, or the **C**ontacts that have been named for the tasks. Choose the **E**ntire Project button to select those recipients for all tasks in the project, not just those currently selected. Choose the **S**elected Tasks button to choose the Resources and Contacts for only those tasks that are selected.

Fig. 15.14
Use the Send Schedule Note dialog box to prepare special notes for special categories of workgroup members.

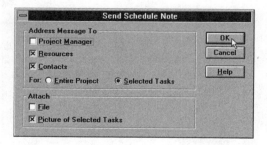

> **Note**
>
> The Contact field is designed explicitly for use with workgroup messaging. You can type the name (which is the address) of any person on your mailing list in the Contact field for those tasks you want that person to be posted on. Then, when you send messages, the Contact person can be included automatically for each of those tasks.
>
> The Contact field does not appear on standard forms or views. You can add the field to a Table in order to assign Contact names to tasks. See Chapter 17, "Using and Creating Views," for instructions on creating Tables.

You can attach the entire project File to the message. You also can choose the Picture of Selected Tasks button to attach a graphic of the way the active view displays the tasks that are selected.

To send a schedule note, follow these steps:

1. If you plan to attach a picture of selected tasks, apply the appropriate view and select the tasks.

2. From the Tools menu, choose Workgroup. Then choose Send Schedule Note. The Send Schedule Note dialog box (see fig. 15.14) is displayed.

3. If you want names of persons who are defined in the project file to receive copies of the message, fill the check boxes for the appropriate categories to be selected: Project Manager, Resources, or Contacts.

   If you fill one or more of the category check boxes, choose whether names are to be selected for those categories from the Entire Project or only from the Selected Tasks.

4. If you want to attach the project file, fill the File check box.

5. If you want to attach a picture of the selected tasks as displayed in the active view, fill the Picture of Selected Tasks check box.

6. Choose the OK button to continue assembling the message. A Mail dialog box will appear (see fig 15.15). The dialog box is initially titled to match the project file, but the title will change to match the Subject of the message.

7. You are free to add or remove names from the To list of direct recipients and the Cc list of copied recipients. Use the Address button to help locate mail addresses.

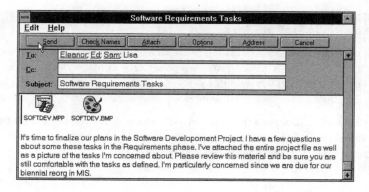

Fig. 15.15
Finalize the
message from
the Send Schedule
Message command
in the mail mes-
sage dialog box.

8. Type the message Subject. The Subject will replace the dialog box title as soon as you leave the field.

9. Type the message text before or after the attachment icons (if there are any).

10. Choose the **S**end button to send the message.

Setting Task Reminders

Use the Set Reminder command to place alarms on tasks in Schedule+. You can choose to have the reminder alarm set to the start or finish dates for the selected tasks, and you can choose how long in advance of the event the alarm will sound.

Caution

If the tasks are subsequently rescheduled, the alarm is not adjusted in Schedule+. Although you can use the Set Reminder command again to capture the new scheduled date, you must manually remove the old alarms in Schedule+.

To set alarms in Schedule+ to give a warning before tasks start or finish, follow these steps:

1. Select the tasks for which you want to set alarms.

2. Choose the Set Reminders button on the Workgroup toolbar, or choose **W**orkgroup from the **T**ools menu, and then select **S**et Reminder. The Schedule+ Reminders dialog box appears.

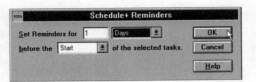

Fig. 15.16
You can set Schedule+ Reminders for the start of finish of tasks.

3. In the "**S**et Reminders for" field, type a number of units and select the unit to be used from the entry list to the right.

4. On the following line choose Start or Finish for the "**b**efore the Start/ finish of the selected tasks."

5. Choose the OK button to set the reminders.

Sending Task Requests

By far the most exciting aspect of the new workgroup environment in Microsoft Project 4 is the feature that allows the project manager to communicate directly with the resources that have been assigned to tasks: to ask them to accept the assignment, to give them revision notices, and to ask them to supply tracking information. All of these messages are composed automatically, and the information supplied by the resource can be inserted into the project as updates without the project manager having to key the responses in. Tracking, long the most time-consuming part of project management and the most neglected phase of project management usage, can now be automated to a significant degree. This section shows you how to notify resources of their assignments and get confirmation that they agree to the assignment.

Composing the Task Request Form

To send a Task Request message, follow these steps:

1. Select the tasks you want resources to confirm.

2. Choose the Send Task Request button, or from the **T**ools menu choose **W**orkgroup and then choose the Send **T**ask Request command. The Task Request dialog box appears (see fig. 15.17).

Fig. 15.17

The Task Request form is automatically generated with a custom message asking resources to confirm their acceptance of task assignments.

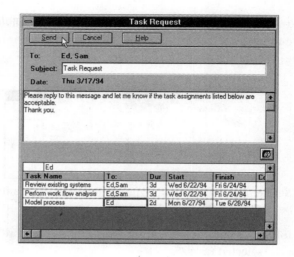

3. Add to or change the Subject if you wish.

4. Add to the message text if you prefer.

5. You also can add to the task assignments with the Resource Assignment button above and to the right of the task list at the bottom of the dialog box.

6. When the dialog box is complete, choose the **S**end button to transmit the request to the resources.

Responding to Task Requests

When the resource receives the request, it will look like figure 15.18. After choosing the **R**eply button, the resource can add to the message text, answer Yes or No to the Accept? column at the bottom of the dialog box, and enter comments in the column to the right of the Finish date.

To respond to the task request, follow these steps:

1. View the mail message, which will be titled Task Request.

2. Choose the **R**eply button to enter your response. The RE: Task Request dialog box will appear (see fig. 15.19).

3. Add to the **M**essage text as necessary.

4. If you must decline a task request, change the "Yes" in the Accept? column to "No."

5. Enter an explanation in the Comments column to the right of the Finish date column.

6. Choose the **R**eply button to send your reply.

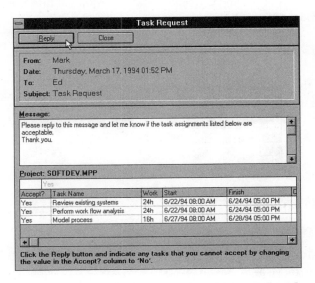

Fig. 15.18
The Task Request dialog box can be used to accept or decline resource assignments.

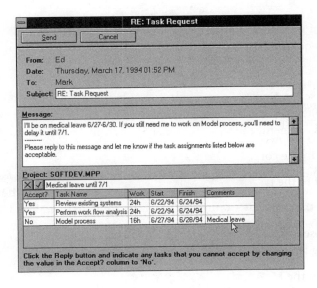

Fig. 15.19
Provide explanations and comments about your acceptance or rejection of task assignments.

Updating the Project

When the project manager receives the reply to the Task Request message, he or she can continue the dialog by adding to the **M**essage text and sending a **R**eply, or the response can be accepted and incorporated into the project with the **U**pdate Project button.

To add the acceptances (or rejections) by resources to the project, follow these steps:

1. View the response from the resource (see fig. 15.20).

Fig. 15.20

The response from the resource about task assignments can become part of a continuing dialog, or it can be used to update the project.

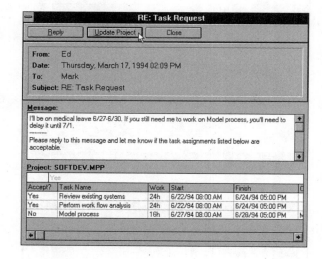

2. Choose the **U**pdate Project button to add the acceptance value and the Comments from the resource to the project file. If the resource accepts the assignment, the task assignment Confirmed field will have the value Yes.

When all resources assigned to the task have confirmed the assignment, the Confirmed field for the task will have the value Yes. If the resource typed text into the Comments field, the comment will be added to the task Note field with attribution to the resource.

Sending Task Updates

As you revise the project in response to actual work or changes in the plan, resources need to be notified of changes in the schedule for the tasks to which they are assigned. The start or finish dates may have changed, or the resource may no longer be assigned to the task. Microsoft Project keeps track of which resources need to be notified because their task assignments have been modified. Use the Send Task Updates command to transmit those changes to the resources that are affected.

To send task updates to resources, follow these steps:

1. Select the tasks for which you want to send updates. If you want to include all tasks, select the column heading for one of the task fields.

2. Choose the Send Task Updates button on the Workgroup Toolbar, or choose **T**ools from the menu, choose **W**orkgroup, and select Send Task **U**pdates. The Task Updates dialog box appears (see fig. 15.21).

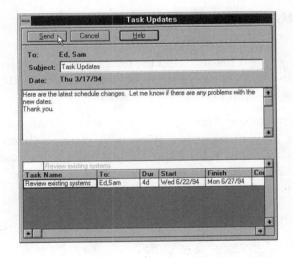

Fig. 15.21
Send schedule revisions to those resources who are affected with the Send Task Updates command.

3. Add to the message text if you wish.

4. Choose the **S**end button to transmit the updates.

Requesting Task Updates

Once the project is underway, it is important that the project manager be informed about progress on individual tasks, and that the schedule be revised to incorporate this information. Only in this way can Microsoft Project help you anticipate the consequences of variances from the planned schedule.

In the past, the project manager has been overwhelmed with the time and effort required to keep the project schedule current by recording actual events. Now, Microsoft Project and Microsoft Mail have been combined to relieve much of that burden. Although you must still find out from resources what the status of tasks is, the response from the resource can now be automatically incorporated into the schedule as actual updates.

As project manager, you now can easily send electronic mail messages to targeted resources requesting progress updates on the tasks they have been assigned to. The message lists the tasks the resource is assigned to work on, and provides fields for recording when work actually started, the amount of work that is completed, the amount of work that remains, and comments (excuses) about the status of the task. The resource merely has to fill in the electronic mail message, like a timesheet, and send the reply back to the project manager.

Sending the Request

To send a request for task updates, follow these steps:

1. Open the project file and select the tasks you want progress reports on. If you have only one task selected, Microsoft Project asks if you want to use all tasks or just the one that is selected.

2. Choose the Request Task Updates button on the Workgroup toolbar or from the **T**ools menu, choose **W**orkgroup, and then choose **R**equest Task Updates. The Update Request dialog box is displayed (see fig. 15.22). Each resource will receive a list showing only those tasks to which it is assigned.

3. Choose the **S**end button to distribute the requests.

Fig. 15.22
Send Update Requests to all resources who should have progress to report to streamline the tracking process.

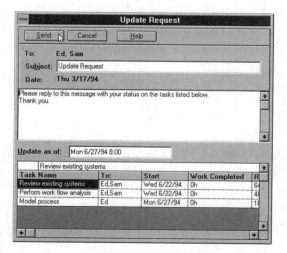

The resource will receive a message like the one in figure 15.23. Responses to the **M**essage can be entered. For each task listed at the bottom of the form, the resource should enter the actual Start, the Work Completed, the Remaining Work, and Comments about individual tasks as appropriate.

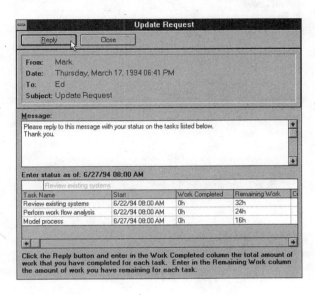

Fig. 15.23
The Update Request message provides fields for the resource to report actual Start dates, work completed, remaining work, and comments for each task.

To reply to the Update Request, follow these steps:

1. Choose the **R**eply button to enter your response. The **R**eply button changes to the **S**end button, and data entry fields open for your input. Data entry fields display question marks to encourage your data entries (see fig. 15.24).

2. Type general comments into the top of the **M**essage box.

3. For each task listed at the bottom of the form, enter the actual Start date, the Work Completed, the Remaining Work, and any Comments you deem appropriate.

4. Choose the **S**end button to send the update information to the project manager.

Shared Project Data

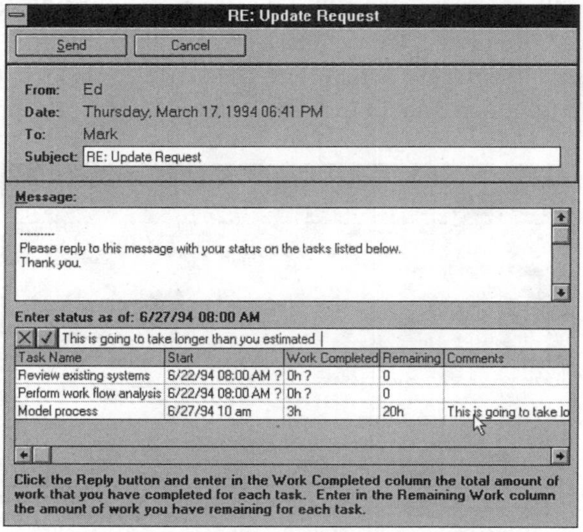

Fig. 15.24
Choosing the
Reply button
opens data fields
for task update
information.

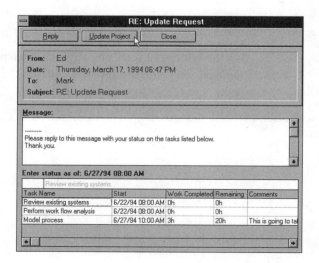

Applying the Updates

When the project manager receives the task updates from resources, she or he
can review them in the mail message window. If further dialog is necessary,
the **R**eply button will send a response back to the resource requesting further
clarification. If the update is acceptable, the **U**pdate Project button will copy
the update information into the appropriate fields for the tasks in the project
file (see fig. 15.25). The Comments for each task will be added to the contents
of the Task Note field, with attribution to the resource that authored the
Comment.

Fig. 15.25
Using the Update
button enters the
responses of the
resources into the
tracking fields of
the project file.

To process the update responses, follow these steps:

1. Open the response message in Microsoft Mail.

2. If further clarification is needed, type the request in the top of the **M**essage box. Choose the **R**eply button to send the request back to the resource.

3. If the update is acceptable, choose the **U**pdate Project button to copy the data into the project's actual fields.

From Here...

This chapter has introduced the new workgroup features of Microsoft Project 4.0. These features are among the most exciting improvements in project management found in Microsoft Project. You have learned to share project data with members of your workgroup. You also have learned how to use Microsoft Mail to notify resources about their task assignments and changes in the schedule for those assignments. Finally, you have learned how to use electronic mail to track progress on the project.

■ For information about combining workgroup projects, see the section on consolidating projects in Chapter 13, "Working with Multiple Projects."

■ For guidelines on distributing printed reports see Chapter 16, "Printing Views and Reports."

■ For information about the special task and resource assignment fields used in workgroup communications, see Appendix A, "The Microsoft Project Field Dictionary."

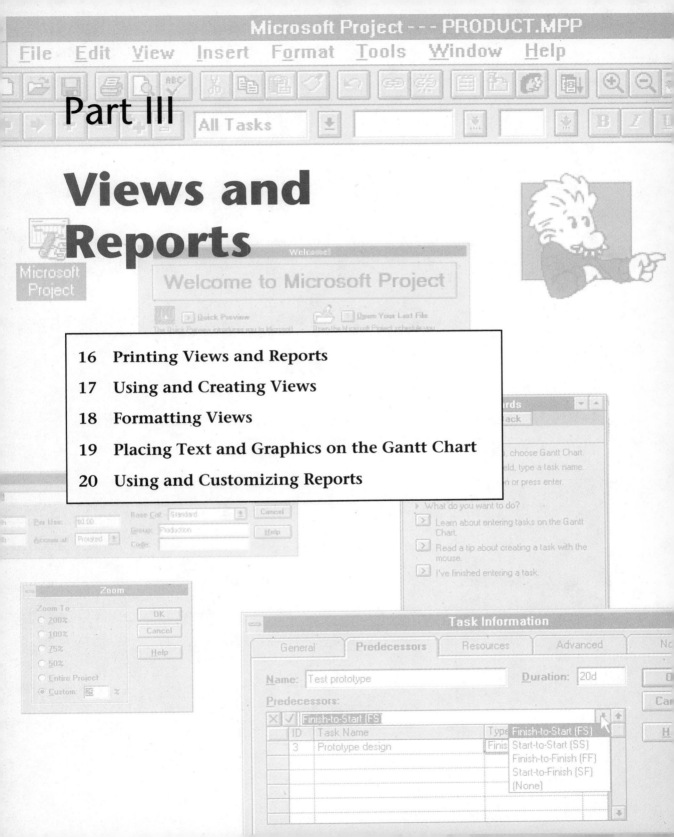

Part III

Views and Reports

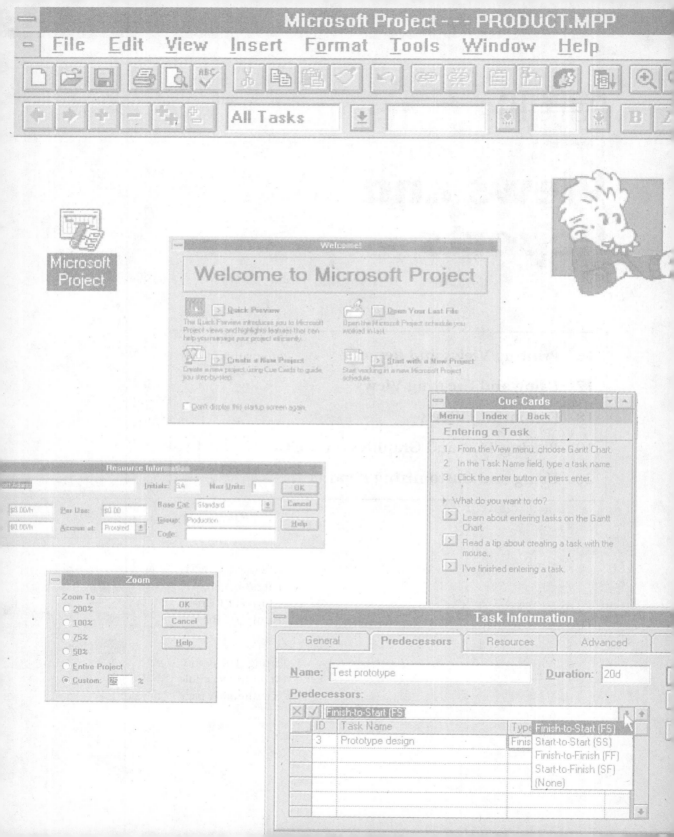

Chapter 16

Printing Views and Reports

One of the main functions of project management software is to print reports that communicate a project plan to others in a clear and informative format.

In this chapter, you learn how to

- Modify the margins and orientation of the page.

- Create and customize headers, footers and legends.

- Use Print Preview.

- Print a standard view or report.

- Control the page or date range that is printed.

There are two ways to print your project data:

- Usually, you just print the view of the data that appears on-screen. The printed version is nearly identical to the display format on-screen. A few views cannot be printed, however, including the Task PERT Chart and the forms (such as the Task Form, the Resource Form, and the Tracking Form).

- Microsoft Project also provides several reports for printing. The report formats include a monthly calendar with tasks shown on the scheduled dates, comprehensive lists of tasks and resources, and a summary page that resembles the Status dialog box.

▶ "Using and Creating Views," p. 463.

▶ "Using and Customizing Reports," p. 563.

III

Views and Reports

Selecting the Print tool sends a copy of the current view to the printer immediately; you do not have a chance to exercise control over the way the report looks. Use the commands in this chapter to make changes to the page setup before using the Print tool.

Using the Print Commands

As in all Windows applications, the printer commands are located on the **File** menu (see fig. 16.1). The Page Set**up** command defines headers, footers, page orientation, and so on, for printed views. You can also use Page Set**up** to select the printer and to change any printer specific options available for your printer. The Print Pre**v**iew and **P**rint commands are used to print views. The reports mentioned in earlier chapters are accessed through the **V**iew **R**eports command. The Page Set**up** and **P**rint buttons found there work the same way the print commands on the File menu do.

Fig. 16.1
The Print
commands.

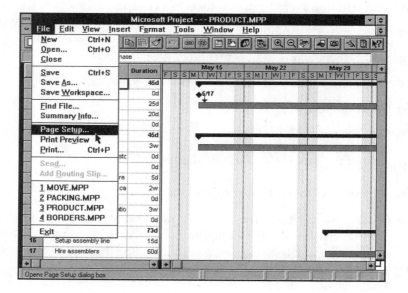

Changing the Printer Setup

You must make sure that you select the correct printer before you start a print job. You can select the default printer for any Windows applications by using programs provided with the Program Manager. These programs include the Print Manager and the Printers program in the Control Panel. You find both programs in the Main Group of the Program Manager.

The default printer is selected when you start to print in Microsoft Project. If you want to use a printer other than the default printer, you can select the printer or the desired printer options with either the **F**ile **P**rint or **F**ile Page Set**u**p command. There is a Printer button available in both of the resulting dialog boxes. Choose the Printer button, and the Print Setup dialog box appears (see fig. 16.2).

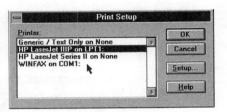

Fig. 16.2
The Print Setup dialog box.

The list of installed printers appears in the Printer selection field. If you only want to change the printer you will be printing to, select the printer you want and choose the OK button. If you want to change the way the printer is set up, choose the printer you want to change the setup for, and then choose the **S**etup button.

Some of the options available may be selecting legal size paper instead of the standard letter size, selecting a paper feeder source, or changing the resolution of graphics objects on a LaserJet printer. You also can change the orientation of the report on the paper from portrait (upright) to landscape (sideways). An information box appears the first time you choose the **S**etup button to advise you that the portrait or landscape orientation setting is managed in the Page Setup dialog box for individual views and reports (see fig. 16.3).

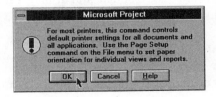

Fig. 16.3
The Print Setup information box.

III

Views and Reports

If the information box appears, choose OK to go on to the Printer Setup dialog box, which displays the options for the printer. Figure 16.4 shows the options for a Hewlett-Packard LaserJet IIIP; your printer may have different options. Select the options you want and choose the OK button when finished. You then need to choose OK on the Print Setup dialog box. Until you change the printer or the options, Microsoft Project continues to use this printer definition as the default.

Fig. 16.4
A sample Printer
Setup dialog box.

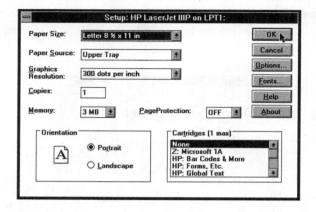

Printing Views

▶ "Formatting
  Views,"
  p. 497.

▶ "Placing Text
  and Graphics
  on Gantt
  Chart,"
  p. 551.

You probably will do most printing by printing the various screen views. This section provides a few pointers about preparing the screen view for printing. Chapters 18 and 19 contain detailed instructions for refining the display with special formatting and graphics features. This chapter focuses on the use of the print commands after the screen presentation is established.

Preparing the View for Printing

The first step is to set up the screen to display the project data just as you want the information to appear on the printed report. You choose from the **V**iew menu, possibly from the **T**ools menu, and (most likely) from the F**or**mat menu to get the combination of data and display features that presents your data in the best way.

Choosing the View Fundamentals

You first must use the **V**iew command to choose the appropriate view: you can view either tasks or resources in either a worksheet table layout or a graphic layout. Moreover, you must choose the pane from which the view is printed. If the view is in the top pane, all tasks or all resources are printed unless you filter the data. If you print from the bottom pane, only the tasks or resources associated with the selection in the top pane are printed. You may decide to print from the bottom pane, for example, if you want to isolate all the resources assigned to a selected task, or you may want to print a list of all the tasks to which a selected resource is assigned.

To establish the basic view, select the pane for the view by using the mouse to select the pane or by using the F6 key to switch from one pane to another. From the **V**iew menu, choose the view you plan to use.

If the view contains spreadsheet-like columns of data, you may need to use the **V**iew Ta**b**le command to choose the most appropriate set of data columns. The various tables were introduced in previous chapters, as tools to use in the process of building and managing a project. Chapter 17 describes how you can create customized tables. To simply change the table that is currently displayed, select the **V**iew menu, choose the Ta**b**le command, and choose the table you want to use.

> ### Note
>
> In views that show a table to the left of a timescale, check the columns of the table that are visible on-screen. Unless you choose the Print All **S**heet Columns option on the View tab of the Page Setup dialog box, the rightmost column that is completely visible is the last column of the table that appears on the printed report. For example, in the initial Gantt Chart view (where the ID, Name, and Duration are the only columns visible), the printed report doesn't show the other columns in the table unless you scroll to display more columns or choose to display all columns on the View tab of the Page Setup dialog box.

Troubleshooting

By default, the ID and Task Name columns are both printed on the Gantt chart. If you want to only print the ID and not the name, you need to edit the table that is currently being used in the view. You need to uncheck the Lock first column check box in the Table Definition dialog box. When this box is not checked, only the first column, ID, will print.

▶ "Creating New Views," p. 464.

Finally, if you want the report to focus on just part of the project, you may want to choose a filter to display only a subset of the tasks or resources. Most of the filters, described in previous chapters, are useful tools in building and managing a project. Chapter 17 describes how you customize filters. To apply a pre-defined filter, select the **T**ools menu, choose **F**iltered for, and choose the appropriate filter.

▶ "Using and Creating Filters," p. 478.

Sorting the Display

After displaying the data you want to print, you may want to rearrange the order of the tasks or resources. To sort the table lists, follow these steps:

III

Views and Reports

1. From the **T**ools menu, choose **S**ort. A drop-down list appears with several sort choices. You may also specify sort choices other than those presented by choosing the **S**ort By option. The Sort dialog box appears.

2. Choose the Sort By field and select the column on which to sort the records.

3. Choose **A**scending or **D**escending for the order of the sort. Add your choices for sorting in the Then By and Then By columns, if desired.

4. Choose the **S**ort button to execute the sort.

► "Sorting the Tasks or Resources in a View," p. 500.

If you printed the report, it would show the data in the order shown on-screen. If at some point you want to return to the default sort order, choose the **R**eset button in the Sort dialog box.

Enhancing the Display of the Text Data

You can format text data to emphasize or highlight selected categories of tasks or resources. For example, you may want to display summary tasks in bold, milestones in italics, or overallocated resources (in a resource view) as underlined. You can customize the display of the gridlines and the column and row separator lines, and in views with a timescale, you can customize the time units and labels used to represent the time units. In graphics views, you can select special graphical features from a *palette*. All these customizing features are covered in detail in Chapter 18. Use these display enhancements selectively to improve the presentation quality of your printed reports.

Setting and Clearing Page Breaks

You can force a page break when printing task and resource lists so that a new page starts at a specific task or resource—even if the automatic page break doesn't occur until further down the list. Page breaks are tied to the task or resource you select when you set the page break. Even if you sort the list or hide a task by collapsing the outline, a new page starts at this task or resource.

Page breaks also affect the printing of the built-in reports. The final dialog box you see just before printing offers an option to use or ignore the page breaks you set manually. This feature prevents you from having to remove all page breaks for one special printout and later having to replace the breaks. You can remove one page break or all page breaks with relative ease.

To set a page break, select the row just below the intended page break. This row becomes the first row on a new page. From the **I**nsert menu, choose **P**age

Break. A dashed line appears above the selected row to indicate the presence of a manually inserted page break.

To remove a page break, reselect the row just below the page break. Select the **I**nsert menu. Notice that when a page break row is selected, the menu choice changes to Remove **P**age Break. Choose Remove **P**age Break to remove the selected page break.

To remove all page breaks, select all of the rows in the active view by clicking the button just above the row numbers and to the left of the Task Name column heading. Choose the **I**nsert menu. The wording of the Page Breaks command changes to Remove All **P**age Breaks. Choose the Remove All **P**age Breaks command.

Note that you cannot set the page breaks on the PERT Chart, but you can move the task nodes to either side of the automatic page breaks. You also can instruct Microsoft Project not to allow a task node to fall on a page break. To display page breaks in the PERT Chart view, open the F**o**rmat menu and choose the **L**ayout command. The Show **P**age Breaks check box controls whether or not lines are drawn on-screen to indicate where the page breaks occur in printing. Select the Show **P**age Breaks option to display page breaks. With the page breaks displayed, you can see where you need to move task nodes relative to the page breaks.

To keep Microsoft Project from placing PERT Chart task nodes on a page break, choose the A**d**just for Page Breaks option from the Layout dialog box. Note that this setting doesn't take effect until you choose Layout **N**ow to redraw the PERT Chart.

Troubleshooting

When you print with manual page breaks defined, if Microsoft Project appears to be ignoring your page breaks, check the Print dialog box and make sure that there is an X in the **M**anual Page Breaks check box.

Changing the Page Setup

You can change features about the appearance of the pages in any view with the Page Set**u**p command. You can change, for example, the margins, the orientation, the headers and footers, and the legend for graphic views. A separate page setup configuration is available for each of the views and reports. For example, changing the header and footer you design for Gantt Charts does not change the header and footer you design for Task Sheets.

III

Views and Reports

To change the page settings for the active view, choose Page Set**u**p from the **F**ile menu or choose the Page **S**etup button in Print Preview. (If the active view cannot be printed, the Page Set**u**p command is not available.) The Page Setup dialog box is displayed for the active view. Figure 16.5 shows the Page tab of the Page Setup dialog box for Gantt Charts. Notice the name of the active view appears in the title bar.

Fig. 16.5
The Page Setup
dialog box.

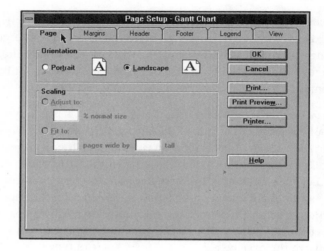

Make the changes described in the following sections, and then choose OK.

Using the Page Setup Dialog Box

▶ "Organizing
Views in
Project Files,"
p. 470.

The current settings on the Page Setup dialog box for any view are saved with the project file. They are not used when you print the view with other project files. If you want to use the settings from another project file, use the Organizer feature of Microsoft Project.

As with other dialog boxes, the Page Setup dialog box has multiple tabs. Each tab at the top accesses a different collection of settings. To see the settings for a particular topic, choose the appropriate tab.

Selecting the Orientation

The Page tab contains options used to set the page orientation to Po**r**trait (upright) or **L**andscape (sideways). This setting overrides the default orientation set in the Print Setup dialog box. If you have a PostScript printer, there will be scaling options available on this tab also. These options allow you to enlarge or reduce the printouts either by a specified percentage or by a given number of pages.

Specifying the Margins

Choose the Margins tab in the Page Setup dialog box to set the margins as appropriate. Note that the **T**op margin is a relative designation, depending on whether the orientation selection is portrait or landscape. The top margin is the empty space above the heading on the page, whether the page is positioned upright or sideways.

Placing Borders

Also on the Margins tab of the Page Setup dialog box are options for placing borders on the printed view. You can use borders to surround the page and separate the body of the report from the header, footer, and legend. For multiple-page PERT Charts that you want to paste together, this capability makes cutting and pasting easier if you place borders around the outer pages only.

To enclose each page in a lined border, choose **E**very Page. To place borders on the outside pages only, choose **O**uter Pages (for PERT Charts only). To suppress all borders, choose **N**one.

Entering Headers and Footers

You can enter up to three lines of header text and one line of footer text to repeat on each page of the printed document. You can type literal text in the header and footer, or you can place codes that are replaced with system variables (date, time, or page number) or with field values from the project file (project name, company name, project file name, start date for the project, and so on). Unless you use alignment codes to specify otherwise, the header and footer appear centered between the margins, as indicated by the center alignment tab.

To enter a header or footer, select either the Header or Footer tab, choose the appropriate alignment tab (if you want it to appear left- or right-aligned), and type the text for the header or footer. Choose the buttons below the text box to include system variables such as date, time, page number, or file name. Alternatively, choose from the pull-down list below for a more extensive list of file specific variables like the project name and manager name. After selecting a variable from the list, choose the Add button. This will add the appropriate code to the Header or Footer text box. Figure 16.6 shows the dialog box entry for a standard header (the project name, the company name, and the project manager's name), all left-aligned.

Tip
The format of the date code is determined by the default date format. To see your default setting, choose **T**ools **O**ptions and choose the View tab.

Formatting of the text in the header and footer is regulated with the Text Styles button on the Page Setup dialog box. For more information, see the section "Formatting Header, Footer, and Legend Text," later in this chapter.

III

Views and Reports

Fig. 16.6
Entering the
header.

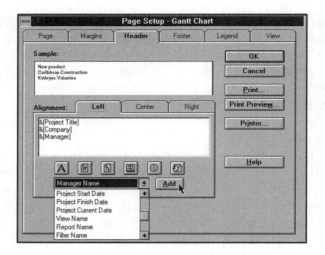

Using Legends

If the view you are printing has graphic elements (as do the PERT Chart, the Gantt Chart, and the Resource Graph), you can place a legend in the report to explain the graphic elements used. Choose the Legend tab to display choices for configuring the display of the legend (see fig. 16.7).

Fig. 16.7
The Legend tab of
the Page Setup
dialog box.

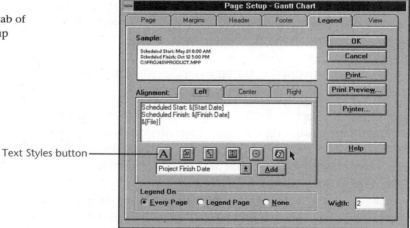

In the Alignment area, you indicate whether you want the legend text to be displayed at the left edge, the right edge, or centered in the legend area. Because each of these presents a different text box below, you should choose this option first. Once you have chosen the alignment, you can enter up to three lines of text in this text box. As with headers and footers, this can be literal text or any of the codes described in the section on headers and footers. The Sample text box at the top of this dialog box shows what your legend will look like.

The text area can occupy up to half of the legend area. You regulate the width of the legend text area by typing a number from 0 to 5 in the **W**idth box; the number represents how many inches of the legend area are devoted to the text. Typing a 0 means all of the legend area is devoted to the graphical legends. Typing a 5 means five inches of the area is reserved for text.

The formatting of the legend text is regulated with the Text Styles button on the Legend tab, in the same manner as header and footer text is.

The last option on the Legend tab enables you to select where to display the legend. You can choose from the following commands:

- **E**very Page prints the legend at the bottom of each page.

- Le**g**end Page prints the legend once on an extra page at the end of the report.

- **N**one suppresses the display of a legend entirely.

Figure 16.7 shows the Legend tab for a legend to be placed at the bottom of all pages. The legend text is used to display the start and finish dates for the project and the project file name. The text area occupies two inches of the legend area width. (Skip to figure 16.11 for a zoomed-in view of the legend text.)

Formatting Header, Footer, and Legend Text

The Text Styles button is available for changing the text formatting of header, footer, and/or legend text. This button appears as a capital A (see fig. 16.7) and is just to the left of the code buttons for inserting file and system variables, as discussed in the section on headers, footers, and legends. Choose this button to display the Text Styles dialog box (shown in fig. 16.8), which you use to apply formatting to the text in the header, footer, and legend. Select an item in the **I**tem to Change field. Use the All selection in the **I**tem to Change field to set the standard font for all text items, and then set variations on this standard by selecting individual lines from the rest of the list.

For each item you select, you can choose a font by selecting the entry list arrow to the right of the **F**ont field. Choose the print attributes you want (bold, italic, or a combination) by selecting from the Font St**y**les list. Turn on Underline by checking the Underline check box. After you choose the font and the font styles, choose the font point size (if multiple sizes are available) by selecting from the Size field. If you are using a color printer or plotter, you also can choose the Color of the text. After all items are formatted, choose the OK button to return to the Page Setup dialog box.

Fig. 16.8
The Text Styles
dialog box.

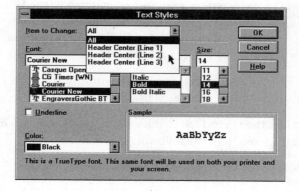

Figure 16.8 shows the selections for the top line of the header that is shown in figure 16.11. The text is set in Courier New 14-point font and is bold. The other lines of the header are set in the same font but smaller sizes, and the manager's name is italicized.

After you configure all page setup options, choose OK to close the Page Setup dialog box. Alternatively, you may choose to view your changes with the Print Preview button or to print directly with the Printer button.

Troubleshooting

If the point size you want doesn't appear to be available, make sure you have chosen the font first. Not all sizes are available for all fonts. Courier for example is only available in 10- and 12-point. It cannot get any larger.

Selecting the Special Options for Views with Sheets

Choose the View tab in the Page Setup dialog box, shown in figure 16.9, to see options specific to views that contain sheets (the Task Sheet and Resource sheet, for example).

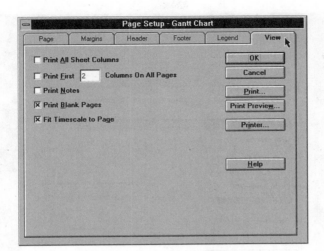

Fig. 16.9
The View tab of
the Page Setup
dialog box.

The following options are available on the View tab of the Page Setup dialog box:

■ Click the Print **A**ll Sheet Columns check box to override the default print all columns of the sheet, whether they are completely visible or not.

■ Select the check box for Print **F**irst *x* Columns On All Pages to override the default of only printing task names on the first column of pages (see fig. 16.12). This option allows you to print a specified number of columns on all pages.

■ Select the Print **N**otes field to print notes that have been entered for Tasks or Resources.

■ Uncheck the Print **B**lank Pages option to suppress the printing of blank pages. The default is for all pages to print.

■ Leave the check box for Fit Timescale to Pa**g**e checked to ensure that a timescale unit (a week, for example) does not break across pages.

Using Print Preview

You can use the Print Pre**v**iew command on the **F**ile menu to preview on-screen the look of the printed document. You also can choose print preview with the Print Previe**w** button in the Page Setup dialog box or the Print Preview tool from the toolbar. Figure 16.10 shows the Print Preview screen for the settings illustrated to this point in this chapter.

Fig. 16.10
The Print Preview
screen.

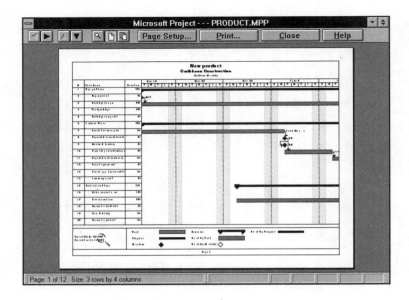

The initial preview screen shows the entire first page of the report. If multiple pages exist, you can use the buttons at the top left of the preview screen to scroll left, right, up, and down one page at a time (see Table 16.1). You can zoom in on the details of a page by choosing the Zoom button or by using the mouse pointer, which changes to a magnifying glass when positioned over a page. Simply click the part of the page you want to see in greater detail. The magnifying glass only appears while the pointer is over the page (otherwise, the pointer is an arrow).

Table 16.1	The Print Preview Tools	
Tool	**Effect**	**Alternate Selection**
◀	Move left one page.	Alt+left arrow
▶	Move right one page.	Alt+right arrow
▲	Move up one page.	Alt+up arrow
▼	Move down one page.	Alt+down arrow

Tool	Effect	Alternate Selection
🔍	Zoom in on one page. (Click area of page to zoom into.)	Alt+1 (one)
📄	View one full page. (Click specific page to view.)	Alt+2
🗐	View multiple pages. (Click area outside of page.)	Alt+3

Use Alt+Z to switch between the zoom, one page, and multiple page views. Alt+1, 2, and 3 are the numbers above the alphanumeric keys, not those on the number pad.

Note

If the Print Blank Pages option on the View tab of the Page Setup dialog box is not checked, pages will be displayed with a gray shaded background.

Figure 16.11 shows the zoomed-in view of the bottom left section of page one of this report. Figure 16.12 illustrates the multiple page preview of the same report. Note that the status line in figure 16.13 indicates that the size of the report preview is 3 rows by 4 columns. Pages are numbered down the columns, starting from the left. Therefore, page 2 of the report is the bottom page in the left column on-screen.

You can open the Page Setup dialog box from the Print Preview screen by choosing the Page Setup button at the top of the preview screen. If you have a question about one of the available options, choose the Help button for context-sensitive on-line help. When you are ready to print, choose the **P**rint button (see the following section). To make modifications, or if you decide against printing at this time, choose the **C**lose button to return to the project view.

Using the Print Command

When the view is refined on-screen and the page setup and printer options are selected, the final step in printing is to choose **P**rint from the **F**ile menu. The **P**rint command prints the current screen view. You also can choose the Print button from the print preview screen or the Print tool from the toolbar. Reminder: the print tool sends the view to the printer directly, without first presenting the dialog box.

Tip
The status line indicator only displays page information if the Status Bar check box is checked on the View tab of the Options dialog box.

III

Views and Reports

Fig. 16.11
The zoomed-in
view.

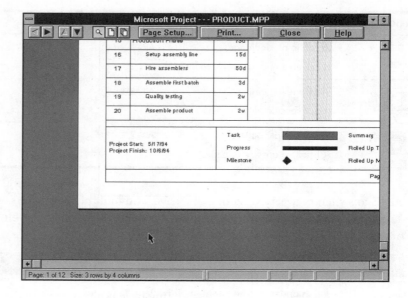

Fig. 16.12
The multiple-page
view.

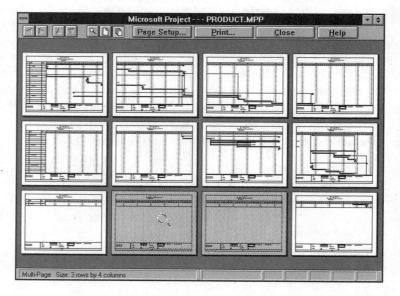

To print reports, you must use **V**iew **R**eports. Once you have viewed them, you can choose the Page **S**etup and **P**rint commands to print the reports (covered in a later section). When you select either of these commands, the Print dialog box appears (see fig. 16.13).

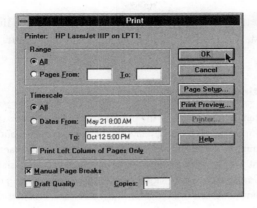

Fig. 16.13
The Print dialog
box.

Some options on the Print dialog box do not apply to all views and are displayed in dimmed mode (are inactive) when printing from these views.

Tip
Ctrl+P is a
shortcut key
combination
that you can
use instead of
selecting the
File menu and
then choosing
Print.

Selecting the Pages To Print

Choose **A**ll to print all pages, or enter the starting page number in the **F**rom field and the ending page number in the **T**o field. To reprint just page 5 of a report, for example, type **5** in both the **F**rom and **T**o fields. On reports that include a timescale, you also can limit the printed output to a specific time span. See the upcoming section, "Printing Views with a Timescale," for details.

If you embedded manual page breaks in a task list or a resource list, these page breaks are not used in printing unless the **M**anual Page Breaks check box is marked. Unmark the check box if you want to ignore the manual page breaks. This procedure is inappropriate if you previously sorted the list for a particular report, and the normal page breaks make no sense in the sorted order.

Selecting the Quality and Number of Copies

Mark the **D**raft Quality check box to speed up printing, or unmark the box to use final quality printing. For multiple copies of a report, enter the number of copies in the **C**opies field. You must collate the multiple copies by hand, because Microsoft Project instructs the printer to print all copies of the first page, and then all copies of the second page, and so on.

Printing Views with a Timescale

For views that contain a timescale, you can print the full date range of the project, from the start date to the finish date of the project, or print the data for a limited range of dates. Choose the **A**ll option button to print the entire

project or choose the Dates From option button to specify a limited range of
dates. Enter the starting date in the From field and the ending date in the To
field.

Troubleshooting

By default, the start and end dates of the project are displayed in the Timescale
section of the Print dialog box. This displays the beginning of the Gantt chart flush
against the columns on the left side of the printed view. You may want to move the
entire Gantt slightly to the right for a better view. You can accomplish this by changing the Dates from: entry to a date slightly earlier than the beginning of the project.
This starts the Gantt timescale at that date, which pushes all task bars slightly to the
right for better display on paper.

Choose the Print Left Column of Pages Only check box to print only the
pages that are on the far left side in Print Preview, Multi-Page Layout. If you
refer to figure 16.13, for example, the two pages that contain the task descriptions are the left column of pages.

Sending the View to the Printer

You can choose the Print Preview button in either the Print dialog box or the
Page Setup dialog box to review the effects of the choices you made. If you
are not currently viewing the Print or Page Setup dialog boxes, you may also
access Print Preview by using the Print Preview tool on the Standard toolbar.
If you selected a limited number of pages to print, the print preview screen
still shows the entire report. Nevertheless, when you are actually printing,
only the selected pages are printed.

In the Print dialog box, choose the Print button to start the print job. Or you
can use the Print tool on the toolbar, which is equivalent to selecting the
Print button on the Print dialog box. Note that selecting the Print tool causes
data to be sent to the printer immediately; you do not get a chance to make
selections in the Print dialog box.

Printing Standard Reports

Five standard categories of reports are available through the **View Report**
command. Choose this command to display the Reports dialog box shown in
figure 16.14.

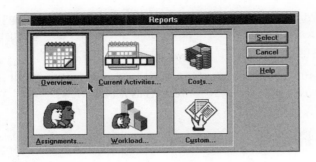

Fig. 16.14
The View Reports
dialog box.

Select the category of reports that you want to view. A subsequent dialog box lists the individual reports that are available for each category. Those individual reports are listed in Table 16.2.

Table 16.2	The Standard Reports
Category	**Report**
Overview	**P**roject Summary
	Top-Level Tasks
	Critical Tasks
	Milestones
	Working Days
Current Activities	**U**nstarted Tasks
	Tasks Starting Soon
	Tasks in Progress
	Completed Tasks
	Sh**o**uld Have Started Tasks
	Slipping Tasks
Co**s**ts	**W**eekly Cash Flow
	Budget
	Overbudget Tasks
	O**v**erbudget Resources
	Earned Value
Assignments	**W**ho Does What
	Who **D**oes What When
	We**e**kly To-do List
	Overallocated Resources
Workload	**T**ask Usage
	Resource Usage

The C**u**stom category accesses a dialog box with numerous pre-formatted reports, many of which were in the categories previously discussed. Select a report, and you are taken to Print Preview. From here you can access the Page

Setup and Print dialog boxes as previously discussed. Customizing these reports and creating new ones will be covered in Chapter 20, "Using and Customizing Reports."

The Page Setup dialog box, the Print Preview screen, and the Print dialog box options are used the same way for reports as for the views.

From Here...

Now that you are familiar with the mechanics of printing views and reports, you are ready to begin customizing views and reports to display your individual project in the manner you prefer. To learn how to customize views and reports as well as format them beyond the default options, refer to the following chapters:

- Chapter 17, "Using and Creating Views," describes how to best display the project information giving you the flexibility of selecting which tasks and or resources to display as well as which fields of information should be shown. You also learn how to create views, tables, and filters of your own design.

- Chapter 18, "Formatting Views," shows you to how to change the way the view appears on-screen to include how the text should be formatted, what order the tasks or resources should be in, and how the various graphical elements of the view should be displayed.

- Chapter 19, "Placing Text and Graphics on the Gantt Chart," illustrates the many ways you can customize printed views by adding your own graphic elements and notations.

- Chapter 20, "Using and Customizing Reports," focuses on the ways you can modify the reports to satisfy your own project needs.

Chapter 17

Using and Creating Views

One of the major strengths of Microsoft Project is the provision of facilities for customizing the standard views and reports and for creating new views and reports to serve specific needs. This chapter shows you how to use the basic building blocks in Microsoft Project to create, customize, and store new views.

In building these views, you will see how to create customized tables of view data, how to modify existing tables, and how to create and modify filters to find specific task and resource information. Finally, you will see how to manage and organize these new view definitions so they become part of the global template file used by Microsoft Project.

The **V**iew Ta**b**le and **T**ools **F**iltered For commands provide options for changing the content of the major views.

Tables and filters are named objects; if you change the fields displayed in a table, all views that use that table name will display the new fields. If you change the criteria specifications of a filter, all views (and reports) that use that filter will display the results of the changed criteria.

In this chapter, you learn how to

- Create new views for the project.

- Organize and manage the views in project files.

- Create and use view tables of data for the views.

- Create and use filters to see only a portion of the view data at one time.

III

Views and Reports

Creating New Views

You can change the views that are available on the **V**iew menu or in the More Views dialog box by editing the standard views or creating new views. If you want to create a new view, you can start by copying an existing view and making changes in the copy (leaving the original view undisturbed), or you can create an original new view. All views use one of a list of basic *screens*, and you cannot change the list of these screens. However, you can combine the basic screens in new ways to produce original views using the Define New View dialog box.

To change views, you begin by choosing **M**ore Views from the **V**iew menu. The **M**ore Views dialog box appears (see fig. 17.1). The **V**iews entry list on the left side of the dialog box is available for use with the **C**opy and **E**dit buttons.

Fig. 17.1
The More Views
dialog box.

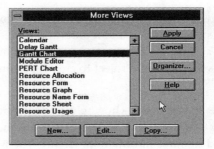

To edit a view or copy the view as a basis for a new view, choose the view from the **V**iews entry list and select either **E**dit or **C**opy. You will see a View Definition box that looks similar to the box in figure 17.2 (if it is a single pane view) or the box in figure 17.3 (if it is combination view). Make changes in the View Definition box using the guidelines provided in the following discussion on defining a new view.

Fig. 17.2
The View Defini-
tion dialog box for
a single pane view.

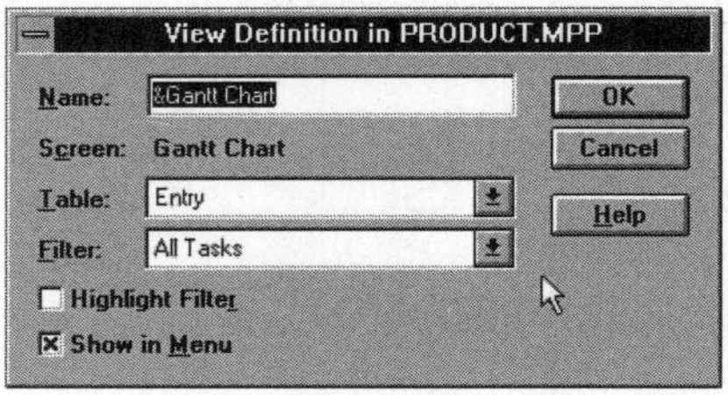

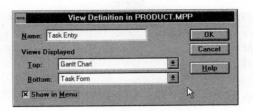

Fig. 17.3
The View
Definition dialog
box for a combi-
nation view.

To create a new view, choose the **N**ew button. The Define New View dialog
box appears (see fig. 17.4).

Fig. 17.4
The Define New
View dialog box.

The purpose of the Define New View dialog box is to give you a place to indicate whether the new view will be a single pane view or a combination view.
A combination view simply displays two views: one in the top and one in the
bottom pane. Single pane views already must be defined for placement in the
combination view definition. To define a single pane view, select the **S**ingle
View button. The View Definition dialog box appears (refer to fig. 17.2).

The View Definition dialog box has entry fields and check boxes for defining
the following options:

■ The **N**ame of the new view.

■ The basic **S**creen that will be used.

■ The **T**able that will be used (if the chosen screen uses a table).

■ The **F**ilter that will be used, and whether it is to be a highlight filter or a
limited display filter.

■ Whether or not the new view appears in the main **V**iew menu.

Entering the Name of the View

You should enter a name that readily identifies the features you are incorpo-
rating into the view. If the view is to appear on the **V**iew menu, you must
mark the Show in **M**enu check box at the bottom of the dialog box. If the
view is to appear in this menu, you may want to designate a letter to use to
choose the view from the menu. Type an ampersand (&) before the chosen

III

Views and Reports

letter when you type the view name. When the view is displayed in the menu, this letter is underlined to indicate that the user can type the letter to select the view. Always make sure that you designate a letter not already used by another view.

Selecting the Screen

▶ "Customizing Toolbars, Menus, Forms, and Cue Cards," p. 615.

Microsoft Project provides a number of basic screens that are used alone or in combination to produce the standard views listed on the **V**iew menu and on the **M**ore Views dialog box. All views must use one of these basic, prefabricated screens.

You cannot change the screen assigned to one of the predefined views listed in the **V**iew menu. You can, however, create custom forms that resemble the basic screens.

The following list shows the basic screens:

Calendar

Gantt Chart

Module Editor

PERT Chart

Resource Graph

Resource Form

Resource Name Form

Resource Sheet

Resource Usage

Task Details Form

Task Form

Task Name Form

Task PERT Chart

Task Sheet

You can modify some of these screens extensively to customize a view; other screens, however, can be changed only in limited ways. You can create your own table to apply to the views that contain tables. You can define a filter that will be permanently attached to the view for all but the PERT Chart views. Format choices can be customized in varying degrees for each of the views, and the format settings can be saved as part of the view.

To define the screen on a new view, first select **Sc**reen from the View Definition dialog box, and then choose a screen from the entry list that appears (see fig. 17.5).

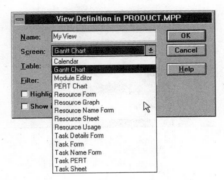

Fig. 17.5
Selecting the screen from the entry list.

Selecting the Table for the View

If the screen that you choose displays a table of field columns, you must define the table to use in the view. To define the table, choose **T**able from the View Definition dialog box, and then choose a table name from the entry list. The entry list contains all tables that are included in the **M**ore Tables menu for the screen type (task or resource) that you have chosen. Figure 17.6 illustrates the selection of a customized table named My Table, which was defined before the view definition was started.

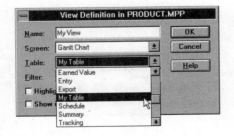

Fig. 17.6
Selecting the table from the entry list.

Selecting the Filter for the View

All views (except the PERT Chart and Task PERT view) have a filter attached. For all the standard views, the filter that is originally attached is the All Tasks or All Resources filter, so that no filter is attached for the standard views until you add one. If you want the view that you are defining to always filter the tasks or resources for a particular purpose, you must define the filter before it can be defined as part of the view. Select the Filter entry list arrow to select one of the defined filters. In figure 17.7, the Cost Overbudget filter is being defined as the filter for the view. This filter will be made a highlight filter only; therefore, all tasks will be displayed, but overbudget tasks will be high-lighted before the dialog box is closed.

Fig. 17.7
Selecting the filter from the entry list.

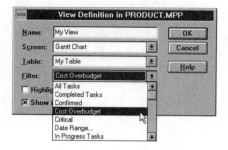

Selecting the Highlight Filter

To stipulate that the chosen filter is to be a highlight filter, mark the **H**igh-light Filter check box at the bottom of the View Definition dialog box. The finished dialog box in figure 17.8 shows the Cost Overbudget filter marked as a highlight filter only.

A highlight filter shows all tasks or resources, but those selected by the filter are displayed with the highlight formatting features bold, italics, underline, and so on, as defined with the Format Text Styles command for highlighted items.

Fig. 17.8
Completing the View Definition dialog box.

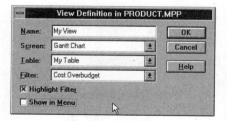

Displaying the View Name in the Menu

To display the view name in the **V**iew menu, mark the Show in **M**enu check box. If you don't want the view to appear in the **V**iew menu, don't mark this check box. The view defined in figure 17.8 doesn't appear in the **V**iew menu because the check box is not marked. All views always appear in the More Views list.

Saving the View Definition

When you have finished using the View Definition dialog box, select the OK button to save your definition. You are returned to the More Views dialog box, where you can take one of the following actions:

- Select the **A**pply button to place the view on-screen immediately. For example, you may want to apply format features to the view, or use the view to edit or view your project.

- Select the Cancel button to leave the current view on-screen but save the view you have just defined.

- Select the **N**ew, **C**opy, or **E**dit buttons to continue working with the list of views.

- Select the **O**rganizer button to save the newly defined view along with all other views to the global file. See the upcoming section, "Organizing Views in Project Files," for more details.

Creating a Combination View

If the view is a combination view (a view that defines other views to be placed in the top and bottom panes), the views for each pane must be defined before you can define the combination view. To define a combination view, access the More Views dialog box by choosing **M**ore Views from the **V**iew menu. Select the **N**ew button to display the Define New View dialog box (refer to fig. 17.4). Then select the **C**ombination View button. The View Definition dialog box that appears is designed for defining a combination view (refer to fig. 17.3).

Choose the **N**ame field and enter a name for the view. In figure 17.3, the name includes an ampersand (&) to designate the selection letter for the view when the name appears on the menu. From the **T**op entry list, choose the view to place in the top pane. All single pane views that have been defined are available for selection. From the **B**ottom entry list, choose the view to place in the bottom pane. All single pane views (except PERT Charts, which cannot appear in the bottom pane) are available for selection. Mark the Show in **M**enu check box if you want the view to appear on the **V**iew menu. Clear this check box if you want the view to appear on the More Views list only.

To complete the view definition, select the OK button. Select the **A**pply button in the More Views dialog box to display the view immediately, or select the Cancel button to save the view but leave the screen unchanged.

If you define a combination view that uses other customized views you have defined, and if these views use customized tables and filters you have defined, you must plan the order in which the customized components are developed. Specifically, you must work from the bottom up. The following sequence is for the most complex case. In this example, you define a combination view that uses new views you have defined; these views use tables and filters you have defined and that contain formatting changes you want to use.

1. Define all new tables that you plan to use. It doesn't matter whether their names appear on the **V**iew Ta**b**le menu. These names appear automatically on the **M**ore Tables menu, which is what matters.

2. Define any new filters that you plan to use. These filters do not have to appear on the **T**ools **F**iltered For menu; appearing on the **M**ore Filters menu is sufficient.

3. Define the views that you want to appear in the top and bottom panes, using the basic screens that are appropriate. Assign to these views the tables and filters that you want the views to use.

4. Format each of the views with the special formatting options that you want to use.

5. Define the combination view by naming the new customized views to be placed in the top and bottom panes. If you want to have this view directly available from the **V**iew menu, place an X in the Show in **M**enu check box. The definitions you have created are saved with the project file.

Organizing Views in Project Files

All the customized changes that you make to the views—whether through defining views, tables, filters, or format specifications—are saved as part of the current project file. If you want these customized views, tables, and filters to be available to all projects, these view definitions must be stored in a global file. The global file for Microsoft Project is GLOBAL.MPT.

When you start Microsoft Project, the view data loads with the project file. When you exit Project, all changes you made to the views are saved with the project file. If you would like to use a customized view you created for another project file, though, it would not be available to you. You can save the view data to the global file, or you can save it with the project file and make these customized views available across all project files created.

To save the view changes to the GLOBAL.MPT file, follow these steps:

1. From the **V**iew menu, choose **M**ore Views and choose the **O**rganizer button.

2. The views available in the GLOBAL.MPT file are on the left of the screen, and the customized and modified views (which are available in the current project file) are on the right (see fig. 17.9).

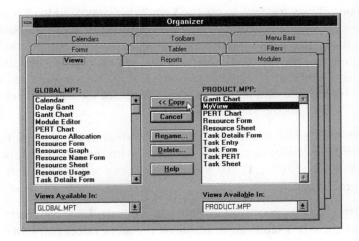

Fig. 17.9
The Organizer screen for managing view definitions.

3. Select the view or views in the project file list that should also be in the global file and click the **C**opy button. This copies these view definitions from the project file over to the global file.

4. The Cancel button changes to close after the Copy is performed. Click the Close button to close the organizer when you are finished copying the view definitions.

If you save the customized views in the global file, anytime you create a new project the views will be available.

You can also use the Organizer to Rename and Delete views from the global or current project files. To delete a view (either customized or standard), perform the following steps:

1. Select the view in the view list from which it should be deleted—either the global file or the current project file.

2. Click the **D**elete button.

3. Click **Y**es to confirm the deletion or **N**o to cancel the deletion.

III

Views and Reports

4. The view will be gone from either the global file (which will affect all projects that used that view) or from the current project file only.

5. Click the Close button to complete the Organizer command.

Using and Creating Tables

This section shows you how to use the **V**iew Ta**b**le command to change the appearance and content of the column data in the sheet views. You can determine the data to be displayed in each column, the width of the column, the alignment of the data within the column, and the title that appears at the top of the column. With the Table Definition dialog box, you can add new columns, delete columns, and make other changes in the definition of the table.

To change the display of a table, select **V**iew Ta**b**le and choose **M**ore Tables. The More Tables dialog box appears on-screen, with the currently displayed table highlighted (see fig. 17.10). You use this dialog box to perform the following procedures:

- Display a table that is not included on the main **T**able command (five additional task tables are available on the More Tables entry list).

- Change the list of tables by adding or deleting tables.

- Change the features of any of the tables on the entry list.

Fig. 17.10
The More Tables
dialog box.

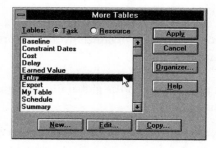

The names of either task tables or resource tables appear on the entry list, depending on the view that was active when you chose the **M**ore Tables command. To switch between task tables and resource tables without leaving the dialog box, choose one of the buttons, **T**ask or **R**esource, at the top of the dialog box.

To apply a table to the current view, choose the desired table from the entry list and choose the **A**pply button. Note, however, that if the current view is a task view, you cannot display a resource table on this view.

To edit an existing table, choose the table from the entry list and choose the **E**dit button. If you want to create a new table that is similar to an existing table, choose the original table from the entry list and choose the **C**opy button.

To create a new table from scratch, choose the **N**ew button.

Whenever you choose the **N**ew, **C**opy, or **E**dit button, the Table Definition dialog box appears. If you choose **N**ew, the fields in the dialog box will be empty. If you choose either **E**dit or **C**opy, the fields will contain the values for the table you selected from the entry list in the More Tables dialog box. Figure 17.11 illustrates a dialog box for a copy of the Entry table. The explanations that follow also apply when you are editing or creating new tables. Using the dialog box options is the same in all three cases.

Tip
If you want to preserve the standard tables in their original form, use the **C**opy command rather than the **E**dit command and edit the copy of the table. You then will have both the original and the revised copies to use.

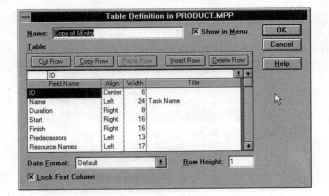

Fig. 17.11
The Table Definition dialog box for making a copy of the Entry table.

Entering a Table Name

If you are creating a new table or editing a copy of another table, you will want to supply a new name for the table. The name can contain up to 49 characters. If the table name is to appear on the table menu, use an ampersand (&) before any character in the name to indicate that this character is used to select the table. If, for example, you enter **&Bid** in the Name box, the Bid table will appear on the menu as **B**id; the user can press B to select the table from the menu. For the table name to be displayed on the table menu, you must mark the check box labeled Show in **M**enu.

III

Views and Reports

Changing the Columns in the Table

You can define up to 92 columns of field names for a table. To place a column in the table, insert a row for the field in the **T**able area of the dialog box.

If you want to use additional fields, scroll down the **T**able area of the dialog box for blank rows. To insert a field between the existing fields, select the row where you want to place the new field, and use the **I**nsert Row button to insert a blank row.

To remove a field from the table, select the row that contains the field name and use the **D**elete Row button. To replace a field with a new field, select the Field Name entry for the old field and replace the name with the new field name.

Use the entry list arrow at the top right of the **T**able area to scroll the list of field names (see fig. 17.12). When you choose a name from the Field Name list, the default Alignment and Width for the field are supplied automatically. You can change the alignment to Left, Center, or Right by typing this specification or by selecting the alignment from the entry list. Type a different Width for the field if you want a width other than the default width.

Fig. 17.12
The Table list of field names, shown in the Table Definition dialog box.

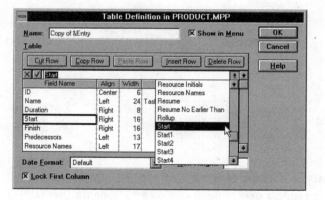

Use the Title column to supply a column name if you want one that is different from the field name. Leave the Title column blank if you want to use the field name as the title.

Completing the Definition of the Table

At the top of the dialog box, the check box labeled Show in **M**enu must be marked if you want the table to appear on the **V**iew Ta**b**le menu (rather than just on the More Tables menu). The **V**iew Ta**b**le menu displays up to 20 table names. The check box acts as a toggle; you mark it to clear it, and you mark it again to fill it.

Mark the check box labeled **L**ock First Column if you want the first column of the table to remain on-screen at all times. In the standard sheet views, the first column is the ID number for the task or resource.

Use the Date **F**ormat area to specify the format for date fields in the table. If you leave the Default entry in place, the date format selected through the **T**ools **O**ptions command is used. Select the entry list arrow to display the other date formats that you can elect to use rather than the default format.

The normal row height in a sheet view is 1, which means that one row of text is displayed for each task or resource *row* in the table. If the row height is greater than 1, long text entries in any column of the table automatically wrap words if the width of the column is insufficient to display them on one line. Choose **R**ow Height and enter the number of text lines to be displayed for each task. Note that additional lines will take up space even if they are blank.

Figure 17.13 shows the definition for a new table named Bid, which displays tasks with ID, Name, Duration, Start date, and Text1 comments. Note that the titles for most of the fields have been changed, the Date **F**ormat has been changed to omit the time of day, and the **R**ow Height has been changed to 3 to facilitate displaying the long text entries that may be found in the Text1 field.

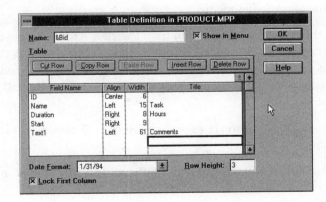

Fig. 17.13
The table definition for the Bid table.

Figure 17.14 shows the Bid table (as defined in fig. 17.13) when applied to the Task Sheet view.

Fig. 17.14
The Bid table
applied to the
Task Sheet view.

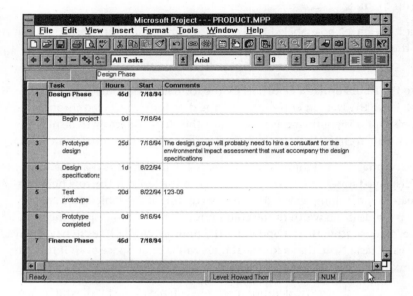

Changing Table Features from the View Screen

Most of the features that you define in the Table Definition dialog box can be changed from the view screen without having to go through the **V**iew Ta**b**le command. For example, you can access the Column Definition dialog box to insert, delete, and edit the definitions of columns directly in the table, without using the More Tables menu.

To change the definition of a column from the view screen, double-click the title of the column. The Column Definition dialog box appears, as shown in figure 17.15, with the current column settings displayed in the selection fields. To redefine a column, change the selections in any of the following entry fields:

- Choose Field **N**ame to view the entry list of field names, and select a field from the list.

- Choose **T**itle if you want to type a different text title to appear at the head of the column.

- Choose **A**lign to change the alignment for the column data.

- Choose **W**idth if you want to set the width of the column manually. Enter the width in number of characters. You also can use the **B**est Fit button to set the width.

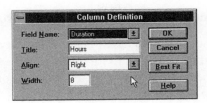

Fig. 17.15
The Column Definition dialog box.

Complete the new definition of the column by choosing either OK or **B**est Fit. Choose OK if you want to apply the new column definition, including the **W**idth setting. Choose **B**est Fit, however, if you want Microsoft Project to calculate the width needed to fully display both the title and the longest data value that initially goes into the column. The **B**est Fit button closes the dialog box and applies the new definition, but with the calculated column width.

To insert a new column, follow these steps:

1. Select the entire column currently located where the new column is to be placed. (You select a column by selecting the column title.)

2. Choose Insert **C**olumn from the **I**nsert menu, or press the Insert (Ins) key. The Column Definition dialog box is displayed with values for the ID field supplied in the definition fields. Select the values for the new column, as previously described.

To remove a column from the table, first select the column (by selecting the column title). Then choose **D**elete Column from the **E**dit menu or press Ctrl+– (the minus key on the numeric keypad).

Caution

Do not use the Delete key for this operation. Pressing Delete erases all the currently selected field values, but doesn't remove the column from the table. If you accidentally use Delete, use the **E**dit **U**ndo command or the Ctrl+Z shortcut to restore the erased values.

You can adjust the column width directly on the view screen by using the mouse. Follow these steps:

1. Move the mouse pointer into the row at the top of the table where the column titles are displayed, and position the pointer on the right gridline of the column you want to adjust.

2. Drag the gridline to the right or left to adjust the column width.

3. Double-click the gridline to have Microsoft Project calculate and adjust the column width to the best fit for the data in the column. The width will be set to the necessary space for a full display of the widest entry found in any row of the column.

Any column width that you set with the mouse is automatically recorded in the Table Definition dialog box. You can change the row height also with the mouse. Drag (up or down) the bottom gridline in the first column (usually the ID column) of the row whose height should be changed. This action adjusts the number of lines to be allocated per row in the table.

If you want your table to appear when you select a view, you must define the view to include the table name. To display the Task Sheet view shown in figure 17.14, you open the **V**iew menu, choose **M**ore Views, and select Task Sheet. Then open the **V**iew menu, choose the Ta**b**le command, and select the Bid table. If you were to choose Task Sheet again, the screen would revert to the table defined for that view—the Entry table. See "Creating New Views," earlier in this chapter, for instructions on defining a view that always displays a custom table.

Using and Creating Filters

All the views except the PERT Chart can have filters automatically assigned to the view. All the standard views have been assigned the all-inclusive filter (All Tasks or All Resources). For details about assigning a different filter to a view, see the earlier section, "Creating New Views."

▶ "Formatting Views," p. 497.

A filter helps you identify and display only the tasks or resources (depending on the view) that match one or more criteria defined in the filter. If a filter is applied as a *highlight* filter, all tasks or resources are displayed, but those selected by the filter are displayed with the highlight formatting features bold, italics, underline, and so on, as defined with the F**o**rmat **T**ext Styles command for highlighted items. Any filter can be applied as a highlight filter or a display-only filter.

▶ "The Microsoft Project Field Dictionary," p. 727.

You define the criteria for a filter by specifying one or more field values that must be matched for a task or resource to be selected by the filter. For example, Microsoft Project maintains a field named Milestone for tasks, and automatically places the value Yes in the field if you define a task as a milestone. The Milestone filter stipulates that the Milestone field must contain the value Yes. You might decide to define a filter that selects all resources with more than 20 hours of overtime work scheduled. Your filter would check the Overtime Work field of the resource database and select all the resources with a value of 20 or more in this field. To create filters, you must have some knowledge of the fields used in the Microsoft Project databases.

In addition to the simple filters just described, filters known as *interactive* filters ask the user to supply the value or values to be looked for in the field. The Date **R**ange filter available through the **T**ools **F**iltered For command, for example, asks the user to enter two dates and then displays all tasks that have a Scheduled Start or Finish date within this range of dates.

Another type of filter, the *calculated* filter, determines what item to display by comparing the values in two fields in the database. For example, the **C**ost Overbudget filter in the Filter list box on the Formatting toolbar compares the value in the Cost field (which is the total scheduled cost for a task) with the value in the Planned Cost field for that same task. If the scheduled cost is greater than the planned cost, the filter selects the task.

Some filters use more than one test for selecting the items to display. For example, the **I**n Progress Tasks filter selects all the tasks that have an Actual Start date recorded (the Actual Start field no longer displays NA) but that also do not have an Actual Finish date recorded (the Actual Finish field still displays NA). In this case, both conditions must be met for a task to be selected: the Actual Start must not have NA, *and* the Actual Finish must still have NA. This kind of criterion is usually called an *and* condition or criterion. For a task to be selected, both this condition *and* that condition must be satisfied.

Another example of a filter that applies more than one test is the Tasks with **F**ixed Dates filter, which is accessed by selecting **T**ools **F**iltered For and choosing **M**ore Filters. This filter locates all the tasks that either have constrained dates (the Constraint Type other than As Soon As Possible) or that already have an actual start date recorded (the Actual Start field no longer shows NA). This filter is useful for helping you resolve scheduling problems caused by fixed dates. In this case, you want the computer to select all the tasks that have a constraint imposed on them *or* that have already started and cannot be rescheduled. This type of criterion is called an *or* condition or criterion. For a task to be selected, either one *or* the other of the conditions must be satisfied.

Using the Standard Filters

Not every view can be filtered, and there are other limitations to using filters. The following points summarize these limitations:

- You can apply only task filters to task views and only resource filters to resource views.

- You cannot apply a filter to a bottom pane view. The reason is that the bottom pane view is already filtered: it displays only the tasks or resources that are associated with the item or items selected in the top pane.

- The PERT Chart cannot be filtered, but the standard filters are available for all other views.

- You cannot apply a highlight filter to a form. Using a filter as a highlight makes sense only for the views that display lists, because the purpose of a highlight is to make selected items stand out from the rest. Thus, only the views that contain a table can accept a highlight filter.

- Each filter considers the entire set of tasks or resources for selections. You cannot use successive filters to progressively narrow the set of selected tasks or resources. For example, if you filter the task list to show Milestones, and then you apply the Critical filter, you will see all critical tasks related, not just critical milestones.

Any view that can accept a filter can have one defined as part of the view: when the view is selected, the filter is automatically applied. All the standard views have the All Tasks or All Resources filters designated as part of the view definition.

Describing the Standard Filters

All Tasks	↕

The standard filters supplied with Microsoft Project provide selection criteria that have been found to be useful to a significant number of users. Tables 17.1 and 17.2 describe the standard task filters and resource filters, respectively. An asterisk marks a filter not found on the standards **T**ools **F**iltered For menu, but which is found instead on the **M**ore Filters menu. All filters are listed in the Filter list box on the Formatting toolbar as well.

Table 17.1   The Standard Task Filters

Filter Name	Purpose
All Tasks	Displays all tasks.
Completed Tasks	Displays tasks that are marked as 100% complete.
*Confirmed	Displays tasks for which the requested resources have agreed to take on the assignment.
*Cost Overbudget	Displays all tasks that have a scheduled cost greater than the baseline cost if the baseline cost is greater than 0.
Critical	Displays all critical tasks.
Date Range	Displays all tasks with a scheduled start date between two dates that you specify in response to prompts.
Incomplete Tasks	Displays all tasks that have a percentage complete of greater than 0, but less than 100%.
*In Progress Tasks	Displays all tasks that have started but have not finished.
*Linked Fields	Displays all tasks that are linked to another application.
Milestones	Displays all milestones.
*Resource Group	Displays all tasks assigned to the resource who belong to the specified resource group.
*Should Start By	Displays all tasks that should have started but have not started by a date supplied by the user.
*Slipping Tasks	Displays all tasks not finished and whose scheduled finish date is later than the planned finish date.
Subprojects Filter	A subproject file specification has been attached to this task.
Summary Tasks	Displays all tasks that have subordinate tasks defined below them.
Task Range	Displays all tasks that have ID numbers within a range specified by the user.
*Tasks with Attachments	Shows tasks that have objects attached, such as a graph or a note in the Notes field.
*Tasks with Fixed Dates	Displays all tasks that have a constraint other than As Soon As Possible or that have already started.
*Top Level Tasks	Displays all highest level summary tasks.

(continues)

Table 17.1 Continued	
Filter Name	**Purpose**
*Unconfirmed	Displays all tasks for which the requested resources have not yet committed to the task.
*Unstarted Tasks	Displays all tasks which have not yet started.
*Update Needed	Displays all tasks that have incurred changes, such as revised start and finish dates or resource reassignments, and need to be sent for update or confirmation.
Using Resource	Displays all tasks that use the resource named by the user.
*Work Overbudget	Displays all tasks with scheduled work greater than the baseline work and greater than 0.

Table 17.2 The Standard Resource Filters	
Filter Name	**Purpose**
All Resources	Displays all resources.
Cost Overbudget	Displays all resources that have a scheduled cost that is greater than the baseline cost.
Group	Displays all resources that belong to the group specified by the user (which have the same entry in the Group field).
*Linked Fields	Displays all resources with fields that are linked to another application.
Overallocated Resources	Displays all resources that are overallocated.
Resource Range	Displays all resources that have ID numbers within the range specified by the user.
*Resources with Attachments	Displays resources that have objects attached or a note in the Notes field.
Work Overbudget	Displays all resources with scheduled work that is greater than the baseline work.

Applying a Filter to the Current View

All Tasks	

To apply a filter to a view, you can use the **T**ools **F**iltered For menu or the Filter list box on the Formatting toolbar. Discussing the menu option first, if the filter that you want is on the **T**ools **F**iltered For menu, select the filter name, and it will be applied immediately. If the filter is not on the **T**ools **F**iltered For menu, first choose **M**ore Filters, and then choose the filter name from the complete list of filters in the **F**ilters entry list (see fig. 17.16). Choose the **A**pply button to apply the filter, so that only filtered tasks or resources— that satisfy the filter—appear. If you want to apply the filter as a highlight filter (so that filtered items are highlighted and all other items remain displayed), choose the **H**ighlight button instead of the **A**pply button.

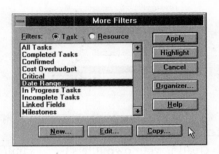

Fig. 17.16
The More Filters
dialog box.

You can apply any filter as a highlight filter by choosing the filter name from the **M**ore Filters entry list and then choosing **H**ighlight. You can apply filters as highlight filters also by holding down the Shift key as you choose the **T**ools **F**iltered For menu and select the filter name.

You can also apply a filter to the current view by selecting the filter name from the Filter list box on the Formatting toolbar (see fig. 17.17). When you select the filter name from the list, the filter is applied immediately. You cannot apply the filter as a highlight filter when using the toolbar list box.

Fig. 17.17
The Filter list box
on the Formatting
toolbar.

III

When you apply a filter, all tasks or resources that satisfy the criteria at that moment are selected by the filter. If you change a value in a field, you may change how this value satisfies the filter criteria. The task or resource will continue to be displayed or highlighted, however, because the filter criteria are evaluated only at the moment the filter is applied. You may need to apply the filter again if you make significant changes in the project.

Tip
You can use Ctrl+F3
to apply the current
filter again. Micro-
soft Project then
recalculates which
tasks or resources
satisfy the filter.

After you have finished using the filtered view, you can remove the filter by selecting the **A**ll Tasks filter or **A**ll Resources filter.

Tip
Use the F3 key to remove the current filter.

After you apply an interactive filter, a dialog box appears in which you must supply the values to be used for testing the tasks or resources. For example, figure 17.18 shows the Using Resource filter dialog box. In this illustration, the filter will select all tasks with an assigned resource that you choose from the entry list.

Fig. 17.18
The Using Resource filter dialog box.

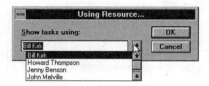

Creating Custom Filters

A good way to begin creating your own filters is to examine the definitions of the standard filters. To look at a filter definition, perform these steps:

1. From the **T**ools menu, choose **F**iltered For and select **M**ore Filters from the list.

2. Select a filter from the entry list.

3. Choose the **E**dit button.

The Filter Definition dialog box appears. Figure 17.19 shows the Filter Definition box for the In Progress Tasks filter.

Fig. 17.19
The Filter Definition dialog box for the In Progress Tasks filter.

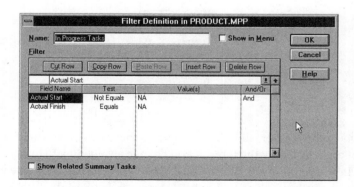

The In Progress Tasks filter applies two tests. The first test examines the Actual Start field to be sure that the value is *not equal* to NA (that is, the task has been started), and the second test examines the Actual Finish field to see whether the value is NA (the task has not finished). The logical operator And has been entered in the And/Or field, meaning that both the first *and* the second conditions must be met for a task to be selected.

Figure 17.20 illustrates the interactive Date Range filter. In this filter, the Finish field is tested to see whether the Finish date value falls after the entered value and whether the Start date falls before the entered value. However, the filter is designed to prompt the user to supply the dates at the time the filter is applied. Note that the *prompt* is written within double quotation marks, and the *pause* for the user to enter a response is defined. Prompts appear with a question mark immediately following the prompt. For multiple prompts, you use a comma (or the list separator specified in the Options dialog box) to separate the values.

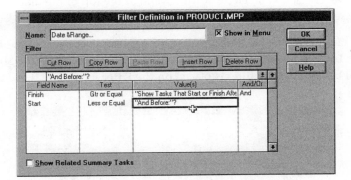

Fig. 17.20
The Filter Definition dialog box for the Date Range filter.

To define a filter, choose **M**ore Filters from the **T**ools **F**iltered For menu. If you want to create a new filter unlike any filter already defined, choose the **N**ew button. Otherwise, select an existing filter name from the **F**ilters entry list if you want to edit or copy an existing filter. In all three cases, the Filter Definition dialog box is displayed. Figure 17.21 shows a new Filter Definition dialog box. The following sections show you how to develop an over budget filter that displays all tasks with a budgeted cost in excess of $1,000.

Fig. 17.21
The Filter Definition dialog box for creating a new filter.

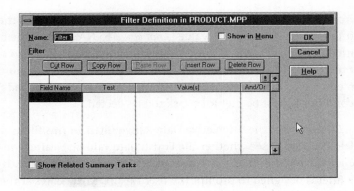

Naming the Filter

Provide a name for the filter by choosing the **N**ame field in the dialog box. If the filter name is to appear in the Filter menu, use an ampersand (&) before the letter that will be underlined (to be used to choose the filter from the menu). The check box labeled Show in **M**enu at the top of the dialog box must be selected for the filter name to appear in the menu.

In the example of the over budget filter, you enter the name as **O&ver Budget by 1000** (with **v** as the selection letter), and you mark the Show in **M**enu box so that the filter is placed on the Filter menu (see fig. 17.22).

Fig. 17.22
The Name field showing the Over Budget by 1000 entry.

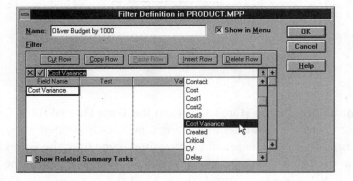

Defining the Filter Criteria

To define the criteria, choose the **F**ilter area. For each test to be imposed on the database, you must fill in a row of this area. Each row must identify a Field Name, the nature of the Test to be conducted in the field, and the Value(s) to be looked for in the field. If multiple tests are to be imposed as part of the filter, the And/Or column must indicate the relationship of the criterion rows.

Selecting the Field Name. Type the field name or use the entry list arrow to select a field name from the entry list. See Appendix C to find out how to learn more about fields. In the example in figure 17.22, the field name is Cost Variance.

▶ "The Microsoft Project Field Dictionary," p. 727.

Selecting the Test. Select the cell in the Test column and use the entry list arrow to view the tests you can select (see fig. 17.23). Select the appropriate test or type the test phrase. In the example, the test is to be *greater than or equal to*, which is represented by the Gtr or Equal phrase on the entry list.

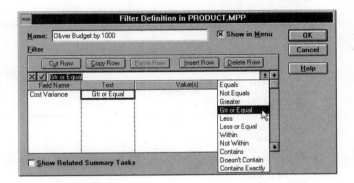

Fig. 17.23
The Test entry list.

Table 17.3 describes the use of each of the items in the Test entry list.

Table 17.3	The Filter Test Options			
Test	**Meaning and Criterion Example**	**Field Name**	**Test**	**Value(s)**
Equals	Field values must match Value(s) entry exactly.			
	Select Critical tasks Code ends with "–12."	Critical Code	Equals	Yes *–12
Not Equals	Field value must differ from Value(s) entry.			
	Task has started	Actual Start	Not Equals	NA

(continues)

Table 17.3 Continued				
Test	**Meaning and Criterion Example**	**Field Name**	**Test**	**Value(s)**
Greater	Field value must be greater than Value(s) entry.			
	Task started after 8/1/92	Actual Start	Greater	8/1/92
Gtr or Equal	Field value must be greater than or equal to Value(s) entry.			
	Budgeted cost $1000 or over	Planned Cost	Gtr or Equal	$1,000
Less	Field value must be less than Value(s) entry.			
	Duration less than 1 day	Duration	Less	1d
Less or Equal	Field value must be less than or equal to Value(s) entry.			
	Task finishes before 9/1/92	Actual Finish	Less or Equal	9/1/92
Within	Field value must lie on or between the range of Value(s) entries.			
	Duration is 5 to 10 days.	Duration	Within	5d,10d
Not Within	Field value must lie outside the range of Value(s) entries.			
	Tasks that are not in the middle of production	% Complete	Not Within	25%, 75%

Test	Meaning and Criterion Example	Field Name	Test	Value(s)
Contains	Field value must contain the string in Value(s).			
	Resource assignment includes Mary Logan	Name	Contains	Mary Logan
Doesn't Contain	Field value must not contain the string in Value(s).	Resource	Doesn't Contain	
Contains Exactly	Field value must contain the exact string in Value(s)			
	Resource assignment includes Mary Logan	Name	Contains	Mary Logan

Entering the Value(s). To enter the value to test for, select the cell in the Value(s) column. Type a value for the test or place an interactive prompt for interactive filters, or use another field name for calculated filters. The entry list for this column is used for calculated filters and contains the names of the fields, with each field name automatically enclosed in square brackets as required by the calculated filters. In figure 17.24, the value is $1,000.

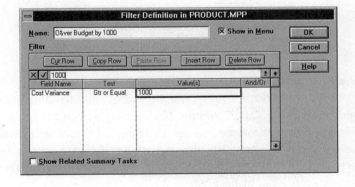

Fig. 17.24
The finished Over Budget by 1,000 filter.

III

Views and Reports

Completing the Filter Definition. Use the **I**nsert Row button to insert a blank row before the criterion rows you have selected. Use the **D**elete Row button to remove the criterion row from the definition.

If the filter is to appear in the Filter menu, be sure that the Show in Menu check box is selected. Mark the Show Related Summary Tasks check box if you want the summary task for any task selected by the filter also displayed.

Choose the OK button to complete the definition and return to the More Filters dialog box. Choose the Apply or Highlight button to apply the filter immediately, or choose Cancel to save the filter definition but not apply the filter at this time.

Using More Filter Criterion Tests

This section illustrates various types of filter criteria. These samples should help you design almost any kind of filter.

Testing for Logical Values

Many of the fields in the databases contain only the logical values Yes or No. For example, the Milestone field contains Yes for Milestone tasks, and No for all other tasks. The standard filter for Milestone tasks looks for the value Yes in the appropriate field (see fig. 17.25).

Fig. 17.25
The Milestone task filter.

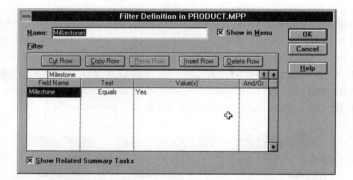

Using the Within and Not Within Tests

Use the Within test to test for values that lie within and including the upper and lower values in the Values column. Use the Not Within test to identify values that fall outside a range of values. The range of values being used in the test is entered in the Value(s) column, with a comma separating the lower and upper values. In figure 17.26, the Finish field is searched to find tasks that finish on 8/10/92 or by 8/15/92.

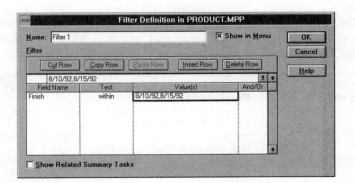

Fig. 17.26
A filter that uses
the Within test.

Using the Contains Test

Some text fields (most notably, Resource Names, Predecessors, and Successors) may contain lists of entries separated by commas. The Resource Names field contains the list of all the resources assigned to a task, and the Predecessors field contains a list of all the predecessors to the task. These are really text fields. The Contains test examines the text to see whether a string of characters that you enter in the Value(s) column is contained within the field contents. Figure 17.27 shows a filter criterion that looks for the resource name Mary Logan to identify the tasks to which Mary is assigned.

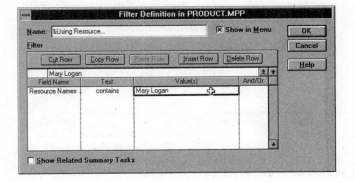

Fig. 17.27
The Contains test.

Using Wild Cards in a Value(s) String

Text field entries can be searched with wild-card characters in the search string. You must use only the Equals or Not Equals test for strings that include wild cards. The wild-card characters in Microsoft Project are similar to wild-card characters used in DOS: the asterisk (*) and the question mark (?). A wild card can match any character that falls in the same place as the wild card in the search comparisons. Therefore, the test string *ab?d* is matched by any character in the third position as long as the *a*, *b*, and *d* are in the right places. The asterisk represents any number of missing characters or no characters, and the question mark represents just one character. Note the following examples:

Test String with Wild Card	Possible Matches
f?d	fad, fbd, fcd, fdd, fed, f2d
f??d	find, ford, food, f23d
f*d	fd, fad, feed, formatted
f*	f, f1, f123, find this text
12-?06	12-A06, 12-106, 12-X06
12-*06	12-A06, 12-06, 12-abc006

The filter in figure 17.28 is defined to search the WBS field for entries that end in –12.

Fig. 17.28
A filter that finds WBS entries ending in –12.

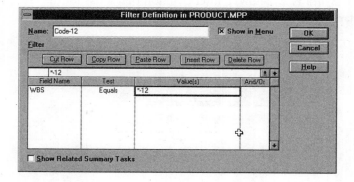

Using Interactive Filters

An interactive filter increases the versatility of a filter that must search for different values in a field from time to time. For example, the filter in figure 17.27 is designed to locate tasks to which Mary Logan is assigned. To search for a different resource name, you must redefine the filter. You can, however, replace the specification of Mary Logan with instructions to ask the user for the name of the resource to be located. Then the filter can be used to locate the tasks for any resource.

Interactive filters are created by placing a message and a question mark in the Value(s) column of the filter definition. When the filter is applied, the message is displayed (in a dialog box) as a prompt for the user, and the question mark causes Microsoft Project to wait for the user to fill a blank that follows the message in the dialog box. For example, the message "Enter resource name:" is a suitable prompt to ask for the resource name to be located. The entry in the Value(s) column of the filter definition would look like the entry in figure 17.29.

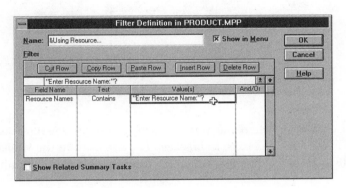

Fig. 17.29
An interactive filter to locate resource assignments.

The filter illustrated in figure 17.26 looks for Finish dates that fall within the range 8/10/92 and 8/15/92. You can replace both of these specific dates with prompts, as shown in figure 17.30.

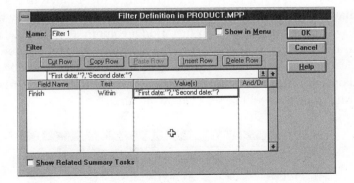

Fig. 17.30
An interactive filter with multiple prompts.

Creating Calculated Filters

A calculated filter compares the value in one field of a task or resource with the value in another field for the same task or resource. For example, tasks that are over budget have in the Planned Cost field a value that is less than the value in the Cost field (which is the currently scheduled cost field). To filter over budget tasks, the criterion needs to compare the Cost field with the Planned Cost field (see fig. 17.31).

Fig. 17.31
A calculated filter.

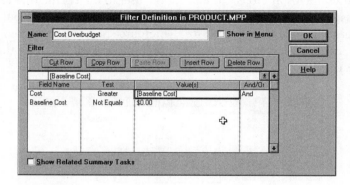

If you are entering a field name in the Value(s) column of the filter definition, the name must be placed in brackets. The entry list for the Value(s) column lists all the field names, which Microsoft Project places within brackets.

Creating Multiple Criteria Filters

If more than one test must be used to create the filter, each test is placed on its own row of the filter definition table. The last column (And/Or) is used to designate how each row is to be used with the row that follows it. If it is necessary that the tests on both rows must be satisfied in order to satisfy the filter, the operator And is placed in the And/Or column. For example, a filter to locate all the critical milestones tests the Milestone field on one row and the Critical field on the next row. Because both requirements must be met, the And operator is placed in the And/Or column (see fig. 17.32). Only Critical *and* Milestone tasks will be selected by the filter.

Fig. 17.32
A filter that uses multiple criterion.

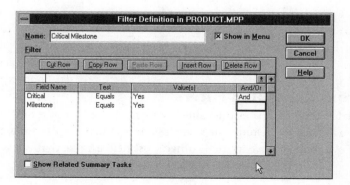

If, however, passing either of the tests is sufficient to satisfy the filter, the operator Or is placed in the And/Or column. If the Or operator is placed in this column in figure 17.32, all critical tasks are selected (whether they are milestones or not), and all milestones are selected (whether they are critical tasks or not).

If more than two rows are used to define a filter, the tests are evaluated from the top down. Therefore, the first two rows are evaluated using the operator on the first row, and then the third row test is added using the operator on the second row, and so on—until all rows have been considered. For example, in figure 17.33, the filter seeks to locate all the critical milestones as well as (or in addition to) all the tasks that are over budget.

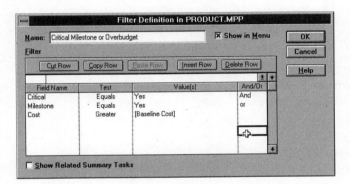

Fig. 17.33
A filter with more than two tests.

From Here...

This chapter described most of the customizing features regarding the layout of views and tables. You also learned how to create and customize filters using the various criteria rules.

The following chapters will provide you with some additional formatting and customization techniques for views and reports:

- Chapter 18, "Formatting Views," discusses the various ways you can format and sort the standard or customized views. Some topics discussed include formatting the text display, formatting timescales, and specific formatting techniques for the commonly used standard views.

- Chapter 20, "Using and Customizing Reports," covers the customization techniques you can use to create and save various reports.

■ Chapter 22, "Customizing Toolbars, Menus, Forms, and Cue Cards," goes into great detail on the ways in which you can customize the layout of the Microsoft Project application window by adding and removing the commands you use most to the toolbars and menus. It also covers the creation and use of custom forms within your project.

Chapter 18

Formatting Views

One of the major strengths of Microsoft Project is the provision for customizing the standard views and reports and for creating new views and reports to serve specific needs. In the previous chapter you saw how to use the basic building blocks included in the standard views to create new views. This chapter shows you how to use menu commands to enhance the appearance and serviceability of the standard views.

In this chapter you learn how to

- Zoom in and out to change the perspective on the project.

- Modify the timescale display to change the perspective on the project.

- Change the font, size, and color of text.

- Change the display of graphical objects on views.

- Change the type of values that are calculated.

- Sort tasks and resources in an order that you specify.

A number of menu commands provide options for changing the appearance and content of the major views. Most of these options are on the Format menu, but you will also find choices on the View, Insert, and Tools menus. Many views share similar customizing options. You use the Format Gridlines command, for example, to change the appearance of the gridlines in all the views that contain gridlines; you use the Format Timescale command in all the views that contain timescales; and you use the Format Text Styles command to change the font, size, and color of text in all views.

▶ "Using and Customizing Reports," p. 563

Using the Format Options in the Standard Views

Unlike tables and filters (described in the previous chapter), the options on the Format menu do not create named objects, but only change the look of the current view. Suppose that you change the timescale on the Gantt Chart to show months instead of days. Until you change the timescale again, this format will be the timescale you see each time you use the Gantt Chart. However, if you switch to another view that also has a timescale (the Resource Usage view, for example), you will find that the timescale in that view does not incorporate the changes in the Gantt Chart timescale, but instead reflects the way the Resource Usage view was last displayed. These changes are saved with the project file only. If you change to another project file, you will not see changes you made in a different file. You can borrow settings from another file or GLOBAL.MPT using the Organizer.

◀ "Organizing Views in Project Files," p. 470

Table 18.1 summarizes the format options for the standard views. The views are listed to emphasize the shared format choices. The same Text Styles formatting options are available, for example, in all views except Forms. With the exception of forms, most of the additional views on the **M**ore Views menu are variations or combinations of these views and have the same format choices as their counterparts in Table 18.1. For example, the Delay Gantt view has the same formatting choices as the Gantt Chart in Table 18.1. These options are displayed in Table 18.2.

Table 18.1   **Format Options for the Standard Views**

	Gantt Usage	Calendar	Resource PERT	Resource Graph	Resource Sheet
Font	X			X	X
Bar	X				
Ti**m**escale	X	X		X	X
Gridlines	X	X	X	X	X
GanttChart **W**izard	X				
Text Styles	X	X	X	X	X
Bar **S**tyles	X	X	X*	X	

	Gantt Usage	Calendar	Resource PERT	Resource Graph	Resource Sheet
Details			X		X
Layout	X	X	X		
Layout **N**ow		X	X		
View **Z**oom	X	X	X		X
Insert **P**age Break	X			X	X
Tools Sor**t**	X	X	X	X	X

The option is actually titled Box Styles.

Table 18.2 Format Options for Additional Views on the More Views Menu

	Delay Gantt	Resource Forms	Task Forms	Task Sheet
Font	X			X
Bar	X			
Ti**m**escale	X			
Gridlines	X			X
GanttChart				
Wizard	X			
Text Styles	X			X
Bar **S**tyles	X			
Details		X	X	
Layout	X			
Layout **N**ow				
View **Z**oom	X			
Insert **P**age	X			X
Break				
Tools Sor**t**	X	X	X	X

Sorting the Tasks or Resources in a View

Sorting is especially relevant for views that display tasks or resources in a table or list layout, but you also can sort the order in which tasks or resources appear in the form views as you scroll with the N**e**xt and Pre**v**ious buttons. The PERT Chart and the Task PERT are the only views in which you cannot sort the displayed items.

The So**r**t command, available on the **T**ools menu, enables you to sort by a number of predefined fields, differing from one view to the next, as well as a combination of up to three columns or fields that you specify. For example, in a resource view, predefined sort fields include by **C**ost, by **N**ame, or by **I**d. The predefined fields in a task view include by S**t**art Date, by **F**inish Date, by **P**riority, by **C**ost, and by I**D**. In addition, for both task and resource views, you can choose the **S**ort by option to specify other fields, a combination of fields, and the order of the sort. You might want to sort first by Group labels; and within each group by the standard rate the resources are paid—but in descending order, so that the highest paid are listed first within each group. If some of the people in the same group are paid the same standard rate, you also can alphabetize these people by name in ascending (normal) order within their rate group.

To sort the entries in a view, choose So**r**t from the **T**ools menu. A cascading menu appears with the predefined sort fields (see fig. 18.1). If you choose from one of these, the tasks or resources will be sorted immediately. If you select the **S**ort by option, the Sort dialog box appears (see fig. 18.2).

Fig. 18.1

The cascading sort list offers easy access to sorting tasks or resources.

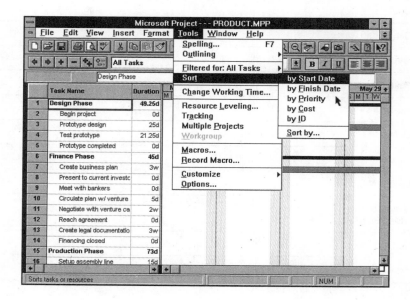

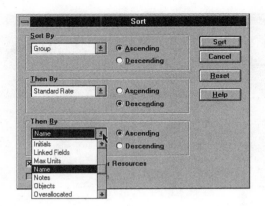

Fig. 18.2
The Sort dialog
box offers more
extensive options
for sorting.

Selecting the Sort Keys

Use the entry list arrow in the **S**ort by area to select the major sort field. Select the **A**scending or **D**escending button to specify the sort order. If you want to further sort the list within the groups that are placed together by the first sort field, choose the two **T**hen by fields, similarly indicating the sort order for each of these fields. In figure 18.2, the Resource Sheet is being sorted by Group name first, in ascending (normal) order. Within each group, the resources are being sorted by their standard pay rate in descending (reverse) order. Notice that the second Then **B**y field is selected so that the entries will be further sorted in ascending order by resource Name.

Selecting the Sort Operation

After you define the fields to sort by, you define the sort operation that you want to take place. For task views, you can mark the **K**eep Outline Structure check box to keep all tasks under their summary tasks, but to sort subordinate tasks within their summary task. To sort all tasks without regard for their position within an outline, uncheck this box.

To sort the list immediately, choose the S**o**rt button. To sort the list and also renumber the tasks or resources, choose the Permanently Renu**m**ber Tasks button. (Notice that this is the default.) To return the sort keys to the standard sort—by ID numbers only—choose **R**eset. Note that Reset will not display the original order of the list if Permanently Renu**m**ber Tasks was selected.

Choosing the Cancel button cancels all changes you may have made to the Sort dialog box and returns you to the workspace.

Figure 18.3 shows the Resource Sheet for the PRODUCT project, after the sort shown in the dialog box in figure 18.2.

Tip
To quickly sort
by date, use the
Sort by Date
tool on the
Standard
toolbar.

III

Views and Reports

Fig. 18.3
Resources are sorted by group, then by standard rate, then by name.

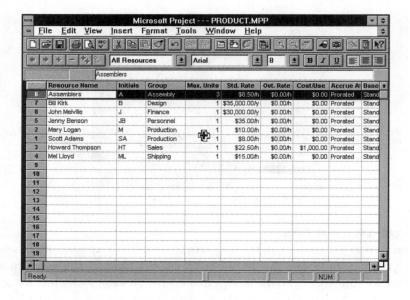

Resource Name	Initials	Group	Max. Units	Std. Rate	Ovt. Rate	Cost/Use	Accrue At	Base
6	Assemblers	A	Assembly	3	$8.50/h	$0.00/h	$0.00	Prorated	Stand
7	Bill Kirk	B	Design	1	$35,000.00/y	$0.00/h	$0.00	Prorated	Stand
8	John Melville	J	Finance	1	$30,000.00/y	$0.00/h	$0.00	Prorated	Stand
5	Jenny Benson	JB	Personnel	1	$35.00/h	$0.00/h	$0.00	Prorated	Stand
2	Mary Logan	M	Production	1	$10.00/h	$0.00/h	$0.00	Prorated	Stand
1	Scott Adams	SA	Production	1	$8.00/h	$0.00/h	$0.00	Prorated	Stand
3	Howard Thompson	HT	Sales	1	$22.50/h	$0.00/h	$1,000.00	Prorated	Stand
4	Mel Lloyd	ML	Shipping	1	$15.00/h	$0.00/h	$0.00	Prorated	Stand

Formatting Text Displays for Categories of Tasks and Resources

Most of the views enable you to choose special format options for displaying text. You can differentiate categories of tasks or resources by the font, type size, style, or color of text used to display the data. For example, you can format critical tasks to be displayed in red, or summary tasks to appear in bold. In table views, you can format the column headings. In timescale views, you can format the unit labels in the timescale. In text formatting, you define the appearance that highlight filters will use to display items selected by the filter.

To change the display of text for categories of tasks or resources in a view, choose **T**ext Styles from the F**o**rmat menu. The Text Styles dialog box is displayed (see fig. 18.4). If the **T**ext Styles command doesn't appear in the F**o**rmat menu, you cannot change the text display in this view. To change the text display for selected tasks or resources that do not fall into any particular category see the section "Formatting Selected Text," later in this chapter.

Selecting the Item To Change

From the **I**tem to Change entry list, choose the item you want. Some items in the list take precedence over others when a task or resource falls into two or more categories. Here are the task items, listed in order of precedence (with the highest priority at the top):

- Highlighted (by a filter)

- Marked

- Summary

- Milestone

- Critical

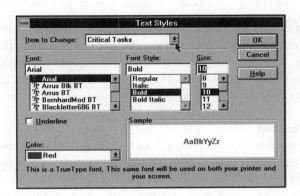

Fig. 18.4
Use the Text Styles dialog box to change text for categories of tasks or resources.

Therefore, if a Milestone task also is a Summary task, the display is governed by the text format for Summary tasks rather than for Milestone tasks. If the same task is selected by a highlight filter, the task shows the Highlight display rather than either the Summary or the Milestone display.

Highlighted tasks are tasks selected by a highlight filter. Use the **T**ext Styles command on the F**o**rmat menu (as described in this section) to determine how highlighted tasks or resources will be displayed. Use the **T**ools **F**iltered for command with the highlight option to display tasks or resources with the highlight format.

Marked tasks have the logical value Yes in the Marked field of the task database. Use the Marked field to manually select tasks without defining a filter (or when there is no logical test that can be expressed for the filter). You can define any task table or custom form to display the Marked field for editing purposes. When you mark tasks, you then can filter or use a special text format for them.

Milestone tasks have the logical value Yes in the Milestone field. The Milestone field is set to Yes when you enter a duration of zero for a task, but you also can designate any task as a Milestone task by checking the **M**ark Task as Milestone check box on the Task Information dialog box, Advanced tab. You also can place the Milestone field in a table for editing purposes.

Tip

You can choose to highlight a filter rather than hide other tasks by pressing the Shift key while choosing **T**ools **F**iltered for.

▶ "Using Custom Forms," p. 642

III

Views and Reports

The All item in the Item to Change entry list is provided so that you can easily make the same change in all items at once. If you make a change in the format options for the All item, this change is made in every other item in the selection list. You may use the All item initially, for example, to set an overall font type or size, leaving all other options clear. This procedure sets the same font type and size in all categories. You then can override the font and size on individual categories. If you later choose the All item again, however, and make a change in the font or point size, all categories change again.

The items listed after the task or resource items are features of the active view. When the Gantt Chart is the active view, for example, the item list includes Column Titles (for the table part of the view), Major Timescale and Minor Timescale (for the unit measures at the top of the timescale), and Bar Text (for displaying field values next to the bars in the bar chart in the timescale).

Changing the Font

Use the Font scroll bar in the Text Styles dialog box to move through the list of font choices for the selected item. The fonts available are the ones that have been installed in Windows for the selected printer. After selecting the font, you may choose the Size (in points) for the selected font from the Size list. You may need to use the scroll bar to move through the list. The reason you must choose the font before selecting a size is that not all sizes are available for all fonts.

Changing the Text Style

Select from the Font Style list to add bold, italic, or a combination of the two to the text. Choose Regular to clear a previous choice. Mark the Underline check box to turn on underlining.

Use the Color entry list arrow to choose the color for the selected item's text. If you don't use a color printer, all the colors print as black (but with different shading on some printers). The clear color option causes an item's text to be transparent in the display, although the row for the item still appears on-screen and on paper. The use of color on-screen still is useful, even if you use a black-and-white printer.

If all items in the Item to Change entry list have the same setting for one of the format features, this setting appears selected when the All item is selected. If all items use the same font, for example, you see the font name displayed when the All item is selected. If one or more items use a different font, however, the font name remains blank when you select the All item. The Underline check box will be marked if all items apply that feature; the box is not marked if no items use the option; and the box is dimmed if at least one, but not all items use the feature.

Formatting Selected Text

There are two additional choices for formatting text: using the Format Font command and using the Formatting Toolbar. The choices available using Format Font are the same as in the Text Styles dialog box, except that you do not have a choice for Item to Change. The toolbar offers entry list arrows for changing the font and point size, as well as buttons for bold, italic, and underline. Additionally, there are three buttons for the alignment of selected text: left, right, and center. The formatting toolbar is displayed in figure 18.5.

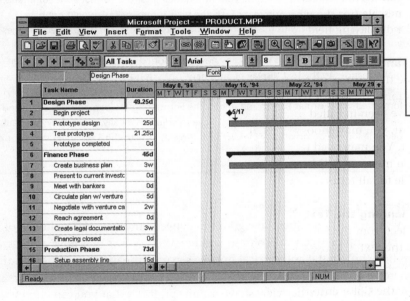

Fig. 18.5
The Formatting toolbar can be useful for formatting **selected** tasks or resources.

———Formatting toolbar

You can copy formatting options that you have created for a single task or resource using the Format Painter tool on the Standard Toolbar. To use this tool, select the task or resource whose format you wish to copy. Click the Format Paint tool. The mouse pointer will change to a cross with a paintbrush attached. Select the tasks or resources that you want to copy the format to. Formatting changes created using this tool are the same as if you used the Formatting toolbar or the Format Font command.

Use caution when using this tool, however, because Undo is not available. If you change your mind about the format, you have to use the Formatting toolbar options or the Format Font command to reset the changes you made.

Caution

The difference between using the Format Text Styles dialog box and using Format Font (or the Formatting toolbar) is significant. When using the latter two options you are making changes to selected text only, not to *categories* of tasks or resources. When additional tasks or resources belonging to a certain category are added, the formatting applied using the Format Font command or the Formatting toolbar are not taken into account. Any text display changes are made only to selected tasks or resources. However, these changes take precedence over changes made using the Text Styles dialog box.

For example, if you manually selected or filtered for Summary tasks, changed the format of the text using either the Formatting toolbar or the Format Font command, and then added another Summary Task, the new Summary Task would not have formatting consistent with the rest of the Summary Tasks. In contrast, when changes are made to the Summary Tasks option in the Text Styles dialog box, they affect all existing Summary Tasks, as well as any new ones added later. Moreover, if you then make changes to the text display of Summary Tasks using the Text Styles dialog box, they will not overwrite the changes made to the Summary Tasks that you previously formatted with Format Font command or the Formatting toolbar. You can easily end up with many format changes that you have to adjust manually, when they could all be done for you automatically by Microsoft Project, as with the Text Styles dialog box options.

Formatting Gridlines

Views that contain tables have gridlines between the rows and columns of the table and between the column and row titles. Views that have a timescale can have horizontal and vertical lines to separate the major and the minor timescale units. The Gantt Chart also can have gridlines between the bars in the bar chart, and other views have unique gridlines that you can choose.

To change the display of gridlines, choose Gridlines from the Format menu. The Gridlines dialog box appears. Figure 18.6 shows the Gantt Chart Gridlines dialog box.

From the Line to Change entry list, choose the kind of line you want to change. The settings in the Normal box are applied to every line of the type that you choose unless a selection in the At Interval box also is active (in which case a different line and color appears at regular intervals). Only a few line categories can be given a distinguishing interval line type and color. Sheet Rows and Sheet Columns in table views, for example, can have intervals, and in the Gantt Chart and the Resource Usage views, rows and columns can have interval colors and line types.

Use the **T**ype entry list arrow in the Normal box to choose one of the five options (clear, solid, dotted, small dashes, and large dashes). Use the **C**olor entry list arrow in the Normal box to choose one of the colors. Select the At Interval line type and color if you want a distinguishing line, if these selections are available. Activate the At Interval **T**ype and Colo**r** fields by choosing an interval. Choose **2**, **3**, or **4**; or choose **O**ther and type the interval number.

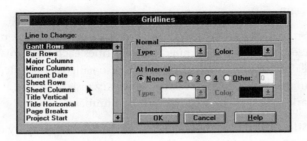

Fig. 18.6
Change the way that lines look using the Gridlines dialog box.

For timescale views, you can define the style of the Current Date line. For table views, you can define the style of page break lines as seen on-screen (page break lines do not print). After you complete the procedure, choose the OK button to accept the changes or the Cancel button to not make the changes.

Using the Outline Options

Views that list tasks (the Gantt Chart and the Task Sheet) can display the tasks in ways that show information about their places in the outline structure. You can hide or display summary tasks, or indent subordinate tasks to show outline level; outline numbers can be displayed next to each task; and summary tasks can be marked with a special symbol to show that these tasks have subordinate tasks.

To change the display of the outlined tasks, choose **T**ools **O**ptions, and then activate the View tab. The Outline display options are presented in figure 18.7. In figure 18.8 you can see the effects of each of these choices when they are marked.

◀ "Outlining the Task List," p. 118

■ If Show Summary Tasks is marked, you see the summary tasks included in the list of tasks. If the check box is not marked, the summary tasks do not appear in the list. If subtasks are currently hidden, they will also be hidden. Notice also that the outlining commands on the Formatting toolbar are no longer available when summary tasks are not shown. If you clear the check box, you also will want to clear the **I**ndent Name check box so that all the subordinate tasks align at the left margin.

III

Views and Reports

■ If Project Summary Task is marked then you will also have an additional summary task at the beginning of the task list that summarizes the entire project. This is useful when consolidating projects. (This topic was covered in Chapter 13, "Working with Multiple Projects.")

■ If the Indent Name box is marked, the tasks are indented to show their subordinate status. If the box is not marked, all tasks are aligned at the left margin.

■ If the Show Outline Number check box is marked, the task names are preceded by an outline number that identifies each task's place in the outline. The outline numbering is in the so-called legal style, with each task number including the related summary task numbers. If this box is not marked, you do not see the outline numbers.

■ If the Show Outline Symbol check box is marked, summary tasks are preceded by a plus sign (+), and nonsummary tasks are preceded by a minus sign (–). The outline symbols are particularly helpful if the outline is collapsed, because you can tell by the plus signs which tasks have hidden subordinate tasks that you can view by expanding this part of the outline. If the Show Outline Symbol check box is not marked, no outline symbols are displayed. This last feature is also accessible using the Outline Symbols tool on the Formatting toolbar. The tool acts as a toggle to turn the outline symbols on and off.

Fig. 18.7
Options for displaying outlines on the View tab of the Tools Options dialog box.

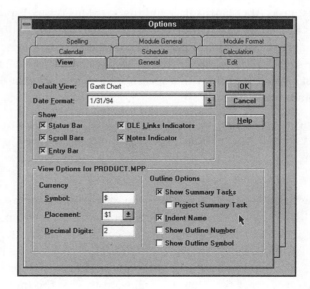

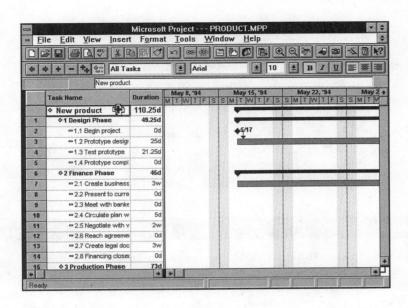

Fig. 18.8
An outline with Project Summary task, Indent Name, Show Outline Number, and Show Outline Symbol turned on.

Formatting Timescales

Views that display a timescale offer you the option of choosing the time units and the date formats for the timescale display. The timescale normally uses two levels of time units, the major units scale and the minor units scale, for clarity in interpreting the timescale. However, you can suppress the display of either scale.

To change the timescale (for views that display a timescale), choose Timescale from the Format menu. The Timescale dialog box appears (see fig. 18.9).

The Timescale dialog box provides areas for defining both the Major Scale and the Minor Scale. Below these areas is a sample display area that shows you instantly what the timescale will look like as you select different options.

Changing the Major Scale

You define the major and minor scales separately. The only requirement is that the units selected for the major scale be at least as large as the units selected for the minor scale.

Selecting the Major Scale Units. To change the Major Scale units, use the Units entry list arrow to choose one of the options provided: Years, Quarters, Months, Weeks, Days, Hours, and Minutes.

Tip
You can access the Timescale dialog box by double-clicking anywhere in the timescale units displayed in the screen view or by pressing the right mouse button while pointing anywhere in the timescale units. Timescale is one of the options available on the Shortcut menu.

III

Views and Reports

Fig. 18.9
Change the time
frame displayed
with the numer-
ous options in the
Timescale dialog
box.

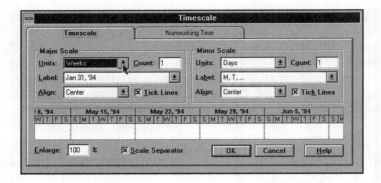

Fig. 18.9
Change the time
frame displayed
with the numer-
ous options in the
Timescale dialog
box.

Note

To change the month that begins the fiscal year (so that Quarter 1 covers the months used by your organization in its reports), you must change the Fiscal Year Starts in option on the Calendar tab of the Tools Options dialog box. Using the entry list arrow, change from the default, January, to the month you want to use. Similarly, if you want the week to begin on Monday instead of Sunday (the default), you must change the Week **S**tarts On item in the same location.

Selecting the Count for the Major Scale Units. To include more than one time period within each major unit, choose the **C**ount field and enter a number other than 1. To have the major scale show fortnights (two weeks), for example, select Weeks as the **U**nits and 2 for the **C**ount. Here, you also could select Days as the **U**nit and 14 for the **C**ount.

Note

If the major scale tick lines that separate the units of the major scale don't change in the sample area immediately after you change the count, you may need to select the **T**ick Lines check box twice to refresh the tick line display. See the upcoming section, "Selecting the Tick Lines," for more information.

Selecting the Label for the Major Scale Units. To choose the label to display in each major scale time unit, use the **L**abel entry list arrow. The list of options is extensive and depends on the units selected for the display. You can use three basic types of labels for any of the time units:

■ The specific time period named, such as the year, quarter number, month name or number, and day number. Many choices are available, including abbreviations, full or partial specifications, numbers, and words. Figure 18.10 shows the list of options available for the Week unit.

■ The number of the time period in the life of the project, starting from the beginning of the project or counting down from the end of the project. These units are designated with either (From Start) or (From End) as part of the label definition. If the unit is Week 1 (From Start), for example, the time periods are labeled Week1, Week 2, and so on, if you are counting from the beginning of the project. If you are counting down from the end of the project, the time periods are labeled Week 40, Week 39, and so on. This labeling scheme is useful in the early planning stages of a lengthy project, before specific start and finish dates are established.

■ No label. If minor scale labeling is sufficient, you can suppress any labeling of the major scale unit. You cannot, however, avoid having a major timescale unit.

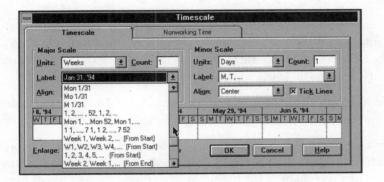

Fig. 18.10
The Major Scale
Units Label
options for Weeks.

Aligning the Units Labels. You can center, left-align, or right-align the time units labels. Use the **A**lign entry list arrow to choose an alignment specification, or just type the specification.

Selecting the Tick Lines. You must mark the **T**ick Lines check box to display tick lines separating the major time units. You use the **C**ount field entry to determine how the tick lines are spaced. If you change the count factor and the **T**ick Lines check box is already marked, you may have to unmark the check box and select again to refresh the display of the tick lines in the sample area.

Tip
When working
with a project
that spans more
than a single
calendar year,
be sure to in-
clude the year
number in the
label.

III

Views and Reports

Changing the Minor Scale

The Minor Scale options are virtually the same as the Major Scale options, with the following exceptions:

■ You cannot have a minor scale unit that is larger than the major scale unit. Specifically, the time span of the minor scale unit, including its count factor, cannot be longer than the timescale of the major scale unit. Microsoft Project will not notify you of this until you choose the OK button.

■ You can choose not to have a minor scale at all by choosing None in the Units entry list.

Otherwise, selecting the minor scale is identical to selecting the major scale.

Completing the Timescale Definition

Notice the two fields at the bottom of the Timescale tab in this dialog box. You use these fields to adjust the overall look of the timescale.

To change the width of the minor timescale units, choose the **E**nlarge field and enter an adjustment percentage. For example, if the values in the Resource Usage view are too large to fit within the cells of the minor timescale units, type **120%** or **150%** to enlarge the minor scale unit space.

You can remove the horizontal line that separates the major scale labels from the minor scale labels. Just unmark the **S**cale Separator check box.

After you enter all the changes, choose OK to put the new timescale format in place. The timescale changes affect only the display of the view that was active when you changed the timescale. Each timescale view has its own timescale format.

Changing the Display of Non-Working Time

Use the Nonworking Time tab in the Timescale dialog box to make changes to the way that Nonworking Time is displayed on the Gantt chart. You can choose F**o**rmat Ti**m**escale and then click the Nonworking Time tab to bring it to the front. Alternatively, you can point at the shaded working time (assuming that it is displayed), press the right mouse button, and then choose Nonworking Time from the Shortcut menu. Or, you can double-click on the shaded working time. The choices are displayed in figure 18.11.

You should first choose the calendar whose nonworking time you will be changing. Use the entry list arrow if you want to select an individual's resource calendar. Otherwise the Standard (Project Calendar) will be used. The options in the Draw section determine the way in which the bars are drawn when spanning nonworking time (evenings and weekends, for example). Nonworking time is shaded with a color and pattern of your choice. Whether or not this time is displayed depends to a large degree on the Timescale format. For example, if your major timescale unit is set to Months, and the minor timescale unit is set to Weeks, you won't be able to see nonworking time.

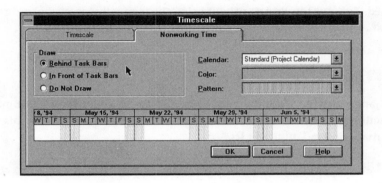

Fig. 18.11
Changing the display of nonworking time on the Gantt chart.

The options for where the shading is drawn include **B**ehind the Task Bars (the default), **I**n Front of Task Bars (leaving a gap in the bars), or **D**o Not Draw. This last option effectively eliminates the shaded display of Nonworking time altogether. Nonworking time is still displayed, but the display is not any different from working time. Task bars that span nonworking time will simply be longer than you might expect from their duration value.

Using Page Breaks

Page breaks were discussed in Chapter 16, "Printing Views and Reports," as part of the printing instructions. Page breaks force the start of a new page when you print the view but have no effect on the screen display (other than an optional dashed line to indicate where the page break falls within the data). You can format the appearance of the page break line with the **G**ridlines command from the F**o**rmat menu.

To force a page break in the views that permit it, select any cell in the row below the intended page break. This row becomes the first row on the new page. Then choose **I**nsert **P**age Break.

To remove a page break, select the row below the page break and choose the **I**nsert menu. The **P**age Break command changes to read Remove **P**age Break because Microsoft Project senses that the selection is on a page break. Choose Remove **P**age Break to remove the break.

To remove all page breaks from the view, select all tasks by clicking the Task or Resource Name column heading before choosing the Insert menu. The Page Break option changes to read Remove All Page Breaks. Choose this option to remove all the page breaks in the view.

The page breaks that you have entered manually are honored by the **P**rint command *only* if the **M**anual Page Breaks check box in the Print dialog box is marked. To print the report without using the manually inserted page breaks, unmark this check box.

Formatting the Gantt Chart

Tip
To use the Short-cut menu, point at any blank portion of the Gantt Chart and press the right mouse button. Double-clicking while pointing anywhere in the background of the Gantt Chart area also accesses the Bar Styles dialog box.

The Gantt Chart is one of the most important presentations in project management reporting. Therefore, many format choices are available for this presentation.

Reviewing the Format Options for the Gantt Chart

The **F**ormat menu for Gantt Charts includes the following options: **F**ont, **B**ar, Ti**m**escale, **G**ridlines, Gantt Chart **W**izard, **T**ext Styles, Bar **S**tyles, and **L**ayout. The options for **F**ont, Ti**m**escale, **G**ridlines, and **T**ext Styles were described in previous sections of this chapter. Refer to the appropriate sections for instructions on using these features. This section shows you several ways to change the look of the bar chart in the timescale section of the Gantt chart view.

Using the Bar Styles Options

One way to change the display of the bar chart section of the Gantt Chart view is to choose Bar **S**tyles from the **F**ormat menu. The Bar Styles dialog box appears (see fig. 18.12).

The top half of the Bar Styles dialog box contains a table with rows for each of the bars and symbols that appear in the Gantt Chart. The bottom half of the dialog box contains two tabs: the bars tab has fields for specifying the formatted look of the bars and symbols, and the Text tab has fields where text can be added in various locations around the bars. You can specify the way a bar will look at the start, end, and in between. The second column in the table at the top of the dialog box displays a sample of the formatted look that you composed.

To insert a new bar within the table, select the row in which you plan to define the bar and select the **I**nsert Row button at the top of the dialog box.

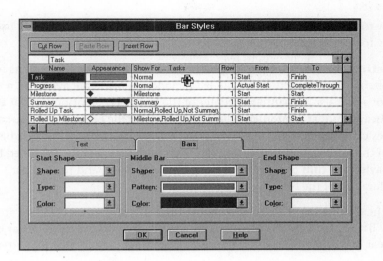

Fig. 18.12
Use the Bar Styles
dialog box to
change the display
of bars in the
Gantt Chart.

To delete a bar from the definition, select the row that defines the bar and choose the C**u**t button. You can paste this definition into a new location; just select the new location and choose the **P**aste Row button. A blank row is inserted, and a copy of the row that you cut is placed in the new row.

To copy a row (for example, to create a bar that closely resembles a bar already defined), C**u**t the row to be copied and immediately **P**aste Row it back to the same location. Then move to the location for the copy and **P**aste Row the row again.

Supplying the Bar Name

Use the first column of the definition table to enter a name for the bar. The bar name can be anything you choose and has no significance, except that the name appears in the legend next to the bar symbol when the Gantt Chart is printed.

Defining the Bar Sample

The second column shows what the bar or symbol looks like when the Palette definition is applied. Change the look of the sample with the Start Shape, Middle Bar, and End Shape fields on the Bars tab at the bottom of the dialog box.

Selecting the Start Shape. You can define the **S**hape, **T**ype, and **C**olor of the start shape at the left edge of the bar. Use the **S**hape entry list arrow to scroll the list for the shape you want. Use the first option, which is blank, if you do not want a symbol to mark the start of the bar. Use the **T**ype entry list arrow to choose Dashed, Framed, or Solid. Finally, use the Color entry list arrow to choose a color.

Selecting the Bar. Use the Shape entry list arrow to view the options for the size and height of the bar. The list includes no bar at all, a full bar, a top half of a bar, a small bar in the center of the bar space, a bottom half of a bar, and heavy lines at the top, middle, and bottom of the bar space. These bar shapes can overlap. The Progress bar (the solid black center of the task bar when the *percentage complete* is greater than zero) for example, is formed by displaying the thin center bar for the progress amount, and the full bar for the duration of the task.

Use the Color entry list arrow to choose the color of the bar. Use the Pattern entry list arrow to choose the fill pattern or shading for the bar. The bar can be clear, have an outline only, be solid, or have any one of nine fill patterns.

Selecting the End Shape. To select the bar end, follow the same procedure as for selecting the bar start. Use the Shape entry list arrow to choose the shape, and the Type entry list arrow to choose the type. Use the Color entry list arrow to choose the color.

The Sample column in the table at the top of the dialog box displays the effect of the choices. You must go through these steps for each bar or symbol that you place on the Gantt Chart.

Selecting the Tasks That Display the Bar

Select the third column (Show For) in the definition table at the top of the Bar Styles dialog box to define the category(ies) of tasks for which the bar is displayed. An entry list now appears on the right side of the entry bar of the Bar Styles dialog box when this column is selected. Choose a bar category from the entry list or type the category in. If you want to use two or more task categories, separate the task categories' names with commas (or the list separator character specified in Window's Control Panel, International Settings).

The entry list contains a large number of task types. All tasks fall into one of the first three categories: they will be a Milestone, a Summary task, or Normal (which is any task that is not a Milestone or a Summary task). You may use these three kinds of tasks in combination with the other types in the list to more narrowly define specific types of tasks, for example, Normal,Critical and Normal,Noncritical instead of just Normal (which includes both Critical and Noncritical). If a task falls into more than one category, it will show the formatting features of both categories. If one formatting feature overwrites another, the feature that is lowest in the definition table will be applied last and will remain visible in the display.

To select all tasks *except* the type named, you can place the word *Not* before the type name. Examples are Not Summary, Not Milestone, and Not Rolled Up.

The Rolled Up type refers to a special field for subordinate tasks that instructs Microsoft Project to show a symbol for the Finish Date of the task on the Summary task bar. You designate tasks as Rolled Up tasks using the Information tool on the Standard Toolbar. This displays the Task Information dialog box. The General tab has a check box for Rollup Gantt Bar to Summary. Figure 18.13 illustrates the use of rollup symbols.

Each of the tasks in the Finance group has been defined as a Rollup task; the **R**ollup Gantt Bar to Summary check box on the Task Information dialog box is selected. The mouse pointer appears as one of the rollup symbols: a small diamond shape. In this example, the date of the rollup marker is displayed above the bar. For more information, see the upcoming section "Placing Text in the Bar Chart." The effect is to show on the Summary task bar what proportion of the total duration is due to each task.

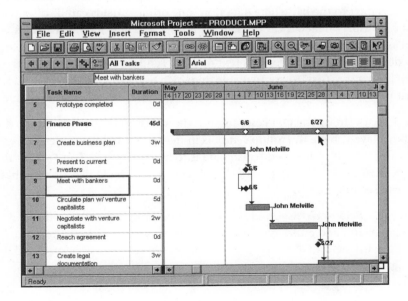

Fig. 18.13
Using rolled up dates to make Summary Tasks more descriptive.

Selecting the Row for the Bar

You can place up to four rows of bars on the Gantt Chart for each task, or you can use the extra rows for displaying text. Notice in the dialog box in figure 18.12 that the Progress bar is placed in Row 1 along with the Task bar. Because the shapes of the bars differ, the effect is to superimpose one over the other. Note, however, that the order in which you list superimposed bars in the definition table is important. The bars in the Gantt Chart are drawn in the order listed in the definition table. If the Progress bar in this example were defined above the Normal bars, the Progress bar would be drawn before the Normal bars, and the larger Normal bars would hide the Progress bar.

Defining the Length of the Bar

The length and placement of every bar or symbol on the Gantt Chart is determined by entries in the From and To columns of the definition table. You can use date fields or one of several measures of time (Percent Complete, Total Slack, Free Slack, and Negative Slack). Choose an entry from the entry bar list or type the designation of the start and stop points (From and To) for the bar or symbol.

Placing Text in the Bar Chart

On the Text tab of the Bar Styles dialog box is a column for designating a position next to the bar where data from one or more fields can be displayed. You can display field data at the left, right, top, and bottom of the bar, as well as inside the bar. You cannot type literal text in these columns; you only can designate fields that contain text display. Ten user-defined Text fields (Text1, Text2, ...Text10) are available, in which you can type text that you want to display in the bar chart. For easy access, place these fields in a table.

Figure 18.14 shows the text columns and the selection that produced the date text displayed above the rollup symbols in figure 18.13. The mouse pointer indicates that the scheduled Finish date is to be displayed as Top Text for the bar defined by the bottom row of the table, which is the Rolled Up row that you can see in figure 18.12.

To select a field to be displayed beside a bar, select the column for the position you want, and either type the field name or select the name from the entry bar list. Select OK to accept your changes or select Cancel to close the dialog box without implementing them.

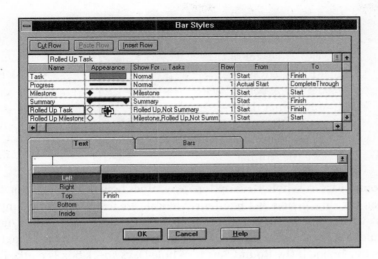

Fig. 18.14
Use the Text tab of the Bar Styles dialog to place text around the bars of the Gantt Chart.

> **Note**
>
> If you want to change the format of specific bars that do not fall into one of the categories available, use the **B**ar option on the F**o**rmat menu. This command has the same options as the Bar Styles dialog box, but it will only apply changes to the selected tasks.

Changing the Layout of the Gantt Chart

The **L**ayout option on the F**o**rmat menu accesses the Layout dialog box (shown in figure 18.15), which offers a number of choices for the way bars are displayed on the Gantt Chart. Where the primary focus of the Gantt Chart is a list of tasks occurring on a timeline, it is often helpful to see the dependency relationships between tasks. In the **L**inks section of this dialog box, you can choose to not have lines drawn to designate the dependency linkages between tasks, or you can choose between two styles of lines.

When dates are displayed as text around the bars, use the Date **F**ormat for Bars entry list arrow to choose from a list of available formats. This will not change the default format for dates displayed elsewhere in the project. The first option on this list is Default, which will return you to the same format as specified on the View tab of the Tools Options dialog box.

Use the **B**ar Height entry list arrow to choose from a list of sizes for the bars.Sizes vary from 6 to 24 points with a default of 12.

Fig. 18.15
Use the Layout
dialog box to
further define the
appearance of the
Gantt Chart.

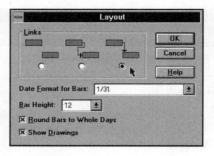

The **R**ound Bars to Whole Days option determines how tasks with a duration less than the time period by the minor timescale are displayed. For example, if a task with a duration of 5 hours is displayed in a Gantt chart with a minor timescale of days, and this box is cleared, then the bar will display a length of exactly five hours. If the **R**ound Bars to Whole Days check box is marked, the bar will extend to a full day. This eliminates any gaps that may be displayed between linked tasks. Only the display of the task is modified, the actual duration and calculated start and finish dates remain the same.

The Show **D**rawings check box enables you to place graphics in the Gantt Chart. This feature will be covered in Chapter 19, "Placing Text and Graphics on the Gantt Chart."

Choose OK to accept your changes or select Cancel to close the dialog box without implementing them.

Using the Gantt Chart Wizard

Microsoft Project includes a feature that makes formatting the bars on the Gantt Chart extremely easy. This automated feature walks through the various formatting options, asking questions about how you would like to have the bars displayed. The options are basically the same as those already covered, but you are taken through the process step by step. To access the Gantt Chart Wizard, you can either choose F**o**rmat Gantt Chart **W**izard or use the Gantt Chart Wizard tool on the Standard toolbar.

You initially are presented with an introductory dialog box with a series of buttons at the bottom. Choose the **N**ext button to see your first set of choices (see fig. 18.16). Notice that the title bar includes the step you are on. There are actually 14 separate steps but you aren't likely to go through each one. As you make your choices, you are taken to the next appropriate step, depending on your choice. Simply choose the desired option, and then choose the **N**ext button to move to the next step. You can **B**ack up, Cancel, or indicate that you are finished at any time.

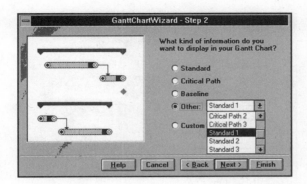

Fig. 18.16
The
GanttChartWizard
walks through the
formatting options
for the Gantt
Chart.

The first question you must answer involves selecting the tasks that are displayed. Your choice here acts as a starting point for setting up the format of the bars on the Gantt Chart.

- Standard uses the same bars that are used in the default Gantt Chart.

- Critical is a helpful view to use when crashing the project.

- Baseline is an appropriate choice when you are tracking a project that is underway.

- The Other radio button offers a list of 13 pre-defined formats that you can use as is or that you can modify as desired (see fig. 18.16).

- Choosing the Custom radio button offers the most extensive choices and will walk through all of the choices for formatting one step at a time. Choosing this option will take your through many if not all of the 14 total steps of the GanttChartWizard. These options include choices for the colors, patterns, and shapes of critical, normal, summary, and milestone tasks. You also have an option for adding bars for baseline information and/or slack.

After you make your initial choice, you are prompted for the kind of text to display in and around the bars. Here again, you have a custom choice which allows for distinct definitions for the text formats of normal, summary, and milestone tasks. The final question involves the kind of link lines that can be drawn to display dependency relationships between the task bars.

Once you have made all of your changes, the GanttChartWizard will do the rest. All you have to do is choose the Format It button (see fig. 18.17). You still have the option of making further changes using the techniques covered in previous sections.

III

Views and Reports

Fig. 18.17
The GanttChart-
Wizard will do all
of the formatting
once you make
your choices.

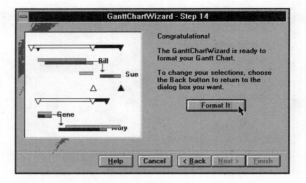

Formatting the Calendar

There are a multitude of ways that you can modify the display of the Calendar View to meet your specific needs. As with other views, you can use the Zoom command on the View menu, or you can use the Zoom In and Zoom Out buttons on the Standard toolbar to cycle through preset options for zooming. You will find this convenient if you have many tasks occurring at the same time.

A number of mouse methods are available for changing the height and width of the date boxes. Point to any vertical line in the calendar, and the mouse pointer changes to a double-headed arrow. Click and drag to narrow or widen the column. Likewise, if you point to a horizontal line, the mouse pointer again changes to a double-headed arrow which you can click and drag to make the date box taller or shorter. This is particularly useful when you have more tasks on a given day than can be displayed at once.

The options that are available on the Format menu for the Calendar view include Timescale, Gridlines, Text Styles, Bar Styles, Layout, and Layout Now. The Text Styles and Gridlines options are the same as discussed in previous sections. The options for Timescale, Bar Styles, and Layout are unique to the calendar view and are discussed in detail here.

Formatting the Timescale for the Calendar

The Timescale dialog box has three tabs that offer choices for headings and titles, for additional data elements that can appear in the date boxes, and for applying shading on certain days.

The Week Headings tab is shown in figure 18.18. Here you have numerous choices of labels for the month, the days of the week, and for each week. This figure shows a label for each week that counts down to the end of the project.

Additionally, you can choose a 5- or 7-day week, and you can choose to show the previous and next month, much like printed calendars do.

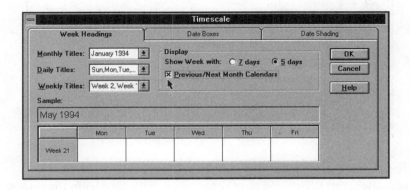

Fig. 18.18
Customize the calendar display with the Week Headings tab on the Timescale dialog box.

The Date Boxes tab, shown in figure 18.19, allows you to place additional data elements in the top and/or bottom row of each individual date box. There are many choices here. The default setting includes an overflow indicator and the day of the year in the top row. The overflow indicator will appear when all tasks scheduled to occur on a given day cannot be displayed with the date box. When printing, overflow tasks will appear on a separate page. A pattern and color can also be chosen for emphasis.

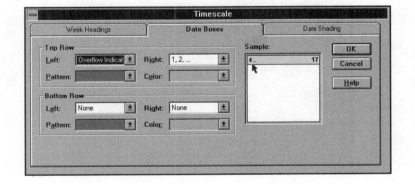

Fig. 18.19
Customize each date box with additional information in the Date Boxes tab of the Timescale dialog box.

Finally, you can shade a variety of categories of working or non-working dates for the base calendar or individual resource calendars. First choose the type of date that you want to shade in the Exception Type list. Then choose a pattern and color from the entry list arrows at the bottom of the dialog box. A sample will be displayed on the right as you make your choices. When you are finished making changes, choose the OK button. You will be returned to the Calendar view to see the effect of your formatting changes.

III

Views and Reports

Fig. 18.20
Indicate working and non-working days on the calendar with options in the Date Shading tab of the Timescale dialog box.

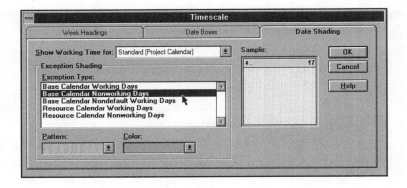

Selecting Calendar Bar Styles Options

As with the Gantt Chart, you have control over how the bars in the calendar appear, including text that can be displayed as part of the bars. Access the Bar Styles dialog box by choosing Format Styles, or point anywhere in a blank spot on the calendar and press the right mouse button to use the Shortcut menu. Select the Bar Styles option, and the Bar Styles dialog box appears (see fig. 18.21).

Fig. 18.21
The Bar Styles dialog box offers choices for changing the display of task bars in the Calendar view.

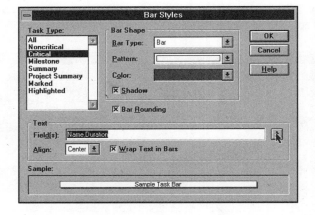

First select the type of bar that you want to modify in the Task Type field. Then use the fields in the Bar Shape box to modify the Bar Type, Pattern, and Color for the bar. You have a variety of choices for pattern and color. As for the bar type, you can have a bar or a simple line extending across the days of the task's duration. If you choose a bar, you can also apply a Shadow for emphasis.

The Bar **R**ounding check box, deals with tasks whose durations are not a whole day (for example, durations of a half day or a day and a half). If the check box is left marked, the bar on the calendar will be rounded to a full day.

In the Text area, you can choose any number of Fiel**d**s to be displayed in the bar either by typing in their names (separated by commas) or by choosing them with the entry list arrow. If you want to have more than one field listed on the bar and you are choosing from the entry list arrow, make sure to deselect the field name and type in a comma before selecting another field from the list. Otherwise, if you choose another field while the first field is still selected, the first field is replaced rather than added to. You can deselect a field name either by pressing the right arrow or by clicking with the mouse at the right end of the field name. Alignment options for the text of these fields can be centered, left, or right. When text is long, it may be useful to check the **W**rap Text in Bars check box.

For all categories of tasks except All, a sample will be displayed at the bottom of the dialog box to show you the effect of your choices. As with text styles discussed earlier in this chapter, when some of the task types have a check box option turned on, the check box will be displayed with a gray shading. When all of the task types have the check box turned on, there will be an X in the check box. When none of the task types have the check box turned on, the check box will be empty.

Choose the OK button when you are finished making your choices. You will be returned to the calendar to see the effect of your changes.

Figure 18.22 shows the calendar view displaying the formatting changes made in the preceding dialog boxes. The bar styles were formatted as follows: summary tasks were changed to a blue line, critical task bars were changed to red with a shadow. Text for these bars includes the task name and duration. Milestones will be displayed as a black square with white text.

Setting the Layout Options for the Calendar View

The Layout dialog box as shown in figure 18.23 can be accessed either through the Format **L**ayout command or the shortcut menu. (To access the shortcut menu, point to any blank area of the calendar and press the right mouse button) The options presented here determine the order of tasks displayed in each date box. The default is to Use **C**urrent Sort Order setting. The alternative to this is to Attempt to **F**it as Many Tasks as Possible without regard for sorting. The check box for **A**utomatic layout determines when the settings will be initiated as tasks are edited, added, or deleted. When **Auto**matic layout is not selected, you must choose Layout **N**ow to apply the changes.

Fig. 18.22
The final calendar view with formatting changes.

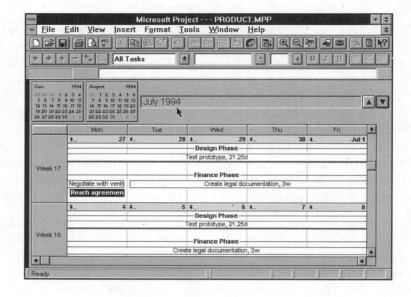

Fig. 18.23
The Layout dialog box allows you to determine how and when tasks are sorted within each date box.

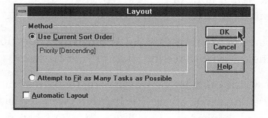

Formatting the PERT Chart

◀ "Moving Task Nodes in the PERT Chart," p. 172

You can customize the PERT Chart by rearranging the layout of the task nodes and by changing the size of the nodes, the borders around the nodes, and the fields displayed within each node.

Reviewing the Format Options for the PERT Chart

The F**o**rmat menu for the PERT Chart view contains the options **T**ext Styles, Box **S**tyles, **L**ayout, and Layout **N**ow. You can also use the **Z**oom option on the **V**iew menu or the Zoom In and Zoom Out buttons on the Standard toolbar.

The use of the Format menu to change the display of text was covered earlier in this chapter. The Zoom, Layout, and Layout Now commands were covered in previous chapters but are summarized here for completeness. The Box Styles commands are covered in detail in the following sections.

Using the Box Styles Options

You can customize the boxes that surround the nodes to display eight border styles and colors. Figure 18.24 shows the seven options and identifies the standard border assignments.

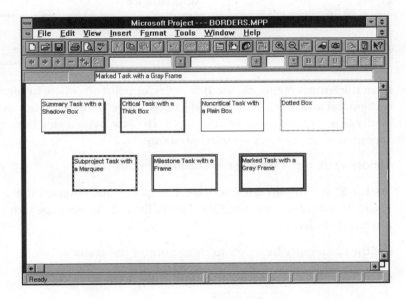

Fig. 18.24

The Borders options for PERT Chart nodes.

You can assign each box one of fifteen colors—sixteen if you count transparent as a color. If you have a color printer or plotter, the use of color can be an effective tool. If you have a black-and-white printer, you cannot distinguish one color from another.

The border styles and colors are assigned by kinds of tasks. Table 18.3 lists the variety of tasks used for border assignments and shows the default border and color assigned to each kind of task. The default color for all critical tasks is red, and the default color for all noncritical tasks is black.

Table 18.3 Border Styles and Colors for PERT Charts		
Task Type	**Critical**	**Noncritical**
Normal	Thick Box, Red	Plain Box, Black
Milestone	Frame, Red	Frame, Black
Summary	Shadow Box, Red	Shadow Box, Black
Marked	Gray Frame, Red	Gray Frame, Black
Subproject	Marquee, Red	Marquee, Black

To assign border styles and colors to tasks in the PERT Chart, follow these steps:

1. From the Format menu, choose **B**ox Styles, or point anywhere in the background area, right-click, and select Box Styles. Or, double-click the border of one of the nodes on the screen. The Box Styles dialog box appears with the Borders tab selected (see fig. 18.25).

2. Choose a task type from the **I**tem to change entry list.

3. Use the **S**tyle entry list arrow to scroll the options and choose a style. The sample display under the Colors entry list will illustrate the style you have selected.

4. Use the **C**olor entry list arrow to choose one of the available colors.

5. After you make all the border selections, choose OK to accept the changes and close the dialog box.

Fig. 18.25
Change the borders for different categories of tasks using the Borders tab on the Box Styles dialog box.

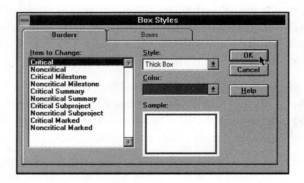

Using the Boxes Options in the Border Styles Dialog Box

You regulate what is displayed within each node, as well as the size of the node, with the Boxes tab. This tab enables you to perform the following procedures:

- Change the fields that appear in each of the five positions.

- Reduce the number of field positions displayed.

- Increase or decrease the size of the task node.

- Change the format for the dates displayed in PERT nodes without having to change the format for dates in other displays.

- Suppress the gridlines that separate the display of the field data.

- Turn on or off the markings that show tasks in progress and tasks completed.

To display the Box Styles dialog box for the PERT Chart, access the PERT Chart view by choosing PERT Chart from the **V**iew menu. Then choose Box **S**tyles from the F**o**rmat menu, or point anywhere in the background of the PERT Chart, right-click, and select Box Styles. Or double-click the background of the PERT Chart screen. Figure 18.26 shows the Box Styles dialog box for the PERT Chart. Note that the layout of the dialog box mirrors a node.

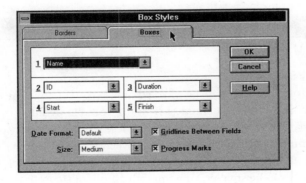

Fig. 18.26
Change the fields displayed in the Boxes tab of the Box Styles dialog box.

III

Changing the Fields Displayed

By default, the PERT nodes display five fields of data: task Name, ID number, Duration, Start and Finish Dates. You can change the field displayed in any node by choosing the field position (**1**, **2**, **3**, **4**, or **5**) and then using the entry list arrow next to the field to choose a field name from the entry list.

If you want the position in the node to remain blank, you can select the blank at the top of the entry list. If both positions **4** and **5** are left blank, these positions on the task node are removed, and the task node shrinks in size accordingly. Likewise, if both positions **2** and **3** are left blank, the task node shrinks even further. By leaving tasks **2** through **5** blank, you can create small task nodes that show only the task name. You then can print PERT Charts that show less detail but display more nodes per page. Figure 18.27 shows a sample PERT Chart with only the task name showing in each node. The size of the node in the figure also is reduced (see the following section).

Fig. 18.27
The PERT Chart showing only the task name.

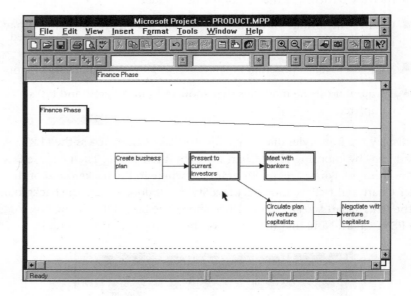

Changing the Node Size

Select the **S**ize field at the bottom of the dialog box to change the size of the node display. You can select Smallest (ID only), Small, Medium, or Large from the entry list, or you can type one of these sizes. You can also use the Shortcut menu to toggle back and forth between Hide and Show Fields. When fields are hidden, nodes are displayed only with the ID field. This causes the nodes to be smaller; subsequently, more of them fit on the screen.

Changing the Date Format

You can change the format for displaying dates in the PERT Chart without changing the default date formats used in other views. Select the **D**ate Format entry list and choose the format that suits you best. The first choice on the entry list is Default. Use the Default option if you want the same date format you have chosen on the General tab of the Tools Options dialog box. You usually will want shorter date formats, which fit in the smaller space available for PERT Chart nodes.

Displaying Gridlines

To display gridlines that separate the field positions in the task node, mark the **G**ridlines check box. Unmark this check box to suppress gridlines.

Selecting Progress Marks

If you select the **P**rogress Marks check box, the nodes for tasks that are completed are displayed with two diagonal lines drawn over the nodes to indicate completion. The nodes for tasks that are in progress but are not completed have a single diagonal line displayed above the nodes. Clear the **P**rogress Marks check box to suppress this display. Figure 18.28 illustrates the use of progress marks.

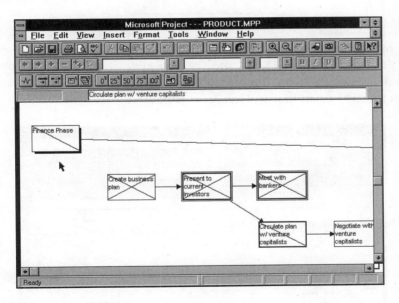

Fig. 18.28
PERT Chart progress marks are used to show progress.

After you have completed the dialog box, choose the OK button to implement the new box and border styles.

Using the Zoom Command

When viewing the PERT Chart, it is often helpful to be able to change the perspective, either pulling back to see the big picture or moving in closer for a more detailed view. This feature is especially useful when you manually move the nodes around to redesign the chart. Microsoft Project offers several ways to access a feature for this purpose. This feature is accessed by selecting the **Z**oom command from the **V**iew menu, by choosing it from the Shortcut menu, or by using either the Zoom In tool or the Zoom Out tool on the Standard toolbar. You can zoom from 25% to 400%. When you use the Zoom In and Zoom Out tools, you are successfully moved through the various zoom levels. When you use either the Shortcut menu or the **V**iew menu, you are presented with the dialog box in figure 18.29.

Fig. 18.29
The Zoom dialog box lets you choose how much to zoom in or out.

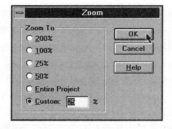

Choose any of the preset zoom values or enter a value of your own choice in the **C**ustom field. Figure 18.30 shows the same PERT Chart that was illustrated in figure 18.28, but it is zoomed out to the maximum extent. You can print the PERT Chart in any of the Zoom levels.

Fig. 18.30
The PERT Chart zoomed to a different perspective.

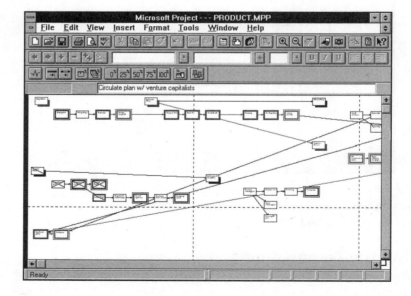

Selecting Layout Options

The Layout **N**ow command on the PERT Chart F**o**rmat menu redraws the PERT Chart according to the following standard rules of node placement:

■ Successor tasks are placed to the right of or below their predecessor tasks.

■ Summary tasks are placed above and to the left of their subordinate tasks.

■ Linked task nodes are connected with straight lines (diagonal lines if necessary), and an arrow is placed at the successor task's end of the line to indicate the direction of the relationship.

■ The Page Setup settings (and consequently where page breaks fall) are not considered in the original layout design of the task nodes.

To some extent, you can modify these rules with the **L**ayout command on the PERT Chart F**o**rmat menu.

The Layout dialog box, shown in figure 18.31, provides several options for changing the way the PERT Chart is drawn by the Layout **N**ow command. To display the dialog box, choose **L**ayout from the F**o**rmat menu. You also can access the Layout dialog box by accessing the shortcut menu. Point to any blank spot on the PERT Chart and press the right mouse button. To close the Layout dialog box, choose the OK button to implement your changes or the Cancel button to ignore them.

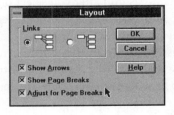

Fig. 18.31
Change the way lines are drawn and how page breaks are handled using the PERT Chart Layout dialog box.

Changing the Type of the Linking Lines

The linking lines that indicate dependency relationships are usually drawn straight from the predecessor to the successor. If the linked tasks are not on the same row or column of the chart, the linking line is drawn diagonally over the shortest distance between the linked nodes. A PERT Chart can become a messy picture if many diagonal lines intersect nodes and other lines. You can choose to have the dependency lines drawn as right-angled (orthogonal) lines only. To select the orthogonal lines, first choose **L**ayout from the F**o**rmat menu. When the Layout dialog box is presented, select the orthogonal diagram by selecting the **L**inks radio button.

You may often need to move nodes manually in the chart to clarify the relationships if you use the orthogonal **L**inks option. Figure 18.32 shows a section of the PERT Chart with diagonal lines.

Fig. 18.32
A PERT Chart
drawn with
diagonal linking
lines can become
confusing.

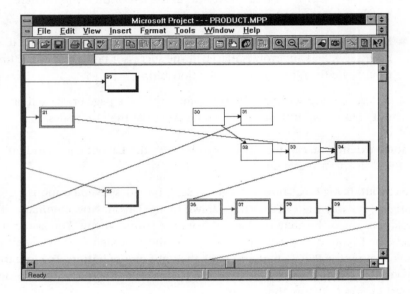

Figure 18.33 shows the same section after you select orthogonal lines. The line leading into task 32 implies that task 21 is a predecessor to task 32. Task 21, however, is the predecessor to task 34, and the line is just passing through task 32 on the way to task 34. Similarly, the line leading from task 31 to task 38 does seem to indicate that task 31 is a predecessor to task 38, yet task 31 really is a predecessor to task 42 (the end of the project).

Figure 18.34 shows the same PERT Chart after manually adjusting the placement of the nodes to clarify the relationships between tasks 21 and 34 and between tasks 31 and 42. You can drag the border of a node to move it. You can also select the node and use the arrow keys.

Showing Arrows, Displaying and Adjusting for Page Breaks
Clear the Show **A**rrows check box to remove the arrows from the successor end of the dependency linking lines. Mark the check box again to restore the display of the arrows.

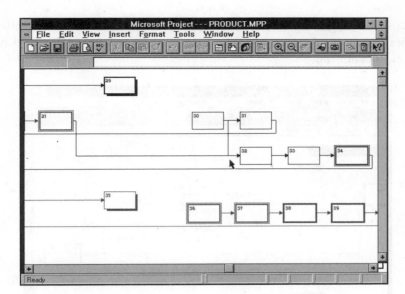

Fig. 18.33
The same PERT
Chart with
orthogonal
linking lines.

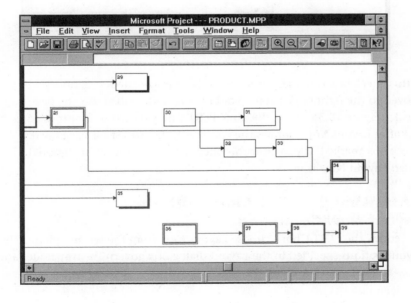

Fig. 18.34
The same PERT
Chart, with task
nodes moved
for clarity.

To see where page breaks will fall, mark the Show **P**age Breaks check box.
This helps you to identify problem areas before printing. Figure 18.35, for
example, shows the page break lines falling across one of the task nodes. If
you print in this manner, getting a clean *paste together* of the split nodes becomes difficult. You can manually move the task nodes away from the page
break lines. You also can mark the A**d**just for Page Breaks check box on the

III

Views and Reports

PERT Chart Layout dialog box to instruct Microsoft Project to avoid placing nodes on page breaks, and then redraw the PERT Chart with the **F**ormat Layout **N**ow command.

Fig. 18.35
The PERT Chart with page breaks displayed highlights where nodes fall on a page break.

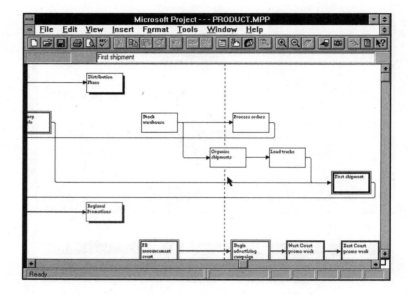

If this check box is marked and Layout **N**ow is executed, task nodes are moved to the right or down to avoid having nodes fall across the page breaks. Figure 18.36 shows the same PERT Chart shown in figure 18.35, but after Layout **N**ow redraws the chart with the A**d**just for Page Breaks check box marked. If you clear this check box, page breaks are ignored when Layout **N**ow is used.

Redrawing the PERT Chart with the Layout Now Command

To redraw the PERT Chart, choose Layout **N**ow from the F**o**rmat menu. The layout options specified in the Layout dialog box govern the way nodes and lines are placed in the chart.

Formatting the Resource Form

Like the other forms, the Resource Form cannot be printed, and the formatting choices are therefore limited. If the form is active in the top pane, you can view all resources with the form. Use the N**e**xt and Pre**v**ious buttons to change the resource displayed in the form. If the form is active in the bottom pane, you can display only resources that are associated with the items selected in the top pane.

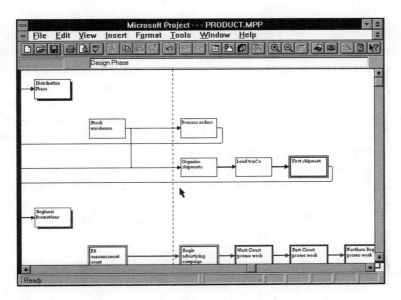

Fig. 18.36
The same PERT Chart, automatically adjusted for page breaks.

To display the Resource Form, select the pane in which you want the form to appear, and then choose **R**esource Form from the **V**iew **M**ore Views menu.

Reviewing the Format Options for the Form Views

The Resource and Task Forms have a limited number of format options. The **T**ools menu for both the Resource and Task Form view provides a Sort option, and the Format menu provides a **D**etails option that offers various entry field tables that you can place at the bottom of the form.

The Sort option changes the order in which resources or tasks appear when you use the N**e**xt and Pre**v**ious buttons. Nevertheless, you can use the Sort option to order the resources, even in the bottom pane.

To sort the resource or task list for display while using the Form view for either, choose **S**ort from the **T**ools menu. Follow the same procedure for using the Sort dialog box (for all views), as described in the earlier section, "Sorting the Tasks or Resources in a View."

Using the Entry Field Options

To select a different set of entry fields for the Resource Form, you can choose other options from the Format Details menu. These options are available and are described in this section.

To display fields for scheduled work on different tasks, choose Schedule (see fig. 18.37). Notice the field named Delay that appears on this entry table. You can use this field to delay the start of work on a task by the resource, which is not the same Delay field that appears on the Delay Table and is displayed on the Delay Gantt Chart. The Delay field on the Delay Table is a delay for the task; this field is a delay for the resource only. If the resource is the only resource assigned to work on a task, the effect of a resource delay has the same effect on the schedule as the effect of a task delay: both choices delay the start of the task. Suppose that several resources, however, are assigned to a task and that one of the resources needs to spend only the last several hours on the task (during the finishing stage, for example). The assignment of this resource to the task can be accompanied by a delay in the Resource assignment to clarify the requirements of the assignment.

Fig. 18.37
Use the Format Details menu to display Schedule fields on the Resource Form.

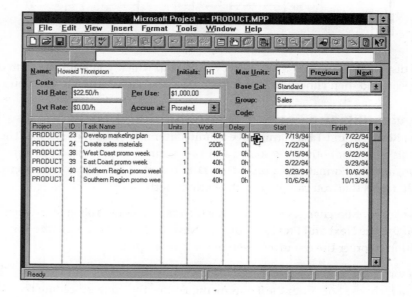

To display the cost fields for the resource for each task to which the resource is assigned, choose Cost from the Format Details menu. Figure 18.38 shows the result of this choice.

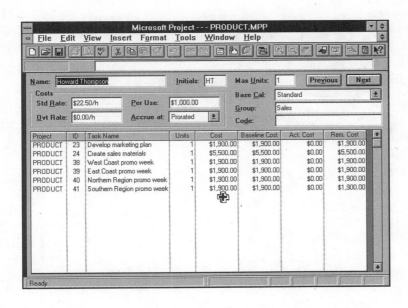

Fig. 18.38
The Costs for each resource by task can be displayed by choosing the Cost fields on the Resource Form.

To display the fields for work on different tasks, choose **W**ork from the F**o**rmat **D**etails menu. Use this version of the form (shown in fig. 18.39) to record the actual work and overtime spent on tasks by the resource.

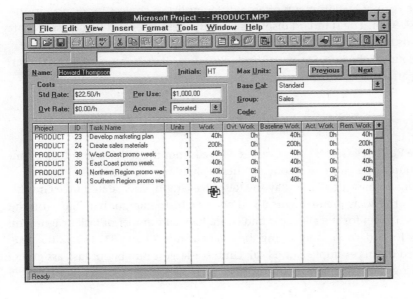

Fig. 18.39
Work hours displayed on the Resource Form.

From the F**o**rmat **D**etails menu, choose **N**otes to display the Notes field for the resource (see fig. 18.40).

III

Views and Reports

Fig. 18.40
The Notes field
on the Resource
Form.

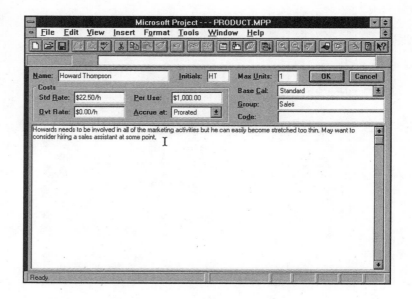

Choose **O**bjects to display objects that were attached to the resource. For
related information see "Placing Graphic Objects on Views," in Chapter 19,
"Placing Text and Graphics on the Gantt Chart."

◄ "Assigning
Resources and
Costs to Tasks,"
p. 205

The F**o**rmat **D**etails menu offers a different list of choices for display in the
Task form. The standard display shows the Resources and Predecessors entry
fields for the selected task. You also can choose to display Successors, the
Resource Schedule, Resource Work, Resource Cost, Notes, and Objects that
are attached to the task.

Formatting the Resource Graph

The Resource Graph shows values derived from the task assignments of one
resource or a group of resources; these values appear as graphical images
along a timescale. To display the Resource Graph, choose Resource Gr**a**ph
from the **V**iew menu. Figure 18.41 shows a histogram, or bar chart, (on the
lower pane) for the allocated and overallocated number of task assignments
for Howard Thompson during the weeks of July 24 and 31. The value measured in this example is the Peak Units, or largest number of task assignments
during each time period (in this case, each day).

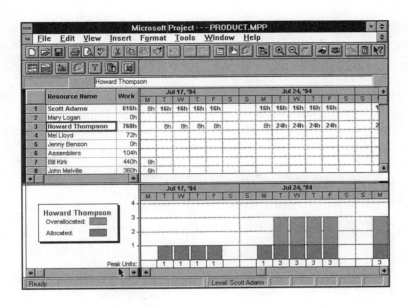

Fig. 18.41
The Resource
Graph showing
peak units
displayed below
the Resource
Usage View.

You can use the graph to show the following measurements for a resource time-period:

- The Peak Units

- The amount of work assigned

- The cost of the assignments

- The overallocation of the resource

- Percent Allocation

- The cumulative work or cost

- The availability of the resource

The graph can show these measurements for one resource, for a group of resources, or for the resource and the group together. The values can be for selected tasks or for all tasks during each time period.

If the Resource Graph is displayed in the bottom pane below a task view, the displayed values are for one resource only. You can show values for this resource's assignment to one task (the selected task) or to all tasks during each period measured on the timescale. Figure 18.41 shows the assignment bars for Howard Thompson for all tasks during each day. This figure provides a quick glimpse of the overassignment in terms of numbers of tasks assigned.

III

Views and Reports

When the Resource Graph is in the top pane, or in the bottom pane but below a resource view, the values displayed are for all tasks and may be for one resource, for a group of resources, or for that one resource compared to the group of resources. If group data is displayed, the group is defined by the filter currently in use. If the All Resources filter (the default filter) is in use, for example, the data summarizes all resources for all tasks. Figure 18.42 shows the total costs associated with Howard Thompson's task assignments, relative to the total costs of all resource assignments in the project.

Fig. 18.42
The Resource Graph for costs associated with Howard Thompson compared to the cost of all other resources.

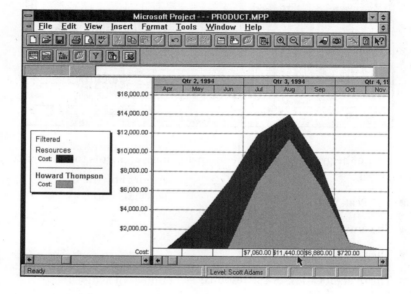

Table 18.4 summarizes the values displayed for different placement locations for the Resource Graph.

Table 18.4 Values Shown in the Resource Graph		
Location of Graph	**Group Value**	**One Resource Value**
Values Displayed		
Top pane or bottom pane below a resource.	Value is for all tasks for all filtered resources.	Value is for all tasks for one view.
Bottom pane below a resource.	Value is for one resource but for all tasks.	Value is for one resource task view but for only the tasks selected in the top pane.

Reviewing the Format Options for the Resource Graph

As with other views, the Zoom command on the View menu is available for the Resource Graph and works as discussed previously in this chapter. Likewise, the Zoom In and Zoom Out tools on the Standard toolbar can be used in this view.

The Format menu for the Resource Graph contains dialog box options described previously in this chapter for formatting the timescale, gridlines, and text styles. The Bar Styles dialog box, however, offers features unique to the Resource Graph. These features are discussed in an upcoming section. The Format menu also provides a Details list of field values and calculated values that you can select to display in the timescale of the Resource Graph. Because the Bar Styles dialog box changes are based on these values the Details options are described first.

Selecting the Values To Display

The unit used in the graph for measuring work (hours, minutes, or days) is determined by the Show Work In option on the Schedule tab of the Tools Options dialog box. The display of costs is determined by the Currency Symbol, Currency Placement, and Currency Decimal Digits choices in the same dialog box, on the View tab.

Displaying Peak Units

Peak Units measures the largest number of units assigned at any moment during each time period on the graph. If the number of assigned units exceeds the available number, the excess is shown as an overallocation. An availability line shows the number of units available.

Note that Peak Units measures *units assigned*, not work assigned. As such, Peak Units may mislead you when it shows an overallocation. Suppose that a person is assigned full-time to two tasks during the same day. The peak units is 2, and because only one unit of a person is usually available per time period, the peak of 2 is an overallocation and is displayed as such. If each of the two tasks is a one-hour task, however, the person should have no problem completing both tasks during the day.

The Peak Units measurement is very useful, however, with multiple-unit resources in which the number of maximum units available is more than one. In these cases, the overallocation warning is more likely to be accurate.

Displaying Work

Work is measured in hours and is the number of units assigned to tasks times the duration in hours of the tasks per time period. The amount of work available to be done by the resource is determined by the number of units of the resource and by the resource calendar during the time unit. If the total work for the time period exceeds the available amount of work, the excess is shown as an overallocation.

Displaying Cumulative Work

Cumulative Work is a measurement of the total work for the resource as of the time unit and since the beginning of the project. This running total includes the work during the time period shown.

Displaying Overallocation

The Overallocation value shows the overallocation of work for the resource for the time period. The Overallocation option shows just the amount of the overallocation. See the section, "Displaying Work," earlier in this chapter for the way work is measured.

Displaying Percent Allocation

The Percent Allocation value is a measurement of the allocated work versus the available work. The Percent Allocation shows the amount of work as a percentage of the amount available. See the previous section, "Displaying Work," for the way in which work is measured.

Displaying Availability

The Availability value is a measurement of the unallocated work for the resource during the time period. The Availability option shows the unused or unallocated work time that is still available. See the section "Displaying Work."

Displaying Cost

The Cost value is the scheduled cost of the resource work during the time period. If the resource cost is to be prorated (as defined in the Accrue At field on the Resource Form), the costs will appear in the time period when the work is done. If there is a Per Use cost associated with a prorated resource, that cost is shown at the start of the task. If the resource cost is to accrue at the start or end of the task, the entire cost will appear in the graph at the start or end of the task.

Displaying Cumulative Cost

The Cumulative Cost display adds each period's cost to the preceding period's cumulative cost to show a running total of costs. You can use this measurement to show total cost over the life of the project if you use only the group graph and include all resources in the group (see the Bar Styles dialog box instructions in the next section).

Using the Bar Styles Dialog Box

When the Resource Graph is displayed, choose Bar **S**tyles from the F**o**rmat menu to display the Bar Styles dialog box. You can also access this dialog box by accessing the shortcut menu available when pointing at a blank portion of the timescale section of the view. A different Bar Styles dialog box will appear for each of the value measurements just described. However, all of these dialog boxes have the same layout and are used the same way. Figure 18.43 shows the Bar Styles dialog box for the Work value. As with all the Resource Graph Bar Styles dialog boxes, this dialog box has four main sections plus three options at the bottom of the box.

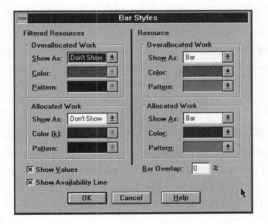

Fig. 18.43
The Resource Graph Bar Styles dialog box for Work values.

You use the two top sections to specify the display of overallocated amounts (if applicable), and the two bottom sections to specify the display of the allocated value up to the maximum available. The sections on the left side of the dialog box are for specifying the display of group data, and the sections on the right side are for specifying the display of one selected resource. You can choose to display or not to display any of the sections on any of the Bar Styles dialog boxes (except that some of the values on the Details menu can display only two of the sections).

Beneath the dialog box, you may see multiple sets of double bars, and in some cases, each bar has an upper and a lower segment. The upper segment, if it exists, is the overallocation measurement. (Note that the top sections in the Bar Styles dialog box also are for the overallocated measurement.) The lower segment is the allocation up to the overallocation level. (The bottom sections in the dialog box are for the allocated, but not overallocated, amount of work.) Where you see pairs of bars, the left bar is the group measurement (again, note the similarity in the dialog box), and the right bar is the selected resource measurement. Recall that the resource group is defined by the filter that is applied when the Resource Graph is in the top pane or as a single pane . In this case, the group represents all resources because no filter has been applied.

Therefore, where you see a pair of bars in the graph, the bar on the right (slightly in front) is the bar for the resource (Howard Thompson in this case), and the left bar (slightly behind) is the bar for the group (all resources in this case). The mouse arrow is pointing to the division between available and overallocated work for Howard Thompson. Note that a horizontal line extends across the graph at this level. This line is the availability line for the resource.

At the bottom of the graph, the work values are displayed in the time periods where the resource is allocated.

All these features are defined by the dialog box. The check boxes at the bottom are marked to show the values and to show the availability line. The bars overlap by 60 percent to show that they are paired.

The shading patterns are determined by the selections in the four sections of the dialog box. For each section, you choose three features that determine how the value is represented. Use the **S**how As entry list arrow to choose the general form of the representation. The Bar is the usual choice, but you also can use lines and areas. The choice Don't Show suppresses all representation of the value. Choose **C**olor to select the color of the image, and choose **P**attern for the pattern that fills the bar or area. (Notice that the highlighted letters for these options are different in each section.)

You manage what is displayed by choosing to display or not to display in each of the four sections of the dialog box. If you want to display only the values for the selected resource, with no representation of the group values, choose Don't Show for both sections on the left. If you want to show only the totals for all resources, choose Don't Show for both sections on the right. When you choose Overallocation on the F**o**rmat **D**etails menu, the Bar Styles dialog box has both of the bottom sections dimmed to show that the sections are unneeded. When you finish making changes, choose OK to implement them or choose Cancel to ignore them.

To prepare the resource graph as shown in figure 18.42 follow these steps:

1. Choose the Format Details command and then Cost from the cascading menu.

2. Choose the Format Bar Styles command.

3. In the Bar Styles dialog box change the Show as option for the Resource Group cost (top left) to area.

4. Set the Show as option for the selected Resource cost (top right) to area. Choose a different color as well.

5. Zoom the timescale to a major scale of quarters and a minor scale of months. You can use the Zoom out tool on the standard toolbar to do this.

Formatting the Resource Usage View

The Resource Usage view shows the same data displayed in the Resource Graph, except that the values appear as number entries in a grid under the timescale. Figure 18.44 shows the Resource Usage view above the Resource Graph to demonstrate the similarity of the data presented. In both views, the value displayed is Peak Units. The Format menu for the Resource Usage view includes text styles, formatting fonts, gridline formatting, and timescale formatting. As with the other views, sorting is also available on the Tools menu, and page breaks can be inserted using the Insert menu. These are all topics covered previously in this chapter under their own headings. See those sections for information about using these format options. At the bottom of the Resource Usage Format menu are the same value choices that were described under the Resource Graph. Select the value to display by selecting one of these options.

If the Resource Usage view is placed in the bottom pane under a task view, the resources that are displayed will be resources assigned to the task that you selected in the top pane. The values displayed for the resource, however, are the total values for all tasks during the time periods shown. If you want the values to reflect only the task (or tasks) you have selected in the top pane, choose Selected Tasks Only on the Format Details menu. You choose that option from the Format Details menu when the Resource Usage view is displayed in the bottom pane.

Fig. 18.44
The Resource
Usage view in the
top pane with the
Resource Graph in
the bottom pane,
both showing
peak units as the
value displayed.

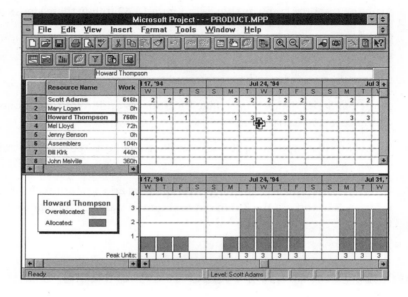

Figure 18.45 shows the Resource Usage view below the Gantt Chart. The values in the usage timescale table show Work assigned to Howard Thompson for all tasks during each time period. The values show that the resource is overallocated for a normal 40-hour work week.

Formatting the Sheet Views

The Task and Resource Sheets both display a table of field values for the list of tasks or resources. The Format menu for both the Sheet views only includes options for changing Fonts, Gridlines, and Text Styles. Also, as before, the Tools menu has a Sorting option, and the Insert menu offers a choice for inserting Page Breaks. These features were discussed previously in this chapter under their own headings. The columns that are displayed depend on the table applied to the sheet. The definition and selection of tables also was covered earlier in the chapter.

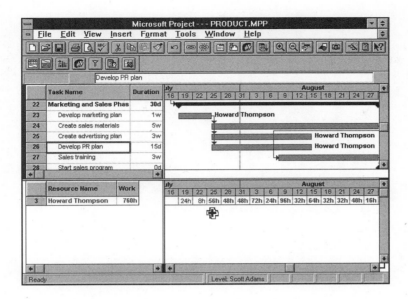

Fig. 18.45
The Resource
Usage view
displayed below
the Gantt chart,
with hours of
Work displayed for
the resource.

From Here...

This chapter described most of the standard customizing features for the
various views in Microsoft Project. In addition to these standard features for
customizing views, you can add text and graphics of your own creation.
There are also numerous options for customizing reports. When you find
yourself using these same features repeatedly, you may want to automate
them with macros. To learn more about these subjects refer to the following
chapters:

■ Chapter 19, "Placing Text and Graphics on the Gantt Chart."

■ Chapter 20, "Using and Customizing Reports."

■ Chapter 21, "Creating and Using Macros."

III

Views and Reports

Placing Text and Graphics on the Gantt Chart

Microsoft Project 4.0 provides a set of drawing tools to help you enhance the appearance of your Gantt Charts. Figure 19.1 shows a text message overlaid on the Gantt Chart, with an arrow directing your attention to the circled tasks the message describes. The drawing tools produce graphic objects that can be moved, resized, placed in front of, along side of, or behind the task bars.

Included among the drawing tools is a text box tool that lets you place free text anywhere in the Gantt Chart display. This chapter will show you how to create and modify graphics and text on the Gantt Chart. Note that graphic objects you have placed on the Gantt Chart will not be displayed when the Gantt Chart is in the bottom pane of a combination view.

In this chapter, you learn how to

- Place geometric figures, lines, arrows, and text on the Gantt chart.

- Move and resize the graphics objects.

- Change the line styles, fill patterns, and colors of the drawings.

- Position objects in front of or behind task bars and other objects.

- Hide and display the objects for different printing needs.

- Attach objects to task bars or to dates on the timeline.

Fig. 19.1
Text and graphics elements can be used to annotate a Gantt Chart or to emphasize one of its aspects.

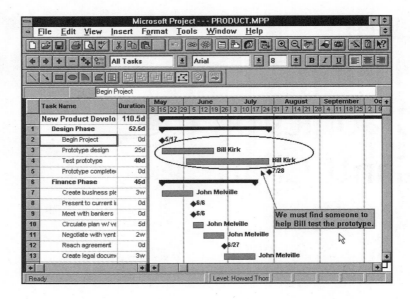

Working with the Drawing Toolbar

◀ "Learning the Basics of Microsoft Project." p. 27

Text and graphic objects are created on the Gantt Chart with the Drawing Toolbar. Once the toolbar is displayed, you can create objects by selecting an object button and creating an example of the object on the Gantt Chart area. Once they are created, you can modify the objects to create the effect you want.

 To display the Drawing toolbar, you can click the Drawing button on the Standard toolbar, or you can choose the **D**rawing command from the **I**nsert menu. The toolbar will be displayed in the workspace area as a floating toolbar. You can move the floating toolbar by dragging its title bar. If you move it to the top of the screen, it will be docked below the menu and the other toolbars.

Descriptions of the Drawing Buttons

The first seven buttons on the toolbar create objects on the Gantt Chart graphic area. The remaining buttons provide access to various editing possibilities.

When you choose one of the first seven buttons, the mouse pointer turns into crosshairs. Position the pointer where you want to begin drawing an object, and drag it to create the object. After it has been created, the object will have small black resizing handles at each corner and along each side. The handles are used to change the dimensions of the object.

Figure 19.2 shows samples of the figures that you can draw. The buttons that draw the objects are described below. These descriptions are brief. See the sections that follow in this chapter for more information about using specific buttons for specific purposes.

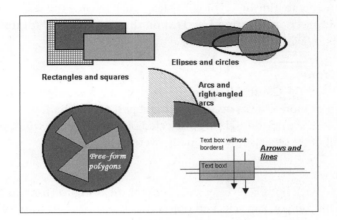

Line

Use the Line button to draw straight lines without arrowheads.

Arrow

Use the Arrow button to draw straight lines with arrowheads.

Rectangle

Use the Rectangle button to draw rectangles, or hold down the Shift key to draw squares.

Ellipse

Use the Ellipse button to draw elliptical figures, or hold down the Shift key to draw perfect circles.

Arc

Use the Arc button to draw arcs with different sized axes, or hold down the Shift key to draw symmetrical arcs.

Polygon

The Polygon button allows you to draw a many-sided figure of any configuration you choose. Each time you click, another line segment is drawn. Double-click to have the computer draw a final line that connects the last point to the starting point, producing a closed figure.

III

Views and Reports

Text Box

The Text Box button draws a box in which you can type free text. Hold down the Shift key to draw a square box. When you release the mouse, and the box is drawn, an insertion point is displayed in the box for you to type in the text. When you are finished typing the text, click outside the text box. See an upcoming section, "Placing Free Text on the Gantt Chart," for instructions about working with text boxes.

Bring to Front

The objects on the Gantt Chart include those you draw, as well as the task bars. If two or more objects occupy the same part of the chart, you can use the Bring to Front button to bring a selected object to the forefront, placing it before all other objects that originally overlaid it.

Send to Back

The Send to Back button reverses the action of the Bring to Front button. With this button you can select an object that is displayed in front of other objects and send it to the back, placing it behind all other objects in the same area.

Move Forward

The Move Forward button allows you to move a selected object in front of another object that is originally in front of it. If multiple objects occupy the same space, this button allows you to position an object between other objects.

Move Backward

The Move Backward button moves the selected object behind the object that is currently behind it. If multiple objects occupy the same space, this button allows you to position an object between other objects.

Reshape

The Reshape button allows you to change the shape of a polygon.

Cycle Fill Color

The Cycle Fill Color button changes the fill color of the selected object, cycling through the palette of color choices each time you click the button.

Attach to Task

This button displays the Size & Position dialog box to allow you to change how the object is tied to the Gantt Chart.

Hiding Objects on the Gantt Chart

The objects you place on the Gantt Chart will remain visible and will print with the Gantt Chart unless you elect to hide them. You can hide them for one printing, for example, and then display them again.

To hide the drawing objects:

1. Choose the Format menu and choose the Layout command. The Layout dialog box will be displayed (see fig. 19.3).

2. Clear the Show Drawings check box at the bottom.

3. Choose the OK button to implement the change.

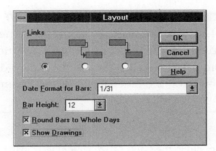

Fig. 19.3
Graphic objects are hidden from view if you clear the Show Drawings check box on the Layout dialog box.

Selecting Objects

When the Gantt Chart is displayed, you can have task fields selected in the table area, you can select a task bar, or you can select objects that you have placed in the graphics area.

You can use the mouse to select objects in the graphics area if you watch the mouse pointer carefully. Move the tip of the pointer to the edge of an object. When a small cross appears below and to the right of the pointer arrow, you can click to select the object. If the object is selected, the small black resizing handles will appear around it.

You also can use the keyboard to select objects. The F6 function key toggles back and forth between selecting the task table and a graphic object. (If a combination view is displayed, the bottom view is also selected in turn by the F6 key.) If you have created multiple objects, once one of them is selected, you can use the Tab key to shift the selection to the other graphic objects one at a time.

Moving Objects

You can move the selected object if you move the mouse pointer to the border of the object. Watch for the small cross to appear to the right of the pointer arrow. Then drag the object to a new position.

> **Caution**
>
> It is very easy to accidentally move a task bar or create a new task bar when your intention is to move or resize an object. If the mouse pointer does not have the cross beside it, you will not be moving the object.

Attaching Objects to a Task Bar or a Date

When you create an object, it is automatically attached to the timescale at the date where you placed it on the Gantt Chart, with a vertical offset to show how far down from the timescale it should be displayed. The object will stay with that date as you scroll the timescale or as you Zoom the timescale.

> **Caution**
>
> Be aware that if you zoom out in the Gantt Chart, your objects may be placed on top of each other due to the compressed timescale.

If the object is attached to the timescale when you move it, it will remain attached to the timescale but at whatever date and vertical position you move it to. You can see the attachment by examining the Size & Position tab of the Format Drawing dialog box for the object (shown in fig. 19.4).

Fig. 19.4
Use the Format Drawing dialog box to attach an object to a task or to the timescale.

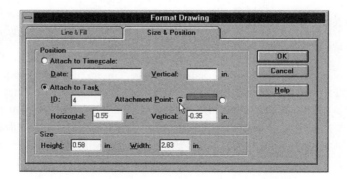

To view the Format Drawing dialog box, select the object and then double-click it. Be sure to double-click the border of text boxes, because double-clicking the center of the box opens the text area for editing.

Alternatively, you can choose the Format menu and choose Drawing. Then choose Properties from the submenu. Or, to use the Shortcut menu, position the mouse pointer over the object so that the pointer displays the small cross to its right. Click the right mouse button to see the Shortcut menu, and select Properties.

To attach the object to a task:

1. Choose the Size & Position tab of the Format Drawing dialog box.

2. Choose the Attach to Task radio button.

3. Enter the task number in the ID field. If you do not remember the ID number, you will have to close the dialog box, find the number, and then come back to the dialog box.

4. Attach the object to the beginning or the end of the task bar by choosing the Attachment Point at the beginning or at the end of the sample task bar.

5. The Horizontal and Vertical fields show the offset from the attachment point where the object's top-left corner will be placed. Although you can enter values in these fields if you want to, it is very difficult to know which measurements will work best. It is not necessary to enter the values here. Once the object is attached to the task, you can move it with the mouse, and the positioning offset will be recorded automatically. The object will remain attached to the task as you move it (until you come back to the Size & Position tab and attach it to the Timescale).

6. Choose OK to return to the workspace.

If you later decide to unlink the object from the task in order to fix it at a particular date, return to the Size & Position tab and choose the Attach to Timescale button. Then move the task with the mouse to the preferred position.

Resizing Objects
Although you can size an object with the Height and Width fields at the bottom of the Size & Position tab in the Format Drawing dialog box (see fig. 19.4), you will find it much easier to use the mouse to achieve the same end.

III

Views and Reports

When a two-dimensional object is selected, its resizing handles will be evident in a rectangular array around the object. The one-dimensional line and arrow display resizing handles at each end of the line. You can change the size of the object by moving the mouse pointer over one of the resizing handles until the pointer changes into a pair of opposing arrows. Drag the handle to the position you desire. The corner handles resize both sides that meet at the corner. The handles along the top and bottom midpoints resize vertically, and the handles along the sides resize horizontally.

 The resizing handles of a polygon disappear when you select the polygon and click the Reshape tool on the Drawing toolbar. Instead you see reshaping handles at the connecting nodes of its line segments. Use these handles to reposition the connecting nodes and thus change the shape of the drawing. To move a connecting node, position the mouse pointer directly over the handle (it will turn into a large plus sign). When you are through reshaping the figure, click the Reshape tool again to display the resizing handles again.

Caution

It is just as easy to accidentally move a task bar or create a new task bar when trying to resize an object as it is when moving an object. If the mouse pointer has not become opposing arrows, you are not resizing the object.

Copying Objects

You can make a copy of an object to display in another area of the chart. To copy an object:

1. Select the original object.

2. Use the **Ctrl** key as you drag away from the original object. You will be dragging a copy of the original.

3. Continue dragging the copy until it is in its new position. The copy will appear in outlined form until you release the mouse button.

4. Release the mouse button when the copy is in position.

You also can use the clipboard to copy an object.

1. Select the original object.

2. Choose the **E**dit menu, and choose the **C**opy command.

3. Choose the **E**dit menu and choose the **P**aste command. A copy of the object will appear at the top left corner of the visible part of the Gantt Chart graphic area.

4. Drag the copy of the object into it desired position.

Changing the Line and Fill Style of an Object

You can change the thickness and color of the lines that surround objects. You can also choose the background pattern and color of the interior of the figure. Both the line and fill are selected on the Line & Fill tab of the Format Drawing dialog box (see fig. 19.5).

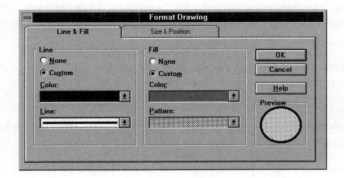

Fig. 19.5
You can customize the attributes of the border lines and the interior fill of objects.

To change an object's border line and fill attributes:

1. Select the object and display the Format Drawing dialog box using one of the methods described in detail in the section titled "Attaching an Object to a Task Bar or a Date." Display the dialog box by double-clicking the object, by choosing F**o**rmat D**r**awing **P**roperties, or by choosing Properties from the Shortcut menu for the object.

2. Choose the Line & Fill tab.

3. If you want the line to be invisible, choose the **N**one button in the Line section. If you select a line color or line style, the Cu**s**tom button will be activated automatically.

4. If you want to select the color for a line, choose a sample color band from the entry list below the **C**olor label.

5. If you want to select the thickness of a line, choose a sample line from the entry list below the **L**ine label.

III

Views and Reports

6. If you want the background of the object to be transparent, so that you can see task bars or other objects behind the object, choose the None button in the Fill section of this tab. If you choose a Color or a Pattern, the Custom button will be activated automatically.

7. If you want to display a fill color in the interior of the object you must select a pattern or else there will be nothing for the color to be attached to. Choose a pattern by selecting a sample from the entry list below the Pattern label. The first pattern in the entry list appears white. It is a "clear" pattern, equivalent to choosing the None button in the Fill section. The second pattern in the entry list is solid black. Choose that band for a solid background in the color you choose from the Color field. The remaining patterns will be displayed against a white background, with the pattern appearing in the foreground in the color you choose from the Color field.

8. Choose a color for the pattern from the sample color bands provided in the entry list below the Color label.

9. Use the Preview box at the lower right corner of the tab to assess the choices you have made. Change the choices until the Preview box looks the way you want the object to look.

10. Choose the OK button to implement the changes. Choose the Cancel button to leave the object unchanged.

Deleting Objects

You can delete objects by simply selecting them and then pressing the Delete key.

Placing Free Text on the Gantt Chart

Use the Text Box drawing button to place free text on the Gantt Chart. After you place the text box on the screen, you enter the text into the box. You can change the attributes and position of the text box as described in the sections above. You can also edit the text and choose the fonts for the text display.

Creating a Text Box

To create a text box:

1. Choose the Text Box button on the Drawing toolbar.

2. Drag the mouse in the Gantt Chart to create a box at the approximate location and of the approximate dimension you will need. An insertion point cursor will blink in the text box.

3. Type the text you want to appear in the box. The text will automatically word-wrap within the current size of the text box. It will also word-wrap automatically when you resize the text box later. Press the Enter key to start new lines in the text box.

4. When you are finished entering text, click outside the text box.

To edit the text in a text box:

1. Select the text box. The mouse pointer will change into an I-beam within the text box.

2. Select the place in the text that you want to edit by clicking the I-beam at that point. (see fig. 19.6)

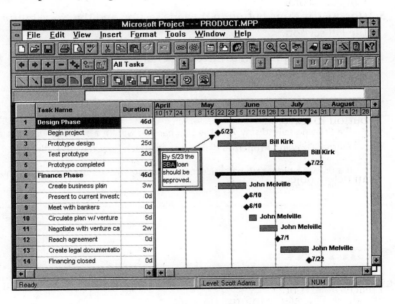

Fig. 19.6
You can use normal editing techniques in a text box.

3. Click outside the text box when you are finished editing.

Note

If you want to move a text box, you must be sure to select its border with the mouse. Unlike the other objects, selecting the interior of the this object does not allow you to move it. Instead, you are allowed to edit the text.

Changing the Text Font

You can choose the font for the text in a text box by selecting the text and box and choosing the F**o**rmat **F**ont command from the menu. You cannot apply different fonts to individual strings within the text box.

Changing the Properties of the Text Box

When you create a text box, it is automatically given a lined border and a white background fill. If you want the text to float freely without lines so that the Gantt Chart shows through, you must choose the None button in both the sections of the Line & Fill tab on the Format Drawing dialog box.

To clear the lines and fill for a text box:

1. Select the text box.

2. Double-click the text box border to display the Format Drawing dialog box.

3. Choose the **N**one button in the Line section and the N**o**ne button in the Fill section.

4. Choose the OK button to effect the change.

Troubleshooting

- If a drawing fails to stay with the task bar you want it associated with, use the F**o**rmat D**r**awing **P**roperties dialog box to attach the drawing to the task.

- If a drawing hides task bars, select the drawing and use the Shortcut menu to move the drawing back.

From Here...

This chapter has demonstrated how to draw graphic objects and text in the Gantt Chart. For related information, see

- Chapter 14, "Exchanging Data with Other Applications," for information on importing objects from other applications.

- Chapter 16, "Printing Views and Reports," for tips about printing the Gantt Chart.

- Chapter 17, "Using and Creating Views," and Chapter 18, "Formatting Views," for ideas on customizing Gantt Charts.

Chapter 20

Using and Customizing Reports

The **R**eports command on the **V**iew menu provides access to five groups of report formats: **O**verview, **C**urrent Activities, Co**s**ts, **A**ssignments, and **W**orkloads. Together these groups contain 22 pre-defined summary, calendar, task, resource, and/or crosstab reports that are all set up and ready to print. However, you cannot edit the content or level of detail of these reports from these groups. A sixth group called **Cu**stom is the doorway to the wide range of options available to you to customize any of the existing pre-defined reports or to create your own reports.

The basic types of reports available in Microsoft Project include project summary, calendars, task lists, resource lists, and crosstab reports. Of these reports, the task lists and resource lists have the most options for customization. In each case, you can select the columns of information to be displayed, the filter to be applied, and the amount of supporting detail about the tasks or resources listed. The crosstab reports are also flexible in allowing you to select which task or resource detail you wish to examine by any given time period. Most of the task, resource, and crosstab reports allow the addition of gridlines and/or gray bands, and all reports allow you to use text formatting to further organize the information for easier reading. This chapter explores the range of options available to those who wish to develop customized reports adapted to their project communication needs.

In this chapter, you learn how to

- Customize any of the 22 standard reports included in Microsoft Project 4.0

- Create new reports based on the standard resource, task, crosstab, and calendar formats included in Microsoft Project 4.0

- Control the display of data in your reports

- Save your custom report formats for use with all your project files and for other users of Microsoft Project 4.0

Using the Basic Custom Report Functions

To print any reports, choose **R**eports from the **V**iew menu. The Reports dialog box appears, listing the available report groups (see fig. 20.1). If you select one of the five pre-defined report groups, you can change only the page setup options (margins, page orientation, header, footer, and legend) before printing; there is no button to edit the content of the report. All changes to reports are done through the Custom group, which will present you with a list of 26 pre-defined reports and buttons for the following actions (see fig. 20.2):

Fig. 20.1

The Reports dialog box.

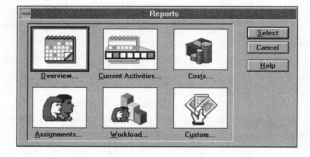

Fig. 20.2

The Custom Reports dialog box.

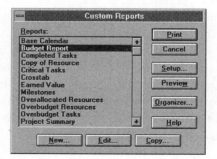

- **P**rint one of the reports in the **R**eports list as the report is currently defined. See Chapter 16, "Printing Views and Reports," for printing instructions.

■ **S**etup the selected report before printing. (This is the same as the Page Setup function, which allows you to set up margins, headers, footers, and so on.)

■ Pre**v**iew one of the reports before printing. The Print Preview screen is activated (see Chapter 16), and you have the option of changing Page Setup before sending the report to the printer.

■ Access the **O**rganizer to copy customized reports to or from the Global template. This **O**rganizer dialog box also allows you to delete reports from your **C**ustom Reports list to keep your list current and uncluttered.

■ **E**dit the report to change the table and filter used and to change the details that are shown (for task and resource reports), the column and row information (for crosstab reports), the sort order for presenting the details (for non-calendar reports), the text formatting used for parts of the report, and the use of border lines in the report. These changes become standard features of the named report.

■ **C**opy an existing report and make modifications in the new report so that you have both the original and the new copy to use when needed.

■ Create a **N**ew report, whose design must follow closely the prefabricated reports on the standard list.

The **N**ew and **C**opy buttons function almost identically to the **E**dit button. The only difference is that the end result for both **N**ew and **C**opy is a new report name to be added to the **C**ustom reports list. In the following sections, the instructions for **E**dit also apply to **N**ew and **C**opy. Use **N**ew to design a report from the ground up. Use **C**opy to use an existing report as a starting point for a new report. In all cases, the instructions begin at the **C**ustom Reports dialog box.

If you choose **N**ew, the Define New Report dialog box appears, asking you to define the type of report you want to create. The dialog box lists the basic report types, Task, Resource, Monthly Calendar, and Crosstab. The Calendar and Project Summary report types do not appear since they are standardized and cannot be customized beyond simple text formatting changes. When you select a report type, the report definition dialog box for the selected report type is displayed. To customize the report, you can choose from a variety of options, as described in the following sections on report types.

Tip

For radical changes or changes that you want to use often but not all the time, you will want to make a copy of the report, give it a descriptive name, and then make your changes on the copy.

III

Views and Reports

You can choose to Print or Preview your custom report from the Define New Report dialog box by clicking on the **P**rint or **P**review buttons and selecting OK.

Customizing the Calendar Reports

The two calendar reports available to you are the Base Calendar and the Working Days reports (available as a pre-defined report under the Overview category of reports). Both calendar reports are identical and show the standard work days and work hours for each base calendar defined in the current calendar file. (The printing of a resource calendar is an optional feature of the Resource reports).

The only option in the Base Calendar report is changing the text formats for the title and details of the report. To edit the Base Calendar report, choose Base Calendar from the reports list in the C**u**stom Reports dialog box. Then choose the **E**dit button. The Report Text dialog box appears (see fig. 20.3). Choose the text format features for the calendar name and the detail section. Select the OK button to close the dialog box. Then choose **P**rint or Pre**v**iew to proceed with printing the report (see Chapter 16 for instructions on printing and previewing).

Fig. 20.3
The Calendar Report Text dialog box.

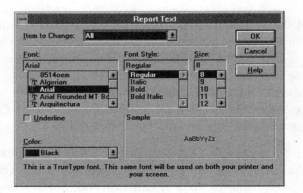

You cannot copy the Base Calendar report, nor can you use its format when creating a new report. Figure 20.4 illustrates the Base Calendar report.

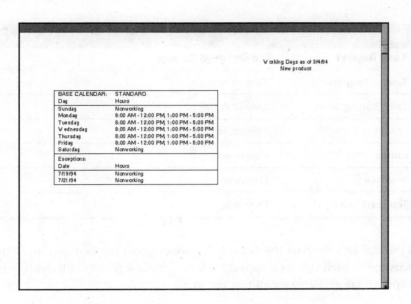

Fig. 20.4
The Base Calendar
report.

Customizing Task Reports

The task reports include all reports that are organized around tasks rather
than resources. Table 20.1 lists all the task reports and the pre-defined group
from the **V**iew **R**eports group in which they are found in their standardized
form.

Table 20.1 Pre-defined Task Reports	
Task Report	**Pre-Defined Group**
Task	*Not in pre-defined group*
Weekly To Do	Assignments
Budget	Cost
Earned Value	Cost
Overbudget Tasks	Cost
Completed Tasks	Current Activities
Should Have Started	Current Activities
Slipping	Current Activities

III

Views and Reports

(continues)

Table 20.1 Continued	
Task Report	**Pre-Defined Group**
Tasks in Progress	Current Activities
Tasks Starting Soon	Current Activities
Unstarted Tasks	Current Activities
Critical	Overview
Milestones	Overview
Top Level Tasks	Overview

All the task reports share the same dialog boxes under the **E**dit button, so the discussion of each option is applicable for all the task reports (although not all options are available for all task reports).

To edit a task report, select the report from the list in the Custom Reports dialog box and click on the **E**dit button. You will see the Task Report dialog box (shown in fig. 20.5). It contains three tabs: Definition, Details, and Sort.

Fig. 20.5
The Task Report
dialog box.

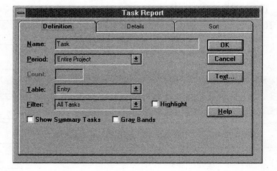

Changing the Definitions for a Custom Task Report

Select the Definition tab to see the current settings for the basic content of the report (the table, filter, and timescale). To change the columns of data to be displayed to the right of each task in the report, select the **T**able box and choose one of the tables from the entry list. The **T**able box lists the standard task tables plus any task tables created with the **V**iew tables command (see Chapter 17, "Using and Creating Views," for more information on creating tables. The standard task tables and the fields these tables display are listed in Table 20.2.

Table 20.2 Standard Task Tables and the Task Table Fields	
Task Table	**Fields**
Cost	Task Name
	Fixed Cost
	Total Cost (Scheduled)
	Baseline Cost
	Variance
	Actual Cost (to Date)
	Remaining (Scheduled Cost)
Entry	Task Name
	Duration
	Scheduled Start and Finish Dates
	Predecessors
	Resource Names
Schedule	Task Name
	Scheduled Start and Finish Dates
	Late Start and Finish Dates
	Free Slack
	Total Slack
Summary	Task Name
	Duration
	Scheduled Start and Finish Dates
	Percent Completion (Duration)
	Cost
	Work
Tracking	Task Name
	Actual Start and Finish Dates

(continues)

III

Views and Reports

Table 20.2 Standard Task Tables and the Task Table Fields	
Task Table	**Fields**
	Percent Completion (Duration)
	Actual Duration
	Remaining Duration
	Actual Cost
	Actual Work
Variance	Task Name
	Scheduled Start and Finish Dates
	Baseline Start and Finish Dates
	Start Variance
	Finish Variance
Work	Task Name
	Work
	Baseline (Work)
	Variance
	Actual (Work)
	Remaining (Scheduled Work)
	Percent Work Completed

To change the time period covered in each group in the report, choose the **P**eriod box and choose years, quarters, months, weeks, or days for the time period. Using the **C**ount box, you can stipulate that each time-period group includes multiple units of the time unit selected. If the resources are paid every two weeks, for example, you may want a list of the related task assignments grouped by pay periods. In this case, you need to set the **C**ount box to 2.

To filter the list of tasks, choose the **F**ilter box and choose a filter from the entry list. If you choose an interactive filter, the interactive prompt appears each time you print or preview the report. As with tables, you can define a task filter to use each time you print the report using the **T**ools **F**iltered for command (see Chapter 16).

To use the filter as a highlight filter only, mark the **H**ighlight check box; tasks which meet the filter criteria will be shaded. To display only the filtered resources, clear this check box.

Mark the Show S**u**mmary Tasks check box if you wish to have each detail task shown with its summary tasks. This is useful if the detail task names are general or are duplicated within the same schedule and need to be associated with a more descriptive summary task to explain them fully for the report reader.

Mark the Print **G**ray Bands check box if you want gray horizontal lines to separate the time periods.

Figure 20.6 shows the Task Report dialog box with customized Definition options. Figure 20.7 displays the resulting report using the Task Report.

Tip
Include the Filter field in your header or footer to keep track of which tasks are highlighted or displayed.

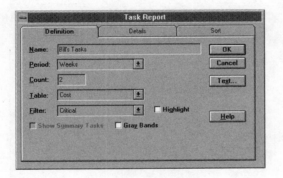

Fig. 20.6
The Task Report definition dialog box.

Changing the Details for a Custom Task Report

Some simple keystrokes can lift details about your tasks from your schedule to include in your report. The Details tab of your Task Report definition dialog box (see fig. 20.8) includes several categories of details that can be selected with checkboxes. These categories are explained on the next page.

III

Views and Reports

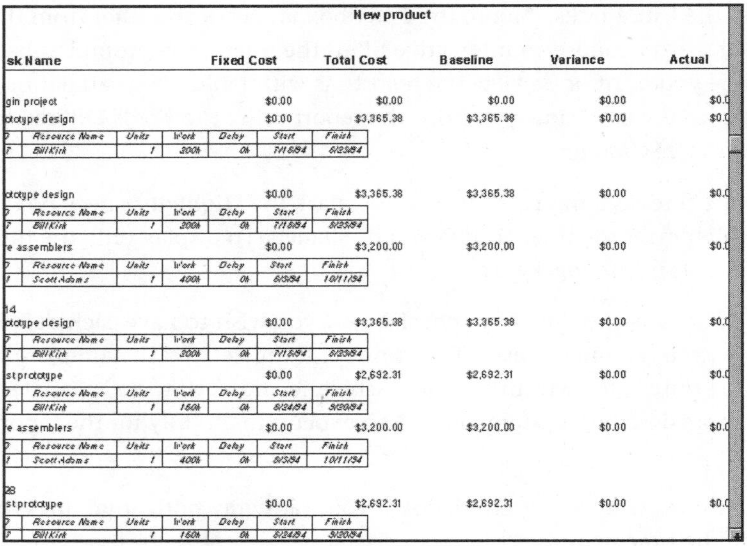

Fig. 20.7
Customized task
report.

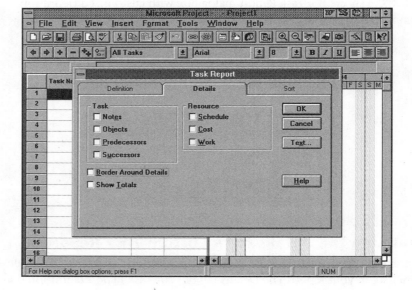

Fig. 20.8
Details tab from
Task Report
definition dialog
box.

1. Select the Details tab to select the task and resource details to be included with each task.

2. Under the Task heading, you can mark one of four boxes:

   ■ Select Notes to include notes you have written for any of your
     tasks (using the Attach Note icon on the Standard toolbar or a
     Notes column in a table).

■ Select Objects if you wish to represent data you have created using another Windows application, such as Microsoft Word or Excel. An example of an object might be a graph done in Microsoft Excel that shows the costs associated with a group of detail tasks under a summary task.

> **Note**
>
> To embed an object in a task to display in a report, it is necessary to use the Task Form or Task Name Form and the Insert Object command. See Chapter 14, "Exchanging Data with Other Applications," for more information.

■ Select the **P**redecessors box if you wish to include a list of the predecessor tasks with Type and Lag information under each task.

■ Select the **Su**ccessors box if you wish to include a list of the successor tasks with Type and Lag information under each task.

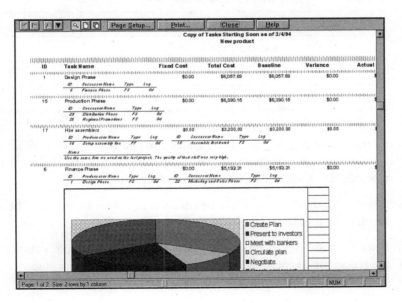

Fig. 20.9
Task report with task details.

III

Views and Reports

3. Under the Resource heading, you can display many kinds of details about each resource by marking the check boxes at the bottom of the dialog box. Mark the Schedule, Cost, and Work check boxes to show detail tables of the task assignments for the resource.

Two fields appear on-screen for the Schedule, Cost, and Work detail tables: Task Name and Units (of Resource Assigned). The following list shows the rest of the fields for each table:

Table	Fields
Schedule	Work (Scheduled Work)
	Delay
	Scheduled Start
	Scheduled Finish
Cost	Cost (Scheduled Cost)
	Baseline Cost
	Actual Cost
	Remaining (Scheduled Cost)
Work	Work (Scheduled Work)
	Overtime Work
	Baseline Work
	Actual Work
	Remaining Work (Scheduled)

If you choose two or three detail tables, the first two may be combined into one table if the report is in landscape. The Work field will not be repeated if the Schedule and Work tables are combined.

4. If you want the detail tables to be enclosed in border lines, mark the **B**orders Around Details check box.

5. Mark the Show **T**otals box if you want to show totals at the bottom of the report for all columns in your table containing numeric information (see fig. 20.10).

Changing the Text Formatting in a Task Report

You can access the Te**x**t button from any of the tabs in the Task Report dialog box. The Text Styles dialog box (shown in fig. 20.11) allows you to select special formatting for a category of tasks and resembles the Format Text

Styles dialog box from the main menu (see Chapter 18, "Formatting Views," for more information on the Format Text Styles command). Use this box to make certain types of information stand out in your report by changing the size, font or formatting of categories of text. The categories available in Task reports are listed in Table 20.3. The default format of each category is 8-point type with no distinguishing characteristics, unless specified in parentheses.

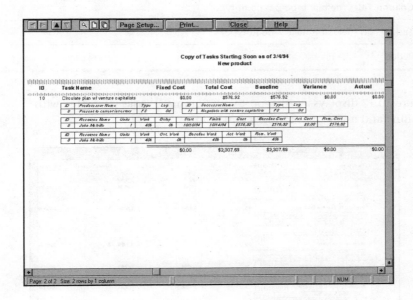

Fig. 20.10
Task Report with resource details and totals.

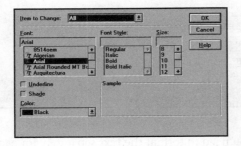

Fig. 20.11
Task report Text Styles dialog box.

III

Views and Reports

Table 20.3 Categories of Tasks Available for Special Formatting in Task Reports

Non-critical tasks

Critical Tasks

Milestones

(continues)

Table 20.3   Continued
Summary Tasks (default is bold)
Marked Tasks
Highlighted Tasks (shaded)
Column Titles (default is bold 9-point type)
Task details (default is italic 7-point type)
Period

Figure 20.12 displays a task report with Summary Tasks formatted with shading and milestones formatted in bold.

Fig. 20.12
Task report with text formatting.

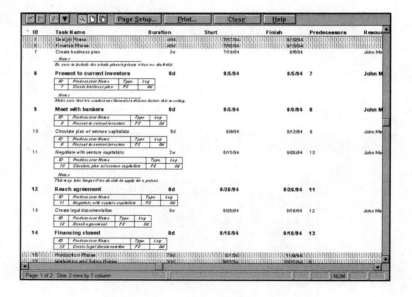

Remember that you need to format the text separately for each individual task report and separately from the text format showing in the current View. For example, even if summary tasks are shaded in your current Gantt view, they will not appear shaded in a task report unless you specify the shading in the Text Styles box from the Task Report dialog box for the individual report.

Sorting Tasks for a Task Report

The Sort tab is identical for all custom reports. See section "Changing the Sort Order for a Report" for more information.

Select OK from any of the dialog box's three tabs to return to your Custom Report dialog box. From there you can Preview and/or Print the report.

Customizing Resource Reports

The resource reports include all reports that are organized around resources. Table 20.4 lists all of the resource reports and the pre-defined group from the View Reports dialog box in which they are found in their standardized form.

Table 20.4 Pre-Defined Resource Reports	
Resource Report	**Pre-Defined Group**
Resource	*Not in pre-defined group*
Who Does What	Assignments
Overallocated Resources	Assignments
Over Budget Resources	Cost

As with the task reports, all the resource reports share the same dialog boxes under the Edit button, so discussion of each option is applicable to all resource reports (although not all options are available for all reports).

Changing the Definitions for a Custom Resource Report

The Definition tab for resource reports (shown in fig. 20.13) is similar to that for the task reports. The Table box lists the standard resource tables plus any custom resource tables created with the View Tables command. Table 20.5 lists the standard resource tables with the fields they display.

Fig. 20.13

The Definition tab of the Resource Report dialog box.

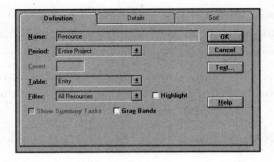

Table 20.5	Standard Resource Tables and Their Fields
Resource Table	**Fields**
Cost	Cost (Total Scheduled Cost)
	Baseline Cost
	Variance
	Actual Cost (to Date)
	Remaining (Scheduled Cost)
Entry	Resource Name
	Initials
	Group
	Maximum Units
	Standard Rate
	Overtime Rate
	Cost/Use
	Accrual Method
	Code
Summary	Name
	Group
	Maximum Units
	Peak Usage
	Standard Rate

Resource Table	Fields
	Overtime Rate
	Cost
	Work
Usage	Resource Name
	Work Resource Name
	Percent Work Complete
	Work
	Overtime
	Baseline (Work)
	Variance
	Actual (Work)
	Remaining (Work)

You can define a resource filter to use each time you print the report. To filter the list of resources, choose the **F**ilter box and then choose a filter from the entry list. If you choose an interactive filter, the interactive prompt appears each time you print the report.

To use the filter as a highlight filter only, mark the **H**ighlight check box; tasks which meet the Filter criteria will be shaded. To display only the filtered resources, clear this check box.

To change the time period covered in each group in the report, choose the **P**eriod box and choose years, quarters, months, weeks, or days for the time period. Using the **C**ount box, you can stipulate that each time-period group includes multiple units of the time unit selected. If the resources are paid every two weeks, for example, you may want a list of the related task assignments grouped by pay periods. In this case, you need to set the **C**ount box to 2.

If you wish to separate time periods with gray bands, mark the Gra**y** Bands box.

Figure 20.14 displays the Resource Report dialog box with customized Definition options. Figure 20.15 displays the resulting report.

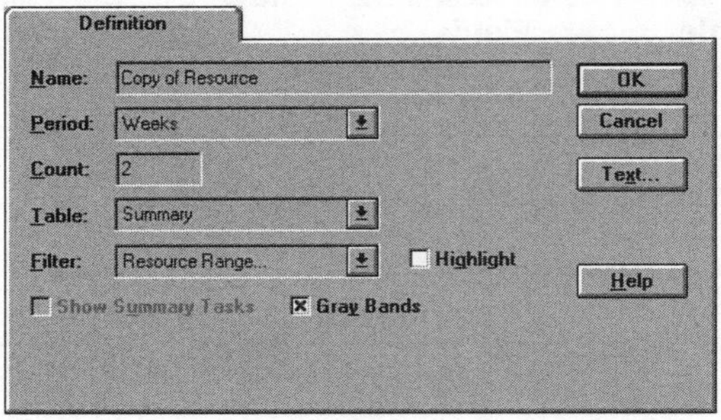

Fig. 20.14
The Resource
Report dialog box.

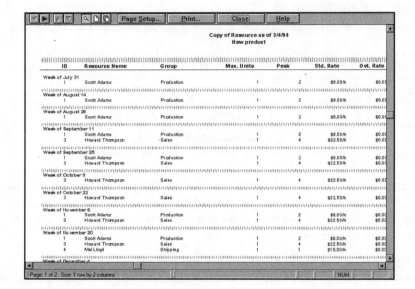

Fig. 20.15
The resulting
resource report.

Changing the Details for a Custom Resource Report

Changing the details included in a custom resource report is much like changing details in a custom task report. Once again, the Details tab of the Resource Report definition dialog box gives you many options. Figure 20.16 shows a resource report with all of the details included.

1. Select the Details tab to select the task and resource details to be included with each task. The options shown on the Details tab for resource reports (see fig. 20.17) vary slightly from those shown for task reports.

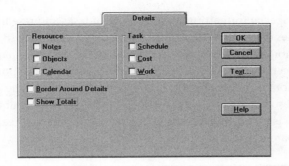

Fig. 20.16
The Details tab
of the Resource
Report dialog box.

2. Under the Resource heading, you can mark one of three boxes:

   Select Notes to include notes you have written for any of your tasks (using the Attach Note icon on the Standard toolbar or a Notes column in a table).

   Select Objects if you wish to represent data you have created using another Windows application, such as Microsoft Word or Excel. An example of an object might be a Microsoft Excel graph of work hours assigned for a group of resources assigned to a group of tasks.

   Select the Calendar box if you wish to include resource calendars in the report.

3. Under the Task heading, you can display many kinds of details about each task (see fig. 20.17). Mark the Schedule, Cost, and Work check boxes to show detail tables of the task assignments for the resource. The fields for each task assigned are the same as those listed under resource details on the Task Reports.

4. If you want the detail tables to be enclosed in border lines, mark the Borders Around Details check box.

5. Mark the Show Totals box if you wish to show totals at the bottom of the report for all columns in your table containing numeric information.

Changing the Text Formatting in a Resource Report

As with task reports, you can access the Text button from any of the tabs boxes in the Resource Report dialog box. The Text Styles dialog box allows you to select special formatting for a category of tasks and resembles the Format Text Styles dialog box from the main menu (see Chapter 18, "Formatting Views," for more information on the F**o**rmat **T**ext Styles command). Use this box to make certain types of information stand out in your report by changing the size, font or formatting of certain categories of text. The categories available in resource reports are listed in Table 20.6. The default format of each category is 8-point type with no distinguishing characteristics, unless specified in parentheses.

Fig. 20.17
Resource report
with task details.

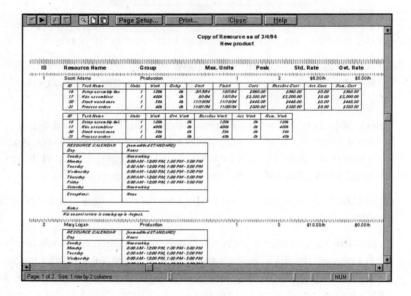

Table 20.6   Categories of Resources Available for Special Formatting in Resource Reports

Allocated Resources

Overallocated Resources

Highlighted Resources (shaded)

Column Titles (default is bold 9-point type)

Resource details (default is italic 7-point type)

Totals

Sorting Your Tasks for Your Resource Report

The Sort dialog box is identical for all custom reports. See the section "Changing the Sort Order for a Report" for more information.

Customizing Crosstab Reports

Crosstab reports show cost amounts or work hours by task or resource in a grid format by selected time period. Table 20.7 lists the pre-designed crosstab reports available for customizing.

Table 20.7 Pre-Defined Crosstab Reports	
Crosstab Report	**Pre-Defined Group**
Crosstab	*Not in pre-defined group*
Who Does What When	Assignments
Weekly Cash Flow	Cost
Resource Usage	Workload
Task Usage	Workload

Crosstab reports share the same dialog boxes under the Edit button, so discussion of each option is applicable to all crosstab reports (although not all options are available for all reports).

Changing the Definitions for a Custom Crosstab Report

Selecting the type of information to be displayed in your crosstab report is done through the Definition section in the Crosstab report definition dialog box. Select the Definition tab to display the Definition box for crosstab reports (see fig. 20.18). The Definition box allows you to indicate whether you wish to list tasks or resources down your rows by selecting one of the two in the **R**ow box. The available information to include in the grid for your row information depends on whether you are working with Tasks or Resources. If you are listing tasks in your rows, the **C**olumn box choices include Cost, Cumulative Cost, Work, and Cumulative Work. If you are listing resources in your rows, your **C**olumn box choices also include Overallocations, Percent Allocation, and Availability. You may also select the time period represented by each column in the grid with the **C**olumn section. Figure 20.19 shows a crosstab report that lists work by resources.

Fig. 20.18
The Definition tab
of the Crosstab
Reports dialog
box.

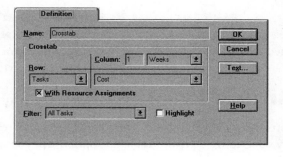

As with resource and task reports, you can select a filter. If you choose to list tasks as your row information, you will be presented with your list of task filters in the **F**ilter box. If you choose to list resources as your row information, you will see your list of resource filters in the **F**ilter box. Remember that if you wish to use a custom filter, you must create it first, using the **T**ools **F**iltered for command (see Chapter 17, "Using and Creating Views").

If you are listing resources in your rows and wish to include details on assigned tasks for each resource, check the **W**ith Task Assignments box. The box changes its label to **W**ith Resource Assignments if you choose Tasks as your **R**ow information, and it will list all assigned resources for the tasks listed in your report. Figure 20.19 shows work by resources with task assignments included.

Fig. 20.19
Crosstab report
showing work by
resources with task
assignments.

			Page Setup...	Print...	Close	Help	

Copy of Crosstab as of 3/4/94
New product

	7/17	7/24	7/31	8/7	8/14	8/21	8/28	9/4	9/11	9/18	9/25	10/2	10/9
Scott Adams			40h	40h	40h	40h	40h	40h	40h	80h	80h	80h	
Setup assembly line										40h	40h	40h	
Hire assemblers			40h	40h	40h	40h	40h	40h	40h	40h	40h	40h	
Stock warehouse													
Process orders													
Mary Logan													
Howard Thompson										40h	120h	120h	160
Develop marketing plan										40h			
Create sales materials											40h	40h	40
Create advertising plan											40h	40h	40
Develop PR plan											40h	40h	40
Sales training													40
West Coast promo week													
East Coast promo week													
Northern Region promo week													
Southern Region promo week													
Mel Lloyd													
Organize shipments													
Load trucks													
Jenny Benson													
Assemblers													24
Assemble first batch													24
Assemble product													
Bill Kirk	40h	40h	40h	40h	40h	40h	40h	40h	40h				16
Prototype design	40h	40h	40h	40h	40h								
Test prototype						40h	40h	40h	40h				
Quality testing													16
John Melville	40h	40h	40h	40h	40h	40h	40h	40h	40h				
Create business plan	40h	40h	40h										

Page: 1 of 2   Size: 1 row by 2 columns | | | | | | NUM |

Changing the Details for a Custom Crosstab Report

Adding details to a custom crosstab reports is done through the same Details tab you see in the custom report dialog box for task and resource reports. However, the details you add to a crosstab report differ somewhat from task and resource reports because the type of information shown in a crosstab report is primarily numeric rather than descriptive. Figure 20.20 shows a crosstab report with all details selected.

1. Select the Details tab to access the other options for your crosstab report (fig. 20.20).

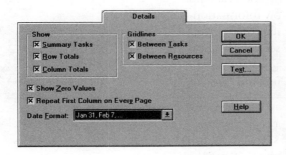

Fig. 20.20
The Details tab of the Crosstab Reports dialog box.

2. The Show section allows you to print **R**ow totals and **C**olumn totals by checking the appropriate box. If both boxes are checked, an overall total is printed at the intersection of the Row and Column totals. If you choose to list tasks as your row information, you have the option of showing **S**ummary tasks. Summary task information will include information from all detail tasks even if they are not displayed on the report (see fig. 20.21).

3. You may show horizontal gridlines between your tasks or resources by clicking on the appropriate box in the Gridlines section.

4. The Show **Z**ero Values box allows you to show or suppress 0's for the grid box representing a time period when the time period's value is 0.

5. Check the Repeat First Column on Ever**y** Page option when your crosstab report extends to more than one page horizontally, and you wish to list the row titles in the first column to repeat on every page.

6. The Date **F**ormat box allows you to specify the date as it will appear along the top of your grid, representing your time period.

III

Views and Reports

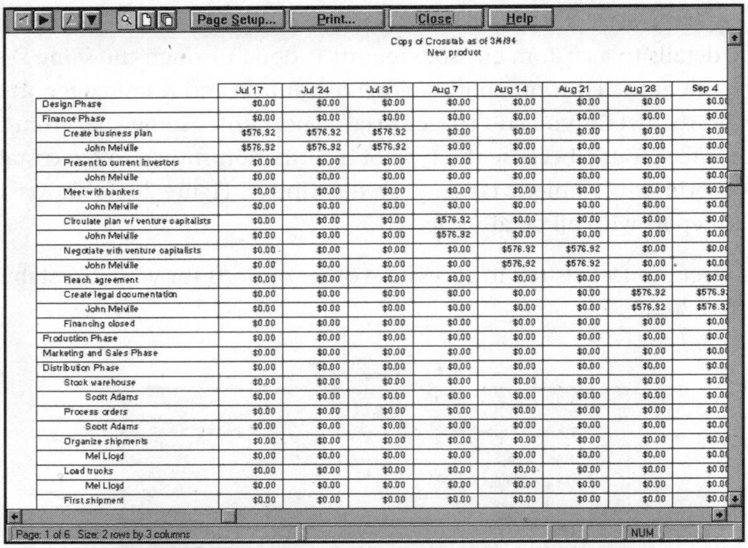

Fig. 20.21
Task crosstab report with details.

Page Setup... | Print... | Close | Help

Copy of Crosstab as of 3/4/94
New product

	Jul 17	Jul 24	Jul 31	Aug 7	Aug 14	Aug 21	Aug 28	Sep 4
Design Phase	$0.00	$0.00	$0.00	$0.00	$0.00	$0.00	$0.00	$0.00
Finance Phase	$0.00	$0.00	$0.00	$0.00	$0.00	$0.00	$0.00	$0.00
Create business plan	$576.92	$576.92	$576.92	$0.00	$0.00	$0.00	$0.00	$0.00
John Melville	$576.92	$576.92	$576.92	$0.00	$0.00	$0.00	$0.00	$0.00
Present to current investors	$0.00	$0.00	$0.00	$0.00	$0.00	$0.00	$0.00	$0.00
John Melville	$0.00	$0.00	$0.00	$0.00	$0.00	$0.00	$0.00	$0.00
Meet with bankers	$0.00	$0.00	$0.00	$0.00	$0.00	$0.00	$0.00	$0.00
John Melville	$0.00	$0.00	$0.00	$0.00	$0.00	$0.00	$0.00	$0.00
Circulate plan w/ venture capitalists	$0.00	$0.00	$0.00	$576.92	$0.00	$0.00	$0.00	$0.00
John Melville	$0.00	$0.00	$0.00	$576.92	$0.00	$0.00	$0.00	$0.00
Negotiate with venture capitalists	$0.00	$0.00	$0.00	$0.00	$576.92	$576.92	$0.00	$0.00
John Melville	$0.00	$0.00	$0.00	$0.00	$576.92	$576.92	$0.00	$0.00
Reach agreement	$0.00	$0.00	$0.00	$0.00	$0.00	$0.00	$0.00	$0.00
Create legal documentation	$0.00	$0.00	$0.00	$0.00	$0.00	$0.00	$576.92	$576.92
John Melville	$0.00	$0.00	$0.00	$0.00	$0.00	$0.00	$576.92	$576.92
Financing closed	$0.00	$0.00	$0.00	$0.00	$0.00	$0.00	$0.00	$0.00
Production Phase	$0.00	$0.00	$0.00	$0.00	$0.00	$0.00	$0.00	$0.00
Marketing and Sales Phase	$0.00	$0.00	$0.00	$0.00	$0.00	$0.00	$0.00	$0.00
Distribution Phase	$0.00	$0.00	$0.00	$0.00	$0.00	$0.00	$0.00	$0.00
Stock warehouse	$0.00	$0.00	$0.00	$0.00	$0.00	$0.00	$0.00	$0.00
Scott Adams	$0.00	$0.00	$0.00	$0.00	$0.00	$0.00	$0.00	$0.00
Process orders	$0.00	$0.00	$0.00	$0.00	$0.00	$0.00	$0.00	$0.00
Scott Adams	$0.00	$0.00	$0.00	$0.00	$0.00	$0.00	$0.00	$0.00
Organize shipments	$0.00	$0.00	$0.00	$0.00	$0.00	$0.00	$0.00	$0.00
Mel Lloyd	$0.00	$0.00	$0.00	$0.00	$0.00	$0.00	$0.00	$0.00
Load trucks	$0.00	$0.00	$0.00	$0.00	$0.00	$0.00	$0.00	$0.00
Mel Lloyd	$0.00	$0.00	$0.00	$0.00	$0.00	$0.00	$0.00	$0.00
First shipment	$0.00	$0.00	$0.00	$0.00	$0.00	$0.00	$0.00	$0.00

Page: 1 of 6   Size: 2 rows by 3 columns   NUM

Customizing the Project Summary Report

The Project Summary report prints details in much the same way as they are printed with the Project Status button on the Microsoft Project 3.0 toolbar. The only change you can make to this report is to change the text formats for the titles and the details. Figure 20.22 shows a Project Summary report. The project name, company name, and project manager name that appear in the header are taken from the fields in the Summary Info dialog box, as is the text for the notes at the bottom of the report. To enter the text for these project values, choose the File menu and select Summary Info. Then choose the Document tab.

To change the text formats for the Project Summary report, choose the report name from the Reports list in the Custom Report dialog box. Then choose the Edit button. The Report Text dialog box is displayed. Change the formats for the project name, company, project manager name, and project details. Select the OK button to return to the Print Report dialog box. The report in figure 20.22 was printed with 14-point text for the project name (New Product), 12-point text for the company name, and 10-point text for the project manager name and details.

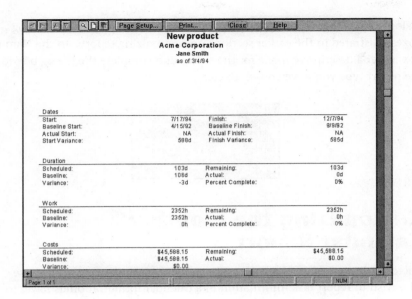

Fig. 20.22
Project Summary
report.

Creating New Reports

You can create a new report either by copying an existing report and making changes or by choosing the **N**ew button from the Custom Report dialog box (accessed by selecting **V**iew **R**eports from the menu) and designing an entirely new report. However, the new report must be modeled on one of the prefabricated report designs already described in this chapter, with the exception of the Monthly Calendar report (see the section "Customizing the Monthly Calendar Report").

If you want to copy an existing report, choose the report name from the **Re**ports list in the Custom Report dialog box, and then choose the **C**opy button. You will see the report definition dialog box for that report, with all features defined as for the original report—except that the **N**ame box displays the name "Copy of" followed by the name of the originating report (for example, "Copy of Critical Tasks Report"). In the **N**ame box, enter a descriptive name for the report and complete the dialog box for the report type you have chosen to copy.

If you choose the **N**ew button in the Custom Report dialog box, you will see the Define New Report dialog box (shown in fig. 20.23). You must select one of the entries in the **R**eport Type list in this dialog box; all reports must be modeled after one of these types. After you select OK, the report definition

III

Views and Reports

dialog box for that report type is displayed. This is one of the same dialog boxes illustrated in the earlier sections on customizing reports. In the **N**ame box, enter a descriptive name for the report and complete the dialog box for the report type you have chosen to create.

Fig. 20.23
The Define New
Report dialog box.

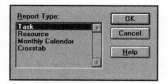

Customizing the Monthly Calendar Report

Microsoft Project offers the option of a monthly calendar report for those who wish to report task information in a calendar format. It offers fewer formatting options than the Calendar View, but can be customized to print any individual's resource calendar (something the Calendar View cannot do). The resource calendar for each individual resource can be customized through the **T**ools C**h**ange Working Time command from the menu (see chapter 8, "Defining Resources and Costs").

The monthly calendar report is accessed only by clicking the **N**ew button from the Custom Reports dialog box. After that, select Monthly Calendar from the Define New Report dialog box, make changes and select OK. You may then select **P**rint or Previe**w**. The Monthly Calendar report produces a page for each month in the life of a project, with project tasks shown on the dates they are scheduled to be in progress. The standard version of this report shows each task as a bar that stretches over the scheduled days for the task. Figure 20.24 illustrates the Monthly Calendar report for September, 1994, for the New Product project.

To customize the Monthly Calendar report, select the **N**ew button on the Custom Reports dialog box and select Monthly Calendar from the **R**eport Type list in the Define New Report dialog box. Then click the OK button. The Monthly Calendar Report Definition dialog box appears (see fig. 20.25).

You can choose any base or resource calendars to use for displaying the working and nonworking days on the report. The advantage of this report over the Calendar View is that it will print any individual's resource calendar, reflecting their working and non-working days. To select the calendar to use for the report, choose the **C**alendar box, and then choose one of the base or resource calendars from the entry list.

You can apply one of the filters on the **F**ilter menu to limit the tasks displayed. You might apply the Using Resource filter, for example, to print a calendar to distribute to this resource, showing the tasks and dates when the resource is scheduled to work on the project.

To apply a filter to the report, choose the **F**ilter box and choose one of the filters from the entry list. To make the filter a highlight filter only, mark the **H**ighlight check box. All tasks will be displayed, but the filtered tasks are displayed with the format chosen for Highlighted Tasks (see the **T**ext choices in the following section). If you select an interactive filter, the interactive prompt appears each time you preview or print the report.

The remaining options on the Monthly Calendar Report Definition dialog box regulate the display of the data, as shown in the following listing:

■ To distinguish working and nonworking days on the calendar, mark the Gray Nonworking Days check box.

■ To show tasks as bars or lines that stretch across the calendar for the duration of the task, mark the **B**ars or **L**ines radio button. To show the scheduled start and stop dates for tasks on the calendar, mark the S**t**art/ Finish Dates radio button.

■ If you decide to display bars for the tasks, you can choose to display breaks in the bars (from one week or month to the next) with dotted or solid lines at the bar ends. Mark the **S**olid Bar Breaks check box if you want solid lines. For dotted lines, leave the check box unmarked.

■ Mark the check boxes for **I**D number, N**a**me, and **D**uration if you want to include these field values in the label for the task. You can use any combination of these three values.

■ If more tasks are assigned on a day than will fit on the calendar, an asterisk is displayed beside the day number, and the unprinted tasks appear in a list at the end of the report. The list is sorted by date. If you want a gray band to separate the dates in the list, mark the **P**rint Gray Bands check box.

■ Choose the Te**x**t button to designate different text formats for parts of the report. You can select unique formats for different kinds of tasks (Noncritical, Critical, Milestone, Summary, Marked, and Highlighted) and for the labels in the calendar.

After you finish defining the Monthly Calendar report, select the OK button to return to the Print Report dialog box. You then can **P**rint or Pre**v**iew the report immediately or use the Close button to save the list of reports and print later.

Figure 20.26 shows an example of a Monthly Calendar report that was filtered to show only the tasks assigned to Howard Thompson. The report also was defined to use the resource calendar for Howard Thompson.

Changing the Sort Order for a Report

You may sort all task, resource, and crosstab reports by their column information. Select the Sort tab to access the Sort options for the report. The Sort dialog box (shown in fig. 20.27) looks similar to the Tools Sort Sort by dialog box on the main menu, allowing you to sort by up to three fields in the report. Remember that the sort order of the tasks in the report does not reflect the sort order of the current view, nor does the sort order selected within a report affect the current screen view. Therefore, you can print a report by a field, such as Priority (for tasks) or Name (for resources), without affecting the task order in your current working view.

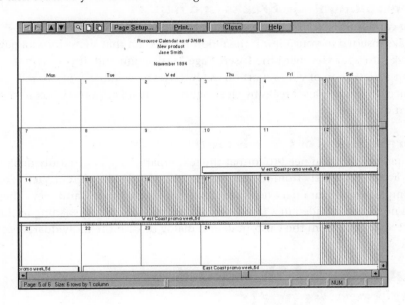

Fig. 20.26
Monthly Calendar report using resource calendar and filter.

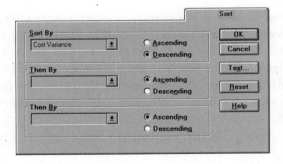

Fig. 20.27
The Sort dialog box for all task, resource, and crosstab reports.

Collapsing Task Detail in a Report

If the outline is collapsed when you print a task or crosstab report, the subordinate tasks that are hidden will not be displayed in the report. You must expand the outline when you print the report if you want all tasks to be displayed. The reports ignore any filter that may have been applied to the current view on-screen, however. You can select filters within the report definitions to be automatically applied regardless of the filter that may or may not be applied to the active view. Note, however, that subordinate tasks hidden by a collapsed outline at the time the report is printed are not included in a report, even though these tasks usually are selected by the defined filter. Collapsing an outline overrides the filter.

Controlling Page Breaks in a Report

You cannot put page breaks in a report, but your report will reflect page breaks inserted in your View if the report is based on that View. Insert a page break into your view with the **I**nsert **P**age Break command. If you wish to print a draft copy of your report on as few pages as possible, you can tell Project to ignore page breaks by clearing the **M**anual Page Breaks box in the Print dialog box.

Formatting Text in a Report

Remember that you need to format the text separately for each individual report and separately from the text format showing in the current View. For example, even if summary tasks are shaded in your current Gantt view, they will not appear shaded in a task report unless you specify the shading in the Text Styles box from the Custom Report dialog box for the individual report.

Saving and Sharing Your Custom Reports

Tip

If you choose to customize a copy of the standard reports (by selecting the **C**opy button from the Custom Reports dialog box), remember to give the copy a unique name so you can copy the report to the global template without overwriting a different report of the same name.

All the reports are saved with your project file, so remember to save your file if you have customized reports—even if you have not changed your task or resource information. If you wish to make your custom reports available to all your project files or to other people sharing the same copy of Microsoft Project, you must copy these reports into the global template file, GLOBAL.MPT, with the Organizer. You can access the Organizer from the View Custom Report dialog box. All reports in the GLOBAL.MPT template file are available to all users of Microsoft Project sharing that GLOBAL.MPT file.

From Here...

The last two chapters dealt with customizing the standard views and reports that come with Microsoft Project. The next chapter shows you how to create graphs of your task and resource data to give further customized emphasis to your data.

In the following chapters, you learn how to create graphs for use with projects that you manage with Microsoft Project.

- Chapter 21, "Creating and Using Macros," goes into great detail on the ways in which you can customize the layout of the Microsoft Project application window by adding and removing the commands you use most to the toolbars and menus. It also covers the creation and use of custom forms within your project.

- Chapter 22, "Customizing Toolbars, Menus, Forms, and Cue Cards," will show you how to attach your macros to toolbar buttons and menu commands.

- Chapter 23, "Using Visual Basic for Applications" will give you much greater depth in macro editing, and will give you a firm foundation to begin using Visual Basic for Applications.

Part IV

Microsoft Project Interface

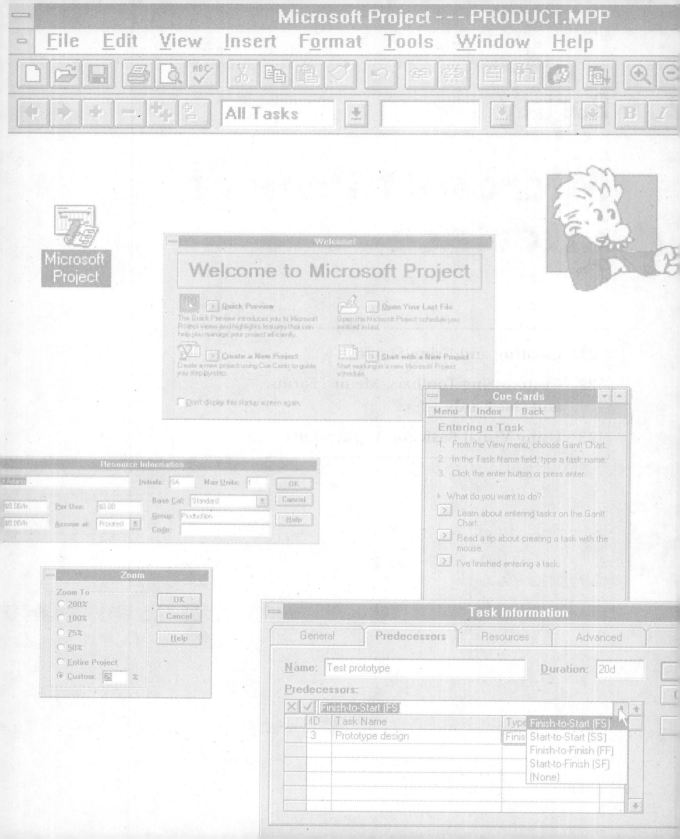

Chapter 21

Creating and Using Macros

A Microsoft Project macro is a written instruction to execute a list of Microsoft Project commands, usually commands that emulate the menu commands or your own selecting and typing actions. When you run the macro it executes all of the commands in the list as a group, one after the other. The macro saves you from having to execute each of the commands by hand and from having to remember the correct sequence of commands that are needed. A macro also can be used to automate a complicated process that beginners, who do not know Microsoft Project well enough to perform the process on their own, can execute.

Microsoft Project 4 includes, for the first time, a full-fledged programming capability, Visual Basic for Applications. Visual Basic for Applications is a version of Microsoft Visual Basic that also includes the command set for Microsoft Project. This is one of the most significant changes in Release 4.0, and it offers users and developers alike the tools they need to create automated applications in Microsoft Project.

In this chapter, you learn how to

- ■ Run macros.
- ■ Use the macros included in Microsoft Project 4.0.
- ■ Record simple macros.
- ■ View and edit macro modules.
- ■ Use your macros from Microsoft Project 3.0.

Introducing Visual Basic for Applications

Though you could write macros in Microsoft Project Release 3.0, you had to write them from scratch. There was no recording feature; so, you had to know the Project macro language. Furthermore, the command set in the project macro language was limited and unique to Microsoft Project. Now you can record macros, though the recording is still in the Project macro language. Furthermore, you can write and run macros in the Visual Basic object-oriented language. There are many good references, readily available training classes, and contract consultants available to give you help with Visual Basic if you need it.

▶ "Using Visual Basic for Applications," p. 679

Visual Basic program structures are *procedures* contained within *modules*. A procedure is simply a unit of macro code that performs a particular function. Each procedure is defined within a module, and you can have many procedures within one module, and many modules attached to a project if you choose. Procedures in the same module can share data conveniently. Microsoft Project 4.0 has a new view, the Module Editor, to let you create, edit, and debug macro procedures.

You can now record macros by having the macro recorder monitor and transcribe your actions that use the mouse and the keyboard. The recorded names of your actions are listed in a procedure in a module that you can edit and enhance with still more powerful programming constructions once you learn Visual Basic.

Running Macros

▶ "Customizing Toolbars, Menus, Forms, and Cue Cards," p. 615

There are several different ways to execute a macro.

- You can execute a macro by choosing the **M**acro command from the **T**ools menu. The **M**acro command displays a list of macros that you can run (see fig. 21.1). The FormatDuration macro is selected in figure 21.1 to be executed with the Run button. This macro is supplied with Microsoft Project 4.0 and is designed to help you change the units used in the durations column so that they all use one consistent unit of time.

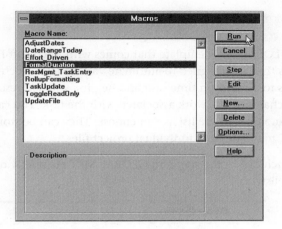

Fig. 21.1
The Macro dialog box displays a list of all macros that are available in the GLOBAL.MPT template and in the current project file.

■ You also can place frequently used macro names in the menu for easy access. In figure 21.2 the Tools menu displays a Format **D**urations command at the bottom which will run the FormatDuration macro.

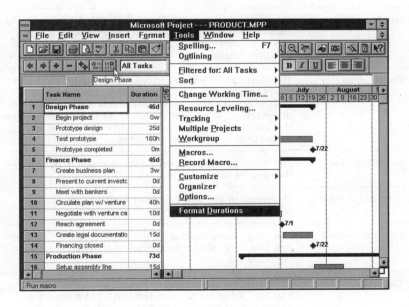

Fig. 21.2
The Format Durations macro has been added to the **T**ools menu for ready access in any project.

■ You also can assign macros to toolbar buttons. In figure 21.2 the mouse pointer is pointing to a customized button that has been assigned to run the FormatDurations macro.

Reviewing the Macros Supplied with Microsoft Project

Tip

See the SAMPLES.WRI file that is copied to your program directory during installation for more information about these macros.

The default GLOBAL.MPT template that comes with Microsoft Project includes macros that are designed to automate various tasks, such as formatting task durations to a common time unit and helping you add resources to a task without changing the work associated with the task. You can add as many macro modules to the list as you choose. They can be stored in the GLOBAL.MPT template or in individual project files.

The macros included in the standard GLOBAL.MPT are briefly described in the following list.

Macro	Description
AdjustDates	This macro helps you change the start or finish date for a project when doing so normally would produce constraint conflicts. Task constraints are adjusted relative to the change in the project start or finish date. You are asked to supply a new start or finish date for the project, and that date is then applied to the project.
DateRangeToday	This macro creates a filter like the Date Range filter (selecting tasks within a date range that you specify) except that you specify the date range as a number of days before and after the current date.
Effort_Driven	This macro allows you to add resource names to a task and have Microsoft Project treat the addition the same as when you increase the number of resource units for a resource driven task. That is to say, the total work for the task remains the same and the duration is adjusted with the work load spread proportionally among the resources.
FormatDuration	This macro asks you to specify a duration unit to be used and then applies that unit to all tasks.
ResMgmt_TaskEntry	This macro displays the Task Entry view with the Resource Schedule in the Task Form in the bottom pane.
RollupFormatting	This macro helps you create a special rollup Gantt Chart, with task names for rollup tasks alternating above and below the Summary task bar.
TaskUpdate	This macro cycles through the project, displaying the Tracking Dialog box for each task that is not a milestone, summary task, subproject, or finished task. It helps you update actual information for all tasks.

Recording a Macro

Writing complex macros is a sophisticated topic and is not covered in depth
in this chapter. Chapter 23, "Using Visual Basic for Applications," shows you
how to get started using Visual Basic. If you are a beginner, however, this
chapter shows you how to record and edit simple macros.

To illustrate recording a simple macro, assume that you want to automate the
process of collapsing the outline in the Gantt Chart to first level tasks only.
To do this manually, you would select all tasks by selecting the column heading over any field, and then you would choose the Hide Subtasks button on
the Formatting toolbar (or use the **T**ools O**u**tlining **H**ide Subtasks menu command). You would probably also select a single task at the end to remove the
highlighted background from having selected all tasks.

To record these actions in a macro, follow these steps:

1. Choose **T**ools and then the **R**ecord Macro command. The Record Macro
   dialog box appears.

2. Choose the **O**ptions button to display the full dialog box (see fig. 21.3).

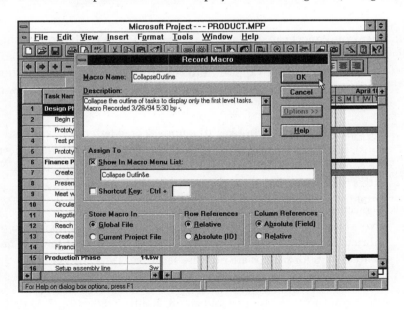

Fig. 21.3
The Record Macro
dialog box lets you
name and display
a new macro in
the menu or attach
it to a shortcut
key.

3. Supply a name for the macro in the **M**acro Name box. In this example, the macro name is CollapseOutline.

4. Use the **D**escription box to provide a brief description of the purpose of the macro. This description appears in the Description box when you select a macro name in the Macros dialog box.

Fig. 21.4
The macro description is very helpful when choosing which macro to run.

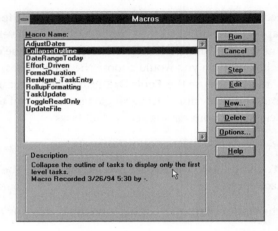

5. Microsoft Project can display a Macro Menu List at the bottom of the **T**ools menu, just like the list of views at the top of the View menu. If you want the macro to appear in the Macro Menu List, mark the **S**how in Macro Menu List check box. Then type the word or phrase you want to appear in the list.

If you want to assign a hot key (the underscored letter in menu options), place an ampersand (&) in this box before the letter that selects the command. Note that the **T**ools menu has already dedicated the letters "ACFHLMOPRSUW" to other commands in the list, so you should avoid using one of those letters.

6. If you want the macro to execute by using a shortcut key, mark the Shortcut **K**ey check box and type the letter that you want to use. The shortcut keys for macros are not case sensitive. Type any keys not already used for menu shortcuts.

The menu shortcut keys to avoid are: **B** (Bold), **C** (Edit Copy), **D** (Fill Down), **F** (Edit Find), **I** (Italics), **N** (File New), **O** (File Open), **P** (File Print), **S** (File Save), **U** (Underline), **V** (Edit Paste), **X** (Edit Cut), and **Z** (Edit Undo). Microsoft Project will not let you use one of those keys for a macro shortcut key.

7. Use the Store Macro In area to designate where the macro is stored. Choose the **G**lobal File button to store the macro in the GLOBAL.MPT template so that it is available in any project document. Choose the **C**urrent Project File button to confine the macro to the current project document. You also can use the Organizer later to copy macro modules between projects and the GLOBAL.MPT template.

8. The last two set of buttons determine how your actions are recorded. Because all views are organized around task or resource rows and field (columns in some views), you may elect to have your macro always act on the same row (task or resource) that you recorded it on or on the same field that you recorded it on. This is "absolute" recording.

Alternatively, you can choose to have the recorded macro treat your actions as general in nature and to be applied to whatever row and field you are in at the time the macro is executed. This is "relative" recording.

Choose **R**elative under Row References to have the macro operate on the currently selected row(s) at the time the macro is run. Choose **A**bsolute (ID) to have the macro always operate on the same ID number when it is run.

Similarly, choose the A**b**solute (Field) button under Column References to have your macro always act on the same field that you recorded it in. Choose the Re**l**ative button to have the macro act on the field or column that is currently selected when the macro is run.

The default settings (**R**elative row and A**b**solute (Field)) will be your most common choice. Macros recorded like this always operate on the currently selected task but go directly to the same field that was used when the macro was recorded.

9. Choose OK when your choices are complete. The recorder is running, and your every keystroke and mouse action is recorded.

Step through all the actions you want in the macro. If you make a mistake, you can stop the recorder (see step 10) or you can remove the mistaken lines of code from the macro later by editing the macro.

For the CollapseOutline macro, you select the column heading of the Task Name column, choose the Hide Subtasks button. Then select the first task to clear the all-task selection.

10. When finished performing the actions for the macro, choose the **T**ools menu and then the Stop **R**ecorder command.

You will now find the macro listed in the Macros dialog box, ready to be run, edited, or deleted (see fig. 14.3). You should test the CollapseOutline macro by displaying all tasks and then running the macro.

If you do not want to keep the new macro, you can delete it. See the section "Deleting a Macro" later in this chapter for instructions on deleting macros and modules.

Viewing the Macro in the Module Editor

The macro Module Editor is a new view in Microsoft Project. The Module Editor lets you view and edit the text of the macro. The text of the macro contains comments and Visual Basic codes. You can add comments to the macro text, and if you know enough about Visual Basic, you can edit the contents of the macro directly. See Chapter 23, "Using Visual Basic for Applications," for more information about the features of the Editor.

To view or edit the macro, follow these steps:

1. Choose **T**ools and then choose the **M**acros command. The Macros dialog box appears.

2. Choose the macro you want to view or edit.

3. Choose the **E**dit button. The Module Editor appears with the Visual Basic toolbar and with the macro text displayed (see fig. 21.5).

Fig. 21.5
The Module Editor shows the Visual Basic code that constitutes the heart of your macro.

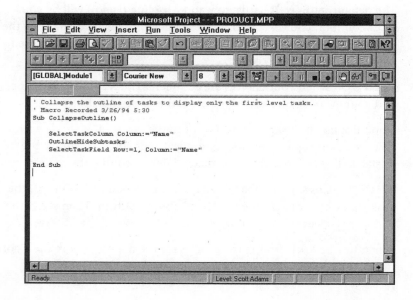

Reading the Macro Text

The lines at the beginning of the macro are comment lines. Those lines begin with a single quote mark.

The macro code begins with the word Sub followed by the name of the macro and a pair of parentheses. In figure 21.5, the macro begins with the line that reads

```
Sub CollapseOutline()
```

The macro ends with the line that reads End Sub. The block of lines between Sub and End Sub provide the instructions that the macro executes.

The codes in this simple macro are fairly easy to understand because the recorder uses commands that are native to the Microsoft Project application.

```
SelectTaskColumn Column:="Name"
```

Represents your selection of the whole column.

```
OutlineHidesubtasks
```

Represents your clicking on Hide Subtasks.

```
SelectTaskfield Row:=0, column:="Name"
```

Represents your selecting the first task name. The argument Row:=0 in the last command reflects your selection of the first row. Visual Basic uses the mathematical origin zero when counting objects; so, task ID 1 is row zero. The argument column:="Name" reflects your choice to record the absolute field used when recording.

Editing the Macro

You can place additional comments in the macro that will not be executed when you run the macro. The comments serve to remind you of the function of the macro, to explain why the macro is designed the way it is, or as general documentation or notes about the macro, the macro's use, or the prerequisites for the macro's use.

Macro comments begin with a single quote mark ('). This is the key to the left of the Enter key on most keyboards. All text on the line following the quote mark is ignored when the macro runs.

You also can begin a comment with the word REM instead of using the quote mark.

You also can add commands and change parts of the recorded commands if you understand the code. Suppose that after recording this macro, you decided to leave the entire project selected when the macro finishes so that you can expand the outline one level at a time with the Show Subtasks button. You would simply select the third line of code (SelectTaskField Row:=1....) and use the Delete key to remove it (see fig. 21.6).

Fig. 21.6
You can add and
delete text in the
macro module.

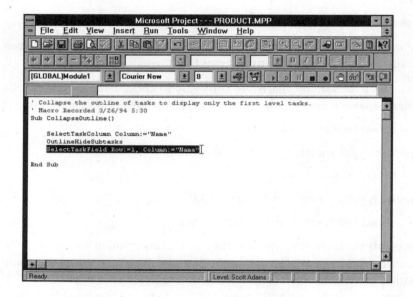

Deleting a Macro

To delete a macro, select the macro name in the **M**acros list and select the **D**elete button. It will be deleted whether it was saved in the active project or in the GLOBAL.MPT template.

To delete a macro, follow these steps:

1. From the **T**ools menu choose **M**acros.

2. Select the macro you wish to delete in the **M**acro Name list (see fig. 21.7).

3. Choose the **D**elete button to remove it. A confirmation dialog box appears (see fig. 21.8).

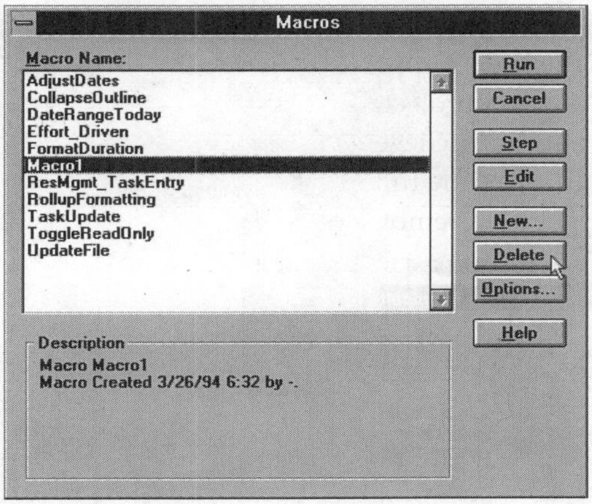

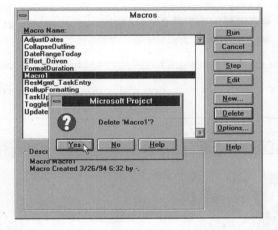

Fig. 21.7
Delete both global
macros and
macros recorded
in the active
project with the
Macros dialog box.

Fig. 21.8
You must confirm
deletions of macros.

4. Choose the Yes button to confirm deleting the macro.

5. Choose the Close button to close the Macros dialog box.

If the deleted macro was the only macro in its module, you will be left with a
module that is empty. Use the Organizer to delete the empty module.

To delete a module, follow these steps:

1. Display the Organizer. One method is to choose the **V**iew menu and
then the **T**oolbars command. Then choose the **O**rganizer button on
the Toolbars dialog box. The Organizer dialog box will appear (see
fig. 21.9).

Fig. 21.9
The Organizer must be used to remove modules from active projects or from the the GLOBAL.MPT template.

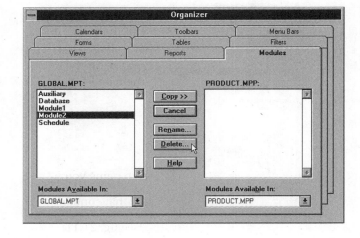

2. Choose the Modules tab to display the macro modules in the GLOBAL.MPT template and the active project file.

3. Select the module you want to delete and choose the **D**elete button.

4. Choose **Y**es in the confirmation dialog box that appears (see fig. 21.10).

Fig. 21.10
You must confirm deleting macro modules in the Organizer.

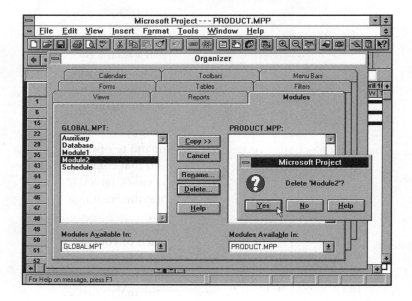

Renaming a Macro

Macro names are determined by the header line in the macro module. The header is the line that begins the macro and that reads Sub *macroname()*. To rename a macro you merely change the *macroname* text in the header line. The moment you change the name in the module, the name will change in the list of macros in the Macros dialog box.

To rename a macro, follow these steps:

1. From the **T**ools menu, choose **M**acros.

2. From the Macros dialog box select the macro name you want to change.

3. Choose the **E**dit button to view the module that contains the macro.

4. Select the macro name in the header line (see fig. 21.11).

5. Replace the selection with the new name.

6. Choose the **V**iew command to return to the project view, or select the **T**ools, **M**acros command to edit other macros.

Translating Release 3.0 Macros

If you created macros in Microsoft Project Release 3.0, you will find that the programming controls are not the same as those in Visual Basic for Applications. If you read your Release 3.0 macros into Microsoft Project 4, the Module Editor translates a fair amount of your code, but you will probably still need to revise the translation to convert to the new control logic.

If you have Microsoft Project Release 3.0 macros that you want to import into Release 4.0, you can use the **F**ile **O**pen command to open the view file (VIEW.MPV or another .MPV file) from Release 3.0 that contains your macros. A new project is created named View. All the views, tables, filters, forms, toolbar buttons, and macros that you saved in that file are imported into the new project.

When you view the Macros dialog box, you see each of your macros, as well as those that were supplied by Microsoft in Release 3.0, listed as [Macro] *macroname* (see fig. 21.11). To have the macro translated into Visual Basic you must Edit the macro. You should try to run the macro first to see how successfully it can be converted to Visual Basic.

Fig. 21.11
All of your
Microsoft Project
3.0 macros can be
imported into
Microsoft Project
4.0 by opening the
View file they were
stored in.

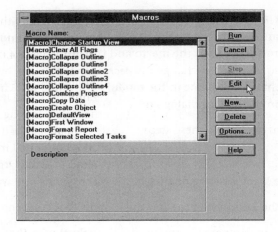

To edit your Release 3.0 macro, follow these steps:

1. Use the **F**ile **O**pen command to open the view file from Release 3.0.

2. Choose the **T**ools **M**acros command to display the Macros dialog box.

3. Choose the macro you want to translate.

4. Choose the **E**dit button. The Module Editor translates the macro as best it can (see fig. 21.12) and places it in a new module named *Modulex*, where "x" is the next available numbered module.

Fig. 21.12
The macro
translation
appears in bold.

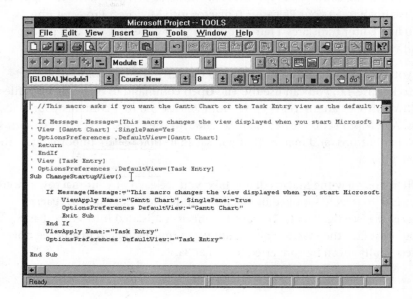

The macro appears in a literal quoted form first, followed by the Visual Basic for Applications translation. You can edit the macro if you know Visual Basic. If not, you can run the macro to see if it works with Release 4.0 project files.

The macro has been added to the GLOBAL template with the name `[GLOBAL]Module1` (or the next available module number). The name appears just above the editing window on the left of the screen (see fig. 21.13). You can open a project file now and try the macro. You are advised to rename the module first. You will quickly lose track of what is contained in each of the macro modules with the module*n* naming scheme. Use the Organizer to rename the macro module.

To rename the macro module, follow these steps:

1. Activate the Organizer from one of the dialog boxes that give access to it. You can use the **T**oolbars command from the **V**iew menu, for example, and choose the **O**rganizer button on the Toolbars dialog box.

2. Choose the Modules tab on the Organizer dialog box.

You see the modules in the GLOBAL.MPT file on the left and those in the current project file on the right, if there are any (see fig. 21.13).

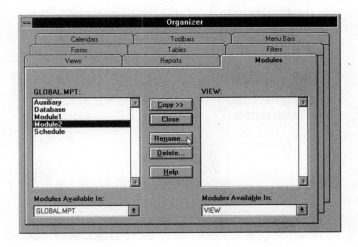

Fig. 21.13
Give macro modules descriptive names by renaming them in the Organizer.

3. Choose Module1 in the GLOBALT.MPT list.

4. Choose the Re**n**ame button. The Rename dialog box appears (see fig. 21.14).

Fig. 21.14
Supply a new
name for the
macro module
in the Rename
dialog box.

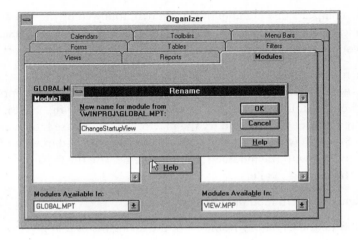

5. Enter the new name. It is important that you use a name that begins
   with a letter. Also, the name must contain nothing but letters, numbers, and underscore characters, and can have no spaces.

6. The new name will appear in the Organizer. Choose the Close button to
   close the Organizer (see fig. 21.15).

Fig. 21.15
The newly named
module appears in
the Organizer list
of modules.

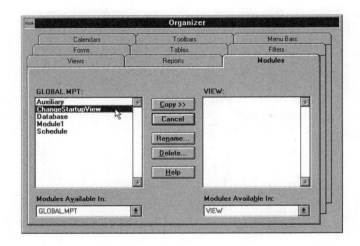

From Here...

In this chapter, you learned how to use macros to speed up your project management. Here's what you can expect in the last two chapters:

■ Chapter 22, "Customizing Toolbars, Menus, Forms, and Cue Cards," shows you how to attach your macros to toolbar buttons and menu commands.

■ Chapter 23, "Using Visual Basic for Applications," gives you much greater depth in macro editing, and gives you a firm foundation to begin using Visual Basic for Applications.

Chapter 22

Customizing Toolbars, Menus, Forms, and Cue Cards

In this chapter, you learn how to

- ■ Customize the display of toolbars.

- ■ Customize buttons on the toolbars.

- ■ Customize the menu bar.

- ■ Use and create custom forms.

- ■ Create custom Cue Cards.

The sections of this chapter all focus on ways to customize the Microsoft Project interface to make your work easier. Changing the toolbars and menus makes your work more efficient because often-used commands and macros can be made more readily accessible. Using custom forms allows you to view and edit project data by focusing on those fields of data that are important to you at the moment. Creating your own Cue Cards gives you the ability to provide instant, on-line instructions for complex tasks for users who are not as familiar with Microsoft Project as you are.

In the beginning of this chapter, bear in mind that the toolbars and menus in Microsoft Project are not contained within the current project file as are views, tables, forms, filters, and so on. If you change the toolbars or the menu bars, your changes are saved in the GLOBAL.MPT template, and they affect all projects you work on.

Although you can use the Organizer to copy toolbars and menu bars into a project file, the only advantage is that you store a copy of the item in the project file. Storing toolbars and menu bars in project files is useful when you want to copy them to another person's Microsoft Project GLOBAL.MPT template. However, you cannot access menu bars or toolbars unless they are stored in the GLOBAL.MPT template.

Creating and Customizing Toolbars

All the toolbar buttons work by executing commands. Buttons simulate using the commands on the Microsoft Project menu bar. For example, the second button on the Standard toolbar displays a picture of a file folder opening; choosing the button displays the Open dialog box, in which you choose a file to open. The command assigned to this button is Open.

You can assign only one command to a button, but one of the available commands, Macro, runs macro modules which can contain many commands. For example, if you create a simple macro named CollapseOutline to select all tasks and collapse the outline to first level tasks only, you can assign a toolbar button to run the macro. You also can have buttons display custom forms so all you have to do is click a button to access frequently used task or resource fields. See the upcoming section, "Using Custom Forms," for more information.

You can customize toolbar buttons to perform any of the commands in the Microsoft Project command set. You also can add new buttons, remove buttons that you don't want, and change the function—as well as the look and the spacing—of the buttons. You can create your own custom toolbars to group together the buttons you use most often.

The Built-In Toolbars

Microsoft Project provides nine built-in toolbars for you to use for different activities as you work on a project. The built-in toolbars are described in the list below:

- The Drawing toolbar provides access to graphics figures and text boxes for placement in the Gantt bar chart.

- The Formatting toolbar gives you access to outlining, filters, and text formatting features. This is the second toolbar in the default display.

- The Microsoft toolbar provides access to other Microsoft applications.

- The Microsoft Project 3.0 toolbar displays the Standard toolbar from Microsoft Project 3.0. Note that the Chart button is omitted because the automated charting feature is no longer supported.

- The Resource Management toolbar provides access to tools for resolving resource overallocations.

- The Standard toolbar gives you access to the main Microsoft Project features.

- The Tracking toolbar provides access to the commands necessary to track progress and reschedule work on interrupted tasks.

- The Visual Basic toolbar provides access to macro controls and Module Editor functions.

- The Workgroup toolbar gives you access to Workgroup features necessary to share project information with others in your workgroup.

To see the name of the button, pause the mouse pointer over the button for a few seconds. The name appears below the button. For descriptions of all the buttons on each toolbar, use the Microsoft Project **H**elp menu. Choose the Help Contents screen, choose Reference Information, and select the Toolbars and Buttons item from the General Reference category.

Displaying Toolbars

You can show and hide toolbars with the Toolbars dialog box or with the Toolbar Shortcut menu.

Using the Toolbar Shortcut Menu

The quickest way to change which toolbars are displayed is to activate the Toolbar Shortcut menu and select one of the toolbars (see fig. 22.1). To activate the Shortcut menu, move the mouse pointer over one of the toolbars and click the right mouse button. The toolbars that are currently displayed have check marks next to them. Choose a toolbar that is not checked to display it. If you choose a toolbar that is checked, the check disappears, and the toolbar is removed from the screen.

At the bottom of the Shortcut menu you see three commands that are used to customize toolbars: Toolbars, Customize, and Customize Tool. These are described in following sections.

You also can show or hide toolbars with the Toolbars dialog box. See the section "Using the Toolbars Dialog Box" later in this chapter.

Fig. 22.1

The Toolbar shortcut menu shows which toolbars are displayed and can be used to display or hide individual toolbars.

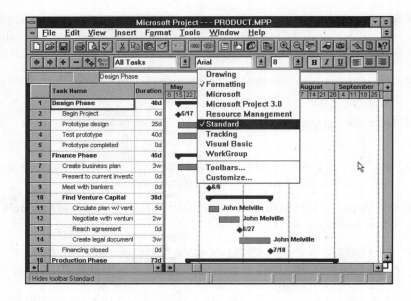

Positioning Toolbars on the Screen

Once a toolbar is displayed, you can move it from the top of the screen to a new position. You can "dock" it at the sides or bottom of the screen or you can "float" it in the middle of the screen as a small window. Toolbars that have combo boxes (buttons with a text box and an entry-list arrow) cannot be displayed on the right or left sides of the screen.

To reposition a toolbar, click the background of the toolbar and drag its outline to a new position. As you drag the outline to an edge of the screen where it can be docked, the outline changes shape to fit that position. Release the mouse when in position. In figure 22.2, the Tracking toolbar has been docked on the right edge of the screen, and the Resource Management toolbar is floating.

A floating toolbar has a title bar and a Close button, as you see in figure 22.2 on the Resource Management toolbar. You can choose the Close button to hide the toolbar.

Using the Toolbars Dialog Box

You can display the Toolbars dialog box by choosing Toolbars at the bottom of the Shortcut menu or by choosing **T**oolbars from the **V**iew menu (see fig. 22.3).

Tip

You also can double-click the toolbar background to make it "float" as a window in the middle of the screen. Double-click the background of a floating toolbar to return it to its docked position.

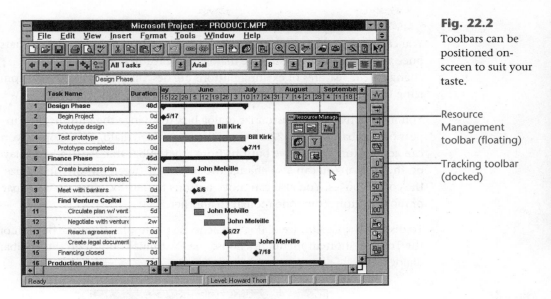

Fig. 22.2
Toolbars can be positioned on-screen to suit your taste.

Resource Management toolbar (floating)

Tracking toolbar (docked)

Fig. 22.3
The Toolbars dialog box can Hide or Show toolbars and is also used to create new toolbars.

When you select a toolbar from the **T**oolbars entry list, the top-right button displays H**i**de if the toolbar is currently displayed and **S**how if the toolbar is currently not displayed. Choose that button to change the display status of a toolbar.

Notice the Show ToolTi**p**s check box at the bottom of the Toolbars dialog box. Clear this check box if you don't want the ToolTips to be displayed when the mouse is over a button.

The other features of this dialog box are described in the sections that follow.

Customizing Toolbars

You can change the buttons that appear on the currently displayed toolbars once you activate the Customize dialog box. Creating new buttons and changing the features of existing buttons are described later in the "Customizing Buttons" section.

You must activate the Customize dialog box to change the buttons that appear on toolbars (see fig. 22.4). Once the Customize dialog box is open, you can add buttons or remove buttons from any toolbar that is already displayed on the screen. You can also change the spacing between buttons and resize the combo boxes. You also can move buttons to new locations on a toolbar or move buttons from one toolbar to another.

To display the Customize dialog box, choose Customize from the bottom of the Toolbar Shortcut menu, or choose the Customize button on the Toolbars dialog box.

Fig. 22.4
Use the Customize dialog box to change the buttons that appear on the active toolbars.

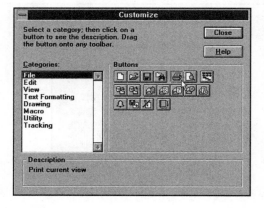

The Customize Dialog box displays the gallery of built-in buttons that you can place on any toolbar.

- The buttons are grouped in categories, and you choose a group from the Categories list on the left.

- Click a button to see its description in the Description area at the bottom of the dialog box. In figure 22.4, the Print button has been clicked, and its description appears at the bottom of the dialog box.

- You can drag the title bar of the Customize dialog box to move it so that you can see the toolbars behind it.

When you drag a button onto a toolbar, it is positioned to the right of whatever lies under the left edge of the new button at the time you release the mouse. The new button is inserted in the toolbar, and other buttons are shifted to the right to make room for the new button. If there are too many buttons on the toolbar, those at the far right end are not visible.

Adding and Removing Buttons

To add buttons to a toolbar:

1. Be sure that the toolbar you want to change is active on the screen.

2. Activate the Customize dialog box using the Toolbar Shortcut menu or the **C**ustomize button on the Toolbars dialog box.

3. Display the button by selecting its group from the **C**ategories field.

4. Drag the button into position on the toolbar. Position the left edge of the new button over the existing button or space that you want to be to its immediate left.

5. Close the Customize dialog box if there are no more changes to be made.

To remove a button from a toolbar, simply drag it off of its toolbar and release it in the center of the screen away from any other toolbars.

Changing the Spacing between Buttons

While the Customize dialog box is active, you can create space between two buttons by dragging the button on the right a little to the right and releasing it. You can remove the space between two buttons by dragging the button on the right to overlap the other button slightly.

Moving Buttons

You can move a button to a new position on the same toolbar or to a different toolbar by dragging the button to its new position. Both toolbars must be displayed, and the Customize dialog box must be active in order to do this.

Resizing Combo Boxes

Combo boxes are those parts of a dialog box that have a text box and an entry-list arrow on the right. The width of the text box can be changed in Customize mode.

To change the width of a combo box:

1. Be sure that the button's toolbar is displayed and that the Customize dialog box is displayed.

2. Move the mouse pointer over the left edge of the text box or over the right edge of the entry-list arrow. The pointer changes to a black cross (see fig. 22.5).

3. Drag the edge of the combo box to the size you want.

4. Close the Customize dialog box if there are no more changes.

Fig. 22.5
The mouse is set to resize the Filter combo box by dragging the left edge of its text box.

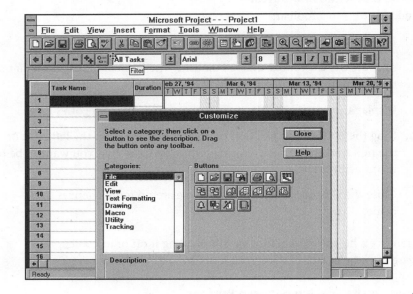

Customizing the Button Face

Tip
You can copy a button from other applications to the Clipboard and then paste it onto a Microsoft Project button.

While you are in Customize mode, each button that is placed on a toolbar (except the combo boxes) can be customized. When you right-click a button that is already placed on one of the toolbars, the Button Shortcut menu appears (see fig. 22.6). You can copy the selected button's face to the Clipboard or paste a button face that is already in the Clipboard onto the selected button. You also can activate the Customize Tool dialog box, which provides even more options for changing the button and is described in detail in the section "Using the Customize Tool Dialog Box" later in this chapter.

Restoring the Built-In Toolbars

You may find that your changes to a toolbar are unsatisfactory and that you want to restore it to its original state. Use the **R**eset button on the Toolbars dialog box to cancel all changes that have been made to a toolbar.

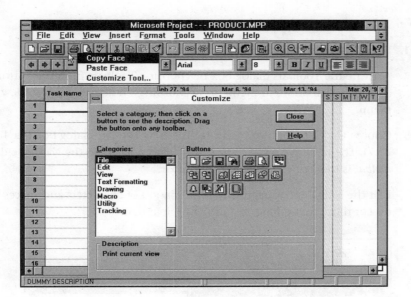

Fig. 22.6
You can use the
Button Shortcut
menu to copy the
button face to the
Clipboard or to
change the button
face.

Caution

Resetting a toolbar removes all customized changes you have ever made to that
toolbar—not just the changes you have most recently made. If you have placed
custom buttons on a toolbar that you plan to reset, you lose the custom buttons.
Drag the custom buttons to another toolbar if you want to preserve them.

Creating New Toolbars

The Toolbars dialog box allows you to create new toolbars. You can make a
copy of an existing toolbar, giving it a new name and making selected
changes, or you can start with a blank toolbar and create a new collection of
buttons on it.

Use the Toolbars dialog box to create new toolbars or to delete the toolbars
you create.

Making a Copy of a Toolbar

If an existing toolbar is similar to one you want to create, make a copy of the
existing toolbar to reduce the number of buttons you have to place on the
new toolbar.

To create a copy of a toolbar:

1. Be sure that the toolbar you plan to duplicate is already on-screen.

2. Activate the Toolbars dialog box by choosing Toolbars from the bottom of the Toolbar Shortcut menu or by choosing **T**oolbars from the **V**iew menu.

3. Choose the Cop**y** button to display the New Toolbar dialog box (see fig. 22.7). The tentative name "Copy of *toolbar*" appears in the Name field; *toolbar* is the name of the built-in toolbar.

   Edit the Name entry, using any combination of characters and spaces except those that duplicate another toolbar name.

Fig. 22.7
Edit the name of a new toolbar in the New Toolbar dialog box.

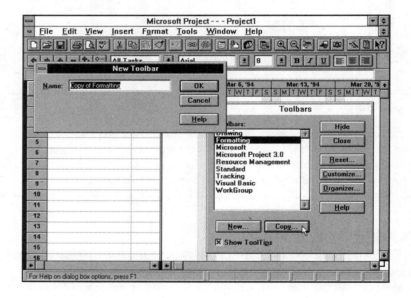

4. Choose OK to finish naming the new toolbar. A copy of the original toolbar appears on-screen, and the name appears in alphabetical order in the **T**oolbars field of the Toolbars dialog box.

   While the new toolbar is selected, the **R**eset button is replaced by a **D**elete button. You can remove the new toolbar with the **D**elete button.

5. Choose the **C**ustomize button on the Toolbars dialog box to begin customizing the new toolbar. See the "Customizing Toolbars" section above for details.

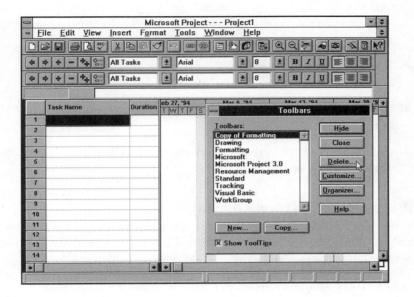

Fig. 22.8
A copy of the
Formatting toolbar
appears beneath
the original
toolbar. Notice the
Delete button that
can be used to
remove the new
toolbar if desired.

Starting a New Toolbar

Creating a new toolbar is almost the same as copying an existing toolbar.
The difference is that the new toolbar appears as an empty floating toolbar
window that you must fill with buttons.

To create a new toolbar:

1. Activate the Toolbars dialog box by choosing Toolbars from the Toolbar
   Shortcut menu or by choosing the **T**oolbars command from the **V**iew
   menu.

2. Choose the **N**ew button. The New Toolbar dialog box appears just as
   it does when you copy a toolbar. The tentative name, however, is
   "Toolbar *number*," where *number* is the next numbered toolbar.

3. Edit the Name field to give the toolbar a distinctive name.

4. Choose OK to begin customizing the new toolbar.

The new toolbar appears at the left of the workspace just under the entry bar.
Drag buttons to it to create the collection you want. You can dock the toolbar
or leave it floating just like other toolbars.

Deleting a User-Defined Toolbar

Toolbars that you create can be deleted. You cannot delete the built-in
toolbars. To delete a user-defined toolbar:

1. Activate the Toolbars dialog box by choosing **T**oolbars from the **V**iew menu.

2. Select the toolbar you want to delete. When selected, the **R**eset button becomes a **D**elete button.

3. Choose **D**elete. A dialog box appears asking you to confirm the deletion of the toolbar.

4. Choose Yes to confirm the deletion and then choose Close to close the Toolbars dialog box.

Adding New Buttons to Toolbars

When you add a new button to a toolbar, it is a blank face and has no command attached to it. Use the Customize Tool dialog box to add features to the new button (see the section below).

To add a new button to a toolbar, follow these steps:

1. Move the mouse pointer over a space in a toolbar or over the background around another button on the toolbar. The new button is inserted in the first space to the right of the mouse position.

2. Press the Ctrl key as you click on the toolbar background. If you click on an existing button, you are editing that button.

   A new, blank button appears on the toolbar and the Customize Tool dialog box appears for you to add features to the button (see fig. 22.9).

3. Use the Customize Tool dialog box as described in the section that follows to define the new button.

> ### Note
> If you create a new button by accident, you can remove it by resetting the toolbar it is on (see the section "Restoring the Built-In Toolbars" earlier in this chapter) or by deleting the button with the toolbar Customize dialog box (see the section "Adding and Removing Buttons" above).

Customizing Buttons

The third level of customizing toolbars is to change the picture on a button, the command it executes, or the ToolTip that is displayed with the button. You can do all three with the Customize Tool dialog box. As an example of a custom button, the following sections illustrate creating a button to run the CollapseOutline macro that was developed in Chapter 21, "Creating and Using Macros." The macro simply collapses the outline in a task sheet or Gantt Chart view to the first level outline tasks.

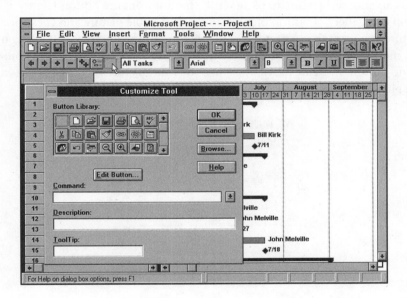

Fig. 22.9
The Customize Tool dialog box lets you create features for new buttons or change the features of existing buttons.

Using the Customize Tool Dialog Box
You can activate the Customize Tools dialog box in several ways.

- It is automatically activated when you create a new button on a toolbar by pressing Ctrl while clicking on the background of the toolbar. The new button is the subject of any changes you effect.

- When you position the mouse over a toolbar button and Ctrl-click on the button, the Customize Tools dialog box is activated, and the button you clicked is the subject of any changes you effect.

- When you position the mouse over a toolbar button and use the right mouse button to activate the Toolbar Shortcut menu, Customize Tool appears at the bottom of the Shortcut menu. The button the mouse pointer was over is the subject of any changes you effect.

- When the Customize dialog box is open and you click the right mouse button over a button on a toolbar, the Button Shortcut menu has Customize Tool as its bottom choice. The button the mouse pointer was over is the subject of any changes you effect.

Each of the sections below describe the options you have for customizing the button.

Add a Picture from the Button Library

You can choose a picture to paste on the button from the Button Library. Scroll this gallery of button pictures to find a suitable picture and click the picture you want to use. If none of the pictures in the library is suitable you can modify one or create an entirely new picture with the **E**dit Button command button. In figure 22.10, the Show All Tasks picture is chosen as a starting picture that is to be edited in the next section.

Fig. 22.10
The Show All Tasks picture is selected as a template to build a new picture.

Editing the Button

To edit the picture you must choose the button labeled **E**dit Button to activate the Button Editor dialog box (see fig. 22.11). The current picture on the button appears enlarged to individual pixels in the Picture box. You can change each pixel in the picture with the mouse.

Fig. 22.11
Use the Button Editor to create or modify button pictures.

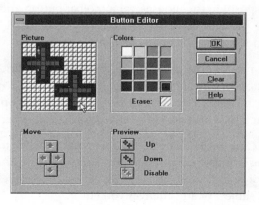

IV

The Colors box is your palette for pasting colored pixels. The Move arrows move the whole picture one row or column at a time. The Preview area shows you how the current picture looks in three different states: Up (the normal look), Down (when clicked on by the mouse), or Disable (when the context makes the button unavailable).

Change the picture with these techniques, applied in any order:

- Change the color of any pixel by clicking a color in the Colors box, and then clicking on the pixel.

- Erase pixels by clicking the erase box and then clicking all pixels you want to clear. You also can simply click a pixel a second time to change its color to the background (semi-gray) color.

- Reposition the picture with the Move arrows if desired. You cannot move colored pixels out of the picture, so you must first clear an area along the edge you want to move into.

- Clear the canvas to start from scratch with the Clear button.

- Cancel changes you have made (for example, if you need to start over) with the Cancel button.

When the picture is satisfactory, choose OK to paste the Picture in the Editor into the Button Library. The picture is selected, and it is the picture for the new button. Figure 22.12 shows the finished picture that will be used for the CollapseOutline macro button.

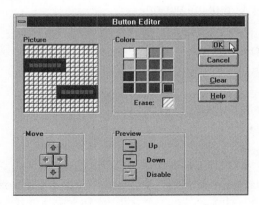

Fig. 22.12
The finished picture for the CollapseOutline button.

Selecting the Command for the Button

The command that the button executes is chosen from the entry list in the **C**ommand field. This list shows all of the Microsoft Project command set that you can choose from to assign commands to buttons.

◄ "Creating and Using Macros," p. 597

To assign a macro module to a button, use the Macro command followed by the macro name in double-quotes. Similarly, to have the button display a custom form, use the Form command followed by the form name in double-quotes. The **B**rowse button lets you review Visual Basic for Applications command words. In the example that follows, the button runs a macro named CollapseOutline (see fig. 22.13).

Fig. 22.13
Macros automatically appear in the list of Commands that can be assigned to a button.

To select the command for a toolbar button, follow these steps:

1. Choose the **C**ommand button.

2. Scroll the list of commands. In this example, the Macro "CollapseOutline" appears in the list because the macro is available in the GLOBAL.MPT template.

3. Choose the appropriate command, in this case Macro "CollapseOutline".

Entering the Description

The **D**escription field automatically shows standard descriptors for most commands. The description appears in the Status bar at the bottom of the screen when the button is chosen. You can edit the **D**escription field as you choose. You can use up to 80 characters in the description (see fig. 22.14).

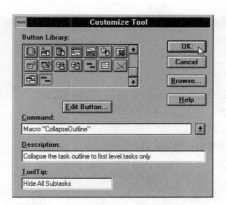

Fig. 22.14
The Description
and ToolTip fields
can be customized
to display your
choice of text for
the button.

Selecting the ToolTip

The ToolTip is the little yellow memo that appears when you pause the
mouse over a toolbar button. You can supply your own ToolTip for your
button. Keep these entries short, as the standard ToolTips are also short (see
fig. 22.14).

When you have supplied the picture, the command, the description, and the
ToolTip for the button, choose OK to close the Customize Tools dialog box.

Managing Toolbars with the Organizer

As stated at the outset of this chapter, toolbars are global objects in Microsoft
Project 4.0. The changes you make in the various toolbar dialog boxes are
saved in the GLOBAL.MPT template. You cannot display a toolbar unless a
copy of it is in the GLOBAL.MPT file.

You can use the Organizer to copy, rename, and delete toolbars. This is, by
the way, the only way to rename a toolbar.

To rename a toolbar, follow these steps:

1. Use the Toolbars Shortcut menu to display the Toolbars dialog box.

2. Choose the **O**rganizer button. The Organizer dialog box appears, with
   the Toolbars tab displayed (see fig. 22.15). The GLOBAL.MPT toolbars
   are listed on the left. The current project file is shown on the right with,
   at least initially, no toolbars included in it.

3. Choose the toolbar you want to rename from the list on the left.

4. Choose the Re**n**ame button. The Rename dialog box appears with the
   current name selected in the **N**ew name field.

Fig. 22.15
The Toolbars tab
of the Organizer
dialog box shows
the named
toolbars, all of
which are
GLOBAL.

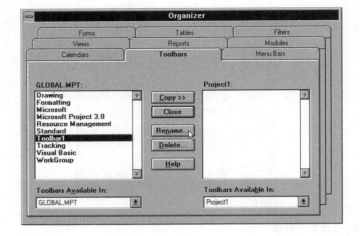

5. Type in a new name, and choose OK (see fig. 22.16).

Fig. 22.16
Provide a new
name for a toolbar
in the Rename
dialog box.

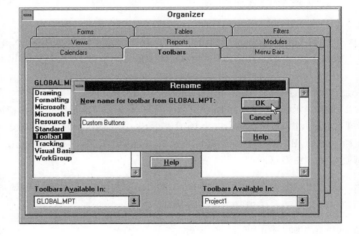

Figure 22.17 shows the newly named toolbar, Custom Buttons, at the top of
the list in the GLOBAL.MPT template.

Although you can copy toolbars into a project file, toolbars stored in project
files cannot be displayed. You would copy a toolbar into a project file merely
for the purpose of being able to copy the toolbar from that project file into
the GLOBAL.MPT template on someone else's computer.

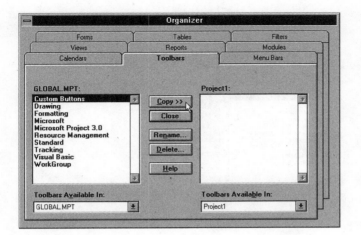

Fig. 22.17
The new name for the toolbar is Custom Buttons.

To copy a toolbar into a project file, follow these steps:

1. Be certain that the project file you want to use is open in memory before you activate the Organizer.

2. Display the Organizer dialog box by choosing the **T**oolbars command from the **V**iew menu, and then select the **O**rganizer button.

3. Select the toolbar you want to copy. You can select multiple toolbars by dragging the mouse. Select multiple toolbars that are not adjacent by using the Ctrl key as you click the additional names you want to copy.

4. If the project file you want to use does not already appear above the right side box, choose it by choosing the Toolbars Available In box at the lower right of the dialog box.

5. Choose the **C**opy button to copy all selected toolbars to the right side of the dialog box.

6. Choose the Close button to close the Organizer dialog box.

Figure 22.18 shows that a copy of the toolbar Custom Buttons has been placed in the Product1 project file.

Fig. 22.18
Toolbars copied into a project file cannot be displayed, but they can be copied into GLOBAL.MPT templates on other computers.

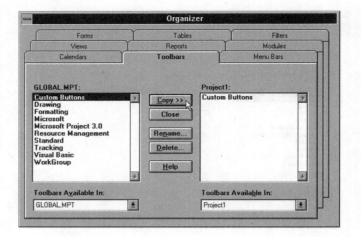

Customizing the Menu Bar

You can change the menu that is displayed in Microsoft Project by customizing the menu bar. As with toolbars, custom menus are global: they are not confined to the project file that is in memory when they are created. Bear in mind, then, that changing the menu is a permanent change that affects all project files you work with.

While working in any project, you can apply any of the defined menu bars. You also can change the name of the menu bar that is the default.

In addition to customizing the menu bar as described in this section, you also can add frequently used views, tables, filters, macros, and so on to the menus that display lists of those objects. See Chapter 17, "Using and Creating Views," for information about placing those objects on the View menu and the Filter menu. See Chapter 21, "Creating and Using Macros," for information about placing macros on the Tools menu.

Tip
When learning to customize menus, start with a copy of the Standard menu bar. If you have trouble, you can keep the copy and work on it while still using the Standard for your work.

Using the Menu Bars Dialog Box

Customize menu bars by starting in the Menu Bars dialog box. From the **T**ools menu choose **C**ustomize and then choose **M**enu Bars. The Menu Bars dialog box is displayed (see fig. 22.19).

All of the menu bars that are currently defined in the GLOBAL.MPT template are listed in the **M**enu Bars list. Figure 22.19 shows the New Product menu bar selected, and the menu at the top of the screen shows its customized choices, **R**eports and **M**acros.

IV

To display a new menu bar, choose the menu bar in the **M**enu Bars box and then the Apply button.

At the bottom of the Menu Bars dialog box a static display shows the name of the Default Menu Bar. You can select a different menu for the Default Menu Bar and for the No Files Open Menu Bar (the menu bar that is displayed when there is no document in the window). Use the De**f**aults button to change these default settings. Figure 22.20 shows the Set Defaults dialog box with New Product chosen as the new **D**efault Menu Bar. In the Menu Bars dialog box, you can see how New Product displays as the Default Menu Bar once it has been set as the default.

At the bottom of the dialog box are the buttons that allow you to change the contents of menu bars.

- Use the **N**ew button to create a new menu from a blank slate.

- Use the **E**dit button to edit the menu that is selected in the **M**enu Bars box.

- Use the **C**opy button to make a copy of the menu that is selected in the **M**enu Bars box. You give the copy a new name and make changes in its structure.

All three buttons open the Menu Bar Definition dialog box. Figure 22.21 shows the Menu Bar Definition dialog box opened with a copy of the Standard menu. The title bar reminds you that you can only work with the menu bars that are defined in the GLOBAL.MPT template.

Fig. 22.21
You can rename and then modify a copy of the Standard menu bar.

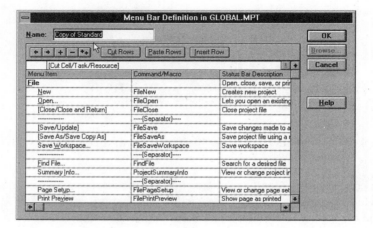

Using the Menu Bar Definition Dialog Box

The Menu Bar Definition dialog box has a **N**ame field, a row of outlining buttons and buttons to manage rows in the menu table, an entry bar, and the menu table. You can use the Cancel button on the right to leave without making any changes.

The menu table displays the entire menu structure as an outline. The menu item text appears in the first column. Some entries in this column are in brackets, for example, [Close/Close and Return]. These are alternatives that change automatically depending on changes or on what is happening in Microsoft Project at the time. (For example, Close and Return appears when Microsoft Project has been invoked by OLE to insert a project object in another application.)

Menu items are flush left and bold. Commands (the items listed under menus in an actual menu) are indented under the Menu items in the first column, and submenus are indented under commands, and so forth. Each element in a menu has a row in the table, including the separator lines.

The second column in the table defines the command from the Microsoft Project command set that is executed by the menu item. These are the same commands you can assign to toolbar buttons or use for macros. When a cell in the second column is selected, the entry-list arrow to the right of the entry bar is active, to show you the possible entries.

The third column can be used to enter the description you want displayed in the Status bar when a menu or command is highlighted.

Resetting the Standard Toolbar

If you edit the Standard toolbar and then want to return it to its original state, use the **R**eset button. The **R**eset button does not appear in figure 22.21 because the Standard menu bar is not being edited. You can see the **R**eset button in figure 22.22 below. Simply choose the **R**eset button to remove all changes and return the menu bar to its original state. A warning dialog box asks you to confirm that you want to restore the original. Choose Yes to restore the original and No to abandon the Reset operation.

Naming the Menu Bar

Use this field to assign a name to the menu bar you are creating or to change the name of a menu bar you are editing.

Using the Outline Buttons

You design the structure of a menu by indenting (shifting to the right) and outdenting (shifting to the left) the rows in the menu table. For example, if you indent the item **O**pen on the third row of figure 22.21, you are making it a submenu item under **N**ew. The **O**pen command would then only appear after the user has chosen **N**ew from the menu. If you were to outdent **F**ind **F**ile on the tenth row, it would then appear as one of the main menu items, and the items indented beneath it would be commands on its drop-down menu.

The outlining buttons at the top of the menu table are used to indent and outdent rows. You also can collapse and expand the outline. Use the buttons as follows:

⬅	Outdent or shift to the left the menu item in the outline
➡	Indent or shift to the right the menu item in the outline
✛	Show subitems for the selected row(s)
▬	Hide subitems for the selected row(s)
✛✛	Show all items for the entire menu

Figure 22.22 shows the entire outline collapsed—all submenu items and commands are temporarily hidden. To hide all but the main menu items as in figure 22.22, select the column heading, Menu Item, and choose the Hide submenu items button. You can then show the subitems for just one main menu item at a time. This arrangement makes it easier to keep your orientation when working with the 170 or so rows of the Standard menu.

Fig. 22.22
You can collapse the menu outline to review the structure of the menu.

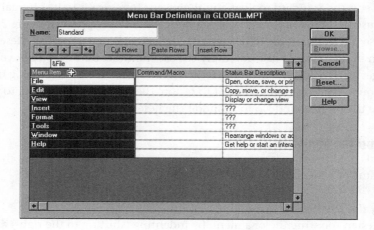

Inserting, Cutting, and Pasting Rows

Use the **I**nsert Row button to insert a blank row for a new menu item. Use the **Cu**t Rows button to cut the selected row(s). You can paste them into another location if desired, or just leave them out of the menu. Use the **P**aste Rows button to paste the rows that were cut into a new location. There is no copy rows button because you obviously would not want the same menu command to appear on the menu twice.

Adding a New Command

The preceding operations are illustrated in this section by inserting a new command in the **T**ools menu to display the Organizer so that the user does not have to find a dialog box with the Organizer box on it every time the Organizer is needed.

The Organizer command is inserted below the **C**ustomize command and above the **O**ptions subcommand. Figure 22.23 shows that section of the menu, with the **O**ptions command selected. Choosing the **I**nsert Row button creates a blank row for the new command.

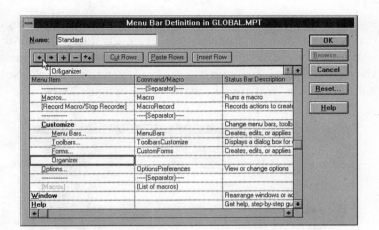

Fig. 22.23
The new Organizer command will be inserted above the **O**ptions command on the Tools menu.

To insert menu command, follow these steps:

1. From the **T**ools menu, choose **C**ustomize. Then choose **M**enu Bars to display the Menu Bars dialog box.

2. Choose the menu bar to be changed in the Menu Bars list.

3. Choose the **E**dit button to display the Menu Bar Definition dialog box.

4. Choose the row where the new menu item is to be placed. The item currently on that row will be below the new menu item once it is inserted.

5. Choose the **I**nsert Row button to create a blank row.

6. Type the new Menu Item text and press Enter. The new command automatically assumes the outline level of the item just above it, as shown in figure 22.24. You may need to indent or outdent it.

   When entering the name, you should consider the use of a *hot key*, a letter or number you can press to select the command from the menu. In figure 22.23 the **O**ptions menu has an underline under the O. Users can activate the Options command by just pressing the O. Notice that in the entry bar of the Menu table there is an ampersand (&) before the letter O. When you enter your menu command name, use an ampersand before the letter you want to have as a hot key. The letter is underlined when the menu is displayed.

Select a letter for the hot key that is not already in use as a hot key on that particular menu. Since the letter O is already the hot key for the Options command, it cannot be used for the new Organizer command. The letter g in Organizer is used as the hot key in this example. Notice the "Or&ganizer" text entry in the entry bar in figure 22.24.

Fig. 22.24

The new menu item Organizer is indented under Customize and will need to be outdented to place it at the same level as Customize and Options.

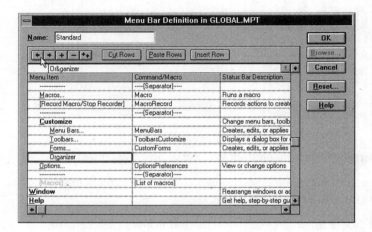

7. Enter the Command to be executed by the new menu item in the second column. The command that is entered in the middle column must be found on the list of commands that is displayed by the entry list arrow at the right of the entry bar (see fig. 22.25).

   The first entries on the entry list are commands in parentheses that provide lists of objects on a menu. Examples are the list of views that appears on the View menu and the list of macros that can be displayed at the bottom of the Tools menu. Below the list commands are the regular commands. The command to display the Organizer is simply Organizer.

8. When the new command is completed, choose OK on the Menu Bar Definition dialog box to return to the Menu Bars dialog box.

9. Choose the Apply button to display the menu. Figure 22.26 shows the **T**ools menu displayed with the new Or**g**anizer command just above **O**ptions.

IV

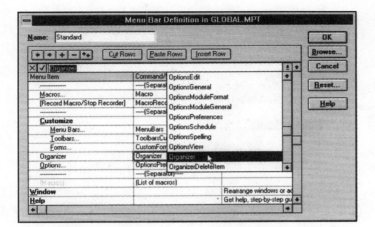

Fig. 22.25
Display the list of commands that can be attached to a menu command with the entry-list arrow to the right of the entry bar.

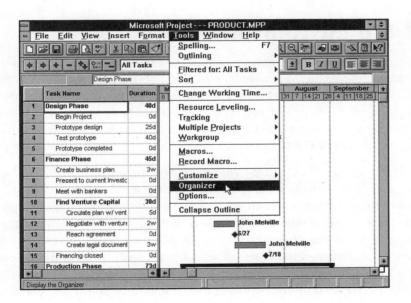

Fig. 22.26
The new **T**ools menu item, Or**g**anizer, is between Customize and Options.

Using the Organizer with Menu Bars

You can rename and delete menu bars on the Menu Bar tab of the Organizer (see fig. 22.27). You also can copy menu bars to a project file in order to carry the menu bar to another computer and copy it to the GLOBAL.MPT template on that computer.

Fig. 22.27
You can rename
and delete Menu
Bars with the
Organizer.

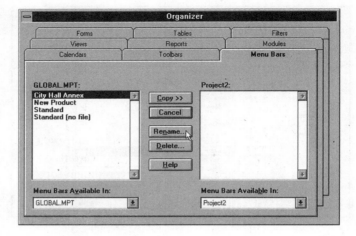

Using Custom Forms

Custom forms are pop-up entry forms that give you quick access to fields that
are not displayed on the current view. A custom form keeps you from having
to change views to access the fields. You also can use custom forms to enter
the same value into one or more fields for multiple tasks or resources. If multiple tasks are selected when a custom form is displayed, all tasks receive the
values that are typed into the form.

Custom forms are similar to the pop-up forms displayed by many of the buttons and menu commands in Microsoft Project. For example, the Update
Task button on the Tracking toolbar displays the Update Task form that gives
you quick access to tracking fields. However, these forms are internal to the
Microsoft Project program, and you cannot delete or change these forms with
the Custom Forms editor. Although you cannot customize the forms supplied
with Microsoft Project, you can design your own custom forms with the Dialog Editor, which is one of the server applications in Windows that you can
use with other Windows applications.

You cannot incorporate custom forms in combination with the other views
supplied by Microsoft Project. These forms can be activated only with the
toolbar buttons, with a menu, or by assigning shortcut keys to them
(Ctrl+*letter*). Therefore, you cannot place a custom form in a pane and then
use the form to scroll through the task list or resource list. You can use custom forms only to edit or view the task or resource that is selected when the
forms are activated. When you select the OK or Cancel button on the form,
the form is removed from display.

You use custom forms, therefore, for the occasional specialty editing or information review. These forms are inappropriate as a primary vehicle for original data entry due to the necessity of having to display the form for each new task or resource. If you need continued access to fields that are not included in a standard view, you must create a View that incorporates a custom table that you design and display in the Task or Resource Sheet view. See Chapter 17, "Using and Creating Views," for guidelines in creating custom views.

The forms discussed in this section are more limited than those you can design with Visual Basic. Although Visual Basic for Applications does not include the Visual Basic forms design module, you can design sophisticated forms with Visual Basic and then use Visual Basic for Applications in Microsoft Project to display and process data with the form. Unfortunately, designing forms with Visual Basic is beyond the scope of this book.

Reviewing the Forms Supplied with Microsoft Project

Microsoft Project includes seven custom task forms and four custom resource forms that were included in Microsoft Project 3.0. You can access the custom forms by choosing the **T**ools **C**ustomize **F**orms command. This command displays the Custom Forms dialog box, which lists the custom forms (see fig. 22.28). The predefined forms are briefly described in the following lists:

Task Forms	Description
Cost Tracking	Tracks costs for tasks that have no resources assigned or that are 100 percent completed.
Earned Value	Examines calculations of comparative cost variances for tasks, based on the planned, scheduled, and actual duration, and work and cost amounts.
Entry	Edits the basic entry values plus the Rollup field.
Schedule Tracking	Tracks the Duration and Percentage Complete. The scheduled dates and variances are shown for your information.
Task Relationships	Edits the list of predecessors and successors for the selected task(s).
Tracking	Tracks the duration and dates for tasks. This is the form that appears when you select the Tracking tool on the toolbar.
Work Tracking	Tracks duration and views the calculated Work tracking fields.

Resource Forms	Description
Cost Tracking	Used to view total cost for a resource (for all tasks).
Entry	An abbreviated entry form.
Summary	Used to view the overall cost and Work tracking information.
Work Tracking	Used to view the Work tracking data.

Fig. 22.28
Select a Task or
Resource form
from the Custom
Forms dialog box.

Using a Custom Form

You can display custom forms with the **T**ools menu, with a toolbar button,
or with a shortcut key.

Using the Menu To Display a Form

To display a custom form with the menu, follow these steps:

1. Select the task or resource that you want to edit with the form.

2. From the **T**ools menu, choose **C**ustomize and then **F**orms. The Custom
   Forms dialog box appears. If a task is selected, the task forms are listed
   (see fig. 22.28). If a resource is selected, the resource forms are listed.

3. Select the form from the list in the **F**orms box.

4. To display the form, choose the Appl**y** button.

5. Use the form to enter data or view the field values.

6. When finished with the form, choose the OK button.

Using a Shortcut Key To Display a Form

To assign a shortcut key to a custom form, follow these steps:

1. From the **T**ools menu, choose **C**ustomize and then **F**orms to display the Custom Forms dialog box.

2. Select the form name on the list in the **F**orms box.

3. Choose the Rena**m**e button to display the Define Custom Form dialog box (see fig. 22.29). You can use this dialog box to change the name of the form or to change the shortcut key assignment.

4. Select the **K**ey box and type the letter that you want to use in combination with the Ctrl key to activate the custom form (numbers cannot be used). The letters are not case-sensitive, so typing an upper- or lower-case letter makes no difference. The shortcut keys already in use that you should avoid are: **B** (Bold), **C** (Edit Copy), **D** (Fill Down), **F** (Edit Find), **I** (Italics), **N** (File New), **O** (File Open), **P** (File Print), **S** (File Save), **U** (Underline), **V** (Edit Paste), **X** (Edit Cut), and **Z** (Edit Undo).

5. To save the key assignment, choose the OK button.

To use the shortcut key, first select the task or resource for which you want to display the form, and then press the shortcut letter while holding down the Ctrl key.

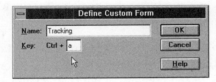

Fig. 22.29
Use the Define Custom Form dialog box to rename a form or assign it a new shortcut key.

Using a Toolbar Button To Display a Form

To assign a form to a toolbar button, follow these steps:

1. Use the Ctrl key while you press the button you want to display the form. If you need to create a button, see the earlier section, "Adding New Buttons to Toolbars."

2. Choose **C**ommand and type **Form** *"form name,"* where *form name* is the name that appears in the list of Custom Forms.

You also can select the entry-list arrow and scroll the Form commands to find the form name listed.

3. Choose the **D**escription field and type the description you want the button to display on the Status line.

4. Choose the **T**oolTip field, and type the ToolTip you want displayed when the mouse pointer pauses over the button.

5. Choose the OK button when the Form command is complete to save the button definition.

To display the form, select the task or resource and then choose the button to which you assigned the form.

Managing the List of Custom Forms

Besides using the Custom Forms dialog box to apply a form, you also can use it to modify the list of forms and to edit the content of the forms. You can use the buttons on the Custom Forms dialog box to rename a form, edit an existing form, and create new forms. You can use the **O**rganizer button to delete forms, rename forms, and copy forms between the Project file in which they are created and the GLOBAL.MPT template or other project files.

To change the name of a form, select the form name in the Custom **F**orms list box and choose the **R**ename button. In the Define Custom Form dialog box, select the **N**ame box and type the new name for the form (see fig. 22.29). Choose OK to save the name.

To change the design of a form, select the form name and choose the **E**dit button. You see the Dialog Editor screen with the definition of the selected form outlined for you to edit. The use of the Dialog Editor is explained in the following section.

To create a new custom form, you can either select the **N**ew button and start with a blank form to create an entirely new form, or you can select an existing form similar to the form you want to create and select the **C**opy button to start with a copy of the existing form. Either way, you first see the Define Custom Form dialog box, which you use to adjust the name of the new form and to define a shortcut key to activate the form (see fig. 22.29).

Choose the **N**ame text box to edit the name, and choose the **K**ey text box to type the letter (numbers cannot be used) that you plan to use to display the form. Choose OK to proceed with editing the form. The Dialog Editor screen appears so that you can create the new form. The form Name appears in the new form's title bar.

Figure 22.30 shows the Dialog Editor screen for a new form named Annotate. The Annotate form is used in the following sections to illustrate the use of the Dialog Editor. The form will be designed to display some useful fields that are not available on any of the standard Views or Tables. The Annotate form will make available for editing tasks all ten Text fields, the Marked field, and all ten of the Flag fields. These fields are frequently used to change the display of the most popular screen views, especially the Gantt Chart and the views that display a table of tasks.

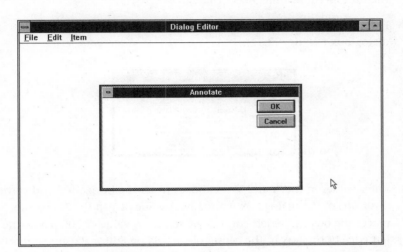

Fig. 22.30
The initial form contains only the OK and Cancel buttons. Add text, fields, and group boxes to complete the form.

In figure 22.30 the form is a task form. Similar forms can be designed for resources. The Annotate form for resources can display only the five Text fields (Text1–Text5).

Using the Dialog Editor

The Dialog Editor screen for a new form displays a small outline of a dialog box in the center of the screen with OK and Cancel buttons already pasted on the blank dialog box form (see fig. 22.30). The name you entered in the Define Custom Form dialog box for the new form appears in the title bar of the form. The size of the form is the size it will be when displayed. You must maximize the Dialog Editor window if you want to maximize the size of the form.

Sizing and Positioning the Dialog Box

You can use the mouse to resize the form's dialog box by dragging the borders or corners of the box to any desired dimension within the Dialog Editor window. When you resize the form initially, it changes symmetrically—the

Tip
If you want to assign a toolbar button or shortcut key to display a similar form for both tasks and resources, assign the same name to both the task form and the resource form. Then, depending on whether you are in a task view or a resource view, the button displays the named form that is appropriate for the current view.

opposite border mirrors the motion of the border that you drag with the mouse. Therefore, the form always remains centered within the Dialog Editor window because the default position of the form is centered. You can reposition the form, without automatic centering, by activating the information box for the Dialog box. To change the position or size settings for the dialog box, follow these steps:

1. Select the dialog box outline by clicking once on the border or, from the **E**dit menu, choose **S**elect Dialog.

2. From the **E**dit menu, choose **I**nfo to display the Dialog Information dialog box (see fig. 22.31).

Fig. 22.31
An Info dialog box can be displayed for the form, or for any item in the form, to position or resize the form or item.

3. Enter values in the **X** and **Y** text boxes to set the horizontal and vertical positions of the dialog box manually. A value of 1 in the **X** text box places the box at the left edge of the screen. A value of 100 places the left edge of the box in the center of the Dialog Editor screen. Similarly, the values 1 and 100 place the top edge of the box at the top and center of the Dialog Editor screen, respectively. However, when the form is displayed, it usually is not displayed in the same location on the Microsoft Project screen as the position to which you moved it in the Dialog Editor screen. This condition is especially true if you move the dialog box to the lower part of the screen.

   If you leave the position on Auto, the form is centered in the Microsoft Project screen when displayed. Mark the Auto check boxes to have the custom form centered on-screen when displayed.

4. Enter values in the **W**idth and **H**eight check boxes to set the dimensions of the form's dialog box. To create a box that completely fills the screen when displayed in Microsoft Project, set the **X** and **Y** boxes to 1 each; set the **W**idth to **360** and the **H**eight to **276**.

All other items that you place on the form can be positioned and sized with their own Information dialog boxes. If the Information form for an item has the Auto check boxes marked, you cannot reposition or resize the item manually with the mouse. If the Auto check boxes are clear, however, you can use the mouse to select—and reposition or resize—the item.

If you resize the form the OK and Cancel buttons may be left in the middle of the form. Use the mouse to drag the buttons into an appropriate position.

Placing Items on the Form

The OK and Cancel buttons are *items* on the form. You place items (including buttons, fields, text, and borders for *groups* of items) with the **I**tem command on the menu.

If the Auto boxes for items are cleared, you can resize or reposition multiple items simultaneously. Select additional items by pressing the Shift key as you click successive items. After all items are selected, change the position or size of one item and all others will follow suit.

Placing Text on the Form

To place text on the form, select the **I**tem command from the menu and choose **T**ext. A small box that contains the characters Text appears on the form, just below the currently selected item. You can begin typing the message that you want to appear in the text item, which replaces the Text displayed as a place holder. The text item expands to accommodate the message that you type. The text item, however, does not word-wrap. You must stop typing when the space is filled and press Enter to end the text for that item. To begin another text item immediately below the line you last typed, just press Enter.

You can reposition a text item either before or after you type the message that you want it to display. You can use the arrow keys or you can use the mouse to drag the text item into position. Use the mouse at the right border of the text item to resize the text item.

You also can double-click the text item to display the related Information dialog box, or select the text item and then choose **I**nfo from the **E**dit menu. If you mark the Auto check boxes, you cannot resize and reposition the text item with the mouse. If you reposition the text item before typing it, you need to begin entering the message by backspacing to delete the Text place holder.

Tip

Use the Shift key to select multiple items to drag together, keeping their positions the same relative to each other.

Figure 22.32 shows the first text item that was added to the form, with the mouse pointer changed to the symbol for dragging the text item to another location.

Fig. 22.32
When an item is placed on the form, it is first placed immediately below the currently select item; you can then move it to a new location.

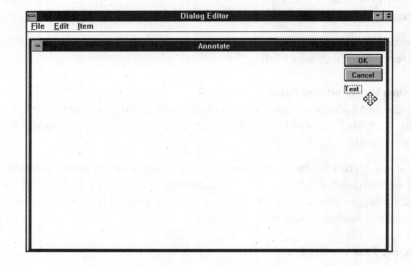

Figure 22.33 shows in the background that the first text item was repositioned and the message "Use this form to enter..." has been typed to explain how to use the form. A text item was placed below that to identify the Task Name field that is to be placed to its right.

Fig. 22.33
Place field information as static text if the user should not attempt to change it.

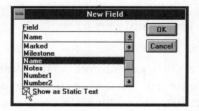

Placing Field Values on the Form

You can display fields from the project file in the form by choosing **F**ields from the **I**tem menu. The New Field dialog box appears for you to select the field name. You also can designate that the field be displayed as Read Only (not editable) by selecting and marking the **S**how as Static Text check box. Type the field name or select the name from the entry list. Choose the OK button to close the dialog box and display the field item. The field is placed below the item that was selected when you created the field.

In the center of figure 22.33, the New Field dialog box has been activated by selecting the **I**tem menu and choosing the **F**ield command. The Name field has been selected to place on the form in order to show the name of the task that was selected when the form was activated. The check box at the bottom has been filled to place the task name as static (non-editable) text. Because the user cannot change the name of the task being edited—that is determined by the task selected when the form was displayed—it's best not to make the field look like it can be changed.

You can reposition the field item or resize the display with the mouse. Double-click the field item or choose **I**nfo from the **E**dit menu to display the Information dialog box for the field item. The Name field was positioned as static text after the text that described it in figure 22.33.

Placing a Group Box on the Form

Use the Group Box to provide a boundary line around fields on the form. The Group Box actually contains the fields that are placed in it; so you can move group items about the form together, by selecting the group and then moving the Group Box. To place a group box on the form, choose **G**roup Box from the **I**tem menu. Enter the text that you want displayed at the top of the Group Box while the new group item is still selected (or at any time when you select the group box), and then use the mouse to position the Group Box mask at the desired location. Do not place the Group Box over any other items on the form. This feature is opaque, so that the items that you cover are hidden from view.

If the Group Box is selected, the fields that you add to the form are placed within the Group Box. Figure 22.34 shows a group box that has not yet been titled but that already contains the first of the Flag fields. The New Field dialog box is positioned to add the next Flag field to the group.

Figure 22.35 shows the Flag Fields group after the group title has been entered and all ten flag fields have been added. The Group Box boundary can be adjusted by selecting the group box and then resizing the box lines. The whole group can be moved together by selecting the group box and then choosing the **E**dit menu and choosing the Select **G**roup command. The whole group of Flag fields was moved to the right side of the form in the finished form (see fig. 22.36).

Fig. 22.34
Place a group box
first, and then
place items
within it.

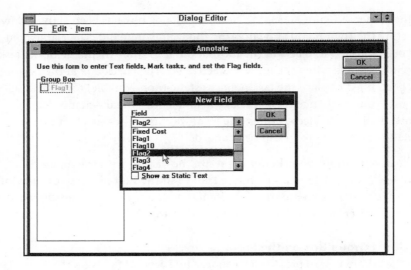

Fig. 22.35
Group boxes are
used to provide
visual orientation
and to make it
easier to reposition
groups of items on
a form.

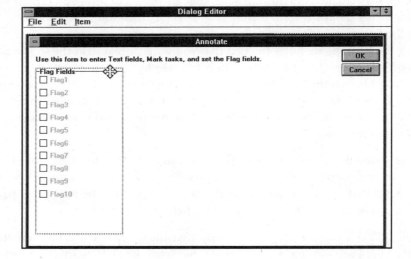

Placing Buttons on the Form

To place a button on the form, from the **I**tem menu, choose **B**utton. You
can choose either an OK button or a Cancel button. You can only have one
button of each type on a form. If you place more than one OK button, the
form only displays the last button you placed in Microsoft Project, even
though all the buttons seem to be positioned on the Dialog Editor screen.
The OK button returns a value of True, and the Cancel button returns a value
of Error if the form is used in a macro IF command. You can change the text
that appears on either button without changing the button's nature.

Both buttons close the dialog box when selected, but the OK button returns a value of True and any changes on the form are saved, and the Cancel button returns a value of Error and all changes are lost.

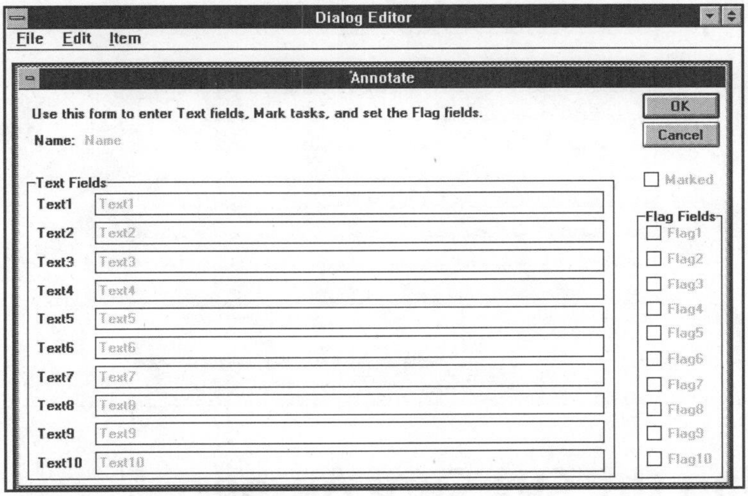

Fig. 22.36
The completed form has the ten Text fields, the Marked field, and the ten Flag fields.

Saving the Form

To save the form and continue working on it, choose **S**ave from the **F**ile menu. After the form is complete, choose E**x**it from the **F**ile menu. If unsaved changes exist, you are prompted to save the form again before exiting.

Once saved, you can apply the form as outlined in the introduction to this section on custom forms. Figure 22.37 shows the Annotate form, applied to the PRODUCT project task "Create Business Plan."

Managing Forms with the Organizer

Custom forms are created in and saved in the project file that is in the active window when you create the form. Use the Organizer to copy a custom form to the GLOBAL.MPT template if you want to use the form in all other project files. To display the Organizer, choose the **T**ools menu, the **C**ustomize command, and the **F**orms command. Then, on the Custom Forms dialog box, choose the **O**rganizer button. The Forms tab is chosen, and you can rename, delete, and copy forms as described in the earlier sections of this chapter.

Fig. 22.37
The custom form
Annotate provides
quick access to the
text and marked
and flag fields for
any task.

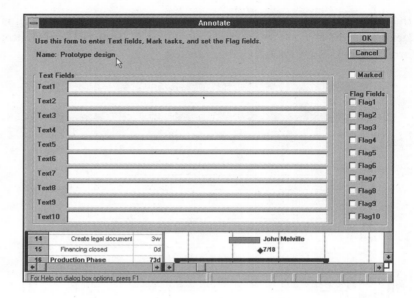

Using the Cue Card Author

Cue Cards are the newest addition to Microsoft's collection of on-line user help features. Like the traditional Help files and the wizards, Cue Cards provide descriptions of activities and definitions of terms. However, Cue Cards differ from the traditional Help screens and the wizards in several ways.

- Unlike the wizards, Cue Cards only provide instructions and information. They make no changes to your project data or to the Microsoft Project working environment.

- Unlike the wizards, Cue Cards remain in their own window on the workspace at all times, but you can go to other windows and return to the Cue Cards at will. You do not have to close the Cue Cards in order to get back to work on your project file.

- Cue Cards remain in front of other windows. You can minimize them or close them, but you cannot remove their "Always On Top" attribute.

- You can create your own Cue Cards. A reduced version of Microsoft's Help File editor is provided with Microsoft Project to create and compile library files that the WINHELP.EXE program can display.

This section shows you how to create your own Cue Cards and how to display them in Microsoft Project. The Cue Cards are actually created in Microsoft Word 6.0 with special templates and macros that guide you through creating the Cue Cards.

Authoring Your Own Cue Card Help File

Follow this sequence of steps to create your own Cue Cards:

■ Outline the topics you want to cover in your Cue Cards in advance.

■ Initialize the Cue Cards *topics file*. This will be a Word Rich Text Format (RTF) text file that you edit to create the text you want displayed.

■ Add your topics to the topics file, including for each topic the descriptive text, pop-up definitions, bulleted items, and "go to" buttons that you want to appear on that topic card.

■ Compile the topic file into a Cue Cards file. The Cue Cards file will have the same file name as the topic file, but it will have the help file extension (.HLP).

■ View the Error File that the compiler creates to see if there are errors you need to fix. If there are, edit the topics file and recompile.

■ Make your Cue Cards available to users by creating a Program Manager icon or a Microsoft Project macro. To run your Cue Cards in Microsoft Project, attach the macro to a toolbar button, menu command, or shortcut key.

■ Run the macro to make sure it does what you want it to.

Outlining the Cue Card Topics

Once you start working in the Cue Card Author, you won't be free to shuffle ideas around as you may like. You will save a great deal of time by creating in advance an outline of the topics you want to cover.

Each topic is a separate screen in the Cue Cards display, and the user should be able to click on buttons to jump to related topics. The advance planning outline should indicate next to each topic a list of other topics that the user can jump to from that topic.

For example, suppose you want to create a set of Cue Cards to provide guidelines for creating custom forms (similar to the guidelines in the previous section of this chapter). The table below shows a tentative list of topic screens. The first column shows the topic titles. The second column contains a label that will be required in the Cue Card Author as a reference name for the topic. The last column contains a list, for each topic, of other topics the user should be able to jump to after reading the topic.

Topic Title	Context String Label	Jump to topics
Working with Custom Forms	Main	Using, Displaying, Creating
How to use a Custom Form	Using	Back to Main
Displaying a Custom Form	Displaying	Back to Main, Menu, Shortcutkey, Button
Displaying a Form with the Menu	Menu	Back to Displaying
Assigning a Shortcut key to display a Form	Shortcutkey	Back to Displaying
Assigning a toolbar button to display a Form	Button	Back to Displaying
Creating a new Form	Creating	Back to Main, Sizing, Text, Fields, Groups, Buttons, Moving, Deleting, Resizing Items
Sizing the Form	Sizing	Back to Creating
Placing Text on the Form	Text	Back to Creating, Sizing, Moving, Resizing items
Placing fields on the Form	Fields	Back to Creating, Sizing, Moving, Resizing items
Placing Group Boxes on a Form	Groups	Back to Creating, Sizing, Moving, Resizing items
Placing buttons on a Form	Buttons	Back to Creating, Sizing, Moving, Resizing items
Moving items	Moving	Back to Creating
Deleting items	Deleting	Back to Creating
Resizing items	Resizing items	Back to Creating, Moving

For example, the first topic, "Working with Custom Forms," is the opening screen (labeled "main"). It will offer the user options to view the screens that are referenced as using, displaying, and creating. If the user chooses to view the "using" topic (How to use a Custom Form), there will then be options to go back to the main topic, or to jump to the topics referenced as "displaying" and "creating."

This outline will help keep the structure of the topics clear while working with the dialog boxes in the Cue Card Authoring system.

Starting a Cue Card Topics File

The first step in actually creating the Cue Cards topics file is to start the Cue Card Author and let it initialize the topics file that will contain the text and controls for your Cue Cards. The Cue Card Author is actually a set of macros and templates in Microsoft Word 6.0 that guide you in creating your Cue Cards.

The Microsoft Project 4.0 Setup program creates a subdirectory named CUECARDS under the WINPROJ directory that it places the program files in. The CUECARDS directory contains Microsoft Word templates (*.dot) and documents (*.doc) that work together to create your Cue Card file. The CUECARDS directory also contains the program file (HCP.EXE) that compiles your topic file into a Cue Cards file.

Open the Word document STARTUP.DOC to initialize the Cue Card Author. After asking you to name the file that will contain your Cue Cards, the Cue Card Author asks you to enter the first *topic title* and its accompanying *context string*. The first topic is like an opening menu; through all other topics, the user should be able to return to the first topic.

Topic titles are the text that appears at the top of each cue card in bold blue letters. Topics are referenced by their context strings, which are nothing more than arbitrary words that you create and assign to each topic as a reference label. Remember these points about context strings:

- Context strings are not case sensitive; it doesn't matter if you use capital letters or not.

- Context strings must not contain any non-alphanumeric characters or spaces.

- The first topic's context string cannot be changed once it has been assigned, or your references back to the first topic from other topics will not work.

- You can edit the name and context string of topics other than the first topic if you want to make changes.

It's easier to build your Cue Cards if you name context strings with words you'll remember, which have some association with the topics they reference.

After creating the first topic, your topics file will be set up and you can go on to add text, buttons, and other elements to that first topic or go on to add other topics.

To initialize the topic file, follow these steps:

1. Start Microsoft Word 6.0.

2. Use the **F**ile **O**pen command to open the file STARTUP.DOC. A Microsoft Word 6.0 dialog box asks you if you want to create a new file or edit an existing Cue Cards file (see fig. 22.38).

Fig. 22.38
You can start a new Cue Cards file or edit an existing file.

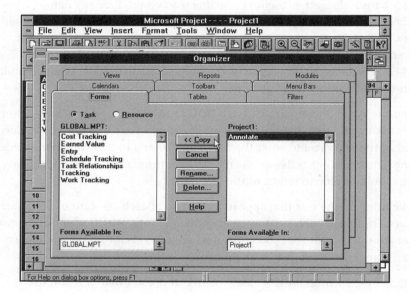

3. Choose the button to Create a New Cue Cards File, and then choose the OK button to proceed. If other Word documents are open, you will be warned that Word must close them, but that it will save any unsaved data before closing the files (see fig. 22.39). If you don't want open files saved or closed, you must choose the Cancel button and start this process again later when there are no other files open that can't be saved and closed.

Microsoft Word then opens the file "CUECARDS.DOC" from the CUECARDS directory, and the file is converted to Rich Text Format (RTF).

> **Note**
>
> If you have filled the **C**onfirm Conversions check box on the File Open dialog box, you will have to confirm the conversion to the RTF format. Choose the OK button, and the Cue Card Author will continue.

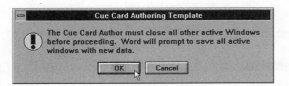

Fig. 22.39
You cannot work on other documents in Microsoft Word while the Cue Card Author macros are running.

4. The next screen shows Cue Cards in the foreground (to help you use the Cue Card Author) and a dialog box in the background for entering the filename that you want to attach to your topics file (see fig. 22.40). Type in the filename you want to use and choose the OK button.

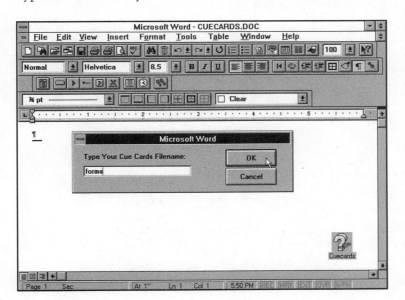

Fig. 22.40
Each set of Cue Cards has its own filename, which you must supply.

Tip
You can review screens and definitions in the accompanying Cue Cards while working with the Cue Card Author. You also can minimize the Cue Cards while typing text to see more. To continue, click the Word document screen or the dialog box currently displayed.

> **Note**
>
> The topics file will be saved with the extension .RTF (Rich Text Format). In the illustration, the name of the file will be FORMS.RTF. Later, when the topics file is compiled, the final Cue Cards file will be named FORMS.HLP. If an inventory of the topics and context strings were generated, the inventory file would be named FORMS.DOC.

5. Next, the Cue Card Author asks you to create your first topic (see fig. 22.41). You must supply both a topic **T**itle and a topic Context **S**tring for the first topic. You can review definitions for those terms by clicking the "title" and "context string" definition terms on the accompanying Cue Cards.

   Enter the first topic title just as you want it to appear. Remember that this will be the title of the introductory cue card that the user will see. In the Cue Cards on the screen, the title "Welcome to Microsoft's Cue Card Author" is the first topic title.

   Enter the context string for the first topic also. Then choose the OK button to continue.

Fig. 22.41
The first topic and its context string must be created before setup is complete.

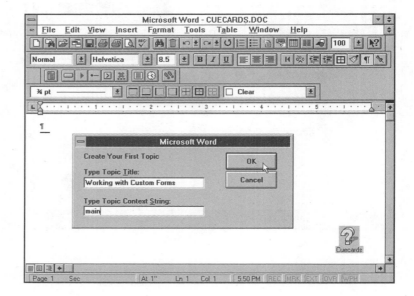

IV

After some processing by the Cue Card Author macros, you see your filename in the title bar with the RTF extension, and the first topic title appears in the text area of the document. Click the OK button on the "Cue Card Setup is Complete" dialog box (shown in fig. 22.42) to proceed.

Fig. 22.42
You can begin entering text once the Cue Cards Setup is complete.

Adding Items to Your Topics File

Once the first topic is defined, you can add text or other Cue Card elements to it. Or you can go on to create other topics and add elements to them. Each topic is a separate page in the topics file.

Inserting Text in a Topic

Select the paragraph marker below the topic title on a topic page to begin entering text. Figure 22.43 shows an explanatory paragraph entered for the first topic.

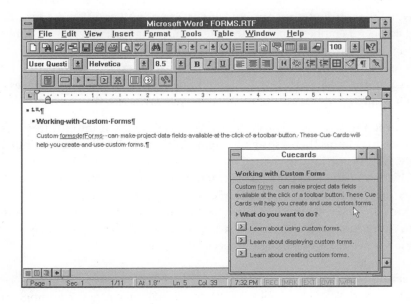

Fig. 22.43
Enter the text for your Cue Cards below the topic title.

Use the Normal style for most paragraph text in your Cue Cards. There is a Numbered List style provided with the Cue Card Author template that you can use on cards where you provide numbered steps as instructions for the user to execute. You can create your own styles if you wish, but there are a few things you must avoid because they have special significance to the styles and macros used in the Cue Card Author:

- You may not use underlining.

- You may not use bullets. There is a special button on the Cue Card Author toolbar to create bulleted items. See the upcoming section "Inserting Bulleted Items."

- You may not use brackets.

- You may not use Word fields or hidden characters.

- You should not change the margins of the topic pages. If you leave the margins alone, the Cue Cards word-wrap effectively within their window.

You may use tabs and paragraph indents in your text, but tab stops generally need to be very close to each other to look good in a cue card window. You may use font attributes such as bold and italics, as well as different font sizes and colors for emphasis in your text. Remember that you may not use underlining. For text that you must enter into dialog boxes (such as bulleted text and user questions), you must apply font formats after the text has been placed on the topic page. Be careful not to disturb any codes within braces ("{}") or any words that are underlined in any way.

In addition to standard paragraph text, you also can insert into the text area of a cue card terms that display pop-up definitions, bulleted item lists, numbered lists, or specially formatted questions for the user, with choice buttons following the question to let the user respond to the question. These text entry options are covered in sections below. Before describing those other options, however, you should know how to add and edit topics and how to get a list of the topics and context strings you have already added. This information is needed for many of the special text items.

Inserting New Topics

 Use the Insert New Topic tool to create additional topic pages. You supply the topic title and context string as described above for the first topic.

Editing Topic Titles and Context Strings

You can change the title of any topic, including the first topic; you can change the context string for any topic except the first topic. If you change a topic's context string, you must search through the topics file and replace all references to the old context string.

To edit the title or context string for a topic:

1. Place the cursor in the page for the topic you wish to change.

2. From the **E**dit menu, choose the **T**opics command at the bottom of the menu. The Topics dialog box appears.

3. Enter the new title or context string.

4. Choose the OK button.

Building and Using the Topic Inventory

As you create topics and their associated context strings, you may lose track of which topic a context string is attached to, or the context strings themselves. This will be especially true if you haven't prepared an outline in advance. The Cue Card Author prepares an inventory of topics and their context strings for you, which you can regenerate as often as you like. The inventory file will have the same filename as the topics file, but it will have the standard .DOC extension used for Word files.

To create the topic inventory, simply click the Create Topic Inventory button on the Cue Card Author toolbar. The inventory file lists each topic and its associated context string, with the topics separated by a double line. Once the inventory is generated, you can print the document to use as a reference as you add more topics and cross-reference topics with their context strings. Choose your topic file (with the RTF format) from the file list at the bottom of the **W**indow menu to return to your topic file for further development of your cue cards.

Inserting Pop-Up Definitions in Text

If you want to provide definitions of key terms within your text, place the term in the text with the Insert Pop-up Definition button. An Insert Definition dialog box appears (see fig. 22.44). This dialog box asks you to type in the term that is to be defined, but it doesn't ask for the definition at this point. You'll enter the definition later as text in a new topic page. At this point, you are merely asked to provide the text for the term itself and a context string to associate with the topic page that will contain the definition.

Fig. 22.44
Supply the term that is to be defined and a context string to reference the topic page that will contain the text of the definition.

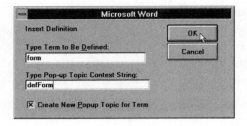

At the bottom of the dialog box, you can fill a check box to create the new topic page immediately. Unless you are cross-referencing a definition that has already been entered, you should fill this check box and create the definition topic page right away.

If you fill the check box to create the topic immediately, a Create Pop-up Topic for Definition dialog box appears (see fig. 22.45). The context string should already be filled in. You need to provide the topic title, which will be the title of the little definition box that appears when the user clicks the pop-up term.

Fig. 22.45
Pop-up definitions are defined as topics with their own title and context strings. The actual definition goes on the topic page as paragraph text.

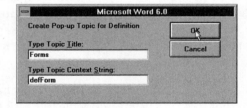

To create a pop-up definition term:

1. Select the place in the text where the term itself is to be displayed. Do not type the term into the text. This procedure will place the term in the text for you, in a special format.

2. Click the Insert Pop-up Definition button on the Cue Card Author toolbar.

3. Type the term in the Type Term to Be **D**efined box, using capitalization as you want it to appear in the text (see fig. 22.44).

4. Type the context string for the definition in the Type Pop-up Topic Context String box. If you created the definition topic earlier, use the context string you assigned to it then. If you haven't created the definition topic, enter the context string you plan to attach to it.

5. Fill the Create New **P**op-up Topic for Term check box if you want to create the topic for the definition now.

6. Choose the OK button to continue. At this point the term is placed in the text of the page where the user will see the term and be able to click it to see the definition. If you filled the check box to create the definition topic now, continue with the next steps. If you didn't fill the check box, skip to the end of this list of instructions.

7. In the Create Pop-up Topic for Definition dialog box (shown in fig. 22.44), you assign the topic title to the definition. In the Type Topic **T**itle text box, type the title you want to appear above the definition when it pops up. The context string should already be filled in for the Type Topic Context **S**tring box.

8. Choose the OK button to complete the creation of the definition topic page.

9. Scroll through the topic file until you find the page headed by the topic title you just entered. Select the empty paragraph marker below the title and type the definition of the term. The term definition cannot itself offer pop-up definitions or any other special jump features.

Figure 22.46 illustrates a pop-up definition. The cue card has the word "form" inserted as a definition term. When clicked, it displays the Forms definition shown in the figure.

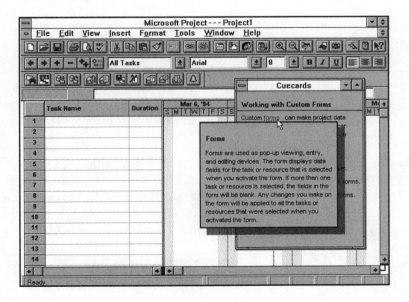

Fig. 22.46
Pop-up definition terms are useful for providing additional information that may not be essential to all users.

Inserting Menu and Next Buttons

You can place a Menu button and a Next button at the top of any cue card to jump to other cue cards. Usually, the Menu button returns the user to a previous cue card where the user clicked a choice button that led to the current cue card. You usually use the Next button to advance the user to the next logical topic instead of having the user choose a jump topic. Both buttons can be used, however, to jump to any topic. You can also place both buttons on the cue card as disabled buttons, just for looks.

To insert buttons at the top of a cue card:

1. Position the cursor anywhere on the page for the topic the button(s) should appear with. The buttons will automatically be positioned at the top of the topic page.

2. Choose the button on the Cue Card Author toolbar that is used to Insert Menu or Next Buttons. A dialog box appears to let you choose the buttons to be placed (see fig. 22.47).

Fig. 22.47
You can insert Menu and Next buttons singly or in combination.

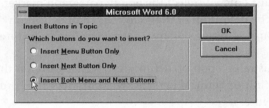

3. Choose to insert a **M**enu button only, a **N**ext button only, or **B**oth buttons.

4. Choose the OK button to continue. For each button, you first choose whether the button is to be active (**J**ump to a new topic) or disabled (**N**othing—Disable the button). If the button is to be active, you then fill a dialog box to define the topic to which the button will take the user.

5. The next dialog box will be labeled "Insert Menu Button" or "Insert Next Button" (see fig. 22.48). For either type of button, choose the **J**ump to a New Topic button or **N**othing — Disable the Button. If you choose to disable the button, you will be finished defining the button. You can go to the end of these instructions.

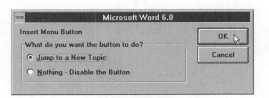

Fig. 22.48
Buttons can actively jump the user to a new topic or they can be disabled so that they do nothing.

6. If the button is to be an active button, you will see a dialog box that requests the context string for the topic to which the button will jump (shown in fig. 22.49). Type the context string into the text box and choose the OK button to conclude the definition of the button.

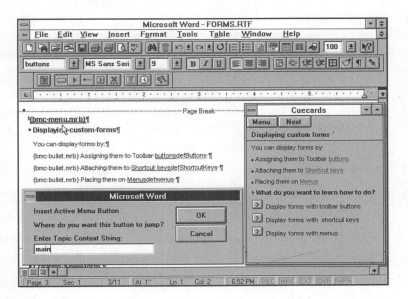

Fig. 22.49
For active buttons, you must define the context string of the topic they will jump to.

7. If you chose to insert two buttons, you will have to repeat steps 5 and 6 above for the second button.

Figure 22.50 illustrates the Menu and Next buttons placed on the custom forms Cue Cards. This figure also illustrates bulleted items, user questions, and choice buttons, all of which are described below.

Fig. 22.50
One of the cue
cards for the
Custom Forms set,
showing buttons,
bullets, user
questions, choice
buttons, and
definition terms.

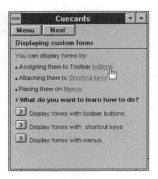

Inserting Bulleted Items

If you want to use bulleted lists on a cue card you must use the Insert Bullet
Point button on the Cue Card Author toolbar instead of using Word's usual
bullet feature. You must go through the steps below once for each bulleted
item you place on a topic. To place bulleted items, follow these steps:

1. Select the place in the topic text where the bulleted list should begin.
   This position should generally be at the beginning of a line, but it can
   follow spaces or tabs.

2. Choose the Insert Bullet Point button on the Cue Card Author toolbar.

3. If you were not positioned at the beginning of a line, a dialog box will
   ask you how you want the bulleted text positioned (see fig. 22.51).

   If you choose Insert Bullet on **N**ext Line, the editor will jump to the end
   of the line you are on and insert a blank line for the bullet and text.

   If you choose Insert Bullet on **P**revious Line, the editor will jump to the
   beginning of the line you are on and insert a blank line for the bullet
   and text.

   If you choose Insert Bullet at **I**nsertion Point, the bullet and text will
   appear at the insertion point in the current line.

Fig. 21.51
If you try to insert
a bullet in the
middle of a line,
the Author asks
for clarification
about its
placement.

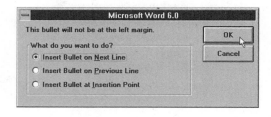

4. Next, a dialog box presents a text box in which you enter the text that you want to appear next to the bullet (see fig. 22.52).

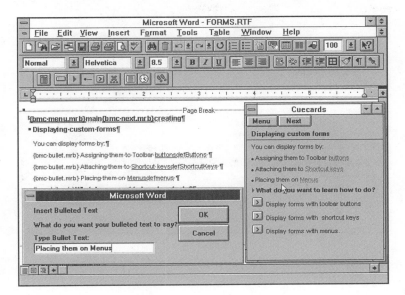

Fig. 22.52
Enter each line of a bulleted list in its own dialog box for bulleted text.

5. Enter the text (without a bullet). The text will scroll if you need to enter more than the text box width.

6. Choose the OK button when the text entry is complete.

Inserting User Questions

The term "user question" is used for text that is displayed with a red triangle bullet to draw attention to it. You can think of placing user questions as using a more dramatic type of bullet. It is intended that you will use this device to display a noticeable prompt before a series of choice buttons.

To enter a user question:

1. Position the cursor in the topic text where the question should be displayed.

2. Choose the Insert User Question button on the Cue Card Author toolbar. A dialog box appears, in which you enter the text of the question (fig. 22.53).

Fig. 22.53
Add user questions with the "Insert User Question" dialog box.

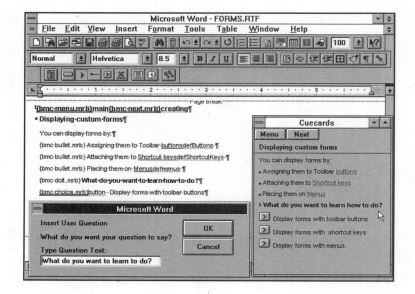

3. Type the text of the question.

4. Choose the OK button to continue.

Inserting Choice Buttons

Choice buttons are used to jump to other cue cards. They are intended to be used after a user question about what the user would like to see next, and they identify topics that you have prepared for the user to view.

To insert choice buttons:

1. Position the cursor at the left margin in the topic text where the buttons should appear. This is usually just after a user question item.

2. Choose the Insert Choice Button button on the Cue Card Author toolbar. A dialog box appears (see fig. 22.54) to ask for the text that is to appear next to the button and for the context string of the topic that should be viewed if the user chooses the button.

3. Type the text that is to accompany the button in the Type Choice Button Text field.

4. Type the context string for the jump topic in the Type Context String of Destination Topic field.

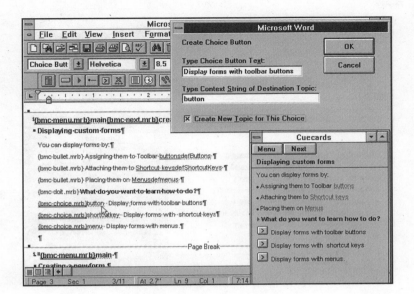

Fig. 22.54
Enter the text that
is to accompany a
choice button,
and the context
string of the topic
the button is to
display.

5. Fill the Create New **T**opic for This Choice check box if the topic is not yet created, and you want to create it now. If you have already created the topic, or if you want to create it later, leave the check box empty. If you leave the check box empty, you can skip the next step in these instructions.

6. If you filled the check box to create a new topic, a dialog box appears for creating the topic (see fig. 22.55). This dialog box is just like other dialog boxes that create new topics. Type the topic **T**itle. The context string should already be filled in from the previous dialog box. You can enter the text of the topic later.

7. Choose the OK button to complete this choice button.

8. Repeat these steps for each choice button on a cue card.

Compiling the Topics File

The topics file must be converted into the format used by the Windows WINHELP.EXE program. The Start Compile button on the Cue Card Author toolbar starts the compiler. If there are no serious errors in the topics file, the result will be a help file with the same name as the topics file, and the .HLP extension. The compiler also produces an error file (with the same filename and the extension .ERR) that lists any errors or warnings about problems with the topics file.

Fig. 22.55
Create choice
button topics just
like you do other
topics: provide a
title and a context
string.

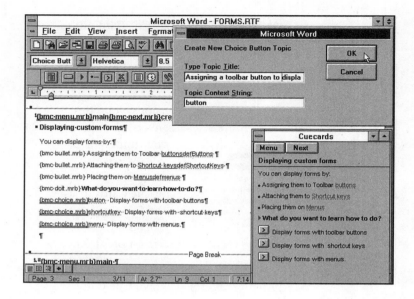

For example, the illustration used in this section created a topics file named FORMS.RTF. The compiler will produce a file named FORMS.HLP and an error file named FORMS.ERR.

You can compile and test your Cue Cards as soon as you have a topic defined. As you add more topics and more features to the topics, compile and view the results as often as you want to verify that you are creating what you intend to create. You can prepare a Word button, a Microsoft Project button, or a Program Manager icon to display the compiled Cue Cards while you are building and testing them; then you can display the Cue Cards easily to see how your work looks. You can keep the Cue Cards displayed as you work on the topics file that generates the Cue Cards. In this way you can view elements that you want to change, review the sequences of jump topics, and so on.

> **Caution**
>
> If you compile and display your Cue Cards and then return to work on the topics file, be sure to close the Cue Cards display before compiling again. Otherwise, the compiler will try to write to a file that is already in use.

To compile your Cue Cards:

1. You must be in the topics file—the file with the RTF extension that shows each topic on a separate page.

2. Choose the Start Compile button from the Cue Card Author toolbar. The compiler will save and close your topics file.

3. When a dialog box appears saying the compilation is complete, choose the OK button to continue.

4. If you have chosen to confirm file conversions, you must choose the OK button when asked to confirm the conversion of the topics file to the RTF format. The compiler will open your topics file again along with the associated error file.

If there are no errors, you can try displaying the Cue Cards to see how they look. If there are errors, use the Cue Cards for the Cue Card Author to read about the errors, and then correct them in the topics file before compiling again. Follow these steps to view the compiler error notes in the Cue Card Author cue cards:

1. From the main menu choose "Create my own Cue Cards."

2. From the "Create my own Cue Cards" topic choose "Compile my Cue Cards."

3. From the "How to Compile a Cue Cards File" topic choose "Check for compiler errors."

4. From the "Check the Compiler Errors" topic choose "Common Compiler Errors and Solutions."

Displaying Your Cue Cards

The end result of the compile process is a help file with the same filename as the topics file and the .HLP extension. You can execute the WINHELP.EXE program with this file from the Program Manager or from an application like Microsoft Project.

Running Your Cue Cards in Microsoft Word 6.0

You can write a simple macro in Word to display your compiled Cue Cards while you work on the topics file. You can run the macro with the **T**ools **M**acro command or you can run it by assigning the macro to a shortcut key, a toolbar button, or a menu command.

To write the Word macro that will run your Cue Cards, follow these steps:

1. From the **T**ools menu in Word choose **M**acro. The Macro dialog box will appear (see fig. 22.56).

Fig. 22.56
Enter a name in
the Macro dialog
box for a macro
you want to create.

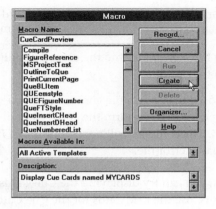

2. Type a name for your macro in the **M**acro Name box. Macro names
   must be start with a letter and must be composed of letters and numer-
   als. You may also type a comment or description in the Descri**p**tion box
   at the bottom of the dialog box as a reminder of what the macro does.

3. Choose the Cr**e**ate button to display the macro module editor (see
   fig. 22.57).

Fig. 22.57
Enter the one-line
macro at the
insertion point in
the macro module
editor.

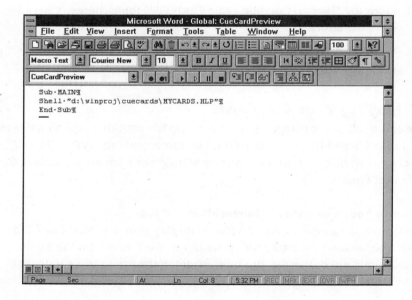

4. The insertion point will be on a blank line between the lines reading "Sub MAIN" and "End Sub." Type the following command at the insertion point, substituting the disk drive and path where you installed the cuecards directory and your own Cue Card file name for the generic "MYCARDS" used in this illustration.

```
Shell "c:\winproj\cuecards\MYCARDS.hlp"
```

5. From the **F**ile menu (or from the Control menu) choose Close.

6. Choose **Y**es in the message box to save your macro (see fig. 22.58).

Fig. 22.58
Choose Yes to save your macro.

You can run the macro, and display your Cue Cards, with these steps:

1. From the **T**ools menu choose **M**acro.

2. Select the macro name in the Macro dialog box (see fig. 22.59).

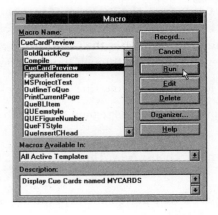

Fig. 22.59
Select the macro you created and choose the **R**un button to play it.

3. Choose the **R**un button to execute the macro.

If you want to attach your macro to a toolbar button, shortcut key, or menu command, see your Microsoft Word documentation for instructions on using the **T**ools **C**ustomize command.

Running Your Cue Cards in Microsoft Project

◀ "Creating and Using Macros," p. 597

You can display your Cue Cards from within Microsoft Project with a one-line macro command. You can attach this command to a toolbar button, to a shortcut key, or to a menu command. For instructions about using macro commands with toolbar buttons see the section "Customizing Toolbars" earlier in this chapter. For instructions about attaching macro commands to menu commands see the section "Customizing the Menu Bar" earlier in this chapter.

The macro command that follows will display the FORMS Cue Cards (the illustration set of cue cards developed in this section).

```
AppExecute command:="winhelp.exe d:\winproj\cuecards\forms.hlp"
```

You would substitute the path and filename of your compiled Cue Cards file in the statement above. The generalized statement is:

```
AppExecute command:="winhelp.exe path\filename.hlp"
```

The same macro command would be used with a custom menu item. If you want your Cue Cards to be displayed with a shortcut key, you must write a named macro that contains the single line shown above, and attach that macro to the shortcut key.

Running Your Cue Cards from the Program Manager

For users who don't know how to start Microsoft Project or open the file or template you want them to open, place the Cue Cards in a group window in the Program Manager to guide them through those opening steps.

To create a program icon to display your Cue Cards:

1. Select the group window in the Program Manager that will contain the icon.

2. From the File menu, choose New. The New Program Object dialog box appears.

3. Choose the Program Item button and then the OK button. The Program Item Properties dialog box appears.

4. Type a label for the icon in the Description field.

5. Type the name of the compiled help file. You must include its complete path. You can use the **B**rowse button to locate the file if you need to.

   The HLP file extension and the Help application file (WINHELP.EXE) must be listed in the Extensions section of your WIN.INI file for this to work.

   There is no need to fill the Working Directory field.

6. Choose the OK button to complete the icon.

Double-click the icon to display your Cue Cards.

From Here...

This chapter showed you how to customize the toolbar and the menu bar, how to create custom forms, and how to create your own customized Cue Cards.

■ If a custom form doesn't meet your needs for accessing fields, see Chapter 17, "Using and Creating Views," for details on creating custom tables to display those fields in a view.

■ See Chapter 21, "Creating and Using Macros," for information about creating macros that the toolbar buttons and menus can activate.

Chapter 23

Using Visual Basic for Applications

In the past, every program with a macro language had a different macro language than every other program. To remedy this, Microsoft has embarked on a program to replace the macro languages in all its mainstream products with a variation of Visual Basic known as Visual Basic for Applications. Visual Basic for Applications makes heavy use of OLE Automation to access and control objects in other OLE Automation VBA-compliant applications.

In this chapter, you will learn

■ How Visual Basic for Applications accesses objects.

■ How to control other programs with Visual Basic for Applications.

■ How to automate tasks with Visual Basic for Applications.

■ How to program in the Visual Basic for Applications language.

What Is Visual Basic for Applications?

Visual Basic for Applications is a programming environment based on the Visual Basic for Windows programming language. However, Visual Basic for Applications currently is fully developed in Excel, and is nearly fully developed in Microsoft Project. Microsoft Project only lacks the elaborate Visual Basic for Applications Forms Designer for creating custom forms. Project does have a custom forms capability, but it is very limited in scope compared to the full Forms creation capability available in Excel. Microsoft Word is compliant with Visual Basic for Applications, and other Microsoft products are expected to be made compliant within the next couple of years.

What's So Special About Visual Basic for Applications?

The difference between Visual Basic for Applications and other Basic programming languages is that it is object oriented. You have already seen objects being exchanged between applications in Chapter 14, "Exchanging Data with Other Applications." Project tables and Gantt Charts can be embedded into other applications such as Microsoft Word. Visual Basic for Applications takes advantage of the capability to control those objects. This capability to control another application using that other application's objects is known as OLE Automation.

Objects and Containers

The objects of Visual Basic are actually blocks of code and data, but you can visualize them as a series of containers (see figure 23.1). The largest container is the Application object. The Application object is the current program you are in, such as Project. In Project, the Application object contains other objects such as Menu objects and Project objects. Within the Project objects are Task and Resource objects. Other applications have similar objects to cover their particular needs. See the documentation and the on-line help for the other applications for a list of the objects each application contains.

Learning More with On-Line Help

Tip
The search capability in on-line help will not locate terms relating to the programming language unless you are in the language section of the on-line Help.

There is a lot more to Visual Basic for Applications than this chapter describes, especially the unique syntaxes and special options of all the commands and functions, and all the programming objects in the different applications. To learn about the details of all these functions, use the on-line help facility. Choose the **H**elp **C**ontents command and select the Visual Basic Reference section. When you are in the language section of on-line help, you can list all of the language elements, or select one of the individual language elements sections to display an alphabetical list of just those elements. You can also use the search capability to locate specific topics.

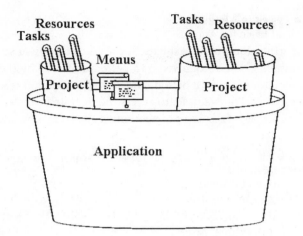

Fig. 23.1

The Visual Basic for Applications object model: containers within containers.

Understanding Objects

Visual Basic for Applications uses an object-oriented programming model. If you understand object-oriented programming (OOP), understanding its implementation in Visual Basic for Applications is easy. If you don't, don't worry—it's not as complicated as it sounds.

Visual Basic for Applications' *objects* are just a convenient way of storing and hiding data and code in a program. Instead of writing a program to manipulate some data values, you encapsulate the data and the code that manipulates that data in an object. From then on, you only have to access the object to use or display its data. You don't write code to manipulate the data—you send the object a message, and it does the work for you.

You see this capability in action when you embed an object from one application into another. The embedded object takes care of itself, and the embedding object has only to give the embedded object a place to display itself. In code, you do much the same thing. You don't try to manipulate an object's data directly, you send it messages and let it do the work.

Visual Basic for Applications' objects include such things as buttons, menu items, tasks, and resources. Most everything you can see on-screen while Project is running is an object.

Accessing Objects

To access a specific object in Visual Basic for Applications, you start with the outermost container object, followed by a period, followed by the next inner container object, followed by a period, and so forth until you reach the object you are interested in. For example, to access the field ResourceNames in a task named Stucco addition in a project named addition, you could use the following reference:

```
Application.Projects("addition").Tasks("Stucco addition"). _
    ResourceNames
```

Because Visual Basic for Applications deals with objects, any application that registers its objects with the Windows operating system makes those objects available to Visual Basic for Applications. Thus, if you are running Visual Basic for Applications in Project, you can access an object in Excel in much the same way you would if you were in Excel itself. The only difference is that you must include the name the other application used when registering itself, to specify which Application object to use. For example, you could use the following in Project to access a cell in Excel:

```
Excel.Application.Workbooks("Book2").Worksheets("Sheet3"). _
    Range("B5")
```

This reference is somewhat cumbersome, so Visual Basic for Applications makes an assumption that allows you to leave out some of these containers. For each container not included on the left side of a reference to an object (such as the Project), Visual Basic for Applications assumes that the currently active object of that type is the one being referenced.

Thus, the Application can almost always be left out, as can the project. Be careful though—be sure you know what objects are active before you leave them out of the specification. Leaving out the containers has the positive effect of making your procedures more portable. If you leave out all but the Task object, your code always applies to the currently active project, so you don't have to change the sheet name in order to apply your code to a different sheet. In addition to the named projects, tasks, and resources, you can use the objects ActiveProject, ActiveCell, or ActiveSelection to reference the currently active objects without having to know their names.

> **Note**
>
> Keep in mind that if you use specific project, resource, and task names in your proce-
> dures, the procedures will only work in those named projects, resources, and tasks.
> By leaving out parts of an object's specification, you make your code applicable to all
> objects of the class you left out.

Understanding Classes and Collections

A *class* of objects is a reference to a general type or classification of objects.
In Visual Basic for Applications, for example, each task in a project is a Task
object, which is an instance of the Task class.

If you combine all the objects of a specific class into a group, that group is
known as a *collection*. Thus, all the projects in the Application object are in
the collection Projects, and all the tasks in a project are in the collection
Tasks.

Accessing Collections

Collections are how you access most objects. To access a specific member of a
collection, follow the collection name by either a string containing the object
name or an integer in parentheses. Thus, `Tasks("Stucco addition")` refers to
the task named `Stucco addition`, and `Tasks(3)` refers to the second task in
the collection of all tasks in the active project. For example, if you want to
access the third task in a project named `Book2`, you could use the following
reference:

```
Projects("Book2").Tasks(3)
```

If you leave out the number and parentheses in the reference to a collection,
the reference is to all the members of the collection.

> **Caution**
>
> Be careful when using numbers to select objects in a collection. If you add or delete
> members from a collection, the numbering of all the other members of that collec-
> tion can change, and your number may select a different object.

Understanding Properties

An object contains data, and data that you can access from the outside of an object is a *property* of that object. Most properties are readable, but not all can be written or changed. See the Visual Basic Reference section of on-line help for a description of each of the properties. In the description of each object is a list of the properties that apply to it.

In the tables in Project, each row is an object, and each column is a property. Thus, for a Task or Resource object (a row), all of the fields are properties. Fields such as the Resource names field are read/write properties; but calculated fields, such as Work, are read only. Properties can refer to the direct data contained in an object, such as the value of a field, or to data values that control how an object looks and behaves, such as color.

Property values can be strings of text, numbers, logicals (True or False), or enumerated lists. An *enumerated list* is a numbered list of options, where the number is used to select a specific option. For example, the Color property of most objects is an enumerated list where 0 is none, 1 is black, 2 is white, 3 is red, 4 is green, 5 is blue, and so forth. For the enumerated lists, Visual Basic for Applications and the other compliant applications in the Microsoft Office contain lists of predefined constants to use in place of the numbers.

Using the constants is much more informative than using the numbers. The constants that are applicable to a property are listed in the description of the property in on-line help. You can get a list of constants by searching for "constants" or "variables" in the on-line help and selecting the "Variables and Constants Keywords Summary," and "Visual Basic Constants" topics. You can also use the Object Browser (described in this chapter) to search the MSProject and VBA libraries for the Constants object.

Accessing Properties

The easiest way to see what properties to set and what values to set them to is to start Project's Macro Recorder, perform whatever changes you want to perform, turn off the recorder, and then copy the recorded property changes into your program.

The syntax for accessing an object's properties is

```
object.property
```

where *object* is the object whose properties you want to change or view, and *property* is the name of the property. If the preceding construct is on the right side of a statement, you are reading the value of the property from the object. If the construct is on the left side of a statement, you are setting the value of the property. For example, to set the value of the ResourceNames property of task Stucco addition to Zachary, you could use the statement

```
Application.Projects("addition").Tasks("Stucco addition"). _
    ResourceNames = "Zachary"
```

To read the same property and store it in the variable theResource, you could use the statement

```
theResource = Application.Projects("addition"). _
    Tasks("Stucco addition").ResourceNames
```

The rules concerning omitting container objects (described previously) apply here. Because you must include an object with the property, you cannot leave off the Task object to get the Resource names in whatever task is the active task. For these and similar cases involving other objects, there are some special properties that return the currently active or selected object. Table 23.1 lists these special properties. For example, the formula necessary to get the first resource name in the Stucco addition task in the Addition project, you could use the statement

```
theResource = Application.Projects("Addition"). _
    Tasks("Stucco addition").ResourceNames(1)
```

If Addition and Stucco addition are the currently active project and task, you could use

```
theResource = ActiveCell.Resource.ResourceNames(1)
```

If Addition is the active project but Stucco addition is not necessarily the active task you could use

```
theResource = ActiveProject.Tasks("Stucco addition"). _
    ResourceNames(1)
```

If you wanted to access the `Resource Names` field on whatever task is active in the `Addition` project, you could use

```
theResource = Projects("Addition").ActiveCell.Task.ResourceNames(1)
```

Everything to the left of the last period must evaluate to an object or a collection of objects.

Table 23.1	Special Properties That Return the Active Objects
Property	**Description**
ActiveCell	The active cell on the active window
ActiveProject	The active project
ActiveSelection	The active selection
ActivePane	The active pane when the window is split
ActiveWindow	The active window, the window on top
Selection	The currently selected object

Understanding Methods

Visual Basic for Applications *methods* are the blocks of code stored in an object that know how to manipulate the object's data. For the `Task` object, for example, the `GetField` method returns the contents of any selected field in the task, and the `Delete` method removes the task from the Tasks collection. As opposed to Properties, which set values, methods do things to objects and the data they contain. To learn more about the specifics of different methods, and to find out what methods apply to what objects, see the Visual Basic Reference section of on-line help. You can also use the Object Browser to see what methods are available for what objects.

Accessing Methods

You access or execute an object's methods in nearly exactly the same way that you access an object's properties. The main difference is that a property is always accessed as part of a formula, but a method need only be part of a formula if it returns a value. For example, the `Resources` method returns a collection containing all the resources in a task. To use it to set the `Cost/Use` property of all the resources in the currently selected tasks to 20, use a formula like the following:

```
Selection.Resources.CostPerUse = 20
```

To get the number of resources in the currently selected tasks, you could use the `Resources` method to return a collection and the `Count` property to return the number of items in the collection:

```
numRes = Selection.Resources.Count
```

Some methods require arguments to make them work. For example, the `GetField` method needs an argument to tell it which field to return. If the method is part of a formula, the arguments must go in parentheses. For example, to get the contents of the third field in task 2, you could use

```
theValue = ActiveProject.Tasks(2).GetField(3)
```

If the method is just being executed, and is not part of a formula, place the arguments to the right of the reference to the method. For example, to use the `Add` method to insert a new resource named Inspectors into the Resources collection, you could use

```
ActiveProject.Resources.Add "Inspectors"
```

Finding Objects with the Object Browser

With all these objects floating around, keeping track of all the names, what properties go with what methods, and what objects are contained in what applications becomes difficult and confusing. The on-line help is a good reference for the objects and methods in the current application. However, to see what applications have made their objects available by registering them with the Windows operating system, use the Object Browser.

Before you can use the Object Browser, you must register any external object libraries (other OLE compliant applications) with Project. To register the external libraries, first open any module with the **T**ools **M**acros command. Choose the **T**ools Re**f**erences command, and the dialog box shown in figure

23.2 appears. In the dialog box, check the check boxes for the object libraries you want to register with Project and choose OK. As more applications support OLE Automation, they will also appear in the References list.

Fig. 23.2
Use the References dialog box to register other object libraries with Project.

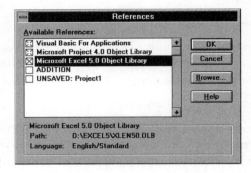

To use the Object Browser, choose the **V**iew **O**bject Browser command. The Object Browser dialog box appears, as shown in figure 23.3. In the **L**ibraries/Projects: box at the top, you select the object library you want to examine, such as Project, VBA (Visual Basic for Applications), any external libraries registered with Project using the References dialog box, or any open projects.

Fig. 23.3
The Object Browser with the Project object library selected. Within the library, the Task object and its GetField method are also selected. The syntax of the GetField method is shown at the bottom.

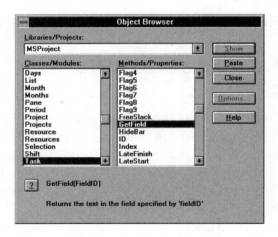

If you select Project, as shown in the figure, all the objects and modules contained in Project appear in the **C**lasses/Modules window on the left. If you select one of the classes, such as the Task class, all the properties and methods appear in the **M**ethods/Properties window on the right. If you select one of the methods or properties, such as GetField, the method—along with its syntax—appears at the bottom. If you press the button with the question mark on it at the bottom left of the window, you are taken directly to the online help topic explaining that method or property. If you select the Paste button, the selected object or method is inserted in the active module at the current insertion point.

Creating Procedures with the Macro Recorder

The best way to learn to use Visual Basic for Applications in Microsoft Project is to create procedures for it using Excel's Macro Recorder. With Project, however, the recorded procedures are still created in a variation of the Project macro language rather than in object-oriented Visual Basic. The macro language commands were added to the Visual Basic for Applications language by attaching them as methods to the Application object. When used, these methods often change the values of task and resource properties, which is not in the purview of the application object, but is the job of the task or resource object being changed.

With that in mind, record some additions to a project and compare the differences between the macro language and Visual Basic. When you turn on the Macro Recorder and create or change a project, the recorder writes code that performs the same actions you are performing by hand.

In the following sections, you record the completion of a project by adding the last few tasks and resources. The project concerns building an addition on a house, and is already mostly complete as shown in figure 23.4.

Starting the Recorder

To actually do this example, you need a partially completed project to which you can add some tasks. Pick any existing project you have available, or create one using figure 23.4 as a guide.

Fig. 23.4
The partially completed Add Addition project.

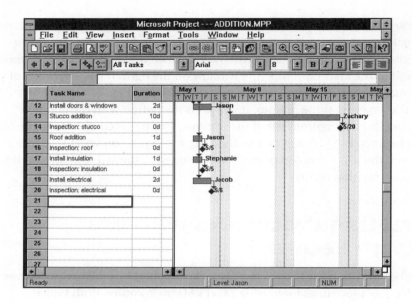

To display the Record New Macro dialog box, follow these steps:

1. Open a project to add tasks to or create one similar to figure 23.4.

2. Display the Record Macro dialog box shown in figure 23.5 by choosing the **T**ools **R**ecord Macro command and then clicking the **O**ptions button.

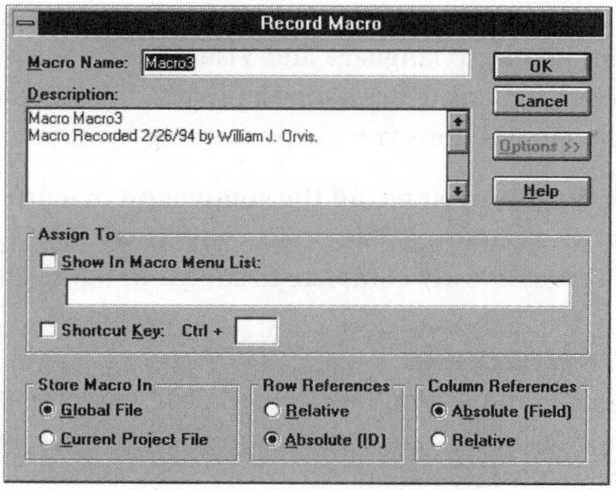

Fig. 23.5
The Record Macro dialog box enables you to set the name and other options for a new procedure.

The Record Macro dialog box, shown in figure 23.5, is where you set the options for the Macro Recorder. You name your macro and add a description for it in the **M**acro Name and **D**escription fields. Including a good, brief description here is important if you intend to keep this macro for more than a few days. If you do not use a good description, you probably will not remember which macro does what the next time you need some capability.

In the Assign To box, you attach the new macro to the Tools menu, or add a Shortcut **K**ey. You do not have to attach a macro to anything, because you can always run it by using the **T**ools **M**acro command. You should only attach macros that you use all the time so you can access them quickly. Also, you do not need to attach the macro now. You can come back later and attach the macro to a menu or button using the **T**ools **M**acro command.

In the Store Macro In box, you specify a place to put this new macro. If you select **G**lobal File, Project attaches the macro to a module attached to Project. Thus, the macro becomes a global macro that is available to all open projects. The **C**urrent Project File option places the macro in a new module attached to the current project.

The Row References and Column References boxes determine how references to rows and columns are stored in the macro. If the **R**elative options are selected, the references are written relative to the currently selected row or column. Use these options when you are applying formatting with a procedure, and you want the procedure to apply to the current selection or to a row or column with a position that is relative to the current selection. Use the **A**bsolute options to have the row reference apply to a specific task ID and the column reference apply to a specific field, no matter what the current selection is.

To fill in the dialog box and start the Macro Recorder, follow these steps:

1. In the **M**acro Name field, type **CompleteProject**.

2. In the **D**escription field, type **Complete the Add Addition project**.

3. Set the Row References to **A**bsolute, set the Column References to A**b**solute, and click OK.

The **T**ools **R**ecord Macro command has changed to **T**ools Stop **R**ecorder, and the Macro Recorder has started recording what you do. It records all your keystrokes and mouse clicks until you select the **T**ools Stop **R**ecorder command.

Recording a Procedure

You now create the procedure by simply changing the project manually as you would normally do. To add three tasks to the project, follow these steps:

1. Open the Gantt chart view and select the first empty Task Name field (row 21 on figure 23.4). Type **Drywall addition.**

2. Select the duration field to its right and type **10**.

3. Select the next empty Task Name field (row 22) and type **Inspection: drywall**.

4. Select the Duration field to its right and type **0**.

5. Select the next empty Task Name field (row 23), and type **Inspection: final**.

6. Select the Duration field to its right and type **0**.

 7. Select rows 20 and 21, and click the Link Tasks button on the standard toolbar.

8. Select rows 18 and 21, and click the Link Tasks button on the standard toolbar.

> **Note**
>
> To select two nonadjacent rows, select the first row, hold down the Ctrl key, and click the second row.

9. Select rows 12 and 21, and click the Link Tasks button on the standard toolbar.

10. Select rows 21 and 22, and click the Link Tasks button on the standard toolbar.

11. Select rows 22 and 23, and click the Link Tasks button on the standard toolbar.

12. Select rows 18 and 23, and click the Link Tasks button on the standard toolbar.

13. Select rows 16 and 23, and click the Link Tasks button on the standard toolbar.

14. Select rows 14 and 23, and click the Link Tasks button on the standard toolbar.

15. Select row 21, scroll to the Resource Names field, and type **Greg**.

16. Choose the **V**iew Resource **S**heet command and find the row with Greg in the Resource Name field.

17. Select the Cost/Use field and type **1500**.

Stopping the Recorder

Stopping the recorder is easy—just select the **T**ools Stop **R**ecorder command. Switch back to the Gantt Chart view, and your project should look like figure 23.6, with the three new tasks added to the project.

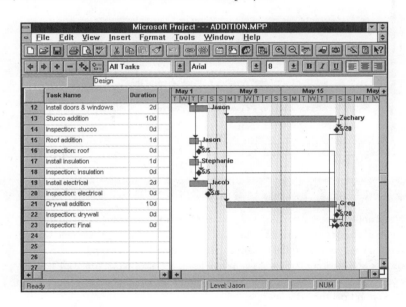

IV

Project Interface

Fig. 23.6
The Add Addition project with three new tasks added at the end.

Restarting the Recorder

To add to a previously recorded procedure, record a new macro and copy its contents to the previously recorded macro.

Examining the Procedure

To examine your newly created procedure, choose the Tools Macros command, select the CompleteProject macro from the list in the Macros dialog box and click the Edit button. Your procedure appears on-screen and looks like figure 23.7.

Fig. 23.7
The Macro Recorder places the recorded commands in a new module as shown here for the CompleteProject procedure.

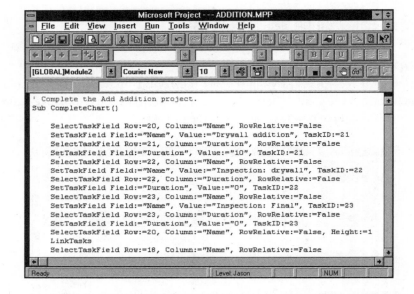

> ### Note
>
> This example was created using the mouse to select tasks and fields. If you use the arrow keys to step over to a particular field instead of using the mouse, you will see a lot more lines containing the `SelectTaskField` or `SelectResourceField` methods. These lines occur because as you step, using the arrow keys, from one field to another, you select every field in between. Using a mouse, you directly select a field, so you don't get the extra lines.

The listing of the procedure is:

```
' Complete the Add Addition project.
Sub CompleteProject()
SelectTaskField Row:=21, Column:="Name", RowRelative:=False
    SetTaskField Field:="Name", Value:="Drywall addition",
```

```
TaskID:=21
    SelectTaskField Row:=21, Column:="Duration", RowRelative:=False
    SetTaskField Field:="Duration", Value:="10", TaskID:=21
    SelectTaskField Row:=22, Column:="Name", RowRelative:=False
    SetTaskField Field:="Name", Value:="Inspection: drywall",
TaskID:=22
    SelectTaskField Row:=22, Column:="Duration", RowRelative:=False
    SetTaskField Field:="Duration", Value:="0", TaskID:=22
    SelectTaskField Row:=23, Column:="Name", RowRelative:=False
    SetTaskField Field:="Name", Value:="Inspection: Final",
TaskID:=23
    SelectTaskField Row:=23, Column:="Duration", RowRelative:=False
    SetTaskField Field:="Duration", Value:="0", TaskID:=23
    SelectTaskField Row:=20, Column:="Name", RowRelative:=False,
Height:=1
    LinkTasks
    SelectTaskField Row:=18, Column:="Name", RowRelative:=False
    SelectTaskField Row:=21, Column:="Name", RowRelative:=False,
Add:=True
    LinkTasks
    SelectTaskField Row:=12, Column:="Name", RowRelative:=False
    SelectTaskField Row:=21, Column:="Name", RowRelative:=False,
Add:=True
    LinkTasks
    SelectTaskField Row:=21, Column:="Name", RowRelative:=False,
Height:=1
    LinkTasks
    SelectTaskField Row:=22, Column:="Name", RowRelative:=False,
Height:=1
    LinkTasks
    SelectTaskField Row:=18, Column:="Name", RowRelative:=False
    SelectTaskField Row:=23, Column:="Name", RowRelative:=False,
Add:=True
    LinkTasks
    SelectTaskField Row:=16, Column:="Name", RowRelative:=False
    SelectTaskField Row:=23, Column:="Name", RowRelative:=False,
Add:=True
    LinkTasks
    SelectTaskField Row:=14, Column:="Name", RowRelative:=False
    SelectTaskField Row:=23, Column:="Name", RowRelative:=False,
Add:=True
    LinkTasks
    SelectTaskField Row:=21, Column:="Resource Names",
RowRelative:=False
    SetTaskField Field:="Resource Names", Value:="Greg", TaskID:=21
    ViewApply Name:="Resource &Sheet"
    SelectResourceField Row:=8, Column:="Cost Per Use",
RowRelative:=False
    SetResourceField Field:="Cost Per Use", Value:="1500",
ResourceID:=8
End Sub
```

If you examine this listing and compare it to the steps you just took, you see that each step results in one or more lines of code inserted in the procedure. The procedure appears in color, with comments in green, keywords in blue, and everything else in black. Along the top of the procedure window is the Visual Basic toolbar. The tool bar can be floating, or can be docked at the bottom or top as shown in the figure. To dock the toolbar, simply drag it to the top (or bottom) of the screen and release it. The function of each button on the toolbar is shown in figure 23.8.

Fig. 23.8
The Visual Basic toolbar contains controls for executing and debugging a program.

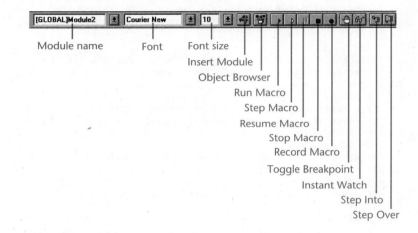

Module name   Font   Font size
                         Insert Module
                         Object Browser
                         Run Macro
                         Step Macro
                         Resume Macro
                         Stop Macro
                         Record Macro
                         Toggle Breakpoint
                         Instant Watch
                         Step Into
                         Step Over

Running the Procedure

To run this procedure, select the Gantt chart view again and delete the last three tasks. Choose the **T**ools **M**acro command. The Macro dialog box shown in figure 23.9 appears, showing all procedures available in this project and on the GLOBAL template. In the dialog box, select the CompleteProject procedure and choose **R**un. The procedure then makes the same additions to the project that you made by hand.

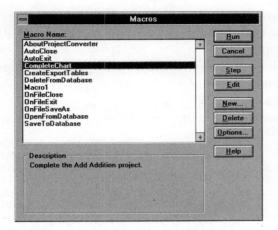

Fig. 23.9
The Macro dialog box allows you to select and execute procedures. The dialog box also provides an easy way to locate, edit, or delete procedures.

Understanding the Procedure

Now go back and take a closer look at the listing of the procedure by choosing the **T**ools **M**acros command, selecting the CompleteProject procedure, and clicking Edit. The first line of the procedure is a comment. Comments are completely ignored by an executing procedure, and can contain any text. Any text following a single quotation mark is a comment, and comments can appear at the beginning of a line, or to the right of any valid Visual Basic for Applications statement.

```
' Complete the Add Addition project.
```

Following the comments is the procedure header, which names the procedure:

```
Sub CompleteProject()
```

Following the procedure header are six pairs of statements that alternately select a field and insert a value into that field. The SelectTaskField method selects a Task field in the current project. The two named arguments Row and Column select the task and the field. The argument RowRelative specifies if the Row argument is relative or absolute. The default is relative, so the RowRelative:=False argument is needed to make it absolute. If RowRelative were omitted or True, the selection would be calculated relative to the current selection.

The `SetTaskField` method changes the contents of a field of a task. As you can see, both the row (`TaskID`) and column (`Field`) are specified in these statements, so the `SelectTaskField` statements could be removed and this procedure would still work. The `Value` argument specifies what to insert into the field.

```
    SelectTaskField Row:=20, Column:="Name", RowRelative:=False
    SetTaskField Field:="Name", Value:="Drywall addition",
TaskID:=21
    SelectTaskField Row:=21, Column:="Duration", RowRelative:=False
    SetTaskField Field:="Duration", Value:="10", TaskID:=21
    SelectTaskField Row:=22, Column:="Name", RowRelative:=False
    SetTaskField Field:="Name", Value:="Inspection: drywall",
TaskID:=22
    SelectTaskField Row:=22, Column:="Duration", RowRelative:=False
    SetTaskField Field:="Duration", Value:="0", TaskID:=22
    SelectTaskField Row:=23, Column:="Name", RowRelative:=False
    SetTaskField Field:="Name", Value:="Inspection: Final",
TaskID:=23
    SelectTaskField Row:=23, Column:="Duration", RowRelative:=False
    SetTaskField Field:="Duration", Value:="0", TaskID:=23
```

The next statements select and link the different tasks. The `SelectTaskField` method is used again to select some tasks to link. First, rows 20 and 21 are selected. The `Height:=1` argument indicates that two rows are selected: row 20, plus the one below it. The `LinkTasks` method then links the currently selected tasks. The next two selections select rows 18 and 21. The `Add:=True` argument on the second `SelectTaskField` method indicates that its selection is to be added to the current selection. The `Height` argument cannot be used here because it would select all the statements between 18 and 21 as well, and link them. The other links follow in the same way.

```
    SelectTaskField Row:=20, Column:="Name", RowRelative:=False,
Height:=1
    LinkTasks
    SelectTaskField Row:=18, Column:="Name", RowRelative:=False
    SelectTaskField Row:=21, Column:="Name", RowRelative:=False,
Add:=True
    LinkTasks
    SelectTaskField Row:=12, Column:="Name", RowRelative:=False
    SelectTaskField Row:=21, Column:="Name", RowRelative:=False,
Add:=True
    LinkTasks
    SelectTaskField Row:=21, Column:="Name", RowRelative:=False,
Height:=1
    LinkTasks
    SelectTaskField Row:=22, Column:="Name", RowRelative:=False,
Height:=1
    LinkTasks
    SelectTaskField Row:=18, Column:="Name", RowRelative:=False
    SelectTaskField Row:=23, Column:="Name", RowRelative:=False,
```

```
Add:=True
    LinkTasks
    SelectTaskField Row:=16, Column:="Name", RowRelative:=False
    SelectTaskField Row:=23, Column:="Name", RowRelative:=False,
Add:=True
    LinkTasks
    SelectTaskField Row:=14, Column:="Name", RowRelative:=False
    SelectTaskField Row:=23, Column:="Name", RowRelative:=False,
Add:=True
    LinkTasks
```

The next two lines select the Resource Names field and insert the name Greg there. Again, the SetTaskField method could be used alone here and the procedure would still work.

```
    SelectTaskField Row:=21, Column:="Resource Names",
RowRelative:=False
    SetTaskField Field:="Resource Names", Value:="Greg", TaskID:=21
```

The ViewApply method changes to the view specified with the Name argument. Here, the Resource Sheet view is selected.

```
    ViewApply Name:="Resource &Sheet"
```

The next two statements select and insert a value in a resource field. Note that the SelectResourceField and the SetResourceField methods work exactly the same as the SelectTaskField and SetTaskField statements, but apply to the Resource list instead of to the Task list.

```
    SelectResourceField Row:=8, Column:="Cost Per Use",
RowRelative:=False
    SetResourceField Field:="Cost Per Use", Value:="1500",
ResourceID:=8
```

The last statement in the procedure is the procedure footer, which marks the end of the procedure.

```
    End Sub
```

Performing the Same Task with Visual Basic for Applications

Now look at the same procedure written with object-oriented Visual Basic for Applications. The listing of the Visual Basic version of the procedure follows.

```
    '
    ' Complete the Add Addition project.
    ' Visual Basic for Applications version.
    '
    Sub CompleteProject2()
      'Add 3 new tasks and durations.
      ActiveProject.Tasks.Add "Drywall addition"
      ActiveProject.Tasks("Drywall addition").Duration = "10"
```

```
ActiveProject.Tasks.Add "Inspection: drywall"
ActiveProject.Tasks("Inspection: drywall").Duration = "0"
ActiveProject.Tasks.Add "Inspection: Final"
ActiveProject.Tasks("Inspection: Final").Duration = "0"
'Link the three tasks to their predecessors.
ActiveProject.Tasks("Drywall addition").Predecessors = _
    Str(ActiveProject.Tasks("Inspection: electrical").ID) & "," & _
    Str(ActiveProject.Tasks("Inspection: insulation").ID) & "," & _
    Str(ActiveProject.Tasks("Install doors & windows").ID)
ActiveProject.Tasks("Inspection: drywall").Predecessors = _
    Str(ActiveProject.Tasks("Drywall Addition").ID)
ActiveProject.Tasks("Inspection: Final").Predecessors = _
    Str(ActiveProject.Tasks("Inspection: drywall").ID) & "," & _
    Str(ActiveProject.Tasks("Inspection: insulation").ID) & "," & _
    Str(ActiveProject.Tasks("Inspection: roof").ID) & "," & _
    Str(ActiveProject.Tasks("Inspection: stucco").ID)
'Set the resource name for the drywalling.
ActiveProject.Tasks("Drywall addition").ResourceNames = "Greg"
'Switch to the resource sheet view.
ViewApply Name:="Resource &Sheet"
'Set the cost for the resource.
ActiveProject.Resources("Greg").CostPerUse = 1500
End Sub
```

> **Note**
>
> The space-underscore (_) at the end of several of the lines in this procedure is the
> Visual Basic for Applications line-continuation character. To make long lines fit on the
> screen, split the lines at a convenient place and insert space-underscore at the split to
> indicate that the current line is joined to the one that follows.

As you examine this procedure, you will see the object-orientedness of the
code. As before, there are comments at the beginning that indicate what this
procedure does. Since it was written by a human instead of a machine, there
are a lot more comments in the body of the procedure, explaining what each
part does:

```
'
' Complete the Add Addition project.
' Visual Basic for Applications version.
'
```

Following the comments is the procedure header, which is identical to that in
the previous version, except that the name has been changed to avoid confusion with the previous procedure.

```
Sub CompleteProject2()
```

The three tasks and durations are added using the Tasks collection instead of the SetTaskField application command. First the Add method is applied to the Tasks collection to add a new member to the collection with the indicated name. This step adds the new task and fills in the Task Name field. The second statement in each pair uses the Tasks collection again, but with the field name as an argument to select a specific task. The Duration property of the selected task is then set to the required value. This step fills in the Duration field. You could use the ID numbers of the three tasks (21, 22, and 23) to specify the task in the Tasks collection, but using the name ensures that you get the correct task, and makes the code more readable.

```
'Add 3 new tasks and durations.
ActiveProject.Tasks.Add "Drywall addition"
ActiveProject.Tasks("Drywall addition").Duration = "10"
ActiveProject.Tasks.Add "Inspection: drywall"
ActiveProject.Tasks("Inspection: drywall").Duration = "0"
ActiveProject.Tasks.Add "Inspection: Final"
ActiveProject.Tasks("Inspection: Final").Duration = "0"
```

The next three statements set the predecessors for the three new tasks. The predecessor's field and property contain the task ID numbers for the tasks linked to the indicated task. The Str() function is used to convert the ID number into a string, and the balance of the string combines those numbers separated by commas. These strings are then equated to the Predecessors property of the selected Task object.

```
'Link the three tasks to their predecessors.
ActiveProject.Tasks("Drywall addition").Predecessors = _
    Str(ActiveProject.Tasks("Inspection: electrical").ID) & "," & _
    Str(ActiveProject.Tasks("Inspection: insulation").ID) & "," & _
    Str(ActiveProject.Tasks("Install doors & windows").ID)
ActiveProject.Tasks("Inspection: drywall").Predecessors = _
    Str(ActiveProject.Tasks("Drywall Addition").ID)
ActiveProject.Tasks("Inspection: Final").Predecessors = _
    Str(ActiveProject.Tasks("Inspection: drywall").ID) & "," & _
    Str(ActiveProject.Tasks("Inspection: insulation").ID) & "," & _
    Str(ActiveProject.Tasks("Inspection: roof").ID) & "," & _
    Str(ActiveProject.Tasks("Inspection: stucco").ID)
```

The next statement inserts the resource name Greg into the ResourceNames property of the selected Task object. This fills in the Resource Name field.

```
'Set the resource name for the drywalling.
ActiveProject.Tasks("Drywall addition").ResourceNames = "Greg"
```

These last few statements switch to the Resource View, select the Greg resource, and set the Cost/Use field to $1,500.

```
    'Switch to the resource sheet view.
    ViewApply Name:="Resource &Sheet"
    'Set the cost for the resource.
    ActiveProject.Resources("Greg").CostPerUse = 1500
End Sub
```

As you can see, in the object-oriented style of programming, each object is selected from its container object, and the values of the objects are changed locally, in the object itself—rather than from above by the application.

Understanding Functions and Procedures

A procedure is the smallest programming object in Visual Basic for Applications. There are two types of procedures in Visual Basic for Applications: Sub procedures and Function procedures.

Sub Procedures

Sub procedures are generally just called procedures. Sub procedures can be sent arguments and can change those arguments. The syntax of a procedure is as follows.

```
Sub procedurename()
    .
' Procedure Body
    .
End Sub
```

Sub procedures always start with a procedure header that starts with the keyword Sub, followed by the procedure name and parentheses. The names of any arguments to be passed to the procedure are placed between the parentheses. Arguments are the data values that a calling procedure is passing to this procedure to work on. They can also contain the values that a procedure is passing back to the procedure that called it. Sub procedures must end with the End Sub procedure footer. Between the procedure header and footer is the procedure body, which can contain declarations, statements, and commands that the procedure executes. You execute sub procedures by selecting them in the Macro dialog box, calling them from another procedure, or pressing a button or other object to which the procedure is attached.

For example, a simple procedure for calculating the tax on an item could be written as follows.

```
' Calculate the tax on an item.
'
Sub GetTax(Cost As Currency, Tax As Currency)
   Const TaxRate = 0.0825
   Tax = Cost * TaxRate
End Sub
```

This procedure is passed the cost of an item, and it calculates the tax on that cost by multiplying it times the tax rate. The calculated tax is then passed back to the calling program in the second argument. The As Currency clauses that follow the argument names in the procedure header indicate the type of data the argument contains. Data types are discussed later in this chapter.

Note

In the GetTax procedure, the constant TaxRate is defined in the procedure using the Const declaration, and then the constant is used in place of the actual number. While this may seem like a needless step, it makes the procedure much more readable. In addition to improving the readability, constants make procedures easier to maintain, as you need only to change the value of a constant to change its value everywhere it is used in a procedure. If you define constants at the top of the module, they are available in every procedure within that module.

User-Defined Functions

Function procedures are very similar to Sub procedures, except that the function's name returns a value. Functions have a procedure header and footer similar to that used for Sub procedures, and they must assign a value to the procedure name before completing.

```
Function functionname()

'   function body

   functionname = value
End Function
```

For example, the following procedure performs the same calculation as the previous example, but does it as a function. The function accepts the cost of an item as an argument. It then calculates and returns the tax on that cost in the function's name.

```
'
' Calculate the tax on an item.
'
Function theTax(Cost As Currency) As Currency
  Const TaxRate = 0.0825
  theTax = Cost * TaxRate
End Function
```

As with the Sub procedure version of this program, the data type of the arguments is specified with an As Currency clause. In addition, the data type of the function itself is specified with an As Currency clause on the right. The function just defined can then be used in another procedure where the tax on an item is needed.

For example, a procedure that uses the theTax function to increase the CostPerUse of a resource by the tax on that cost could be written as follows:

```
'
' Increase the cost per use by the tax.
'
Sub AddTax()
  ActiveCell.Resource.CostPerUse = ActiveCell.Resource.CostPerUse + _
    theTax(ActiveCell.Resource.CostPerUse)
End Sub
```

A cell in a resource view must be selected in order for this to work. The ActiveCell object must be a cell on the row containing the resource you want to change. The Resource property of the ActiveCell returns the resource object containing the ActiveCell. This may seem like a backward reaching reference, since it would seem that a cell should be contained in a resource and not the other way around. However, it works because the ActiveCell is contained in the Application object and not in the active project. This is because the application takes care of activating and deactivating objects. The Resource then follows from this ActiveCell.

Understanding Variables and Assignment Statements

Variables are named places in memory for storing data. Like naming cells on a worksheet, using variables to name storage locations in memory makes a program much more readable. You don't have to explicitly name a specific location in memory to use a variable—Visual Basic for Applications takes care of that for you. Simply using a name in a formula causes Visual Basic for Applications to define storage for it. Once defined, you can use a variable in assignment statements to store data.

An *assignment statement* consists of a variable or property name on the left, an equals sign, and a constant value or formula on the right. A formula can consist of a single constant value or a mixture of variables, constants, mathematical operators, and functions. The following are all assignment statements:

```
myName = ActiveCell.Task(3).Name
Selection.Resources.CostPerUse = 20
myVariable = 17
someThing = Log(3.5)
yourVariable = myVariable * 33
```

Creating an Application

Now that you know all about objects, properties, and methods, you can start putting some of that together to create a simple application. The application you are going to create is a scanner for locating overallocated resources. The program searches all the resources in the current project, and displays a dialog box when it finds an overallocated resource. It then gives you the option of searching for the next overallocated resource, or of opening the resource sheet and selecting the overallocated resource.

To create the procedure, perform the following steps:

1. Select the **T**ools **M**acro command and click the **N**ew button to insert a new module.

2. In the dialog box that appears, name the procedure **FindOverallocated**, insert the description **Find overallocated resources and switch to the resource.**, and click OK.

3. Type the procedure in the following listing into the module.

```
Option Explicit
'
'  Find overallocated resources and switch to the resource.
'
Sub FindOverallocated()
  Dim NumRes As Integer, I As Integer
  Dim Answer As Integer, aMsg As String
  NumRes = ActiveProject.Resources.Count   'Get the number of
resources.
  For I = 1 To NumRes  'Loop over all the resources in the active
  'project. Check each resource to see if it is overallocated.
    If ActiveProject.Resources(I).Overallocated = True Then
      'If it is overallocated, tell the user and ask if he wants to
      'see the resource or look for another.
      aMsg = ActiveProject.Resources(I).Name & _
        " is over allocated, switch to Resource Sheet?"
      Answer = MsgBox(aMsg, vbYesNo, "Overallocation")
      If Answer = vbYes Then 'See if the user answered yes.
        'If the user answered yes, then switch to the resource
        'sheet, select the overallocated resource, and quit.
        ViewApply Name:="Resource &Sheet"
        SelectResourceField Row:=I, Column:="Name",
RowRelative:=False
        Exit Sub
      End If
      'If the answer was no, then look for another overallocated
      'resource.
    End If
  Next I
  MsgBox "Search complete.", , "Overallocation"
End Sub
```

4. Execute the **T**ools **M**acros command again, select the FindOverallocated procedure, and click the Options button.

5. In the Options dialog box, check the **S**how in Macro Menu List check box, and type the menu name **Find O&verallocated**. This menu item is now at the bottom of the Tools menu, and is linked to the FindOverallocated procedure. The ampersand (&) in the name makes the following character (in this case "v") the speed key for selecting the command from the keyboard.

6. Select the **T**ools Find O**v**erallocated command. If a resource is overallocated, the dialog box shown in figure 23.10 appears giving you the option of looking for another overallocated resource or switching to the one the procedure has found.

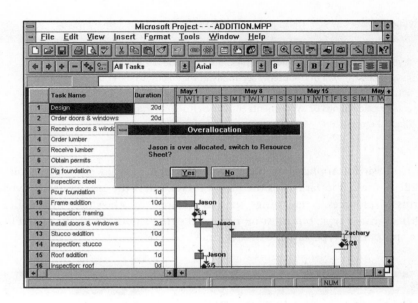

Fig. 23.10

The dialog box that appears when an overallocated resource is found.

Using Declarations and Visual Basic for Applications Data Types

Not all data values are the same type in Visual Basic for Applications. If you don't declare any variables, then all variables have a data type of Variant. The Variant type is useful because it can store anything from strings to pictures to floating point numbers. The problem with a Variant type variable is that in order to be able to hold anything, it must check every time to see what kind of data is being stored in it—and have a lot of memory available to store it. Thus a variable of the Variant data type wastes time and memory. For a few small items, this waste won't matter, but it becomes important if you are storing many data items.

If you declare the type of a variable before you use it, Visual Basic for Applications does not have to check every time to see what it is, and then reserve space for it. If it is declared, the type is known, and the space is reserved ahead of time. Another reason to declare all variables is to help ensure that you have not misspelled something, creating a program *bug*. Visual Basic for Applications does not force you to declare everything, but you can do it yourself by placing an Option Explicit at the top of a module (see the start of the previous listing). If you do this, Visual Basic for Applications forces you to explicitly declare the data type of every variable in that module before you use it.

> **Note**
>
> If you have not yet encountered a program bug, you are living a charmed life. But, never fear, you will undoubtedly see many in the near future. A bug in a program is actually an error of some sort caused by using improper syntax (syntax errors), improper calculations or assignments (runtime errors), or improper program logic (logical errors).

Visual Basic for Applications has several built-in data types, shown in Table 23.2. Of these, the Variant is the most general, but is the least conservative in terms of resources. A few things, such as pictures, must be stored in variables with a Variant type, but most numeric and string values should be stored in the appropriate type variable to save time and space.

Table 23.2 The Built-In Data Types in Visual Basic for Applications.

Data Type	Size (bytes)	Digits	Range
Boolean	2	1	True or False
Integer	2	5	-32,768 to 32,767
Long	4	10	-2,147,483,648 to 2,147,483,647
Single	4	7	-3.402E38 to 3.402E38
Double	8	15	-1.797E308 to 1.797E308
Currency	8	19	-9.22E14 to 9.22e14
Date	8		1/1/100 to 12/31/9999
String	1 per character + 1		
Object	4		
Array	Depends on type and number of elements.		
Variant	Depends on the type of data stored in it.		

To declare the type of a variable, use the Dim statement. At the top of a procedure or module, type the keyword Dim followed by a variable name, and then type the keyword As followed by the variable's data type. If the type is not specified, the variable is the `Variant` type. You can put more than one variable type declaration on a single line, separated by commas. The following are all variable declaration statements:

```
Dim theProject As Object
Dim OutputRange As Object
Dim theItem As String, theCost As Currency
Dim theRow As Integer, NumItems As Integer
```

Variables passed as arguments to a procedure are declared in the procedure header. For example, the following procedure header defines the arguments being passed to a procedure as an integer and a string:

```
Sub myProcedure(aVariable As Integer, AnotherVariable As String)
```

The type of value returned by a function procedure is declared by placing the type at the right side of the function header. For example, the following function takes a `Single` type value as an argument and returns a `Double` type value.

```
Function myFunction(aVariable As Single) As Double
```

Arrays

Arrays are not really a new data-type, but are lists of one of the existing types, such as Integer or String. An *array* is an indexed list of values (elements), where the array name is followed by one or more integers in parentheses. The integer selects the specific *element* of the array. The number of integers in the parentheses determines the *dimension* of the array.

A one-dimensional array has a single-integer index and is a linear list of values. The index selects which element of the list to use, counting from the beginning. For example, the statement

```
Dim myArray(10) As Integer
```

declares a list of 11 memory elements for storing integers (elements 0 through 10). In a formula, the value `myArray(3)` selects the fourth integer in that list and `myArray(7)` selects the eighth.

Note

Everything may seem to be off by one when examining array indices. This occurs because the default starting point for an array index is 0, which makes the number of elements in an array one more than the value of the upper limit specified in the `Dim` statement. You can modify the default property by placing an `Option Base 1` statement at the top of a module, which changes the default starting point to 1. You can also use constructions like `Dim anArray(5 to 7)` to force the index to range between specific limits.

A two-dimensional array uses two integers in the parentheses and is a two-dimensional table of numbers with the first index selecting the row and the second selecting the column. Higher order arrays are allowed, but they are a little difficult to imagine once the dimension goes over three. The following are declarations for arrays.

```
Dim anArray(5) As Single, thedigits(50,2) As Integer
Dim anOther(5,3,10) As Long
```

User-Defined Types

In addition to the built-in data types, you can define your own data types to make it more convenient for you to store your data. For example, in an address book type program, you want to store names, addresses, and phone numbers. A name takes at least one string, and an address usually takes three, plus the phone number. This makes five strings that are all bound to the same entry. You could store them in five different variables, but it makes sense to create a new data type that combines them into a single *user-defined type*. A user-defined type is a data type that you create to fit the specific circumstances of whatever program you are creating. A user-defined type can be nearly any combination of the existing data types, including other user-defined types.

To create a user-defined data type, place a Type statement at the top of the procedure or module that needs the type. The Type statement consists of a Type header containing the keyword Type followed by the new type name, one or more named subvariables with As-type clauses, and an End Type statement. For example, for an address book program, create a compound variable type that stores all the parts of the address in a single variable. A user-defined data type to do this is defined as follows:

```
Type myType
    Name As String
    Company As String
    Address As String
    City As String
    State As String
    Zip As Integer
    Phone As String
End Type
```

To use this type, you must declare a variable in a Dim statement and use the new type name as the type. For example,

```
Dim theData(100) As myType
```

creates an array of 101 elements of `myType` variables. To access the parts of a user-defined type, follow the variable name with a period and the part name. For example, to get the ZIP code part from element 34 you would use:

```
theData(34).Zip
```

The Scope of Variables

Variable declarations can be placed at the top of the module outside of the procedures, or within the procedures themselves. The type definitions and variable declarations placed at the top of a module are available to all the procedures within the module. If the declarations are placed within a procedure, then the values stored in the variables are only available within that procedure. The same variable could be defined in several different procedures, and each of those variables would be completely independent from the others, even though they have the same name. If you have more than one module in a program, and you want a variable to be available to all the procedures in all the modules, you must declare that variable at the module level and use `Public` instead of `Dim` in the declaration.

Note

You can have many different variables with the same name but in different procedures, but it is poor programming proctice because of the confusion it can cause to anyone trying to figure out what you are doing.

Constants

Another declaration that is often placed at the top of modules and procedures is a constant declaration like the following.

```
Const MaxNumItems = 10
```

An entry of this type declares a constant. When a constant is declared at the top of a module, it is available to all the procedures in that module. Note that a constant is not a variable, so you cannot change its value in a running program. When you use a constant, it behaves exactly as if you had typed the value of the constant everywhere the name is used. Using constants makes programs easier to understand and easier to change. In the `GetTax` function procedure, if you want to change the tax rate, you need only change the value of the constant.

Branching and Decision Making

As you read down the listing of the FindOverallocated procedure, you come across the following line:

```
If ActiveProject.Resources(I).Overallocated = True Then
```

This line is an If statement that tests the value of the Overallocated property of a resource to see if it is True. The property is normally False, but becomes True if the indicated resource is overallocated. The If statement tests the value of the property and executes the following block of code only if the value is True. If the property is False, the block of code is skipped. Thus, the If statement controls a branch in the structure of the program.

Block *If* Structures

A block If structure allows you to use a logical condition equation to make a decision as to which block of code to execute. The syntax of a block If structure is as follows:

```
If condition1 Then
    statements1
ElseIf condition2
    statements2
Else
    statements3
End If
```

When the If statement is executed, *condition1* is tested, and if it is True, the block *statements1* is executed. If *condition1* is False, *condition2* is tested, and if it is True, the block *statements2* is executed. There can be multiple ElseIf clauses, and each is tested in turn looking for one whose condition is True. If none of the conditions are True, the statements following the Else clause are executed. Only the block of statements following the first condition that returns True is executed; all the others are skipped, even if their conditions would have returned True.

Logical Formulas

The conditions used in the If statements are logical values, formulas that result in a logical value, or numeric formulas that result in a value of 0 (False) or non-zero (True). Logical formulas are usually created by comparing two values using one of the comparison operators shown in Table 23.3. Logical expressions may also be combined with the Boolean operators given in Table 23.4. Search for "comparison operators" and "logical" in the Visual Basic Reference section of on-line help for more information.

Table 23.3	The Comparison Operators
Operator	**Description**
=	Equal to
<>	Not equal to
>	Greater than
<	Less than
>=	Greater than or equal to
<=	Less than or equal to

Table 23.4	The Logical Operators
Operator	**Description**
And	Logical and
Eqv	Logical equivalence
Imp	Logical implies
Not	Logical negation
Or	Logical or
Xor	Logical exclusive or

Select Case

The Select Case structure performs a function similar to the block If structure, in that an expression is used to select a particular block of statements. In Select Case, the expression returns a value, and that value is used to determine which block of statements to execute.

```
Select Case expression
Case list1
    statements1
Case Else
    statements2
End Select
```

When the Select Case statement is executed, *expression* is evaluated. Following the Select Case statement are one or more Case statements. The value of *expression* is compared to the comma-delimited list of values *list1*. If one of the values matches, the block *statements1* is executed. Otherwise, it skips over that block to the next Case statement. If none of the Case statements result in a match, the block *statements2* following the Case Else statement is executed. As with the block If statement, only one of the blocks of statements is executed.

Calling Procedures

The ViewApply method is an example of a procedure that is called by other procedures. The FindOverallocated procedure needs to change the view, and calls the ViewApply procedure to do so. User-defined Sub procedures are called in the same manner.

The GetTax procedure described earlier calculates the tax on an item and returns that number.

```
'
' Calculate the tax on an item.
'
Sub GetTax(Cost As Currency, Tax As Currency)
  Const TaxRate = 0.0825
  Tax = Cost * TaxRate
End Sub
```

The procedure needs two arguments, the Cost of an item, and the Tax. Both Cost and Tax are Currency type variables. The value in the Cost argument is passed to the procedure, and the value in the Tax argument is passed back to the calling program. You would call this procedure in another procedure with a statement like the following:

```
GetTax aCost, aTax
```

Because this procedure call is not part of a formula, there are no parentheses required around the argument.

The function version of this procedure, theTax, is called by the AddTax procedure as part of a formula.

```
'
' Increase the cost per use by the tax.
'
Sub AddTax()
  ActiveCell.Resource.CostPerUse = ActiveCell.Resource.CostPerUse + _
    theTax(ActiveCell.Resource.CostPerUse)
End Sub
```

```
' Calculate the tax on an item.
'
Function theTax(Cost As Currency) As Currency
   Const TaxRate = 0.0825
   theTax = Cost * TaxRate
End Function
```

To use this procedure, switch to a resource view, select a resource and run the procedure. The procedure selects the Cost/Use field and increases the value of the field by the tax due on that amount.

In AddTax, the function is passed the value of the property CostPerUse as an argument. This variable points to a memory location, and that memory location is passed to the theTax procedure where it is named Cost. Both names point to the same memory location, so if the value of Cost were changed in theTax, the value of CostPerUse would be changed in AddTax when the procedure returned.

In some cases, you want to make sure that a procedure does not change an argument, so you must pass the argument as a value instead of a memory address. You can do this in the procedure heading or in the calling program. For example, in a procedure heading, precede the argument with the keyword ByVal:

```
Function theTax(ByVal Cost As Currency) As Currency
```

The other way is to turn the argument in the calling program into a formula. Instead of the addresses of any of the variables, the address where the result of the formula is stored is then sent to the procedure. You make a variable into a formula by simply surrounding the variable name with parentheses:

```
ActiveCell.Resource.CostPerUse = ActiveCell.Resource.CostPerUse + _
   theTax((ActiveCell.Resource.CostPerUse))
```

Using Loops

The FindOverallocated procedure has to search through all the resources in a project to locate any overallocated ones. If you were to write out formulas for all the resources, you could locate the overallocated one that way, but you probably don't want to spend your time typing the same statement over and over again. To handle cases like this, you use loops.

For/Next

A For/Next loop is a counted loop that executes a block of statements a specified number of times. The syntax of the For/Next loop follows:

```
For loopvariable = start To end Step stepval
.
.statements
.
Next loopvariable
```

In the For/Next loop, *loopvariable* is a standard variable. The first time the loop executes, *loopvariable* has the value *start*, and all the statements down to the Next statement are executed. The second time the loop executes, *stepval* is added to *loopvariable* and that value is compared with *end*. If *loopvariable* is greater than *end*, the loop terminates; otherwise the statements within the loop are executed again. The Step *stepval* clause can be omitted, in which case the *stepval* is 1. If *stepval* is negative, the loop counts down instead of up, until *loopvariable* is less than *end*.

The FindOverallocated procedure uses a For/Next loop to scan through all the resources that might be overallocated.

```
    For I = 1 To NumRes  'Loop over all the resources in the active
    'project. Check each resource to see if it is overallocated.
      If ActiveProject.Resources(I).Overallocated = True Then
         'If it is overallocated, tell the user and ask if he wants to
         'see the resource or look for another.
         aMsg = ActiveProject.Resources(I).Name & _
            " is over allocated, switch to Resource Sheet?"
         Answer = MsgBox(aMsg, vbYesNo, "Overallocation")
         If Answer = vbYes Then 'See if the user answered yes.
            'If the user answered yes, then switch to the resource
            'sheet, select the overallocated resource, and quit.
            ViewApply Name:="Resource &Sheet"
            SelectResourceField Row:=I, Column:="Name",
RowRelative:=False
            Exit Sub
         End If
         'If the answer was no, then look for another overallocated
         'resource.
      End If
    Next I
```

In this example, I is the loop variable, and it ranges from 1 to NumRes. Each time the loop executes, a different resource is selected using the Resources collection.

Do/Loop

The Do/Loop loop calculates a block of statements until a condition changes from True to False, or False to True. Because the condition can be either True or False, and can be tested at the beginning or end of the loop, there are four vairations of the syntax for this loop. The syntax of the Do/Loop loop follows:

```
Do While condition
    .
    .statements
    .
Loop
```

or

```
Do Until condition
    .
    .statements
    .
Loop
```

or

```
Do
    .
    .statements
    .
Loop While condition
```

or

```
Do
    .
    .statements
    .
Loop Until condition
```

The Do/Loop loop uses a condition to determine how many times to execute the loop. The condition can be tested at the beginning or the end of the loop, and the loop can continue While the condition is True or Until the condition becomes True (while it is False).

For Each

The For Each loop is used to perform some action for all the elements of an array or collection. The syntax of the For Each loop follows:

```
For Each element In group
    statements
Next element
```

The For Each loop applies to arrays and collections only. The loop executes
once for each element in the array or collection. This loop is very useful
when you don't know (or don't care) how many elements there are in a collection. The loop variable *element* is of the data type of the elements in the
group collection. Each time the loop is calculated, *element* takes on the value
of another member of the collection.

The FindOverallocated procedure can be rewritten using the For Each statement instead of the For Next statement. The For Each statement actually
produces simpler code, because you don't need to determine the value of the
number of resources in the Resources collection.

```
Option Explicit
'
'  Find overallocated resources and switch to the resource.
'  For Each version.
'
Sub FindOverallocated2()
  Dim aRes As Object
  Dim Answer As Integer, aMsg As String
  'Loop over all the resources in the active project.
  For Each aRes In ActiveProject.Resources
    'Check each resource to see if it is overallocated.
    If aRes.Overallocated = True Then
      'If it is overallocated, tell the user and ask if he wants to
      'see the resource or look for another.
      aMsg = aRes.Name & " is over allocated, switch to Resource Sheet?"
      Answer = MsgBox(aMsg, vbYesNo, "Overallocation")
      If Answer = vbYes Then 'See if the user answered yes.
        'If the user answered yes, then switch to the resource
        'sheet select the overallocated resource, and quit.
        ViewApply Name:="Resource &Sheet"
        SelectResourceField Row:=aRes.ID, Column:="Name",
RowRelative:=False
        Exit Sub
      End If
      'If the answer was no, then look for another overallocated
      'resource.
    End If
  Next aRes
  MsgBox "Search complete.", , "Overallocation"
End Sub
```

Accessing Disk Files

Often you will store or calculate data in a program, and need to save it for another time. For example, in the tax calculation program, you probably want to keep track of how much tax has been collected, so you can fill out your tax forms. You could go back and recalculate everything, or you can save the data in a disk file and retrieve it later. In this example, add code to the theTax function procedure to store the amount of tax collected at the end of a data file as shown here. The added lines are in bold.

```
'
' Increase the cost per use by the tax.
'
Sub AddTax()
  ActiveCell.Resource.CostPerUse = ActiveCell.Resource.CostPerUse + _
     theTax2(ActiveCell.Resource.CostPerUse)
End Sub
'
' Calculate the tax on an item.
'
Function theTax2(Cost As Currency) As Currency
  Const TaxRate = 0.0825
  theTax = Cost * TaxRate
  'Save the data.
  Open "c:\examps.dat" For Append As #1
  Write #1, Cost, theTax
  Close #1
End Function
```

Use this program as before: switch to the resource view, select a resource, and run the procedure.

In the added lines, the file is opened for appending using a file number of 1. Appending places each new entry at the end of the file. The Write statement writes the Cost and the amount of tax paid to the file. The program still appears to work the same, but now the data is saved every time the tax is calculated. If you open the data file EXAMPS.DAT, after running the program several times, you will see something like the following:

```
18.25,1.5056
25.45,2.0996
1.25,.1031
```

Note how the Write statement delimits the data in the file by placing commas between items written to disk. If strings are written to disk, they are surrounded with quotation marks. These delimiters make it easy for the Input statement to be used to read the data back into a program for further processing. If you use Print instead of Write, the text and strings are written to the file without delimiters, creating a text file suitable for printing rather than for reading back into another program.

For more information about reading and writing files, search for "input" in the Visual Basic Reference section of on-line help, and select the topic "Input and Output Keyword Summary."

Using Built-In Dialog Boxes

Visual Basic for Applications has two built-in dialog boxes that you can use in your programs to send data to the user and to get data from the user. The two dialog boxes are created with the MsgBox() and InputBox() functions. You have already used the MsgBox() function to display a dialog box as shown in figure 23.10. The InputBox() function displays a similar dialog box that contains an area in which you can type the answer to a question rather than just clicking on a button. Both functions take one or more arguments to set the prompt text, box title, number and type of buttons, and so forth. See the on-line help for a complete list of arguments.

Using the Debugging Tools

Program bugs are a fact of life for computer programmers. No matter how careful you are, bugs almost always show up and must be found and removed from your codes. The simplest bugs are syntax errors where you have put a comma in the wrong place or used a key word improperly. Syntax errors are normally found by Visual Basic for Applications as soon as you type them. Next are the runtime errors, which are caused by using the wrong type of variable, or by performing an improper numeric calculation (for example, taking the square root of –1). These errors are also found by Visual Basic for Applications as soon as the improper statement is executed. Lastly are the logical errors, where a program runs just fine, but does not do what you want it to. Logical errors are the most difficult to find because everything seems to work—it just works wrong.

Visual Basic for Applications has a built-in set of powerful debugging tools to help you find and correct program bugs. You can set breakpoints anywhere in your programs to force them to stop executing at that point. After you stop your program, use the Instant Watch command to view the value of any variable or expression. You can then continue executing a program or step through it one statement at a time until you find your problems. You can also set watchpoints that automatically break a program when a variable or expression reaches a certain value.

Using Break Mode

Break mode is where an executing program is halted with all its variables still intact. A running program enters break mode when you press Ctrl+Break, when it encounters an error, or when it encounters a breakpoint or watchpoint. When a program enters break mode (when it encounters an error or when you press Ctrl+Break), the Macro Error dialog box appears as shown in figure 23.11, giving you the choice to quit or to open the Debug window.

Fig. 23.11
The Macro Error dialog box.

Setting Breakpoints

Breakpoints and watchpoints also put a program into break mode. A breakpoint is a marker on a line of code that forces a program to stop executing when Visual Basic for Applications attempts to execute the marked line. A watchpoint is a marker on the value of a variable or a simple formula. When the value of a watchpoint changes in some specific way, the program is stopped and placed in break mode.

To set a breakpoint, open the module containing your procedure and select the line of code where you want the program to stop. Select the **R**un Toggle **B**reakpoint command or click the Toggle Breakpoint tool to set a breakpoint. Select the command again to remove a selected breakpoint, or select the **R**un **C**lear All Breakpoints command to remove all of them. Then run your code. When it reaches a breakpoint, it stops and enters break mode. When a program enters break mode (when it encounters a breakpoint or watchpoint), it goes directly to the debug window discussed next.

The Debug Window

If you select **D**ebug on the Macro Error dialog box, or if the program encounters a breakpoint or watchpoint, the Debug window appears. The Debug window (see fig. 23.12) is a split window, with the currently executing procedure in the Code pane at the bottom and either the Immediate pane or the Watch pane at the top. In the bottom half of the window, you can select lines of code, add or remove breakpoints, and select code for watchpoints. The Debug window shown in figure 23.12 shows the code stopped at an error intentionally inserted in the procedure (a = 1/0, a division-by-zero error). The statement where the procedure stopped is boxed in the Code pane. The Watch pane shows the current value of Cost, and Cost*TaxRate as watch variables. At this point, you can continue execution of a procedure, set or delete more watchpoints, examine the value of variables, or step through the procedure, one statement at a time.

Fig. 23.12
The Debug window showing the Watch and Code panes. The Immediate pane is behind the Watch pane, and is selected with the tab at the top. The boxed line of code in the Code pane is where the program stopped execution. The Watch pane shows Watch variables and their current values.

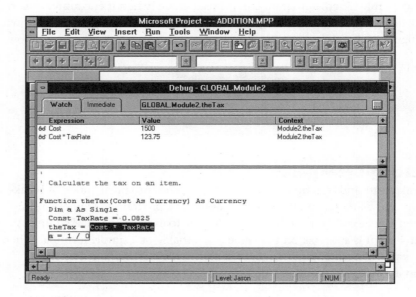

The Immediate Pane

In the Immediate pane of the Debug window, you can type and execute almost any Visual Basic for Applications command. The only restriction is that it must be only one line long. The Immediate pane also receives any printed values caused by the Debug.Print statement, used to print values from a running program.

The Watch Pane and Watch Variables

The Watch pane displays the current value of watchpoints and watch variables. Watchpoints, watch variables displayed in the Watch pane—continuously show the value of the variable or expression. The difference between these two is that while both show the value of a variable, a watchpoint can stop your code if the selected value changes in some specified way. The Instant watch is used to show the current value of a variable or expression without placing it in the Watch pane. Figure 23.13 shows the results of selecting the variable `theTax` in the Debug window and selecting the **T**ools Instant **W**atch command (or clicking the Instant Watch toolbar tool). If you select the Add button, the instant watch variable is changed into a watch variable and added to the Watch pane.

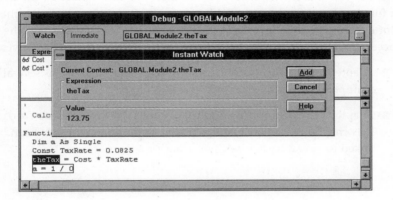

Fig. 23.13
An Instant Watch dialog box.

The Step Commands

There are two step commands that you can use at this point to execute one line of your program and stop again in break mode: **R**un Step **I**nto and **R**un Step **O**ver. The **R**un Step **I**nto command makes the program execute one line at a time. If the program reaches a procedure call, the next step occurs in that called procedure.

The **R**un Step **O**ver command is similar, but when it reaches a procedure call, it executes the procedure completely before stopping and going into break mode again. Thus, the Step Over command appears to step over procedure calls in the procedure you are executing.

The Calls Window

The Calls window is on the upper right side of the Debug window shown in figure 23.12. The Calls window shows the name of the procedure that contains the current point of execution. If you select the Calls window, it expands and lists all the active procedures in this program. Active procedures are those that have not finished running yet, either because they contain the current execution point or because they were one of the calling procedures that eventually called the procedure that contains the execution point.

From Here...

One of the best sources of information for the syntax and usage of the Visual Basic for Applications commands and functions is the on-line help. Be sure to select the Visual Basic Reference section; then you can explore all the different functions and methods available there. The Object Browser is another helpful feature because it looks at the actual library files and extracts the real procedure names and properties directly from the procedures themselves.

- Chapter 21, "Creating and Using Macros." This chapter has several examples of working macro programs.

- Chapter 22, "Customizing Toolbars, Menus, Forms, and Cue Cards." This chapter discusses creating custom forms and menus that can be linked to Visual Basic for Applications programs.

Appendixes

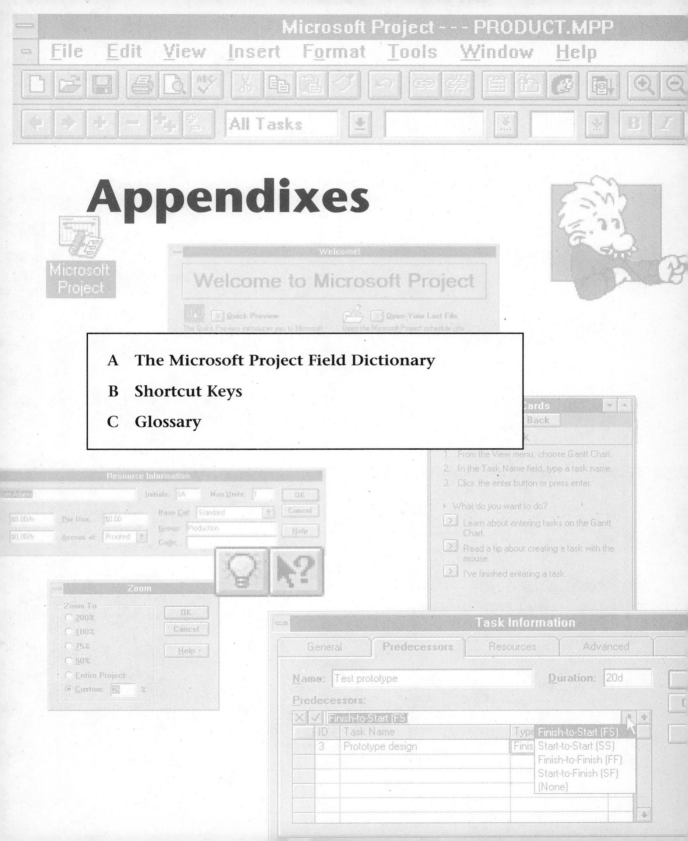

- **A**   **The Microsoft Project Field Dictionary**
- **B**   **Shortcut Keys**
- **C**   **Glossary**

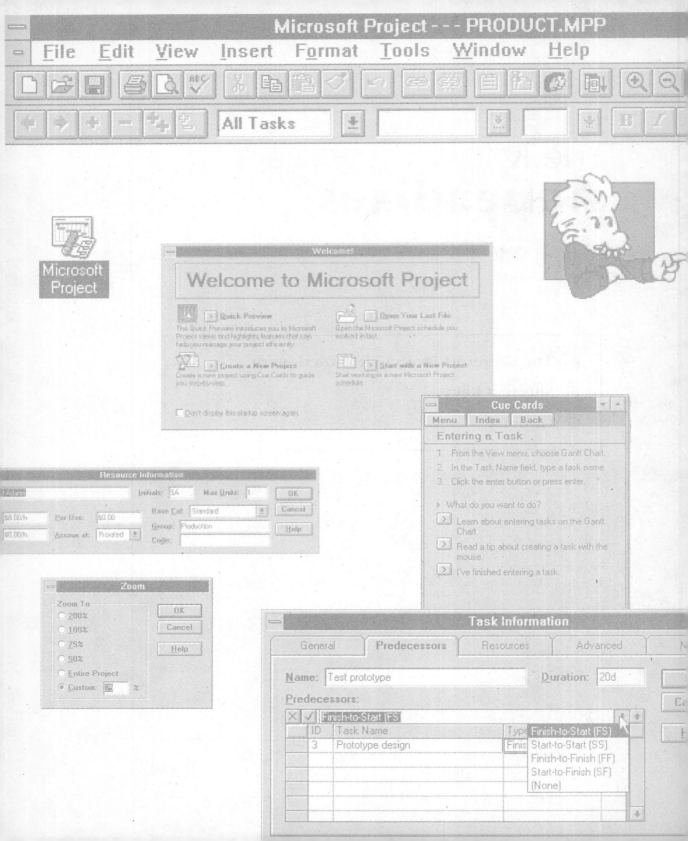

The Microsoft Project Field Dictionary

This appendix is designed to help you understand how to use the Microsoft Project fields when using and customizing filters, tables, and forms, and also in creating macros and Visual Basic applications.

The Organization of this Appendix

There are two tables in this appendix. The first (Table A.1) is a table of descriptions for the fields. The second (Table A.2) is an alphabetized list of all the field names. The fields in Table A.1 are grouped in a functional order to help you understand how the fields interact. If you are looking for a specific field, you can locate its name in Table A.2 and then use the accompanying Index number to locate its description in Table A.1.

For still more detailed information about individual fields, use the on-line Help file in Microsoft Project. To view the Help screen for a field, choose the **H**elp **C**ontents command. Choose the Reference Information topic; then choose the Views, Filters, Tables, & Fields topic; and then choose the Fields topic. From the Fields screen, choose the type of field (Task, Resource, Resource Assignment), and finally choose the specific field topic from the alphabetized list.

There are three groups of fields used in Microsoft Project databases:

■ The *task database fields* appear on task tables and forms. These fields define the tasks and the schedule in the project and calculate summary statistics for resource assignments for each task.

- The *resource database fields* appear on resource tables and forms. These fields define the individual resources in the resource pool and calculate summary statistics showing all work assignments for each resource.

- The *resource assignment fields* appear only at the bottom of task and resource forms. These fields define the exact work assignment for each resource on each task.

You can display almost all of the task or resource fields on custom tables and forms. The resource assignment fields cannot be added to tables or forms. They are only available by applying the Format Details command to one of the standard task or resource forms.

The resource assignment fields provide the link between individual resources and tasks, defining the work assignments and providing the detail work and cost statistics that are summed by the summary statistics fields in the task and resource databases.

The Organization of Table A.1

Table A.1 presents the fields in an order that follows the flow of data as you develop a project and as Microsoft Project uses your entries to compute calculated fields. The table is divided into functional groups as described below.

Task Definitions This table describes the basic fields that are most often used to define the essential characteristics of tasks. Also included are some fields that are maintained by Microsoft Project automatically as the schedule is calculated. Additional task fields are included in other groups below. For example, the task's Baseline Start and Finish dates are included in the Tracking Group.

Resource Definitions This table describes the basic fields that are used to define the resources in the resource pool. Other resource fields are included in other tables.

Resource Assignments This table describes the resource assignment fields and related fields in the task and resource databases that sum the resource assignment details.

Tracking This table contains the fields that record baseline data and calculate variances, as well as the fields that record actual values for tasks, work, and costs.

Other   The final section contains fields that let you record additional information about tasks and resources or let you select task or resources for sorting, filtering, and formatting.

The Columns Used in Table A.1

The fields are defined in five columns in Table A.1. The first three provide a cross-reference to Table A.2 and to the on-line Help text in Microsoft Project. The last two columns describe how the field data is generated, what type of data it must be, and a description of the field's use and relationship to other fields.

The Index Column

The sequential numbers in the Index column can be used with Table A.2 to locate a field definition quickly. Find the field name in the alphabetical listing of Table A.2. Use the Index number that accompanies the field name in Table A.2 to find the field in Table A.1.

The Source Column

This column merely identifies the Microsoft Project database in which the field is found. Look in the database section of the Help screens to locate additional information about a field. The source codes used are:

T   Task database

R   Resource database

RA   Resource assignment database

The Field Name Column

This is the official name of the field as used in Microsoft Project.

The Type Column

This column displays two different kinds of information about the field: whether the field is calculated by Microsoft Project or entered by the user, and what data type is used in the field.

1. The top row contains one of three codes to describe whether the field is calculated by Microsoft Project, entered by the user, or both.

   C   Calculated by Microsoft Project. No direct entry by the user is permitted.

   E   Entered by the user.

CE   Calculated by Microsoft Project but can be overwritten by the user.

2. The second row identifies the data type used by the field.

A   Alphanumeric (any letters or numbers may be entered).

A*   Alphanumeric (an entry list of acceptable values is available).

N   Numeric (a simple number with no units attached).

NT   Numeric with a time unit attached.

D   Date or date and time.

L   Logical (Yes/No values only).

The Description Column

The description column provides a definition of the purpose of the field, how its value is calculated, or how the field is used with other fields in scheduling and tracking a project.

Table A.1   Microsoft Project Field Descriptions

Index	Source	Field Name	Type	Definition
The Task Definition Fields				
1	T	**NAME**	E A	The name you enter to describe the task. The name can contain up to 255 characters and may contain any of the letters, numbers, or symbols on the keyboard. Names do not have to be unique (the Unique ID number identifies each task).
2	T	**CREATED**	C D	This normally hidden field is automatically filled with the current date at the time you create the task. The date is taken from the Project tab of the Summary Info dialog box.
3	T	**UNIQUE ID**	C N	A sequential number assigned to tasks as they are created. The Unique ID is never associated with any other task— even if you delete the task to which it is originally assigned.
4	T	**ID**	C N	The ID number is automatically assigned to indicate the position of the task in the task list. The ID number will be adjusted if tasks are inserted or deleted, or if you choose to sort the tasks and renumber them to match the new sort order. The Unique ID number, however, never changes. Because of the way ID numbers are maintained, you can have duplicate task names or even unnamed tasks.

Index	Source	Field Name	Type	Definition
5	T	**PROJECT**	C A	The name of the project file is automatically recorded in this field for all tasks. This field is useful for identifying tasks by project when multiple projects are in memory atthe same time.
6	T	**DURATION**	CE NT	Duration measures the number of time units on the working calendar scheduled for (occupied by) the task. All tasks are initially given a default duration of one day (measured in minutes, hours, days, or weeks). You can enter any duration using a number followed by one of the four time unit abbreviations: **m** (minutes), **h** (hours), **d** (days), **w** (weeks). If work on a task continues around the clock without regard to the calendar (e.g., a continuous chemical process), the duration is entered as ELAPSED DURATION (**em**, **eh**, **ed**, or **ew**). If you enter elapsed duration, Microsoft Project automatically makes the task a Fixed duration task.
7	T	**MILESTONE**	CE L	A logical field (Yes/No) that defines a task as a milestone. Microsoft Project automatically makes any zero-duration task a milestone. The Milestone field appears as a check box on the Task Edit Form. Change this field to Yes (by filling the check box) to make any task into a milestone. Remove the milestone status of a zero-duration task by clearing the check box.
8	T	**FIXED**	E L	A logical field (Yes/No) that defines a task as Fixed Duration instead of Resource Driven (the default). Changes in resource assignments do not affect the duration of Fixed tasks. The Fixed field appears as a text box on the Resources tab of the Task Information dialog box as well as on the various task forms. All elapsed duration tasks are automatically Fixed. Use the Schedule tab of the Tools Options dialog box to change the default status of new tasks from Fixed Duration to Resource Driven.
9	T	**CONSTRAINT TYPE**	E A*	This field defines the existence of a constraint on the scheduling of a task. The constraint type "As Soon As Possible" (which means there is no constraint) is set by default when a task is first entered. Acceptable values may be selected from a pull-down selection list. The field appears on the Advanced tab of the Task Information dialog box.
10	T	**CONSTRAINT DATE**	E D	If any Constraint Type other than As Soon As Possible or As Late As Possible is selected, this field must be filled to define the effective date of the constraint. If no date is entered, the current date is used by default. If the Constraint Type is returned to As Soon As Possible or As Late As Possible, this field is cleared automatically.

(continues)

Appendixes

Table A.1 Continued				
Index	**Source**	**Field Name**	**Type**	**Definition**
The Task Definition Fields				
11	T	**OUTLINE LEVEL**	C N	Microsoft Project supports outlining up to ten levels (nine subordinate levels). This field contains an integer from 1 to 10 that represents the outline level for the task. First level tasks are numbered 1, their immediate subordinates are numbered 2, etc. Use this field in filters to select tasks by their level in the outline.
12	T	**OUTLINE NUMBER**	C N	This number shows the exact location of a task within the outline. This is the number you see displayed in the Name field when you choose Show Outline Number on the View tab of the **T**ools **O**ptions dialog box. The Outline Number is automatically supplied to the WBS (Work Breakdown Structure) code field, but the WBS code also can be changed by entering a code manually.
13	T	**SUMMARY**	C L	This is a logical (Yes/No) field that is automatically set to Yes if a task has subtasks demoted under it.
14	T	**WBS**	CE A	This field stores the Work Breakdown Structure code assigned to a task. If you do not enter a WBS code, the field is automatically calculated to show the current Outline Number for the task. Once you enter a WBS code that differs from the Outline Number, the field is not recalculated.
15	T	**PREDECESSORS**	E A	This field identifies the ID numbers of all the task's predecessors. The field is displayed at the bottom of the task forms as an entry table when one of the Predecessor choices is selected from the Fo**r**mat **D**etails command. The same display is also available on the Resources tab of the Task Information dialog box. Each predecessor appears on a separate row, with columns for the ID, Name, dependency Type, and Lag. The predecessor types are Finish-to-Start, Start-to-Finish, Start-to-Start, and Finish-to-Finish. Lag time is entered as a number followed by a time unit (m,h,d,w). Lead time is entered as a negative number in the Lag column. The predecessor field also appears as a column in the GANTT Chart view. In a table, a PERT node, or a form, this field is displayed as a comma separated list of the ID numbers for predecessor tasks (along with the partial dependency codes if the dependency is any other than Finish-to-Start with zero Lag).
16	T	**SUCCESSORS**	E A	This field identifies the ID numbers of all the task's successors. Presentation of the field is the same as the presentation of Predecessors. See the description of Predecessors for more details.

Index	Source	Field Name	Type	Definition
17	T	**UNIQUE ID PREDECESSORS**	C A	This field is the same as the Predecessors field except that Unique ID numbers are used to identify the predecessors.
18	T	**UNIQUE ID SUCCESSORS**	C A	This field is the same as the Successors field except that Unique ID numbers are used to identify the successors.
19	T	**EARLY START**	C D	The earliest possible start date for the task, given the schedule for its predecessors, the calendar, and any constraints that may be imposed on the task. If there is no Delay, the Scheduled Start is the same as the Early Start. Once the Actual Start field is used, this field is calculated from the Actual Start.
20	T	**EARLY FINISH**	C D	The earliest possible finish date for the task, given its Early Start date, its Duration, the calendar, the scheduling method, and any constraints. Once the Actual Finish field is used, this field is calculated from the Actual Finish. The latest Early Finish date among all tasks determines the finish date for the project.
21	T	**LATE START**	C D	The latest start date for the task that would not delay the finish of the project. Once the Actual Start field is used, this field is calculated from the Actual Start.
22	T	**LATE FINISH**	C D	The latest finish date for the task that would not delay the finish of the project. Once the Actual Finish field is used, this field is calculated from the Actual Finish.
23	T	**DELAY**	E NT	An arbitrary amount of time by which the Scheduled Start of the task will be delayed after its Early Start date. This field uses **elapsed** time units (em, eh, ed, or ew). Selecting the **T**ools Resource **L**eveling command and choosing the **L**evel now button calculates this field to delay one or more tasks that are competing for a resource. You can enter your own delay values in the Delay GANTT view. Enter a zero to remove the delay for a task. The **C**lear Leveling button on the Resource Leveling dialog box resets the Delay field to zero for all or selected tasks.
24	T	**SCHEDULED START**	CE D	This field shows the currently scheduled start date and time for a task. It is calculated by adding the Delay (if any) to the Early Start date. If you enter a date and time into this field, Microsoft Project changes the task Constraint Type to Must Start On. Once the Actual Start date is set, this field is calculated as equal to the Actual Start field.
25	T	**SCHEDULED FINISH**	CE D	This field shows the currently scheduled finish date and time for a task. It is calculated from the Early Finish and Delay fields. If you enter a date and time into this field, Microsoft Project changes the task Constraint Type to Must Finish On. Once the Actual Finish date is set, this field is calculated as equal to the Actual Finish field.

Appendixes

(continues)

Table A.1 Continued				
Index	**Source**	**Field Name**	**Type**	**Definition**
The Task Definition Fields				
26	T	**TOTAL SLACK**	C NT	Total Slack is the amount of time that a task's finish can be delayed without delaying the finish of the project or causing a successor task's constraint to be violated. It is calculated by subtracting the task's Early Finish from its Late Finish. Critical Tasks are defined as those tasks with zero or negative Total Slack. If Total Slack is negative, the task is not scheduled in time to allow a successor constraint to be satisfied.
27	T	**FREE SLACK**	C NT	Free Slack is the amount of time that a task can be delayed without affecting the schedule of any other task. If the task has no successors, Free Slack is equal to Total Slack.
28	T	CRITICAL	C L	This is a logical (Yes/No) field that identifies critical tasks. The field is automatically set to Yes if Total Slack is less than or equal to the amount entered in the Schedule tab for the "Show As critical If Slack <=" field. Normally, that value is set to zero and any task with zero or negative slack is shown as critical.
29	T	**FIXED COST**	E N	A cost amount that is to be associated with a task but which is independent of the duration or the resource assignments to a task.
30	T	**PRIORITY**	E A*	This field determines a task's likelihood of being chosen for a delayed start during the leveling operation. Set a priority of Do Not Level for those tasks that should never be delayed. This field appears on the General tab of the Task Information dialog box.
31	T	**SUBPROJECT FILE**	E A	If the schedule for another project file (subproject) is to be included in the schedule for the current project, create a task that will represent the subproject and attach the subproject to the task by supplying the subproject name in this field. The duration of the task will equal the duration of the subproject. This field appears as the field labeled **F**ilename on the Advanced tab of the Task Information dialog box.

Index	Source	Field Name	Type	Definition
The Resource Definition Fields				
32	R	**NAME**	E A	The name you enter for a resource.
33	R	**UNIQUE ID**	C N	A sequential number assigned to resources as they are created. The Unique ID is never associated with any other resource—even if you delete the resource to which it is originally assigned.
34	R	**ID**	C N	The ID number is automatically assigned to indicate the current position of the resource in the resource list. The ID number will be adjusted if resources are inserted or deleted, or if you choose to sort the resources and renumber them to match the new sort order. The Unique ID number, however, never changes.
35	R	**INITIALS**	E A	An abbreviated reference to the resource name. Use the initials in reports where the full resource names take up too much room. You also can use the initials when assigning resources in the Task Form.
36	R	**GROUP**	E A	The entries in this field are used merely for sorting and filtering in views and reports. Microsoft Project does not aggregate the resources that have the same Group field entry. Enter any combination of characters and numbers.
37	R	**MAX UNITS**	E N	Enter in this field the maximum number of units of a resource (0–100) that are available at any one time. If you assign more units than the maximum available, you will see the Leveling message.
39	R	**STANDARD RATE**	E NT	Enter the rate to be used per unit of time for calculating the cost of resource work. The default unit is **h**ours, but you can also define the rate per **m**inute, **d**ay, **w**eek, or **y**ear. This rate will be applied to work performed during the calendar hours.
40	R	**OVERTIME RATE**	E NT	Enter the rate to be used per unit of time for calculating the cost of resource work that is to be done in overtime, outside the hours defined on the calendar.
41	R	**COST PER USE**	E N	This amount is multiplied by the number of units of the resource that are assigned to a task and added to the cost of the task. This cost is charged to all tasks to which the resource is assigned.
42	R	**ACCRUE AT**	E A*	Choose Start, End, or Prorated (the default) for this field in order to define at what point in the work on a task the resource costs will be recorded as having been incurred.

(continues)

Appendixes

Table A.1 Continued				
Index	**Source**	**Field Name**	**Type**	**Definition**

The Resource Definition Fields

43	R	**CODE**	E A	This field is provided for sorting and filtering. It is commonly used to tag the resource with its appropriate cost accounting code.
44	R	**BASE CALENDAR**	E A*	This field identifies the base calendar to which the resource calendar is linked. All changes made to the base calendar are automatically extended to the resource calendar unless exceptions have been defined for the resource calendar.
45	R	**EMAIL ADDRESS**	E A	When the electronic mail features are used to communicate task information, the Name of the resource is normally used as the electronic mail address. If there is an entry in this field, that entry is used for the electronic mail address instead of the Name. If the entry "None" is placed in this field, no electronic mail is sent to the resource.

The Resource Assignment Fields

The first group of fields in this table record the work assignment for individual resources on individual tasks. The fields that follow provide automatic summaries of the individual work assignments by task and then by resource. These fields can only be viewed on the standard forms provided by Microsoft Project. You cannot place them on tables or custom forms.

46	RA	**ID**	CE N	On a task form, this field shows the ID number for the resource assigned to the task. On a resource form, it shows the ID number of the task to which the resource is assigned. The Resource ID is calculated when you enter the resource Name.
47	RA	**RESOURCE NAME**	CE A	This field appears on a task form when one of the resource assignment field tables has been selected with the Format menu. It shows the names of the resources assigned to a task.
48	RA	**TASK NAME**	C A	This field appears on a resource form when one of the resource assignment field tables has been selected with the Format menu. It shows the name of the task to which assignments are being made.
49	RA	**PROJECT**	C A	This field identifies the project that contains the task to which the resource is assigned. It appears next to the task name on the resource form in the assignment field tables.

Index	Source	Field Name	Type	Definition
50	RA	**UNITS**	E N	The number of resource units assigned to a task. Values can be from 0 to 100, with no fractions smaller than hundredths.
51	RA	**WORK**	CE NT	This is the assigned work for one resource name for one task. If you leave this field blank when assigning a resource, the Work value is computed by multiplying the task Duration and the number of resource Units. If you enter a value for the assigned Work, Duration is recalculated (unless the task is a Fixed duration task) as the assigned Work divided by the number of resource Units. The assigned Work field is only available for data entry on the Task Form and the Task Detail Form. Work is denominated in hours **(h)** usually, but also can be entered and displayed in minutes **(m)**, days **(d)**, or weeks **(w)**.
52	RA	**OVERTIME WORK**	E NT	Enter the amount of the assigned Work that the resource will do outside the time defined on the resource calendar. Only work that is not overtime is scheduled within the calendar, and the Scheduled Start and Finish of the task will only reflect the work that is not done in overtime.
53	RA	**COST**	CE N	This field shows the cost of the assigned resource Work on the task, based on the standard, overtime, and per use rates for the resource and the work assigned. Until the task is marked as 100% complete, this field is calculated only. Once the task is complete, you can enter the actual cost in this field.
54	RA	**DELAY**	E NT	Use this field to delay the scheduled work on a task of one resource while other resources start on the Scheduled Start date for the task.
55	RA	**SCHEDULED START**	C D	This field shows when the resource is scheduled to start work on the task. This field is equal to the scheduled start of the task plus the resource assignment Delay field.
56	RA	**SCHEDULED FINISH**	C D	This field shows when the resource assignment on the task will be finished. The Scheduled Finish for the task is computed as the latest of these Scheduled Finish dates for any of the resources assigned to the task.

These fields provide summaries of resource assignments by task.

Index	Source	Field Name	Type	Definition
57	T	**RESOURCE NAMES**	CE A	The names of resources assigned to work on the task are displayed in a comma separated list in this field. If the number of units assigned is not one (1), the unit assignment will be displayed in square brackets immediately after the name.

(continues)

Appendixes

Table A.1	Continued			
Index	**Source**	**Field Name**	**Type**	**Definition**

The Resource Assignment Fields

Index	Source	Field Name	Type	Definition
58	T	RESOURCE INITIALS	E A	The initial(s) of resources assigned to the task are displayed in a comma separated list in this field. The Resource Initials are preferred in some reports since they take up less space than the full Resource Names.
59	T	RESOURCE GROUP	C A	This field displays a comma separated list of the resource groups to which the individual assigned resources belong. The field can be included in a table or a report to use for sorting or filtering.
60	T	WORK	CE NT	This field sums the Work assignments of all resources assigned to the task. The default unit is hours. If you enter a value in the task Work field after resources are assigned, Microsoft Project will recalculate the work assigned to each resource, with the total work divided among the resources in the same proportion as before.
61	T	COST	C N	The total cost of a task, including Fixed Cost and resource costs (resource work multiplied by the Standard or Overtime Rate for the resource).

These fields summarize for each resource the total assignments of that resource to all tasks. This includes all tasks in all projects that are open in memory that use the same resource pool.

Index	Source	Field Name	Type	Definition
62	R	WORK	C NT	This field is displayed on the Work table for Resource Sheet views. It summarizes by resource all work assignments for all tasks for all projects in memory.
63	R	OVERTIME WORK	C NT	This field sums all of the overtime work assigned to a resource for all tasks in all projects that are open in memory.
64	R	COST	C N	This field sums for each resource all costs for all tasks in all projects that are open in memory.
65	R	PEAK	C N	This field shows, for the displayed time period, the largest simultaneous Units assignment during the time period.
66	R	OVER ALLOCATED	C L	This logical (Yes/No) field is Yes if the Peak units exceeds the Max Units for the resource at any point in time.

Index	Source	Field Name	Type	Definition

The Tracking Fields

The Baseline fields are copied from corresponding Scheduled values when you use the Tools Tracking Save Baseline command. The Baseline fields retain their values even though the schedule is subsequently modified. The Variance fields are calculated by comparing the Baseline and Scheduled fields.

Index	Source	Field Name	Type	Definition
67	T	BASELINE START	E D	This field shows the baseline start for the task.
68	T	BASELINE FINISH	E D	This field shows the baseline finish for the task.
69	T	BASELINE DURATION	E NT	This field shows the baseline duration for the task.
70	RA	BASELINE WORK	E NT	This field records the baseline work for one resource on one task.
71	RA	BASELINE COST	E N	This field records the baseline cost of the work for this resource on this task.
72	T	BASELINE WORK	CE NT	This field sums the work fields for all resources on the task.
73	T	BASELINE COST	CE N	This field sums the cost for all resources for the task.
74	T	START VARIANCE	C NT	Scheduled Start Date minus the Baseline Start Date for the task.
75	T	FINISH VARIANCE	C NT	This field shows the difference calculated by subtracting the Baseline Finish date from the Scheduled Finish date for the task.
76	T	DURATION VARIANCE	C NT	This field shows the difference calculated by subtracting the Baseline Duration from the Scheduled Duration for the task.
77	T	WORK VARIANCE	C NT	The Scheduled Work minus the Baseline Work for the task.
78	T	COST VARIANCE	C N	Scheduled Cost for the task minus the Baseline Cost for the task.
79	R	BASELINE WORK	C NT	The sum of the Baseline Work for all tasks the resource is assigned to.
80	R	WORK VARIANCE	C NT	Scheduled Work on all tasks minus the Baseline Work on all tasks the resource is assigned to.
81	R	BASELINE COST	C N	The sum of the Baseline Cost for the resource for all tasks it is assigned to.

Appendixes

(continues)

Table A.1 Continued

Index	Source	Field Name	Type	Definition
The Tracking Fields				
82	R	COST VARIANCE	C N	Scheduled Cost (for all assigned tasks) minus Baseline Cost.
83	T	START1–START5	E D	Up to five different Baseline Start dates for a task can be stored.
84	T	FINISH1– FINISH5	E D	Up to five different Baseline Finish dates for a task can be stored.

Actual Fields

The Work and Cost fields in this group include actual values for the individual resource-task assignment, as well as summaries of those assignment values by task and by resource.

Index	Source	Field Name	Type	Definition
85	T	ACTUAL START	E D	This field contains "NA" until an entry is made in it. If no entry is made in this field but an entry is made in any actual field that implies that work on the task has started, then the Scheduled Start is copied (not calculated) into this field.
86	T	ACTUAL DURATION	CE NT	The actual duration of work on the task to date. The three fields Actual Duration, Remaining Duration, and Percent (%) Complete are interdependent. Entering one of the three defines the values of the other two (for a given Duration). Entering an Actual Duration that is greater than the scheduled Duration causes scheduled Duration to be set equal to the Actual Duration and the other two fields to show that the task is complete.
87	T	PERCENT (%) COMPLETE	CE N	Actual Duration as a percentage of Scheduled Duration.
88	T	REMAINING DURATION	CE NT	Scheduled Duration minus Actual Duration.
89	T	STOP DATE	C D	This field contains NA except while work is in progress on the task (after the Actual Start and before the Actual Finish). It shows the date and time at which the last recorded actual work stopped on the task.
90	T	RESUME DATE	C D	This field contains NA except while work is in progress on the task (like the Stop field). This field shows the date and time when the remaining work on the task is scheduled to resume, and that is computed as the later of the dates in the Stop Date field (when recorded work stopped) and the Resume No Earlier Than field (an arbitrary resume date).

Index	Source	Field Name	Type	Definition
91	T	RESUME NO EARLIER THAN	E D	This field is used to enter a date for the resumption of the remaining work on a task. It is set using the Reschedule Work button on the tracking toolbar, or by selecting the Tools Tracking Update Project command to display the Update Project dialog box and using the field labeled Reschedule Uncompleted Work to Start.
92	RA	ACTUAL WORK	CE NT	Recorded work for a given resource on a given task. This field is computed by applying the Percent (%) Complete field for the task to the Scheduled Work for the resource as long as the Updating Task Status Updates Resource Status check box is filled on the Schedule tab of the Tools Options dialog box. If that check box is cleared, you can enter actual work directly for each resource assignment.
93	RA	REMAINING WORK	CE NT	Scheduled Work for the resource on this task minus Actual Work.
94	T	ACTUAL WORK	CE NT	The sum of the resource assignment Actual Work fields for all resources assigned to the task.
95	T	PERCENT (%) WORK COMPLETE	CE N	The task Actual Work field as a percentage of the task Scheduled Work.
96	T	REMAINING WORK	CE NT	The task Scheduled Work minus the task Actual Work.
97	RA	ACTUAL COST	CE N	The product of the Actual Work for each resource assigned to the task and the cost rates for the resources.
98	RA	REMAINING COST	CE N	The Scheduled Cost for this assignment minus the Actual Cost.
99	T	ACTUAL COST	CE N	The sum of the Actual Costs for all resource assignments for this task.
100	T	REMAINING COST	CE N	The Scheduled Cost for the task minus the Actual Cost.
101	T	ACTUAL FINISH	E D	This field contains "NA" until an entry is made in it. If no entry is made in this field but an entry is make in any actual field that implies that work on the task is complete, then the Scheduled Finish is copied into this field.
102	R	ACTUAL WORK	C NT	This field summarizes the Actual Work values for all task assignments for the resource.
103	R	PERCENT (%) WORK COMPLETE	C N	This field divides the Actual Work for the resource by the Work (scheduled) field for the resource to compute the percentage completed. (Actual Work/Work) * 100.

(continues)

Appendixes

Table A.1 Continued				
Index	**Source**	**Field Name**	**Type**	**Definition**
Actual Fields				
104	R	REMAINING WORK	C NT	This field subtracts the Actual Work from the Work field.
105	R	ACTUAL COST	C N	This field sums the Actual Cost fields for all tasks the resource is assigned to.
106	R	REMAINING COST	C N	This field subtracts the Actual Cost from the Cost field for the resource.

The next four fields are calculations that appear on the Earned Value task table. They are used to compare the baseline (budgeted) cost as of the report date versus the actual cost as of that date. The actual cost of a task as of any given date may differ from the baseline cost of the task as of that date either because the task is ahead or behind schedule (this is what is measured by the SV field) or because the resource work for the task differs from the baseline resource work (this is what is measured by the CV field).

107	T	BCWP	C N	Budgeted Cost of Work Performed or *Earned Value*.
				This field helps to assess the extent to which actual costs differ from the plan due to differences between baseline (planned) work and actual work. BCWP is computed by multiplying the Percent (%) Complete field (the percentage of task duration completed) by the Baseline Cost field. The result is the Baseline Cost that should have been incurred at this stage of completion of the task. Baseline Cost is also known as "Budget At Completion" or BAC.
				BCWP = Baseline Cost * Percentage (%) Complete
108	T	BCWS	C N	Budgeted Cost of Work Scheduled (sometimes called the *Planned Earned Value*).
				This field measures how much of the Baseline Cost of the task should have been incurred by today's date if the task had started as planned. The "planned percentage complete" (the percentage of the baseline duration that should have been completed by today's date) is multiplied by the Baseline Cost of the task to get BCWS. Note that the "planned percentage complete" is calculated using elapsed time.
				BCWS = Baseline Cost * "Planned Percentage Complete"
109	T	CV	C N	CV (Earned Value Cost Variance) CV = Actual Cost – BCWP
				This field compares Actual Cost for the task thus far with BCWP. If Actual Cost at this point is greater than BCWP, then costs are running above schedule for the duration completed. Actual Cost is labeled ACWP (Actual Cost of Work Performed) on the Earned Value table.

Index	Source	Field Name	Type	Definition
110	T	SV	C N	Earned Value Schedule Variance SV = BCWP – BCWS The actual cost of a task as of any given date may differ from the baseline cost of the task as of that date either because the task is ahead of or behind schedule. This is what is measured by the SV field.

Miscellaneous Information Fields

Index	Source	Field Name	Type	Definition
111	T	**NOTES**	E A	The Notes field can be used to save comments or notes about the task. Notes can contain over 3,000 characters. The field is displayed as the Notes tab on the Task Information dialog box. Use the Format Details command to display the Notes field on any of the Task forms.
112	R	**NOTES**	E A	The Notes field can be used to save comments or notes about the resource. Notes can contain over 3,000 characters. Use the Attach Note button on the Standard toolbar to display the resource Notes dialog box. Use the Format Details command to display the Notes field on any of the resource forms.
113	T	**TEXT1– TEXT10**	E A	These ten text fields can be used to associate any kind of random text with tasks. One use of these fields is to attach them to task bars on the GANTT chart, thus displaying the user's text entries next to the bar for the task. You must customize a table or form to display these fields.
114	R	**TEXT1–TEXT5**	E A	Use these fields to attach text to resources.
115	T	**NUMBER1– NUMBER5**	E N	These fields can be used to track any number data for tasks that the user chooses.
116	T	**COST1–COST3**	E N	These fields can be used to store cost information that you want to have for reference but that are not real costs to be included in the cost calculations of the task or the project.
117	T	**DURATION1– DURATION3**	E NT	These fields can be used to store duration estimates that you want to have for reference but that are not to be used for scheduling the task.
118	T	**FLAG1– FLAG10**	E L	These ten logical fields are used to tag tasks for selection by filters and to identify tasks for special GANTT chart bars.
119	T	**MARKED**	E L	Use this field to select random tasks for filtering or for special print formats. The Format Text command provides a special text formatting for marked tasks. You must customize a table or form to display this field for editing.

(continues)

Appendixes

Index	Source	Field Name	Type	Definition
Table A.1	**Continued**			

Miscellaneous Information Fields

Index	Source	Field Name	Type	Definition
120	T	**RECURRING TASK**	C L	If a task is a recurring task, this field is set to Yes. It otherwise has the value No.
121	T	**HIDE BAR**	E L	If this field is set to Yes, the task's bar on the GANTT Chart will be hidden. This field appears as a check box on the General tab of the Task Information dialog box.
122	T	**ROLLUP**	E L	This field appears on the General tab of the Task Information dialog box, and is used when displaying GANTT charts. If you fill the check box for a subtask, it will appear as a marker on the task bar for its summary task. You can customize the display of the task on its summary task bar with the Format Bar Styles command.
123	T	**CONTACT**	E A	This field is used to associate an electronic mailbox name with the task. This would be a person other than one of the resources assigned to the task to whom you wish to send Schedule Notes about the task. It could be, for instance, a person who is responsible for monitoring the task or a supervisor. Use the Tools Workgroup Send Schedule Note command to send messages to the Contact addresses.
124	T	**LINKED FIELDS**	C L	This field contains Yes if any field in the task receives its value via a link to another project or to another Windows application.
125	T	**OBJECTS**	C N	This field shows the number of objects that are attached to the task. Display the objects in any task form by selecting the Format Details command and choosing Objects.
126	R	**LINKED FIELDS**	C L	This field contains Yes if any field for the resource receives its value via a link to another project or to another Windows application.
127	R	**OBJECTS**	C N	This field shows the number of objects that are attached to the resource. Display the objects in any resource form by selecting the Format Details command and choosing Objects.

The following fields are used by the Tools Workgroup commands to send electronic mail to resources about the tasks to which they are assigned, and to use their responses to update the project. With one exception (Update Needed), these fields cannot be placed in a table or form. They can only be accessed directly through the Module Editor.

Index	Source	Field Name	Type	Definition
128	RA	**UPDATE START**	C D	This field contains the last start date that was sent to resources assigned to the task. When this field differs from the current Scheduled Start date for the task, the Update Needed field is set to Yes. This field can only be accessed through the Module Editor.

Index	Source	Field Name	Type	Definition
129	RA	**UPDATE FINISH**	C D	This field contains the last finish date that was sent to re-sources assigned to the task. When this field differs from the current Scheduled Finish date for the task, the Update Needed field is set to Yes. This field can only be accessed through the Module Editor.
130	RA	**UPDATE NEEDED**	C L	If either the current Scheduled Start or the Scheduled Finish date differs from the Update Start or Update Finish fields, this field contains Yes. Otherwise, it contains No. If the field contains Yes, the **T**ools **W**orkgroup Send Task **U**pdates command will be triggered to include this task and its assigned resources in the next task update that is broadcast.
131	T	**UPDATE NEEDED**	C L	If any of the resource assignments for this task have a Yes in their UPDATE NEEDED field, this field shows yes for the entire task. If the field contains Yes, the **T**ools **W**orkgroup Send Task **U**pdates command will be triggered to include this task and its assigned resources in the next task update that is broadcast. This field can be displayed in tables and on custom forms.
132	RA	**PENDING RESPONSE**	C L	A Yes in this field indicates that the resource assigned to the task has yet to respond to the electronic mail request to work on the task. A No indicates that the response has been received. This field can only be accessed directly through the Module Editor.
133	RA	**CONFIRMED**	C L	This field contains a Yes only if the resource that has been asked to work on the task has returned a Yes response. This field can only be accessed from the Module Editor.
134	T	**CONFIRMED**	C L	This field contains a Yes only if all resources that have been asked to work on the task have returned Yes responses. This field can only be accessed from the Module Editor.
135	RA	**SCHED+ ID**	C A	This field contains the unique identifier assigned to the task by the Microsoft Schedule+ calendar and scheduling program. The field is used to assure that task information is sent to the correct task on the resource's scheduler. This field can only be accessed by the Module Editor.

Appendixes

Table A.2 Alphabetized List of Fields Used in Microsoft Project	
Field Name	**Index to Table A.1**
Task Definition Fields	
Actual Cost	99
Actual Duration	86
Actual Finish	101
Actual Start	85
Actual Work	94
Baseline Cost	73
Baseline Duration	69
Baseline Finish	68
Baseline Start	67
Baseline Work	72
BCWP	107
BCWS	108
Confirmed	134
Constraint Date	10
Constraint Type	9
Contact	123
Cost	61
Cost Variance	78
Cost1, Cost2, Cost3	116
Created	2
Critical	28
CV	109
Delay	23
Duration	6
Duration Variance	76

Field Name	Index to Table A.1
Duration1, Duration2, Duration3	117
Early Finish	20
Early Start	19
Finish Variance	75
Finish1, Finish2, ..., Finish5	84
Fixed	8
Fixed Cost	29
Flag1, Flag2,..., Flag10	118
Free Slack	27
Hide Bar	121
ID	4
Late Finish	22
Late Start	21
Link Fields	124
Marked	119
Milestone	7
Name	1
Notes	111
Number1, Number2, ..., Number5	115
Objects	125
Outline Level	11
Outline Number	12
Percent (%) Complete	87
Percent (%) Work Complete	95
Predecessors	15

(continues)

Appendixes

Table A.2 Continued	
Field Name	**Index to Table A.1**
Task Definition Fields	
Priority	30
Project	5
Recurring Task	120
Remaining Cost	100
Remaining Duration	88
Remaining Work	96
Resource Group	59
Resource Initials	58
Resource Names	57
Resume Date	90
Resume No Earlier than	91
Rollup	122
Scheduled Finish	25
Scheduled Start	24
Start Variance	74
Start1, Start2, …, Start5	83
Stop Date	89
Subproject File	31
Successors	16
Summary	13
SV	110
Text1, Text2, …, Text10	113
Total Slack	26

Field Name	Index to Table A.1
Unique ID	3
Unique ID Predecessors	17
Unique ID Successors	18
Update Needed	131
WBS	14
Work	60
Work Variance	77

Resource Definition Fields	
Accrue At	42
Actual Cost	105
Actual Work	102
Base Calendar	44
Baseline Cost	81
Baseline Work	79
Code	43
Cost	64
Cost Per Use	41
Cost Variance	82
Email Address	45
Group	36
ID	34
Initials	35
Linked Fields	126
Max Units	37
Name	32
Notes	112

(continues)

Appendixes

Table A.2 Continued	
Field Name	**Index to Table A.1**
Resource Definition Fields	
Objects	127
Overallocated	66
Overtime Rate	40
Overtime Work	63
Peak	65
Percent (%) Work Complete	103
Remaining Cost	106
Remaining Work	104
Standard Rate	39
Text1, Text2, ..., Text 5	114
Unique ID	33
Work	62
Work Variance	80
The Resource Assignment Fields	
Actual Cost	97
Actual Work	92
Baseline Cost	71
Baseline Work	70
Confirmed	133
Cost	53
Delay	54
ID	46

Field Name	Index to Table A.1
Overtime Work	52
Pending Response	132
Project	49
Remaining Cost	98
Remaining Work	93
Resource Name	47
Sched+ ID	135
Scheduled Finish	56
Scheduled Start	55
Task Name	48
Units	50
Update Finish	129
Update Needed	130
Update Start	128
Work	51

Appendix B

Shortcut Keys

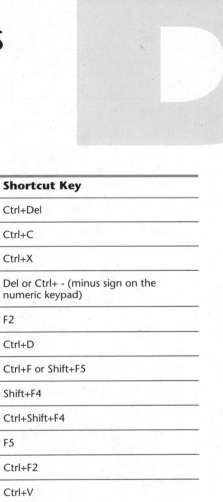

Menu Command or *Function*	Shortcut Key
Edit: Clear Contents	Ctrl+Del
Edit: Copy selection	Ctrl+C
Edit: Cut selection	Ctrl+X
Edit: Delete Task or Resource	Del or Ctrl+ - (minus sign on the numeric keypad)
Edit: Entry bar to edit text in a field	F2
Edit: Fill Down	Ctrl+D
Edit: Find	Ctrl+F or Shift+F5
Edit: Find Next	Shift+F4
Edit: Find Previous	Ctrl+Shift+F4
Edit: Go To ID number or Date	F5
Edit: Link Tasks	Ctrl+F2
Edit: Paste	Ctrl+V
Edit: Resource Assignment dialog box	Alt+F8
Edit: Resource Information dialog box	Shift+F2 (when in Resource views)
Edit: Task Information dialog box	Shift+F2 (when in Task views)
Edit: Undo	Ctrl+Z
Edit: Unlink Tasks	Ctrl+Shift+F2
Editing: Show Entry List	Alt+down arrow

(continues)

Menu Command or *Function*	Shortcut Key
File: Close document window	Ctrl+F4
File: New	Ctrl+N or F11
File: Open	Ctrl+O
File: Print	Ctrl+P
File: Save	Ctrl+S
File: Save As dialog box	F12 or Alt+F2
Help: Context-sensitive Help pointer	Shift+F1
Help: Open Help	F1
Insert: Insert task or resource row	Ins or Ctrl++ (plus sign on the numeric keypad)
Menu bar: On/Off	F10 or Alt
Scroll timescale to Date for current task	Ctrl+Shift+F5
Selection: Add To Selection mode	Shift+F8
Selection: Extend Selection mode	F8
Selection: Other pane in combination view	F6
Selection: Reduce selection to a single field	Shift+Backspace
Selection: Select drawing object	F6
Selection: Select field tables at bottom of form	Alt+1 (first), Alt+2 (second)
Tools Filter: Apply Same filter again	Ctrl+F3
Tools Filter: Display All tasks or All resources	F3
Tools Options Calculate: Calculate All open projects	F9
Tools Options Calculate: Calculate Active project	Shift+F9

Menu Command or *Function*	Shortcut Key
Tools Options Calculate: Turn Auto Calculate On/Off	Ctrl+F9
Tools Sort: Reset sort to ID order	Shift+F3
Tools Sort: Sort again using current sort order	Ctrl+Shift+F3
Tools: Indent task in outline	Alt+Shift+right arrow
Tools: Outdent task in outline	Alt+Shift+left arrow
Tools: Spelling	F7
View Table: Column Definition dialog box	Alt+F3
Window: Next/Previous project window	Ctrl+F6, Ctrl+Shift+F6
Window: Split bar	Shift+F6

Appendix C

Glossary

The following Glossary contains a short list of common project management terms:

Actual   Aspects of the project that have actually happened, as opposed to being Planned or Scheduled or predicted. Includes recorded dates, duration, work, and/or cost data for tasks and for resource work done on tasks.

Base calendar   A calendar used as the primary CALENDAR for the whole project or multiple resources, and that specifies work and non-work time.

Baseline   A copy of the schedule dates, work, and cost data as of a moment in time that's used for comparison purposes when tracking project progress. Usually the final plan just before work begins on the project.

Calculated filter   A filter that compares values in two fields for a task or resource as a basis for selecting the task or resource.

Calendar   A list of time periods during which work can be scheduled. It consists of the normal working days in a week, the normal working hours on those days, and a list of nonworking days and hours that are exceptions to the normal times. *See* BASE CALENDAR and RESOURCE CALENDAR.

Collapsed outline   A view of the task outline where the subtasks for one or more of the summary tasks are hidden from view. *See* EXPANDED OUTLINE.

Combination view   A view having two panes. The bottom pane view always shows a detailed view of the selection in the top pane view.

Constraint   A limitation set on the scheduling of the start or finish of a task. Normally, all tasks are scheduled to start and finish as soon as possible. Constraints can be placed on the start or on the finish of a task. They may be expressed, for example, as "must start on, must finish on, start no earlier than, finish no later than," and so on.

Cost   The total scheduled cost for a task, resource, resource assignment, or project. Includes FIXED COST and RESOURCE COST.

Criteria   Conditions that must be met in a filter for a task or resource to be selected.

Critical path   A sequence of tasks, each of which must finish on schedule for the project to finish on time.

Critical task   A task which, if its finish date were delayed, would delay the finish of the project.

Dependency relationship   General term that describes the relationship between a DEPENDENT TASK and its PREDECESSOR. *See* also LAG TIME, LEAD TIME, and PARTIAL DEPENDENCY.

Dependent task   A task whose scheduled start or finish date must be set to coincide with or be linked to the scheduled start or finish date of some other task (its PREDECESSOR).

Driving resource   One among multiple resources assigned to a task, whose work takes the longest duration to complete. The duration for the task is "driven" by this resource.

Duration   The number of working time units (minutes, hours, days, or weeks) between the start and the finish of a task or group of tasks. The working time units are defined by the base or resource calendar that governs the scheduling of the task.

Example: If a task has a duration of four hours and is started during the last hour of a working day, the remaining three hours of work will be scheduled for the next three working hours on the scheduling calendar, whenever that may be (the next day, after the weekend, after vacation, etc.). Its total duration of four hours on the scheduling calendar may take place over many more hours of actual time. *See* ELAPSED DURATION.

Elapsed duration   The actual clock time (not the working calendar time) that elapses between the start and finish of a task. This is based on a 24-hour day and a 7-day week.

Expanded outline   An outline view in which all of the subtasks are displayed. *See* COLLAPSED OUTLINE.

Field   A data entry point in a table or on a form. All tasks and resources, for example, have a *Name* field in which you can record a name for the task or resource.

Filter   A criterion or set of criteria that is applied to all tasks or resources to differentiate those that meet the criteria from those that do not. A filter can operate in two ways: it can hide all tasks that fail to match the filter criteria or it can show all tasks but *highlight* those that match the criteria.

Fixed cost   Fixed costs are assigned directly to tasks and remain constant regardless of task duration or work performed.

Fixed date tasks   Tasks that have constrained dates or that already have a recorded Actual Start Date cannot be rescheduled by Microsoft Project and are called fixed date tasks.

Fixed task   Also called *fixed duration task*. A task whose duration will not be affected by increasing or decreasing the quantity of resources assigned to do work on the task. *See* RESOURCE DRIVEN TASK.

Gridlines   Lines that separate rows and columns in a table or timescale view. Also used in graphs to mark value levels against an axis.

Interactive filter   A filter that first prompts the user for one or more values that are then used in selecting the tasks or resources to display in the short list.

Lag time   A delay that must be observed between the scheduling of a task and the scheduled date of its PREDECESSOR task. *See* DEPENDENCY RELATIONSHIP.

Lead time   An amount of time by which a DEPENDENT task can be scheduled to overlap or anticipate the scheduled start or finish of its PREDECESSOR task.

Legend   A reference on a graphic image that defines the graphic elements (markers, patterns, colors, shapes, etc.) in terms of the data represented.

Leveling   The process of delaying tasks in order to *level out* the demands on resources so that the resources are no longer overallocated.

Linked tasks   Tasks that have a DEPENDENCY RELATIONSHIP.

List separator character   The character (initially the comma) that is used to separate items on a list when they are typed on the same line. Defined in the PREFERENCES list.

Macro   An automated list of instructions that you create to replicate an operation on command. Macros are maintained with Visual Basic for Applications.

MAPI   Messaging Application Programming Interface is the Microsoft protocol for sending user messages from one application to another.

Master project   A project that contains one or more tasks that are linked to other projects (subprojects) and whose duration, work, and costs are a summary of the entire duration, work, and cost of the subproject they represent.

Milestone   A task whose purpose is to record a significant accomplishment or event in the life of the project—not to schedule work that must be done. If a task is given a duration of zero, it is automatically marked as a milestone. However, any task, even a summary task, can be marked as a milestone.

Node   The box device used in the PERT Chart to represent each task.

Operator   A device used in filters to link multiple criteria. If multiple criteria must all be met to satisfy the filter, the And operator is used. If meeting any one of the multiple criteria will satisfy the filter, the Or operator is used.

Outline   A structured presentation in Microsoft Project that allows tasks to be grouped under SUMMARY TASKS to show functional relationships. Detailed, subordinate subtasks are demoted under their summary tasks to produce a traditional outline appearance.

Partial dependency   A dependency relationship where the two tasks overlap or where there is a specified gap of time between the two tasks. *See* DEPENDENCY RELATIONSHIP.

Percent complete   A measurement of the actual duration or work that has been completed on a task. Measured as the ratio of actual work or duration to scheduled work or duration.

PERT Chart   A network chart used in project management to illustrate the dependency relations among tasks. Each task is represented by a box (or node) and is connected by a line to each predecessor or successor task to show the sequencing of tasks.

Plan   Technically, the plan is the BASELINE (the finalized plan, prior to commencing work on the project). The term is sometimes ambiguously (and mistakenly) used to refer to the current schedule.

Predecessor   If the scheduled start or finish of task A is determined by the scheduled start or finish of task B, then B is the predecessor task for task A. "Predecessor" is an unfortunate term, because the term implies chronological precedence when the important point is that the scheduling of task A is dependent on the scheduled date for task B. *See* DEPENDENCY RELATIONSHIP, SUCCESSOR.

Priority   A task field whose value is used to determine the likelihood of the task being selected as one of the tasks to be delayed during the LEVELING process. The higher the priority value, the less likely the task will be delayed.

Recurring task   A task that is repeated at regular intervals during all or part of the project.

Reschedule tasks   A Microsoft Project command that you can use when part of the work on a task has been done but the remainder must be rescheduled to a later time.

Resource allocation   The assignment of a resource to do work on a task.

Resource calendar   A list of the working days and hours for a specific resource. It is composed by defining a base calendar as a reference and listing all of the exceptions to the base calendar.

Resource conflict   The conflict that results when a resource is scheduled to do more work in a given time period than the resource is available to deliver.

Resource cost   The sum of all resource costs for a task. Resource cost includes the sum of the work times the cost rate for the resource (standard and overtime) as well as the cost per use for the resource if defined.

Appendixes

Resource driven task   A task whose duration is driven or determined by the number of resource units assigned to work on the task. *See* FIXED TASK.

Resource group   There are two meanings. 1. The Group field in the resource database can be used to enter names of groups to which resources belong.
2. A single resource name may refer to multiple units of a type of resource called a *group resource*, such as a group of trucks, a group of painters, and so on.

Resource pool   The list of resources that are available for assignment to tasks. A project can have its own resource pool, or it may use the resource pool that is already defined in another project file.

Resource view   A view that displays resources instead of tasks (*see* TASK VIEW). The standard resource views include the Resource Sheet, Graph, Form, Allocation, and Usage views.

Resources   The people, equipment, facilities, vendors, and suppliers that do the work of the project.

Roll up task   To display a marker on a summary task bar in a Gantt Chart to show a date for one of the subtasks.

Schedule   Often called the *current plan*. The current set of actual (already completed) and predicted (yet to complete) dates, durations, resource assignments, and costs for the project.

Selecting   Before you can use commands on a field or piece of data, you must select it. Selected data is highlighted or marked in some way to show that the data is selected.

Single-pane view   A view that uses only the top pane.

Slack   "Total" slack is the amount of time by which a task can be delayed without delaying the finish of the project. "Free" slack is even more restrictive: it is the amount of time a task can be delayed without delaying the schedule for any other task.

Slippage   A measure of the amount of time by which a task's schedule is behind its baseline or planned dates.

Subproject   A project file that is represented as a single task in another project file. The master or *superproject* project file uses the start and finish of the subproject as the start and finish of the task which represents the subproject. Thus the subproject schedule is fitted into the master project schedule.

Subtask   A task that is indented under a Summary task.

Successor   In a DEPENDENCY RELATIONSHIP, the dependent task is often called the *Successor task* and the task it depends on is called the *PREDECESSOR* task. The tasks may actually overlap in time, however, and you shouldn't assume that the successor task comes after the PREDECESSOR task.

Summary task   A task whose sole function is to encompass and summarize the duration, work, and costs of other tasks (called *subtasks*).

Table   A Table defines the columns that appear in a view of project data that is laid out in columns and rows, like a spreadsheet. The Table defines which columns are included in the view, the data field that is to be displayed, the column title, the alignment, and the width of the column.

Task   A normal task is an essential job or operation that must be completed in order for a project to be completed. Milestones and Summary tasks are special types of tasks.

Task view   A view of the project data that is organized around the defined tasks. The standard task views include the Calendar, the Task Sheet, Task Forms, the GANTT Chart, and the PERT Chart.

Timescale   An area in a view that marks chronological dates along the top of the view and shows data for tasks or resources placed in the appropriate time periods.

Variance   The difference between the baseline and currently scheduled data. Variances for tasks usually refer to dates, while those for resources usually refer to work and costs.

View   A screen display of project data. The View command is used to select the display or view that is most appropriate for your work with the project.

Visual Basic for Applications   A complete programming language that you can use to automate your work in Microsoft Project, as well as to automate interactions between Microsoft Project and other Microsoft applications.

Wild card   In a FILTER, a wild card is one of two symbols ("?" or "*") that can be used in Equals and Not Equals criteria to take the place of one or more unspecified parts of a search string. For example, if you wanted to find all the task names that begin with a "t" and end with a "p," you would use the filter string "t*p." When the asterisk ("*") wild card is used, the filter will find entries that have any number of unspecified characters in the position where the asterisk is placed. Thus, the filter "t*p" would find "top," "tp," and "Train supervisors to setup." When the question mark ("?") wild card is used, there must be exactly one character in the position where each question mark is placed, but there are no restrictions on what those characters must be. The filter string "t??p" would select "trip" and "tarp," but it would reject "tip" and "tulip."

Work Breakdown Structure (WBS)   A method of organizing a project by which tasks are grouped into a hierarchical structure featuring major phase groups, with sub-groups at many levels. Tasks are assigned a code that identifies the group, sub-groups, and individual task within each group. Microsoft Project uses *outlining* to achieve the same organizational objective.

Working time   The days and hours on a base calendar or a resource calendar during which work on tasks can be scheduled.

Index